CW00631625

MASTERING™ WINDOWS 98 SECOND EDITION

Robert Cowart
0-7821-2618-9
928 pp.
$39.99 US

This updated edition of *Mastering Windows 98* not only covers Microsoft's newest 32-bit operating system from beginning to end but also covers the latest additions and enhancements, such as Web View, "live" Internet connectivity, and the new Internet Explorer 5 interface. *Windows 98 Second Edition* also ties into the Internet with the new Active Desktop and channels and includes enhanced security, major bug fixes, expanded networking features, and support for hundreds of new peripherals. This is the book for everyone who wants to become immediately productive with the latest version of the Windows operating system. Includes an exclusive CD previously available only with *Mastering Windows 98 Premium Edition!*

THE INTERNET: NO EXPERIENCE REQUIRED™

Christian Crumlish
0-7821-2385-6
496 pp.
$19.99 US

The explosive growth of the Internet makes having the skills to use it essential to just about anyone with a computer. Here is a no-nonsense, skills-based guide to communicating with e-mail, browsing, chatting, and publishing on the Web. Four new and unique chapters on troubleshooting make this book the most valuable and essential survival guide available. Consider it a great introduction to the Internet that also leads you through the most exciting new possibilities in e-mail, push technologies, Usenet, multimedia, and much more.

PC COMPLETE
Second Edition

SYBEX® SAN FRANCISCO ▸ PARIS ▸ DÜSSELDORF ▸ SOEST ▸ LONDON

Associate Publisher: Roger Stewart

Contracts and Licensing Manager: Kristine O'Callaghan

Acquisitions Editor: Diane Lowery

Developmental Editor: Pat Coleman

Compilation Editor: Anamary Ehlen

Editors: Douglas Robert, Shelby Zimmerman, Pat Coleman, Anamary Ehlen, Kim Wimpsett, Bonnie Bills, Brenda Frink, Dann McDorman, Lee Ann Pickrell

Technical Editors: Mark Kovach, Rima Regas, Maryann Brown, Doug Smith, Doug Langston, Steve Bigelow, Dale Wright, Juanita Tischendorf, Elizabeth Shannon, Tyler Regas

Desktop Publisher: Franz Baumhackl

Production Editor: Bronwyn Shone Erickson

Associate Production Editor: Molly Glover

Indexer: Nancy Guenther

Cover Designer: DesignSite

Cover Photographer: Mark Johann

Screen reproductions produced with Collage Complete.

Collage Complete is a trademark of Inner Media Inc.

SYBEX is a registered trademark of SYBEX Inc.

Mastering, Expert Guide, Premium Edition, and No Experience Required are trademarks of SYBEX Inc.

First Edition Copyright © 1999

Copyright © 2000 SYBEX Inc., 1151 Marina Village Parkway, Alameda, CA 94501. World rights reserved. No part of this publication may be stored in a retrieval system, transmitted, or reproduced in any way, including but not limited to photocopy, photograph, magnetic or other record, without the prior agreement and written permission of the publisher.

Library of Congress Card Number: 00-102135

ISBN: 0-7821-2778-9

Manufactured in the United States of America

10 9 8 7 6 5 4 3 2 1

TRADEMARKS:

SYBEX has attempted throughout this book to distinguish proprietary trademarks from descriptive terms by following the capitalization style used by the manufacturer.

Netscape Communications, the Netscape Communications logo, Netscape, and Netscape Navigator are trademarks of Netscape Communications Corporation.

Netscape Communications Corporation has not authorized, sponsored, endorsed, or approved this publication and is not responsible for its content. Netscape and the Netscape Communications Corporate Logos are trademarks and trade names of Netscape Communications Corporation. All other product names and/or logos are trademarks of their respective owners.

Internet screen shot(s) using Microsoft Internet Explorer version 5 reprinted by permission from Microsoft Corporation.

PC Novice, the PC Novice logo, Smart Computing, and the Smart Computing logo are trademarks of Sandhills Publishing.

The author and publisher have made their best efforts to prepare this book, and the content is based upon final release software whenever possible. Portions of the manuscript may be based upon pre-release versions supplied by software manufacturer(s). The author and the publisher make no representation or warranties of any kind with regard to the completeness or accuracy of the contents herein and accept no liability of any kind including but not limited to performance, merchantability, fitness for any particular purpose, or any losses or damages of any kind caused or alleged to be caused directly or indirectly from this book.

Photographs and illustrations used in this book have been downloaded from publicly accessible file archives and are used in this book for news reportage purposes only to demonstrate the variety of graphics resources available via electronic access. Text and images available over the Internet may be subject to copyright and other rights owned by third parties. Online availability of text and images does not imply that they may be reused without the permission of rights holders, although the Copyright Act does permit certain unauthorized reuse as fair use under 17 U.S.C. Section 107.

ACKNOWLEDGMENTS

This book incorporates the work of many people, inside and outside Sybex.

Gary Masters and Peter Kuhns hammered out the original idea of an inexpensive compilation including the widest possible range of topics for PC users. They defined the book's overall structure and contents. Pat Coleman compiled and adapted all the material for publication in this book.

A large team of editors, developmental editors, project editors, and technical editors helped put together the various books from which *PC Complete,* Second Edition, was compiled: Sherry Bonelli, Tracy Brown, Ellen Dendy, Brenda Frink, Linda Lee, and Diane Lowery handled developmental tasks; Mike Anderson, Raquel Baker, Pat Coleman, Ed Copony, Donna Crossman, Anamary Ehlen, Shannon Murphy, Linda Lambert Orlando, Doug Robert, Laurie Stewart, Benjamin Tomkins, and Kristen Vanberg-Wolff all contributed to editing or project editing; and the technical editors were Mark Kovach, Maryann Brown, Donald Fuller, Susan Glinert, James Kelly, Doug Langston, Rima Regas, and Doug Smith.

A special thanks to the *PC Complete,* Second Edition, production team of designer and desktop publisher Franz Baumhackl, production editors Bronwyn Shone Erickson and Molly Glover, and illustrator Tony Jonick who all worked with incredible speed and gusto to turn the manuscript files and illustrations into the handsome book you're now reading.

Finally, our most important thanks go to the contributors who agreed to have their work excerpted into *PC Complete,* Second Edition: Mark Cohen, Pat Coleman, Gini Courter, Robert Cowart, Christian Crumlish, Peter Dyson, Ben Ezzell, Guy Hart-Davis, Rhonda Holmes, Annette Marquis, Mark Minasi, Erik B. Sherman, Alan Simpson, and Gene Weisskopf. Without their efforts, this book would not exist.

CONTENTS AT A GLANCE

CONTENTS

Chapter 3 □ **Installing Windows 98 Second Edition on Your Computer**   **57**

Chapter 6 □ Managing Files and Folders   171

Chapter 7 □ Windows Multimedia   197

Part IV ▸The Internet   497

Chapter 16 □ Understanding Internet and World Wide Web Basics   499

Part V ▶Gaming and Music   635

Chapter 21 ▢ An Introduction to Gaming and Your PC   637

Part VI Home Networking   757

Chapter 23 □ Home Networking   759

Part VII ▶PC Complete User's Reference   807

Appendix A □ Vendor Guide   809

Appendix B □ Complete Hardware Dictionary   855

INTRODUCTION

First published in 1999, *PC Complete* quickly became a popular choice among PC users at all levels. As you may have heard, computer years are sort of like dog years. For every calendar year, the world of computing racks up seven technological years. And so it was time to bring *PC Complete* up-to-date. This Second Edition draws on the strengths of the First Edition—breadth of content and low price, but you'll find that we've included new technologies and that the book is based on the latest consumer version of Windows—Windows 98 Second Edition.

This 1000-page compilation of information from more than a dozen Sybex books provides comprehensive coverage of related hardware and software issues and Internet and Windows topics. This book, like its predecessor, was created with several goals in mind: first to offer at an affordable price a thorough guide covering all the important user-level features of your PC; second to help you become familiar with the essential hardware and software topics so you can choose your next PC book with confidence. The book's third goal is to acquaint you with some of our best authors—their writing styles, teaching skills, and the level of expertise they bring to their books—so you can easily find a match for your interests as you delve deeper into your PC and the realms of software and hardware it opens up to you. *PC Complete, Second Edition,* is designed to provide all the essential information you'll need to get the most from your computer, while at the same time inviting you to explore the even greater depths and wider coverage of material in the original books.

If you've read other computer "how-to" books, you've seen that there are many possible approaches to the task of showing how to use software and hardware effectively. The books from which *PC Complete* was compiled represent a range of the approaches to teaching that Sybex and its authors have developed—from the quick, concise *No Experience Required* style to the exhaustively thorough *Mastering* style. These books also address readers at different levels of computer experience, from *To Go* to *In Record Time.* As you read through various chapters of *PC Complete,* you'll see which approach works best for you. You'll also see what these books have in common: a commitment to clarity, accuracy, and practicality.

You'll find in these pages ample evidence of the high quality of Sybex's authors. Unlike publishers who produce "books by committee," Sybex authors are encouraged to write in individual voices that reflect their own experience with the software at hand and with the evolution of today's personal computers. Nearly every book represented here is the work of a single writer or a pair of close collaborators; when Mark Minasi, for example, says, "I once helped troubleshoot a network that had been installed...," you know you are getting the benefit of *his* direct experience. Likewise, all the Windows chapters are based on their authors' firsthand testing of prerelease software and subsequent expertise with the final product.

In adapting the various source materials for inclusion in *PC Complete*, the compiler preserved these individual voices and perspectives. Chapters were edited only to minimize duplication, omit coverage of non-Windows tools, and update or add cross-references so that you can easily follow a topic across chapters. A few sections were also edited for length so that other important topics could be included.

Who Can Benefit from This Book?

PC Complete, Second Edition, is designed to meet the needs of a wide range of computer users. Your PC contains a wealth of features, with some elements that everyone uses, as well as tools that may be essential to some users but of no interest to others. Therefore, while you could read this book from beginning to end—from hardware installation and software issues through application features and the Internet—you may not need to read every chapter. The table of contents and the index will guide you to the subjects you're looking for.

Beginners   Even if you have only a little familiarity with computers and their basic terminology, this book will get you up to speed with the ins and outs of your PC. You'll find step-by-step instructions for installing and maintaining hardware and for the operations involved in running application programs and managing your computer system, along with clear explanations of essential concepts.

Intermediate users   Chances are, you already know how to do routine Windows tasks. You know your way around a few productivity applications, use e-mail extensively, browse the Web a little, and maybe have a favorite game or two. You also know there is always more to learn about working more effectively, and you want to get up to speed on the ins and outs of your PC. Throughout this book you'll find instructions for just about anything you want to do. Nearly every chapter has nuggets of knowledge from which you can benefit.

Power users   Maybe you're a hardcore multimedia freak looking to upgrade your hardware to take advantage of the expanded capabilities of Windows 98 SE, or maybe you're the unofficial guru of your office network. If you're responsible for maintaining your own computer and for deciding what components to upgrade and when, our experts provide time- and money-saving tips for you. You'll learn how to protect your computer from physical hazards, and you'll get some guidelines for getting the most from your hardware accessories. If you don't want to spend hundreds of dollars to get a system that's ready for Windows 98 SE and the Internet, check out the chapters on adding RAM, multimedia, and modems.

This book is for people using a PC in any environment. You may be a "SOHO" (small-office/home-office) user, working with a stand-alone computer or a simple peer-to-peer network with no administrators or technical staff to rely on. In that case, you'll find plenty of information about maintaining, troubleshooting, and upgrading your computer and about sharing resources. Or you may be working within a larger network, and simply want to get a leg up, quickly and inexpensively, as your office migrates to the new operating system.

How This Book Is Organized

PC Complete has 7 parts, consisting of 23 chapters and 2 appendices.

Part I: Windows Basics   The eight chapters in Part I cover all the Windows essentials—installing Windows 98 SE, touring the Desktop, creating shortcuts to programs and files you use frequently, using Control Panel to customize your computer system, working with printers, and much more. You'll learn about extensive support of Windows 98 SE for multimedia and about tools for keeping your computer trouble-free. Anyone migrating from a previous Windows version (3.1, 95, or 98) will benefit greatly from this comprehensive guide to the new features of Windows 98 SE.

Part II: Hardware and Troubleshooting   Not surprisingly, a large portion of owning and using a PC is about maintenance. The second section of the book is devoted to teaching you how to maintain and troubleshoot your PC's hardware. The four chapters in Part II cover all your hardware essentials—touring your PC's hardware, avoiding expensive service costs with preventive maintenance, installing memory, and installing hard drives and cards. In Chapter 10 you'll learn expert tips for supporting your hardware accessories, how to solve common hardware issues, and how to keep your computer trouble-free. With very little money and the expertise you'll gain here, you just might give your current PC another couple of years of useful life.

Part III: Office Basics The three chapters in this section help you understand and master the most essential file operations and applications in the Office environment. In Chapter 14, you'll learn how to create and save a Word document; you'll also learn how to format your document and use a variety of Word tools with ease. Chapter 15 explains how to create worksheets and workbooks, how to enter data, and how to format Excel spreadsheets.

Part IV: The Internet The extensive Sybex library of Internet books has already helped guide hundreds of thousands of users into cyberspace. Part IV is a comprehensive look at the Internet and the tools you use to browse the Web and exchange e-mail. You'll learn how to connect to the Internet using your PC and modem. You'll also learn about Netscape Communicator, the most popular alternative to Internet Explorer.

Part V: Games and Music The real reason you bought a computer? Maybe not, but our gaming expert may persuade you otherwise. In this section, Mark Cohen guides you through the garden of delights that await you in the computer games department—how to prepare your computer for gaming, the practicalities of hardware choices, and descriptions of major computer game categories and sub-categories, including reviews of the best classic and current games and those you can look forward to in the near future. And, then, to put the icing on the cake, Guy Hart-Davis explains MP3, the technology for compressing and transferring music files that has become so popular it has brought some university computer systems to a screeching halt. Find out what MP3 can do, what you need to know about the legalities involved in this technology, how to find the music you want, organize it, and play it, and much, much more.

Part VI: Home Networking Did you know that for relatively little money and not much time you—yes, you—could network together all the computers in your house or apartment? In this part of the book, Erik Sherman tells you how in plain English, step-by-step fashion. We've compiled a collection of tricks, tips, and how-to advice from his book, *Home Networking! I Didn't Know You Could Do That....*

Part VII: PC Complete User's Reference   The appendices here are designed for quick lookup—or casual browsing. There's a complete listing of contact information for vendors of hardware and utility software and an alphabetic reference to your computer's hardware.

A Few Typographical Conventions

When an operation requires a series of choices from menus or dialog boxes, the ➢ symbol is used to guide you through the instructions, like this: "Choose Programs ➢ Accessories ➢ System Tools ➢ System Information." The items the ➢ symbol separates may be menu names, toolbar icons, check boxes, or other elements of the Windows interface or an application—any place you can make a selection.

`This typeface` identifies Internet URLs and HTML code, and **boldface type** is used whenever you need to type something into a text box.

You'll find these types of special notes throughout the book:

TIP

You'll see a lot of these—quicker and smarter ways to accomplish a task, which the authors have based on many, many months spent testing and using your system's hardware and software.

NOTE

You'll see these Notes, too. They usually represent alternate ways to accomplish a task or some additional information that needs to be highlighted.

WARNING

In a very few places you'll see a Warning like this one. There are few because it's not easy to do irrevocable things in Windows 98 SE or Windows applications unless you work hard at it. But when you see a warning, do pay attention to it.

YOU'LL ALSO SEE "SIDEBAR" BOXES LIKE THIS

These boxed sections provide added explanation of special topics that are noted briefly in the surrounding discussion, but that you may want to explore separately. Each sidebar has a heading that announces the topic so you can quickly decide whether it's something you need to know about.

So Where Can I Get These Great Books?

All the Sybex books used to compile *PC Complete,* Second Edition, are available at book and computer stores worldwide. If you can't find a book you're looking for (or can't easily get to a bookstore), don't worry. All Sybex books are available for purchase online at the Sybex Web site, at

    http://www.sybex.com

or through online booksellers, such as Computer Literacy, at

    http://www.cbooks.com

and Amazon.com, at

    http://www.amazon.com

For More Information...

See the Sybex Web site, www.sybex.com, to learn more about all the books that went into *PC Complete,* Second Edition. On the site's Catalog page, you'll find links to any book you're interested in.

We hope you enjoy this book and find it useful. Happy computing!

PART I
WINDOWS BASICS

Windows 98

Chapter 1

INTRODUCING THE PC

There are millions of reasons for wanting to learn to use a computer. Maybe you want to use the Internet. Or maybe you plan to write the great American novel. Perhaps you want to play games. Maybe you want to use a computer to help manage a business. Regardless of what you plan to do with your PC, your first step to getting *anything* done will be to learn to use Windows. This chapter will explain why.

Adapted from *Windows 98 to Go*
by Alan Simpson
ISBN 0-7821-2493-3   258 pages $6.99

Windows 98 SE Makes Computing Easy

If your first experience with computers was way back in the days of command-line interfaces (such as DOS and Unix), or if you failed miserably at programming with archaic languages such as Fortran and COBOL, stop worrying. Those days are long gone. Windows 98 SE offers a much simpler point-and-click approach to computing. You point to whatever you want (using the mouse) and then click on that item. No weird commands to memorize and type.

Of course, you do need to know *how* to point and click. And you need to know *what* to click and *when*. Randomly clicking items on the screen won't do you any good. The PC can't read your mind and "guess" what you want it to do. (Bummer, I know.) But fear not! The Windows basics described in this part of the book will take all the guesswork out of your computing.

What Is Windows 98 SE?

To understand why one might want to learn to use Windows, it helps to understand what Windows actually is. Simply stated, Windows 98 SE is that thing that waits around for you to tell the computer what to do. When you first turn on a computer, it whirs and buzzes, and technical-looking information goes by on the screen. Then it finally settles down and doesn't do anything but show some little pictures on the screen. That screen is called the Windows 98 SE *Desktop,* and it usually looks something like the example in Figure 1.1.

To use a computer, you need to know how to work that Desktop, which is exactly what this part of the book teaches you. But first, a little better description of what Windows really is and how it got that weird name.

FIGURE 1.1:   The Windows 98 SE Desktop

Windows 98 SE Is a Program

If you walk into any computer store or even a large office supply store, you'll find dozens of *programs* that you can buy and use on your PC: games, educational programs, programs for the home, programs for business, and so on.

Windows 98 SE is a program, too. However, it isn't a game. And it isn't something you use to keep track of your bills. Instead, it's sort of the *master program* that gives you access to all other programs and all the different things a computer can do.

Most new PCs come with Windows 98 SE already installed. So if you bought (or plan to buy) such a PC, you don't have to buy Windows separately. If you have an older PC with some other *operating system* on it, such as Windows 3.1 or Windows 95, you can upgrade to Windows 98 SE simply by purchasing the upgrade version at any computer store.

WHY NEW VERSIONS ALL THE TIME?

You may be aware that there are different versions of Windows around, such as Windows 3.1, 95, 98, and 98 SE. Each version is an improvement over the previous version, with Windows 98 SE being the most recent. And in case you're wondering, there weren't 92 versions between versions 3.1 and 95. It's just that in 1995, Microsoft, the maker of Windows, decided to start identifying versions by the year they were released, as the automobile industry does. After all, everyone knows what "version" of car a 1995 Chevy is!

Some people think that different software versions are a plot by software companies to make you keep buying the same product over and over again. The common misconception is that software manufacturers intentionally put *bugs* (errors) in programs so that people will have to buy the next version of the program when it becomes available, to get rid of the bugs.

Fortunately, that's not the way it works. Nobody is trying to trick you into buying anything. The main reason that new versions of programs become available is that computer science is still a very young technology. It's growing and evolving all the time. New versions of software are created and sold mainly to take advantage of these new technologies as they become available.

Windows 98 SE is no exception. Although on the surface Windows 98 SE looks and acts much like its predecessors, Windows 95 and 98, there's new support—or better support—for technologies that have evolved since Windows 95 was first released. For instance, Windows 98 SE has much better support for using the Internet and for multimedia technologies.

Windows 98 SE Is an Operating System

Unlike games and business programs, Windows is a special type of program called an *operating system*. (That's pronounced with the emphasis on the "op", as in *OP-erating system*). The letters *OS* are its abbreviation. Two things make an operating system different from the other kinds of programs lining the shelves of your local Nerds-Are-Us or other computer store:

▶ The operating system doesn't let you do a specific job, such as write or draw pictures. Rather, it makes it so that you can *operate* the computer to get to the programs that allow you to do those jobs.

▶ Although *application programs* (such as games, business programs, and so on) are optional, every PC *must* have an operating system in order to function. It's mandatory.

Windows 98 SE isn't the only operating system on the market. You may have heard of some of the others, such as DOS, Unix, or Mac OS for the Mac. Though not the only OS, Windows is certainly the most popular operating system for that class of computers we call the PC.

Windows 98 SE Is Home Base

The term *newbie* applies to someone who is just starting to learn something new, such as Windows. I've sat next to many a newbie who's trying to work a PC without having a clue as to what they're doing. It's not a pretty sight. They tend to ask questions—directed at no one in particular—as they stare at the screen with a puzzled expression:

▶ What did I just do?

▶ Where am I?

▶ How did I get here?

▶ How do I get back?

A few minutes of that is enough to turn anyone away from computers. This is too bad, because if you have at least some clue as to what you're supposed to do, it's easy. Once you realize that the Windows 98 SE Desktop is your home base and always at your beck and call, you need never feel lost or intimidated again.

Windows 98 SE Skills Are PC Skills

All Windows programs follow a standard set of rules that define how users (people like you) interact with their computers. This standardization among programs is great news because it means that the skills you acquire while learning Windows 98 SE will apply *to virtually every program you ever run on your PC*. As a simple example, in Windows you can press the F1 key at any time to get help. When you start using some other program, you can rest assured that pressing F1 will bring up help for that particular program. You don't have to go digging through the program's manual trying to find out how to get to its help screens.

WHY IT'S CALLED WINDOWS

Back when Windows was quite new, I was having a conversation with a couple of people, one of whom mentioned that he had gotten Windows for his computer. When that guy left, the other person in the conversation looked at me with a puzzled expression and asked, "What are windows, and why would you want them on a computer?" In my mind, I pictured little curtained windows on the sides of peoples' monitors. Maybe he did too.

Anyway, the question should be, What *is* Windows? And we know the answer to that now. Microsoft Windows (with a capital *W*) is an operating system for PCs. Understanding *how* Windows got its name might help explain why someone would want it on their PC.

In the olden days, most computers would run only one program at a time. You would start the program, and it would take over the entire screen. Before you could use some other program, you'd have to close the one you were in. The next program would then hog up the entire screen like the first one did. There was no way to have two programs on the screen at once.

This got to be a drag when people realized they might want to combine stuff from different programs. For example, suppose you typed up a magazine article in your word-processing program. You also had some digital photos that you wanted to add to the article and a graphics program that let you display and retouch those photos. Cool.

The problem was that getting the picture out of the graphics program and into your magazine article would be like trying to pull teeth from an irate emu. If not outright impossible, it took considerable experience to make it happen.

Windows changed it all. Instead of letting each individual program devour the entire screen, Windows made each program run in its own little *window* on the screen. And you could have as many of those *windows* on the screen as you liked.

So a window, then, is just a box on the screen that displays a program. No curtains. Each window sits on top of the Desktop, like sheets of paper on your real (wooden) desktop. You can even stack them up and shuffle them around like sheets of paper on a real desktop.

In Figure 1.2, I'm running two programs on the Windows 98 SE Desktop, each in its own window. One program is called WordPad, a mini word-processing program used for typing. The other program is named Kodak Imaging, and it's used to display and work with pictures.

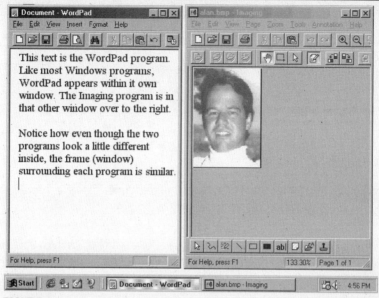

FIGURE 1.2:   Most Windows programs run inside a small window on the screen.

So that's how Windows got its name. Windows allowed you to run more than one program at a time, each in its own little *window* on the screen. For future reference, when you see *Windows* with a capital *W*, I'm referring to the program named Windows. When you see *windows* with a lowercase *w*, I'm referring to two or more programs, each in its own window, on the Desktop.

Cut-and-Paste

Along with the ability to have two or more windows on the screen at a time, Windows took care of the irate emu problem as well. No longer would you have to jump through technological flaming hoops to get your photos into your typed document. Instead, you could do it naturally—by *copying* the photo from the graphics program and then *pasting* it into the word-processing program. For example, in Figure 1.3 I copied the picture from the Imaging program into my typed WordPad document.

The procedure described is commonly referred to as *cut-and-paste*. But we're getting way ahead of ourselves. Before you can start doing all that fancy stuff, you have to be able to turn the darn computer on and get to your Windows 98 SE Desktop. And before you do that, you might want to learn a little about your PC and what all that stuff attached to it is for.

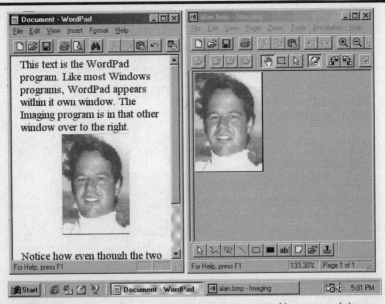

FIGURE 1.3: A photo from my imaging program pasted into a typed document

HARDWARE AND SOFTWARE

To really understand what Windows does for you, it helps to understand a little bit about how that mess of plastic and wires we call a PC works. If you're new to computers and don't know a megabyte from a philodendron, you'd do well to give yourself a crash course in computer fundamentals. Not only will this give you some perspective, but it will take away some of the intimidation caused by the techno terms you'll inevitably come across. You'll also be able to impress people when the cocktail party chit-chat turns to (yawn) computer stuff.

A complete computer system consists of some *hardware* and some *software*. The software is the invisible stuff that makes the computer hardware do what you want it to do. All programs, including Windows 98 SE, are software. Pretty much everything else—the stuff you can actually see and rap your knuckles against—is hardware.

The main components that make up a typical PC are the system unit, monitor, keyboard, and mouse. In a desktop PC, these various components are separate, and all plug into the large *system unit,* as shown in Figure 1.4. A laptop computer contains all the same components, but they're all combined into a single, portable unit.

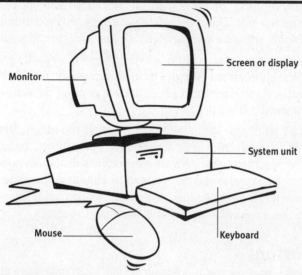

Monitor

Screen or display

System unit

Mouse

Keyboard

FIGURE 1.4: The hardware components that make up a typical PC

Every component plays a particular role in helping you get your work done. Before you can really learn to use Windows, you need to know a little about each of those components.

The Monitor

The PC's *monitor* is the part that looks like a TV. It's there so you can see what the heck you're doing. Many monitors have their own on/off switch; that switch must be on for the monitor to work. Most monitors also have Brightness and Contrast controls, like a TV. Many have additional controls that let you size and position the picture on the screen. You can use those to fine-tune the appearance of your screen at any time.

The part of the monitor that looks like a TV screen is, amazingly enough, called the *screen* or *display*. The screen is your "virtual desktop," where you do all your work. Every time you do something with the mouse or keyboard, the screen provides some feedback. Learning to keep your eyes on the screen is an important part of learning to use a PC.

The Mouse

Old-fashioned computer operating systems such as DOS and Unix used what's called a *command-line interface*. In order to get something done, you had to type some weird, cryptic command such as **DIR *.exe /p**, and then press Enter to get a result. This was really a pain because if you didn't know the right command, you were completely stuck. Guessing would surely fail.

Today's operating systems, including Windows 98 SE, sport a *graphical user interface,* abbreviated GUI and pronounced *gooey.* A GUI provides a "point-and-shoot" interface in which options appear on the screen, and you choose the ones you want.

But you don't point and touch with your finger. If you had to do that, your arm would get really tired after a while. And you'd forever be squinting through the fingerprint smudges all over your screen. No, to point and shoot at the screen, you use the *mouse* or some similar *pointing device*, such as a trackball. These are simply devices that let you point to and activate things on the screen without actually touching the screen.

Mouse Buttons

The mouse is the most common pointing device. Most mice have at least two buttons on them. The button on the left is called the *primary mouse button,* or just the *mouse button.* That's the button you use most often when working with your PC. It's sort of the "Go" button.

 LEFT-HANDED REMARKS ABOUT MICE

If you're a lefty, you can reverse the mouse buttons so that the primary button is on the right side and the secondary button is on the left side. Then, when your left hand is resting on the mouse, your index finger naturally rests on the primary mouse button, as it does for right-handed people. To make the change, you'll need to use the Mouse icon in Control Panel. You'll learn more about Control Panel in Chapter 4. (The terms *right-click* and *click* remain the same, no matter which hand you use.)

The other button is called the *secondary mouse button,* or *right button*. You mainly use the secondary mouse button when you want to know what options are available for some doodad on the screen. The secondary mouse button is less aggressive than the primary mouse button. It doesn't shout, "Go!" Rather, it says, "Tell me more." You'll see some examples as we progress through this book.

TRACKBALLS AND TOUCHPADS

Technically, a mouse is a *pointing device*, so named because it allows you to point to items on the screen and click on them. Though a mouse is the most common pointing device, there are others. You can use a trackball or a touchpad rather than a mouse, if you prefer. These devices also have primary and secondary mouse buttons. If you have such a device, you'll probably be able to figure out which button is which by experimenting for a few minutes on your own. If you need help, you'll need to refer to the instructions that came with that particular device.

Using a mouse is simple but takes a little practice. First, be aware that you do not have to touch the mouse to the screen. Nor do you have to pick up the mouse and aim it at the screen like a ray gun. (I've seen people try both approaches.) Instead, leave the mouse sitting on your desktop. Or better yet, leave it on a *mouse pad,* which is a piece of rubber that gives the mouse wheel some traction. Then, rest your right hand comfortably on the mouse, with your index finger resting on the left mouse button, as shown in Figure 1.5.

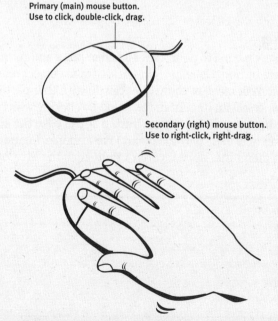

Primary (main) mouse button.
Use to click, double-click, drag.

Secondary (right) mouse button.
Use to right-click, right-drag.

FIGURE 1.5: How to hold a mouse

Pointing

To use the mouse, you roll it around on the mouse pad. A little *mouse pointer* on the screen moves in whatever direction you move the mouse. To *point* to something, rest the mouse pointer on it. The mouse pointer might change to a little pointing hand when it touches something that can be clicked on, but that's not important now. All you need to know is that the phrase *point to an object* generally means to rest your mouse pointer on that object.

Clicking

To *click* something (or *click on* something), press and release the primary mouse button without moving the mouse. The idea is to keep your hand still and relaxed and give the primary mouse button a gentle click with your index finger. Exactly what happens when you click an object on the screen depends on the object, as you'll learn.

WARNING

It's important to keep your hand relaxed on the mouse. I've seen people so tense that when they click the mouse button, the whole mouse moves, and they end up clicking on something other than they intended. The result is total confusion!

Right-Clicking

To *right-click* an object means to point to it and then press and release the secondary mouse button. Usually, right-clicking some object on the screen displays a *shortcut menu* of things you can do with that particular object. You can then select an item from the menu by clicking whichever option you want using the primary mouse button again. (Use the secondary mouse button only to display the menu.) For example, Figure 1.6 shows the shortcut menu that appears after I right-click the My Computer icon.

FIGURE 1.6: Right-clicking an object displays that object's shortcut menu.

As you'll learn, the shortcut menu that appears when you right-click an object is a useful tool. It gives you a quick idea of the different things you can do with that object. It also provides access to the object's *properties*, or *characteristics*. Things like size and color, for example, are properties. You can usually change an object's properties simply by right-clicking that object and choosing Properties from the shortcut menu that appears.

TIP

It may help to think of the primary (left) mouse button as the "do something" button, and the secondary mouse button as the "tell me more" button.

There are still other things you can do with the mouse and plenty of buzzwords to describe. To get you started, here are some basic terms:

Drag   To point to something and hold down the primary mouse button while you move the mouse.

Right-drag   To point to something and hold down the secondary mouse button while you move the mouse.

Drop   To release the mouse button after dragging an item.

Mouse Wheel

Some mice have a wheel in the middle. When working with a lengthy list that sports *scroll bars* (discussed in Chapter 4), you can spin the wheel to scroll up and down through the text. You can also use the mouse wheel as a third mouse button. To determine what happens when you click the mouse wheel, you need to check, and possibly change, your mouse settings. You can do that via the Mouse icon in Control Panel. (See Chapter 4 for information about Control Panel.)

The Keyboard

The *keyboard* is the thing that looks like a typewriter keyboard. Like the mouse, it's a means of interacting with your PC. But unlike the mouse, the keyboard is there mainly so you can type, if and when you ever need to type. A few special keys on the computer keyboard let you "do things" beyond typing letters and numbers. The locations of those keys are shown in Figure 1.7, and a brief description of what each key does follows. Don't worry about memorizing the function of every key right this minute. I'll tell you when something important comes along. For now, familiarize yourself with the locations of the keys, and remember that when pressed, these keys don't type anything on the screen. Instead, they make the computer *do* something.

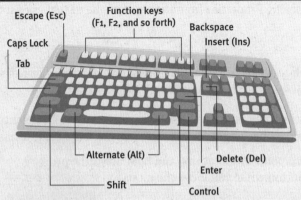

FIGURE 1.7: Special keys on a computer keyboard

Function keys   The function keys labeled F1 through F10 or F12 all provide some special service. The F1 key is usually the key to press when you need help. Other keys' functions vary from program to program.

Esc (Escape)   As the name implies, this key lets you "escape" from unfamiliar territory into more familiar territory on your screen. My motto is "If in doubt, Escape key out."

Tab   This key is sometimes shown with two opposing arrows. Tab lets you move from one option to the next in screens that present many options to choose from.

Ctrl (Control)   This key is used only in combination keystrokes (discussed shortly) to send certain commands to the computer.

Alt (Alternate)   Like Ctrl, this key is used in combination keystrokes to send special commands to the computer.

Shift   Generally, you hold this key down while typing to type uppercase letters or the punctuation marks above the numbers across the top of the keyboard.

Caps Lock   Press once, and every letter you type will be in uppercase. Press again, and all letters you type go back to lowercase.

Backspace   After typing something, pressing the Backspace key erases the letter you just typed.

TIP

Most keys on your keyboard are *typematic*, which means you have to hold the key down to repeat it. For example, to backspace through 20 characters, it's not necessary to press the Backspace key 20 times. Instead, you can simply hold down the Backspace key until the 20 characters are erased.

Enter   This key is used to end paragraphs when typing, but it can also be used as a means of completing commands typed at the keyboard. (This key is also called *Return* because it's where the Carriage Return key is on a typewriter.)

Ins (Insert)   When typing, the Insert key toggles between Insert and Overwrite modes. For example, suppose I've typed ABCDEFG, and I put the cursor after the C. If I type **XXX** in Insert mode, those letters are inserted, resulting in ABCXXXDEFG. In Overwrite mode, the new letters would *replace* the existing letters, resulting in ABCXXXG.

Del (Delete)   This key erases the character that's at the cursor position. (Backspace erases the character to the left of the cursor.)

Most keyboards also have some special groups of keys. Keyboards specifically designed for Windows (called *Windows Enhanced Keyboards* or *Windows Keyboards*) also sport a couple of extra keys named *Window* and *Application*. Figure 1.8 points out the groups of special keys and the Windows keyboard keys.

NOTE

Any keyboard will work with Windows—you don't need to own a Windows keyboard. The extra Windows and Application keys on the Windows keyboard are handy, though certainly not necessary.

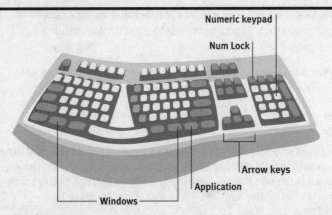

FIGURE 1.8: Groups of special keys are available on some keyboards.

Arrow keys   These keys let you move the *cursor* around when you're typing and editing text. The cursor is *not* the same as the mouse pointer!

Numeric keypad   This section of the keyboard has numbers and math symbols (+, -, /, and *, the last for multiplication) arranged like an adding machine's, for those of you who are familiar with adding machines. The numeric keypad works only when the Num Lock key is turned on. When the Num Lock key is off, the numeric keypad's keys act as arrow keys.

Num Lock   This key allows the numeric keypad's keys to function either as arrow keys or as numeric keys on an adding machine.

Windows   This key is only on Windows keyboards. When pressed, it displays the Windows Start menu. Like Ctrl and Alt, the Windows key can also be used in combination keystrokes (discussed shortly).

Application   The Application key is available only on Windows keyboards. Its function varies from program to program.

Combination Keystrokes (*key* + *key*)

Unlike regular typewriters, computers also support *combination keystrokes* in which you hold down one key while pressing another to tell the computer to do something. Combination keystrokes are written using this format:

key + *key*

Part i

To type such a keystroke, you hold down the first *key,* tap (press and release) the second key, and then release the first key. For example, the instruction to "press Alt+F4" means "Hold down the Alt key, press and release the F4 function key, and then release the Alt key."

Most combination keystrokes duplicate things you can do with your mouse—the idea being that if you happen to be typing up a storm and need to issue some command, you can do so without taking your hands off the keyboard. People who can *really* type appreciate this feature because they can leave their fingers on the home keys at all times.

Some examples of combination keystrokes and the jobs they perform are listed in Table 1.1. However, they're presented only as examples to give you a sense of what I'm talking about. You don't need to memorize those keys right now. In fact, you may never need to use them.

TABLE 1.1: Examples of Combination Keystrokes and Their Functions

COMBO KEYSTROKE	FUNCTION
Alt+F4	Close current window
Alt+Tab	Display a list of running programs
Ctrl+S	Save your work
Ctrl+O	Open previously saved work
Ctrl+Alt+Delete	Get unstuck
Ctrl+Escape	Display the Start menu

PRESS VS. CLICK

It's become standard practice in the computer industry to use the word *press* when referring to something you do on the keyboard. For example, "press Enter" means to press and release the Enter key on the keyboard. The word *click* always refers to something you do with the mouse, as opposed to the keyboard. So...

▶ When you see the instruction to *press* something, think *keyboard.*

▶ When you see the instruction to *click* something, think *mouse.*

The System Unit

The *system unit* houses all the stuff that does the actual work taking place on your screen. In fact, the system unit *is* the computer. The rest of the stuff that's attached to it with cables—monitor, keyboard, mouse, and so on—are *peripheral devices* (also called *peripherals*). In addition to those plug-in components, the system unit has a few important components of its own built in.

The Floppy Disk Drive(s)

Most computers have at least one *floppy disk drive*, usually placed right on the front of the computer. That drive is used to read stuff from and write stuff to 3.5-inch floppy disks (sometimes called *floppies*). As a rule, you only use floppy disks to copy stuff from one computer to another. Occasionally, new programs you buy will be stored on floppy disks. To use such a program, you first *install* that program from those floppy disks.

To insert a floppy disk into the floppy disk drive, hold the disk with the label pointing up and the sliding metal door facing the computer. Push the disk in until it clicks into place. To remove a floppy disk, press the little Eject button on the drive door, shown in Figure 1.9.

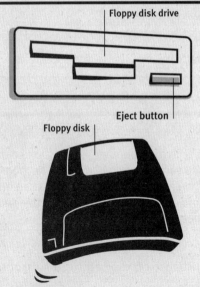

Floppy disk drive

Eject button

Floppy disk

FIGURE 1.9:   A floppy disk and floppy disk drive

Most of the time, you'll leave the floppy disk drive empty. As a rule, you need to remove any floppy disks from that drive before starting your computer. Otherwise, the PC won't start correctly.

If you're wondering why it's called a floppy disk, it's because the actual disk inside the plastic case is very thin and floppy. You never handle that little disk directly with your hands because if you did, you'd ruin it. The floppy part needs to stay inside its hard plastic shell to survive.

NOTE

Really old PCs use 5.25-inch floppy disks, which are rare these days. If your computer has a 5.25-inch floppy drive, you can have it swapped out for a 3.5-inch drive at any computer store.

The CD-ROM Drive

The *CD-ROM drive* is similar to a floppy drive in that it's used mainly to transport stuff from one computer to the next. Many software manufacturers use CD-ROMs, rather than floppies, to deliver their programs, because a single CD can hold as much information as 500 floppy disks. It is a lot cheaper to deliver a single CD than it is to deliver a big stack of floppy disks.

NOTE

Unlike floppy disks, which you can use to store files, a CD-ROM is *read-only*. This means you can copy stuff from the CD, but you cannot add new files to it nor change its contents in any way.

To use a CD, open the CD-ROM drive by pressing its Eject button. Lay the CD label (painted) side up in the drive. Then press the Eject button again, as shown in Figure 1.10, to close the door. You can also gently push the door shut, if you prefer.

Some CDs start automatically. After you insert a CD-ROM into its drive, you might want to wait half a minute or so before doing anything else. If some program doesn't appear on your screen after that time, you'll have to start the CD manually.

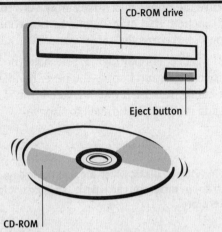

FIGURE 1.10: A CD-ROM and CD-ROM drive

The Hard Disk (or Fixed Disk)

The reason that you can leave your floppy and CD-ROM drives empty most of the time is because everything that's in your computer is actually stored on a *hard disk,* or *fixed disk,* hidden inside the system unit. Unlike floppy disks and CD-ROMs, which are *removable* media, the hard disk is nonremovable. You can't pop a hard disk out of its drive; you can't even see the hard disk because it needs to stay sealed in its own little drive inside the system unit.

NOTE

Some people think that the little 3.5-inch floppy disks are the hard disks because the disk is wrapped up inside a hard plastic shell. However, the term *hard disk* refers specifically to the disk inside the system unit, which you never actually see or handle directly.

Your PC's hard disk is really the "filing cabinet" of your PC. In a real office, you use a filing cabinet to store all the things you need, or *might* need, to do your job. When you want to work with a file, you pull it out of the filing cabinet and take it to your desktop where you can work on it. When you've finished with that file for the time being, you put it back into the filing cabinet, where it's out of the way but can be easily found again in the future.

In a computer, your hard disk is your filing cabinet, where you keep stuff you need, or might need, to do your work. When you create and save something on a PC, that item is saved in a *file* on the hard disk. Should you want to see or work on it in the future, you yank a copy off the hard disk, just like a filing cabinet. Exactly *how* you go about doing that is something you'll learn in this part of the book. But rest assured that it's not nearly as difficult or scary as it sounds.

Every program that you use (including Windows 98 SE) and every new program that you purchase and install is stored on that same hard disk. Whenever someone refers to something that's "in the computer," they're actually referring to something that's stored on the hard disk inside the system unit.

Random Access Memory (RAM)

Random Access Memory (*RAM* for short) is the electronic equivalent of your desktop. Whereas all the stuff you might need is filed away on the hard disk, RAM stores only the stuff you are working on right now. In a sense, your screen is a reflection of what's stored in RAM at the moment.

You might wonder, if everything is already stored on the hard disk, why do you need a separate area for stuff you're working on right now? Good question, and there are several answers. The simple, nontechnical answer is that this approach resembles how we do things in real life. We use one medium (a filing cabinet or hard disk) to store stuff we may need access to in the future. We use another medium (our desk or RAM in a computer) to store the stuff we are working on right now.

The technical reasons for why things are done this way are several. RAM is great for doing work because it's very fast. There are a couple of downsides to RAM, however:

► RAM is expensive.

► RAM is volatile, meaning that it loses its memory when it loses power.

The fact that RAM is expensive encourages us not to put too much of it into a PC: it keeps the cost down. However, the main problem is that RAM is volatile. RAM needs electricity to store information. The moment the electricity goes, everything stored in RAM exists no more. Poof! Gone in the blinking of a eye. This is not a good type of memory to use for long-term storage, like a file cabinet.

Disk memory, on the other hand, is magnetic and doesn't need electricity to keep its memory. Pulling the plug makes the disk stop spinning, but the information on the disk remains unharmed, which makes it a good filing cabinet. In addition, disk storage is much cheaper than RAM, so you can have lots and lots of it without driving up the cost of the PC significantly.

Megs, Gigabytes, and All That

There are units of measure, such as ounces, quarts, and gallons, to describe how much stuff RAM and disks can store. The single unit of measure is a *byte,* which is the amount of storage it takes to store one character, such as the letter *c* or *j*. For example, to store the word *Hello* in a computer requires five bytes, one byte for each letter.

Most computers can store thousands, millions, even billions of characters (bytes). The buzzwords that describe these units of measurement are listed in Table 1.2.

TABLE 1.2: Units of Measure for Computer Information Storage

WORD	ABBREVIATION	PRONUNCIATION	APPROXIMATE CHARACTERS
Byte	B	*bite*	1
Kilobyte	K or KB	*kay*	1,000
Megabyte	M or MB	*meg*	1,000,000
Gigabyte	G or GB	*gig*	1,000,000,000

The CPU

Whereas RAM and disks *store* information, the *central processing unit* (*CPU*) does the actual work of making things happen. Other names for this little gizmo include the *microprocessor,* the *processor,* or just the *chip.* Like the hard disk and RAM, the CPU can't be seen because it's inside the system unit. But it's always there doing its thing. Some popular brand-name microprocessors for today's PCs include the Pentium, Pentium II, and Celeron, all manufactured by Intel Corporation, and the K6, manufactured by AMD.

TIP

Some people call the system unit the CPU. However, that's not the correct term. The CPU, like the disk drives and RAM, is contained *within* the system unit.

Because the processor does work (not store information), we measure its abilities by the speed at which it can perform that work. The unit of measure is *MHz* (*megahertz*). Suffice it to say, the higher the number, the faster (and more expensive) the processor. For example, a 400MHz Pentium chip can do the same job a 200MHz Pentium chip can do, but in half the time (or twice as fast). So a job that takes 10 seconds for a 200MHz chip to do could be done by a 400MHz chip in only 5 seconds. (Wow, you get to save a whole 5 seconds!)

WHAT WINDOWS 98 SE NEEDS

Most software products, including Windows, can only perform on PCs that meet certain hardware requirements. As a rule, though, any computer that can run Windows 98 SE can probably run about any other program you put on that machine. Table 1.3 lists the minimum hardware requirements needed to run Windows 98 SE. The Suggested column indicates values that will give you better performance than the minimum requirements.

TABLE 1.3: Windows 98 SE Minimum and Suggested Hardware Requirements

COMPONENT	MINIMUM	SUGGESTED
Processor	486DX at 66MHz	Pentium, Celeron, or K6 at 200+ MHz
RAM	24MB	32MB
Disk Storage	210–400MB, depending on system configuration and installed options	1.5GB or more

HOW IT ALL WORKS

When you start your computer, it does a little self-testing, and then it goes out to the hard disk to see whether it can find an operating system. If it finds an operating system, it loads it (or a significant portion of it) into RAM. Whatever is in RAM gets to bark orders at the CPU, telling it what to do. So at first, Windows gets to bark the orders.

Let's say that you, sitting at the computer, do some clicking to run a program. Windows will go to the hard disk, find the requested program, and load a copy into RAM. Once in RAM, *that* program can also tell the CPU what to do. If you start yet another program, that program also gets squeezed into RAM, and it too gets to boss the CPU around. Whichever program you happen to be using at the moment usually gets top priority. Ultimately, you're the one who's actually deciding which program gets its CPU processing needs attended to first.

Storing just the programs you're using at the moment in RAM explains why one PC can do a ton of seemingly unrelated tasks—manage your business, teach toddlers their ABCs, let teens play Alien Angst across the Internet, and more. It's all because the PC really doesn't do *anything* by itself. It does whatever the program currently in RAM tells it to do.

OPTIONAL GOODIES

If you've ever been in a computer store, you probably know that there's a lot more than mouse, monitor, and keyboard to plug into a PC. Other optional equipment that you can purchase and install includes:

Printer   Makes a printed paper copy of anything you can see on your screen.

Modem   Makes it possible to connect to other computers and/or the Internet via a telephone line. Internet access also requires an account with an Internet Service Provider (ISP).

Sound card   A sound card adds audio capabilities to your computer. Although not absolutely necessary, a sound card does make computing more fun and interesting.

Zip drive   Similar to a floppy disk, but it holds as much information as *hundreds* of floppy disks.

Digital camera Lets you take pictures without film and view, edit, and print them from your PC.

Joystick These are devices used to play certain kinds of games only. You can't do much of anything in Windows via a joystick.

NOTE

Some of this stuff may have come with your computer when you bought it.

There you have it—enough information and buzzwords about PCs to tread into the real hands-on world of Windows. You may also know enough to hold your own at a computer store or cocktail party.

WHAT'S NEXT?

This chapter has not told you everything there is to know about a PC (that would take a library of books), but it has told you everything you *need* to know to get started using your computer. In the next chapter, Alan Simpson continues to build on this information with an introduction to Windows 98 SE. Chapter 2 is a hands-on approach, and if you are at your computer and have Windows 98 SE installed, you can follow along as you use Windows.

Chapter 2

INTRODUCING WINDOWS

Now that you know what Windows is and what the various gizmos that make up your PC are for, you can start learning how to use Windows. In this chapter, you'll learn how to start Windows 98 SE on your PC. Then, you'll learn what all the various doodads on the screen are about and how to use them. Many of the skills you learn in this chapter will apply not only to Windows but also to the vast majority of programs that you'll use on your PC. In fact, what you'll really be learning here is how to use a PC! If you have Windows 98 SE installed on your computer, you can follow along at your computer. If you have not installed Windows 98 SE, you might want to do so and then go through this chapter. (See Chapter 3 for information on how to install Windows 98 SE.)

Adapted from *Windows 98 to Go*
by Alan Simpson
ISBN 0-7821-2493-3   258 pages $6.99

How to Start Windows 98 SE

Windows 98 SE starts automatically whenever you first turn on your PC. Well, let me clarify that. When you first turn on your PC, it does some self-testing to make sure everything is in place. Then, it *loads* the Windows 98 SE program from your hard disk into RAM and displays the Windows 98 SE Desktop on your screen. This process of automatically loading the operating system at start-up is called *booting up*. Anyway, here are the exact steps to follow to fire up your PC and start Windows 98 SE:

1. First, make sure both the floppy disk drive and the CD-ROM drive are empty. (Press the little Eject button on the front of each drive, and if any disks pop out, remove them). This step ensures that the computer will boot from the internal hard disk on which Windows 98 SE is stored.

2. Turn on any devices that are attached to the computer, such as your monitor, printer, modem, and anything else that has its own on/off switch.

3. Turn on the main power switch. This will be on the system unit.

4. Wait as the computer goes through its self-test phase. You can ignore the techno-babble that appears on the screen during this time.

5. It might take a minute or more, but eventually you'll start seeing Windows appear on the screen.

Exactly what happens next depends on how your computer is configured. The sections that follow cover some of the possibilities.

Entering a Password

If your computer is brand new, is set up to accommodate multiple users, or is connected to other computers in a network, the first thing you'll see as Windows starts up is a *dialog box* asking for a user name and password. (A dialog box is a little box that appears on the screen that asks for information.)

At this point, you have two main choices:

▶ If this is your personal computer, there's no need to enter a password. Click the OK button or press the Enter key on your keyboard to proceed.

▶ If this computer is at work and someone there gave you a user name and password, you should type those in now. If you have any trouble doing that, ask someone at work to help you. Press Enter or click the OK button to proceed.

Hey, I Didn't Type ****

Be aware that when you type a password, you can't see the actual letters you type. Each character you type appears as an asterisk (*). For example, if your password is *sesame,* when you type it on the screen, it will appear as ******. This is to keep people from looking over your shoulder and discovering your password.

Case-Sensitivity

You also need to be aware that passwords are *case-sensitive,* which means that uppercase letters and lowercase letters are *not* considered the same. For example, if your password is *sesame* (all lowercase letters) and you type *Sesame* or *SESAME* as your password, you will not be allowed onto the computer. Only *sesame,* typed in all lowercase letters, will work. (Because you can't see the letters you're typing, this is tricky.) Unless your password is in all uppercase letters, you want to make sure the Caps Lock key is off before you type your password.

TIP

When the Caps Lock key is on, every letter you type will be in UPPERCASE. The Shift key works in reverse with letters. Holding down the Shift key while typing a letter displays that letter in lowercase. Numbers and punctuation marks are not affected by the Caps Lock.

The Windows 98 SE Desktop

Once you get past the password dialog box, you'll be taken to the Windows 98 SE Desktop. Depending on how your computer is configured, you might also see a Welcome to Windows screen, as in Figure 2.1.

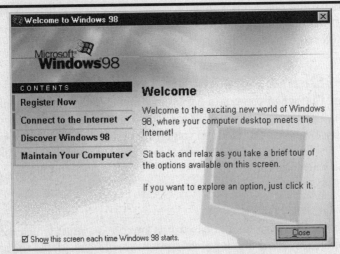

FIGURE 2.1: The Windows 98 SE Welcome window

Clean Up Your Act

One of the first things you'll want to learn is how to keep your Desktop organized and uncluttered. You can start by learning how to close windows (programs) that you're not using at the moment. The procedure is simple: click the Close (X) button near the upper-right corner of the object you want to close, as illustrated below.

When you close something, it goes back to the file cabinet from which it came (your hard disk), thereby leaving room for other projects on your Desktop. For example, Figure 2.2 shows the Windows 98 SE Desktop after closing the Welcome to Windows screen that appeared automatically at start-up. To close the Welcome screen, I clicked the X button in its upper-right corner. What remains on the screen is called the Windows 98 Desktop. The items pointed out in Figure 2.2 are described below.

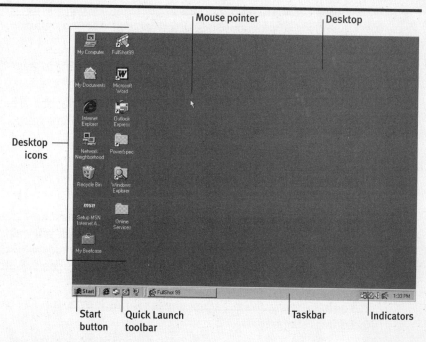

FIGURE 2.2: The Windows 98 SE Desktop

Desktop The large background area is the Windows 98 SE Desktop. Everything else on the screen lies "on top" of the Desktop, like a piece of paper atop a normal wooden desktop.

Mouse pointer The little arrow that moves in whatever direction you move the mouse.

Desktop icons The little pictures on the Desktop are called *icons*. Each represents a program you can run. When you *open* an icon, its contents are displayed in a *window*. To open an icon, you click or double-click it, depending on which navigation style you choose, as discussed later in this chapter.

Taskbar Similar to the top drawer in your desk, the Taskbar is a handy place to store stuff you use often. You'll learn how to do that a little later in this chapter.

Start button An easy way to start any task on the PC—just click the Start button.

Quick Launch Toolbar This toolbar shows icons for frequently used programs so that you can start those programs with a single mouse-click.

Indicators These show the current time, according to your PC's internal clock, and perhaps some icons.

If anything is missing from your screen, don't worry about it. The Windows Desktop is flexible, and you have a lot of leeway in how you go about setting it up.

USING THE START BUTTON

To get your PC to do something, you generally start whatever program is best suited to the job you want to perform. For example, if you want to type up and print a letter, a word-processing program would be best. To work with photos or other graphic images, a graphics program would be best.

The simplest way to start a program is via the Start menu. The basic procedure is simple:

1. Click the Start button near the lower-left edge of the screen.

2. Click whichever option you want. Keep doing so until you find the item you want, and click it.

If you look closely at the Start menu, you might notice that some options have a little right-pointing triangle to the right. Those options lead to a submenu rather than to a specific program. If the option has a right-pointing triangle next to it, a submenu follows. To view a submenu, you don't have to click the Menu option. You can point to it instead. For example, in Figure 2.3, I clicked the Start button and then pointed to Settings to display the Settings submenu.

Any and all programs that are installed on your PC are available from the Programs option on the Start menu. Finding a program and starting it is simply a matter of looking through the options available from the Programs submenu until you find the option to start the program you want.

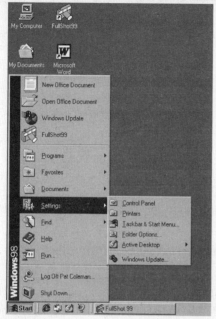

FIGURE 2.3: The arrow points to the Settings submenu.

Using the Start Menu from the Keyboard

If you prefer to use the keyboard instead of the mouse (perhaps because you're an awesome typist and hate to take your hands off the keyboard), you can open the Start menu by pressing Ctrl+Escape. If you have a Windows-style keyboard, you can press the Windows key (the one with the flying windows on it) to open the Start menu. Once the menu is open, you can move the selection highlight around by using the arrow keys. To select the currently highlighted option, press the Enter key.

Bailing Out of Menus

If you ever get befuddled while going through the menus and want to go back to square one, you can click some neutral area outside the menu. (By "neutral area," I mean some empty spot on the Desktop.) You can also press the trusty Escape (Esc) key to back out of the current menu, or tap the Alt key to bail out of all the menus.

TIP

The Escape (Esc) key is the universal "get me out of here" key. If you can remember the saying "When in doubt, Escape key out," you'll find it easier to back out of any unfamiliar territory that you happen to land in.

Menu Sequences

In many computer books, including this one, it's customary to use a sort of shorthand notation for describing a series of menu selections. For example, rather than saying, "Click the Start button, then point to Programs on the Start menu, then point to Accessories, and then click the WordPad option," the shorthand notation might look something like this:

Choose Start ➤ Programs ➤ Accessories ➤ WordPad

You can use whichever method you want to make the selections. For example, you can click the Start button, point to Programs, point to Accessories, and then click WordPad. You can also use the keyboard to open the Start menu and work your way through the series of menu options.

ALL ABOUT ICONS

As I mentioned earlier, the little pictures on the Desktop and down in the Taskbar are called *icons*. Each represents some program that you can open. Many of the same programs are also available from the menus. The little icons on the Desktop and Taskbar are there for convenience. They provide easy one-click access to frequently used programs so that you don't have to go through a series of menus. As you'll learn later in this chapter, you can easily decide for yourself which programs you use most frequently and which ones you want quick one-click access to.

The icons on the Taskbar (see the "Using the Taskbar" section later in this chapter) have little hidden *ToolTips* (also called *pop-up descriptions*) that provide a bit more information about what the icon has to offer. To see a ToolTip, rest your mouse pointer on that icon for a couple of seconds. That ToolTip will appear right at the mouse pointer.

NOTE

If none of your icons display ToolTips, it's probably because that feature is turned off on your PC. No big deal. You can turn that feature back on via the Show Pop-up Description For Folder And Desktop Items option in the Folder Options dialog box. We'll discuss that dialog box under "To Click or Double-Click?" later in this chapter.

Arranging Icons

If your icons get spread randomly about the Desktop, you can put them into nice, neat rows again by following these simple instructions:

1. Right-click the Windows 98 SE Desktop (not on an icon, just the Desktop.)

2. From the shortcut menu that appears, choose Arrange Icons ➤ By Name.

The icons will arrange themselves neatly, though not quite in alphabetic order as the option "By Name" implies. Permanent icons such as My Computer and Recycle Bin never change their positions when you choose this command, although you can move them manually by dragging them.

Opening Icons

I wish I could say, "To open an icon, just click it." However, it's not quite that simple. In the early days of Windows, you had to double-click icons to open them. Now you have a choice. You can use "Classic Windows"-style navigation and double-click icons to open them, or you can switch to Web view and open any icon by clicking it once. This style of navigation is patterned after the World Wide Web on the Internet, where a single click is all it ever takes—hence the name "Web view."

To Click or Double-Click?

If you're accustomed to older versions of Windows, you might want to continue to use the Classic navigation style, because that's what you're accustomed to. If you're a beginner or an experienced user who's tired of double-clicking, you'll probably want to use the simpler Web view. To choose one or the other, you need to get to the Folder Options dialog box and make your selections. Here's how:

1. Choose Start ➢ Settings ➢ Folder Options. The Folder Options dialog box appears as shown in Figure 2.4.

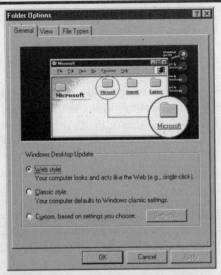

FIGURE 2.4: The Folder Options dialog box

2. Choose which navigation style you want by clicking the little round button next to that option. For example, in the figure I've chosen Web Style.

3. After making your selection, click the OK button.

The dialog box closes, and you're returned to the Desktop. When you're sitting at any computer, it's really easy to tell if that computer is set up for Classic or Web style navigation:

▶ If you point to an icon and the mouse pointer changes to a little pointing hand, as shown on the left in Figure 2.5, you can single-click that icon to open it.

FIGURE 2.5: The mouse pointer on an icon in Web view (left) and Classic view (right)

▶ If you point to an icon and the mouse pointer doesn't change, as on the right side of the picture, you need to double-click to open that icon.

Regardless of whether you're using Classic- or Web-style navigation, you can always right-click an icon and choose Open from the shortcut menu to open it. As I mentioned, right-clicking the icon will also show you other things you can do with that icon.

NOTE

Some people think that "Web view" means that their computer is somehow connected to the Internet's World Wide Web. Not true. Web view simply means that icons on the Windows 98 SE Desktop look and act like links in Web pages. You can use Web view whether or not you have Internet access from your PC.

What Happens When You Open an Icon

Opening an icon by clicking or double-clicking almost always produces the same result—something opens up on the screen in its own *window*. For example, clicking the My Computer icon opens the window shown in Figure 2.6.

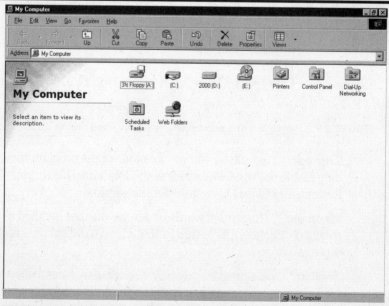

FIGURE 2.6: Results of opening the My Computer icon

It's more important to pay attention to the frame and other stuff surrounding that window. You want to learn about that frame because virtually every program you ever run will appear inside a frame that's similar to My Computer's frame. That frame gives you all the tools you need to size and position the window and much more.

Managing Open Windows

As I've mentioned, almost every program that you run will appear on the Desktop in its own window. If you ignore the specific program being displayed inside the window, you'll notice that the windows surrounding these programs all have the elements shown in the mostly empty window (see Figure 2.7). The items labeled in this figure are described below.

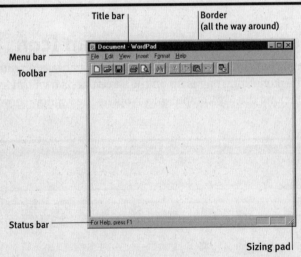

FIGURE 2.7: Elements that are common to most windows

Title bar   The title bar shows the name of the program running inside the window, as well as the Minimize, Maximize, Restore, and Close (X) buttons for the window.

Menu bar   The strip of words under the title bar is called a *menu bar*. Clicking any option in that menu bar displays a dropdown menu.

Toolbar   Some programs display a series of pictures, called a *toolbar*, under the menu bar. Icons on the toolbar provide quick, one-click access to frequently used menu options.

Border   The border around a window not only makes a nice visual frame, but it also lets you size the window. To size a window, drag any border.

Sizing pad   If you have a tough time sizing a window from its border, you can drag the window's sizing pad instead.

Status bar   The gray strip along the bottom of a window is the status bar. This bar displays information from the program that's contained within the window.

In Windows, you can have as many programs open as you like. Each of them will occupy a window on the screen. To keep your screen from getting disorganized, you can use various tools on each window's border to size and position the window, as I'll discuss in a moment.

Every program that you open will also display its own button in the Taskbar at the bottom of the screen. For example, in Figure 2.8, two program windows are open, one named Imaging, the other named WordPad. You can see a button for each in the Taskbar. In addition, you'll see a button for FullShot 99, the program I used to capture screens for this book. FullShot is open but is running in its minimized state.

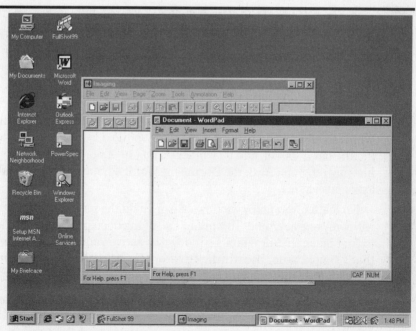

FIGURE 2.8: Two windows open on the Desktop

WANNA TRY?

If you happen to be sitting at a computer and would like to try out some of the techniques described here, you can open WordPad and Imaging right now. To start Imaging, click the Start button and choose Programs ➤ Accessories ➤ Imaging. Then click the Start button again and choose Programs ➤ Accessories ➤ WordPad.

The Active Window

If only one window is open on the Windows 98 SE Desktop, that window is, by nature, the *active window*. When several windows are open on the Desktop, only one of them is the active window. The program in the active window is the only one that's capable of accepting input from the keyboard. (If *all* open windows could accept keyboard input at the same time, you'd end up typing the exact same thing into all open programs, which is generally *not* something you want to do.)

When multiple windows are open on the screen, it's easy to tell which one is the active window and is capable of accepting keyboard input:

▶ The title bar of the active window is colored differently than the title bars of inactive windows.

▶ If several windows are open and stacked up on the Desktop, the active window is always at the top of the stack.

▶ The Taskbar button for the active window looks pushed-in.

For example, looking back at Figure 2.8, which is displaying both WordPad and Imaging, you can see that WordPad is the active window. Its title bar is darker, and its window is on top of the window for the Imaging program. Also, the Document-WordPad button in the Taskbar looks pushed in.

No matter how many windows are open on the screen, you really work with only one at a time. To work in one of the open programs, you need to first make that program's window the active window. Fortunately, that's simple to do. Use whichever technique below happens to be most convenient at the moment:

▶ Click anywhere in the window that you want to make the active window.

▶ If that window is covered by other windows on the screen, click the window's Taskbar button.

▶ If you prefer to use the keyboard, hold down the Alt key and press the Tab key until the name of the program you want is framed, as in Figure 2.9. Then release both keys.

FIGURE 2.9:   Press Alt+Tab to switch among open programs.

No matter which approach you use, the specified window will instantly become the active window.

Sizing a Window

You can adjust the size of most windows to take up as much or as little space on the screen as you feel that program needs at the moment. One way to size a window is by using the buttons near the upper-right corner of the window's title bar, as shown below.

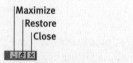

Buttons that appear in a maximized window

Buttons that appear in a nonmaximized window

Minimize   When clicked, this button makes the window occupy *no* space on the screen. Only the Taskbar button for that window remains. To bring the window out of hiding, you need to click its Taskbar button.

Maximize   Click the Maximize button to expand the window to full-screen size and make it the active window. The Maximize button is available only if the window is not already maximized.

Restore   When a window is maximized, the Maximize button is automatically changed into a Restore button. Clicking the Restore button puts back the maximized window to its previous size.

TIP

Here's a little trick you can use to maximize and restore a window without using the little buttons. Double-click the window's title bar to expand it to full-screen size or reduce it to its previous size.

Drag to Size

You can also size a window by dragging any border. If the window is maximized, you'll first need to shrink it a bit by restoring it to its unmaximized size. Then, follow these simple steps:

1.   Rest the mouse pointer on the window border. When positioned correctly, the mouse pointer turns into a two-headed arrow.

2.   Drag the mouse pointer in either direction indicated by the arrows to expand or shrink the window.

When the window frame (or ghost image of the window) is the size you want, release the mouse button. Couldn't be easier!

NOTE

The ghost image I refer to is just an empty frame that's the same size as the window you're moving. No, you won't see a little picture of a ghost!

Close vs. Minimize vs. Delete

Earlier I mentioned that you can minimize a window by clicking its Minimize button. When you *minimize* a window, the program in that window stays open, and the program itself remains in RAM. In a sense, you've taken the window (sheet of paper) off your desktop and tucked it into your desktop drawer (the Taskbar), where it's out of the way but not actually "filed away." To reopen the window, you have to click its Taskbar button.

When you *close* (rather than minimize) a window, you essentially put that whole thing back in the filing cabinet. Both the window itself and the Taskbar button disappear. The copy of the program that was in RAM is removed, making room for other programs. However, a copy of the program remains on the hard disk, so nothing is really lost. Because no Taskbar button remains though, the only way to reopen the window is by opening its icon or by going through the Start menu again.

WARNING

Some people are scared to death of computers because they fear that they'll inadvertently do something terrible that ruins other peoples' work or even the whole PC. This is not likely! Unless you purposefully go about deleting things that you don't recognize, it's impossible to cause any harm. There is no secret "Delete Everything" or "Blow Up The World" icon or keyboard key that you might accidentally click or press.

Do Not Delete

Finally, a word of caution. The term *delete* does not mean the same thing as "close" or "minimize." The term *delete* means to completely remove the item from your hard disk. The equivalent action in the real world would be to pull a file from your file cabinet and then burn it. Deleting something is generally not good unless you know exactly what it is you're deleting and what the effects of that deletion will be.

For now, be aware that before the computer lets you delete something, it almost always puts up a message on the screen asking, "Are you sure you want to delete *whatever*?" You can then decide if you really do want to delete the item.

Moving a Window

To move a window to some new location, you first need to make it the active window. Also, you have to make sure the window isn't maximized. Then, drag the window by its title bar to its new location on the screen, and drop it there. Here are the exact steps:

1. Click the title bar or Taskbar button of the window you want to move to make sure it's the active window. If the window you want to move is maximized, you can double-click the title bar to shrink the window to a moveable size.

2. With the mouse pointer still on the window's title bar, hold down the primary mouse button, and drag the window (or the ghost image of the window) in whatever direction you please.

3. When you've found a good location for the window, release the mouse button to drop it there.

Easy as can be!

Closing a Window

I mentioned earlier that you can close any open window by clicking the Close (X) button in the window's upper-right corner. You can also use a couple of other techniques:

- ▶ Right-click the window's Taskbar button, and choose Close.

- ▶ Press Alt+F4 to close the active window.

- ▶ Choose File ➤ Exit from the program's menu bar.

Moving, Sizing, and Closing with the Keyboard

Though the mouse is by far the easiest way to move, size, and close windows, you can also do all those activities right from the keyboard. First, remember that the keyboard keys affect only the active window. If the window you want to move, size, or close is not the active window, you'll need to click the window or its Taskbar button first or press Alt+Tab to make that window active. You can then use the techniques below to move, size, or close the active window from the keyboard:

1. Press Alt+spacebar to open the window's Control menu, which is shown in Figure 2.10.

FIGURE 2.10:   The active window's Control menu appears when you press Alt+spacebar.

2. Select an option from the menu by using the arrow keys to move the highlight. Press Enter when the highlight is on the option you want. What you do next depends on the option you chose from the menu:

- ▶ If you selected Close, the window closes and nothing else happens.

- ▶ If you selected Restore, Minimize, or Maximize, the window is sized accordingly and nothing else happens.

- ▶ If you selected Move, you can then position the window by pressing the arrow keys. Press Enter after you've found a good position.

- ▶ If you selected Size, you can then use the arrow keys to size the window. When the window is the size you want, press the Enter key.

But I Can't See the Title Bar!

It's sometimes possible to drag a window so far to the edge of the screen that you can no longer see its title bar. Don't worry; you can still operate that window. Here's how:

1. Right-click the window's Taskbar button, and choose Move.

2. Press the appropriate arrow key until the window's title bar is visible on the screen.

3. Click the mouse button to complete the movement.

As an alternative to that approach, you can cascade, tile, or open windows, as I'll discuss next.

QUICK SHUFFLES

If you do work with many open windows on your Desktop, here are some techniques that will further help you keep things organized.

Hide All Windows

The Show Desktop button in the Quick Launch toolbar hides all open windows on the Desktop, giving you a clear view of your Desktop again. (The icon is supposed to be a pen resting on a notepad, but it looks more like a paint brush without the aid of an electron microscope.) When you see that, you're supposed to think "Desktop." When you rest the mouse pointer on that button, the ScreenTip reads Show Desktop, as shown below.

Working the button is simple:

▶ To instantly hide all open windows on your Desktop, click the Show Desktop button.

▶ To bring those open windows back out of hiding, click the Show Desktop button a second time.

▶ Optionally, you can bring a single window out of hiding by clicking its Taskbar button.

Arrange All Open Windows

The Taskbar's shortcut menu also offers some options for arranging open windows on the Desktop. To use those options, you need to do the following:

1. Right-click some neutral area of the Taskbar (not on a button or icon). The shortcut menu shown below appears.

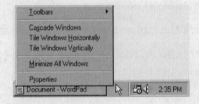

2. Choose whichever option best describes how you want to arrange the open windows on your Desktop. (The options will be available only if there are open windows on the Desktop.)

Cascade Windows   Stacks the windows like sheets of paper, with only their title bars showing. You can bring any window to the top of the stack by clicking its title bar.

Tile Windows Horizontally   Gives each window an equal amount of screen space, and tiles the windows horizontally so that they don't overlap.

Tile Windows Vertically   Gives each window an equal amount of screen space, and tiles the windows vertically so that they don't overlap.

Minimize All Windows   Hides all open windows; same as the Show Desktop button in the Quick Launch toolbar.

Undo Minimize All   Available only after choosing Minimize All Windows, this option brings all the windows back
out of hiding.

Working the Menu Bars

Many (though not all) programs have their own *menu bar,* which gives
you access to the features and capabilities of that particular program. As
a rule, a program's menu bar appears under its title bar. Each option has
an associated drop-down menu. To see a menu option's drop-down menu,
you can do either of the following:

▶ Click the menu bar option you want.

▶ If you prefer to use the keyboard, you can hold down the Alt key
and press the underlined letter.

For example, to open the WordPad File menu shown in Figure 2.11, you
could click File in the menu bar. Or, you could press Alt+F on the keyboard.

FIGURE 2.11:   A sample File drop-down menu

Once a drop-down menu is open, you can click whichever option you
want to select that option. When you do, the menus disappear, and the
requested option appears on the screen. If you prefer the keyboard, you
can use the arrow keys to move the highlight around the menus. When
the option you want is highlighted, press Enter to select that option.

TIP

If you get into some menus and can't find what you're looking for or you want
to bail out without making any selections, you can click some neutral area outside the menus. You can also press the Escape (Esc) key to close the menu without making a selection.

USING THE TASKBAR

The Taskbar is a handy tool that plays many roles in Windows. As I mentioned earlier, it maintains a button for each and every open window on the Desktop. You can make any window on the Desktop the active window simply by clicking its Taskbar button. The Taskbar is also home to the handy Start button, the Quick Launch toolbar, and various indicators, as shown in Figure 2.12.

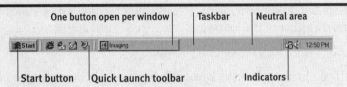

FIGURE 2.12:   The Windows 98 SE Taskbar

You can size, position, and display the Taskbar in many ways. As a beginner, you'll want to keep the Taskbar visible somewhere on the Desktop. Let's take a look at how you can control the appearance of the Taskbar.

Moving the Taskbar

No rule says that the Taskbar has to be along the bottom of the screen. You can *anchor* (attach) it to any edge of the screen simply by dragging it there. More specifically, you have to do the following:

1. Move the mouse pointer so it's touching the Taskbar (not the Start button, not an icon, but the Taskbar itself).

2. Hold down the primary mouse button, and drag the mouse pointer to any edge of the screen. A ghost image of the Taskbar appears along that edge of the screen.

3. Drop the Taskbar by releasing the mouse button.

Sizing the Taskbar

The width of the Taskbar isn't fixed either. You can make it wider or narrower by following these steps:

1. Move the mouse pointer so it's touching the edge of the Taskbar. When the mouse pointer is correctly positioned, it changes to a two-headed arrow, as shown here.

2. Hold down the primary mouse button, and drag the edge in either direction indicated by the mouse pointer's arrows.

3. When the object (or its ghost image) is at the width or height you want, release the mouse button.

If you size the Taskbar so small that you can no longer see it, don't panic. Move the mouse pointer to the very edge of the screen where you anchored the Taskbar. Then hold down the mouse button, and drag toward the center of the screen.

TIP

The steps described for sizing the Taskbar are just about universal in Windows. If ever you need to make something wider or narrower, taller or shorter, try resting the mouse pointer on the edge of that item. If the two-headed arrow appears, you can drag that edge to size the item.

Hiding and Viewing the Taskbar

In the preceding sections, you learned how to change several characteristics, or *properties*, of the Taskbar, such as its position and size. The Taskbar has other properties that you can fiddle with, as well. To get to those other properties, you first need to get to the Taskbar's *Properties dialog box*. As a rule, you can get to any object's properties simply by right-clicking the object and choosing Properties from the menu that appears.

Here are the exact steps to follow in order to get to the Taskbar's properties:

1. Right-click the Taskbar. (Be sure to click right on the bar itself, not on the Start button or any icons.)

2. Choose Properties from the shortcut menu that appears.

A *dialog box* named Taskbar Properties appears on the screen (see Figure 2.13). The various *controls* that appear in that dialog box let you control the appearance and behavior of the Taskbar.

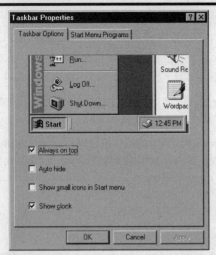

FIGURE 2.13:   The Taskbar Properties dialog box

The picture at the top of the dialog box is called the *preview*. As you make selections from the controls below the picture, the preview illustrates how those changes will affect the actual Taskbar. This lets you test the effects of a selection before actually committing to that selection.

The check boxes are the actual *controls* that let you decide which properties or features are activated (checked) and which are deactivated (cleared). Each check box acts as a *toggle* that you control with the mouse. Click an empty check box, and a check mark appears. Click it again, and the check mark disappears. Simple.

The properties that you can turn on or off using those check boxes are summarized below. If you're sitting at a computer, you might try clicking each check box a few times and watch how the preview picture changes to show you the effects of the current setting.

Always On Top   If selected, nothing else on the screen can cover the Taskbar. If deselected, other items on the screen can cover the Taskbar.

Auto Hide   If you select this option, the Taskbar shrinks to a thin gray line whenever the mouse pointer isn't touching it. To bring it out of hiding, point to that thin gray line. Leaving this option deselected prevents the Taskbar from going into hiding.

Show Small Icons In Start Menu   When selected, reduces the size of the Start menu by showing smaller icons. Keeping this option deselected shows the larger icons on the menu.

Show Clock   When selected, shows the current time in the Indicators section of the Taskbar. When cleared, the clock doesn't show.

If you're following along with a computer nearby, I suggest that you set up your Taskbar properties as shown in the previous figure. That is, select Always On Top and Show Clock. Leave the other two options deselected.

OK, Cancel, and Apply

One thing you need to understand is that the selections you make in a dialog box are not applied to the actual object until you click the OK button or the Apply button. This allows you to change your mind and get out of the dialog box without applying your settings. The options available to you when you've finished making selections are usually on three buttons near the bottom of the dialog box, labeled OK, Cancel, and Apply:

OK   To apply your selections and close the dialog box, click the OK button.

Cancel   To bail out without applying any selections and close the dialog box, click the Cancel button. If you clicked the Apply button during this session, only changes made since that time will be ignored.

Apply   To apply your selections and leave the dialog box open so you can make still more selections, click the Apply button. Once you click the Apply button, however, the Cancel button will no longer cancel out those selections.

Mouse Pointer Hints

As you may have noticed by now, the mouse pointer doesn't always look the same. It changes from time to time to give you information. For example, when the computer is really busy, the mouse pointer turns into a little hourglass. That's your cue to wait (don't do anything) until the mouse pointer returns to normal. Similarly, when you rest the mouse pointer on something that can be moved or sized, the mouse pointer changes to arrows. Table 2.1 summarizes the meaning of the various mouse pointer shapes.

TABLE 2.1: Meaning of Various Mouse Pointer Shapes

POINTER	MEANING
	Point and click normally.
	Click this item to open it.
	Drag left or right to size.
	Drag up or down to size.
	Drag diagonally to size.
	Use arrow keys to move in any direction.
	Please wait, computer is busy.
	PC is a little busy. You can use the mouse normally, but performance will be sluggish until the other job is finished.
	Click the item you want help with.
	Can't drop that item here.

SHUTTING DOWN YOUR PC

Before you turn off your PC, you should shut down Windows 98 SE. Doing so allows Windows to do some last-minute housekeeping and also gives you the opportunity to save any work in progress. Shutting down Windows is a simple task:

1. Click the Start button.

2. Choose Shut Down.

3. Choose the Shut Down option in the Shut Down Windows dialog box.

4. Click the OK button.

5. Follow any instructions that appear on the screen (though there may not be any).

Some computers will shut themselves down completely at this point. You don't even need to turn off the PC. If your PC cannot shut itself down, the screen will display a big message, "It is now safe to turn off your computer." Go ahead and turn off the PC as well as connected gadgets that have their own on/off switches.

LEAVE ON OR TURN OFF?

Some people never turn off their PCs. I know people who have had PCs running for years that they've never shut down. The PC consumes so little energy when not in use, there's really no reason to shut it down. Some PCs will automatically go into a "sleep mode" when left alone for an hour or so. To get it back running, you have to move the mouse around or press some key on the keyboard. Within a few seconds, the Windows 98 SE Desktop will appear.

If you're not comfortable leaving your PC on all the time, that's fine too. Feel free to shut down your PC whenever you won't be using it for a while. You won't do any harm.

WHAT'S NEXT?

If you have been reading this away from your computer and have not yet installed Windows 98 SE, you might want to revisit this chapter after you install Windows 98 SE. In the next chapter are all the instructions. Robert Cowart takes you step by step through the process.

Chapter 3

INSTALLING WINDOWS 98 SECOND EDITION ON YOUR COMPUTER

C hances are good that your computer came installed with Windows 98 Second Edition already, in which case reading this chapter isn't necessary for you. On the other hand, if you are still using Windows 3.x, Windows 95, or the first edition of Windows 98, or if you have no version of Windows on your computer at all, you'll want to read this chapter. If at some point after you install Windows you discover that you are missing some of the components discussed in this book, you can install them later from the Windows Control Panel's Add/Remove Programs applet.

Adapted from *Mastering Windows 98 Second Edition* by Robert Cowart

ISBN 0-7821-2618-9   893 pages $39.99

There are several basic scenarios when installing Windows 98 Second Edition:

▶ Installing on a new or newly formatted hard disk

▶ Installing over Windows 3.*x*

▶ Installing over Windows 95

▶ Installing over Windows 98 (first edition)

NOTE

Not sure which version of Windows 98 you have? Right-click My Computer, and choose Properties from the shortcut menu. On the General tab of the System Properties dialog box, you should see a version listed. If you already have Windows 98 Second Edition, you should see the words "Second Edition" under System. The version number for Second Edition is 4.10.2222 A.

Within each scenario, there are subscenarios, based on the source of the installation programs:

▶ Local CD-ROM or hard disk

▶ Installation files copied to your hard disk

▶ Network CD-ROM or hard disk

In the vast majority of cases, you'll be installing from a local CD-ROM drive, over an existing Windows installation.

NOTE

If you have a previous version of Windows on your computer, you can install from a DOS prompt, but Microsoft recommends installing from within Windows.

Although I don't recommend it, you can choose to install Windows into a directory other than the existing Windows directory. This lets you install a "clean" version of Windows 98, with no settings pulled in from the earlier installation. Although this assures you of having a fresh Registry and might make you feel safer about trying out the new version, it will be a hassle in the long run. What I *do* recommend is upgrading *over* your existing Windows directory, by which I mean installing into the same directory; typically this would be C:\Windows. Besides, when you install over an existing version of Windows, you are offered the option of saving your old system files, so you can effortlessly revert to the old system if you want. (But be warned that if you're currently running Windows 95 or 98, it can take as much as 110MB of additional space to perform this save.)

When you opt to install over an existing Windows version (that is, 3.*x*, 95, or 98—see the note below about Windows NT and Windows 2000), various important settings—such as program INI settings, file locations, program associations, program groups, and so forth—are transferred into your new version. The most important advantage of this approach is that you won't have to install all your applications (such as Microsoft Office) again for Windows 98 Second Edition. (If you install to a separate directory, things get complicated, because with two separate versions of Windows on the same computer, the changes you make in one version don't carry over to the other.)

NOTE

If you are installing on a computer that has Windows NT or Windows 2000 on it, read the NT/2000 section at the end of this chapter. You cannot install over NT/2000, though 98 can coexist with NT/2000 on the same drive.

Microsoft has done a laudable job of making the Windows 98 SE installation process rather painless, thanks to the Setup Wizard, which provides a pleasant question-and-answer interface. It's been made even simpler than in Windows 95 by asking only a few questions up front and then doing the rest of the work on its own without your intervention. Therefore, I'll spare you the boredom of walking you through *every* step here on paper. Rather, I'll get you going and discuss some of the decisions you'll have to make along the way.

TIP

Setup requires approximately 210MB of hard disk space to complete. The exact amount will depend on the setup options you choose, as well as on the configuration of the hard drive on which you are installing Windows 98 SE. For additional information about space requirements, see the file \Win98\setup .txt on the Windows 98 Second Edition CD-ROM before you begin installation.

WARNING

Microsoft strongly suggests that you back up any important existing data and programs before you install Windows 98 SE, just to be safe. Also, be sure to take Setup's advice about making a new Startup disk. Startup disks that you may have created with earlier versions of Windows are not compatible with some features of Windows 98 SE.

Part i

Easiest Approach: A Full Upgrade from an Earlier Version of Windows

First off, you'll need to decide whether you are going to install from a CD-ROM or your local area network. I highly recommend using a CD (or networked CD or hard disk if one is available). If you choose to copy the installation files to your hard disk, see \Win98\setup.txt on the Windows 98 Second Edition CD-ROM for special instructions.

Before beginning, make sure you have at least 210MB of free hard disk space on the drive you're going to install Windows on. You can use Windows Explorer or the DOS dir command to check this.

To begin the setup process:

1. Boot your computer into Windows.

2. Insert the CD into the CD-ROM drive.

TIP

As I mentioned earlier, if you're using the CD, the CD-ROM drive needn't be on your local computer. Furthermore, you can install over a local area network or dial-up connection from a shared directory or drive that contains the CD (or a copy of all of its files). You simply switch to that directory (via File Manager in Windows 3.x or Windows Explorer in Windows 95 or 98) and run setup.exe.

3. I recommend you read through three text files that contain last-minute information about Windows 98 SE. These files might provide special tips about your brand of computer or cards, printers, and other accessories. The files are called readme.txt, setuptip.txt, and setup.txt. The first two can be found in the root directory of the CD-ROM, and setup.txt can be found in the \Win98 directory. To read these files, just get to them via the File Manager or Windows Explorer, and then double-click them.

4. If you're running Windows 3.x, switch to the File Manager or Program Manager, open the File menu, and choose Run. If you're running Windows 95, choose Start ➢ Run. Then enter whichever of the following commands is appropriate for your

Part i

circumstance (that is, depending on whether you're installing from a CD-ROM, hard disk, or network):

- ▶ If installing from a CD, enter **d:\win98\setup**.
- ▶ If installing from a network, click Browse, and navigate to the network computer and CD-ROM drive where the disk is located.

(You may have to replace d: in the above statement with the appropriate drive letter for your machine.) Alternatively, in File Manager or Windows Explorer, you can look around for setup.exe and double-click it. In a few seconds, you'll be greeted with a fancy blue screen and some directions about installation (as in Figure 3.1).

NOTE

If you install from the DOS prompt instead of from Windows, you will have more questions to answer than the ones you're asked from this series of screens, relating to your choice for the destination directory for Windows and concerning which components to install. If you're interested in this approach, see the section "Installing to a Fresh Disk or New Directory."

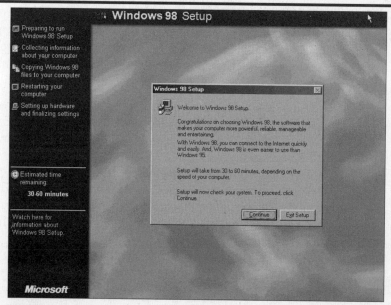

FIGURE 3.1:   The first welcome screen when installing over an existing version of Windows

5. Click Continue to let Setup check out your computer. If you
   have too little disk space, you'll be alerted.

   ▶ You'll also be alerted to quit other programs if they are
     running. This is because Setup might bomb, in which
     case any work you have open in those programs could be
     lost. Switch to any program in which you have open work,
     save the work, close the program, and switch back to
     Setup.

   ▶ If you see a warning pertaining to your antivirus soft-
     ware, follow the instructions on screen. Ideally you
     should disable the antivirus software before proceeding
     with the installation.

6. Next, you'll see a license agreement. If you agree to the terms,
   click Yes, and then click Next. You will be prompted to enter
   the Product Key, which is a 25-digit number you should have
   received with your Windows 98 Second Edition CD. Click
   Next again when you have entered it.

7. Setup now checks out what hardware is in your computer and
   initializes the system's Registry file. It will check for installed
   components if you are upgrading from a previous version of
   Windows, and it will check to see that you have enough hard
   disk space. Assuming there is enough disk space (you
   checked for that earlier, didn't you?), you won't see any error
   messages about that. If you do, see the "Removing Uninstall
   Files to Free Disk Space" section later in this chapter.

   You'll also be asked at this point if you want to save your "system files." This is so that you can uninstall Windows 98 SE if
   it doesn't work, or if you decide you don't like it, or if for some
   other reason you want to be able to go back to your old operating system. (See the "Reverting to the Previous Operating
   System" section later in this chapter.) Click Yes or No. If in
   doubt, click Yes, and then click Next. If you have more than
   one hard drive, you will also be asked which disk you want the
   uninstall files saved on.

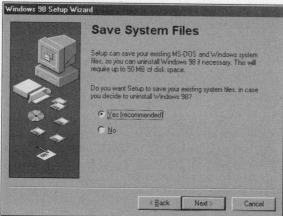

8. Your current system files will be backed up to a hidden, compressed file. If doing that would leave too little space for installation of Windows 98 SE, you'll be alerted and given the option of skipping the backup in order to save disk space.

9. Next you're asked about your location. This will allow Windows to more easily set you up to receive local news and information via the Internet "channels." For now, just click the country you are in, and then click Next. (Scroll the list if necessary.)

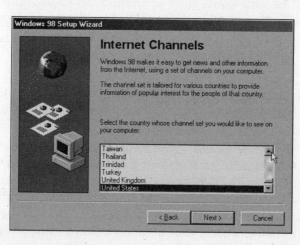

10. At this point, Setup offers the opportunity to create an emergency startup disk. This is for starting your computer in case

the hard disk is damaged or some system files get lost or corrupted. Since these are problems that could happen to even the best of machines, it's a good idea to make such a disk and keep it in a readily accessible drawer near your computer. This disk is also necessary for uninstalling Windows 98 SE in case the installation bombs. Just read the screen, and then click Next. Setup creates the list of files that will be put on the startup disk, but it doesn't make the disk yet.

11. You'll be prompted to insert a floppy disk in the disk drive and click OK to make the disk. Anything on the floppy disk will be erased, so don't use one with something important on it. You can skip this procedure by clicking Cancel, but I don't recommend it.

WARNING

For reasons given earlier, it's a very good idea to create the startup disk now. However, if you don't have a floppy with you, you can cancel this process for now and continue with the rest of the installation. You can always return to Setup at some other time (even after you've been using Windows 98 SE for months) to make a startup disk. However, if setup crashes for some reason, you could be left with a computer that won't boot.

12. Now you'll move on to the main stage of the installation process: the copying of files from the source to your hard disk. This is the portion that takes the most time. Click Next to start this process. A status bar keeps you abreast of the progress of the file-copying operation.

At this point, your computer will reboot. Remove the floppy disk, if you haven't already, and let the computer restart. If nothing happens for an extended period, you may have to turn the machine off and then on again. It *should* pick up where it left off.

Upon restarting, a Windows 98 SE screen appears with blue clouds on it and the words "Getting ready to run Windows for the first time." This screen may stay there a *long time* (15 minutes or more) and your hard disk may sound like a garbage disposal (lots of activity), but that's okay. Really. Setup is doing some major housekeeping and possibly defragmenting your hard disk. Just sit tight.

NOTE

I've actually had to sit for 20 minutes while waiting for Windows to do its initial housecleaning. As long as the hard disk light is still on or you hear hard disk activity, all is well. Don't despair unless everything goes silent for multiple minutes.

Now you're in the phase in which hardware drivers are installed. Plug-and-Play devices are detected first, and then older, non-Plug-and-Play hardware is detected.

The system may then reboot again in order to load the hardware drivers it just set up. Devices such as PCMCIA (PC Memory Card International Association) cards should initialize. Again, if the system hangs (nothing happens for a long period of time), turn the computer off and on again using the power switch.

Next, a number of other things are adjusted:

▶ Control Panel options are set up.

▶ Programs on the Start menu are set up.

▶ Windows Help is installed.

▶ MS-DOS program settings are adjusted.

▶ Applications are set to start faster.

▶ Some system configuration is optimized.

The last activity, updating system settings, can take a bit of time, like 5 to 10 minutes. But a progress bar lets you know how it's going. A few files may be copied from the CD at this time, so make sure the CD is still available.

Again the system restarts. The blue clouds will appear. It may take a couple of minutes for the Windows Desktop to appear. If you were updating from a previous version of Windows, you should see the same Desktop background or wallpaper you had before. You'll be prompted to enter your user name and password.

TIP

You may choose a user name and password now and enter it if you like. Remember the password for the next time you log in to Windows 98 SE. If you don't enter a password, you won't be prompted for a name and password during startup in the future.

After that, the computer may even restart one more time. Once it does, you're up and running.

INSTALLING TO A FRESH DISK OR NEW DIRECTORY

You may prefer to install Windows 98 SE into a new directory for one of three reasons:

▶ You have no version of Windows on the machine.

▶ You have an existing version of Windows on the machine, but want to keep that version and set up Windows 98 SE too. Then, by changing directory names or using some third-party utility program such as Partition Magic or BootCom, you can choose which version boots up. (This option is for confident, advanced users.)

▶ You want to control what components of Windows get installed. When you install to a new directory, you have many more options than when upgrading over an existing installation.

To control the destination directory, you must (1) run Setup from a DOS prompt, and (2) boot in such a way as to have access to the CD-ROM drive, or, if you're installing across a network, to the network drive. If you have Windows 95 on the machine, the best way to do this is to create a Windows 95 emergency startup disk and boot from that. (To create this disk, go to Control Panel, choose Add/Remove Programs to open the Add/Remove Programs Properties dialog box, and click the Startup Disk tab.) If you had a CD-ROM drive available to you when you created the startup disk, it should have CD driver support files on it. Once you've booted to DOS, switch to the Setup source disk, and run `setup.exe`.

When running Setup from DOS, ScanDisk runs first, checking the hard disk media. Assuming that all is OK (see the following section if it's not), exit ScanDisk by typing **X** (for Exit) when prompted. Setup will proceed, temporarily in character mode, then in a GUI mode with graphics, blue background, and mouse functionality.

After accepting the terms of the license agreement, you'll be given the option of choosing a hard disk directory for your Windows 98 SE installation. The default will be the existing Windows directory if there is one, but you can create a different directory at this point by typing a name for it. Next, you'll see a series of screens asking for your input or verification concerning the following tasks:

▶ Choose which set of Windows 98 SE components to install: Typical, Portable, Compact, or Custom (your choice).

- ▶ Provide your name and company name.
- ▶ Select specific components.
- ▶ Provide or verify your network ID: computer name, workgroup, and workstation description.
- ▶ Verify your computer settings: Keyboard, Language, Regional Variants, and User Interface (Windows 98 or 3.1).
- ▶ Choose your Location. (You can simply choose the country at this point.)
- ▶ Create a Windows 98 Emergency Startup disk.

The rest of the installation will go as explained in the previous section.

TIP

If you have a situation that requires additional setup options—for example, you may be a LAN administrator and want remote setup capabilities—refer to the Microsoft Windows 98 Resource Kit.

FINDING AND FIXING HARD DISK PROBLEMS DURING INSTALLATION

The Setup program automatically runs ScanDisk to check for problems on your hard disk before proceeding. If it finds problems on your hard disk, the setup process won't continue until they are fixed. It's also possible that you'll see a message during a later stage of the setup process that says you have to run ScanDisk to fix the problems.

WARNING

The MS-DOS–based version of ScanDisk that Setup runs may detect long-file-name errors, but it can't correct them. These errors will not prevent Setup from proceeding, but once it completes, you should run the new Windows version of ScanDisk from within Windows 98 SE to correct these errors.

To run ScanDisk:

1. Exit the Setup program (and quit Windows if it's running).

2. Boot to a DOS prompt that offers access to the drive you're installing from.

3. Insert the CD into the drive, and from a DOS prompt, type the following:

   `d:scandisk.exe /all`

   (replacing the `d:` with the letter for the drive that contains the setup disk; for example, `e:` if that is the letter for your CD-ROM drive).

4. Follow the instructions on your screen to fix any problems that ScanDisk finds.

5. Run Setup again (from Windows if it's available on your machine; otherwise, run it from a DOS prompt).

TIP

If you have problems or questions about Setup that are not covered in this chapter, check out the file called `setup.txt` on the Windows 98 SE CD. On the CD, you'll find it in the `Win98` directory.

REVERTING TO THE PREVIOUS OPERATING SYSTEM

Assuming you opted during your Windows 98 SE setup to save your previous version's system files, you can revert to that version of Windows in case of a failed or an unappreciated installation. (For exceptions to the "Saving System Files" scenario, see the upcoming sidebar.)

To uninstall Windows 98 SE and completely restore your system to its previous versions of MS-DOS and Windows 3.x or Windows 95 or 98, follow these steps:

1. Choose Start ➤ Settings ➤ Control Panel.

2. Double-click Add/Remove Programs to open the Add/Remove Programs Properties dialog box.

3. On the Install/Uninstall tab, click Uninstall Windows 98 Second Edition, and then click Add/Remove.

If you can't even get to the Start menu to begin the steps above (because of problems starting Windows 98 SE), use your startup disk to start your computer, and, from a DOS prompt, type **a: uninstal**, and press Enter. Here are a few notes to be mindful of when running Uninstal:

▸ The Uninstal program needs to shut down Windows 98 SE. If your computer starts to run Windows 98 SE again on reboot, try restarting it again, and this time quickly pressing F8 when you see the message "Starting Windows 98." (Note, though, that you might only have a fraction of a second to do this, depending on how fast your machine is. Another approach that may work, depending on your computer, is to hold down the Shift key during the bootup process.) Then choose Command Prompt Only, and run Uninstal from this command prompt.

▸ If you've misplaced your startup disk but can get to the DOS prompt, you can run Uninstal from the hard disk instead. There should be a copy of the Uninstal program in your Windows directory on the hard disk.

▸ If you saved your files on a drive other than C, you can use the /w option to specify the drive where the files are located. For example, if your system files were saved to drive E during installation, type **uninstal /w e:** to access them on that drive.

WHY YOU CAN'T ALWAYS SAVE YOUR SYSTEM FILES

The option of saving your system files for a future uninstall is not always offered during setup. Here are some situations in which Setup does not offer the option:

▸ You are upgrading over an earlier version of Windows 98 itself.

▸ You are installing to a new directory (in which case, you don't need to revert to your previous version; instead, you can simply boot to the previous version's directory to run that version).

▸ You are running a version of MS-DOS earlier than 5.0 (in which case, your system is automatically updated with the version of DOS that is used in Windows 98 SE).

CONTINUED ➡

Part I

In most other situations, you are given the option to save your system files. When you choose this option, Setup saves your system files in a hidden, compressed file on your local hard drive. (They cannot be saved to a network drive or a floppy disk.) If you have multiple local drives, you will be able to select the one you want to use.

If you are not in one of the above exception situations, but you see a message during setup about not being able to save your system files, refer to the "Setup Error Messages" section of the setup.txt file in the CD's Win98 directory or on the floppy installation disk.

REMOVING UNINSTALL FILES TO FREE DISK SPACE

If you want to free an additional 50 to 100MB of disk space, you can remove the Uninstall files by following the steps below. Please note, however, that without the Uninstall files, you will no longer be able to uninstall Windows 98 SE. In short, save this operation until you're sure you're going to keep Windows 98 SE.

Here are the steps for removing the Uninstall files. Note that Windows 98 must be running to perform this operation.

1. Choose Start ≻ Settings ≻ Control Panel.

2. Double-click Add/Remove Programs to open the Add/Remove Programs Properties dialog box.

3. On the Install/Uninstall tab, click Delete Windows 98 Second Edition Uninstall Information, and then click Add/Remove.

INSTALLING ONTO A COMPRESSED DRIVE

If you have used compression software to compress your hard disk, or if a host drive or partition for your startup drive is compressed, you may get a

Part I

message during setup that there is not enough space on the host partition of the compressed drive. If you get this message, you should free
some space on the specified drive and then run Setup again. Note that if
the drive was compressed with SuperStor or Stacker, you'll have to decompress the drive and remove the compression program before you can install
Windows 98 SE. If you used Microsoft DriveSpace, you were smart: you
don't have to decompress in order to free extra space—you just tell it to free
the space.

Here are some other steps to freeing space for your installation:

▶ If you are setting up Windows on a compressed drive, try setting
it up on an uncompressed drive if possible.

▶ Delete any unneeded files on your host partition.

▶ If you are running Windows 3.1 and have a permanent swap file,
try making it smaller. In Control Panel, click the 386 Enhanced
icon, and then click Virtual Memory. Then modify the size of your
swap file.

▶ Use your disk compression software to free some space on the
host drive for the compressed drive.

And don't forget to check out the following subsections concerning
particular compression programs.

WARNING
If you create a startup disk during setup, make sure you do not use a compressed disk for the startup disk.

SuperStor or Stacker Compressed Drive

If you have compressed your hard disk by using SuperStor, Setup may not
be able to find your startup drive and install Windows 98 SE. If you get a
message about this during setup, uncompress your disk, remove Super-
Stor, and then run Setup again.

Windows 98 SE will not run on a Stacker-compressed hard drive. If
you currently have Stacker version 4.1 installed on your computer, uninstall Stacker before you upgrade to Windows 98 SE.

DriveSpace or DoubleSpace Compressed Drive

1. Quit Windows and get to a DOS prompt.

2. Run Drvspace.exe or Dblspace.exe (probably in your DOS or Windows directory).

3. Select the compressed drive on which you want to free some space.

4. On the Drive menu, select Change Size.

NOTE

If you notice a discrepancy between the amount of free space reported by Setup and the amount of space you think is available on your host drive, it may be because Windows is reserving some space for a swap file.

XtraDrive Compression

If you have compressed your hard disk by using XtraDrive and you are upgrading over a previous version of Windows, you'll have to turn off XtraDrive's *write cache* before doing the install. Here's how to do that:

1. Exit Windows and get to DOS.

2. Run Vmu.exe (XtraDrive's Volume Maintenance Utility).

3. Click Advanced Options, and then press Enter.

4. Set the EMS cache size to **0**.

5. Set the Conventional cache size to **1** (the minimum).

6. Set Allow Write Caching to **No**.

7. At the confirmation prompt, click Yes. You will see a message saying that you must restart your computer for the changes to take effect.

8. Quit the Volume Maintenance Utility, and then restart your computer.

9. Start Windows, and then run Windows 98 SE Setup again.

HOW TO INSTALL WINDOWS 98 SECOND EDITION ON A MACHINE RUNNING WINDOWS NT OR 2000

Although you can install Windows 98 SE on a machine that is already running Windows NT or Windows 2000, you must install it to a separate partition—you cannot install 98 SE *over* NT or 2000. Although you can have NT or 2000 and Windows 98 SE on the same computer and boot either operating system as you like, they won't share INI settings, installed applications, or other settings. This may change in the future, but in the meantime, it's simply an annoyance, because it means you'll have to install most applications twice—once for NT or 2000 and once for Windows 98 SE.

If you're configured to multi-boot MS-DOS and Windows NT or 2000   Boot to MS-DOS, and then run Windows 98 SE Setup from either MS-DOS, Windows 95, or Windows 98. You will not be able to install Windows 98 SE to a partition with a shared Windows 95/Windows NT configuration; you will need to install Windows 98 SE to a different partition.

If you're not configured to multi-boot MS-DOS and Windows NT or 2000   You must first configure your computer to multi-boot MS-DOS and Windows NT/2000, and then follow the instructions above.

If you were planning to boot to MS-DOS from a floppy disk and then run Windows 98 SE Setup   This approach permits you to install Windows 98 SE as you wish; however, you will no longer be able to boot to Windows NT or 2000. You can *restore* Windows NT, however, by booting from the Windows NT boot/repair disk and then selecting the Repair option.

NOTE

Windows 98 Second Edition Setup will not run on OS/2. You need to boot to MS-DOS and then run Setup from the MS-DOS prompt. For more about installing over OS/2, see the setup.txt file on floppy disk 1 or in the readme directory on the Windows 98 CD.

MULTI-BOOTING WINDOWS 98 SECOND EDITION WITH LINUX

If you currently have a version of Linux installed on your computer and want to be able to multi-boot Windows 98 SE, you must install Windows on its own DOS partition. Create the partition using Disk Druid, and then run a normal MS-DOS prompt installation of Windows, as described earlier.

When the installation is complete, reboot using your Linux boot floppy. The Windows 98 SE setup program erases LILO (the Linux Loader program), so you will have to reinstall it by running /sbin/lilo. LILO can then be configured to ask you which operating system you want to boot during startup.

WHAT'S NEXT?

Now that Windows 98 SE is up and running on your computer, it's time to take a look around. In the next chapter, Robert Cowart takes you on a guided tour of the Windows interface—the parts and pieces of the Desktop, the parts of a window, bars, buttons, boxes, and so on—and shows you how to use them effectively.

Chapter 4

AN INTRODUCTION TO THE WINDOWS INTERFACE

In this chapter, I'll begin explaining Windows so you can start using your computer to get your work done. If you're an experienced Windows user, you can skim this chapter just to get the gist of the new features of Windows 98 SE. If, on the other hand, you're new to Windows, you should read this chapter thoroughly because it will introduce you to essential Windows concepts and skills that you'll need to have no matter what your line of work is or what you intend to do with your computer.

Adapted from *Mastering Windows 98 Second Edition* by Robert Cowart
ISBN 0-7821-2618-9   893 pages $39.99

WINDOWS 101

Windows owes its name to the fact that it runs each application or document in its own separate *window*. A window is a box or a frame on the screen. Figure 4.1 shows several such windows.

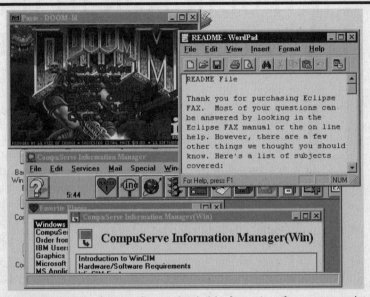

FIGURE 4.1: Windows are frames that hold information of some sort on the screen.

You can have numerous windows on the screen at a time, each containing its own program and/or document. You can then easily switch between programs without having to close one down and open the next.

Another feature that Windows has is a facility—called the *Clipboard*—that lets you copy material between dissimilar document types, making it easy to *cut* and *paste* information from, say, a spreadsheet into a company report or a scanned photograph of a house into a real-estate brochure. In essence, Windows provides the means for seamlessly joining the capabilities of very different application programs. Not only can you paste portions of one document into another, but by using an advanced document-linking feature—for example, OLE or DCOMM—those pasted elements remain *live*. That is, if the source document (such as some spreadsheet data) changes, the results will also be reflected in the secondary document (such as a word-processing document) containing the pasted data.

In addition to expediting the way you use your existing applications, Windows comes with quite a handful of its own little programs. For example, there's a word-processing program called WordPad, a drawing program called Paint, an e-mail program, Internet connectivity programs, several games, utilities for keeping your hard disk in good working order (or even doubling the amount of space on it), and a data-backup program—just to name a few.

Before Moving Ahead...

Before going on in this book, make sure you've installed Windows correctly on your computer. Then, while experimenting with Windows on your computer, you should feel free to experiment (if with some caution) as I explain things you can do, offer tips, and so forth. Experimentation is the best way to learn. I'll try to warn against things you shouldn't do, so don't worry. Experience really is the best teacher—especially with computers. Contrary to popular belief, they really won't blow up if you make a mistake!

If at any time while reading this chapter you have to quit Windows to do other work or simply because you want to turn off your computer, just jump to the end of this chapter and read the section called "Exiting Windows." Also, if at any time you don't understand how to use a Windows command or perform some procedure, go to the newly improved Help facility available within Windows and any Windows application.

If you truly get stuck and don't know how to escape from some procedure you're in the middle of, the last resort is to reboot your computer and start up Windows again. Though this isn't a great idea, and you may lose part of any documents you're working on, it won't actually kill Windows or your computer. There are several ways to do this, but always try this one first: click the Start button, and choose Shut Down. Then choose Shut Down from the dialog box of shut-down options.

If that doesn't work, try pressing the Ctrl, Alt, and Delete keys simultaneously (in other words, press Ctrl and hold, press Alt and hold both, then tap Delete.) A box should appear, offering you a Shut Down button to click (no, Enter doesn't work). If your computer is really stuck, sometimes you might have to press Ctrl, Alt, and Delete again (that is, twice in a row). This will likely restart Windows.

The most drastic but surefire way to reboot the computer is by pressing the reset switch on your computer or turning your computer off, waiting about five seconds, and then turning it on again. This will almost invariably get you out of what you were doing and make the computer ready to use again.

NOTE

All but the first method are last resorts to exiting Windows and can result in losing some of your work! It's better to follow the instructions at the end of this chapter (in the section entitled "Exiting Windows").

Starting Windows

To start Windows and get to work, follow these steps:

1. Remove any floppy disk from the computer's floppy disk drive.

2. Turn on your computer, monitor, and any other stuff you're likely to use (for example, an external CD-ROM drive or external modem).

3. Wait. Unlike in the old days of Windows 3.1, the DOS prompt (C:>) will not appear. Instead, after a few seconds you'll see the Windows 98 SE start-up logo, which may seem to sit there a long time. You'll see some action on the screen, such as the blue bar moving across the bottom of the screen. This means, "Don't worry, your computer is still alive." Windows takes quite a while to load from your hard disk into RAM. You just have to wait.

TIP

If you have 16-bit device drivers included in your autoexec.bat file, you may see a command prompt instead of the Windows 98 SE logo while Windows 98 SE loads. Also, if you press Escape while the Windows 98 SE logo is displayed, the logo will disappear, and you'll see a listing of your config.sys lines as they load.

4. After about 15 seconds or so, the Windows sign-on dialog box appears and asks you to type your user name and password.

By pressing Escape or clicking the Cancel button, you tell Windows that you will not be using a password. On subsequent startups, you will not be asked to enter a password. If you want a little more security or will be using your computer on a network, enter a name and a password at this point. If you upgraded from Windows 95 or Windows for Workgroups, your old user name and password should work just as it did before. Then click OK (or press Enter).

NOTE

Clicking means positioning the mouse pointer on the item in question and then clicking the *left* button once (or, if you've custom configured your pointing device, whichever button you've assigned as the *primary* button). The middle and right (or secondary) mouse buttons won't cut it unless I mention them specifically—they are used for other things! *Double-clicking* means clicking an item twice in quick succession.

5. If you are hooked up to a local area network (LAN), and Windows detected the network and installed itself for network activities, you may be prompted to enter your network password, like this:

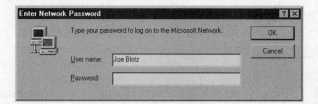

This might seem redundant, as you entered a password already. No, it's not Fort Knox. It's just that there are two possible password requirements—one that gets you into your own computer and into a workgroup, and another one for signing you onto a network domain. A typical peer-to-peer network of Windows 98 SE machines is considered a workgroup. If your workgroup machine is interconnected with a Windows NT or 2000 Server, the second password will be used by Windows 98 SE to authenticate you on the Microsoft Network domain. If you don't already have a network user name and password, invent one now. You'll be prompted to confirm it.

NOTE

The sequence of boxes that prompt you for your user name and password the first time you run Windows 98 SE will likely be different from subsequent sessions. You'll have fewer steps after signing in the first time because you won't be asked to confirm your password.

6. Click OK (or press Enter).

Now the Windows 98 SE starting screen—the Desktop—appears, looking approximately like that in Figure 4.2. Take a look at your screen and compare it with the figure. Your screen may look a bit different, but the general landscape will be the same. You may see a Welcome to Windows 98 box and hear some jazzy music asking if you want to take a tour of Windows or get some help about Windows. Just click the Close button (the X in the upper-right corner of the box) to close it. You can explore the Help system and take the Windows Tour later. If you do not want the Welcome box to reappear every time you restart Windows, click to remove the check mark next to where it says Show This Screen Each Time Windows 98 Starts" before you close it.

NOTE

If you or someone else has used your Windows 98 setup already, it's possible that some open windows will come up on the screen automatically when Windows boots (starts up). It's also possible that you'll see more icons on the Desktop than what's shown in Figure 4.2. That depends on what options you chose when Windows 98 SE was installed.

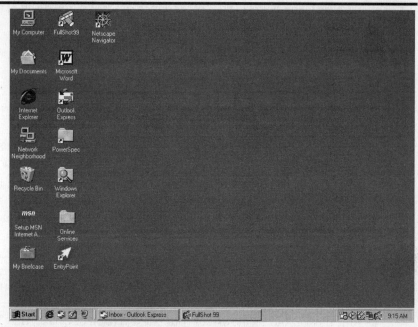

FIGURE 4.2: The initial Windows 98 SE screen. This starting screen is called the Desktop—the place where you can organize your work and interact with your computer a bit like the way you use your real desk.

PARTS OF THE WINDOWS SCREEN

Now let's take a quick look at the basic parts of the Windows start-up screen: the Desktop, icons, and the Taskbar. Once you understand these three essential building blocks (and one other—a *window*—which you'll see in a few minutes), you'll begin to get a feel for how Windows works.

The Desktop

The *Desktop* is your overall work area while in Windows. It's called the Desktop because Windows uses your whole screen in a way that's analogous to the way you'd use the surface of a desk. As you work in Windows, you move items around on the Desktop, retrieve and put away items (as if in a drawer), and perform your other day-to-day tasks. You do all of this using graphical representations of your work projects.

November   Music School   Letters
Budget   Logo

The analogy of the Desktop falls a bit short sometimes, but it's useful for understanding how the program helps you organize your activities.

You can put your favorite (for example, most oft-used) items on the Desktop so that getting to them requires less hunting around. Each time you run Windows, those items will be right there where you left them. This is a great feature of Windows 98 SE.

In Figure 4.2, which displays a rather "virgin" system, several items are ready to go. (Remember, you may have slightly different items, depending on options you chose when installing Windows.) We'll get to what those items are for, but you get the picture. When you add your own items, such as your thesis, your recipe list, or your latest version of Quake, they'll be represented by little graphics, also known as *icons*, in the same way that the items above are represented.

Icons

An *icon* is a graphical symbol that represents something in your computer. To get your work (and play) done, you interact with these little graphics. Notice the icons along the left side of your Desktop. The icons have names under them. Windows 98 SE uses icons to represent folders, documents, and programs when they are not currently opened and running. Below are a couple of icons.

My Computer   Research for
Thesis

Icons that look like file folders are just that—folders. Folders (just like on the Mac) are used to keep related documents or programs together. You can even have folders within folders, a useful feature for really organizing your work from the top down.

NOTE

Folders were called *directories* in DOS and Windows 3.*x* terminology. As of Windows 95, the help system and manuals refer to directories (and program groups as well) as *folders*.

There's another kind of icon-ish sort of thing you'll need to know about. Technically, it's called a *minimized window*. When you want to get a window off the screen temporarily but within easy reach, you minimize it. This lets you do work with a document that's in another window without any extra clutter on the screen. When a window is *minimized* in this way, it's as if its program or document is shoved to the bottom of your desk for a moment and put in a little box on the Taskbar.

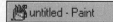

We'll cover this kind of icon later, when I discuss the Taskbar and running your programs.

There are several variations on these boxes, but the upshot is the same: the program or document's window will pop up again if you simply click or double-click it (more about double-clicking later).

NOTE

Incidentally, while minimized, the program or document will actually be running. It's just that you can't interact with it while it's shrunken. This means that a spreadsheet could still be calculating, a database could be sorting, or a communications program could still be sending your e-mail while it's minimized.

Understanding Windows

Just in case this whole "windows" thing is eluding you, here's the scoop on what a window is and the various types of windows. Because there are different types, people can get somewhat confused when looking at a bunch of windows on the screen. You'll want to learn what they are and how they work, or the screen can be confusing.

It's actually simple. When you want to do some work, you open up a program or document with the mouse or keyboard, and a window containing it appears on the Desktop. This is similar to pulling a file folder or notebook off the shelf, placing it on the desk, and opening it up. In Windows, you do this for each task you want to work on.

Just as with a real desktop, you can have a number of project windows scattered about, all of which can be in progress. You can then easily switch between your projects, be they letters, address lists, spreadsheets, games, or whatever, as you see in Figure 4.3. This approach also allows you to copy material from one document to another more easily by cutting and pasting between them.

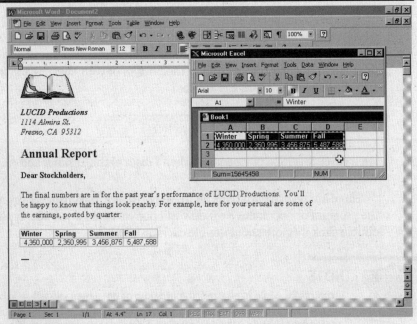

FIGURE 4.3: Windows let you see documents simultaneously.

Another feature designed into Windows is that it can be instructed to remember certain aspects of your work setup each time you quit. For example, if you use a certain group of programs regularly, you can set up Windows to come up with those programs already running—or ready to run with just a click of the mouse. Programs you use less frequently will be stored away within easy reach without cluttering your Desktop.

TYPES OF WINDOWS

Now let's look a little more closely at the various parts of the Desktop. While working, you'll encounter three types of windows: *application windows, document windows,* and *folder windows.* In the following two sections, I'll discuss application and document windows. Chapter 6 explains folder windows.

TIP

If you want to place a window on the screen that you can play with a bit as you read the next section about window sizing, double-click the My Computer icon.

Application Windows

Application windows are those that contain a program that you are running and working with, such as Word, Excel, Paint, WordPerfect, and so on. Most of the work that you do will be in application windows. Figure 4.4 shows a typical application window, sometimes called a *parent window*.

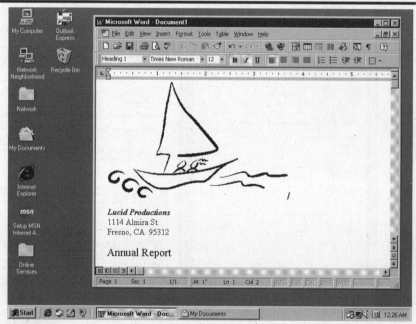

FIGURE 4.4:   An application window is a window in which a program is running.

Document Windows

Some programs let you have more than one document open within them at a time. What does this mean? Well, take the spreadsheet program

Microsoft Excel, for example. It allows you to have several spreadsheets open at once, each in its own document window (sometimes called a *child window*). Instead of running Excel several times in separate application windows (which would use up too much precious RAM), it just runs once and opens several document windows within Excel's main window. Figure 4.5 shows Excel with two document windows open inside it.

NOTE

Document windows make sense, but ironically, Microsoft is changing the way they work. Some newer programs such as Word 2000 and Excel 2000 open a separate program window for each document, meaning each one has its own button on the Windows Taskbar.

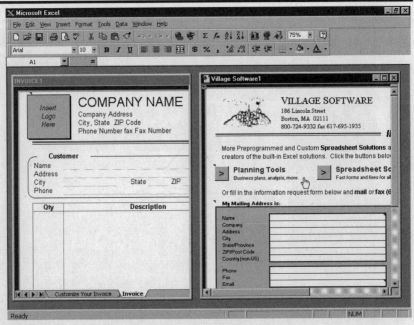

FIGURE 4.5:   Two document (child) windows within an application (parent) window

ANATOMY OF A WINDOW

Now let's consider the parts of a typical window. All windows have the same elements in them, so once you understand the anatomy of one window, others will make sense to you. Of course, some programs have extra stuff like fancy toolbars built in, but you learn about those things as you experiment with the particular program. Here we're talking about the elements common to any kind of window.

The Title Bar

OK. Let's start from the top and work down. The name of the program or document appears at the top of its respective window, in what's called the *title bar*. In Figure 4.5, notice that the title bars read Microsoft Excel, INVOICE1, and VILLAGE SOFTWARE1. If you were running another application, such as PageMaker or Paint, its name would be shown there instead.

Sometimes an application window's title bar also contains the name of the document being worked on. For example, here Notepad's title bar shows the name of the document being edited:

The title bar also serves another function: it indicates which window is *active*. Though you can have a lot of windows on the screen at once, only one window can be active at any given time. The active window is the one in which you're currently working. When a window is made active, it jumps to the front of other windows that might be obscuring it, and its title bar changes color. You make a window active by clicking anywhere within its border.

Minimize, Maximize, and Close

At the right end of the title bar are three small buttons with small graphics in them—the Minimize button, the Maximize or Restore button, and the Close button. These are little control buttons with which you can quickly change the size of a window or close the window completely, as I'll explain in a moment.

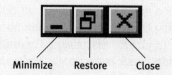

Minimize   Restore   Close

The button with the skinny line in it is the *Minimize* button. The one to its right is the *Restore* button. (It changes to a *Maximize* button when the window is less than its full size—you can see the Maximize button in the graphic in the preceding section.) The third button is called the *Close* button.

NOTE

3.*x* users: In Windows 3.*x* the Minimize, Maximize, and Close techniques varied too much between applications and thus were confusing to users. Now you can close any application (including a DOS box) with a single click on the "X" button.

After a window has been maximized, the Maximize button changes to the *Restore* button. Restore buttons have two little boxes in them. (Restored size is neither full-screen nor minimized. It's whatever size it was when it was last *between* minimized and maximized.)

Essentially, a window can have three sizes:

Minimized   The window becomes an icon on the Taskbar (or on the application's window if it's a document or child window), where it's ready to be opened again but takes up a minimum of screen space.

Normal   The window is open and takes up a portion of the Desktop, the amount of which is determined by how you manually size the window, as explained in a later section. This is also called the *restored* size.

Maximized   The window takes up the whole Desktop. When you maximize a document window, it expands to take up the entire application window. This may or may not be the entire screen, depending on whether the application's window is maximized.

Here are the basic mouse techniques to quickly change the size of a window. To try these techniques, you'll first want to open a window on your screen. If you don't already have a window open, you can open one by double-clicking the icon called My Computer. I'll explain this icon's purpose later. But just for discussion, try double-clicking it. If nothing happens, you didn't click fast enough. Make sure you're clicking the left mouse button (on a standard right-handed mouse or trackball).

TIP

In Web view, double-clicking is replaced with single-clicking and makes the whole interface act much like a Web page. When you install Windows 98, Web view isn't the default setting; the so-called Classic view is. But you can turn on Web view if you want. I'll cover that later in this chapter.

To Minimize a Window

1. First, if you have a number of windows open, click inside the perimeter of one you want to work with. This will activate it.

2. Position the mouse pointer (the arrow that moves around on the screen when you move the mouse) on the Minimize button (the one with the short line in it), and click.

The window reduces to the size of an icon and "goes" down to the bottom of the screen in the Taskbar. The window's name is shown beside the icon so you know what it is. Notice here it says "My Computer." Sometimes this kind of icon is called a "button."

To Restore a Window from an Icon

Now suppose you want to get the window back again. It's simple. The window is waiting for you, minimized down on the Taskbar.

1. Move the mouse to position the pointer just over the little My Computer button (icon) down at the bottom of your screen, in the Taskbar. (Unless for some reason your Taskbar has been moved to one of the other edges of the screen, in which case, use that.)

2. Click the button. The window is now restored to its previous size.

TIP

In Windows 98 SE, you can alternately restore and minimize a window by clicking its button on the Taskbar. If a window is minimized, clicking the button restores it to the screen. Click the button again, and the window is minimized.

To Maximize a Window

You maximize a window when you want it to be as large as possible. When maximized, a window will take up the whole screen. Unless you have a very large screen or need to see two application windows at the same time, this is the best way to work on typical documents. For example, in a word-processing program, you'll see the maximum amount of text at one time with the window maximized.

1. Activate the window by clicking within its perimeter.

2. Click its Maximize button:

The window expands to fill the entire screen. If you're maximizing a child window (remember, that means a window within a window), the window can be only as big as its parent, so it might not be able to get as large as the screen; you'd have to maximize the parent window first. You have to look carefully to find the location of Maximize and Minimize buttons for child windows. Don't confuse them with the buttons for the parent application window. As an example, see Figure 4.6.

After you maximize a window, its Maximize button changes to a Restore button.

Clicking this button will restore the window to its "restored" size, which is neither full nor minimized; it's the intermediate size that you either manually adjusted it to (see the next section), or the size that it originally had when you opened the window.

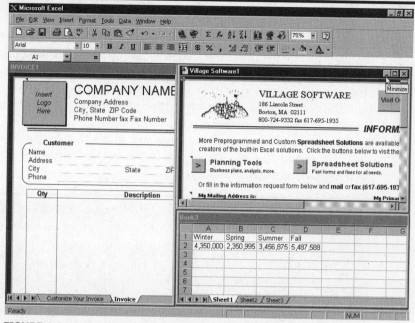

FIGURE 4.6: Document windows have their own Minimize, Maximize, Close, and Restore buttons. Don't confuse them with the buttons for the parent application in which they're running.

To Manually Adjust the Size of a Window

Sometimes you'll want to adjust the size of a window manually to a very specific size. You might want to arrange several windows side by side, for example, so that you can easily see them both, copy and paste material between them, and so forth.

TIP

Clicking and dragging a window's corner allows you to change both the width and height of the window at the same time.

NOTE

Dragging simply means keeping the mouse button pressed while moving the mouse.

Here's how you manually resize a window: Carefully position the cursor on any edge or corner of the window that you want to resize. The lower-right corner is easiest on windows that have a little triangular tab there, designed just for resizing. (You'll see this feature only on newer programs, though not all of them. You can still resize a window if it's not there. Just click on any side or corner of a window.) When you are in the right position, the cursor shape changes to a two-headed arrow, as you can see in Figure 4.7. Press the left mouse button and hold it down. A "ghost" of the window's outline moves with the arrow to indicate that you are resizing the window. Drag the window edge or corner to the desired position and then release the mouse button.

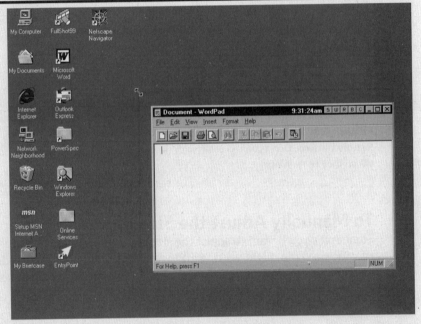

FIGURE 4.7:   Change a window's size by dragging its corner.

TIP

Instead of seeing a "ghost" line while resizing, you can set Windows to actually resize the contents as you drag the border. I'll cover this later in this chapter, but if you're impatient, right-click the Desktop, choose Properties from the short-cut menu, click the Effects tab, and check the Show Window Contents While Dragging check box.

TIP

Moving a whole window: You can drag an entire window around the screen (to get it out of the way of another window, for example) by dragging its title bar. Simply click the window's title bar, keep the mouse button pressed, and drag it around. Release the mouse button when the window is where you want it. (For this to work, the window can't be maximized, since that wouldn't leave any screen room for moving it.)

The Control Box

Every title bar has a little icon at its far left side. This is the *Control box*. It has two functions. First, it opens a menu, called the Control menu. Figure 4.8 shows a Control box with its Control menu open. This is the same menu you get when you single-click a minimized window. This menu comes up from the Control box only when you single-click. Most of the commands on a Control menu let you control the size of the window, so you rarely have to use them. (Menus are covered in detail later in this chapter.) But some programs put special items on their Control menus.

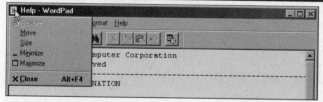

FIGURE 4.8:   Single-clicking the Control box displays the Control menu.

Second, the Control box for a program or document will close the window (terminate the program or close the document) when you double-click on it.

TIP

Pressing Alt+hyphen opens the Control box of the active child window; pressing Alt+spacebar opens the Control box of the active parent window.

Scroll Bars, Scroll Buttons, and Scroll Boxes

On the bottom and right edges of many windows, you'll find *scroll bars*, *scroll buttons*, and *scroll boxes*. These are used to "pan across" the information in a window: up, down, left, and right. This is necessary when there is too much information (text or graphics) to fit into the window at one time. For example, you might be writing a letter that is two pages long. Using the scroll bars lets you move around, or *scroll*, within your document to see the section you're interested in, as two full pages of text won't be displayed in a window at one time. Scrolling lets you look at a large amount of data through what amounts to a small window—your screen. Figure 4.9 illustrates this concept. Many Windows operations—such as listing files on your disks, reading Help screens, or displaying a lot of icons within a window—require the use of scroll bars and boxes.

FIGURE 4.9: Scrolling lets you work with more information than will fit on your screen at one time.

Scroll bars have a little box in them called the *scroll box*, sometimes called an *elevator*. Just as an elevator can take you from one floor of a building to the next, the scroll bar takes you from one section of a window or document to the next. The elevator moves within the scroll bar to indicate which portion of the window you are viewing at any given time. By moving the elevator with your mouse, you cause the document to scroll.

TIP

If you have a "scrolling" mouse, such as the Microsoft Intellimouse, you can scroll the window by simply turning the little roller on the mouse using your index finger.

Try these exercises to see how scroll bars and boxes work:

1. If you haven't already double-clicked the My Computer icon, do so now. A window will open. (We'll discuss the purpose of the My Computer windows later. For now just use one as an example.) Using the technique explained above, size the window so that it shows only a few icons, as shown below. A horizontal or vertical scroll bar (or possibly both) appears on the bottom edge of the window. This indicates that there are more icons in the window than are visible because the window is now so small. What has happened is that several icons are now out of view.

2. Click the elevator with the left mouse button, keep the button held down, and slide the elevator in its little shaft. Notice that as you do this, the elevator moves along with the pointer, and the window's contents are repositioned. (Incidentally, this mouse technique is called *dragging*.)

Part I

3. Now try another approach to scrolling. Click the scroll buttons (the little arrows at the ends of the scroll bar). With each click, the elevator moves a bit in the direction of the button you're clicking on. If you click and hold, the elevator continues to move.

4. One more approach is to click within the scroll bar on either side of the elevator. Each click scrolls the window up or down a bit. With many programs, the screen will scroll one entire screenful with each click.

This example used only a short window with relatively little information in it. In this case, maximizing the window or resizing it just a bit would eliminate the need for scrolling and is probably a better solution. However, with large documents or windows containing many icons, scrolling becomes a necessity, as you'll see later.

ALL ABOUT MENUS

The *menu bar* is a row of words that appears just below the title bar. (It appears only on application windows. Document windows do not have menu bars.) If you click one of the words in the menu bar (called a menu *name*), a menu opens up, displaying a series of options that you can choose from. It is through menus that you tell all Windows programs what actions you want carried out.

Try this as an example:

1. With the My Computer window open and active, click on the word *File* in the menu bar. A menu opens, as you see in Figure 4.10, listing seven options. You can see why it's called a menu; it's a bit like a restaurant menu listing things you can order.

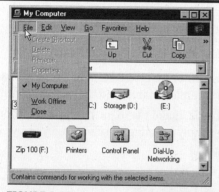

FIGURE 4.10: Open a menu by clicking its name in the menu bar.

TIP

You could also have pressed Alt+F to open the File menu. If there is an underlined letter in any menu's name, holding down the Alt key (either one, if your keyboard has two) and pressing that letter opens the menu.

2. Slide the mouse pointer to the right to open the other menus (Edit, View, Go, Favorites, and Help) and examine their choices.

As you might surmise, each menu contains choices somewhat relevant to the menu's name. The names on menus vary from program to program, but there are usually a few common ones, such as File, Edit, and Help. It may take a while for you to become familiar with the commands and which menus they're located on, but it will become more automatic with time. In any case, it's easy enough to look through the menus to find the one you want.

Selecting Menu Commands

Once a menu is open, you can select any of the commands in the menu that aren't dimmed (dimmed choices are explained soon).

NOTE

At this point, don't select any of the commands just yet. We'll begin using the commands in a bit.

When a menu is open, you can select a menu command in any of these ways:

▸ By typing the underlined letter in the command name

▸ By sliding the mouse down and clicking a command's name

▸ By pressing the down-arrow or up-arrow keys on your keyboard to highlight the desired command name, and then pressing Enter

You can cancel a menu (that is, make the menu disappear without selecting any commands) by simply pressing the Escape key or by clicking anywhere outside the menu.

Special Indicators in Menus

Menus often have special symbols that tell you a little more about the menu commands. For example, examine the menus in Figure 4.11. Notice that many of these commands have additional words or symbols next to the command name. For example, the Options command has ellipses (three dots) after it. Other commands may have check marks, triangles, or key combinations listed beside them. In the following sections, I'll tell you what these words or symbols mean.

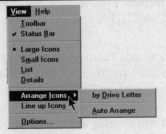

FIGURE 4.11: Typical menus

A Grayed (Dimmed) Command Name

When a command is shown as *grayed*, or *dimmed*, this choice is not currently available to you. A command can be dimmed for a number of reasons. For example, a command for changing the typestyle of text will be grayed if you haven't selected any text. Other times, commands will be grayed because you are in the wrong program mode. For example, if a window is already maximized, the Maximize command on the Control menu will be dimmed because this choice doesn't make sense.

Ellipses (...)

Ellipses next to a command means that you will be asked for additional information before Windows or the Windows application executes the command. When you select such a command, a dialog box will appear on the screen, asking you to fill in the needed information. (I'll discuss dialog boxes in the next section of this chapter.)

A Check Mark (✔)

A check mark preceding a command means the command is a *toggle* that is activated (turned on). A toggle is a command that is alternately turned off and on each time you select it. It's like those old high-beam switches on the car floor that you step on to change between high beams and low beams. Each time you select one of these commands, it switches from *active* to *inactive*. If there is no check mark, the command or setting is inactive. This is typically used to indicate things like whether selected text is underlined or not, which font is selected, what mode you are in within a program, and so on.

A Triangle (▶)

A triangle to the right of a menu command means that the command has additional subchoices for you to make. This is called a *cascading menu* (because the next menu starts to the right of the previous one and runs down from there, a bit like a waterfall of menus). You make selections from a cascaded menu the same way you would from a normal menu. The left example in Figure 4.11 shows a cascaded menu. The Taskbar also uses cascading menus, but we'll get to that in a moment.

A Dot

A dot to the left of the command means that the option is currently selected and is an exclusive option among several related options. For example, in Figure 4.11, the center section of one of the menus contains the options Large Icons, Small Icons, List, and Details. Only one of these options can be selected at a time. The dot indicates the current setting. By simply opening the menu again and clicking one of the other options, you set that option on.

A Key Combination

Some menu commands list keystrokes that can be used instead of opening the menu and choosing that command. For example, in the My Computer's Edit menu, shown below, notice that the Cut command could be executed by pressing Ctrl+X, the Copy command could be executed by pressing Ctrl+C, and the Paste command with Ctrl+V. These alternative time-saving keystrokes are called *shortcut keys*.

NOTE

A keystroke abbreviation such as Ctrl+C means to hold down the Ctrl key (typically found in the lower-left corner of your keyboard) while pressing the C key.

RIGHT-CLICKING IN WINDOWS

Right-clicking on objects throughout the Windows 98 SE interface displays a shortcut menu that has options pertaining to the object at hand. The same options are typically available from the normal menus, but are more conveniently reached with a right-click.

NOTE

These button names will, of course, be reversed if you are left-handed or have reversed the mouse buttons for some other reason. If you have a trackball, a GlidePoint, or other nonstandard pointing device, your right-click button may be somewhere unexpected. You may have to experiment a little to find which button activates the right-click menus.

Right-clicking isn't just part of the Windows 98 SE interface; it's been incorporated into many Windows programs too. For example, Microsoft Office programs such as Word and Excel have had right-click menus for some time. Some of the accessory programs supplied with Windows 98 SE have context-sensitive right-click menus too. In general, the contents of the right-click menus depend on the type of object. Options for a graphic will differ from those for a spreadsheet cell, text, a Web page, and so on.

As a rule, I suggest you start using the right-click button whenever you can. You'll learn through experimentation which of your programs do something with the right-click and which don't. Some older 16-bit Windows programs won't even respond to the click; others may do the unexpected. But in almost every case, right-clicking results in a pop-up menu that you can close by clicking elsewhere or by pressing Escape; so don't worry about doing anything dangerous or irreversible.

A good example of a right-clickable item is the Taskbar. Right-click an empty place on the Taskbar, and you'll see this menu:

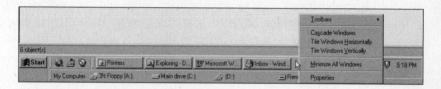

Now right-click the Start button, and you'll see this menu:

Here are a few other right-clicking experiments to try:

▶ Right-click My Computer and notice the menu options.

▶ Right-click a document icon. If you click a word-processing document, you can often print it directly from the right-click menu!

▶ When you right-click a printer in the Printer's folder, you can quickly declare the printer to be the default printer or to work offline (not actually print yet, even though you print to it from your applications) or go online with accumulated print jobs. Right-click the Desktop to change the screen properties, and so forth.

- ▸ Right-click any program's title bar, and notice the menu for resizing the window or closing the application.

- ▸ Right-click a minimized program's button down in the Taskbar. You can close the program quickly by choosing Close.

- ▸ Right-click the time in the Taskbar, and choose Adjust Date/Time to alter the date and time settings for your computer.

Right-click menus will often have Cut, Copy, Paste, Open, Print, and Rename choices on them.

Many objects, such as folders, printers, and Network Neighborhood, have a right-click menu called Explore that displays the item in the Windows Explorer's format (two vertical panes). This is a super-handy way to check out the object in more detail. You'll have the object in the left pane and its contents listed in the right pane. In some cases, the contents are print jobs; in other cases they are fonts, files, folders, disk drives, or computers on the network.

Sharable items, such as printers, hard disks, and fax modems, will have a Sharing option on their right-click menus. The resulting dialog box lets you declare how an object is shared for use by other users on the network.

USING PROPERTIES DIALOG BOXES

Just as most objects have right-click menus, many also have *Properties dialog boxes*. Properties pervade all aspects of the Windows 98 SE user interface, providing you with a simple and direct means for making settings for everything from how the screen looks to whether a file is hidden or what a shared printer is named.

Virtually every object in Windows 98 SE—whether a printer, modem, shortcut, hard disk, folder, networked computer, or hardware driver—has a Properties dialog box containing such settings. These settings affect how the object works and, sometimes, how it looks. And Properties dialog boxes not only *display* the settings for the object, but usually allow you to easily *alter* the settings.

You've probably noticed that many right-click menus have a Properties choice down at the bottom. This choice is often the quickest path to an object's Properties dialog box—not that there aren't other ways. Many dialog boxes, for example, have a Properties button that will display the object's settings when clicked. And Control Panel is used for setting numerous properties throughout Windows 98 SE. Still, as you become more and more comfortable with Windows, you'll find the right-click approach most expedient.

The Properties option is always the last command on a right-click menu. For example, if you right-click My Computer, you'll see this menu:

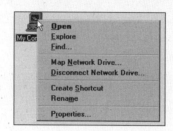

Or right-click the time in the Taskbar, and you'll see this:

Here's another everyday example. Suppose you're browsing through some folders (or the Windows Explorer) and come across a Word document. Wondering what it is, when it was created, and who created it, you just right-click and choose Properties. The file's Properties dialog box pops up, as shown in Figure 4.12. This dialog box has several tabs because Word specifically stores additional property information in its files.

Properties dialog boxes for other kinds of files may have only a single tab with less than a copious amount of information. In fact, most document Properties dialog boxes are truly useful only if you want to examine the history of the file, determine its shorter MS-DOS filename, or set its DOS attributes, such as whether it should be read-only (to prevent others from using it), hidden from view in folders, or if its *archive bit* should be set. (A check mark in the Archive box means the file hasn't been backed up since it was last altered or since it was created.) My point is that you can usually only *view* the status of the document, not *alter* the information about the document.

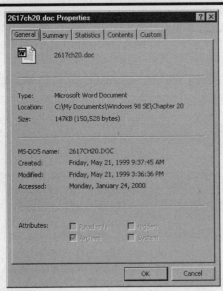

FIGURE 4.12: A typical Properties dialog box for a document file. This one is for a Word 2000 file, so it has several tabs listing its editing history, who created it, keywords, title, and so forth.

WORKING WITH DIALOG BOXES

As I said earlier, a dialog box will always appear when you select a command with an ellipsis (...) after it. Dialog boxes pop up on your screen when Windows or the Windows application program you're using needs more information before continuing. Some dialog boxes ask you to enter information (such as filenames); others simply require you to check off options or make choices from a list. The list may be in the form of additional sub-dialog boxes or submenus. In any case, after you enter the requested information, you click OK, and Windows or the application program continues on its merry way, executing the command.

Though most dialog boxes ask you for information, other boxes are only informative, alerting you to a problem with your system or an error you've made. Such a box might also request confirmation on a command that could have dire consequences or explain why the command you've chosen can't be executed. These alert boxes sometimes have a big letter *i* (for "information") in them or an exclamation mark (!). A few examples are shown in Figure 4.13.

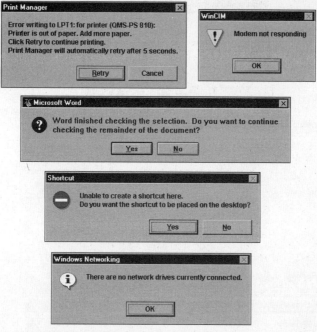

FIGURE 4.13: Dialog boxes are used for a wide variety of purposes. Here are some examples of dialog boxes that are informative only, and do not ask you to make settings or adjust options.

More often than not, these boxes ask you only to read them and then click on OK (or cancel them if you decide not to proceed). Some boxes have only an OK button. Let's look at some typical dialog boxes and see how they work.

Moving between Sections of a Dialog Box

As you can see in Figure 4.14, dialog boxes often have several sections to them. You can move between the sections in three ways:

- ▶ The easiest way is by clicking on the section you want to alter.

- ▶ If you are using the keyboard, you can press the Tab key to move between sections and press the spacebar to select them.

- ▶ You can also use the Alt key with the underlined letter of the section name you want to jump to or activate. Even when you are using a mouse, the Alt-key combinations are sometimes the fastest way to jump between sections or choose an option within a box.

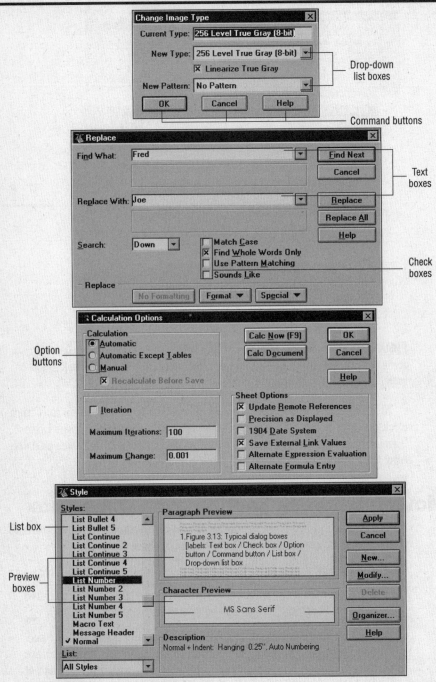

FIGURE 4.14: Typical dialog boxes

Notice that one of the dialog boxes here has a Preview section. This is a feature that more and more dialog boxes will be sporting as applications become more *user friendly*. Rather than having to choose a formatting change, for example, and then OKing the dialog box to see the effect on your document, a Preview section lets you see the effect in advance. This lets you "shop" for the effect you want before committing to it.

Many newer Windows programs have dialog boxes with *tabs*, a new item introduced around the time of Windows 95. Tabs keep a dialog box to a reasonable size while still letting you adjust a lot of settings from it. To get to the tab you want, simply click it. Figure 4.15 illustrates this concept. I've clicked the View tab of Word's Options dialog box.

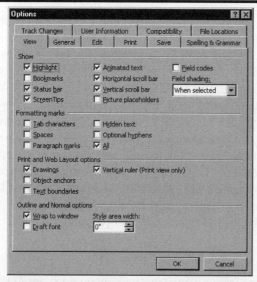

FIGURE 4.15: Newer dialog boxes have multiple tabs that make the boxes easier to understand and appear less cluttered. Click a tab, and a new set of options appears.

Entering Information in a Dialog Box

Now let's look at how you enter information in dialog boxes. Dialog boxes have seven basic elements:

- ▶ Text boxes
- ▶ Check boxes

- ▶ Option buttons

- ▶ Command buttons

- ▶ List boxes

- ▶ Drop-down list boxes

- ▶ File dialog boxes

Once you've jumped to the correct section, you'll need to know how to make choices from it. The next several sections explain how to use each kind. (Please refer to Figure 4.14 during the next discussions.)

Text Boxes

In this sort of section, you are asked to type in text from the keyboard. Sometimes text will already be entered for you. If you want to keep the text as is, just leave it alone. To alter the text, simply type new text. If the existing text is already highlighted, the first key you press will delete the existing entry. If it is not highlighted, you can backspace over it to erase it. You can also edit existing text. Clicking once on highlighted text will *deselect* it and cause the *insertion bar* (a vertical blinking bar) to appear when you put the pointer inside the text area. You can then move the text cursor around by using the arrow keys or the mouse, and insert text (by typing) or delete text (by pressing the Delete key). Text is inserted at the position of the insertion bar. Text boxes are most often used for specifying filenames when you are saving or loading documents and applications, or specifying text to search for in a word-processing document.

Check Boxes

Check boxes are the small square (or sometimes diamond-shaped) boxes. They indicate nonexclusive options. For example, you might want some text to appear as bold *and* underlined. Or, as another example, consider the Calculation Options dialog box from Excel shown in Figure 4.14. In this dialog box, you can set any of the settings in the Sheet Options section on or off. These are toggle settings (as explained previously) that you activate or deactivate by clicking the box. When the box is empty, the option is off; when you see an x, the option is on.

Option Buttons

Unlike check boxes, which are nonexclusive, option buttons are exclusive settings. Sometimes called *radio buttons*, these are round rather than square or diamond shaped, and only one option can be set on at a time. For example, using the same Calculation Options dialog box referred to above, you may select Automatic, Automatic Except Tables, *or* Manual in the Calculation section of the dialog box—not a combination of the three. Clicking a button turns it on (the circle will be filled) and turns any previous selection off. From the keyboard, you first jump to the section, and then use the arrow keys to select the option.

Command Buttons

Command buttons are like option buttons, except that they are used to execute a command immediately. They are rectangular rather than square or circular. An example of a command button is the OK button found in almost every dialog box. Once you've filled in a dialog box to your liking, click the OK button, and Windows or the application executes the settings you've selected. If you change your mind and don't want the new commands on the dialog box executed, click the Cancel button.

There is always a command button that has a thicker border; this is the command that will execute if you press Enter. Likewise, pressing the Escape key always has the same effect as clicking the Cancel button (that's why there's no underlined letter on the Cancel button).

Some command buttons are followed by ellipses (...). As you might expect, these commands will open additional dialog boxes for adjusting more settings. Other command buttons include two >> symbols in them. Choosing this type of button causes the particular section of the dialog box to expand so you can make more selections.

List Boxes

List boxes are like menus. They show you a list of options or items from which you can choose. For example, when choosing fonts to display or print text in, WordPad shows you a list box. You make a selection from a list box the same way you do from a menu: by just clicking on it. From the keyboard, highlight the desired option with the arrow keys, and then press Enter to choose it. Some list boxes are too small to show all the possible selections. In this case, a scroll bar will be on the right side of the box. Use the scroll bar to see all the selections. Some list boxes let you make more than one selection, but most allow only one. To make more than one selection from the keyboard, press the spacebar to select or deselect any item.

TIP

You can quickly jump to an option in a list box by typing the first letter of its name. If there are two choices with the same first letter and you want the second one, press the letter again, or press the down-arrow key.

Drop-Down List Boxes

Drop-down list boxes are indicated by a small arrow in a box to the right of the option. The current setting is displayed to the left of the little arrow. Clicking the arrow opens a list that works just like a normal list box and has scroll bars if there are a lot of options. Drop-down list boxes are used when a dialog box is too crowded to accommodate regular list boxes.

File Dialog Boxes

A dialog box like one of the three shown in Figure 4.16 often appears when you're working in Windows programs. (Figure 4.17 shows a file dialog box from Windows 98 SE.) This type of box is called a *file dialog box*, or simply *file box*. Though file boxes are used in a variety of situations, you're most likely to run into file boxes when you want to open a file or when you save a document for the first time. For example, choosing File ➤ Open from almost any Windows program will display such a box asking which document file you want to open.

NOTE

If you're new to Windows, you may want to mark this section of the book with a paper clip and refer to it when you have to save or open a file for the first time.

File dialog boxes vary somewhat from program to program, even though they perform the same job. Some boxes, as you will note in Figure 4.16, allow you to open a file as Read Only, for example, or help you search for a file with a Find button or a Network button (if you're connected to a network). The file box went through a major redesign by Microsoft after they finally figured out that novices were thoroughly confused by it. Now the new design is much more intuitively obvious and is very similar to the file boxes used on the Mac. Because the older two boxes and new type are pretty different from one another, I'll explain the steps for the newer style boxes here.

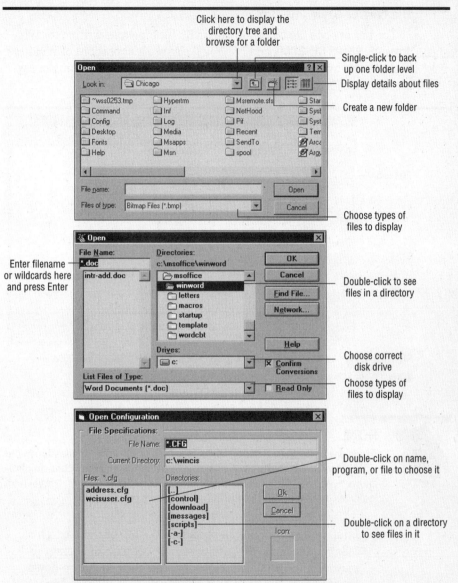

Click here to display the directory tree and browse for a folder

Single-click to back up one folder level

Display details about files

Create a new folder

Choose types of files to display

Enter filename or wildcards here and press Enter

Double-click to see files in a directory

Choose correct disk drive

Choose types of files to display

Double-click on name, program, or file to choose it

Double-click on a directory to see files in it

FIGURE 4.16: A file dialog box lets you scan through directories to load or save a document. Here you see three typical file dialog box types. The upper one is the newer Windows 95/98 style. The middle one is the Windows 3.x style, and the lowest one is the moldy, oldy 3.0 style.

Part i

The Newer-Style File Box

The newer-style file box shows up in 32-bit programs written for Windows 95, 98, 98 SE, 2000, and NT. You'll also see it in portions of Windows itself. Here's how to use this type of file box when you're opening or saving files (see Figure 4.17).

FIGURE 4.17: This newer file box is used by many 32-bit applications in Windows 98 SE.

NOTE

To see one of these new dialog boxes, you can run the Paint application found in the Accessories folder by clicking the Start button and then choosing Programs ➤ Accessories ➤ Paint. Now choose File ➤ Open. (The ➤ symbol here indicates a chain of choices you make from the menus.)

1. First, notice the Look In section at the top of the box. This tells you the name of the folder whose contents are being displayed in the window below. You can click this drop-down list to choose the drive or folder you want to look in.

2. If the file is in a folder whose icon is displayed in the Places bar, click the icon to display the folder's contents.

3. You can create a new folder using the Create New Folder button in the dialog box's toolbar if you want to save something in a

folder that doesn't already exist. This can help you organize your files. The new folder will be created as a subfolder to the folder shown in the Look In area. (After creating the new folder, you'll have to name it by typing in a new name just to the right of the folder.)

4. The object is to display the target folder in the window, and then double-click it. So, if the folder you want is somewhere on your hard disk (typically drive C), one way to display it is to choose C: from the Look In area. All the folders on your C drive appear in the window. *Don't forget about scrolling! You might have to scroll the contents of the window to display the folder you want, if there are too many folders to fit in the window.*

5. In the large window, double-click the folder you want to look in. If you don't see the folder you're aiming for, you may have to move down or back up the tree of folders a level or two. You back up a level by clicking the Up One Level button. You move down a level by double-clicking a folder and looking for its subfolders to then appear in the window. You can then double-click a subfolder to open that, and so on.

6. Finally, click the file you want to open. Or, if you're saving a file for the first time, you'll have to type the name of the file. Of course, if you are saving a file for the first time, the file won't exist on the drive yet, so it won't show up in the list of files; you'll be giving it a name. To do this, select the drive and directory as outlined above, and then click in the File Name area and type the filename. Make sure to delete any existing letters in the text area first, using the Backspace and/or Delete keys.

7. If you want to see only certain types of files, open the Files Of Type box to select the type of files you want to see (such as a certain kind of document or all files). If the options offered don't suit your needs, you can type in DOS-like wildcards in the File Name area, and then press Enter to modify the file list accordingly. For example, to show only Lotus 1-2-3 worksheet files, you'd enter ***.WK?** in the File Name area and press Enter.

8. Once the file you want is visible in the file box at the left, double-click it or highlight it, and click OK.

TIP

Here's a trick I use all the time. Instead of scrolling around to find a file or folder that I know I'm heading for, I can jump to it, or close to it, quickly. Just click once on a folder or file in the box (any one will do), and then type the first letter of the item you're looking for. That will jump the highlight to the first item that starts with the letter and probably bring your target into view. Successive key-presses will move through each item that starts with that letter.

USING THE WINDOWS 98 SE WEB VIEW

The use of the Internet and the World Wide Web (sometimes called "WWW," "W3," or simply "the Web") has escalated beyond anyone's wildest imaginations. You can't read a magazine, watch a TV commercial, or watch the evening news without seeing Web addresses. You can't even listen to the radio without hearing the words "dot com" in half the commercials. Quite a few of my friends have their own Web sites, and so do I, for that matter (www.cowart.com).

Since so many of us are using our computers to look at the Web, Microsoft decided to come up with an adjustment to the Windows interface to make for a more seamless meshing of stuff that's in your computer with stuff that's out there on the Internet. For instance, on Web pages, you click once on a link to go to a new Web page. In the optional interface to Windows 98 SE, you can also click once to go to files and launch programs.

The new look is called *Web view*, for obvious reasons. It's pretty nice, and I have to say I like it a lot. It cuts down on clicking (and resultant finger and carpal tunnel wear over the course of a day's work), and I don't have to remember if I'm on a Web page or looking at folders and files on my hard disk. Now everything works much more similarly.

Technically the Web view option is a feature of Internet Explorer, the Web browser from Microsoft. You might have heard of Netscape Navigator, the competition. But Netscape Navigator doesn't have this feature. Even though lawsuits and Federal Trade Commission investigations are raging as of this writing, Internet Explorer 5 (IE5) continues to be shipped with Windows 98 SE, and so you have Web view as an option in your copy of Windows 98 SE. (See Chapter 19 for more about Internet Explorer.) Despite the Microsoft bashing, IE is a terrific Web browser and integrates with Windows 98 SE very nicely, as you'll see.

Internet Explorer 5 changes the look and feel of Windows. Here are the main points:

▶ Folder windows have *Back* and *Forward* buttons. The Windows Explorer also has these buttons. These buttons let you easily review a sequence of folders that you've recently been examining, without having to traverse the directory tree.

▶ The toolbars in Folder and Explorer windows are customizable, just like those in IE are. You can add an "address bar," for example—type in a Web address while you're exploring your hard drive's contents, press Enter, and the window becomes a Web browser. It connects to the Internet and displays the page. (See Chapter 6 for more about Windows Explorer.) Type a local hard disk name in the address bar (**C:** for example), and folders are displayed again.

▶ Files and folders can act like "hot links" on a Web page: one click activates them.

▶ All folders can have a specialized Web page "look" that you can customize using a background or custom HTML code. With a single menu choice, even nonprogrammers can choose a default Web view that has some useful features, including a display that shows thumbnail views (of pictures, local Web pages, text documents, and so on).

▶ Your Desktop can be made "active," displaying data streaming in from the Internet (such as stocks, news, entertainment listings, and so on).

In this section, I'll cover only those effects that are related to the overall interface.

Turning On Web View

Want to try Web view? Good. You just might like it. Of course, if you're in a business in which you use lots of other people's computers and they aren't using Web view, you might confuse yourself a bit by mixing up your habits, but it's not really that mentally difficult to switch between them.

1. Choose Start ➤ Settings ➤ Folder Options to open the Folder Options dialog box.

2. Click the Web Style radio button to turn on the option.

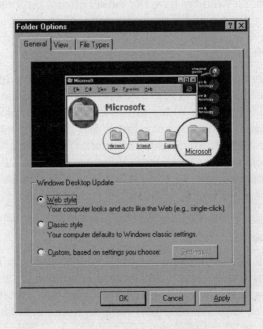

3. Click OK. You'll be prompted to make sure this is what you want to do.

Now your Desktop should have changed its look, as you see in Figure 4.18.

Notice that the My Computer window now looks fancier and has a description. Most any folder window (including stuff like Printers or Control Panel, which you can reach now by single-clicking them in the My Computer window) will have a spiffed-up look, complete with descriptions.

FIGURE 4.18:   After turning Web view on, icons, folders, and other documents have a line under them like Web links.

An important skill with Web view is "pointing." See, in Classic view (the traditional view you're using when you're *not* using Web view) you select an object by clicking on it. But with Web view on, you select an object by just pointing to it. You don't click. Try out this example:

1. Adjust the My Computer window to a larger size, to give you some room to navigate.

2. Simply move the pointer to one of the icons such as Control Panel. Don't click; just keep the pointer still over the Control Panel icon. The window should change to look like Figure 4.19. Notice also that the pointer takes the shape of a pointing hand.

3. Try pointing to the C drive. You'll see a little pie chart indicating the amount of free space on the disk and some other drive statistics. Pretty spiffy, eh?

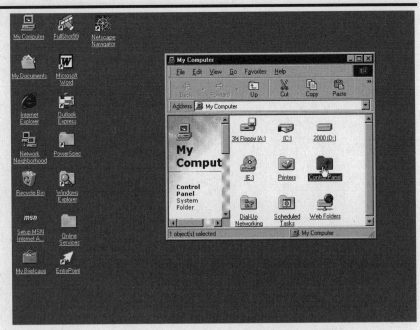

FIGURE 4.19: In Web view, you simply point to an object to select it.

WARNING

This pointing technique has some important consequences. In Web view you have to be careful not to click on things unless you are ready to execute some action. That's because a single click is now the same as a double click in Classic view. Clicking a folder opens it. Click a file, and it opens. Click a program, and it runs. And so forth. This also affects the selection of a *range* of objects, such as files or folders. Whereas in Classic view you click the first item in the range, hold down the Shift key, and then click the last item, in Web view you point to the first item, wait a second for it to be selected, and then press Shift and—you guessed it—*point* to the last item in the range.

TIP

Are you the nit-picky type? Want to control some of the details of Web view settings? You can do it. Select the Custom option in the Folder Options dialog box, click the Customize button, and change any settings that you would like to change. (Some of these are pretty technical though. If you don't understand a setting, don't touch it.) Personally, I think the standard Web style settings are right for most people. However, I do like the setting that eliminates the underline until you point to an object.

MESS-O-ADJUSTMENTS

There's a bushel of adjustments you can make to the user interface that I'm not going to go into here. But if you're brave or anxious to know, check them out by doing this:

1. Open any folder in a window.

2. From that folder's menu bar, choose View ➤ Folder Options to open the Folder Options dialog box.

3. Click the View tab. You'll see a list of options.

Study and remember these options. They could come in handy. Most germane to this discussion regarding the look of the interface are the last two options (you'll probably have to scroll down to see them):

Show Window Contents While Dragging   I mentioned this earlier in this chapter. If this check box is on, you can make the innards of a window move around with your mouse as you resize it or drag it.

Smooth Edges Of Screen Fonts   This smooths out some smaller letters on screen that might otherwise look blocky, filling in the gaps with a sort of thin, grayish blur. It's a nice feature and makes the screen easier on the eyes.

To activate one of these items, click it so that a check mark appears, and then click Apply or OK.

If you later decide that you've messed up the settings in this dialog box, click the Restore Defaults button. Everything will be set back to the way it came from the factory.

Returning to Classic View

If you decide you don't like Web view, it's cool. You can easily return to regular old Windows operation:

1. Open the Folder Options dialog box as we did in the preceding examples.

2. Click the General tab, and choose Classic Style.

3. Click OK.

EXITING WINDOWS

When you're finished with a Windows session, you should properly shut down Windows before turning off your computer. This ensures that Windows saves your work on disk correctly and that no data is lost. Even if you are running an application in Windows and you close that application, you *must* exit Windows too before turning off your computer.

WARNING

Exiting Windows properly is very important. You can lose your work or otherwise foul up Windows settings if you don't shut down Windows before turning off your computer. If you accidentally fail to do so, the computer probably won't die or anything, but the hard disk will be checked for errors the next time you turn it on.

Here are the steps for correctly exiting Windows:

1. Close any programs that you have running. (This can almost always be done from each program's File menu—choose Exit from the menu—or by clicking the program's Close button.) If you forget to close programs before issuing the Shut Down command, Windows will attempt to close them for you. This is fine unless you were working on a document and didn't save your work. In that case, you'll be prompted by a dialog box for each open document, asking you if you want to save your work. If you have DOS programs running, you'll have to close them manually before Windows will let you exit. You'll also be reminded if this is the case by a dialog box telling you that Windows can't terminate the program and you'll have to do it from the DOS program. Quit the DOS program and type **exit** at the DOS prompt, if necessary.

SAVE ENERGY! THE SUSPEND OPTION FOR LAPTOPS AND DESKTOPS WITH ONNOW

If your computer has Advanced Power Management (APM) or Advanced Configuration and Power Interface (ACPI) built in, you may have a Standby option in the Shutdown dialog box. This is like shutting down, only it lets you come right back to where you were

CONTINUED ➡

working before you suspended. This means that you don't have to exit all your applications before turning off your computer. You only have to choose Standby. It also means that you can get right back to work where you left off without rebooting your computer, finding the document(s) you were working on, and finding your place in those documents. You can just press a key or button (depending on your computer), and in a few seconds you are up and running right where you left off.

An increasing number of laptop computers now support this Standby (sometimes called Suspend) function. There is a limit to the amount of time a laptop computer can stay in a suspended state. If the battery runs out, the computer will have to be rebooted when you turn it on, and your work may be lost. If you're going to standby on a laptop for very long, you should use the Hibernate function, if your laptop supports it (check the manual). Most new ones do. There is no time limit with Hibernate, though it takes a little longer to revive the machine (like about 15 seconds). Still, the effect is the same—you start working from where you left off.

My experience is that Toshiba computers hold the record in terms of how long they will stay in Suspend mode. I have had five Toshibas thus far, precisely for their well-engineered *Auto Resume* feature. A typical Toshiba laptop will stay suspended on a full battery charge for several days to a week or more. Most other brands won't stay suspended for more than a few hours. You'll want to check with the manufacturer of your computer about how long theirs will stay "alive" in a suspended state if you plan to use the Windows 98 SE Standby option.

Due to the growing popularity of this idea on laptops, and the desire by the U.S. Department of Energy for us all to conserve power, the latest breed of desktop computers have OnNow technology built in. This means that they, too, can be put in a suspended state, lowering power consumption considerably. That saves you lots on your electric bill (way too many offices leave their PCs on all the time) and keeps the air cleaner (did you know that 80 percent of our power comes from burning fossil fuels and garbage?). If your desktop machine supports this feature, you'll have a Standby option in

CONTINUED ➡

your Shutdown dialog box. Some machines, such as ones from Compaq, have a hardware button on the keyboard or computer box to engage Standby mode, too.

WARNING

If you do have Standby capability on your computer, you should save your work before suspending. You don't necessarily have to close the applications you're using, but you should at least save any documents you're working on.

2. Next, click the Start button and choose Shut Down. You'll now see a dialog box like that in Figure 4.20.

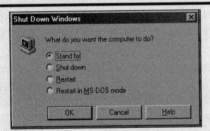

FIGURE 4.20: The Start ≻ Shut Down command offers a variety of ways to end your Windows session.

3. Choose Shut Down or Standby (if available), depending on which you want.

4. Click OK. Now take one of two actions:

    ▶ If you chose Standby, in a few seconds the computer will appear to shut off. There may be some indication that it's still semi-alive, such as a little light somewhere or an indicator on an LCD panel or something (depending on the brand and model of your computer). If it's a laptop computer, you can now close the cover and pack it up if you need to take to the streets.

► If you chose Shut Down, wait until Windows completely shuts down and tells you it's OK to turn off your computer. This can take up to about 15 seconds. Just wait until the screen says, "It's now safe to turn off your computer."

Then turn off the computer, printer, monitor, and other stuff you have attached. You're home free.

What's Next?

Understanding the interface is your first step in taking charge of your Windows computer. You need this information in order to run your Windows applications properly and easily, which is the topic of the next chapter in this section. Robert Cowart takes a look at the various ways to run programs and discusses how to use Desktop shortcuts, customize the Taskbar, switch between applications, and share data between applications.

Chapter 5

GETTING DOWN TO BUSINESS: RUNNING YOUR APPLICATIONS

I f you're upgrading from Windows 3.1 or Windows 95, you already know a lot about how to use Windows and Windows applications. A few things will be different with Windows 98 SE, but you'll probably pick those up quickly. If you're new to Windows, getting used to the turf might take a little longer, though you'll have an advantage—you won't have to unlearn any bad habits that Windows 3.*x* veterans have ground into their craniums.

Adapted from *Mastering Windows 98 Second Edition* by Robert Cowart

ISBN 0-7821-2618-9   893 pages $39.99

NOTE

In this chapter, I'm going to assume that you're running Windows 98 SE in Web view rather than in Classic view. (See Chapter 4 if you forget the difference, or for how to change views.) Although Classic view is the default setting until you change it, I think that Web view is the wave of the future. When something I'm talking about looks radically different in Classic view, I'll mention it in a note or an aside.

RUNNING PROGRAMS

As with many of the procedures you'll want to do while in Windows, starting your programs can be done in myriad ways. Here's the complete list of ways to run programs. You can:

- ▶ Choose the desired application from the Start button's menus.

- ▶ Add the application to the Quick Launch toolbar, and click it to run.

- ▶ Open My Computer, walk your way through the folders until you find the application's icon, and double-click it.

- ▶ Run Windows Explorer, find the application's icon, and double-click it.

- ▶ Find the application with the Find command, and double-click it.

- ▶ Locate a document that was created with the application in question, and double-click it. The application runs, and the document opens.

- ▶ Right-click the Desktop or a folder, choose New, and then choose a document type from the shortcut menu. This creates a new document of the type you specify. Double-clicking the icon runs the application.

- ▶ Open the Documents list from the Start button, and choose a recently edited document. The document opens in the appropriate application.

- ▶ Enter command names from the MS-DOS prompt. In addition to the old-style MS-DOS commands that run MS-DOS programs and batch files, you can run Windows programs right from the MS-DOS prompt.

▶ Click a program icon on the Windows Desktop. Many programs place shortcut icons on the Desktop to make launching them easy, and you can also create your own Desktop icons.

In deference to tradition, I'm going to cover the approaches to running applications in the order listed above. All the approaches are useful while using Windows, and you will probably want to become proficient in each of them.

Running Programs from the Start Button

Certainly the easiest way to run your applications is with the Start button. That's why it's called the Start button.

When you install a new program, the program's name is almost always added to the Start button's Program menu system. You simply find your way to the program's name, choose it, and the program runs. If you want to run Notepad, for example, follow these steps:

1. Click the Start button.

2. Choose Programs because you want to start a program. Up comes a list of programs similar to what's shown in Figure 5.1. Your list may differ because this is the list of programs on *my* computer, not yours. Any selection that has an arrow pointer to the right of the name is not actually a program but a program *group*. If you've used Windows 3.*x*, you'll know that program groups are the collections of programs and related document files that were used to organize your programs in Windows 3.*x*'s Program Manager. Choosing one of these opens another menu listing the items in the group.

3. I happen to know that the Notepad program lies among the accessory programs that come with Windows 98 SE. Slide the pointer up or over to highlight Accessories. A list of accessory programs appears. Slide the pointer down to Notepad and click, as shown in Figure 5.2.

You've successfully run Notepad. It's now sitting there with a blank document open, waiting for you to start typing. To close Notepad, click the Close button, or open the File menu and choose Exit.

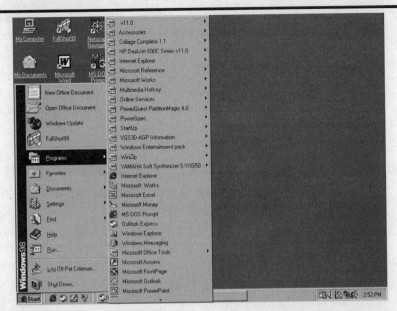

FIGURE 5.1: The first step in running a program is to click the Start button and choose Programs from the resulting list.

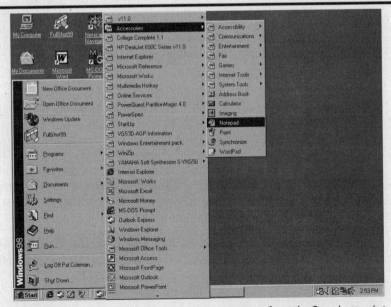

FIGURE 5.2: The second step in running a program from the Start button is to choose the program itself from the resulting Program list, or to open a group such as Accessories and then choose the program.

Because Windows 98 SE lets you nest groups of applications and documents into multiple levels, you might occasionally run into multiple levels of cascading menus when you're trying to launch (that's computerese for *run*) an application. In the example above, I had to open the Accessories group to find Notepad. If you open the Accessories group, you'll notice several groups within Accessories up at the top: Accessibility, Communications, Entertainment, Games, Internet Tools, and System Tools. Sometimes because of the length of a list, the list might need to scroll off the screen. In this case, you'll see arrows at the top or bottom of the list, like this:

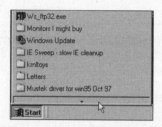

Just click the arrow to scroll the list, release the mouse button when you see the one you want, and then click it.

TIP

Sometimes spotting a program in a list is a visual hassle. Computers are smart about alphabetizing, so notice that the items in the lists are in order from A to Z. Folders appear first, in order, and then programs follow. This ordering is something you'll see throughout Windows. To make things even simpler, you can press the first letter of the item you're looking for, and the highlight will jump to it. If multiple items start with that letter, each key press will advance one in the list. This works fairly reliably unless the pointer is sitting on an item that has opened into a group.

TIP

Often you will accidentally open a list that you don't want to look at—say, Documents. Just move the pointer to the one you want—let's say, Programs. The Document list will close, and the Programs list will open. It takes a little getting used to, but you'll get the hang of it. Another way to close unwanted program lists is by pressing the Escape key. This has the effect of closing open lists one at a time. Each press of Escape closes one level of any open list. To close all open lists, just click anywhere else on the screen, such as on the Desktop or another window, and all open Start button lists will go away.

Running Programs from My Computer

At times, you might want to do a little sleuthing on your hard disk using a graphical approach, as opposed to hunting for a name in the Start list. The My Computer icon lets you do this. My Computer is usually situated in the upper-left corner of your Desktop. Clicking it reveals an interesting entry point to all the elements of your computer—hardware, software, printers, files, and folders.

NOTE

Just a reminder: If you are using Classic view, a double click is going to be necessary to open a folder, run a program, and so on. I'm going to try to use consistent language in this chapter, which, as I mentioned earlier, is based on Web view. Sometimes I'll just simplify matters by saying "Open the folder," "Run the program," or whatever, and you can decide how you're going to open it based on which view you're using.

The My Computer icon is the entry point for the file system and other parts of your computer, including Control Panel, Dial-Up Networking, and Printers. It's a very Mac-like way of moving through the stuff in your computer. Getting to a program you want can be a little convoluted, but if you understand the MS-DOS directory tree structure, or if you've used a Mac, you'll be able to grasp this easily. Try it out by following these steps:

1. Get to the Desktop by minimizing any windows that are on the screen. You can do this by clicking each window's Minimize button, but the fastest way is by clicking the Show Desktop icon to the right of the Start button (this is a great little time-saver).

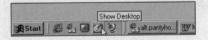

TIP

Yet another way to minimize all your windows and display the Desktop is to right-click the time in the Taskbar and choose Minimize All Windows.

2. Now open My Computer (you know, double-click it, or single-click if in Web view). A window appears, looking something like the following.

3. Typically, drive C is where your programs are located. Open the drive icon, and your hard drive's contents will appear (in the same window if you are in Web view, or in another window in Classic view), as shown in Figure 5.3.

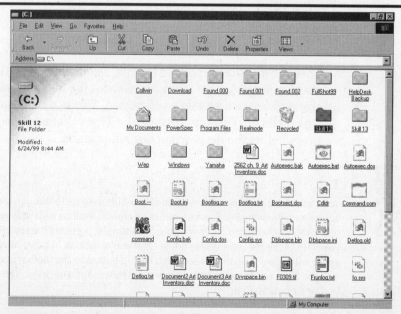

FIGURE 5.3: Opening a drive icon displays its contents in a window. Here you see a portion of what I have on my C drive. Notice that folders (which used to be called directories in Windows 3.*x*) are listed first. Scrolling the listing would reveal files. Here we are in essence looking at the root directory of my C drive. Clicking a folder will reveal its contents.

4. The object is to locate the folder containing the program you want and open it. (Some programs are so hidden away that it's difficult to find them. You may have to search around a bit.) The standard setting shows folders and files as *large icons*. If you want to see more folders on the screen at once to help in your search, you have several options. The Large Icon view can be annoying because it doesn't let you see very many objects at once. Check out the View menu, as shown below, and choose Small Icons, or better yet, click the little arrow next to the View button in the toolbar.

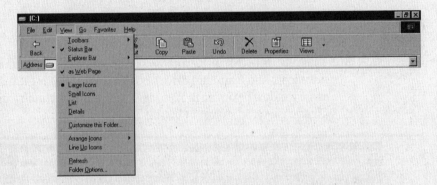

5. Choose Small Icons, List, or Details. *Details* will show the sizes of files and other information about the files and folders, such as the date they were created. This is useful when looking for applications, because the Type column will indicate whether the file is an application program.

TIP

You can simply click repeatedly on the View button to cycle through the available views. Pressing Backspace while in any folder window will move you back one level. While in the C drive window, for example, pressing Backspace takes you back to the My Computer window. Or, if you're looking at a directory, Backspace will take you up to the root level. The Up button on the toolbar works too. And the Back and Forward buttons move you forward and back through folders you've already visited.

6. When you see the program you want to run, click it. For example, in Figure 5.4 I've found Microsoft Word.

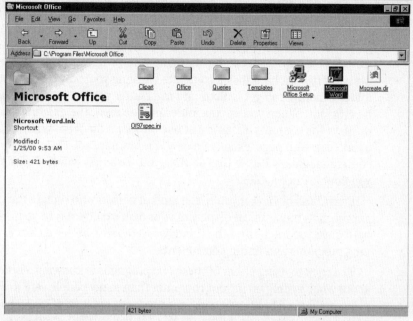

FIGURE 5.4: Run a program by clicking its icon. Regardless of whether you're displaying Large Icons, Small Icons, List, or Details view, clicking (or double-clicking in Classic view) will run it.

Many of the files you'll find in your folders are *not* programs. They are documents or other kinds of files that are used by programs. Programs tend to have specialized icons such as the one for Microsoft Word in Figure 5.4. Documents, as you will learn later, tend to look a bit different.

TIP

Normally, files with some specific extensions (the last three letters of a file's name) are hidden from display. Files with dll, sys, vxd, 386, drv, and cpl extensions will not display. Nor will "hidden" system files and folders display. Microsoft made this decision to prevent cluttering the display with files that perform duties for the operating system but not directly for users. Hiding these files also prevents your meddling with files that could affect how the system runs. If you want to see all the files and folders on your machine, do this: from a folder's window choose View ➤ Folder Options to open the Folder Options dialog box, click the View tab, and then click the Show All Files option button.

Running Programs from Windows Explorer

On the Mac, all you get to work with to organize your documents and programs are folders—essentially the same arrangement the last section illustrated. This approach can be annoying when what you want is a grand overview of your hard disk's contents. Working your way through a lot of folder windows can get tedious and can clutter up the screen too much to be efficient. When you open a folder in Web view, the existing window displays the contents. (This is just like browsing the Web. When you click a link on a Web page, usually no new window appears. Only the window's content changes.) But in Classic view, you see a new window each time you double-click a folder.

Regardless of view, if you're the kind of person who prefers the tree approach (a hierarchical display of your disk's contents) to your PC's hard disk, you might find the Windows Explorer a better means of running programs and finding documents.

The trick to using either of these two programs is knowing a little more about what's going on in your computer than many people care to. Principally, you'll need to know where your programs are located and what their names are. For example, Microsoft Word is really called `word.exe` on the hard disk and is typically stored in the `Program Files\Microsoft Office\Office` directory.

NOTE
Although not featured, the old-style Windows 3.*x* File Manager is actually supplied as part of Windows 98 SE. It's not listed on the Start button menu, but it's most likely on your hard disk. Click Start ➤ Run, type **winfile**, and press Enter. Ye olde File Manager opens on your screen.

Here's how to use Windows Explorer to run your programs:

1. Because Windows Explorer is a program itself, you have to run it before you can use it to run other programs. So click the Start button, choose Programs, and point to Windows Explorer, as shown in Figure 5.5.

TIP
Another way to run Explorer is to right-click My Computer or a drive's icon in the My Computer window, and choose Explore.

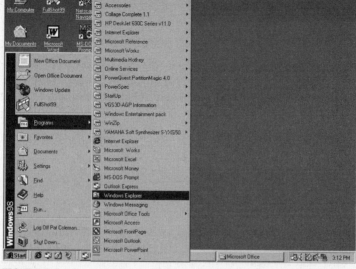

FIGURE 5.5: To run Windows Explorer, click Start, click Programs, and then click Windows Explorer.

> **2.** When the Windows Explorer window opens, adjust the window size for your viewing pleasure. It should look something like Figure 5.6.

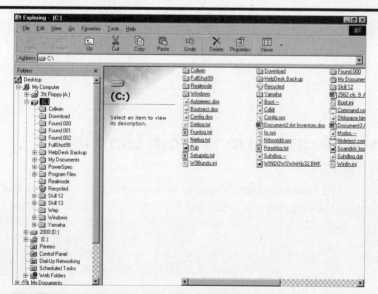

FIGURE 5.6: The Windows Explorer, in Small Icons view

3. The items on the left side are folders. Scroll down to the folder that contains the program you're looking for (folders are in alphabetic order). If a folder has a plus sign next to it, it has subfolders. Clicking the plus sign displays the names of any subfolders.

4. Single-click the folder containing the program you want to run. Its contents will appear in the right side (called the right *pane*) of the window.

5. Click or double-click the program. Here I'm about to run Microsoft Works.

Notice that the items in the right pane are displayed as large icons. Just as when using folders, you can change the appearance of listed items by clicking the View button, using the little list next to the View button, or opening the View menu and choosing Large Icons, Small Icons, List, or Details. It's easier to see which file is a program when the display is set to Large Icons (because you can see the icon clearly) or Details (because the third column will say *application* if the file is a program).

Running Applications from the Find Command

As with Windows Explorer, the Find command helps if you know the file-name of the program you're looking for, but at least it cuts you some slack if you don't know the whole name. You can specify just part of it. Find will search a given disk or the whole computer (multiple disks), looking for something that is similar to the program (or other file, such as a document) name you tell it. Once found, you can double-click the program in the resulting list, and it will run. Pretty spiffy.

TIP

Using the Run box (described earlier in this chapter) is easier than using Find if you know the exact name of the program. But the catch is that Run requires the program to be in the MS-DOS *search path*. If it's not, the program won't run, and you'll just get an error message saying the program can't be found. Of course, if you know the drive and directory the program is in, you *can* enter its entire path name, in which case it will probably run.

Here's an example. I have the program called Dunmon somewhere on my computer. It's a program that doesn't have its own setup program, so it never got added to my Start menus. I could add it manually, as you'll learn how to do later, but I'm too lazy to do that for all the programs I have. So I use the Find command. Why not the Run command? Well, the Run command won't run this program, because Dunmon is stored in a folder that's not in my MS-DOS search path. All I get when I try to find it is this message:

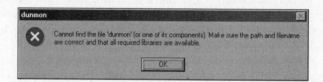

So I cancel the Run dialog box and try the Find command. Here's how:

NOTE

From here on out, I'm going to rely more heavily on the shorthand notation to describe making multiple menu choices. For example, instead of "Click the Start button, choose Programs, then choose Accessories, and then choose Paint," I'll say, "Choose Start ➢ Programs ➢ Accessories ➢ Paint."

1. Choose Start ➢ Find ➢ Files Or Folders.

2. The Find dialog box appears, and I fill in the top part with at least a portion of the name of the file I'm looking for. (See Figure 5.7—I've enlarged the Find window to show you as much information as possible.) As a default, Find searches the C drive, which is usually fine unless you have multiple hard disks on your computer and want Find to comb through them all.

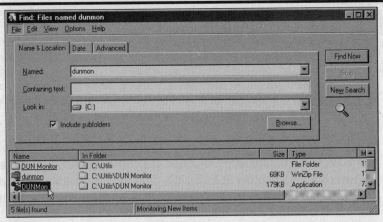

FIGURE 5.7: Choosing Find from the Start menu lets you search the computer for a program (or any file for that matter).

3. I click Find Now. In a few seconds, any files or folders matching the search request show up in the bottom pane, as Figure 5.7 illustrates. Several Dunmon files were located, but only one is an application (a program).

4. I click the Dunmon application, and it runs.

If you're running in Classic view, be careful not to double-click a filename slowly (click once, second click). Doing so tells Windows that you want to change the object's name. You know this has happened when a little box appears around the name of the file, like this:

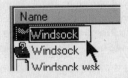

Just press Escape to get out of editing mode. To be safe, it's better to click any item's icon (the picture portion) when you want to run it, open it, move it, and so forth.

Running a Program via One of Its Documents

As I mentioned earlier, some documents will open when you click their icons—if they are *registered*. Windows 98 SE has an internal Registry (basically just a list) of file extensions that it knows about. Each registered file type is matched with a program that it works with. When you double-click any document, Windows scans the list of registered file types to determine what it should do with the file. For example, clicking a bmp file will run Paint and load the file.

The upshot of this is that you can run an application by clicking (or double-clicking in Classic view) a document of a known registered type. For example, suppose I want to run Word. All I have to do is spot a Word document somewhere. It's easy to spot one, especially in Large Icons view, because all Word documents have Word's telltale identifying icon. Unregistered documents have no discernible icon. Check out Figure 5.8. There I'm about to double-click a Word document that I came across in a folder.

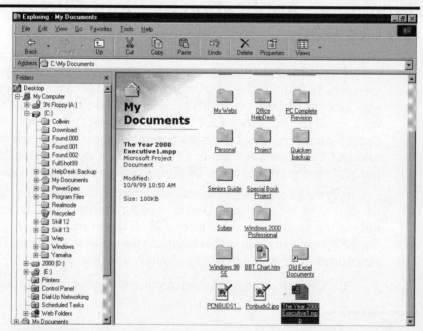

FIGURE 5.8: Double-clicking a file of a registered type runs the program that created it.

Once the program runs, you may decide you don't want to work with the actual document that you used as a trick to get the program going. That's OK, because most programs will let you close the current document (try choosing File ➢ Close) and then let you open a new document (usually via File ➢ New) or an existing one with File ➢ Open.

TIP

Try clicking the Start button and choosing Documents to see a list of the files you've recently edited. Depending on what's on the list, you may be able to run the program you're looking for.

NOTE

By default, file extensions of registered files are not displayed on screen. This cuts down on visual clutter, letting you see simple names that make sense, such as 2000 Report instead of 2000 Report.wk3.

Running an Application by Right-Clicking the Desktop

When you don't want to bother finding some favorite program just to create a new document, there's an easier way. How often have you simply wanted to create a To Do list, a shopping list, a brief memo, a little spreadsheet, or what have you? All the time, right? Microsoft figured out that people often work in just this way—they don't think: "Gee, I'll root around for Excel, then I'll run it, and then I'll create a new spreadsheet file and save it and name it." That's counterintuitive. On the contrary, it's more likely they think: "I need to create a 'Sales for Spring Quarter' Excel spreadsheet."

Simply create a new *empty* document of the correct type on the Desktop, and name it. Clicking the Desktop icon for the file you just created will run the correct program. Windows 98 SE takes care of assigning the file the correct extension so that internally the whole setup works. Try an experiment to see what I'm talking about. Follow these steps:

1. Clear off enough windows so you can see your Desktop area.

TIP

Remember, you can click the Show Desktop button in the Taskbar to minimize all the open windows. You can reverse the effect and return all the windows to view by clicking the button again.

2. Right-click anywhere on the Desktop. From the resulting shortcut menu, choose New. You'll see a list of possible document types. The types in my computer are shown in Figure 5.9 as an example.

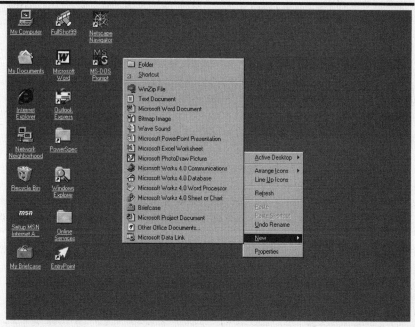

FIGURE 5.9: You can create a variety of new document types by right-clicking the Desktop. This creates a blank document that you then name and run.

3. Choose a document type from the list by clicking it. A new document icon appears on your Desktop, such as this one that appeared when I chose Text Document:

4. The file's name is highlighted and has a box around it. This means you can edit the name. As long as the whole name is highlighted, whatever you type will replace the entire name. When you create a new document this way, you don't have to worry about entering the extension. For example, a text file normally has a `txt` extension, but you could just type **Shopping List** for the name and press Enter (remember, you

have to press Enter after typing the name to finalize it). The actual filename will be Shopping List.txt, because Windows 98 SE adds a hidden file extension for you.

5. Click (or double-click) the icon to run its associated program. In the case of the text file, the Notepad program will run, open the new file, and wait for me to start typing my shopping list.

Using the Documents List

As I mentioned in a Tip earlier in this chapter, choosing Start ➤ Documents lists the documents you've recently created or edited. It's an easy way to revisit projects you've been working on. This list is maintained by Windows 98 SE and is *persistent*, which means it'll be there in subsequent Windows sessions, even after you shut down and reboot. Only the last 15 documents are remembered, though, and some of these won't be things you'd think of as documents. Some of them might actually be more like programs or folders. Check it out and see if it contains the right stuff for you. Figure 5.10 shows my list the day I wrote this section.

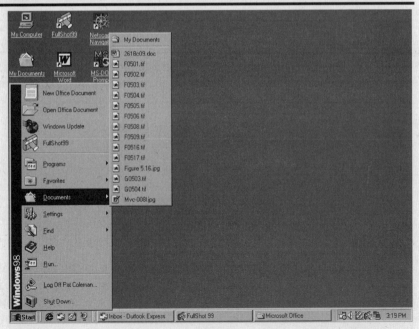

FIGURE 5.10: The Documents list from the Start button provides a no-brainer path to ongoing work projects, but only the last 15 documents you viewed or edited are shown.

Part I

Notice the My Documents choice at the top of this list. This is a short-cut to the My Documents folder on the Desktop. That's a folder that some programs use to store documents you've created. Office 2000, for example, defaults to storing your documents in the My Documents folder.

TIP

Many Windows programs have a similar feature that lists your most recently edited documents at the bottom of their File menus. Because many of my favorite programs sport this feature, I tend to rely on that more than on the Documents list.

TIP

You can clear the items in the Documents list and start fresh if you want to. Click the Start button, choose Settings ➢ Taskbar & Start Menu to open the Taskbar Properties dialog box, click the Start Menu Programs tab, and click the Clear button.

Running DOS Programs

Although DOS applications are by no means the preponderant genre of PC programs being sold these days, they certainly were for many years. Consequently, tens of thousands of useful and interesting programs exist for the IBM-PC DOS environment. Some of these programs are not easily replaced with popular Windows programs, because they were specialized programs custom designed for vertical market uses, such as point of sale, transaction processing, inventory, scientific data gathering, and so on. It's safe to say that after a corporation invests significantly in software development, testing, implementation, and employee training, conversion to a Windows-based version just because it looks groovier isn't a very attractive proposition. As a result, much of the code that was written 10 to 15 years ago and ran in DOS programs is still doing its job in companies and other institutions today.

The great thing about Windows 98 SE is that you can still run all those wonderful DOS programs, even multiple ones at the same time. And each can have its own DOS environment, task settings, window size and font, and so on.

RUNNING APPLICATIONS FROM THE COMMAND PROMPT

One of the nicest features of Windows 98 SE is that you can run any application—even those designed for Windows instead of DOS—from the MS-DOS command prompt. You can open an MS-DOS Prompt window from the Start menu (choose Start ≻ Programs ≻ MS-DOS Prompt). If you use the command prompt frequently, you might want to create a shortcut on the Desktop to make access to the command prompt faster. To do so, follow these steps:

1. Right-click the Desktop.

2. From the shortcut menu, choose New ≻ Shortcut to open the Create Shortcut dialog box.

3. In the Command Line box, enter **command.com**.

4. Click Next.

5. Because a Program-Information File already exists for this program, the Select A Title For The Program dialog box's Select A Name For The Shortcut box should already have MS-DOS Prompt listed, but if it doesn't, go ahead and enter it now. If you want another title to be displayed, you can enter that instead.

6. Click Finish. A new shortcut should now be displayed on the Desktop.

7. At this point, you can change the default start-up directory (the MS-DOS Prompt's default directory) by right-clicking the program icon and selecting Properties. In the MS-DOS Prompt Properties dialog box, choose the Program tab, and then change the entry in the Working box to your desired directory. I often change this to C:\ instead of the default C:\Windows so that I can browse from the root directory.

If you use a long filename directory, remember to enclose the entire text string in quotes. For example, if you want to start your command prompt in the Program Files directory, the Working box should contain C:\Program Files.

Once you have a command prompt, you can use your familiar MS-DOS commands, such as cd to change directories or md to make a new directory, or you can run your programs (any bat, pif, com, or exe file). You can run either MS-DOS or Windows programs. Simply

CONTINUED ➤

type the program name to start the program. For instance, if you want to run the Windows 3.*x* version of File Manager, type **winfile**, and press Enter, as we did earlier in this chapter. Or, to run Windows Explorer, type **explorer**, and press Enter.

I'll explain briefly how you run DOS programs here.

First off, you can run DOS programs using most of the same techniques explained earlier in this chapter:

- ▶ Click the program's name in a folder (pretty good method) in Windows Explorer.

- ▶ Enter the program's name at the Run command (an acceptable method, but cumbersome, since the DOS path may be needed in the command).

- ▶ Run a "DOS session," and then type the program's name at the DOS prompt.

- ▶ Double-click a document file with an extension that you've manually associated with the DOS program.

I explained the first two of these techniques earlier, when I told you how to run Windows programs. The only difference between running Windows programs and running DOS programs using those techniques is that DOS programs don't normally have an identifying icon, such as a big "W" for Word. Instead, they tend to have a boring, generic icon that looks like this:

Xtgold

Therefore, you have to rely on the icon's name alone. This one is for XTree-Pro Gold, but because the actual program's name on disk is Xtgold.exe, that's what you see. Well, actually, you don't see the exe part, because as I mentioned earlier, exe extensions are normally hidden from view.

To run a DOS session and start a DOS program, follow these steps:

1. Click the Start button.

2. Choose Programs ➤ MS-DOS Prompt, as shown in Figure 5.11.

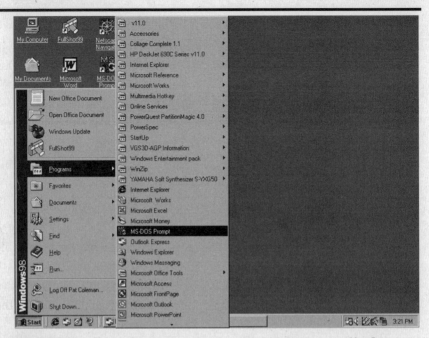

FIGURE 5.11: Choose Start ≻ Programs ≻ MS-DOS Prompt to display
the MS-DOS Prompt window.

3. The result will be what's called a *DOS box*—a window that operates just as if you're using a computer running DOS. Try typing **DIR** and pressing Enter. You'll see a listing of files on the current drive, as shown in Figure 5.12. Both short and long filenames are displayed. Long filenames are in the rightmost column, with corresponding short filenames over on the left.

4. Enter the command **exit** when you are finished running DOS programs or executing DOS commands. This will close the DOS window and end the session.

NOTE

If no DOS program is actually running, clicking the Close button will also end the DOS session. If a DOS program is running, clicking the Close button results in a message prompting you to quit the DOS program first.

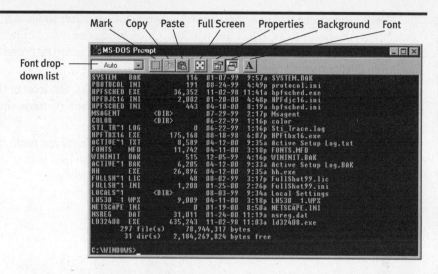

FIGURE 5.12: The DOS box lets you enter any standard DOS commands and see their output. Here you see the end of a DIR listing and the DOS prompt that follows it.

Options While Running a DOS Session

While running a DOS session, you can make several easy adjustments that are either cosmetic or that actually affect the performance of the program. You can easily do any of the following:

- ▶ Toggle the DOS session between full screen and windowed.
- ▶ Turn the toolbar on or off.
- ▶ Adjust the font.
- ▶ Resize the DOS box.
- ▶ Allow the DOS session to work in the background.
- ▶ Cause the DOS session to take over the computer's resources when in the foreground.

Let me briefly discuss each of these options. Refer to Figure 5.12 for toolbar buttons.

First, if the DOS window is taking up the whole screen (all other elements of the Windows interface have disappeared) and you'd like the

DOS program to run in a window so that you can see other programs, press Alt+Enter to switch it to a window. Once windowed, you can return to full-screen mode, either by clicking the Full Screen button or pressing Alt+Enter again.

If you don't see the toolbar shown in Figure 5.12, click the icon in the upper-left corner of the DOS window, and choose Toolbar. (Choose the same command again, and the toolbar will turn off.)

A nice feature in Windows 98 SE is the adjustable TrueType fonts that you can use in a DOS box. The easiest way to change the font is to open the Font drop-down list (rather than clicking the Font tool).

Fonts are listed by the size of the character matrix (in pixels) that constitutes each displayed character. The larger the matrix, the larger the resulting characters (and consequently the DOS box itself). Setting the size to Auto has the effect of scaling the font automatically if you resize the DOS box from its lower-left corner. When resizing, don't be surprised if the mouse pointer jumps around a bit wildly. The box is not infinitely adjustable as Windows programs are, so as you're adjusting, the outline of the window jumps to predetermined sizes.

NOTE

The Font button on the toolbar lets you choose whether only bit-mapped fonts, TrueType fonts, or both will appear in the Fonts listing on the left. By default, both types are available, giving you more size choices.

We'll leave the Properties button alone for the time being. Selections you make here are rather complicated and require some detailed discussion. So, moving right along, the other button of interest is the Background button, which determines whether the DOS program will continue processing in the background when you switch to another program. By default, this setting is on. You can tell it's on because the button looks indented.

You can turn it off if you want your DOS program to temporarily suspend when it isn't the active window (that is, when it isn't the window in which you're currently working).

TIP

The Exclusive button, seen on DOS boxes in Windows 95, was removed for Windows 98. That button determined whether your DOS program, when in the foreground, would receive all of your CPU's attention, running as though there were no other programs running in the computer. Some programs—such as data-acquisition programs that expect total control of the computer, the screen, keyboard, ports, and so forth—may require this. If that's the case with your program, you'll have to run it in "MS-DOS mode" outside Windows. The next section talks about more esoteric DOS-box settings such as this.

TIP

You can, of course, run multiple DOS sessions at the same time in separate windows. This lets you easily switch between a number of DOS programs.

NOTE

You can copy and paste data from and to DOS applications, using the Windows Clipboard. See the section "Sharing Data between Applications" later in this chapter for details.

Additional Property Settings for DOS Programs

DOS programs were designed to run one at a time and are usually memory hogs. They often need as much as 560KB of free RAM, and some may require some additional expanded or extended memory to perform well. Since DOS programs think they don't have to coexist with other programs simultaneously, running a DOS program with several other programs (particularly other DOS programs) under Windows is conceptually like bringing a bunch of ill-mannered guests to a formal dinner.

The upshot is that Windows has a lot of housekeeping to do to keep DOS programs happy. When running from Windows, DOS programs don't really "know" that other programs are running, and they expect to have direct access to all the computer's resources: RAM, ports, screen, keyboard, disk drives, and so on.

In most cases, Windows 98 SE does pretty well at faking out DOS programs without your help, using various default settings and its own memory-management strategies. However, even Windows isn't omniscient, and you may occasionally experience the ungracious locking up of a program or see messages about the "system integrity" having been corrupted.

TIP

In reality, what Windows is doing when running DOS programs is giving each of them a simulated PC to work in called a *VDM* (Virtual DOS Machine).

If a DOS program doesn't run properly under Windows 98 SE or if you want to optimize its performance, you must modify its PIF (Program Information File), declaring certain settings that affect the program within Windows. With Windows 3.*x*, making PIF settings for a program required using a program called the PIF Editor—a cumbersome program supplied with Windows. Things became simpler with Windows 95, and this carries over to Windows 98 Second Edition. Here's how it works: The first time you run a DOS program, a PIF is automatically created in the same directory as the DOS program. It has the same name as the program but looks like a shortcut icon. Examining the properties of the icon will reveal it has a pif extension.

To adjust a program's PIF settings, simply open the Properties box for the DOS program and make the relevant changes. You can do this by running the DOS program in a window and clicking the Properties button on the toolbar or, without running the program, by right-clicking its PIF icon and choosing Properties (but this requires finding the icon first, which is a hassle). When you close the Properties box, the new PIF settings are saved. From then on, those settings go into effect whenever you run the program from within Windows.

The PIF settings affect many aspects of the program's operation, such as, but not limited to:

▶ The filename and directory of the program

▶ The font and window size

▶ The directory that becomes active once a program starts

▶ Memory usage, including conventional, expanded, extended, and protected-mode memory usage

▶ Multitasking priority levels

- Video-adapter modes

- The use of keyboard shortcut keys

- Foreground and background processing

- Toolbar display

- Program-termination options

I discussed some of these options earlier, and you can make quick adjustments using the toolbar in the DOS box; other adjustments are not as easy to make. Here are some ways to fine-tune the DOS environment for running a program.

- If the program will run without bombing, follow these steps:

    1. Run it as explained earlier.

    2. If it's not in a window, press Alt+Enter.

    3. Click the Properties button if the toolbar is displayed; if the toolbar is not displayed, click the Control box in the upper-left corner of the window, and choose Properties.

- If the program won't run without bombing, follow these steps:

    1. Navigate with My Computer or Windows Explorer to the folder containing the DOS program.

    2. Find the program's icon, and click it.

    3. Choose File ➢ Create Shortcut. A new icon will appear in the folder, called "Shortcut to [*program*]."

    4. With the new shortcut highlighted, choose File ➢ Properties.

Now you'll see the DOS program's Properties dialog box, from which you can alter quite a healthy collection of settings (see Figure 5.13). Unfortunately, there isn't room in this book for an explanation of all the settings available from this box. Remember, you can get some basic information about each setting via the ? button in the upper-right corner. Click it, and then click the exact button, line, or option in question.

Simply adjust your settings as necessary. When you're happy with them, click OK in the Properties dialog box to save the settings. The next time you run the program by double-clicking the shortcut or the program's icon, the settings will go into effect.

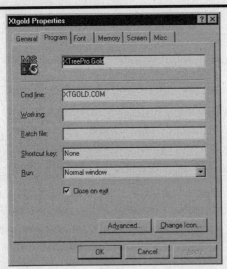

FIGURE 5.13: The Properties dialog box for the program XTreePro Gold

Using Desktop Shortcuts

When it comes to running your programs, Windows 98 SE has a spiffy feature called *shortcuts*. (If you haven't used Windows 95 or a Mac, this will be a new concept.) Shortcuts are alias icons (icons that represent other icons) that you can add almost anywhere, such as in folders, on the Desktop, or on the Taskbar's Quick Launch toolbar (later for that). The neat thing about shortcuts is that since they're really only a link or pointer to the real file or application they represent, you can have as many as you want, putting them wherever your heart desires, without duplicating your files and using up lots of hard disk space. So, for example, you can have shortcuts to all your favorite programs right on the Desktop. You can then run them from there without having to click the Start button, walk through the Program listings, and so forth, as we've been doing.

Many of the icons that are automatically placed on your Desktop when you install Windows are actually shortcuts. The icon for Outlook Express is a good example.

Notice the little arrow in the lower-left corner of the icon. This indicates that the icon is actually a shortcut to the program file for Outlook Express. Click it (or double-click in Classic view) to open the program.

SWITCHING BETWEEN APPLICATIONS

Remember, Windows lets you have more than one program open and running at a time. You can also have multiple folders open at any time, and you can leave them open to make getting to their contents easier. Any folders that are open when you shut down the computer will open again when you start up Windows again.

People often think they have to shut down one program before working on another one, but that's really not efficient nor true. When you run each new program or open a folder, the Taskbar gets another button on it. As you know, simply clicking a Taskbar button switches you to that program or folder. For the first several programs, the buttons are long enough to contain the names of the programs or folders. As you run more programs, the buttons automatically get shorter, so the names are truncated. For example:

You can resize the Taskbar to give it an extra line or two of buttons if you want to see the full names. On the upper edge of the Taskbar, position the cursor so that it turns into a double-headed arrow (this takes some careful aiming). Then drag it upward a half inch or an inch and release. Here I've added an additional line for my current set of buttons:

Obviously, as you increase the size of the Taskbar, you decrease the effective size of your work area. On a standard VGA (Video Graphics Adapter) screen, you'll be cutting into your work area quite a bit if you go to two or three lines. On SVGA (Super Video Graphics Array) screens, the impact will be less.

Another nice feature is that you can set the Taskbar to disappear until you move the mouse pointer down to the bottom of the screen. This way, you sacrifice nothing in the way of screen real estate.

TIP

If you prefer, you can also position the Taskbar on the right, left, or top of the screen. Just click any part of the Taskbar other than a button, and drag it to the edge of your choice.

Here's how to set the Taskbar options:

1. Choose Start ≻ Settings ≻ Taskbar & Start Menu to open the Taskbar Properties dialog box, as shown in Figure 5.14.

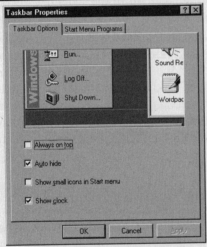

FIGURE 5.14: You set the Taskbar options from this dialog box. The most likely choice you'll make will be Auto Hide.

2. Click Auto Hide to turn that option on—this is the one that makes the Taskbar disappear until you move the pointer to the edge of the screen where you've placed the Taskbar.

TIP

A quick way to get to the Taskbar's property settings is to right-click an empty area of the Taskbar and choose Properties from the shortcut menu.

3. If you'd like to see smaller icons in the first Start-up menu, set that option on too.

4. Click OK, and the Taskbar will disappear. Try the Auto Hide setting: move the pointer down to the bottom, and see how the Taskbar reappears.

NOTE
Even when set to Auto Hide, the Taskbar still uses one or two pixels (a very small area) at the edge of the screen to indicate where it is and to act as a trigger zone to pop up the Taskbar when the pointer touches it.

Switching with Alt+Tab

Don't like the Taskbar? Are you a habituated Windows 3.x user? Okay. As you may know, there's another way to switch between programs and folders—the Alt+Tab trick. Press the Alt key and hold it down. Now, press the Tab key (you know, that key just above the Caps Lock and to the left of the Q). You'll see a box in the center of your screen showing you an icon of each program or folder that's running, like this:

Each press of the Tab key advances the outline box one notch to the right. The outline box indicates which program you'll be switched to when you release the Alt key. If you want to back up one program (that is, move the outline box to the left), you can press Alt+Shift+Tab. The name of the program or folder is displayed at the bottom of the box, which is especially useful when choosing folders, because all folders look the same.

Sharing Data between Applications

One of the greatest features of Windows 98 SE is the ability to share pieces of information between your programs. You can mix and match a great variety of document types, such as text, sound, graphics, spreadsheets, databases, and so forth, thus constructing complex documents.

Windows 98 SE offers three internal vehicles for exchanging data between programs:

▶ The Windows Clipboard

▶ Object Linking and Embedding (OLE)

▶ Dynamic Data Exchange (DDE)

I'll concentrate on using the Windows Clipboard here because it's the concept you will use most often.

NOTE

Many of my examples in this chapter refer to Microsoft products. This isn't necessarily my endorsement of Microsoft products over other competing products! Competition in the software marketplace is a healthy force, ensuring the evolution of software technology, and I highly support it. But, because so many of you are bound to be familiar with the Microsoft product line, I use products such as Word, Excel, Graph, and Access in my examples in hopes of better illustrating the points I'm trying to make here.

Using the Windows Clipboard

Though it's not capable of converting data files between various formats, such as xls to wk3 or rtf to doc, the Windows Clipboard is great for many everyday data-exchange tasks. Just about all Windows programs support the use of the ubiquitous cut, copy, and paste commands, and it's the Clipboard that provides this functionality for you.

The Clipboard makes it possible to move any kind of material—text, data cells, graphics, video, or audio clips—and OLE objects between documents and, since Windows 95, between folders, the Desktop, the Explorer, and other portions of the interface. The actual form of the source data doesn't matter that much, because the Clipboard utility and Windows together take care of figuring out what's being copied and where it's being pasted, making adjustments when necessary—or at least providing a few manual options for you to adjust. The Clipboard can also work with non-Windows (DOS) programs, albeit with certain limitations that I'll explain later.

How does the Clipboard work? It's simple. The Clipboard is built into Windows and uses a portion of the system's internal resources (RAM and virtual memory) as a temporary holding tank for material you're working with. For example, suppose you have cut some text from one part of a document in preparation for pasting it into another location. Windows stores the text on the Clipboard and waits for you to paste it into its new home.

The last item you copied or cut is stored in this no-man's-land somewhere in the computer until you cut or copy something else, exit Windows, or intentionally clear the Clipboard. As a result, you can paste the Clipboard's contents any number of times.

You can examine the Clipboard's contents using the Clipboard Viewer or Clipbook utility supplied with Windows. If you've used Windows for

Workgroups or Windows NT, you'll be familiar with these applications. You can also use these applications to save the Clipboard's contents to disk for later use or to share specific bits of data for use by others on your network.

To place information in the Windows Clipboard, you simply use each application's Edit menu (or the Edit menu's shortcut keys) for copying, cutting, and pasting (see Figure 5.15).

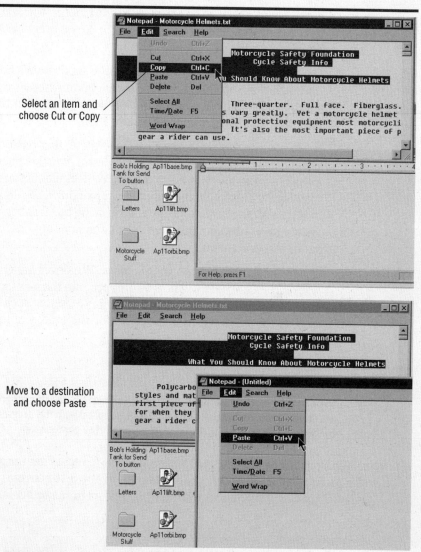

FIGURE 5.15: Copying and pasting in a Windows program

Here are the steps for cutting, copying, or pasting within a Windows program:

1. First, arrange the windows on screen so you can see the window containing the source information.

2. Now *select* the information you want to copy or cut, such as text, a graphic, spreadsheet cells, or whatever. In many programs, simply clicking an object, such as a graphic, will select it. Other programs require you to drag the cursor over objects while pressing the left mouse button.

3. Once the desired area is selected, open the application's Edit menu and choose Copy or Cut, depending on whether you want to copy the material or delete the original with the intention of pasting it into another location.

4. If you want to paste the selection somewhere, first position the cursor at the insertion point in the destination document (which may or may not be in the source document) you're working in. This might mean scrolling up or down the document, switching to another application using the Taskbar, or switching to another document within the *same* application via its Window menu.

5. Open the Edit menu and choose Paste. Whatever material was on the Clipboard will now be dropped into the new location. Normally, this means any preexisting material, such as text, is moved down to make room for the stuff you just pasted.

TIP
There may be some shortcuts for cut, copy, and paste in specific programs, so you should read the manual or help screens supplied with the program. Generally, pressing Ctrl+X cuts, Ctrl+C copies, and Ctrl+V pastes.

When pasting in graphics, you'll typically have to reposition the graphic *after* pasting, rather than before. For example, Figure 5.16 shows a graphic just after pasting it into a Paint window. It appears in the upper-left corner, waiting to be dragged to its new home.

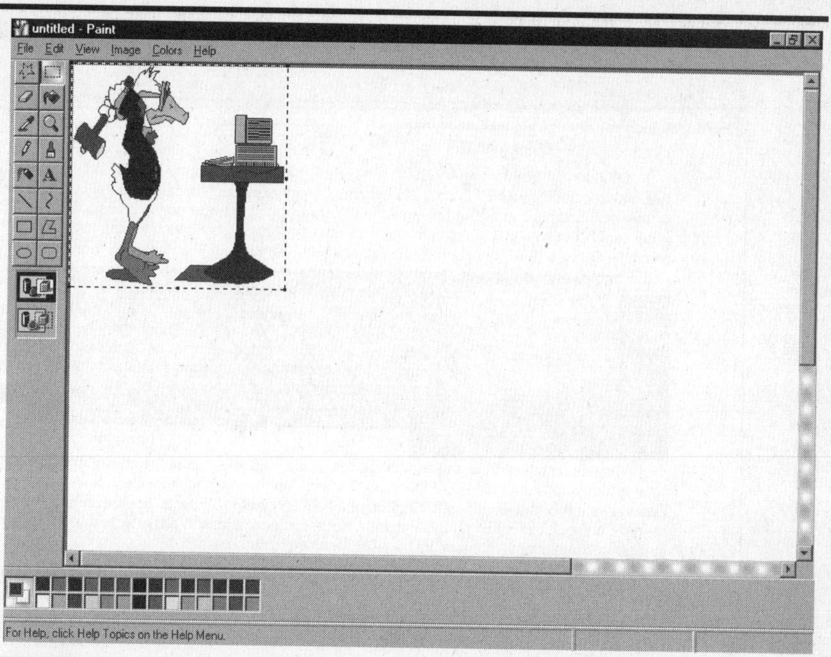

FIGURE 5.16: Graphics applications typically accept pasted information into their upper-left corner, where they wait to be repositioned.

Right-Click Shortcuts for Cut, Copy, and Paste

As mentioned earlier, the cut, copy, and paste scheme is implemented throughout Windows 98 SE, even on the Desktop, in Windows Explorer, in folder windows, and so forth. This is done using right mouse-button shortcuts. Many applications offer this feature too.

Right-clicking a file in a folder window and choosing Copy puts a pointer to the file on the Clipboard. Right-clicking another location, such as the Desktop, and choosing Paste drops the file there (for example, on the Desktop). Try clicking the secondary (normally the right) mouse button on icons or on selected text or graphics in applications to see if there is a shortcut menu. Figure 5.17 shows an example of copying some text from a Word document by using this shortcut.

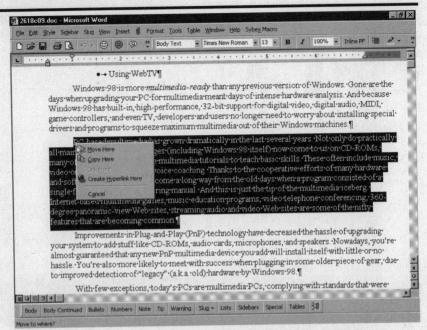

FIGURE 5.17: Shortcuts for cut, copy, and paste are built into much of Windows 98 SE via the right-click menu. Windows applications are beginning to implement this feature too, as you see here in Word.

Copying Text and Graphics from a DOS Window

Copying selected graphics from DOS programs is also possible. This is a pretty nifty trick for lifting material out of your favorite DOS program and dropping it into a Windows document. There's only one caveat: the DOS program has to be running in a window, not on the full screen.

When you cut or copy selected material from the DOS box, it gets dumped into the Clipboard as text or graphics, depending on which mode Windows determines the DOS box (*box* means window) was emulating. Windows knows whether the application is running in character mode or graphics mode and processes the data on the Clipboard accordingly. If text mode is detected, the material is copied as characters that could be dropped into, say, a word-processing document. If the DOS application has set up a graphics mode in the DOS box (because of the application's video requests), you'll get a bit-mapped graphic in the destination document when you paste.

Because of the DOS box's toolbar, the procedure for copying is simple to learn. You can use the toolbar almost as if you were using another Windows program. Figure 5.18 illustrates the simple technique. Here are the steps:

1. First, switch to the DOS application and display the material you want to work with.

2. Make sure the application is running in a window, rather than running full screen. If it's not, press Alt+Enter. (Each press of Alt+Enter toggles any DOS window between full and windowed view.)

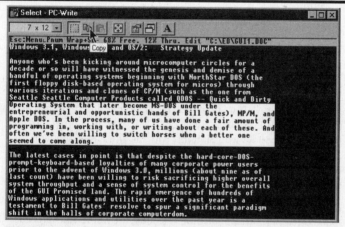

FIGURE 5.18:   Copying text from an MS-DOS box is a simple procedure. Click the Mark button, click and drag across the desired text, and click the Copy button.

3. If the DOS box's toolbar isn't showing, turn it on by clicking in the upper-left corner of its window (on the MS-DOS icon) and choosing Toolbar.

4. Click the Mark button.

5. Holding the mouse button down, drag the pointer over the desired copy area, dragging from upper left to lower right. As you do so, the color of the selection will change to indicate what you're marking.

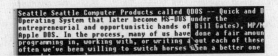

6. Release the mouse button. The selected area will stay high-lighted.

7. Click the Copy button. The information is now on the Clipboard.

NOTE

Notice that there isn't a Cut button, because you can't cut from a DOS application in this way. Cutting has to be done using the DOS program's own editing keys, and these keys won't interact with the Windows Clipboard.

TIP

As soon as you click the Mark button, the DOS box's title bar changes to read *Mark*. Once you start marking the selection, the word *Select* precedes the program's name in the title bar, indicating that you're in select mode. Pressing any letter on the keyboard terminates the selection process.

That's all there is to copying information from an application that's running in the DOS box. Of course, the normal procedure will apply to pasting what was just copied. You just switch to the destination application (which, incidentally, can be a DOS *or* a Windows program), position the cursor, and choose Edit ➢ Paste to paste in the Clipboard's contents at the cursor position. (For a DOS application as the destination, you'd use the Paste button on the DOS box's toolbar. This is explained later in this chapter.)

Working with the Clipboard Viewer

Once data is on the Clipboard, you might not want to paste it immediately, or you might want to see what's there. There's a program supplied with

Windows that makes this really easy. Clipboard Viewer can be found in the Accessories folder (choose Start ➤ Programs ➤ Accessories ➤ System Tools ➤ Clipboard Viewer). This program lets you do some useful Clipboard-related things, such as:

- ▶ View the Clipboard's contents.

- ▶ Save and retrieve the Clipboard's contents to/from a file.

- ▶ Clear the Clipboard's contents.

NOTE

If you don't see the Clipboard Viewer in your System Tools menu, you might need to install it.

Let's look at each of these simple tasks in order.

Viewing the Clipboard's Contents

Sometimes you'll simply forget what information is on the Clipboard because you won't remember what you cut or copied last. And before you go ahead and paste it into an application (especially if that application doesn't have an Undo command), you might want to check out what's going to get pasted. Another time when viewing is useful is when you're trying to get a particular item into the Clipboard and don't know how successful you've been. Opening the Viewer and positioning it off in the corner of the screen can give you instant feedback as you cut and copy.

NOTE

Actually, there are two different utilities that let you examine the Clipboard's contents: Clipboard Viewer and Clipbook Viewer. You won't have Clipbook Viewer, however, unless you installed Windows 98 SE as an upgrade over an earlier version of Windows (3.11 or 95).

Here's how to view the Clipboard's contents.

1. Click on the Start button and choose Programs ➤ Accessories ➤ System Tools ➤ Clipboard Viewer to open the Clipboard Viewer.

2. The Clipboard Viewer displays the Clipboard's current contents. Figure 5.19 shows typical Clipboard contents; in this case, a portion of an image that I just copied from a graphics program.

FIGURE 5.19: The Clipboard's contents being displayed

Let's take an example. A Paint picture can be passed on to another application as what Windows calls a *bitmap*, a picture, or a Windows Enhanced Metafile. (In addition to this, there can be information that pertains to Object Linking and Embedding, but these aspects don't appear in the Viewer window.)

When you first view the Clipboard's contents, the Viewer does its best to display the contents so they look as much as possible like the original. However, this isn't a fail-safe method, so there may be times when you'll want to try changing the view. To do this:

1. Open the Display menu.

2. Check out the available options. They'll vary depending on what you've got stored on the Clipboard. Choose one, and see how it affects the display. The Default setting (called *Auto*) returns the view to the original display format in which the material was first shown. However, none of the options will affect the Clipboard contents—only its display.

NOTE

When you actually go to paste into another Windows application, the destination program tries to determine the best format for accepting whatever is currently on the Clipboard. If the Edit menu on the destination application is grayed out, you can safely assume that the contents are not acceptable. (Changing the Clipboard's view format as described above won't rectify the situation, either. In fact, it doesn't have any effect on how things actually get pasted.)

Storing the Clipboard's Contents in a File

When you place new material onto the Clipboard, reboot, or shut down the computer, the Clipboard contents are lost. Also, because the Clipboard itself is not *network aware* (meaning it can't interact with other workstations on the network), you can't share the Clipboard's contents with other networked users. However, there is one trick left. You *can* save the Clipboard's contents to a disk file. Clipboard files have the extension clp. Once the Clipboard's contents are stored in a disk file, it's like any other disk file—you can later reload the file from disk. If you do a lot of work with clip art and bits and pieces of sound, video, text, and the like, this technique can come in handy. Also, if you give network users access to your clp file directory, they can, in effect, use your Clipboard.

TIP

The Clipboard clp files use a proprietary file format that is readable by virtually no other popular programs. So, to use a clp file, you have to open it in Clipboard and *then* paste it where you want it to appear. This might all seem like a hassle, and it is. The Clipbook Viewer, if you have it, offers a hassle-free way to archive little things you regularly want to paste.

In any case, here's how to save a Clipboard file:

1. Make sure you have run the Clipboard Viewer, as explained above.

2. Choose File ➢ Save As. A standard Save As dialog box will appear.

3. Enter a name. As usual, you can change the folder, name, and extension. Leave the extension as clp, because Clipboard uses this as a default when you later want to reload the file.

4. Click OK. The file is saved and can be loaded again as described below.

As I mentioned, once the clp file is on disk, you can reload it. Follow these steps:

WARNING

When you reload a clp file, anything currently on the Clipboard will be lost.

1. Run the Clipboard Viewer.

2. Choose File ➢ Open. The Open dialog box will appear.

3. Select the file you want to pull onto the Clipboard. (Only legitimate clp files can be opened.)

4. If there's something already on the Clipboard, you'll be asked if you want to erase it. Click OK.

5. Change the display format via the View menu if you want to (assuming there are options available on the menu).

6. Paste the contents into the desired destination.

Clearing the Clipboard

To clear the contents of the Clipboard, open Clipboard Viewer, choose Edit ➤ Delete, and click Yes when you are asked if you want to clear the contents.

WHAT'S NEXT?

In this chapter, we really did get down to a lot of business. And, as we looked at the ways you can run your DOS and Windows applications, I mentioned the terms *files* and *folders* often. The next chapter will get down to some more business, with a detailed look at how you manage the files and folders on your computer—saving them, moving them, deleting them, and so on. You need this kind of information if you want to be able to find and use the information on your computer effectively.

Chapter 6

MANAGING FILES AND FOLDERS

by Pat Coleman

I f you are a new PC user, it won't be long before you realize that you need to impose some order on the documents, graphics, games, applications, and so on that you create or install on your system. The reason for this is really quite simple: if you don't, you aren't going to be able find things when you need them, or, at least, you aren't going to be able to find things easily or quickly.

My friend Janis is a perfect example. Janis contributes articles on local history topics to several publications, but because she didn't understand how to manage the files and documents she was creating, she had to use the Find command every time she wanted to open an existing document. Now, there's nothing wrong with using the Find command, but you have much better ways to locate and open files. (I'll discuss the Find command later in this chapter.)

In this chapter, we'll look at what you need to know about files and folders in Windows 98 SE, and we'll start with the essential tool for dealing with files and folders, Windows Explorer.

USING WINDOWS EXPLORER

From the Desktop, you can start Explorer in several ways:

- ▶ Right-click Start and select Explore.
- ▶ Choose Start ➢ Programs ➢ Windows Explorer.
- ▶ Right-click any Desktop icon other than Connect To The Internet, and choose Explore.

The view in which Explorer opens depends on which commands you used. For example, if you open it from the Start menu, the Start Menu folder is selected, the title bar displays Start Menu, and the contents of the Start Menu folder are displayed in the right pane, as is shown in Figure 6.1.

You can use the following techniques to display files and folders within a folder:

- ▶ In the Folders pane, select a folder to display its contents in the right pane.
- ▶ In the Folders pane, click the plus (+) sign to display a list of what it contains.
- ▶ In the right pane, double-click a folder to display subfolders or files.

If you can't see all the items in the hierarchical Folders pane, drag the horizontal scroll bar to the right or drag the vertical scroll bar up or down.

In this section, we have rather quickly covered Explorer basics. As we discuss the other tasks related to managing files, we'll look at the other ways you can use Explorer to navigate and organize your system.

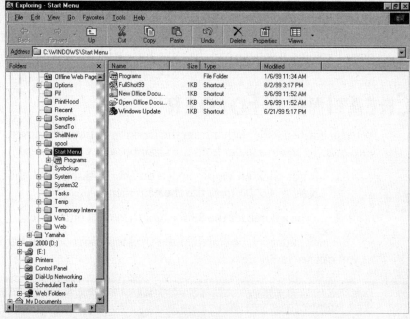

FIGURE 6.1: Windows Explorer in Details view

PLACE A SHORTCUT TO WINDOWS EXPLORER ON THE DESKTOP

If you use Windows Explorer frequently, you'll probably want to place a shortcut to it on your Desktop. To do so, follow these steps:

1. Choose Start ≻ Programs.

2. Right-click Windows Explorer, and drag the icon out onto your Desktop.

3. Release the mouse button to display the following shortcut menu:

4. Choose Copy Here or Create Shortcut(s) Here.

OPENING FILES AND FOLDERS

To open any file or folder, simply double-click it in the right pane of Windows Explorer. It will open in the program in which it was created.

CREATING A FOLDER

You can create a folder either from the Desktop or from Windows Explorer. To create a folder from the Desktop, follow these steps:

1. Right-click an empty space on the Desktop, and choose New ➤ Folder from the shortcut menu.

2. Type a name for the folder, and then click outside it.

This new folder will be stored in the Desktop folder on your hard drive, as you can see in Figure 6.2.

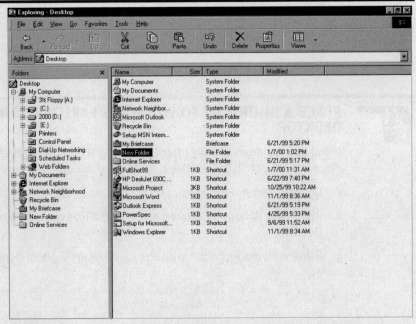

FIGURE 6.2:   A new folder created on the Desktop is stored in the Desktop folder.

To create a folder inside another folder in Explorer, follow these steps:

1. Select the folder.

2. Choose File ➤ New ➤ Folder.

3. Type a name for the folder, and click outside it.

TIP

If you're ever in doubt about where to save a file, simply put it in your My Documents folder. You can always move it later, and if you get in the habit of placing files in this folder, you'll always know where to find them.

If you're trying to set up a common-sense system for organizing files and folders, it's probably a good idea to create folders in Explorer so that you can see the relationships. You can, however, easily move a folder that you create on the Desktop, as you'll see shortly.

NAMING FILES AND FOLDERS

Filenames can contain a maximum of 255 characters and can contain spaces, commas, semicolons, equal signs (=), and square brackets ([]). Filenames can be in upper- and lowercase letters, but they cannot contain the following characters: / \ : * ? " < > |.

In Explorer, 255 characters is the equivalent of a rather longish paragraph, and you'll be hard-pressed to display it easily on the screen, so don't get carried away. Be sure, though, to give files and folders names that you will easily recognize several months hence when you're trying to clean up your hard drive or when you need to send someone the monthly sales report for April of last year.

CREATING A FILE

You can create a file in three ways:

▶ From the Desktop

▶ From Windows Explorer

▶ From within an application

To create a file from the Desktop, follow these steps:

1. Right-click an empty space on the Desktop, and choose New.

2. From the submenu, select the type of file you want to create.

3. Type a name for the file, and then click outside it on the Desktop.

This file is stored in the Desktop folder on your hard drive.

To create a file from within Explorer, follow these steps:

1. Open the folder that will contain the new file.

2. Right-click in a blank space in the right pane of Explorer.

3. Choose New, and then from the submenu, select a file type.

4. Type a name for the file, and then click outside it in a blank space.

You'll probably most often create a new file from within an application. For purposes of example, here are the steps for creating a new file in Notepad:

1. Choose Start ➤ Programs ➤ Accessories ➤ Notepad to open Notepad:

2. Choose File ➤ Save As to open the Save As dialog box:

3. Select a folder in which you want to save the document.

4. Enter a name in the File Name box.

5. Click Save.

NOTE

To save a file the first time, you choose File ➤ Save As. To save it again later after you've edited it, choose File ➤ Save to save it with the name you originally gave it. Choose File ➤ Save As to save it under a new name.

UNDERSTANDING FILE TYPES

Regardless of how you create or save a file, Windows gives it an extension that identifies its type. When you create a file from the Desktop or Explorer, you select a type from the shortcut menu's submenu. For example, selecting Rich Text Format creates a file that has the rtf extension, and selecting Bitmap Image creates a file that has the bmp extension. To see a file's extension in Explorer, choose View ➤ Details.

Part I

DISPLAYING AND SETTING PROPERTIES

In Windows 98 SE, every item you see on the screen is an object, and each object has properties. For example, all the following are objects and have properties:

- ▶ Modems

- ▶ Folders

- ▶ Files

- ▶ Shortcuts

- ▶ Other computers on the network

The properties for each object are collected together and displayed in a special Properties dialog box. To open the Properties dialog box for an object, you right-click the object (for example, a filename in Windows Explorer) and then choose Properties from the shortcut menu. Figure 6.3 shows the General tab of the Properties dialog box for the file that contains the text for a chapter in this book, which was created in Microsoft Word.

FIGURE 6.3: The Properties dialog box for the Chapter 5 file

Windows automatically supplies some of the information in the Properties dialog box, such as the file size and type, the creation date, the modification date, and so on, and you cannot change this information. You can, however, modify certain settings. Which settings you see depends on the complexity of the object.

TIP

In many Windows applications, you can display a file's Properties dialog box by opening the document and then choosing File ➢ Properties.

COPYING AND MOVING FILES AND FOLDERS

You can copy or move a file or a folder in four ways:

- ▶ By dragging and dropping with the right mouse button
- ▶ By dragging and dropping with the left mouse button
- ▶ By copying and pasting or cutting and pasting
- ▶ By using the Send To command

Which method you use depends on your personal preference and, to some extent, on the circumstances. When you can see both the source and the destination, dragging and dropping is easiest.

To copy or move a file or folder using the right mouse button, follow these steps:

1. Locate the file or folder in Explorer.

2. Right-click it, and then drag it to its destination.

3. Release the mouse button, and then choose Copy Here or Move Here from the shortcut menu.

If you change your mind en route, press Escape.

To copy a file when the source and destination are on different drives using the left mouse button, left-click the file and drag it to its new location. If you use the left mouse button to drag and drop and the source and destination are on the same hard drive, the file is moved rather than copied. To move a file when the source and destination are on different drives, click the file with the left mouse button and hold down Shift while you drag the file.

To copy or move a file using the Cut, Copy, and Paste commands, follow these steps:

1. Right-click the source file, and choose Cut or Copy from the shortcut menu.

2. Right-click the destination folder, and choose Paste from the shortcut menu.

Another way to copy a file to a new location, such as a floppy disk or another hard disk, is to right-click the file and choose the Send To command on the shortcut menu. If the shortcut menu doesn't include a destination you want to use regularly, you can add it. Follow these steps:

1. In Explorer, locate your Windows folder, and then locate the Send To folder within it.

TIP

If you don't see the Send To folder, choose View ➤ Folder Options to open the Folder Options folder, and click the View tab. In Advanced Settings, scroll down and click the Show All Files option. We'll look at the Folder Options dialog box in detail later in this chapter.

2. Select the Send To folder, and then choose File ➤ New ➤ Shortcut to open the Create Shortcut dialog box:

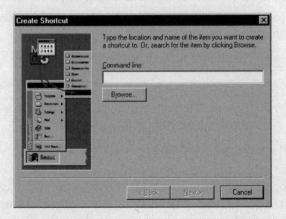

3. Enter the name of the shortcut you want to add, or click Browse to find it.

4. Click Next.

5. Type a new name for the shortcut if you want, and then click Finish.

RENAMING FILES AND FOLDERS

You can easily rename a file or a folder in two ways:

▶ Left-click twice (wait about a second between clicks) on the name of the file or folder, and enter a new name in the highlighted box.

▶ Right-click the name of a folder, choose Rename from the shortcut menu, and then type a new name.

If you change your mind about the new name, you can click Undo, or you can re-rename the file or folder.

DELETING FILES AND FOLDERS

You can delete a file or a folder in three ways:

▶ In Explorer, right-click the name of the file or folder, and then choose Delete from the shortcut menu.

▶ In Explorer, left-click the name of the file or folder, and then press Delete or click the Delete button on the toolbar.

▶ If the Recycle Bin is visible on the Desktop, click the name of the file or folder and drag it to the Recycle Bin.

TIP

To bypass the Recycle Bin and permanently erase the file or folder from your hard drive, hold down Shift when choosing or pressing Delete.

To restore a file you've sent to the Recycle Bin, follow these steps:

1. Double-click the Recycle Bin to open the Recycle Bin dialog box shown in Figure 6.4.

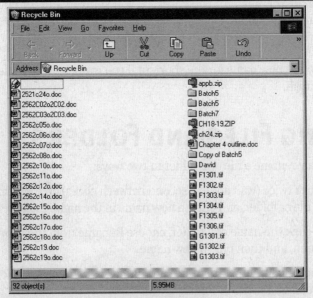

FIGURE 6.4:   The Recycle Bin dialog box

2.   Right-click the file, and choose Restore from the shortcut menu.

The file is restored to its original location.

WARNING

You cannot use the Undo command to retrieve a file that you delete from the Recycle Bin.

USING THE UNDO COMMAND

While you can't use Undo to retrieve a file you've deleted from the Recycle Bin, you can use it to fix a lot of other missteps. For example, if you delete a file from a folder and it goes to the Recycle Bin, simply click Undo to get it right back. You can click the Undo button on the toolbar, or you can right-click an empty area of the screen and choose Undo Delete from the shortcut menu.

In addition, you can choose Undo from the Edit menu. Here and on the shortcut menu, the Undo command will always include the immediately preceding action, such as move, delete, copy, and so on.

FINDING FILES AND FOLDERS

If you can't remember where you stored a file or what you named it, you can try to locate it in a couple of ways. You can scroll endlessly through Explorer, or you can right-click a drive in Windows Explorer and choose Find from the shortcut menu. (You can also choose Start ➤ Find ➤ Files Or Folders.) In the Find: All Files dialog box, shown in Figure 6.5, you can search for the filename, and you can search for a file containing the contents you specify.

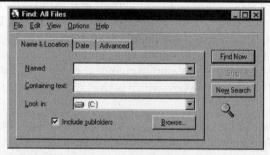

FIGURE 6.5: Use the Find: All Files dialog box to find files and folders.

To find a file if you know its name or even part of its name, follow these steps:

1. Open the Find: All Files dialog box.

2. In the Named box, enter your search term.

3. Specify a drive to search.

4. Click Find Now.

All files matching the criteria you entered are displayed in the bottom section of the dialog box. To open a file, simply click it. If you want to search on file contents, enter your text in the Containing Text box.

TIP

You can also use the wildcard characters * and ? when you're searching. The asterisk represents one or more characters, and the question mark represents a single character. For example, ***.doc** will find all files that have the doc extension; **chap?** will find *chaps* and *chap1* but not *chapter*.

Sometimes you may not remember the filename or part of the filename, but you do remember when you created or last edited the file. To search for a file by date, click the Date tab, and enter your criteria. You can click the Advanced tab to locate a file by its type or size.

CHANGING THE FOLDER VIEW

In any folder, you can specify how you want information to be displayed by using the options on the View menu. You can opt to display less or more information about specific files or folders, and you can choose to display a folder as a Web page or in classic Windows view. The options you select apply only to the open folder. If you want to change the view of all folders, you use the Folder Options dialog box, which is the topic of the next section in this chapter.

To see how this works, we'll take a look at the My Computer folder in the various views. To display this folder as a Web page, follow these steps:

1. From the Desktop, double-click My Computer.

2. In the My Computer folder, choose View ➤ As Web Page. You'll see something similar to Figure 6.6.

In addition to displaying a folder as a Web page, you can display files and folders as large or small icons, you can display files and folders as simple lists, or you can display details about files and folders (the most comprehensive view). Figure 6.6 shows large icons, and Figure 6.7 shows small icons. Figure 6.1, earlier in this chapter, shows the Start Menu folder in Windows Explorer's Details view. To see the list display, simply open a folder, and choose View ➤ List.

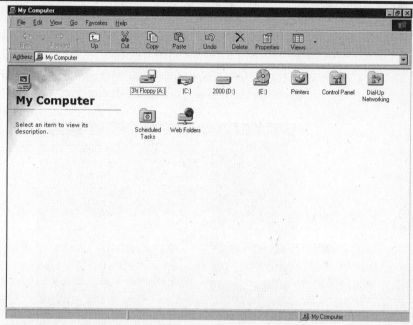

FIGURE 6.6: The My Computer folder when viewed as a Web page

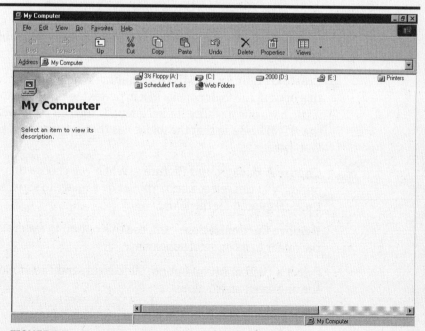

FIGURE 6.7: The My Computer folder in Small Icons view

Customizing a Folder

When you are working in Web view, you can customize the appearance of any folder. To do so, follow these steps:

1. With the folder open, choose View ➤ Customize This Folder to open the Customize This Folder dialog box:

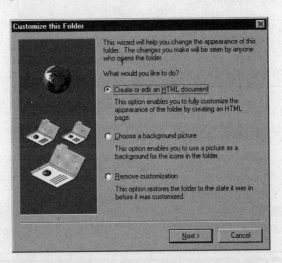

2. On the first screen of the Wizard, you have the following options:

   Create Or Edit An HTML Document   When you choose this option, the folder opens in a hypertext template editor, if you have one installed, or in Notepad. You can then edit the HTML code so that the folder has the appearance of a Web page.

   Choose A Background Picture   When you choose this option, you can select a bmp, jpg, or gif image to serve as the background for the folder.

   Remove Customization   Choose this option to restore the folder to its original appearance.

   Select a customization option, click Next, and then follow the on-screen instructions.

Enabling Thumbnail View

The term *thumbnail* has been borrowed from the world of graphic arts and denotes a tiny representation of the larger real thing. If you've had any film developed lately, you probably got a print that included thumbnails of each photo so that you could select which pictures to reprint. It's much easier to select from a thumbnail than from a bunch of negatives.

In Windows 98 SE, Thumbnail view shows graphic representations of the files in a folder. The file can be of any type, but Thumbnail view is probably most useful for graphics files. As you can see in Figure 6.8, even a Large Icons view of the graphics files in a folder is not a lot of help in determining what's in each file.

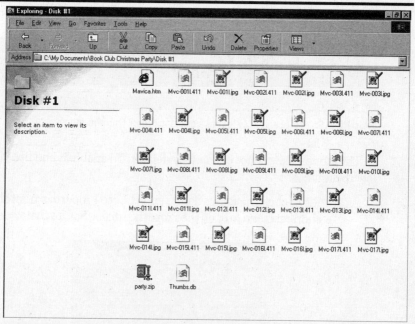

FIGURE 6.8: The Large Icons view doesn't reveal what's inside a graphics file.

On the other hand, in Thumbnail view, you can tell exactly what's in each file, as you can see in Figure 6.9.

FIGURE 6.9: You can easily locate a specific file in Thumbnail view.

Thumbnail view is not enabled by default. To enable it and use it, follow these steps:

1. Right-click the folder name, and choose Properties from the shortcut menu to open the Properties dialog box for that folder:

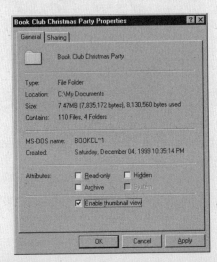

Part I

2. At the bottom of the dialog box, click the Enable Thumbnail View check box, and click OK.

3. Choose View ➤ Thumbnails. You'll see something similar to Figure 6.9.

Even if Thumbnail view is not enabled, you can see a thumbnail of a single image file if the folder is open in Web page view. Simply click the file, and the thumbnail of that file will appear on the left side of the screen:

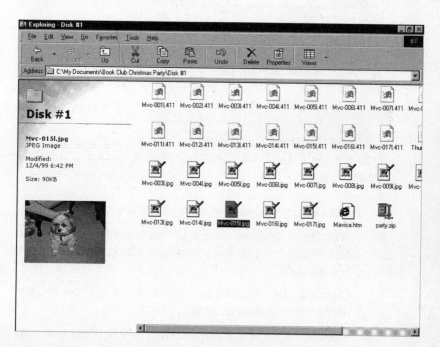

UNDERSTANDING AND USING FOLDER OPTIONS

When you want to specify how all folders are displayed (rather than only the open folder), you use the Folder Options dialog box. To open the Folder Options dialog box, choose Start ➤ Settings ➤ Folder Options. You'll see the dialog box shown in Figure 6.10, which opens at the General tab.

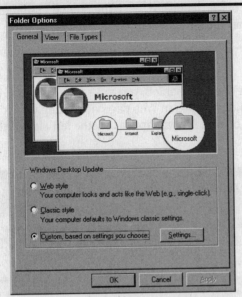

FIGURE 6.10: Use the Folder Options dialog box to specify how files and folders are displayed.

On the General tab, you can choose from the following options:

Web Style   Folders open in the same window in Web view. Names and icons act like hyperlinks, which you can open with a single click.

Classic Style   Each folder opens in a new window, and you double-click to open an item.

Custom   Choose Custom and then click Settings to specify some combination of Web and Classic style for your folders.

Select the View tab, as shown in Figure 6.11, to specify how and which folders are displayed. Earlier in this chapter, we used this tab to tell Windows to display hidden files in Explorer. In the Advanced Settings section, use the scroll bar to check out the other options. If you have already made some changes and want to display all folders as they were when you installed Windows, click Reset All Folders. If you have made changes to the Advanced Settings and want to restore this area as it was when you installed Windows, click Restore Defaults.

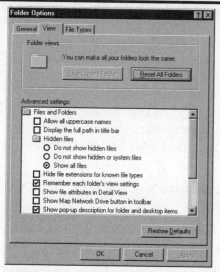

FIGURE 6.11: Specify which files to display and how in the Advanced Settings section of the View tab.

Select the File Types tab to display the screen shown in Figure 6.12. Here you see a list of filename extensions and associated file types and applications that are registered with Windows. You can add, delete, and change items on this list.

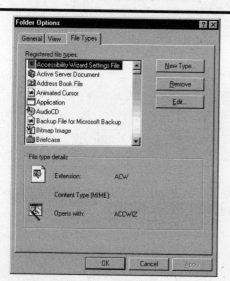

FIGURE 6.12: The File Types tab in the Folder Options dialog box

I mentioned earlier in this chapter that when you click to open a file in Windows Explorer (or any other folder, for that matter), Windows opens it in the application with which it was created—usually, that is. Normally, when you install an application, Windows registers the file types associated with the program. For example, Microsoft Word files have the extension doc, and when you click to open a doc file, Windows opens that file in Word.

In some cases, however, you may find that files don't open in the application you expect, and so you need to change the registered file type. You do so using the File Types tab in the Folder Options dialog box. Follow these steps:

1. In the Folder Options dialog box, select the File Types tab, as shown in Figure 6.12.

2. In the Registered File Types list, select the type of file you want to change, and then click Edit to open the Edit File Type dialog box:

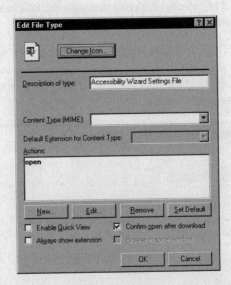

3. In the Actions list, select Open, and then click Edit to open the Editing Action For Type dialog box.

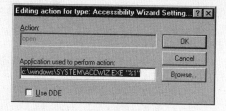

4. In the Application Used To Perform Action box, enter the path to the application, or click Browse to locate it.

5. Click OK when you are finished.

Now the document will open in the application you specified.

TIP

If you want to change the icon associated with a file type, click the Change Icon button in the Edit File Type dialog box, and in the Change Icon dialog box, select another icon, and click OK.

HANDLING FLOPPY DISKS

Whether you work on a stand-alone system, you're connected to a local area network, or you live and breathe via the Internet, you probably also use *sneakernet* from time to time. On a sneakernet, you copy files to a floppy and schlepp the disk over to a co-worker. Some of you may think this is tantamount to programming with a pen and quill, but since it's still a fact of life, let's complete this chapter by looking at how you format and copy a floppy.

Formatting a Floppy Disk

Unless you buy formatted disks, you must format a disk before you can store information on it. Formatting a disk that already contains files deletes those files. Follow these steps to format a floppy:

1. In Windows Explorer, scroll up in the Folder pane until you see the icon for the floppy, and then right-click it.

2. Choose Format from the shortcut menu to open the Format dialog box:

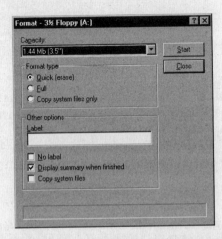

3. Ensure that the correct options are selected, and then click Start. A bar at the bottom of the dialog box will indicate the progress of the format.

4. When Windows says Format Complete, click OK and close the Format dialog box.

Copying a Floppy Disk

To copy a floppy disk, follow these steps:

1. In Windows Explorer, scroll up in the Folders pane until you can see the icon for the floppy drive, and right-click it.

2. In the shortcut menu, choose Copy Disk to open the Copy Disk dialog box:

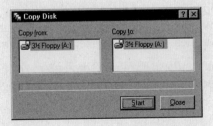

3. When prompted, place the disk you want to copy in the floppy drive, and click OK.

NOTE

If you have more than one floppy drive, you can specify the From and To disks. If you're on a network, you may be lucky to have one floppy drive, much less two. For security purposes, network computers often have no floppy drive.

4. When Windows has finished reading the source disk, it will ask you to insert the destination disk. Do so, and click OK.

5. When the copy is completed, click Close.

WHAT'S NEXT?

With the information you've acquired in this chapter, you're in good shape to handle the files and folders on your computer and to organize whatever you want to add in the future, which will likely include the topic of the next chapter—multimedia. At its simplest, multimedia is simply the simultaneous play of two or more types of media—for example, audio and video. With Windows 98 SE, however, you're good to go in more ways than that, including DVD, 2-D and 3-D graphics, Surround Video, and Web casts. In the next chapter, Robert Cowart takes you on a multimedia tour and gives you tips for getting the most out of your computer's multimedia capabilities.

Chapter 7

WINDOWS MULTIMEDIA

Windows 98 SE is more *multimedia-ready* than any previous version of Windows. Gone are the days when upgrading your PC for multimedia meant days of intense hardware analysis. And because Windows 98 SE has built-in, high-performance, 32-bit support for digital video, digital audio, MIDI, game controllers, and even TV, developers and users no longer need to worry about installing special drivers and programs to squeeze maximum multimedia out of their Windows machines.

Adapted from *Mastering Windows 98 Second Edition* by Robert Cowart
ISBN 0-7821-2618-9   893 pages $39.99

PC-based multimedia has grown dramatically in the last several years. Not only do practically all mainstream software packages (including Windows 98 SE itself) now come to us on CD-ROMs, many of them also have online multimedia tutorials to teach basic skills. These often include music, video, or animation, as well as voice coaching. Thanks to the cooperative efforts of many hardware and software engineers, we've come a long way from the old days when a program consisted of a single floppy disk and a big, boring manual. And this is just the tip of the multimedia iceberg. Internet-based multimedia games, music-education programs, video telephone conferencing, 360-degree panoramic-view Web sites, and streaming audio and video Web sites are some of the nifty features that are becoming common.

Improvements in Plug-and-Play (PnP) technology have decreased the hassle of upgrading your system to add stuff like CD-ROMs, audio cards, microphones, and speakers. Nowadays, you're almost guaranteed that any new PnP multimedia device you add will install itself with little or no hassle. You're also more likely to meet with success when plugging in some older piece of gear, due to improved detection of "legacy" (a.k.a. old) hardware by Windows 98 SE.

With few exceptions, today's PCs are multimedia PCs, complying with standards that were primarily developed by Microsoft and a few other industry giants. The "multimedia PC standard" proposed a few years back has been widely adopted by PC makers, partly by design and partly as the result of mass popularity of specific pieces of hardware. (For example, most PC sound systems are "SoundBlaster" compatible. Manufactured by Creative Labs, Inc., SoundBlaster was one of the first add-in sound cards. Even without being endorsed by other hardware and software companies, it has become a de facto industry standard thanks to the sheer number of installed units in the field.) Windows 98 SE has helped solidify the standards for multimedia by adding multimedia APIs (Application Program Interfaces) that serve as a set of building blocks for anyone making multimedia programs for Windows. By writing their code around the APIs, software developers have to write only one version of a program regardless of the hundreds of possible combinations of video, audio, MIDI, or other multimedia hardware that might be included in users' computer systems. Windows and the installed device drivers take care of the rest.

A multimedia PC equipped with Windows 98 SE can:

▶ Display cable and broadcast television in a resizable window or full screen with better-than-TV quality, and even capture the closed-captioning text of a show to a text file for later perusal.

- ▶ Play DVD movies, complete with display of embedded textual or other material that the producer may add.

- ▶ Record, edit, and play sounds in a variety of formats from highly compressed monaural voice grade to CD-quality stereo.

- ▶ Play MIDI sequences on your synthesizer or other MIDI device.

- ▶ Play fancy CD-ROM titles such as interactive encyclopedias that talk or adventure games such as *Myst*.

- ▶ Display streaming video and audio from Web broadcasts such as live concerts or news shows.

- ▶ Display live video and audio teleconferencing over the Internet using NetMeeting or other compatible programs.

All such capabilities, and the hardware and software that make them work, fall into the category of *Windows multimedia*. This chapter will answer your questions about the multimedia abilities of Windows 98 SE and show you how to best take advantage of them. Please keep in mind while reading this chapter that talking about Windows multimedia is like shooting at a moving target. Changes are taking place so rapidly in the field that book publishers would need unrealistically brisk turn-around times (akin to that of magazines) to accurately reflect the state of the industry. Therefore, to spare you the annoyance of reading out-of-date material, I'll focus this chapter on the multimedia features of Windows 98 SE itself and deal only fleetingly with issues of secondary, aftermarket products.

Exactly What Is Multimedia?

Multimedia—alias *interactive media* or *hypermedia*—is difficult to define, which accounts for much general confusion on the topic. The practical definition changes each time I write a book about Windows, and that's about every year or so. Actually, multimedia simply means two or more simultaneous types of display. Regular old TV is a good example—it's a multimedia device since it integrates audio and video. Computers are capable of even more advanced levels of multimedia, amalgamating animation, graphics, video, MIDI, digitally recorded sounds, and text. Computers can also interact with people as they view the presentation.

It's interesting to chronicle the breakneck rate of multimedia advancements. Just a few years ago, updating a system to multimedia meant adding a CD-ROM drive. Today, any decent PC and even most laptops have them built in, along with speakers and even accelerated video display cards capable of 30-frame-per-second high-speed animation and texture mapping.

Some multimedia programs are *interactive,* and some are not. Interactivity means that through some input device such as a keyboard, mouse, voice, or external controller—for example a Musical Instrument Digital Interface (MIDI) keyboard—you interact with the system to control aspects of the presentation. Most of today's software is still primarily based on text display, though it's increasingly permeated with graphics, charts, and clip art. With the added capabilities of stereo sound, animation, and video, multimedia computing offers a rich and efficient means of conveying information. As an example of a simple interactive program, consider the Windows tour, which demonstrates Windows fundamentals for the newcomer. (You launch it by choosing Start ➣ Programs ➣ Accessories ➣ System Tools ➣ Welcome To Windows. Then click on Discover Windows 98.) The tutorial demonstrates rudimentary multimedia, integrating animation, text, and voice. It does not incorporate live-action video clips. Now imagine expanding such a tutorial to include music, realistic 3-D animation, and moving video images just as if you were watching TV. As you probably know by now, animators, musicians, designers, writers, programmers, audio engineers, industry experts, and video producers have joined forces to create multimedia applications such as:

▶ A word-processing document that lets you paste in video clips (with audio); instead of displaying just a still graphic, the document will be "alive" with sight and sound.

▶ A music-education program on a CD-ROM from Microsoft that plays Beethoven's Ninth Symphony while displaying informative and educational text about each passage and about the composer.

▶ A dictionary, thesaurus, book of quotations, and encyclopedia on a CD-ROM from Microsoft that not only contains a huge amount of textual information but actually pronounces the dictionary entries; reads quotations aloud in the voices of Robert Frost, Carl Sandburg, T. S. Eliot, e. e. cummings, Dylan Thomas, and John F. Kennedy; and illustrates scientific phenomena with animation.

▶ Programs that teach you how to play the piano using a MIDI keyboard connected to your PC. The computer senses whether you play the lesson correctly and responds accordingly with a recorded high-quality voice. Similar programs teach music theory.

▶ Interactive company annual reports, product demonstrations, presentations, or corporate training manuals for new employees.

▶ *Moving catalogs* from mail-order houses, displaying everything from cars to coats via high-quality video and audio.

▶ An interactive geography test used at the National Geographic Society Explorer's Hall in Washington, D.C.

▶ Interactive high-speed, random-access books, newspapers, or catalogs for the blind, using high-quality voice synthesis or recorded voices.

▶ Interactive training for hard-to-teach professions such as medical diagnosis, surgery, auto mechanics, and machine operation of various types.

▶ Complex interactive games and children's learning programs that incorporate stereo sound effects, flashy visuals, and the ability to move through synthetic virtual worlds.

These multimedia products and more already exist. The explosion of multimedia CD titles has been enormous in the last few years.

WHAT'S NEW IN WINDOWS 98 SE MULTIMEDIA

Windows 98 SE adds some new features and enhances some of the multimedia features of Windows 98:

Windows Media Player 6.1   Enables playback of several multimedia formats, including streaming media such as Windows Media and MP3.

NOTE

MP3 is an abbreviation for MPEG layer 3, a compression format for audio files. MP3 filenames include the mp3 file extension. For all the details about MP3, see Chapter 22.

Enhanced IEEE 1394 Support   IEEE 1394 is a protocol that provides a high-speed, Plug-and-Play–capable bus that eliminates the need for peripherals to have their own power supplies and provides support for isochronous data transfer. For more information about IEEE support and Windows 98 SE, go to www.microsoft.com and search on IEEE 1394.

NOTE

IEEE (pronounced "eye-triple-e") is the abbreviation for the Institute of Electrical and Electronics Engineers, an organization that coordinates computing and communications standards.

WebTV for Windows Updates   Provides wider support for analog television tuner cards and AVTEF (Advanced Television Enhancement Forum) standards for HTML-based enhanced programming.

DirectX API 6.1   Enhances audio and video synchronization.

Windows NetMeeting 3   The latest version of this conferencing application that you can use for video conferencing, audio conferencing, sharing applications, chatting, and more.

In this chapter, we'll look at some of these new features and also look at multimedia features that have become Windows standards.

UPGRADING TO MULTIMEDIA

With Windows 3.x, working with multimedia required purchasing Microsoft's Multimedia upgrade kit or buying an expensive and hard-to-find MPC (multimedia PC). Beginning in Windows 95, Microsoft started to bundle multimedia drivers with their operating systems and include related utility programs (such as Sound Recorder) in the hope that this would accelerate the development of multimedia Windows applications. Establishing the MPC specification helped set some standards for what a multimedia PC should look and act like, and the PC add-on market did the rest. Multimedia hardware, applications, and utilities are now widely available, and many are incorporated into Windows 98 SE.

The magazines now inundate us with ads for newer and faster CD-ROM and DVD-ROM drives, 128-bit co-processed video cards, high-resolution energy-efficient monitors, and fancy sound cards—some even have samples of real orchestral instruments built in. The MPC moniker has fallen by the wayside, and now what's really more important is whether a system is fully Windows 98/98 SE compatible. After that, the rest is icing on the cake: how big is the screen, how good do the speakers sound, how clear is the image, and, overall, how fast does the *whole system* perform (not just the CPU chip)? You'll have to rely on the magazines for these kinds of test comparisons. Don't rely on the guys in the store. One brand of 400MHz Celeron machine might actually be faster than another one that's got a 450MHz Pentium III under the hood, because of the vagaries of hard-disk controllers, type of internal bus, memory caching, or speed of the video card.

If you already own a multimedia-ready machine with a couple of speakers and a CD-ROM drive, you might as well skip this section and move down to the next major section in this chapter, "Supplied Multimedia Applications and Utilities." But if you don't have such a machine, and you're thinking about endowing your machine with the gift of gab, some fancy video graphics capabilities, and the ability to play TV or DVDs, stay on track here.

You can upgrade your computer in three basic ways:

▶ Buy a whole new computer.

▶ Buy an "upgrade-in-a-box."

▶ Mix and match new components that exactly fit your needs.

As of this writing, you could choose from about 20 upgrade-in-a-box products. You'll typically get a CD-ROM drive, speakers, a sound card, a microphone, and maybe some CDs in the package. The sound card has the SCSI (Small Computer Systems Interface, pronounced "scuzzy") connector that hooks the CD-ROM drive to the computer. Mixing and matching is for us total control-freak geeks, who must have the best or who don't like the idea of other people controlling our purchase decisions. The obvious downside is that sorting through the sea of components in the marketplace is a big waste of time. I've spent too many hours testing video boards, trying to get a SCSI upgrade to my sound card to work with my CD-ROM drive, or running around listening to speakers. In any case, here are a few points about the pros and cons of the three upgrade routes.

In your shopping, you may wonder what the minimal requirements of a multimedia system should be. With the technology changing so quickly, it's hard to predict what the pickings will look like a year from now or what the latest and greatest version of *Riven* (or some other multimedia game you'll want as your major distraction from work) will crave in the way of MM nuts and bolts. Still, here's Bob's rule of thumb about buying new computer stuff: the best balance between price and performance lies just in the wake of the technology wave.

That is, if price is an issue, eschew the cutting edge! State-of-the-art gear is too expensive and usually still has some bugs to be worked out or ends up becoming an "industry standard" with a half-life of about nine months before being dropped like a hot potato. When a product hits the mainstream, that's the time to buy; prices usually take a nosedive at that point, often about 50 percent. Table 7.1 outlines and explains the three approaches I listed earlier in this section.

TABLE 7.1: Approaches to Multimedia Upgrading

QUESTION	NEW COMPUTER	KIT IN A BOX	MIX AND MATCH COMPONENTS
What is it?	A whole computer system that is designed for Windows 98 SE multimedia from the ground up and includes a fairly zippy computer, color screen, speakers, microphone, sound card, fast video display card capable of TV tuning and video capture, built-in Zip drive, and a CD-ROM drive. Options will be CD writers and DVD players.	A box of stuff you get at a computer store or by mail order. Everything works together and costs less than $200. Includes a sound card, CD-ROM drive, microphone, and speakers. (For more money you can get a DVD drive instead of a CD-ROM drive. Most DVD drives can play normal CDs as well as DVD discs.)	CD-ROM drive, optional DVD drive, sound board, speakers, microphone, cabling, and possibly necessary software drivers. Purchase parts separately. $200–$400. Add an additional $150 minimum for a CD writer.
Who should buy?	Owner of an older computer who has already decided to purchase a new computer either because existing computer isn't worth upgrading to a faster CPU and larger hard disk or because an additional computer is needed.	Average owner of nonmultimedia computer that's acceptably endowed in terms of the CPU and hard disk (e.g., at least a Pentium and a 2GB hard disk or larger) but needs multimedia capability to run multimedia games and standard productivity applications.	Power user who wants the best selection of components—or who already has one or two essential components, such as a CD-ROM drive, and now wants the rest. May be a professional (such as a musician, application developer, or graphic artist) who needs one element of the multimedia upgrade to be of very high quality.

TABLE 7.1 continued: Approaches to Multimedia Upgrading

Question	New Computer	Kit in a Box	Mix and Match Components
How much hassle?	No hassle. Everything is installed and working. Get the system with Windows 98 Second Edition installed and working, and you're really set.	You'll have to remove the cover of the computer, remove some screws, insert a couple of cards, hook up some cables and the CD-ROM drive (if the drive is the internal type), and then hook up the speakers. If the cards and computer are not Plug-and-Play compatible, you'll have to make IRQ (interrupt request) and DMA (direct memory access) settings. This may take some homework. You might have conflicts with existing hardware; if so you should have Windows 98 SE detect and install drivers for the new hardware, or use supplied drivers.	About the same amount of hassle as a box upgrade, but you'll have to deal with separate documentation for each component and figure out how to get everything working together, unless they are Plug-and-Play components. IRQ and DMA conflicts are likely otherwise.
Advantages?	Low hassle factor. You can start getting work done instead of poring over magazines and manuals. Your church (or kid) gets your old computer (which means you get an easy tax write-off), and you get more sleep and have only one vendor to deal with at service time.	You don't have to sell your existing computer. You might even get some free CD-ROM software in the box.	You can have exactly what you want. 24-bit TrueColor graphics, direct video capturing, video conferencing, great sound, superfast display at 1600 by 1280—you name it.

TABLE 7.1 continued: Approaches to Multimedia Upgrading

Question	New Computer	Kit in a Box	Mix and Match Components
Disadvantages?	You have to buy a whole new system. You'll probably be compromising somewhat on the components for the low hassle factor.	It will take some work to install it, unless it comes from the same people who made your computer (e.g., a Dell upgrade to a Dell computer). Again, some compromise on the components is likely. You may not have the best-sounding speakers, fastest video, greatest color depth, or CD-ROM drive.	Price and installation hassle can be high, but PnP is making things much easier. Multiple dealers to reckon with at service time.
Price?	Less than $1500 for most systems, which is not much more for a multimedia system than for those without multimedia. A few hundred additional dollars is typical. Tricked-out systems with all options and lots of memory and large hard disk will be between $2500 and $4000.	Typically between $100 and $250 for fast CD-ROM or DVD drive, 3-D sound card, speakers, and a few extras.	Difficult to predict. Bottom-of-the-line but functional clone parts could run you as little as a few hundred dollars. Or you could pay well into the thousands for the best brands.

What does this mean in the current market? Well, the now old and crusty MPC specification requires a machine with at least 4MB of RAM, a 130MB hard disk, and a fast processor such as a 486 or Pentium. But that's now a joke. You won't find a PC with that little RAM these days. On the next few pages are my suggestions to keep in mind when you're shopping for multimedia components and systems.

Computer   I'd suggest at *least* a Pentium MMX CPU, a local bus video card, and a 2GB hard disk—EIDE (Enhanced Integrated Drive Electronics) or SCSI—with 32MB (preferably 64MB) of RAM. A SCSI hardware interface is even better because you can also hook up as many as seven devices to most SCSI controllers, not just hard disks, and they run faster. But the bulk of machines these days have EIDE hard disks, and they are fast enough for most purposes short of doing real-time video capture. Remember, this is a minimum configuration.

Of course, if you're buying a new computer, you're probably going to get at least a Pentium II or Celeron 400 (or equivalent) with a 4GB hard disk. For any serious work (or play) I'd recommend that kind of speed or faster.

CD-ROM Drive   Get at least a 16X speed drive. (The X means how many times faster the data can be read from the disk relative to the first CD drives, which are considered 1X.) As of this writing, affordable 40X drives are common. Windows 98 SE caches your CD-ROM drive data so that slower drives can keep up with the data-hungry demands of applications that display video, for example.

If you want to be able to connect to a laptop or move the drive between computers, get a lightweight portable external job, maybe even a Zip or Jaz drive. Many computer manufacturers offer optional Zip drives for less than $100. Make sure the drive supports multisession Kodak photo format. This lets you not only view photographs in CD-ROM format on your computer but also take an existing photo CD-ROM to your photo developer and have them add new pictures to it. You might want up-front manual controls on the player so you can listen to audio CDs without running the CD Player program that comes with Windows.

PHOTOS AND WINDOWS 98

If you're among the gadget happy, you'll probably be procuring yourself a digital camera soon or at least want your photos on disk or in your computer somehow. That way, you can futz with your pictures using nifty software such as Adobe PhotoShop, Goo Power Tools, or other programs that let you make art out of common photographs. Or, so you can e-mail pictures of your pet iguana to your friends back home.

The easiest way to get your pix into the computer is to take your next roll of film down to the photo finisher's and request your snaps back on disk as well as on paper. Though some will give them to you on floppies, most services will provide the shots on CD. The standard format is the Kodak CD format.

CONTINUED ➡

Once you get the CD, check it for the info that tells you how to view the pictures. If all else fails, you may be able to simply click on the picture files using Windows Explorer, but better to use some software front-end to do it. The pictures usually show up as jpg or gif files, and there may be numerous resolutions for each picture (thus, a set of files for each picture).

Digital cameras always come with Windows software and instructions for getting your pictures from the camera into your computer. I like using the cameras that have a pop-out memory card that I can plug into the PC card slot on my laptop. Then I don't have to hassle with wires (and thus the relatively slow download speed of the pictures over a wire). Two of the cameras I've tested (Panasonic Cool Shot and Kodak DC 210) used these cards, and they were interchangeable. I just took some pictures and then popped the card out of the camera and into the computer. Windows 98 SE recognizes the card automatically and treats it like a disk drive, which makes it easy to display the contents in Windows Explorer or in a Browse box from a photo display program or other imaging program.

NOTE

There are two flavors of Photo CD you should know about: *single-session* and *multi-session*. With a multi-session Photo CD, you can just take your existing CD to your photo finisher's shop and ask them to add your new pictures to the same disk. Single-session doesn't let you do that; it's a write-once format.

CD Writer   Among the latest goodies in the CD-ROM drive market are the now-affordable writers that will "burn" (record) a custom CD for you. These used to cost thousands of bucks, and only recording and software magnates could afford them. Now, creating your own music CDs (I create CD compilations of my fave dance tunes for parties) or backing up tons of data on CDs is something anyone can do. All you need is a CD-R (CD Recordable) or CD-RW (CD ReWritable) drive. The blank discs cost only a few dollars, and you can put 650MB on one. The drives that record them, though, are about three times the price of a standard CD-ROM reader.

I bought a CD-R kit recently (called the "Smart and Friendly" kit) for just a few hundred dollars at Costco/Price Club. Such a deal. It installed with only a little hassle, and the bundled Adaptec Easy CD Pro software was simple to use. Check the magazines and get a kit that has everything you might need, right in the box. You might be buying more than you need, but you'll be avoiding headaches in the long run. For example, I paid for the extra SCSI card they bundle with the drive (I already have a faster one), just so I knew I had a complete one-stop solution. Also note that CD-R drives tend to be slower at reading CD-ROMs than regular read-only drives. Mine reads at only 6X and writes at a measly 2X. So I have two CD drives: a regular 24X and the CD-R at 2X/6X. Many CD-Rs require a SCSI interface, but not all do. Many EIDE units are also available. Most of the SCSI units come with a simple SCSI adapter card. It doesn't have to be a fancy fast SCSI card (fast/wide/ultra or any of that), since speed isn't an issue. If you already have a SCSI card, it will likely work with a CD-R drive.

NOTE

The CD-R format allows you to record once, and that's all. Once a CD is written, it can't be erased and rewritten. With some formats you can add more data later, until the disc is full, but you can't erase. Another format, CD-RW (rewritable) uses slightly more expensive media to allow you to write and rewrite discs again and again.

DVD   DVD drives are the new hot item on the market. However, DVD is a technology in such an emerging state that manufacturers can't even agree what DVD stands for. (Some say digital video disc while others say digital versatile disc.) Regardless, we're seeing a lot more of them every day. Many households in the United States have DVD players in their computers and on their TV set tops already. As of this writing, set-top DVD players run about $250 and support lots of nifty features such as:

▶ 500 lines of horizontal resolution (more than twice as sharp as standard TV)

▶ 8 sound tracks (for different languages, instruction, and so on)

▶ 32 sets of subtitles

▶ Multiple movie-viewing formats (standard, letterbox) and angles

▶ Theater sound

▶ 2 hours of video per side (up to 4 hours max)

▶ Dolby digital sound

Adding a DVD drive to your PC lets you view movies and educational titles on the PC, with the superior resolution of your computer's monitor (instead of the pretty funky resolution of a standard TV). In addition, you'll be able to interact with DVD titles designed for computers. Windows 98 SE supports DVD drives and has a DVD player program (similar to its CD player program) for playing DVD titles.

A number of DVD add-in kits are available today for your PC. More and more PCs come equipped with DVD as an option or standard fare, and writable DVDs should appear soon. Currently they are expensive. But once those appear, editing your own homebrew movies will be a snap.

Speakers   The larger the better, usually. Little speakers will sound tinny, by definition. Listen before you buy if possible. Listen to a normal, speaking human voice—the most difficult instrument to reproduce. Does it sound natural? Then hear something with some bass. If you're going to listen to audio CDs, bring one with you to the store and play it. Speakers that are separate (not built into the monitor) will allow a nicer stereo effect. Separate tweeter and woofer will probably sound better, but not always. It depends on the electronics in the speaker. Magnetic shielding is important if the speakers are going to be within a foot or so of your screen; otherwise, the colors and alignment of the image on the screen will be adversely affected. (Not permanently damaged, though. The effect stops when you move the speakers away.)

Of course, instead of buying speakers, you can use your stereo or even a boom box if it has high-level (sometimes called *auxiliary*) input. Some boom boxes and virtually all stereos do have such an input. Then it's just a matter of using the correct wire to attach your sound card's *line* output to the stereo's or boom box's AUX input and setting the volume appropriately. The easiest solution is to purchase a pair of amplified speakers designed for small recording studios, apartments, or computers. For about $100 you can find a good pair of smaller-sized shielded speakers (4- or 5-inch woofer, separate tweeter) with volume, bass, and treble controls. For $300 you can get some that sound very good. If you like real bass, shell out a little more for a set that comes with a separate larger subwoofer you put under your desk.

Sound Board   This should have 64-bit sound capability for CD-quality sound. You'll want line-in, line-out, and microphone-in jacks at least. Typical cards also have a joystick port for your game controller. The card should be compatible with Windows 98 SE, with the MIDI specification, and with SoundBlaster so it will work with popular games. This means it should have protected-mode 32-bit drivers for Windows 98 SE, either supplied with Windows 98 SE or with the card. If it doesn't, you'll be stuck using 16-bit drivers that take up too much conventional memory space, preventing many DOS-based games and educational programs from running. I've seen this problem with cards, such as the SoundBlaster Pro, that prevent a number of games such as the Eagle-Eye Mystery series from running. Fancy cards such as those from Turtle Beach don't sound like cheesy synthesizers when they play MIDI music because they use samples of real instruments stored in *wave tables* instead of using synthesizer chips, but you'll pay more for them. Wavetable cards are easy to find now for less than $40.

Video Card and Monitor   The video card goes inside the computer and produces the signals needed to create a display on the monitor. A cable runs between the video card and the monitor. For high-performance multimedia, you'll want a *local bus* video card, typically VLB (VESA–Video Electronics Standards Association–local bus) or PCI (Peripheral Component Interconnect), capable of at least 256 colors at the resolution you desire. If your motherboard has an AGP (Accelerated Graphics Port) adapter, get an AGP video card for best performance.

TIP

Local bus cards only work in computers that have a local bus connector slot, so check out which kind of slots your computer has before purchasing a video card upgrade.

Standard resolution (number of dots on the screen at one time, comprising the picture) for a PC is 640 (horizontal) by 480 (vertical). Most new video cards these days will support that resolution at 256 colors. If you have a very sharp 15-inch screen or a 17-inch screen, you may opt for a higher resolution, such as 800 by 600 or 1024 by 768. When shopping for a video card, make sure it displays at least 16-bit color (and preferably 24-bit) at the resolution you want *and has at least a 70Hz noninterlaced refresh rate at that resolution and color depth*. The correct refresh rate prevents screens from flickering, which can cause headaches and/or eye fatigue. Video cards with graphics coprocessor chips on them will run faster than those that don't. High speed is necessary when you move objects around on the screen or display video clips.

Make sure the board will work well with Windows 98 SE, preferably with the 32-bit video driver that comes with Windows 95, 98, and 98 SE, not an old driver designed for Windows 3.x. You don't have to worry about any monitor's ability to display colors because any color monitor will display all the colors your card can produce. What you *do* have to check on are a monitor's dot pitch, controls, and refresh rate. The monitor should ideally have a dot pitch of .25 or .26, be at least 17 inches (though 15 inches will do), and run all your desired resolutions at 70Hz or higher refresh to avoid flicker. Beware of the refresh-rate issue: false or misleading advertising is rampant. Many monitors and video cards advertise 72Hz or higher refresh rates, but the fine print reveals that this is only at a low resolution such as 640 by 480. Bump up the resolution, and the refresh rate on cheaper cards or monitors drops to a noticeably slow 60Hz. Get a monitor that has low radiation emissions, powers down automatically when it isn't being used (a so-called green monitor), and has a wide variety of controls for size, picture position, brightness, contrast, color, and so forth.

TIP

If you expect to view lots of TV or play the latest games, get a video card with 2-D and 3-D acceleration, video capture, a TV tuner, and video in and out. The ATI All-In Wonder is currently my card of choice. It works well with the Windows 98/98 SE TV tuner programs, has a slew of video resolutions, and works right out of the box with Windows 98/98 SE. Street price is about $140.

That's the basic rundown on multimedia upgrading. Now let's look at what's supplied with Windows 98 SE in the way of multimedia programs and utilities.

SUPPLIED MULTIMEDIA APPLICATIONS AND UTILITIES

Windows 98 SE comes with several multimedia programs and utilities:

Sounds   This Control Panel applet lets you assign specific sound files (stored in the wav format) to Windows system events such as error messages, information dialog boxes, and e-mail notification.

Windows Media Player   This application (choose Start ➤ Programs ➤ Accessories ➤ Entertainment ➤ Windows Media Player) lets you play a variety of multimedia files on the target hardware. If a device contains data, such as a CD-ROM or video disc, Windows Media Player sends commands to the hardware, playing back the sound or video therein. If the data is stored on your hard disk (as are MIDI sequences, animation, and sound files), Windows Media Player will send them to the appropriate piece of hardware, such as a sound board, MIDI keyboard, or other device.

TIP

The Media Player only works with MCI (Media Control Interface) devices and thus requires MCI device drivers.

Sound Recorder   This is a simple program for recording sounds from a microphone or auxiliary input and then editing them. Once recorded, sound files can be used with other programs through OLE (object linking and embedding). Sound files also replace or augment the generic beeps your computer makes to alert you to dialog boxes, errors, and so forth. Sound Recorder is also the default program used to play back wav files.

TIP

You can find more elaborate wav file editors. For my CD recording projects I use a shareware program called Cool Edit, which you can find and download from the Web. Another capable shareware wav file program is called WaveWorks.

CD Player   Assuming your computer's CD-ROM drive and controller card support it (most do), this accessory program lets you play back standard audio CDs. This can be a great boon on long winter nights when you're chained to your PC doing taxes or writing that boring report. You'll find coverage of this program later in the chapter.

DVD Player   If the DVD drive you purchase, whether by upgrade or built-in, says it is Windows 98 or 98 SE compatible, it will come with a DVD player program. Whether you choose to use that player or the one supplied with Windows 98 SE is up to you; they all work similarly. You just have to compare their respective features, as some have more bells and whistles than others. In this chapter, I'll cover the player that comes with Windows 98 SE.

Adding Drivers   The System and Add New Hardware applets in Control Panel let you install drivers for many add-in cards and devices such as CD-ROMs, MIDI interface cards, and video-disc controllers if they are not detected automatically once you plug them in. Drivers for most popular sound boards such as the SoundBlaster (from Creative Labs, Inc.) and Ad Lib (Ad Lib, Inc.) and popular MIDI boards such as the Roland MPU-401 (Roland Digital Group) are supplied. Other drivers can be installed from manufacturer-supplied discs using this option. Even if your hardware is physically installed, it won't work unless the proper driver is loaded.

Volume Control   The Volume Control accessory, available from the Taskbar, simply lets you control the balance and volume levels of the various sound sources that end up playing through your computer's speakers. Right-click the icon to adjust the volume via a slider bar. To make more specific adjustments, double-click the icon to open the Volume Control dialog box, in which you can change various volume aspects as well as mute your computer.

MIDI Mapper   This was included as a separate Control Panel applet in Windows 3.1 and NT, but has been hidden in Windows 98/98 SE because it is rarely used. Its purpose was to declare settings for your MIDI device, such as channel assignment, key remapping, and patch-number reassignment for nonstandard MIDI instruments. The assumption now is that most MIDI instruments comply with the MIDI standard for these parameters and thus the Mapper is rarely needed. If you have a nonstandard MIDI instrument that you're running from Windows programs (this won't affect DOS programs), open the Multimedia applet in Control Panel, and in the Multimedia Properties dialog box, click the MIDI tab. Click Custom Configuration, and then click the Configure button to open the MIDI Configuration dialog box, which contains some rather complex remapping facilities.

Doing It All with DVD Player

As I mentioned earlier in this chapter, Windows 98 SE includes support for DVD (digital versatile disc / digital video disc) drives. DVD and CD-ROM use very much the same technology (micro laser to read the disc), so besides being able to play DVD discs on your computer, you should be able to use a DVD drive to read your current CD-ROM and audio CD disc (this depends, however, on how early you buy; first-generation DVD drives could not read as many CD formats as the current generation). Price wise, this will be an almost unnoticed transition, at least for new system buyers. A computer equipped with a DVD drive will probably cost only $100 to $150 more than one equipped with a CD-ROM drive instead. (If it weren't for the need for a decoder card to play DVD movies on your computer, the difference would be less.) DVD drives are now offered as standard equipment in many PCs as they begin to replace CD-ROM drives.

Some DVD Specifics

I already sang the praises of DVD earlier in the chapter. However, as there is some confusion about different generations of DVDs, I want to make sure you have the basics understood before I discuss the DVD Player program supplied with Windows 98 SE.

DVD is becoming the content-providing medium of choice. Sure, CDs will still be around, but even with the giganto capacity of 650MB on a CD, some programs (such as Microsoft's own Office 2000) actually require multiple CDs! In addition, mega-databases such as national phone directories, the catalog of the Library of Congress, the complete Oxford English Dictionary, photo stock house collections, museum and gallery holdings photographed in high resolution, and font packages span multiple CD-ROMs. These are all prime candidates for appearing on DVD.

And then, of course, we've got movies—the hands-down winners of the disc-consumption sweepstakes. With a maximum capacity of 17GB (yes, gigabytes), an innocent DVD (which looks almost identical to a CD) can store two hours of video that displays more clearly (and has groovier options) than VHS, LaserDisk, or video CD-ROMs. DVD movies boast multichannel surround sound, subtitles, multiple alternative audio tracks (for different languages), multiple video playback formats, and even, in some cases, user-selectable camera angles.

How does a DVD pack all that information onto a 5-inch disc? Well, first, the optical pits on a DVD disc are stuffed in twice as close to one another as on a CD, and so are the tracks. Also, more of the surface is recorded on. *And* error correction is more rigorous! All this increases the data storage capacity from a CD's 650MB to a DVD's 4.3GB. But wait! That's only for one layer! DVDs can have *two* layers per side. By focusing the read laser carefully, a second layer can be used, adding another 4.3GB, for a one-side total of approximately 8.4GB. But wait! DVDs can have data written on *both sides*, so by flipping the disc over, the 8.4GB is doubled.

Another compelling point about DVD is its versatility. CD-ROM suffers from a plethora of competing and often incompatible formats: multisession, Photo CD, Mode 1, Mode 2, Joliet, CD-I, and CD+, to name but a few. The DVD spec is, well, versatile (as the name implies: digital versatile disc). A new disc file format that was devised for DVD, called Universal Disc Format (UDF), ensures compatibility between disc and player, regardless of content. (Well, almost. As the saying goes, some limitations apply.) A single DVD drive should be able to read most existing CDs, as well as text, data, and video DVD formats. Even CD-R (recordable CD) and CD-RW (rewritable CD) discs should be readable by most second-generation DVD drives.

Shop Carefully!

If you're thinking about buying a DVD drive, check the specs thoroughly, and ask around before you drop your cash. Third-generation drives are widely available, so you'll probably want to skip buying a first- or second-generation drive. The differences lie mostly in the formats they can read. Second-generation drives can read CD-R and CD-RW, whereas first-generation drives can't. Third-generation drives read a greater variety of recordable and re-recordable formats.

As for speed, don't worry. As long as they can play back a movie, you'll have speed to burn. The latest crop of DVD drives (5X DVD) plays CDs at the equivalent speed of a 32X CD-ROM drive.

Installation of DVD can be tricky. I suggest you purchase a complete upgrade kit or purchase a computer with the DVD built in. I upgraded piece by piece. It cost me more and was a hassle to get working. Read the requirements for an upgrade carefully. Typically you'll need at least a 166MHz Pentium with 16MB of RAM; you'll also need a bus-mastering PCI slot, an empty drive bay for the drive, and an open EIDE connector. (Although some DVDs are SCSI drives, most are EIDE. Besides, most motherboards support four EIDE drives, and you probably don't have four hard disks connected; so why buy a SCSI disk controller if you don't need it?) Most DVD drives don't care whether they are "slave" or "master" drives.

TIP

As a rule, just look for a kit or computer that is compatible with Windows 98/98 SE, and follow the instructions supplied with the unit.

In addition, until you can buy a video card that is tailored to support DVD video playback, you'll need a *decoder card* to be able to watch DVD movies on your computer. (If you aren't planning to play video DVD discs, neither of these is necessary.) The decoder card plugs into the PCI bus (typically) and connects to your existing video card (via a ribbon cable) to translate the video data into the analog signals needed for display on your monitor. Among other things, such as decoding Dolby Surround-Sound audio and handling copy-protection schemes, the decoder decompresses the MPEG-1 or MPEG-2 compressed video in real time. This takes some serious computing speed. Some DVD drives come with "software" decoders which they say can be used instead of a decoder card, but don't expect smooth performance from them, even on a fast Pentium machine. The computer's CPU just can't keep up with the data stream very well and ends up dropping frames to keep up.

Running the DVD Player

Typically the DVD player that comes with the drive will have all the basic controls found on a VCR, plus some number of additional bells and whistles, such as searching tools, audio controls for bass, treble, and volume, a viewing angle selector, child-proofing locks, video format selector, "chapter" and "title" features, and so on. Most of them are used in similar ways; you'll just have to compare the features of each. In this section, I'll provide the basic instructions for running the player that comes with Windows 98 SE.

First, I'll assume that you've got your hardware installed (or someone at the factory did it for you), as discussed earlier. If your drive is in working order, here are the basics of running the Windows DVD Player:

1. Insert a DVD disc as you would insert a disc into any other drive, and shut the door. Windows will detect the disc; if the disc is a video disc, DVD Player will start; if it's an audio disc, CD Player will start (as discussed earlier in this chapter).

2. If a disc has been inserted and nothing happens, run DVD Player explicitly by choosing Start ➤ Programs ➤ Accessories ➤ Entertainment ➤ DVD Player. Then click Options

button, and choose Select Disk to open the Load DVD File dialog box:

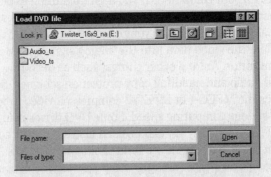

3. If you've set the option that prevents someone from running a movie without authorization (see the Tip following this step), you'll see the Show Logon Box Selection dialog box:

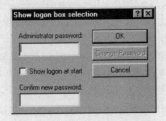

TIP

You can create a new logon password by choosing the Options button on the player. Typically, you might create a password to prevent children from playing your discs.

4. To start playing a disc, click the Play button on the player toolbar (the right-pointing triangle). You should experiment with the other controls by clicking them as well, just as you might in the CD player application or on a VCR. You can play, stop, pause, fast forward, fast rewind, eject, and so on. (You'll also find buttons here for Very Fast Forward and Very Fast Rewind.) If you're better with words than icons, you can

display a textual list of all the commands available from the player toolbar by right-clicking any one of the controls:

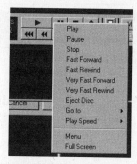

To see a full-screen view of the movie you are watching, click the little icon of the television set in the toolbar. The toolbar disappears. You can access the tools again by right-clicking anywhere on the screen, which pops up the following menu:

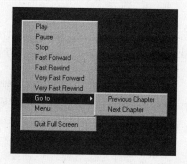

Choose the Quit Full Screen command to display the toolbar again, or choose any of the other commands as you wish. Alternatively, to cancel this menu and return to full-screen view, click anywhere outside the menu.

Chapters and Titles   Typically you'll watch video DVDs just as you would a VHS tape; that is, you'll start it, pause it once in a while to get up for more popcorn, then sit down and click Play to start it up again. But as more interesting DVDs start to hit the market, you may want to jump to specific *titles* and *chapters*. Think of a title as, say, one of several shows on the disc. A chapter, then, is a subset of a title: perhaps a lesson, a scene in the movie, or a section of a tutorial, for example. Once a disc is inserted, you can quickly choose to search for sections by title or chapter by right-clicking the display, as shown here:

▶ If you choose Search Title, this handy little box lets you jump to a specific title and to any portion of the title track by entering its time value:

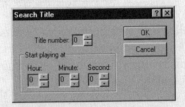

▶ If you choose Search Chapter, you'll see the following dialog box, which also expects you to enter a time value:

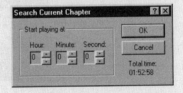

Just enter the hour, minute, and second of the spot you want to jump to (and if you're in the Title box, enter the title number), and click OK.

Selecting Language and Subtitles   Some discs will have subtitles (nice for when you're talking on the phone; that way nobody can hear what's distracting you), and some discs will have multiple languages (that is, multiple alternative audio tracks), as I mentioned earlier. You can make choices for these features by clicking the Options button.

The procedure is a no-brainer:

1. Click Options.

2. Choose SubTitles or Language.

3. Set the subtitle or language option as desired, and click Close.

For example, suppose I wanted to see English subtitles (assuming my disc offered them). Choosing the Options ≻ SubTitles command might show the following choices:

I'd just click English and then click the Show Subtitles check box. For language choice, I might see the following little dialog box. I'd just choose the audio language I'm interested in listening to:

Ending a DVD Session   When you're finished listening to, using, or viewing the disc, you can either press the Eject button on the front of the drive or click the Eject button on the DVD Player toolbar. Then close the DVD Player program.

Assigning Sounds with Control Panel's Sounds Utility

You can use Control Panel's Sounds utility for assigning sounds to system events, such as warning dialog boxes, error messages when you click in the wrong place, and so on. Once you've installed a sound board, you can personalize your computer's beep to something more exciting. If your computer had a sound card when you installed Windows 98 SE, it's likely Windows established a default set of rather boring sounds for your system, most of which you're probably tired of already. Besides making life more interesting, hearing different sounds for different types of events is also more informative, because you can assign sounds to many more events than Windows does by default. You know when you've made an error as opposed to when an application is acknowledging your actions, for example.

Of course, to add basic sounds to your Windows setup, you need a sound card that is compatible with Windows 98/98 SE. The sounds you can use must be stored on disk in the wav format. Most sounds that you can download from the Internet or get on disk at the computer store are in this format. Also, the Sound Recorder program explained later in this chapter records sounds as wav files. Windows 98 SE comes with more than a few sound files. In fact, just as with the color schemes you can create and save with Control Panel's Display applet, you can set up and save personalized sound schemes to suit your mood. Microsoft has supplied us with several such schemes, running the gamut from happy nature sounds to futuristic, mechanistic robot utterances to the sonorities of classical musical instruments.

NOTE
You have to do a Custom installation to get all the sound schemes loaded into your computer. You can do this after the fact by opening Control Panel and choosing Add/Remove Programs ➢ Windows Setup. Then click Multimedia to select it, and click the Details button. The Multimedia Sound Schemes are located near the middle of the list.

Despite this diverse selection, you may still want to make or acquire more interesting sounds yourself or collect them from other sources.

To record your own, you'll need a sound board that handles digital sampling. I have messages in my own voice, such as, "You made a stupid mistake, you fool," which—for a short time—seemed preferable to the mindless chime. If your system lets you play audio CDs, you should be able to directly sample bits and pieces from your favorite artists by popping the audio CD into the computer and tapping directly into it, rather than by sticking a microphone up to your boom box and accidentally recording the telephone when it rings. Check out the Volume Control applet, and adjust the slider on the mixer panel that controls the input volume of the CD. Then use the Sound Recorder applet to make the recording.

TIP

Any time your sound isn't working correctly (if there's no sound, for example), check the following: Are your speakers connected and turned on? Is the volume control on them (if they have it) turned down? Has the sound worked before? If so, it's probably the mixer settings that are wrong. Right-click the Volume icon near the clock in the Taskbar, and choose Open Volume Controls to open the Volume Control dialog box. Check the settings. Don't forget to choose Options ➤ Properties and poke around. Don't change the mixer device, but notice that you can choose to see the Recording mixer controls, and choose which sliders are on either the recording or playback controls. Make sure the source that isn't working properly isn't muted.

Like any good sound-o-phile, I'm always on the lookout for good wav files. You'll find them everywhere if you just keep your eyes open: cheap CDs at the local Compu-Geek store, on the Internet, on CompuServe, even on other people's computers. Usually these sound files aren't copyrighted, so copying them isn't likely to be a legal issue. Most wav files intended for system sounds aren't that big, either. But do check out the size, using the Explorer or by showing the Details view in a folder, before copying them. Sound files *can* be super large, especially if they are recorded in 16-bit stereo (about 172KB per second of CD-quality audio). As a rule you'll want to keep the size to a minimum for system sounds because it can take more than a few seconds for a larger sound file to load and begin to play.

Once you're set up for sound and have some wav files, you assign them to specific Windows events. Here's how:

1. Open Control Panel, and click the Sounds applet to open the Sounds Properties dialog box, which is shown in Figure 7.1.

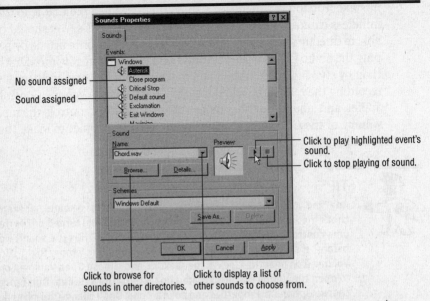

Click to play highlighted event's sound.

Click to stop playing of sound.

No sound assigned

Sound assigned

Click to browse for sounds in other directories.

Click to display a list of other sounds to choose from.

FIGURE 7.1: Use this dialog box to choose which sounds your computer makes when Windows events occur.

2. The top box lists the events that can have sounds associated with them. There will be at least two classes of events—one for Windows events and one for Explorer events. (Scroll the list to the bottom to see the Explorer events.) As you purchase and install new programs in the future, those programs may add their own events to your list. An event with a speaker icon next to it already has a sound associated with it. You can click it and then click the Preview button to hear the sound. The sound file that's associated with the event is listed in the Name box.

3. Click any event for which you want to assign a sound or to change the assigned sound.

4. Open the drop-down Name list, and choose the wav file you want to use for that event. Some of the event names may not make sense to you, such as Asterisk, Critical Stop, or Exclamation. These are names for the various classes of dialog boxes that Windows displays from time to time. The sounds you're most likely to hear often will be Default Sound, Menu Command, Menu Popup, New Mail Notification, Question, Open Program, Close Program, Minimize, Maximize, Start Windows, and Exit Windows.

TIP

The default directory for sounds is the \Windows\Media directory. That's where the wav files that come with Windows 98 SE are stored. If you have wav files stored somewhere else, you'll have to use the Browse button to find and assign them to an event. I find it's easier to copy all my wav files into the \Windows\Media directory than to go browsing for them when I want to reassign a lot of sounds.

5. At the top of the Name list is an option called (None) that has the obvious effect—no sound will occur for that event. Assigning (None) to all events will effectively silence your computer for use in a library, church, and so forth. You can also quickly do this for all sounds by choosing the No Sounds scheme as explained in the next section.

6. Repeat the process for other events to which you want to assign or reassign sounds.

7. Click OK.

Keep in mind that different applications will use event sounds differently. You'll have to do some experimenting to see when your applications use the default beep, as opposed to the Asterisk, Question, or Exclamation.

Clicking the Details button displays information about the wav file, such as its time length, data format, and copyright information (if any).

Loading and Saving Sound Schemes

Just as the Display applet lets you save color schemes, the Sounds applet lets you save sound schemes so you can set up goofy sounds for your humorous moods and somber ones for those gloomy days—or vice versa. The schemes supplied with Windows 98 SE are pretty nice even without modification.

To choose an existing sound scheme:

1. Click the Schemes drop-down list button, down at the bottom of the Sounds Properties dialog box:

2. A list of existing schemes will appear. Choose a sound scheme. Now all the events in the upper part of the box will have the new sound scheme's sounds. Check out the sounds to see if you like them.

3. If you like the sound scheme, click OK.

You can set up your own sound schemes by assigning or reassigning individual sounds, as I've already explained. But unless you *save* the scheme, it will be lost the next time you change to a new one. So, the moral is: once you get your favorite sounds assigned to system events, save the scheme. Then you can call it up any time you like. Here's how:

1. Set up the sounds the way you want. You can start with an existing scheme and modify it or start from scratch by choosing the No Sounds scheme and assigning sounds one by one.

2. Click the Save As button:

3. In the Save Scheme As dialog box, enter a name for the scheme. For example, here's one I made up and saved:

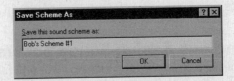

4. Click OK, and your scheme is saved. Now you can create additional schemes and save them or just OK the large dialog box to activate the new scheme.

You can delete any existing sound schemes by choosing the doomed scheme from the list and then clicking the Delete button. You'll be asked to confirm the deletion.

Playing Multimedia Files with Windows Media Player

Windows Media Player is a little application that plays multimedia files, such as digitized sounds, MIDI music files, and video files. It can also send control information to multimedia devices such as audio CD players or videodisc players, determining which tracks to play, when to pause, when to activate slow motion, and so on.

The capabilities of Windows Media Player have been upgraded for Windows 98 Second Edition, primarily to allow it to handle a wider variety of media formats than previous versions. Microsoft now claims that the Media Player can play virtually all standardized formats of audio, video, and streaming signals, but some media providers may still require you to use a specific player. This is especially true for streaming audio, which most often uses RealNetwork's RealPlayer (`www.real.com`), and for streaming video, which often utilizes QuickTime 4 from Apple (`www.apple.com`).

Obviously, you can only use Media Player on devices installed in your system and for which you've installed the correct device drivers, so first see to that task. Then follow these instructions for playing a multimedia file:

1. Choose Start ➤ Programs ➤ Accessories ➤ Entertainment ➤ Windows Media Player to open Media Player:

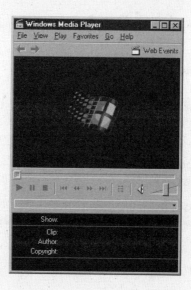

2. Choose File ➤ Open to open the media file you want to play.

3. In the Open dialog box that appears, type the address (or path) of the file. If it's located on disk, it will probably be easiest to click on Browse and navigate to the file from there. When the correct file address appears in the Open dialog box, click OK. The Media Player's appearance will change slightly based on the type of media file you opened. In the example shown below, a wav sound file has been opened. Since the file contains only sound, the video playback section of the Media Player is automatically hidden:

TIP

You can jump to a particular location in the piece by dragging the scroll bar, clicking at the desired point in the scroll bar, or using the arrow keys and the Page Up and Page Down keys. Also, check the Device menu for options pertaining to the device you are using.

4. Now you can use the buttons in the dialog box to begin playing the piece. The buttons work just as on a VCR or cassette deck; if in doubt, point to a button to display a ToolTip.

5. When you're done playing, close the application from the File menu.

Media Player has a few options worth noting. Check out the View ➤ Options dialog box. Choose Repeat Forever to keep playing the media file over and over.

Recording and Editing Sounds with Sound Recorder

Sound Recorder is a nifty little program that lets you record your own sounds and create wav files. To make it work, you need a digital sampling card such as the SoundBlaster and some kind of input device, such as a microphone. The program also lets you do some editing and manipulation of any wav files you might have on disk. You can do this even if you don't have a microphone.

The resulting wav files can be put to a variety of uses, including assigning them to system events or using them with other multimedia applications, such as Media Player. Once a file is recorded, you can edit it by removing portions of it. Unfortunately, you cannot edit from one arbitrary spot to another, only from one spot to either the beginning or the end of the file. You can also add an echo effect to a sample, play it backward, change the playback speed (and resulting pitch), and alter the playback volume.

Playing a Sound File

To play a sound file, follow these steps:

1. Make sure your sound board is working properly. If it's been playing sounds, such as the one that plays when Windows starts up, it probably is. If not, check that you've installed the correct driver and that your sound board works.

2. Run Sound Recorder by choosing Start ➤ Programs ➤ Accessories ➤ Entertainment ➤ Sound Recorder. The Sound Recorder dialog box will appear, as shown here:

3. Choose File ➤ Open to open the Open dialog box, and select the file you want to play. Notice that the length of the sound

appears at the right of the window and the current position of the play head appears on the left.

4. Click the Play button or press Enter to play the sound. As it plays, the wave box displays the sound, oscilloscope style. When the sound is over, Sound Recorder stops. Press Enter again to replay the sound. You can click Stop during a playback to pause the sound, and then click Play to continue.

5. Drag the slider bar (see below), and notice how the wave box displays a facsimile of the frequency and amplitude of the sample over time:

You can also click the Seek To Start and Seek To End buttons to move to the start and end of the sample or press the Page Up and Page Down keys to jump the play head forward or backward in longer increments.

Recording a New Sound

This is the fun part, so get your microphone (or line input) ready. Suppose you want to make up your own sounds, perhaps to put into an OLE-capable application document such as WordPad or Word so that it talks when clicked. Here's how:

1. In Sound Recorder, choose File ➤ New.

2. You may want to check the recording format before you begin. Choose File ➤ Properties. In the Choose From drop-down list, select Recording Formats, and then click Convert Now to open the Sound Selection dialog box, which is shown in Figure 7.2. A combination of data-recording format (for example, PCM, ADPCM, and so forth) and sampling rate (for example, 8KHz 8-bit mono) are shown. Together these constitute a format scheme.

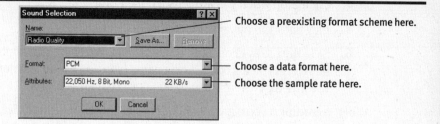

Choose a preexisting format scheme here.

Choose a data format here.
Choose the sample rate here.

FIGURE 7.2:   Choosing a data scheme for a new sound recording

NOTE

The Attributes list shows the amount of disk space consumed per second of recording. You'll want to consider this when making new files, because recording in high-fidelity stereo can suck up precious disk room, rendering sound files quite unwieldy. Also, for most purposes, you are best served by choosing one of the preexisting sound schemes—CD Quality, Radio Quality, or Telephone Quality—for your recordings. All three use the PCM recording technique but employ different sample rates. If you are recording only voice, use either the Radio or Telephone setting. The CD Quality setting will only use up more disk space than you need to. If you are planning to record from an audio CD player, you'll probably want to choose the CD Quality setting unless you want to conserve disk space. If you accidentally record at a higher quality level than you wanted to, don't worry. You can convert to a lower quality and regain some hard disk space by choosing File ≻ Properties ≻ Convert Now. You can save recording and playback settings with the Save As button in the dialog box.

3. Click the Record button. The clock starts ticking, counting the passing time. Begin talking into the microphone that's plugged into your sound card, playing whatever is connected to your AUX input (a.k.a. *line in*) on the sound card, or playing the audio CD that's in the CD-ROM drive. You'll have to use the Volume Control applet to set the relative balance of the various devices. Typically you'll be able to mix these disparate audio sources into a single recording if you use the mixer deftly. The maximum recording time will vary, depending on your recording format. In the default setting (PCM, 22,050Hz 8-bit mono), you can record for up to one minute. Be cautious about the length of your sounds, as they tend to take up a large amount of disk space. For example, a one-second sample at CD Quality in stereo consumes about 172KB.

4. Click Stop when you are finished recording.

5. Play back the file to see if you like it.

6. Save the file by choosing File ➤ Save As. You'll see the familiar Save As dialog box. Enter a name (you don't have to enter the wav extension; the program does that for you).

When recording a voice narration, be sure to speak loudly and clearly, particularly if you notice that playback is muffled or buried in noise.

Editing Sounds

You can edit sound files in several ways. For instance, you can:

▶ Add echo to a sample.

▶ Reverse a sample.

▶ Mix two samples together.

▶ Remove unwanted parts of a sample.

▶ Increase or decrease the volume.

▶ Increase or decrease the speed and pitch.

▶ Convert it to another format for use by a particular program.

NOTE
You may run out of memory if your file becomes very long because of inserting files into one another. The amount of free physical memory (not virtual memory) determines the maximum size of any sound file.

To edit a sound file:

1. Open the sound file from the File menu.

2. Open the Effects menu to add echo, reverse the sound, increase or decrease volume, or increase or decrease speed. All the settings except echo can be undone, so you can experiment without worry. You undo a setting by choosing its complementary setting from the menu (for example, choose Increase Volume instead of Decrease Volume) or by choosing Reverse. Some sound quality can be lost by doing this repeatedly, however.

3. To cut out the beginning or ending of a sound—that is, to eliminate the lag time it took you to get to the microphone or

click the Stop button—determine the beginning and ending points of the sound, get to the actual starting position of the sound, and choose Edit ➢ Delete Before Current Position. Then move the slider bar to the end of the desired portion of the sample, and choose Edit ➢ Delete After Current Position.

4. To mix two existing sounds, position the cursor where you'd like to begin the mix, choose Edit ➢ Mix With File, and choose the filename. This can create some very interesting effects that are much richer than single sounds.

5. To insert a file into a predetermined spot, move to the spot with the slider bar, choose Edit ➢ Insert File, and choose the filename.

6. To place a sound on the Clipboard for pasting elsewhere, choose Edit ➢ Copy.

7. To return your sound to its original, last-saved state, choose File ➢ Revert.

Not all sound boards have the same features. Some won't let you save a recording into certain types of sound files. Also, the quality of the sound differs from board to board. Some boards sound "grainy," others less so. This is determined by the sampling rate you've chosen, the quality of the digital-to-analog converters (DAC), and the analog amplifiers on the board.

Some programs require a particular sound file format to use sounds. For example, the Voxware plug-in for Web browsers (which lets you put sound clips on your Web pages) expects sound files in its proprietary Voxware format. To convert an existing sound file, follow these steps:

1. Open Sound Recorder.

2. Choose File ➢ Properties to open the Properties For Sound dialog box.

3. Click Convert Now to open the Sound Selection dialog box.

4. Select the correct setting from the Format list.

5. Click OK, and then save the file.

NOTE

Typically, programs that require proprietary sound formats supply their own conversion tools, and it's often better to use those tools when they are available than a little accessory such as Sound Recorder.

Playing Tunes with CD Player

The CD Player accessory turns your computer's CD-ROM drive into a music machine. With it, you can play standard audio CDs with all the controls you'd expect on a "real" CD player, and then some. Of course, you'll need speakers (or at least a pair of headphones) to hear the music. Here's what CD Player looks like:

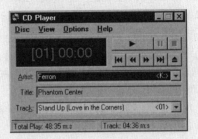

With CD Player, you can:

► Play any CD once through or continuously while you work with other programs.

► Play the tracks in sequential or random order, or play only the tracks you like.

► Move forward or in reverse to any desired track.

► Fast forward or rewind while a track is playing.

► Stop, pause, and resume playback and (if your CD-ROM drive has the capability) eject the current CD.

► Control play volume if you're playing the CD through a sound card (this only works with some CD-ROM drives).

► Control the contents of the time display (you can display elapsed time, time remaining for the current track, or time remaining for the entire CD).

► Catalog your CDs (after you've typed in the title and track list for a CD, CD Player will recognize it when you load it again, displaying the titles of the disk and the current track).

Getting Started with CD Player

To run CD Player, begin from the Start menu and choose Programs ➤ Accessories ➤ Entertainment ➤ CD Player. Load your CD-ROM drive with an audio CD, turn on your sound system or plug in the headphones, and you're ready to go.

CD Player can tell when your CD-ROM drive is empty or doesn't contain a playable audio CD. In this case, it will display the message:

```
Data or no disc loaded
Please insert an audio compact disc
```

in the Artist and Title areas in the middle of the dialog box.

Basic Playing Controls

The CD Player dialog box looks much like the front panel of a typical CD player in a sound system. The large black area at the top left displays track and time information. On the left, the faux LED readout tells you which track is currently playing, while on the right it keeps a running tally of how many minutes and seconds have played in the track.

If you've ever worked a standard CD player, the control buttons (to the right of the track and time display) should be immediately familiar:

On the top row are the essential stop/start controls:

Play   The largest button with the big arrow starts or resumes play.

Pause   The button with the two vertical bars pauses play at the current point in the track.

Stop   The button with the square stops play and returns you to the beginning of the current track.

On the second row, the first four buttons have double arrows pointing to the left or right. These let you move to other parts of the disc.

TIP

You can move directly to a specific track by choosing it from the list in the Track area near the bottom of the CD Player dialog box. See "Playing Discs with the Play List" later in the chapter.

Previous and **Next Track**   At either end of this set of four buttons, the buttons with the vertical bars move to the beginning of the previous or next track. The one at the left end—with the left-pointing arrows—moves to the beginning of the previous track (or if a track is playing, to the beginning of the current track). The one at the right—with the right-pointing arrows—moves to the beginning of the next track.

Skip Backwards and **Skip Forwards**   The two center buttons in the set of four have double arrows only; these are for moving quickly through the music while the disc plays in the reverse or forward direction.

Eject   This is the last button at the far right of the second row, with the upward-pointing arrow on top of a thin rectangle. Click here to pop the current disc out of your CD-ROM drive. Of course, this will only work if your drive is capable of ejecting automatically.

Display Options

Like other Windows programs, CD Player has a toolbar with buttons for other common commands (we'll cover these in a moment). The toolbar may not be visible when you first run the program; choose View ➤ Toolbar to turn it on and off. Here's how the CD Player window looks with the toolbar visible:

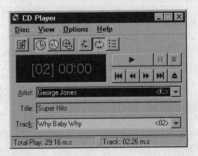

When the toolbar is displayed, you can get a brief description of each button's function by placing the mouse pointer over the button.

Two other elements of the CD Player dialog box can also be turned off and on via the View menu. These are the status bar and the area displaying the artist and disc and track titles.

When visible, the status bar runs along the bottom of the window. It offers Help messages when the mouse pointer passes over a menu choice or rests over a button on the toolbar. Otherwise, it displays the total play time for the disc and current track. To turn the status bar off or on, choose View ➤ Status Bar.

Once you've cataloged a disc, CD Player displays the artist, disc title, and title of the current track in the middle of its window. If you want to hide this information, perhaps to make the window small enough to stay on your screen while you work with another program, choose View ➤ Disc/Track Info.

TIP

You can choose between two font sizes for the numerals in the track and time readout. See "Setting CD Player Preferences" later in this discussion.

You can also control the display of time information in the main readout of the CD Player window. The standard setting shows elapsed time for the track currently playing. If you prefer, you can instead see the time remaining for the current track or for the entire disc. To select among these options, open the View menu and choose one of the three relevant options: Track Time Elapsed, Track Time Remaining, or Disc Time Remaining. The currently active choice is checked on the View menu. Or, if the toolbar is visible, you can click the button corresponding to your time-display choice.

Other Play Options

You have several commands for determining the play order of a disc's tracks. Three of these are available as items on the Options menu or as buttons on the toolbar:

Random Order   Plays the tracks randomly. This is often called *shuffle* mode on audio-only CD players.

Continuous Play   Plays the disc continuously rather than stopping after the last track.

Intro Play   Plays only the first section of each track. You can set the length of this intro with the Preferences command, covered later in this section.

NOTE

If you have a multiple-disc CD-ROM drive, you'll find an additional Multidisc Play choice on the Options menu. Select this if you want to hear all the discs loaded in the drive rather than only the currently active disc.

You can select these playback options in any combination. To turn them on or off, open the Options menu and choose the desired item; they are active when checked. Alternatively, click the button for that command (the button appears pressed when the command is active). Here are the buttons you use:

If none of these commands are active, CD Player plays the tracks in full and in sequence, stopping after the last track.

Other play options include whether the current disc keeps playing when you close CD Player (covered in "Setting CD Player Preferences," later in this chapter) and playing a custom list of tracks, covered in the next section.

Cataloging Your CDs and Creating Play Lists

If you're willing to do a little typing, CD Player will keep a "smart" catalog of your disc collection. Once you've entered the catalog information, such as the disc title, the artist, and the track titles, CD Player automatically displays these details whenever you reload the disc:

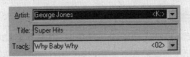

If you have a multidisc CD-ROM drive (or more than one unit), you can choose from the available drives by letter, using the list in the Artist area.

Cataloging a Disc   When you load a disc that hasn't been cataloged, CD Player displays generic disc information. The Artist area reads *New Artist*, and the Title area says *New Title*. Tracks are titled by number (*Track 1*, *Track 2*, and so on).

To enter the actual information for the current disc, choose Disc ➤ Edit Play List, or, if the toolbar is visible, click the corresponding button. The Disc Settings dialog box shown in Figure 7.3 will appear.

FIGURE 7.3: The Disc Settings dialog box

The top area in this dialog box, labeled Drive, identifies the location of the disc being cataloged. If you have a multidisc player, you can double-check whether you're working with the correct disc here.

Type the name of the artist and the title of the CD in the appropriate areas at the top of the dialog box. To enter track titles, follow these steps:

1. Select a track in the Available Tracks box.

2. Type the track title in the Track area at the bottom of the dialog box.

3. Click the Set Name button to change the current name.

You can change any of this information at any time. When you're satisfied with your entries, go on to create a play list as described below or click OK to return to CD Player. The disc information will appear in the appropriate areas of the dialog box.

Creating a Play List   The typical CD has some great selections, a few that are good to listen to but aren't favorites, and one or two that are just terrible. CD Player lets you set up a custom play list for each disc so you never have to hear those dog selections again. If you like, you can even play your favorites more often than the others (be careful, you might get sick of them).

Here's how to create a play list:

1. In the Disc Settings dialog box (see Figure 7.3), the Play List box on the left side of the window displays the tracks in the play list. Initially, the box displays all the tracks on the disc in order.

2. If you just want to remove one or two tracks, drag each track off the list as follows: point to the track's icon (the musical notes) in the Play List box, hold down the mouse button, and drag to the Available Tracks box. Alternatively, you can highlight each track in the Play List box and click the Remove button. To remove all the tracks and start with an empty list, click Clear All.

3. You can add tracks to the play list in two ways:

   ▶ Drag the track (or tracks) to the Play List box using the same technique for deleting tracks but in the reverse direction: starting from the Available Tracks box, drag the track to the desired position in the Play List. You can add a group of tracks by dragging across them to highlight them, releasing the mouse button, and then dragging from the icon area to the play list.

   ▶ Use the Add button: highlight one or more tracks in the Available Tracks box, and click Add. In this case, the added track always appears at the end of the list.

4. If you want to start again, click Reset. The Play List box will again show all the tracks in order.

5. Click OK when you've finished your play list to return to the main CD Player dialog box.

Playing Discs with the Play List   CD Player always selects the tracks it plays from the play list. Before you make any modifications, the play list contains all the tracks on the disc, and you'll hear every track when you play the disc. Once you've created your own play list, though, CD Player plays only the tracks on the list. If you select Random Order play, the program randomly selects tracks from the play list, not from all the tracks on the disc.

The play list tracks are accessible individually in the Track area near the bottom of the CD Player dialog box. To move to a particular track, just select it in the list. If the disc is already playing, the selected track will start. Otherwise, click the Play button to start it.

Setting CD Player Preferences

Use the Preferences dialog box to change miscellaneous CD Player settings. To display it, choose Options ➣ Preferences. Here's what the Preferences dialog box looks like:

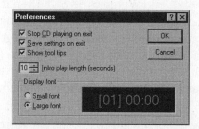

Here are the available preference settings and their effects:

Stop CD Playing On Exit   The CD stops playing when you close CD Player.

Save Settings On Exit   When this box is checked, the settings you make on the View and Options menus and in the Preferences dialog box are saved when you close the program. If you clear this box, changes in settings affect only the current session—the previous settings are restored the next time you start CD Player.

Show Tool Tips   Check this box if you want pop-up descriptions (also known as ScreenTips) and Help messages in the status bar when the mouse pointer rests on a button. Clear it if you find these messages annoying.

Intro Play Length   Use the arrow controls to set the number of seconds at the beginning of each track that CD Player will play when you activate the Intro Play command.

Display Font   Choose a large or small font for the LED-like track and time readout by choosing the appropriate radio button.

Web TV

One of my favorite multimedia applications in Windows 98 SE is Web TV, formerly known as the TV Viewer. It's probably not installed in your system, because it's an option. To install it from the CD, open Control Panel, and choose Add/Remove Programs ➢ Windows Setup ➢ Web TV For Windows. You may be prompted to reboot the computer several times before the installation is complete, so close any work in advance.

Web TV works in conjunction with special TV cards and video capture cards/drivers that are compatible with DirectShow 2.0 and WDM (drivers that are built into Windows 98 SE). Even if you don't have a video capture card or TV display card, you can still take advantage of the program listing guide, which downloads TV listings from the Web and displays them in various formats that put *TV Guide* (even the online version) to shame. You can search for shows, times, show types (sci-fi, drama, specials, and so on), and set reminders so your computer reminds you not to miss a show.

With the appropriate hardware, you can select and tune among hundreds of analog (broadcast and cable) or digital satellite television programs, and navigate to Web channels and other information broadcast through these networks. For satellite reception, drivers specifically written for the Broadcast Architecture are required. Check with your satellite TV provider to see whether their service is compatible with Web TV.

You will need a PC system capable of running Microsoft Windows 98 SE, including:

- A Pentium-class PC with at least 24MB RAM
- An additional 65MB of free hard disk space
- Television or standard VGA monitor (large screen monitor optional)
- Supported TV tuner and video card(s)
- Wireless remote control device (optional)
- Modem and Internet connection (optional)

TIP

For more information on supported hardware, search the Microsoft Web site for Broadcast Architecture.

What's So Cool about Web TV?

For starters, you watch TV either on the whole screen or in a window while you work, and the quality is very high. The picture is much sharper than on a standard TV, and some of the TV cards perform "line doubling," drawing twice as many lines on the screen as on a normal TV. This results in a better-looking picture, especially since you are typically watching from just a couple of feet from your screen. Most TV tuner cards decode stereo sound, so the sound will be good as well. Further, you also get the benefit of *enhanced TV* viewing. Here are some of the potential benefits of enhanced TV viewing (once this technology is more firmly developed):

- ▶ News and weather reports can be accompanied by local or other specialized information that satisfies the needs of limited audiences.

- ▶ Educational programs could spice things up with references and links to other programs and locations on the Web.

- ▶ When watching dramas and comedies, you could read cast information, recaps of past episodes, links to related Internet and bulletin board sites, and other such background information.

- ▶ When watching sporting events, you could read statistics, or even create your own data sheets for personalized tracking of favorite players or teams. You could hear or read additional syndicated commentary.

- ▶ Music-only channels can add background graphics containing title, album, and artist information, so you know what you are listening to and how to find it again.

- ▶ Shows can be enhanced by letting the viewer respond and interact. Viewers can then play along with game shows, enter contests, take quizzes, vote on issues presented in the show, express opinions, and take part in polls. Consumers using a back channel can actually investigate and purchase things from the comfort of their living rooms.

NOTE

Of course, your Internet connection must be correctly configured and working to download Program Guide information from the Web and to interact with shows. To verify your connection, confirm that you can successfully view content from some popular Web pages such as http://www.microsoft.com with Internet Explorer.

How It Works

At its simplest, Web TV simply picks up TV signals from an antenna or cable TV input plugged into your TV tuner card and displays the result in a resizable window. Windows 98 SE provides the TV tuner program to make this happen. If your TV tuner card is supported, Windows 98 SE supplies all the drivers. If not, you'll get them in the box with the card.

Going a step beyond that, if you're on a digital satellite system, you'll probably have to get a special accompanying card (either external or mounted inside the PC) that decodes the digital signals and then pumps them into the TV card.

You can download your program listings either from a broadcast channel or over the Web. It's much faster over the Web. The Web TV program is set up to decode the broadcast listings from Gemstar and load them into the Program Guide.

Using TV Viewer

To run the program, first install it as I explained above. Then run it either by clicking the TV set icon in the Quick Launch bar or choose Start ➣ Programs ➣ Accessories ➣ Entertainment ➣ Web TV For Windows. The first thing you'll notice upon running the program is that it takes a bit of time to load. You'll see the TV Viewer "splash screen" first, and after a little wait you'll be walked through setting up the program the first time. There a man's voice will tell you what to do. Just listen and follow the instructions.

If you're already hooked up to a good TV source (antenna, cable, satellite), have the Wizard scan for channels. I have found that when I'm using a cheesy antenna, I have to input the channels manually or they don't get registered because the signals aren't strong enough. (I'll show you how to do that shortly.) And if you have a Web connection, choose that as the source for your Program Guide data, not the broadcast option, which can take hours to download, though you may be able to do this in the background. If you download from the Web, you'll have to answer a few questions about your zip code and perhaps specify your source of TV signal (which cable company, which local broadcast area), as in Figure 7.4.

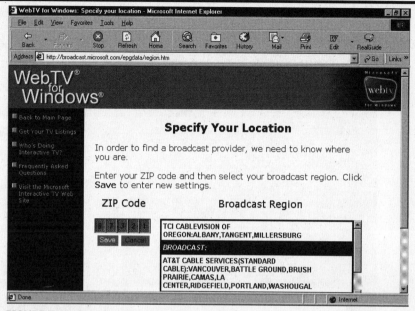

FIGURE 7.4: Specifying your broadcast medium when using the Gemstar Program Guide Web download

After a few minutes of downloading, the Web page should tell you that the process is complete. You can start using the program, and you'll see something like what I have in Figure 7.5. It looks totally unlike anything else in Windows 98 SE, so get ready, since the interface is completely new and a little annoying at first. But it's easy to learn, so don't worry.

TIP

You may not have program listings, either because you aren't connected to the Web and therefore can't download them from the Net, or you don't live in an area that broadcasts the listings over the air. Not to worry. If you don't have program listings, you can still watch TV. You just click the TV channel number over to the left, or press the Page Up and Page Down keys to change channels. If you have no channels except 1 and 99 showing, you have to add your channels manually. See the next section, "Adding (and Removing) Channels Manually."

NOTE

Only the shows displayed in green are being broadcast currently. Other times are displayed with a blue background. Clicking them does nothing.

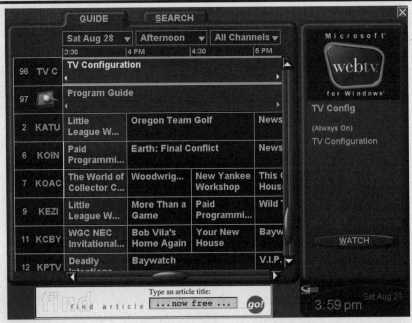

FIGURE 7.5: Typical Program Guide appearance. Click a green area to preview a show on the right.

Adding (and Removing) Channels Manually

Just like when you set up a new TV or VCR, the automatic scan option can add channels you don't want or can skip over weak channels and not add them. To manually add or remove channels, do this:

1. With the Web TV window active (or full screen), press Alt or F10 to display a big toolbar with a few icons on it.

2. Click Settings in the toolbar. In the resulting dialog box, click Add Channels. Add and enter the number, as you see in Figure 7.6. To remove a channel, select it, and click on Remove.

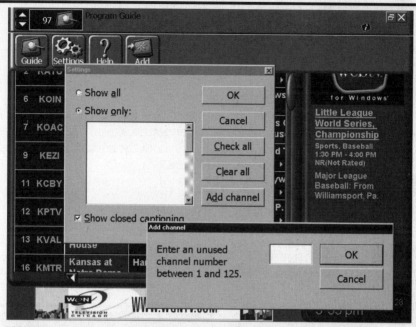

FIGURE 7.6: You can add or remove channels using the Settings dialog box. You also choose which channels to display in the Program Guide.

Tips for Using Web TV

Here are some tips to make using Web TV easier.

Access Online Documentation

Use the online help. It's pretty good. Just press F1 while you're in Web TV.

Avoid Channel 1

Channel 1 is the Setup channel. Choosing it by clicking it, or (more likely) by landing on it while pressing Page Up and Page Down to channel-surf, runs the Wizard again and starts talking you through the setup routine. Unless you want to hear all that and download the Program Guide again, or choose your video options (like for assigning a VCR or camera to a channel), just skip to another channel quickly.

TIP

Channel 99 is always the Program Guide.

Scroll the Display

Note the scroll buttons on the display. You can grab them and slide just as you do with other windows. When you do so, you'll see an indication of where you're headed. They work in both the horizontal (time) and vertical (channel) directions. (See Figure 7.7.)

TIP

You can size the display to any size you want, including full screen. The correct height/width proportion of the image is maintained as you resize. See the keystroke table (Table 7.2) later in this chapter for how to toggle between full screen and a window. While in a window, size it just as you would any other.

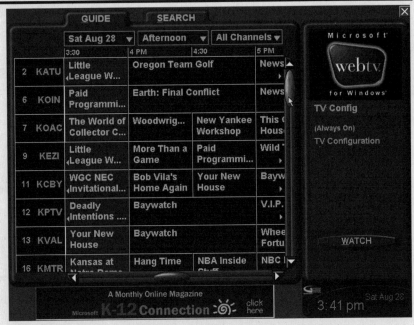

FIGURE 7.7:   Use the scroll bars to get around in your Program Guide.

Search for a Show

How many times have you wondered, "Hey when is *X-Files* (or *Who Wants to be a Millionaire?*, or something else) on? Now you don't have to scan the whole *TV Guide*. Just use the Search option.

1. Click the Search tab near the top of the TV Viewer window.

2. Click the Search area at the bottom left.

3. Enter the show you're looking for. Then click Search.

You'll see shows that match the name, on all stations in your area. You can then choose to set reminders (see below) or tune to the show immediately. You can also click Other Times to display a list of other times and channels when the same program will air.

Look for a Category of Shows

Looking for a drama, something educational, maybe a musical? Instead of just channel surfing and taking pot luck with a regular TV remote control, why not search by category and get what you're really looking for, like when you go to the video store? Follow these steps:

1. Click the Search tab.

2. Click the desired category in the left pane.

3. Pull down the left time menu at the top:

4. Choose a time slot.

TIP

After choosing a time slot, you'll only see listings for that time. The time slot you choose stays active until you change it or go back to the Guide Page by clicking the Guide tab. So, clicking other categories will also display only shows in the chosen time slot.

Read about a Program

Wondering if you've seen the program before? A spiffy feature of the Program Guide is that it also contains lots of information about shows it lists. You can click a show in the Program Guide, and over to the right, under the preview screen, you'll see some stuff about the show, such as the rating, whether it's a rerun, a synopsis of the content, and more. Figure 7.8 shows an example.

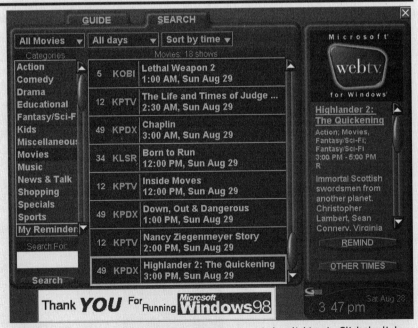

FIGURE 7.8: You can read about a program or movie by clicking it. Click the link (if you're online) to search for Web pages that contain the name.

If you're online with the Internet, you can click the name of the program just under the preview window to quickly conduct a search of pages that contain the name of the show. Sometimes you get useful information about the show, fan pages, and so on.

Set Reminders

Want to be alerted before a show comes on, so you can tape it or watch it? Easy. You just set a reminder:

1. Click a program in Program Guide.

2. Click the Remind button in the lower right to open the Remind dialog box:

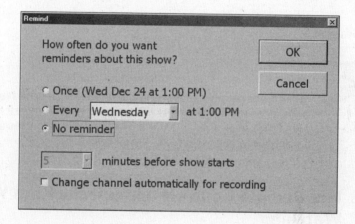

3. Fill in the relevant info, and click OK.

A dialog box will appear on the screen to remind you of the upcoming show, at the time(s) you choose.

NOTE
The Web TV program has to be running in order to give you reminders.

Add Favorite Channels to Your Toolbar

You can place as many as five favorite channels in your toolbar, making it easy to switch between favorite channels. If you have five and add another, the oldest one disappears and is replaced by the new one. Follow these steps:

1. Display the toolbar.

2. Select a channel you want, using one of the various techniques.

3. Click Add:

The new channel appears on the toolbar. Click it now to switch to that channel.

TIP

When you're viewing full screen, just move the pointer to the top of the screen and wait a second. The toolbar will appear. If you then move it away from the top of the screen, the toolbar will disappear after a few seconds. Pressing Escape always makes the toolbar go away too.

Use Remote Controls and Special Keys While Watching

Web TV is designed to work with remote controls available (or to-be-available) from your computer manufacturer. (Not your standard TV remote!) If you don't have a computer remote control, you're not alone. As an alternative, you can use the keystrokes listed in Table 7.2 with Web TV: the most frequently used keys are listed first.

TIP

If you have a Gateway Destination entertainment system, your remote control will work with Web TV. The only exception is that the Recall button on the Gateway remote control has no function.

TABLE 7.2: Keystroke Controls for Web TV

KEYSTROKE	ACTION
F10	Displays the toolbar menu (favorites, guide, logins, preferences, and other options are accessible from the toolbar).
F6	Toggles windowed/full screen mode. Windowed mode is useful for displaying video while using desktop applications.
0–9	Changes channels. Channels are three digits.
Enter	Confirms selection.
↑, ↓, ←, →	Scrolls up/down and left/right when viewing programming grid.
Win	Displays the Start menu.
Win+Ctrl+Shift+z	Displays the Program Guide (grid view).
Win+Ctrl+z	Displays Web TV if not yet started; otherwise, toggles between Desktop and full screen.
Win+Ctrl+v	Volume Up (on Master Mixer).
Win+Shift+v	Volume Down (on Master Mixer).
Win+v	Toggle Mute (on Master Mixer).
Win+Ctrl+Alt+z	Channel Up.
Win+Ctrl+Alt+Shift+z	Channel Down.
Win+Ctrl+Alt+Shift+f	Arrow Left (some applications may interpret as Rewind).
Win+Ctrl+Alt+Shift+p	Arrow Up (some applications may interpret as Play).
Win+Ctrl+Alt+f	Arrow Right (some applications may interpret as Forward).
Win+Ctrl+Alt+Shift+g	Recall (some applications may interpret as Eject).
Win+Ctrl+Alt+p	Arrow Down (some applications may interpret as Stop).
Win+Ctrl+Alt+g	Pause.

* "Win" means the Windows key on your keyboard if it has it. Older keyboards do not have this key.

MANAGING MULTIMEDIA DRIVERS AND SETTINGS

When you add a new piece of hardware to your system, such as a sound board, CD-ROM controller, MIDI board, or other piece of paraphernalia, you'll have to alert Windows to this fact by installing the correct software device driver for the job. Some drivers simply control an external player as though you were pushing the buttons on the device's control panel by hand. These types of devices are called Media Control Interface (MCI) devices and include audio CD players, videodisc players, MIDI instruments, and others. Other drivers actually send the sound or video data to the playback card or hardware, as well as control the playback speed and other parameters.

You use the Add New Hardware option in Control Panel to install the device driver. Drivers for popular multimedia items are included with Windows and will often be detected when you've added the hardware, especially if the hardware is Plug-and-Play compatible.

TIP

As a rule, when you're purchasing new stuff, avoid non–Plug-and-Play hardware like the plague.

If you are having trouble running your multimedia hardware or need to make adjustments to it, you'll have to examine the properties of the item and its driver. Device Properties dialog boxes can be reached from several locations. For example, the Edit menu in the Sound Recorder applet will take you to your sound card's Properties dialog box, though you could also use the System applet in Control Panel to get there.

When in doubt, always contact the manufacturer of your multimedia hardware to obtain drivers and driver updates for use with Windows 98 SE. You can often download new drivers over the Web, but not always. Sometimes a phone call is required.

WHAT'S NEXT?

If you don't happen to have all the hardware bells and whistles described in this chapter, you may have been making a shopping list as you were reading. And adding hardware to your computer makes it even more important that you take care of regular maintenance chores. In Chapter 8, you'll learn about the Windows maintenance tools you can use, you'll find out how Windows helps you to make backups, thus ensuring that you don't lose information, and you'll get an overview of computer viruses—how to avoid them and what to do if one infects your computer system.

Chapter 8

MAINTAINING YOUR SYSTEM

by Pat Coleman

Although we might wish it were so, our computers did not come with a maintenance-free guarantee. Maintaining your computer system won't take nearly as much time as maintaining your automobile or residence, but unless you regularly clean up your hard drive, back up files and folders, get rid of unnecessary files and folders, and so on, you won't be operating at maximum efficiency.

In this chapter, we'll take a look at how to use the Windows tools to maintain your system, and I'll walk you through the steps that you can use to schedule routine maintenance so that Windows does some of the work for you automatically.

USING THE WINDOWS SYSTEM TOOLS

To access all the Windows 98 SE system tools, choose Start ➤ Programs ➤ Accessories ➤ System Tools. You'll see the menu shown in Figure 8.1.

FIGURE 8.1: The Windows System Tools menu

Before you start using these tools though, you need a way to get information about your system—for example, how much free space is available on your hard drive, how much RAM your system has, which applications are installed on your system, and so on. An easy way to display a complete overview is to select System Information from the System Tools menu, which opens the Microsoft System Information dialog box shown in Figure 8.2.

The information that is displayed depends, of course, on your system. To display more information, click the plus (+) sign next to an item in the left pane. A lot of the data in this dialog box is very technical and is of use primarily when technical personnel are trying to troubleshoot a system problem. But now you know how to get it when you need it.

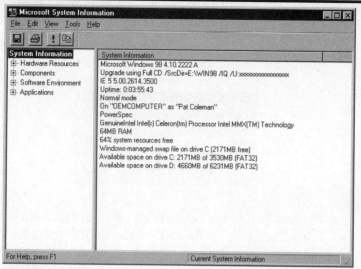

FIGURE 8.2: The Microsoft System Information dialog box

NOTE

Another source of information about your system is System Monitor, which tracks kernel processor usage and which is also on the System Tools menu. The *kernel* is the core of the operating system, and it manages such things as memory, date and time, and system resources.

Now, let's get down to the nitty-gritty of how to use the system tools to maintain your computer so that it operates as efficiently as possible.

Cleaning Up Your Hard Drive

In the process of managing your computer, the Windows 98 SE operating system creates a number of temporary files on your hard drive. These can include files that speed the performance of the graphical interface, temporary Internet files, temporary setup files, and other types of files that no longer serve a specific purpose and can be deleted.

If you are pressed for hard-disk space, you'll want to be rather zealous about identifying and deleting these unnecessary files whose names are inscrutable and whose purpose is usually unknown. Disk Cleanup is your tool of choice here. It checks your system for files that can safely be deleted and then presents you with a list. You can choose to delete all or only selected files. To run Disk Cleanup, follow these steps:

1. Choose Start ➢ Programs ➢ Accessories ➢ System Tools ➢ Disk Cleanup to open the Select Drive dialog box:

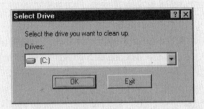

2. Select the drive you want to clean up and then click OK. Disk Cleanup checks the selected drive and then opens the Disk Cleanup dialog box:

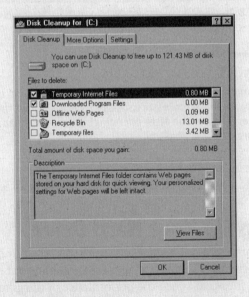

3. Place a check by the categories of files you want to delete, and then click OK.

Although you certainly can delete all the files that Disk Cleanup has identified as unnecessary, you may not really want to do so. Here are some of the categories that Disk Cleanup identifies. It's up to you to decide which you want to delete.

Temporary Internet Files   When you visit sites on the Web using Internet Explorer, these pages are stored on your computer in the Temporary Internet Files folder. When you want to revisit a site whose page is stored in this folder, any content that has not changed since the previous visit will open directly from the Temporary Internet Files folder. This is a considerable time savings over once again retrieving the page from the server. However, you certainly don't want to keep these files indefinitely. With the Temporary Internet Files category selected, click View Files to open the folder. Figure 8.3 shows the list of temporary Internet files on my computer. If necessary, choose View ➤ Details, and then click the Last Accessed heading to sort the files by date. At the very least, delete any that are more than six months old.

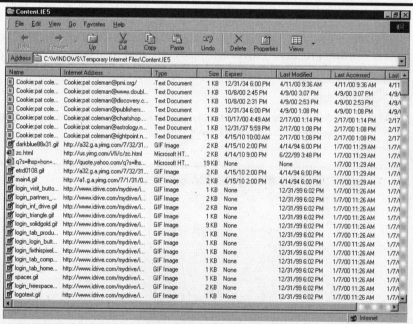

FIGURE 8.3: The temporary Internet files on my drive C

Downloaded Program Files   These files were downloaded from Web sites that you visited so that you could run ActiveX or Java applets.

Offline Web Pages   These are files that you specified to work with offline (perhaps because you know that the content is static rather than dynamic).

Recycle Bin   If the size of your Recycle Bin is set correctly, you shouldn't need to manually delete these files. (See Chapter 6 for information about managing files and folders and the Recycle Bin.)

Temporary Files   These files are routinely created by Windows and Windows applications and are normally deleted in the course of time by the operating system. If Disk Cleanup finds any of these temporary files, you can safely delete all of them.

Delete Windows 98 Uninstall Information   You can obviously get rid of these files after Windows 98 SE is installed and up and running.

If you want to free more space by deleting Windows components that you don't use or by deleting applications that you don't use, select the More Options tab, as shown in Figure 8.4. Click Clean Up to open the Add/Remove Programs Properties dialog box, and then delete what you want.

NOTE

The More Options tab simply provides another route to the Add/Remove Programs applet in Control Panel.

FIGURE 8.4: The More Options tab in the Disk Cleanup dialog box

If you want to automatically run Disk Cleanup when disk space is getting low, select the Settings tab, and then click the If This Drive Runs Low On Disk Space, Automatically Run Disk Cleanup check box.

If you bought your computer within the last year or so, you may well have more hard drive space than you'll ever need. I still recommend that you run Disk Cleanup every two or three months. It's just tidier to get rid of stuff that's totally and completely useless.

Defragmenting Your Hard Drive

The term *defragmenting* sounds techie, but it describes a really straightforward process that rounds up the bits and pieces of files that are scattered about on your hard drive and organizes them so that applications can find and load them faster.

How did these bits and pieces of files get spread around in the first place? Well, when Windows writes a file to your hard drive, it puts the file anywhere it finds room. Over time, any one file can have a piece here, a piece there, a piece somewhere else, and so on. Windows always knows the locations of the pieces (the *fragments*), but access tends to be slower because the system has to go to several places to pick up the fragments. Running the Disk Defragmenter fixes this problem.

In general, you should run Disk Defragmenter about once a month. To do so, follow these steps:

1. Choose Start ➤ Programs ➤ Accessories ➤ System Tools ➤ Disk Defragmenter to open the Select Drive dialog box.

2. Select the drive you want to defragment, and then click OK.

If you want to specify particular options for the defrag process, click the Settings button in the Select Drive dialog box to open the Disk Defragmenter Settings dialog box:

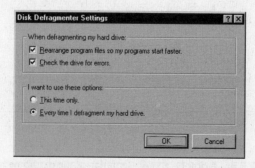

As you work, Windows 98 SE tracks which programs you start most often and which files are required. If you want Disk Defragmenter to optimize the location of these files for faster access, click the Rearrange Program Files So My Programs Start Faster check box. If you want Disk Defragmenter to check your hard drive for errors before it starts to defragment, click the Check The Drive For Errors check box. If Disk Defragmenter finds errors, it will notify you and then won't continue. Run ScanDisk, fix the error, and restart Disk Defragmenter. (See the next section in this chapter for information about how to run ScanDisk.)

When the defragmentation process starts, you'll see a dialog box like that in Figure 8.5, which contains a progress bar that shows the percentage of the job that is complete. For a graphical representation of the process, click the Show Details button. You'll see something similar to the screen in Figure 8.6. To return to a nongraphical view, click the Hide Details button. For an explanation of what the various colors and symbols mean, click the Legend button to display the Defrag Legend dialog box, which is shown in Figure 8.7.

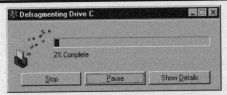

FIGURE 8.5: The progress bar shows the percentage of defragmenting that is complete.

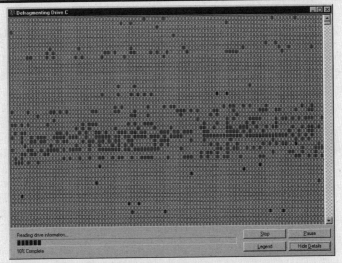

FIGURE 8.6: A graphical representation of the defragmenting process

FIGURE 8.7: The Defrag Legend dialog box

Running ScanDisk

ScanDisk is a tool that checks your hard disk for logical and physical errors and repairs any damaged areas it finds. You may have seen ScanDisk run even though you haven't manually chosen to do so. If Windows shuts down and the proper sign-off procedure is not observed (for example, when the system reboots as a result of a power glitch), ScanDisk will run upon restart of the system.

NOTE

A *logical error* is usually a mistake in the way that information about the files on your hard disk is stored. Such an error might cause a fragment of a file to become isolated from the main part of a file and thus effectively lost. A *physical error* occurs when a part of your hard disk is defective.

In general, you should run ScanDisk with its Standard setting about once a week so that an accumulation of little problems doesn't turn into a serious big problem. Once a month or so, run ScanDisk with its Thorough setting turned on. The Standard setting checks files and folders, and the Thorough setting checks files and folders as well as the disk surface. To run ScanDisk, follow these steps:

1. Choose Start ➢ Programs ➢ Accessories ➢ System Tools ➢ ScanDisk to open the ScanDisk dialog box:

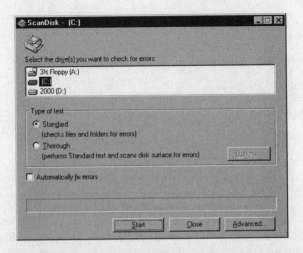

2. Select the drive you want to check, select a type of test (Standard or Thorough), and then click the Advanced button to open the ScanDisk Advanced Options dialog box:

In this dialog box, you have several options regarding how found errors will be handled.

Display Summary   By default, ScanDisk produces and displays a report of what it finds (the Always option). Choose Never if you don't ever care to see a report, or choose Only If Errors Found if you want to display a summary only when ScanDisk locates problems. Figure 8.8 shows a summary report.

Log File   By default, ScanDisk creates a new activity log each time it runs. To create one continuous log, select Append To Log; if you don't care about the log, select No Log.

Cross-Linked Files   A cross-linked file occurs when two or more files attempt to share the same area of your hard disk. When an application tries to access a cross-linked file, it will probably read the wrong information. You can choose to delete, copy, or ignore such files.

Lost File Fragments   A lost file fragment is a fragment that can't be linked to an existing file. If you leave Convert To Files selected, ScanDisk converts the fragment to a file so that you can verify whether you want to retain it or delete it. These files are given names such as FILE0001 and are stored in your root directory. I usually select the Free option here, which simply deletes a lost fragment, and I've never lost anything important. But if you want to err on the side of caution, keep Convert To Files selected. Just be sure to check out the files and delete them if they really are useless.

Check Files For   By default, ScanDisk searches for invalid filenames. In addition, you can check for invalid dates and times and duplicate names. If you select all three of these options, ScanDisk will warn you that this may slow performance. Actually, the check does run slower but not a lot slower.

Check Host Drive First   A host drive is an uncompressed drive on which a compressed drive is stored, and a host drive may be hidden. Since errors on a compressed drive are often caused by errors on its host drive, you'll want to leave this option selected.

Report MS-DOS Mode Name Length Errors   Check this box if you want ScanDisk to report any filename errors.

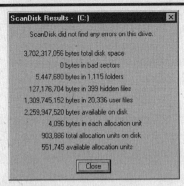

FIGURE 8.8:   A summary report produced by ScanDisk

3. Click OK after you have specified option settings, and then in the ScanDisk dialog box, click Automatically Fix Errors if you want ScanDisk to do so. If you don't select this option, ScanDisk will notify you when it finds an error and give you an opportunity to decide how you want to deal with the error.

4. Click Start to begin the scanning process.

OPTIONS WHEN PERFORMING THE THOROUGH TEST

If you select the Thorough setting in the ScanDisk dialog box, you can click the Options button to open the Surface Scan Options dialog box:

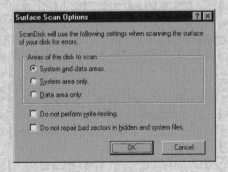

CONTINUED ➡

In this dialog box, you can specify the settings that are in effect when doing a Thorough scan. You have the following options:

System and Data Areas   This is the most commonly used option; selecting it checks the entire disk for errors.

System Area Only   Checks only that part of the disk on which Windows system files reside. Most of these files cannot be relocated, and so ScanDisk cannot repair any problems in this area.

Data Area Only   Checks only that portion of the disk on which applications and their data reside.

Do Not Perform Write-Testing   During write-testing, ScanDisk reads the contents of each sector of the disk and then writes the contents back to verify that the disk can be read from and written to correctly. Click this option if you do not want your disk write-tested.

Do Not Repair Bad Sectors in Hidden and System Files   Repairing bad sectors involves moving files to good sectors of the disk. Moving the data in hidden or system files may cause some programs to work incorrectly.

Using the Maintenance Wizard

We have now taken a look at three of the most important tools you can use when maintaining your system—Disk Cleanup, Disk Defragmenter, and ScanDisk. You can choose to run each of these tools yourself as the need arises, or you can let Windows take care of this for you and run each tool according to a schedule that you specify.

To establish a maintenance schedule that occurs automatically, you use the Maintenance Wizard. You can choose the Express setup that the Wizard suggests, or you can specify a Custom setup. We'll look at the Express setup first, and then I'll point out how you can use the Custom setup to vary the settings.

1. Choose Start ≻ Programs ≻ Accessories ≻ System Tools ≻ Maintenance Wizard to start the Maintenance Wizard:

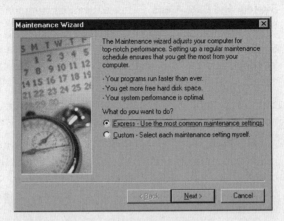

2. Accept the default choice of Express, and click Next to open the screen from which you can select a schedule:

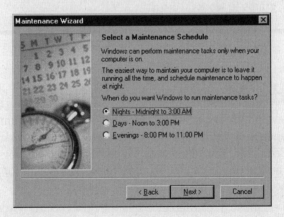

Obviously, you need to select a time when your computer is up and running and when you don't need to use it. The Wizard suggests a time during the night, but if that doesn't work for you, you can select one of the other times.

3. Select a time, and then click Next to open the last screen of the Wizard, which lists the tasks that will be performed:

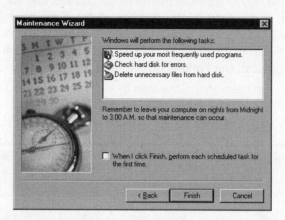

Speed Up Your Most Frequently Used Programs   Disk Defragmenter will run weekly with the option set so that files are arranged so that programs run faster.

Check Hard Disk For Errors   ScanDisk, with its default settings, will check your hard drive weekly.

Delete Unnecessary Files From Hard Disk   Disk Cleanup will run monthly and delete all unnecessary files.

4. If you want to run these three maintenance tools right away, click the check box at the bottom of the Wizard's last screen, and then click Finish. If you don't click this check box, these tools will run at the time you have specified in the Wizard.

If you prefer to exercise more control over when and exactly how these maintenance tasks are performed, select the Custom option in the first screen of the Maintenance Wizard. Then click Next, and in the following three screens you can specify a time for the tool to run (or specify that it not run) and specify exact settings, such as whether to defragment all drives or only a certain drive. The Wizard's final screen will display the schedule of tasks that you've established.

Using Task Scheduler

Another way to schedule maintenance tasks so that they run automatically is to add them to the Task Scheduler. If you have used the Maintenance Wizard to establish a maintenance task schedule, those tasks will also appear in the Scheduled Tasks folder, and the Task Scheduler icon will appear in the Taskbar on your Windows Desktop.

You can open Task Scheduler by clicking its icon in the Taskbar or by choosing Start ≻ Programs ≻ Accessories ≻ System Tools ≻ Scheduled Tasks. You'll see a folder similar to that in Figure 8.9.

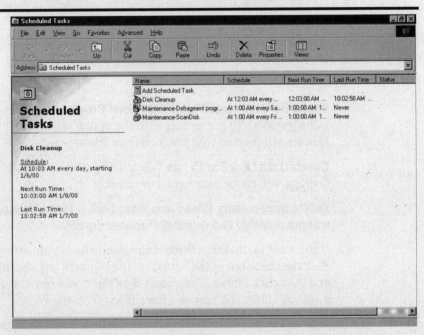

FIGURE 8.9:   The Scheduled Tasks folder

To add a task to the Task Scheduler, follow these steps:

1. In the Scheduled Tasks folder, double-click Add Scheduled Task to start the Scheduled Task Wizard.

2. Click Next to open a screen that displays a list of programs and applications on your system.

3. Select a program, and then click Next to display a list of times that you can choose to run the program:

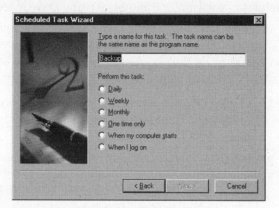

4. Select a time period, click Next, select the specific day and time, click Next, and then click Finish.

To delete a scheduled task, select it in the Scheduled Tasks folder, and press Delete.

TIP

You can also use Task Scheduler to specify that a specific program always start when you start your computer. Simply select the program from the Wizard's list, and then choose When My Computer Starts.

Saving Space on Your Hard Drive

As I mentioned earlier in this chapter, if you've bought a personal computer recently, say, within the last year or two, you may well have more space on your hard drive than you can ever fill up. On the other hand, I've thought that before and within a year was scrambling for any and all ways to make room on the drive.

Windows 98 SE includes a couple of features that you can use to effectively create some extra space on your hard drive: DriveSpace and Drive Converter (FAT32). DriveSpace is a utility that compresses the information on a hard drive so that storage space is increased, and Drive Converter (FAT32) is a file allocation system that can increase storage space on a hard drive by as much as several hundred megabytes.

Before we get into how you use each of these though, you need to be aware that these features are mutually exclusive; that is, if you convert your hard drive to FAT32, you cannot then compress it using DriveSpace. Likewise, if your hard drive was formatted with the FAT32 system when you bought it, you cannot compress it using DriveSpace.

In a later section, I'll go into detail about FAT32 and explain how it got its name as well as how it works. First, however, we'll look at Drive-Space. Before we do that, you need to determine how your hard drive is formatted, if you don't already know. Follow these steps:

1. On the Desktop, right-click My Computer, and choose Prop-erties from the shortcut menu to open the System Properties dialog box.

2. Click the Performance tab:

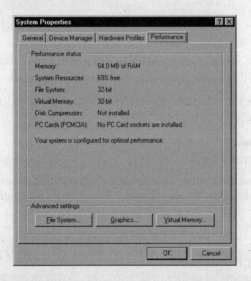

If your hard drive is formatted to FAT32, you'll see 32-bit next to the File System listing. If it is not formatted to FAT32, you'll see 16-bit next to the File System listing.

Using DriveSpace

DriveSpace is most appropriate for use on a hard drive that is about a giga-byte or less in size. Here's how it works. If you compress, for example, your drive C, the result is a new drive called drive H, which is a host drive. When you start your system, a DriveSpace command tells the system to look for drive H and load it so that it looks exactly like the uncompressed drive C. The difference is that, after compression, drive C can contain about twice as much information. When you open an application, save a document, or perform any other disk operation, DriveSpace automatically decompresses or compresses as required, without any intervention on your part.

TIP

You can't read the host drive, nor should you mess with it; so it's a good idea to hide it. To do so, click that option in the Properties dialog box for the host drive.

To compress a drive, follow these steps:

1. Choose Start ➢ Programs ➢ Accessories ➢ System Tools ➢ DriveSpace to open the DriveSpace 3 dialog box:

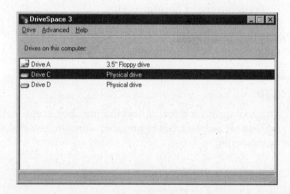

2. To specify the compression method you want to use (that is, the trade-off between free disk space and system speed), choose Advanced ➢ Settings to open the Disk Compression Settings dialog box:

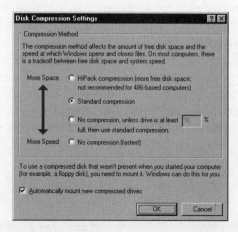

3. Select an option, and click OK.

4. Select the drive to compress from the Drives On This Computer list.

5. Choose Drive ➤ Compress to open the Compress A Drive dialog box, which shows a graphical representation of the disk before and after compression.

6. Click Start.

7. Click Back Up Files, and follow the on-screen instructions.

8. Click Compress Now. A progress indicator will display the percentage of compression.

Depending on the size of the drive and the number of files, the compression process could take some time—more than an hour in most cases.

TIP

To uncompress a drive, follow the previous steps, selecting Uncompress instead of Compress. But be prepared—uncompressing takes even longer than compressing.

Converting to FAT32

FAT stands for *file allocation table* and is the data structure that is created on a hard disk when the disk is formatted. In essence, the FAT is a list that Windows maintains to manage disk space used for storage. As I mentioned in the "Defragmenting Your Hard Drive" section earlier in this chapter, a single file can be stored in several separate areas on your hard drive. The FAT maps the available storage space so that it can find and link the pieces of a file.

The system that MS-DOS used and that Windows 95 used initially is now referred to as FAT16. It divided a hard drive into 65,536 allocation units; as hard drives became available in larger and larger sizes, the allocation units in the FAT16 system also had to become larger. The down side to this is that large allocation units waste disk space.

Thus, in 1996, Microsoft introduced FAT32, an enhancement to FAT16. FAT32 allows for a much larger file allocation table, which means smaller allocation units and much less wasted space. Initially, FAT32 was available only to computer manufacturers who installed it on new machines running

Windows 95. With the release of Windows 98, however, DriveConverter (FAT32) was made available so that anyone who wanted to do so could convert a FAT16 drive to FAT32. And, of course, now all new Windows machines are formatted to FAT32.

If you are running an older machine and seem to be constantly running out of hard disk space, I strongly suggest that you convert to FAT32. The first time I did so, I almost doubled the available space on my hard drive.

To convert your hard drive to FAT32, follow these steps:

1. Choose Start ➤ Programs ➤ Accessories ➤ System Tools ➤ Drive Converter (FAT32) to start the Drive Converter Wizard:

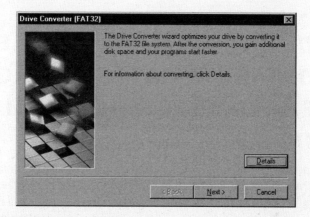

2. Click Next, select the drive to convert, and click Next again.

3. After Windows checks your system for anything incompatible with FAT32 and resolves any issues that arise, click Next.

4. Back up your files if you have not yet done so, and then click Next twice. Your computer will reboot to MS-DOS, run the conversion, restart Windows, and run Disk Defragmenter.

Although the Drive Converter Wizard will warn you that the conversion process will take a few hours, the conversion is actually accomplished rather quickly. What could take a few hours is running Disk Defragmenter, so don't schedule conversion at a time when you could conceivably need your computer system for business or production activities. You can pause Disk Defragmenter, but system performance will be degraded until you completely defragment the disk you have just converted.

SOME OTHER WAYS TO FREE UP DISK SPACE

When you're desperately searching for more disk space, don't forget about some of the obvious solutions:

▶ Back up and remove all your old, unneeded document files.

▶ Remove any Windows components that you don't use.

▶ Remove any applications that you never use.

▶ Purchase and install the biggest hard drive you can afford.

ACQUIRING AND USING SOME IMPORTANT MAINTENANCE TOOLS THAT AREN'T INCLUDED WITH WINDOWS

Windows 98 SE comes with an impressive arsenal of system tools, but at the very least you'll want to investigate acquiring a few others. First, you should check out a virus-scanning application. A *virus* is a malevolent program that can attach itself to your computer system without your knowledge or permission and wreak havoc that ranges from a minor annoyance all the way to total destruction of your system.

Computer viruses are not airborne; they travel from system to system via infected diskettes, e-mail, files that are downloaded from the Internet, and even shrink-wrapped software. After a virus attaches itself to your system, it can be triggered into action by a date or by running a particular program.

The best way to protect against computer viruses is to acquire and run antivirus software regularly. Sometimes a new PC will come with a virus-scanning program, but normally it includes only a couple of free upgrades to a database of known viruses. This is insufficient because new viruses are being discovered all the time, and your antivirus software needs to know about them.

Your best bet is to buy a full-powered antivirus program and keep it upgraded. The two most popular such programs are McAfee's VirusScan (available from www.mcafee.com) and Norton AntiVirus (available from www.symantec.com).

TEN TIPS THAT CAN HELP YOU AVOID COMPUTER VIRUSES

1. Be cautious about opening e-mail from unknown senders. To be on the ultra-safe side, delete such messages without opening them.

2. Don't download a file or open an e-mail attachment if you don't know the source.

3. Don't double-click e-mail attachments; save and scan them first.

4. Keep your antivirus software current.

5. Turn on Macro Virus Protection. In a Microsoft Office 2000 program, choose Tools ➢ Macro ➢ Security to open the Security dialog box, select High or Medium, and then click OK.

6. Consider whether downloading free software from the Internet is worth the risk.

7. Do not give out important personal information unless you know exactly who is asking for it and that it is necessary for a transaction.

8. Protect the integrity of your home computer and your office computer. It is common to catch a workplace virus and bring it home or to acquire a virus at home and then infect the office network.

9. Never give out your password over the phone or online.

10. Don't believe everything you hear. There are as many hoaxes about viruses as there are viruses. To get the facts, go to one of the antivirus software vendor's sites or check Network Associates' list at www.avertlabs.com.

The second tool you might think about acquiring is an uninstaller program. Although Windows 98 SE includes the Add/Remove Programs applet in Control Panel, you will eventually find that you want to get rid of programs that aren't listed there. You'll also find that when you install some programs, you can't uninstall some features of them. For this you need a third-party tool such as Norton's CleanSweep and McAfee's Uninstaller. Both these programs search your hard drive and delete the pesky files that are taking up space but doing nothing helpful. In addition, these programs can delete temporary files and even transfer programs between drives or between computers.

Finally, I need to tell you about one other type of tool. If you are a serious but novice PC user and nervous about messing with anything under the hood, you might want to purchase a utility suite. This type of program is designed to track down and fix problems. Look into McAfee Office 2000, Ontrack's SystemSuite 2000, or Norton SystemWorks 2000.

BACKING UP AND RESTORING

It's been said that the universe of computer users is divided into two groups—those whose hard disk has crashed, and those whose hard disk hasn't crashed yet. Another oft-quoted aphorism is that the only files you ever lose are those you can least afford to be without. I could probably dredge up more sage expressions that aptly describe why you should be compulsive about backing up, but you are probably aware that backing up your data files needs to be a part of your daily routine and that you need to establish some sort of schedule for routinely backing up the rest of your computer system.

If you want to back up a single file, you can simply copy it to another medium—a floppy disk, a tape backup system, a hard drive on another computer if you are on a network, and so on. (See Chapter 6 for information about copying files.) If you want to back up more than a single file, however, you'll want to use the Microsoft Backup program, which you'll find on the System Tools menu.

The first time you use Backup, a welcome dialog box asks what you would like to do. Your choices are to create a new backup job, open an existing backup job, or restore backed-up files. Most likely you want to create a new backup job so that you can back up some files. A *backup job* is not the backup itself; it is the set of instructions that you create which tell Backup what to back up, where to back up, when to back up, and how to back up.

You can create a backup job using the Backup Wizard or simply the Backup program itself. Because using the Wizard is a quick and easy way to get started, I'll use it to walk through the steps. After you become familiar with the process, you can use the Wizard or work with Backup directly.

BACKUP PRACTICALITIES

How often you should back up and what you back up depend on several things. For starters, think about how long it would take you to replicate a lost file, if you could even do so. If your data is

CONTINUED ➡

irreplaceable or if the cost of replacing it would be prohibitive, you not only need to back it up regularly, but you need to ensure that the backup is in a safe place.

A friend of mine is writing the great American novel—a project that is now in its seventh or eighth year—and he lives in an earthquake-prone area of California. About once a quarter he sends me a backup of his project (I live in Texas), just in case.

Whether you're creating an important work of fiction or an annual report for a Fortune 500 company, make your regular backups, but also be sure that you store them where they won't be damaged. Right next to your computer is probably not the best place, and I wouldn't leave a backup floppy in its drive either. Mission-critical files are often stored off-site, whether that means out of the confines of your home office or away from corporate headquarters.

You can also use a Web service to back up important files. One such service, i-drive (www.idrive.com), starts you out with 25MB of free space, and you can get more by visiting their partners MP3.com and Epitonic.com.

Using the Backup Wizard

Once you've decided it's backup time and you know what you need to back up and where, follow these steps:

1. Choose Start ➤ Programs ➤ Accessories ➤ System Tools ➤ Backup to open the welcome screen:

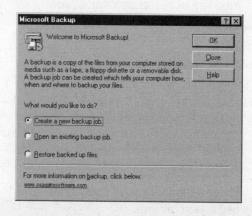

2. Select the Create A New Backup Job option, and then click OK to start the Backup Wizard:

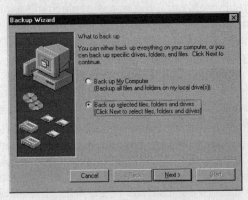

3. You can use Backup to back up your entire computer system or selected files and folders. For this example, let's make it easy and back up a single folder. Select the Back Up Selected Files, Folders And Drives, and then click Next.

4. Click the check box next to the item you want to back up, and then click Next.

5. Now, you can specify that all the selected files be backed up, or you can specify that Backup back up only those files that are new or that have changed since the last backup. Since this is theoretically the first backup, click the All Selected Files option and click Next.

6. Specify a destination for your backup. If necessary, click the folder button to open the Where To Back Up dialog box, and browse for the location. Click Next.

NOTE

Backup files are given the `.qic` extension.

7. In this next screen, you specify how to back up. You can verify that the backed-up files exactly match the originals, you can compress the backup files, or you can do both. When you've checked your preference(s), click Next to open a screen that summarizes your instructions for the backup job.

8. Enter a name for your backup job, and then click Start to begin your backup.

The Backup Progress dialog box, shown in Figure 8.10, will indicate the elapsed time and display a message when the backup is complete.

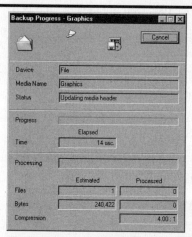

FIGURE 8.10:   The Backup Progress dialog box

Using the Backup Program

To back up using the Backup program rather than the Wizard, follow these steps:

1. Choose Start ➢ Programs ➢ Accessories ➢ System Tools ➢ Backup, and click Close at the Welcome screen. You'll see the Microsoft Backup dialog box:

2. In the Backup Job box, enter a title for your backup job.

3. In the What To Back Up section, choose to back up all selected files or only those files that are new or changed.

4. Click the plus (+) sign next to the disk that contains the file or folder you want to back up.

5. Scroll down the list and click the box next to the file(s) you want to back up to place a check in the check box.

6. In the Where To Back Up section, specify the destination where you want the backup stored.

7. In the How To Back Up section, click the Options button to open the Backup Job Options dialog box:

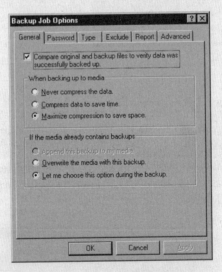

8. Select your backup options, and then click OK.

9. Click Start to begin the backup.

10. When the backup is complete, save it.

Backing Up an Existing Backup Job

Once you've created a backup job (sometimes called a backup file set), you can use it to back up those files and folders again later. Follow these steps:

1. Choose Start ≻ Programs ≻ Accessories ≻ System Tools ≻ Backup, and click Close at the Welcome screen.

2. In the Microsoft Backup dialog box, click the drop-down arrow in the Backup Job box, and select the existing job.

3. Click Start to begin the backup.

Restoring a Backup

Restoring a backup involves copying the files from the medium to which they were backed up back onto your hard drive. Most obviously, you restore files when the current files on your system have become damaged or lost, but you can also restore files that you have backed up and removed from your system to save space.

You can use the Restore Wizard to restore a backup, or you can use the Restore tab in the Microsoft Backup dialog box. To use the Restore Wizard, click the Restore Backed Up Files option on the Welcome screen, click OK, and then follow the instructions on the screen. To use the Restore tab, follow these steps:

1. Start Backup, and at the Welcome screen, click the Close button.

2. In the Microsoft Backup dialog box, click the Restore tab:

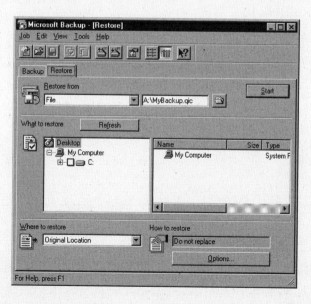

3. In the Restore From section, select the file you want to restore.

4. In the What To Restore section, click the check box next to each item you want to restore.

5. In the Where To Restore section, click the drop-down arrow to specify the destination. The default is the original location, but you can also select a different location.

6. Be sure the medium containing the backup is mounted, and then click Start.

WHAT'S NEXT?

In this chapter, we've taken a look at the software tools you can use to maintain your system. In the next major part of this book, we'll look at how to maintain and troubleshoot your computer's hardware. Hardware is commonly defined as any computer component that you can stub your toe on. In the next chapter, Gini Courter and Annette Marquis will describe those components in detail.

PART II
HARDWARE AND
TROUBLESHOOTING

Chapter 9

THE INS AND OUTS OF PERSONAL COMPUTER HARDWARE

The personal computer revolution has created an insatiable market for faster, easier-to-use, and more powerful components and peripherals. This chapter provides an overview of personal computer input and output devices and focuses on the amazing developments in hardware that make personal computing unique. After you read this chapter, you will be able to do the following:

- Classify each type of peripheral appropriately as input, output, or input-output (I/O)
- Delineate reasons for using a particular input or output device
- Compare impact and nonimpact printers
- Name three types of monitors currently in use
- Discuss several methods for entering data in a computer
- Name and explain several devices that retrieve information from a PC

Adapted from *The Learning Guide to Computers*
by Gini Courter and Annette Marquis
ISBN 0-7821-1968-9   416 pages $24.99

An Overview of Input and Output

Input, output, memory, and storage devices are called *peripherals*, because they are peripheral, or outside, the processor. An input device allows you to enter programs or data into a computer and issue commands—in short, to tell the computer what to do. An output device provides a way for people to view the results of computer processing and for other computers to use computer-generated information for additional tasks. Some peripherals, such as a fax modem, are input *and* output (I/O) devices, because they both receive and send data.

Input Devices

A vast array of input devices are available for entering text and graphics, issuing commands, inputting audio and video, and inputting data. Some of these devices have multiple functions, but, generally, a device is specially designed for the type of input a task requires. Several input devices are shown in Figure 9.1.

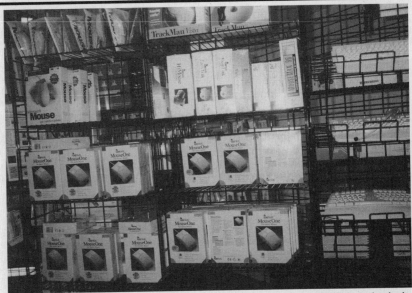

Courtesy of Twilight Technologies

FIGURE 9.1: Common input devices

Text-Entry Devices

Much of the input a computer receives originates as text-based data. A *keyboard* is the device most commonly used for entering text into a computer. A keyboard allows you to enter text by pressing alphabetic and numeric keys (see Figure 9.2).

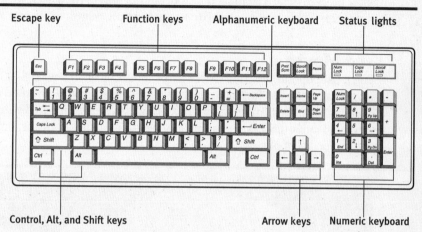

FIGURE 9.2:   A computer keyboard

Keyboards differ from typewriters in a number of ways. Computer keyboards contain special keys not found on a typewriter, including the Caps Lock and arrow keys that are used to move within a document. The Caps Lock key (usually located to the left of the letter *A*) is called a *toggle* key—press Caps Lock once and it's on, press again and it's off. The Caps Lock key was originally included on computer keyboards for programmers using programming languages that required uppercase letters. Command keys can be customized for entering commands in programs. The Escape (Esc) key is often programmed so that it can be used to cancel a command or to exit an undesirable situation. You use the Control (Ctrl) and Alt keys, located in the bottom row of keys next to the spacebar, in combination with other keys to enter commands. The function keys (F1, F2, and so on) are located across the top of a keyboard.

Although keyboards work well for typists, they are a barrier for other users. To use a keyboard, you must be able to read in the language used to label the keys and have a certain amount of physical dexterity. Other input devices have been designed to simplify computer use and reduce errors. Many of these devices fall into the category of pointing devices.

Pointing Devices

Pointing devices come in many varieties but have essentially the same objective, which is to allow users to control the movements of a small pointer on the screen. Rather than having to type commands, users can point to different areas of the screen and click to enter commands. Some pointing devices allow users to issue a command by touching an area of the screen with a finger; others allow users to create drawings or graphics by drawing on a tablet.

The Mouse

The most popular pointing device is the *mouse*, a small device that fits into your hand. The first mouse, shown in Figure 9.3, was invented by Douglas Engelbart in the early 1960s. Engelbart experimented with a variety of input devices, including foot pedals and knee controls, before settling on the mouse.

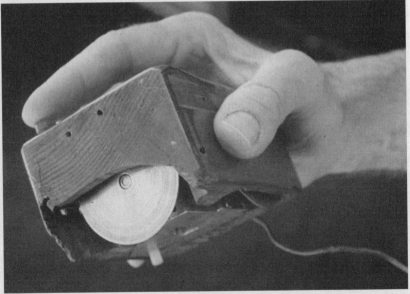

Provided by Douglas C. Engelbart and the Bootstrap Institute

FIGURE 9.3: Douglas Engelbart demonstrates the first mouse, which was actually made of wood.

Generally, the mouse is connected to a port by a cable; however, wireless mouse devices, which use infrared technology to send messages to the computer, are becoming common. Moving the mouse on the desktop rotates a small ball on the underside of the mouse. Sensors register the movement of the ball and send an electronic message to the computer about the mouse's position. The mouse pointer on the screen moves to correspond with the movement of the mouse.

Mouse devices, such as those shown in Figure 9.4, are so easy to use even very young children can master them. By moving the mouse, you can point to objects on the computer screen and then click a mouse button to send a command to the computer. You can also hold down the mouse button and drag objects around the screen to reposition them. Dragging is an especially valuable skill when working with graphic images.

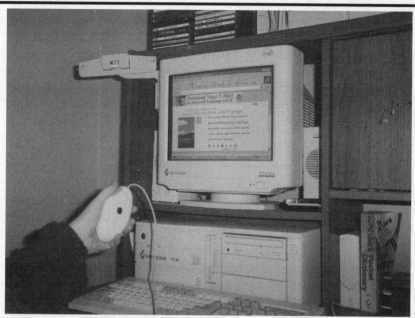

FIGURE 9.4: The mouse easily fits into a child's hand.

One of the newer mouse-type devices on the market is designed specifically for surfing the Internet. The GyroPoint by Gyration, shown in Figure 9.5, uses gyroscope technology so that users can point, click, and scroll without rolling the mouse on the desktop. The GyroPoint has a lengthy cord so that you can sit back and relax while cruising around.

FIGURE 9.5: GyroPoint allows users to surf the Internet without being tied to a mouse pad.

Pointing Devices for Laptop Computers

Some users, especially those who use laptops, find mice inconvenient because they require desktop space. Users who find mice a nuisance often prefer *trackballs*, which are essentially upside-down mice. The trackball stays stationary, and you rotate the ball with your thumb. Trackballs are built into some full-sized keyboards and laptop computers and are also sold as external pointing devices, such as the ones shown in Figure 9.6.

Laptop manufacturers are experimenting with a number of other pointing devices. Some laptops have a *trackpoint* or *GBH button* (so named because it is mounted at the intersection of the G, B, and H keys on the keyboard). Trackpoints are commonly referred to as *eraser-heads* because they resemble pencil erasers. You manipulate an eraser-head with your index finger like a miniature joystick; the trackpoint's command buttons are built into the laptop case. With other portable computers, your index finger actually becomes the pointing device. To move the pointer on screen, you drag your index finger across a small square pad called a *touch pad*. To click, you simply tap your finger on the pad. All the pointing devices take a little getting used to, and you'll find that once you try several, you'll develop a definite preference.

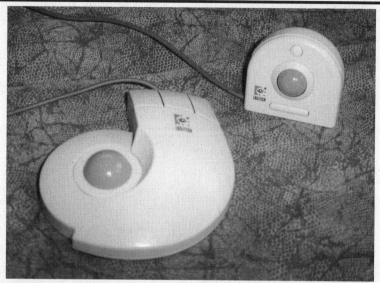

FIGURE 9.6: Logitech trackballs

Touch Screens

Another pointing device that lets your fingers do the walking, a *touch screen*, is most commonly seen at tourist information areas, malls, museums, and airports. You touch areas of the screen with your fingers to issue commands or call up information. An example of a touch screen application is located in a kiosk at Circle Centre Mall in downtown Indianapolis. By pressing different buttons or icons on the screen, you can discover what's happening in Indianapolis and find out what there is to do around town. Touching one button may take you to another series of buttons where you can narrow your choices according to your particular interests, budget, age group, and other criteria. Results are displayed on the screen. Another touch screen application is found in restaurants; employees touch a screen to enter patrons' orders. In some fast-food restaurants, you can enter your own order on a touch screen.

Joysticks

A *joystick* is a common pointing device used with computer games. Based on the controls found in airplanes and helicopters, joysticks are hand-sized sticks mounted on a base unit. You can pull and push the sticks in all directions, making the joystick a very versatile pointing device for flying futuristic spacecraft through enemy territory, playing a game of basketball, or controlling the "point-and-kill" movements of adventure game characters. Joysticks have a number of buttons programmed to control different activities—such as firing a weapon, shooting a ball, or picking up a secret message—depending on the game being played. The boy in Figure 9.7 is using Microsoft's SideWinder 3D Pro joystick to play Megagames' *Tyrian*.

FIGURE 9.7:   Microsoft's SideWinder 3D Pro joystick

Other Input Devices

Light pens are penlike devices. When you touch a light pen to the computer screen, a light cell in the tip of the pen senses light from the screen and indicates the pen's location. You can use the pen to draw on the screen, or you can tap it on the screen to register choices or issue commands. Light pens are a common input device for personal digital assistants.

Graphic tablets and *digitizers* are pointing devices that graphic designers, architects, and artists use to create images that appear on the computer screen. The images created on the tablet are converted to digital signals and transmitted to the computer. Other occupations require even more specialized input devices. For example, an engineer might use calipers to input the dimensions of a physical object into a computer-aided design (CAD) program.

All the pointing devices discussed in this section have the advantage of making certain types of input easy for users. However, they also have the disadvantage of taking the user's hands away from the keyboard. Speed typists complain that pointing devices slow them down; many would prefer to use keyboard commands whenever possible. Pointing devices also have the added disadvantage of creating muscle strain if reaching is involved. When using any input device, change positions periodically, and exercise your arm and hand to get the blood flowing again and relax the muscles.

Audio, Video, and Graphics Input

Advances in technology have led to multimedia-capable computers that can produce dynamic sound, crisp graphic images, and full-motion video. Accordingly, peripherals dedicated to multimedia input are becoming more common and of higher quality.

You can use a small, inexpensive microphone to talk into your computer and then convert your voice to digital sound waves. You can then attach these digital sounds to documents or to multimedia presentations or transmit them through the Internet to a loved one around the world. Voice input is becoming a more common form of medical and legal dictation. Rather than a transcriptionist typing tape-recorded notes, the doctor or lawyer can use a good microphone and speech-to-text software that immediately converts their words to text. Voice technology is also being used on a limited basis in other ways, for example, as a security tool to prevent unauthorized entry to high-security locations. By matching a person's voice pattern to a previously recorded sample, voice technology can determine if the voice of the person requesting entry is authorized. Command applications allow users to control the computer through the use of specific words such as "open," "save," "print," "close," and "exit." This technology is especially valuable when you don't have the use of your hands, either because of a disability or because you are operating some other equipment at the same time in an industrial setting. Voice input may also be used for data entry. Users can complete a form verbally, usually using pre-established numbers or letters to respond to questions.

Part ii

NOTE

Voice technology is used instead of motion sensors to open the doors of many urban storefronts in Japan. As you approach a door, say "Open, please" in English or Japanese. If you forget to say "Please," you run into a closed door—Miss Manners goes high tech.

Speech technology is one of the most talked-about computer-related developments on the horizon. Since we can talk much faster than we can type, it might not be long before the computer keyboard becomes completely obsolete. Not only do microphones and other voice input devices hold promise as the most convenient input device, they offer a new type of freedom. A simple phone call to a computer would be all it would take to get information, place an order, or conduct myriad other operations.

Although voice input devices provide exciting ways to input facts into a computer, we are also a visual society; we want to be able to enter graphic images easily. With a digital camera, you can take photos and input them directly into your computer. A digital camera uses no film; instead, images are recorded on the camera's SRAM and then uploaded (transferred electronically) to a computer. You can then insert the photographs as graphic images in documents or display them on the computer's monitor.

The two types of video input devices are *fixed-image* and *full-motion*. A fixed-image (or still-image capture) device is connected between a video camera or VCR and a computer and converts the video signal into a graphic image much like a photograph. Video capture boards, installed in an expansion slot, have a port into which a VCR or a camera can be plugged. Capture boards support full-motion video by digitizing and storing the video and audio signal to create a video "movie" that can be played on a PC.

Source Data Automation Input Devices

Much of the data we want to computerize already exists as hard-copy (paper) source documents. Rather than retyping all this data, which not only takes time but risks the introduction of errors, several input devices have been developed that scan (read) hard copy into the computer. *Scanners* have become increasingly popular with businesses and individuals.

If you want to scan full pages of information, you can use a *flatbed* scanner, which allows you to feed in source documents as you would with a copy machine. *Hand-held* scanners are useful when the data you need is not on a sheet of paper. For example, you might need to scan inventory labels attached to all the equipment in your office. You could move from chair to filing cabinet, just carrying a hand-held scanner and a laptop or hand-held computer. Hand-held scanners are frequently used in industrial settings to scan labels in warehousing and manufacturing.

Scanned documents are stored as graphic images and cannot be manipulated without special software. *Optical character recognition (OCR)* was a process developed to enable a scanner to recognize text printed in special block type styles. With OCR, the scanned text could then be edited, reformatted, and stored by a computer. Although character recognition software does not always recognize 100 percent of the text, it converts most of it and then identifies the unrecognizable characters.

Two other types of character recognition, Optical Mark Recognition (OMR) and Magnetic Ink Character Recognition (MICR), are used for very specific purposes. OMR is used to process the #2 pencil marks on all those standardized tests you've had to take in your life. (The forms used in these tests are often called "bubble forms" because the user fills in circles.) Similar forms are also used for other types of questionnaires, including health histories in physicians' offices and customer surveys sent through the mail.

MICR is most commonly used on turn-around documents (documents that are returned to the source with additional information on them) such as checks. Special magnetic ink is used when checks are printed to record the check number, bank number, and account number. When the check is processed, the check amount is also magnetically printed on the face of the check. All this data is then scanned into the bank's computer system through special MICR scanners. With MICR, banks have greatly improved the speed, efficiency, and accuracy of check processing.

You can use flatbed or hand-held scanners to scan photos taken with traditional nondigital cameras. But some manufactures are building special photo scanners into their personal computers. To scan a photo, you simply insert it into a photo reader mounted in the computer case. The photo is scanned, and you can then use the image as a graphic, perhaps in a company newsletter or an electronic presentation.

Bar codes are a type of optical code that represents data through different thicknesses of vertical lines and spaces. Between retail stores and the U.S. Post Office, bar codes have become quite commonplace. Bar codes can represent numbers or numbers and letters, depending on which bar code system, or symbology, is used. One of the most familiar symbologies is the universal product code (UPC), the bar code you see on retail products that identifies the manufacturer and the product number. Typically, these numbers are scanned into computers using bar code readers, devices designed to interpret these symbols into characters. Bar code readers come as hand-held guns, penlike devices called wands (see Figure 9.8), and flatbed readers like those in most grocery stores. A combination of a reader and a computer terminal or PC is called a point-of-sale (POS) system.

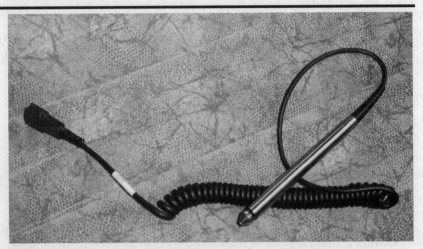

FIGURE 9.8: Bar code wand reader

Output Devices

Inputting a bunch of data into your computer won't do you any good unless you have some sort of output device that allows you to retrieve the information your computer has processed. The most common forms of output are produced by monitors and printers. Monitors and their video cards display text, graphics, and still video. More-capable video cards can send full-motion video to the monitor. Printers produce text and graphic output—everything from clip art (noncopyrighted graphic images available for use in documents) to highly specialized computer-aided design. Speakers—considered a standard peripheral device on multimedia personal computers—output music, human voice, and electronic sounds.

Monitors

The first output you encounter when you use a personal computer is what you see on the video monitor. A monitor is part of the computer's interface and is integral to human interaction with computers. *Monochrome* monitors display a single color on a lighter or darker color background, and *grayscale* monitors display various shades of gray. But as the price of color monitors has decreased, monochrome and grayscale monitors have become less common. Most video monitors and cards used today can produce at least 256 colors. However, because they use less power, cost less, and require less-capable (read: "cheaper") video cards, monochrome and grayscale monitors still serve a valuable purpose in some business applications.

The size of monitors is measured diagonally, just as a television is. Fifteen-inch monitors are the standard on most desktop computers. But because of the growing interest in computer-generated graphics and videos, 17-, 19-, and 21-inch monitors are becoming more popular. Monitors are typically wider than they are tall. However, some of the larger monitors are designed so that they are, in effect, standing on their sides. This allows users to clearly see full-page documents on one screen, making design and publication work much easier.

CRT Monitors

Most desktop monitors are similar to televisions in that their pictures are produced using a cathode ray tube. A *cathode ray tube (CRT)* is a vacuum tube that forms the screen display at one end and has a socket at the other end. The monitor image is produced by electron beams (which are invisible, by the way) that are generated in the neck of the CRT and shot against colored phosphors on the face of the CRT. When the invisible electron beam strikes a colored phosphor (red, green, or blue), the corresponding color is liberated. Using three synchronized electron beams to excite each color phosphor in the desired proportion, almost any color can be produced.

There are also some significant differences between CRT monitors and television sets. For one, monitors can produce much higher resolution than most television sets. *Resolution* determines the clarity, quality, and detail of the picture displayed on a screen. Resolution is discussed in terms of *pixels*—individual spots on the screen that can display a particular color. Higher resolution not only makes images clearer but reduces the possibility of eyestrain that can occur after long periods of time looking at a monitor. In the computer industry, monitor resolution is often defined as the total number of pixels in height and width. For example, a 15-, 17-, or 21-inch monitor can be set to a resolution of 1024 pixels wide by 768 pixels high, or 1024 by 768. The resolution of scanners and printers is still defined in pixels per inch, as opposed to the total number of horizontal and vertical pixels displayed at one time.

Resolution is not the only measurement of image quality—color is the other defining characteristic. For example, a 1024 by 768 image at 256 colors can be much more detailed than a 1024 by 768 image at 16 colors, and a 1024 by 786 image at 16 million colors is virtually indistinguishable from a photograph.

CRT monitors also differ from televisions in how they draw pixels on the screen. Televisions draw every other line of pixels, and when they reach the bottom of the screen, they begin again at the top and fill in the missing lines. This process is called *interlacing,* and the staggered redrawing can cause a visible flicker. Noninterlaced computer monitors draw lines of pixels one at a time from the top of the screen to the bottom, a process that is repeated multiple times per second. The actual number of redraws is called the *refresh rate.* Faster refresh rates result in crisper, more fluid images.

CRT monitors and televisions also produce some undesirable output—low-levels of radiation, called *extremely low frequency (ELF) radiation.* As with many forms of radiation, the long-term impact of ELF radiation has yet to be determined. However, monitor manufactures are beginning to incorporate safety standards into new monitors. Interestingly enough, the U.S. FCC (Federal Communications Commission) standards for monitors are considered the least stringent in the world; the MPR II Swedish standards are the toughest. To protect yourself from ELF radiation, you can purchase an ELF radiation guard that fits over the front of your monitor to block some of the emissions. It is also considered safer if you stay an arm's length away from your monitor and view the monitor directly rather than from the side, since most ELF is radiated from the sides and rear of the monitor. If you sit near several computers in an office, sit at least 4 feet from the sides of other users' monitors.

Video Cards

A video adapter, or video card, provides the output to a computer monitor. Originally, video cards were special expansion cards. Today, basic video adapters are generally built into the system board, although you can purchase better boards to enhance video output. These adapters, which conform to standards developed by the Video Electronics Standards Association, control the resolution and number of colors that can be displayed by a monitor.

The most common video cards in use today are VGA (Video Graphics Adapter) and SVGA (Super Video Graphics Array). Traditionally, VGA is 640 by 480 by 16 colors; SVGA is loosely defined as any resolution or color depth higher than that.

Other Video Displays

In addition to CRT monitors, two other types of visual output devices are commonly used:

- ▶ LCD displays
- ▶ Gas plasma displays

Most laptop computers today use a *liquid crystal display (LCD)*. The two types of LCD panels are active matrix and passive, or dual-scan, matrix. Active matrix uses more transistors to generate an image, making active matrix displays easier to read and much more expensive.

A *gas plasma display* consists of three sheets of glass separated by a gas called plasma. When electricity is sent through a point in the display, it charges the plasma, and the plasma gives off energy in the form of orange-colored light in the same way that a fluorescent light bulb emits white light. Gas plasma displays are occasionally used in laptops because they are very thin and are easy on the eyes. Because they do not have a size limit, glass plasma displays can also be used for large wall-sized displays. However, plasma displays use a large amount of energy and can't display multiple colors.

LCD Projectors and Panels

If you're asked to give a presentation for a group of people today, using an LCD panel or projector will set you apart from the crowd. An LCD panel is an output device that sits on top of an overhead projector (where a transparency would go) and connects to a personal computer. Whatever you display on the computer is displayed on the LCD and projected onto a screen by the overhead. Using special presentation software, you can display images or video. An LCD projector works like an LCD panel, except it contains a built-in projector. Either device combined with a laptop computer makes a practical and useful tool for the occasional presenter or full-time lecturer.

Part II

Printers

The market for printers changed dramatically in the 1990s. Until recently, high-quality printing was expensive, and color printing was out of the question for most PC owners. Today, more and more home computer users are purchasing excellent quality color printers at affordable prices. As computers have moved into the mainstream, the caliber of printers has increased and prices have continued to drop. Printers for personal computers fall into two categories:

▶ Impact printers—dot-matrix printers, letter-quality printers, and plotters

▶ Nonimpact printers—laser printers, ink-jet printers, thermal printers, and dye-sublimation printers

Impact Printers

Impact printers make an image by hitting a print head or key against a ribbon and were the most common type of printer available for personal computers until the early 1990s. Today, impact printers, such as the HP 5000 shown in Figure 9.9, are largely used to quickly print paychecks, invoices, and other reports generated by a network or mainframe computer.

Dot-matrix printers form an image by using columns of small pins in 9-, 18-, or 24-pin configurations that strike a ribbon to form a pattern of small dots on a page. Because dots are used to create the image, dot-matrix printers can easily create both characters and graphics; however, the print quality of these printers is relatively low. Because impact printers actually strike the paper, they are primarily used today to print multiple-part forms.

Letter-quality printers, which are closely related to the typewriter, use a daisy wheel or a thimble hitting against a ribbon to produce text. Letter-quality printers cannot produce graphic images, and type styles depend on the availability of interchangeable print heads. Letter-quality printers produce a better quality type than dot-matrix printers. Both dot-matrix and letter-quality printers are slow and noisy, making them unattractive in business settings.

Large architectural or engineering drawings may be printed on another type of impact printer called a *plotter*. A plotter is a printer that uses a series of pens filled with ink that switch on and off to reproduce an image. Drum plotters have pens that only move horizontally and use two drums to move the paper vertically against the pens. Electrostatic plotters are drum plotters that use a row of electrodes rather than a pen to create images on

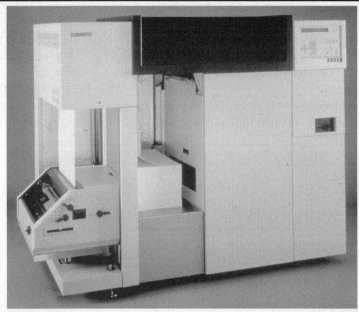

Photo courtesy of Hewlett-Packard Company

FIGURE 9.9: High-quality print for high-volume production print applications is available in the HP 5000 family of printers. These printers can produce from 100 to 210 printed pages per minute (ppm) on fan-folded (continuous forms) paper.

specially charged film or paper. Flatbed plotters resemble Etch-A-Sketch machines with pens mounted on a set of arms so that they can move both horizontally and vertically. The larger flatbed plotters, used in the automobile industry, can produce a full-size drawing of a vehicle.

Nonimpact Printers

Nonimpact printers, with their high-quality output, speed, low noise, and graphics capability, have quickly taken over the printer market. *Laser printers* generally produce the best output and, as a result, are commonly used in business settings. Laser printers produce an image the same way a copy machine does—by directing a laser beam onto a round drum. This charges a pattern of particles on the drum. As the drum rotates, it picks up an electrically charged powder called *toner*. The toner adheres to the paper and creates the text or graphic image. Laser printers print an average of 6 to 10 pages per minute (ppm). However, high-speed laser printers used in commercial applications can print as many as 500 pages per minute.

Printer resolution quality is measured in dots per inch (dpi). Extremely high-quality laser printers can print in resolutions as high as 1200dpi. Most laser printers print at 300dpi; however, 600dpi laser printers are coming down in price and becoming more common. Color laser printers, such as the HP Color LaserJet 5 shown in Figure 9.10, continue to be quite expensive. In order to print in color, the paper has to pass through the printer once for each color. This requires the paper-feeding mechanisms to be extremely accurate so that the paper is precisely lined up on each pass.

Photo courtesy of Hewlett-Packard Company

FIGURE 9.10: Low cost per page and industry-leading network-printing capabilities make this HP Color LaserJet 5 printer ideal for workgroups.

Fortunately, color printing is not limited to high-cost laser printers. Another type of nonimpact printer, called an *ink-jet printer*, is quite affordable for home use. And the quality of ink-jet printers isn't bad either—many produce high-quality, nearly photographic images.

Ink-jet printers, such as the HP DeskJet 660C shown in Figure 9.11, print by spraying a fine jet of ink onto the paper; this ink can be black or a combination of black, yellow, red, and blue. Like laser printers, black ink-jet printers are rated by the number of pages they print per minute. Color printers may be rated by *minutes per page* (mpp) rather than pages per minute, because whole numbers are more convenient than fractions.

Photo courtesy of Hewlett-Packard Company

FIGURE 9.11:   HP's DeskJet 660C printer is designed for convenience and ease-of-use. Black and color cartridges sit side by side in the printer, making it convenient to print in true black and color on the same page without swapping cartridges.

With ink-jet printers, you choose the quality of the print by selecting draft, normal, or high-quality output. The quality of the output directly influences the speed of the printer—the higher the quality, the longer you wait for it.

Thermal printers use heat to transfer an image onto specially treated paper. The early thermal printers used a shiny paper once common in older calculators, and the quality of the printing was generally poor. Newer models of thermal printers, which use a process called *thermal wax transfer,* are of a much higher quality. Ink is injected into wax on a ribbon, and then heat is applied to the ink-filled wax so that it melts onto the paper at 66dpi. *Dye-sublimation printing* works the same way as thermal wax transfer except that it smoothes the dots of ink once they are placed on the page; this changes the tones and produces photo-quality images. Both thermal wax transfer and dye-sublimation printing are much faster than color laser printing and produce a better quality image at a lower cost. These printers are generally used for full-color publishing, including magazines.

Sound Output Devices

The voice, music, and other sounds produced by computers are amplified and projected by speakers or through external jacks that can be connected to headphones or recording devices. Most PCs include small, cheap speakers like those found in the worst of clock radios. Multimedia PCs and multimedia kits that you add to your existing PC usually come with speakers of reasonable quality. But speaker quality varies, just as it does in home audio systems. For truly dynamic sound, consider purchasing a separate audio card and speakers or a multimedia kit manufactured by a major audio company such as Altec Lansing, Yamaha, or Sony.

INPUT/OUTPUT DEVICES

Some hardware is actually two devices in one: an input device and an output device. This class of peripherals is called *I/O devices*. Storage devices such as disk drives are sometimes included in lists of I/O devices.

Sound and Motion

You can use video cameras and camcorders with video input jacks, VCRs, and optical disk players to transfer graphic images to and receive images from a computer. You can transfer the images as static images or as moving pictures. With the addition of a video capture card, you can store computer actions on video tape or edit home videos and add text to them. Using animation software and supporting hardware, you can create "movies," which can also be transferred to tape.

The biggest roadblock to full-motion video becoming commonplace is the size of the files video requires. Because video is such a storage hog, developers are focusing on developing better methods of file *compression*, in which repetitive and unnecessary bytes are removed before video files are stored, resulting in smaller, more compact files. As compression improves, we will see an explosion of video use in computer applications.

You can attach specially designed electronic music keyboards, and wind, string, and percussion instruments to a computer as input devices. Through the use of a standardized interface called *MIDI (Musical Instrument Digital Interface)*, computers, synthesizers, and instruments can communicate. With the addition of specialized software, whatever is played on an instrument can appear as sheet music on the screen. You can create MIDI compositions on screen with software and then output to an instrument through a MIDI port.

Musicians have found that computerized instruments have other advantages too. Because MIDI is a universal standard, sound input from one MIDI instrument can be played back with the sound of another instrument so that the computer becomes a sophisticated synthesizer to create new and different kinds of music. MIDI provides composers with the ability to develop as many as 16 tracks (16 sequences of code) that can be played simultaneously. A high-quality sound card can support enough tracks to create the effect of a full orchestra. Since MIDI code is very compact, it can be stored in significantly less space than the same recording in high-fidelity, digital sound. Surprisingly, MIDI sounds do not sound electronically produced. They accurately reflect the characteristics of the instruments they represent, and, consequently, the recording industry regularly uses MIDI to enhance or even originate musical compositions.

NOTE

The first music played on a computer was the tune "Daisy," played by a computer at Bell Labs in 1957. This bit of computer "musical trivia" is subtly referenced in the film *2001: A Space Odyssey.* Astronaut Dave Bowman sequentially removes memory modules to shut down HAL, an artificial intelligence computer. As the modules are removed, HAL loses more of its capabilities until, finally, HAL sings a few lines from "Daisy" and then lapses into silence.

Fax Machines and Modems

When Douglas Engelbart first revealed his vision of personal computing in 1968, he demonstrated a computer communicating with another computer located at his laboratory 30 miles away. In his mind, computers were meant to talk to each other. Never has this been more evident than in the explosion of online communication in the 1990s. Commercial online services and the Internet have become a primary reason that many people are buy-ing personal computers. Businesses are connecting satellite offices to headquarters with wide area networks and customized versions of the Internet called *intranets*.

> A personal computer without a telephone line attached to it is a poor, lonely thing.
>
> —Stewart Brand, founder, *Whole Earth Catalog*

A significant amount of traditional postal service delivery, commonly referred to as "snail mail," has been replaced by electronic mail. All this communication is made possible by a device called a modem. A *modem* allows computers to communicate with each other by connecting through regular telephone lines.

Phone lines transmit analog signals—signals that travel as a wave, as sound does. Computers generate digital signals. Analog devices can handle varying values of signals within a certain range, or set of frequen-cies. Digital devices can handle only two values: 0 and 1. In order for a computer-generated digital file to be transmitted over analog phone lines, it must first be converted or modulated. When a digital signal is modulated, 0s and 1s are replaced with low- and high-frequency tones. When the analog signal is received by the remote computer, the signal must be demodulated, or reconverted back to a digital signal. The term *modem* comes from a combination of the two terms, *mo*dulate and *dem*odulate. Different types of modems are shown in Figure 9.12.

Facsimile, or *fax*, technology allows images to be transmitted over tele-phone lines by converting text, characters, and graphics into a pattern of small dots. Fax modems combine the technology of modems with the tech-nology of facsimile transmission to create a multifaceted device capable of sending documents to other computers or to facsimile machines at other locations. Recent improvements in technology have produced multipur-pose machines that include a fax, a scanner, and a copier all in one.

NOTE

Incredible as it sounds, fax machines are actually older than telephones! The first patent on a fax machine was granted in Great Britain in 1843. Of course, this machine couldn't use telephone lines, and the technology was quite different, but the purpose was essentially the same. A French news report with a photo-graph was first sent by fax in 1914. By 1924, faxes were a regular part of the newspaper business.

FIGURE 9.12:   Internal, external, and PCMCIA fax modems

Modems and fax modems are available on expansion cards as internal modems. External modems are connected to the computer's serial port. The phone line is connected directly to the modem, and lights on the modem indicate the status of the modem at all times.

A *PCMCIA card* is a plug-in for laptop computers. About the size of a credit card, it is based on standards developed by the PC Memory Card International Association. Laptops include a PCMCIA port that can receive the cards. PCMCIA cards provide a variety of add-on options for laptop owners, including sound adapters, flash memory, network cards, and fax modems.

The most important factor in evaluating a fax modem is the data transmission speed. Early modems transmitted at a speed of approximately 300 bits per second (bps). Using a unit of measure for signal speed called *baud*, this was referred to as 300 baud. Since more than one bit can be sent per second, however, baud does not always correspond to the number of bits per second. Today's modems encode a signal using changes in several aspects of an audio analog signal. For example, a 28.8Kbps modem can send and receive about 115,000 (115K) bits per second. To access the Internet without frustration, modems need to transmit a minimum of 14,400bps, or 14.1Kbps. Modems of 28,800bps (28.8Kbps) or faster provide users with less wait time and greater reliability in data transfers.

NOTE

The ultimate vision of the "information superhighway" is the creation of a complex network of digital communication lines that would allow computers to communicate without the use of modems.

WHAT'S NEXT?

In the next chapter, Mark Minasi offers valuable guidance on preventive maintenance—simple things you can do to keep your computer hardware running smoothly and to protect it from physical hazards ranging from dust and static electricity to flooding.

Chapter 10

AVOIDING SERVICE: PREVENTIVE MAINTENANCE

The most effective way to cut down your repair bills is by good, preventive maintenance. There are things in the PC environment—some external, some created in ignorance by you through inattention—that can drastically shorten your PC's life.

Adapted from *The Complete PC Upgrade & Maintenance Guide* by Mark Minasi
ISBN 0-7821-2606-5   1,620 pages $49.99

Now, some of the things that affect your PC's life are common-sense things; I don't really imagine that I've got to tell you not to spill soft drinks (or, for that matter, hard drinks) into the keyboard. But other PC gremlin sources aren't quite so obvious; so, obvious or not, we'll get to all the environmental hazards in this chapter. A few factors can endanger your PC's health:

▶ Excessive heat

▶ Dust

▶ Magnetism

▶ Stray electromagnetism

▶ Power surges, incorrect line voltage, and power outages

▶ Water and corrosive agents

HEAT AND THERMAL SHOCK

Every electronic device carries within it the seeds of its own destruction. More than half the power given to chips is wasted as heat—but heat destroys chips. One of an electronic designer's main concerns is to see that an electronic device can dissipate heat as quickly as it can generate it. If it cannot, heat slowly builds up until the device fails.

You can help control your PC's heat problem in several ways:

▶ By installing an adequate fan in the power supply or adding an auxiliary fan

▶ By installing a heat sink

▶ By adjusting your box design for better ventilation

▶ By running the PC in an area that is within a safe temperature range

Removing Heat with a Fan

In general, laptops don't require a fan, because enough heat dissipates from the main circuit board all by itself. But most desktop and tower PCs will surely fail without a fan.

When designing a fan, engineers must trade noise for cooling power. Years ago, power supplies were quite expensive, running in the $300 range for the cheapest, so great care was exercised in choosing the right fan. Nowadays, power supplies cost less than $25, and I doubt that most engineers at PC companies could even tell you what kind of fan is sitting in their machines, any more than they could tell you who makes the case screws.

Now, that's a terrible shame, because the $3 fan that's sitting in most PC power supplies is a vital part. If it dies, your PC will cook itself in just a few hours.

And they *do* die.

The more stuff that's in your PC, the hotter it runs. The things that make PCs hot inside include:

- ▶ Chips, memory chips, and CPUs in particular, because they have the greatest number of transistors inside them.

- ▶ Drive motors in hard disks, floppies, and CD-ROMs. Some CD-ROMs run quite warm, such as the Plexor 4-Plex models. Large hard disks run *extremely* hot. I've seen an old Maxtor 660MB ESDI drive run so hot that it almost burned my fingers; I've seen the same thing more recently on my 1.7GB Fujitsu drive. Newer drives in the 3½-inch half-height or third-height format run much cooler. Some circuit boards can run quite hot, depending on how well (or how poorly) they're designed.

Truthfully, heat buildup inside a PC is much less a problem than it was in the mid-1980s. In those days, every drive was a full-height drive, and every computer had 640K of memory built up from 90 separate 64K chips. Add one of those early hot 8087 coprocessors, and it was common to find the inside of a PC running 30 degrees F (16 degrees C) warmer inside its box than in the outside room.

Removing Heat with a Heat Sink

For years, electronic designers have had to struggle with hot components on circuit boards. Sometimes a fan just isn't enough, so they need more help cooling an infernal chip. They do it with a *heat sink*. A heat sink is a small piece of metal, usually aluminum, with fins on it. The heat sink is glued or clamped to the hot chip. The metal conducts heat well, and the fins increase the surface area of the heat sink. The more area on the heat sink, the more heat that can be conducted off to the air and thereby removed from the PC.

The standard Pentium II and Xeon processor packages have a heat sink and a fan integrated with the chip. The idea is that the heat sink pulls the heat off and the fan disperses it. The Celeron doesn't come with a heat sink, but that doesn't mean that it's not a good idea to think about putting one on a hot chip. You can find heat sinks in electronics supply catalogs. Adding a fan can really increase the heat sink's ability to cool its chip. I've noticed that many of today's motherboards have connections to power a couple of auxiliary fans, and you can buy fans that attach to those connections from PC clone parts places (look in the back of *Computer Shopper* for them).

Good and Bad Box Designs

It's frustrating how totally unaware of heat problems many computer manufacturers are. The first tower computer I purchased was from a company named ACMA, and they put together an impressive machine. There were two fans in the case—a very nice touch—as well as a CPU fan. I've got to say that they spoiled me. A later (1994) purchase, from an outfit called Systems Dynamics Group, was somewhat less enjoyable. The back of the PC chassis had room for two fans, but there was only one fan in the system. There's nothing intrinsically wrong with that, except that the cutout for the second fan—which is right next to the first fan—was left empty. The result was that the fan just sucked in air from the cutout a few inches away from it and blew it back out. Made the fan happy, I suppose, but didn't do much for the CPU.

I noticed this pointless ventilation system rather quickly, so I took some tape and covered up the extraneous cutout. Within seconds, the air being pumped out the back of the Pentium got 10 degrees warmer. If I'd left the extra cutout uncovered, the only ventilation that my Pentium system would have gotten was just the simple convection from the heated boards and drives. Even at that, however, the Pentium system—which included a 1GB drive, 80MB of RAM, a CD-ROM, video capture board, video board, SCSI host adapter, and Ethernet card—only ran 10 degrees hotter inside the box than outside the box.

Things could have been a bit worse if the case was like some I've seen, with the fan *on the bottom of the tower*! This is not too common, fortunately, but it's worth asking so you can avoid it when purchasing a PC. This setup puts the circuit boards on the top of the tower and the fan on the bottom. I have no idea who designed this case, but it's nice to know that the banjo player kid from *Deliverance* finally has someone to look down upon. The point I'm making here is, take a minute and look at the airflow in the box. Of course, even if you have a good box, you can still run into heat problems.

Dead Fans

Years ago (around 1995), I installed Freelance Graphics on my system. Pulling the first floppy out of my A drive, I noticed that the floppy was warm. My memory flashed back to 1982, when something similar had happened—so I knew what was going on. My system's fan had died.

Fortunately, I found the problem early and shut down the computer. I had to travel to Europe for a few weeks to teach classes and consult, but I figured, no problem—I'll just leave the computer off.

Unfortunately, while I was gone, one of my employees helpfully started up the computer—reasoning that I always leave my computers on all the time, so what the hey? So, despite the "do not turn it on" sign I'd left on it, the computer merrily melted itself down while I lectured in Amsterdam. By the time I returned, the hard disk had self-destructed, as had the Ethernet card in it.

It's actually amazing what *didn't* die in the system. The CPU (a 50MHz 486DX) ran for a couple of years afterward (until it became too slow to be of value), and the Adaptec 1742 SCSI host adapter is still in service in an old server.

Heat Sensor Devices

Now, I could have avoided this problem altogether with a 110 Twinalert from a company called PC Power and Cooling Systems. They're a name to know when you're buying power supplies. The 110 Twinalert is a circuit board about the size of a business card that plugs into a floppy power connector. When the PC's internal temperature gets to 110 degrees F, it starts making an annoying squealing noise. At 118 degrees F, it just shuts the computer down. The device is under $50, and every network server should have one.

While I'm on the subject of PC Power and Cooling, I should mention that this company also makes an interesting variety of power products for the PC, including power supplies with very quiet fans, power supplies with built-in battery backup, and high-quality PC cases. I use their stuff when I want to increase the odds that my PC will be running when I need it.

My introduction to PC Power and Cooling came with a hot 386. When I say "hot," I mean that this PC ran 25 degrees warmer inside than the temperature outside. PC Power and Cooling sells the Turbo Cool, a power supply that claimed at the time to cool your PC by 35 to 40 degrees (all Fahrenheit). Now, obviously, my 386 could not be cooled by 35 degrees, because it ran only 25 degrees over ambient—the best that a fan can do is to lower the temperature inside the machine to the surrounding temperature. However, buying PC Power and Cooling Systems' Turbo Cool cooled my machine from 25 degrees over ambient to only *four* degrees over ambient. You can find PC Power and Cooling Systems' address in the Vendor Guide (Appendix A).

Safe Temperature Ranges for PCs

Electronic components have a temperature range within which they are built to work. IBM suggests that the PC, for instance, is built to work in the range of 60 to 85 degrees F. This is because the circuit boards can run as hot as 125 degrees, but a typical machine may be as much as 40 degrees hotter *inside* than outside. And 125 minus 40 yields 85 degrees, the suggested maximum temperature.

Obviously, if you've got a good fan, the acceptable range of room temperatures expands considerably. If you had a really good fan, the inside of the machine would be close to the same temperature as the outside. You don't want the inside of the PC to get any hotter than 110 degrees—hard disks can fail at that point, although, again, circuit boards can function in higher temperatures than that.

Since the temperature inside the PC is the ambient temperature plus some constant, you can cool the inside of the PC in two ways—either lower the constant with a good fan or lower the ambient temperature. If you keep the room cooler, the PC will be cooler.

Heat also aids the corrosion process. Corrosion is a chemical process, and inside a computer, corrosion can roughly *double* in speed when the temperature of the process is raised by 10 degrees C (about 18 degrees F). Chips slowly deteriorate, the hotter the faster.

How do you measure temperature and temperature changes in your PC? Simple—get a *digital temperature probe*. Radio Shack markets one for about $30. Or you can buy one from Edmund Scientific Corp., whose address is listed in Appendix A.

The easy way to use the probe is to tape it over the exit vents by the fan's power supply. An indoor/outdoor switch lets you quickly view the PC's inside temperature and the ambient temperature.

Duty Cycles

I said before that a device should get rid of heat as quickly as it creates it. Not every device is that good, however. Devices are said to have a *duty cycle.* This number—expressed as a percentage—is the proportion of the time that a device can work without burning up. For example, a powerful motor may have a 50-percent duty cycle. This means that it should be active only 50 percent of the time. A starter motor on a car, for example, must produce a tremendous amount of power. Powerful motors are expensive to produce, so instead, cars use a motor that can produce a lot of power for a very short time. If you crank the engine on your car for several minutes at a stretch, you will likely damage or destroy the car's starter motor. Floppy disk drive motors are a similar example: if you run a floppy motor continuously, you'll likely burn out the motor. *Hard* disk motors, on the other hand, run continuously and must be designed with a 100-percent duty cycle.

Duty cycle is used to describe active versus inactive time for many kinds of devices, although this definition could be misleading, since it implies that all devices can be continually active without problems. Not all devices are designed to be active all the time. Some desktop laser printers, for example, will not run well if they are required to print continuously.

Thermal Shock

Because a PC is warmer inside than outside, changes in room temperature can multiply inside a PC.

This problem leads to a hazard called *thermal shock.* Thermal shock comes from subjecting components to rapid and large changes in temperature. It can disable your computer due to expansion/contraction damage. The most common scenario for thermal shock occurs when the PC is turned on Monday morning after a winter's weekend. Many commercial buildings turn the temperature down to 55 degrees over the weekend: your office may contain some of that residual chill early Monday morning. Inside the PC, though, it may still be 55. Then you turn the machine on. Within 30 minutes some PCs can warm up to 120 degrees. This rapid, 65-degree rise in temperature brings on thermal shock.

This is an argument for leaving the PC on 24 hours a day, seven days a week. (We'll see some more reasons to do this soon.) The temperature inside the PC will be better regulated. By the way, you can't leave portable PCs on all the time, but you should be extra careful with portables to avoid thermal shock. If your laptop has been sitting in the trunk on a cold February day, be sure to give it some time to warm up before trying to use it. And give it some time in a *dry* place, or water vapor will condense on the cold disk platters. Water on the disk platters is a surefire way to reduce your drive's life.

Sunbeams

Another heat effect is caused by sunbeams. Direct sunlight isn't a good thing for electronic equipment. A warm sunbeam feels nice for a few minutes, but if you sit in one for an hour, you'll understand why PCs don't like them. Direct sunlight is also, of course, terrible for floppy disks. Find a shadowy area, or use drapes.

DEALING WITH DUST

Dust is everywhere. It consists of tiny sand granules, fossil skeletons of minuscule creatures that lived millions of years ago, dead skin, paper particles, and tiny crustaceans called dust mites that live off the other pieces. Dust is responsible for several evils.

First, it sticks to the circuit boards inside your computer. As dust builds up, an entire board can become coated with a fine insulating sheath. That would be fine if the dust was insulating your house, but thermal insulation is definitely a bad thing for computers. You seek, as we have seen, to minimize impediments to thermal radiation from your computer components. To combat this, remove dust from inside the computer and from circuit boards periodically. A good period between cleaning is a year in a house and six months in an office. A simpler approach is to use the "while I'm at it" algorithm—when you need to disassemble the machine for some other reason, clean the insides while you're at it. A tool that can assist you is a can of compressed air. Just as effective for the case and inside support assemblies is a dust-free cloth dampened with a little water and ammonia (just a few drops). Don't use the cloth on circuit boards—get a can of compressed air and blow the dust off.

Actually, *compressed air* isn't actually compressed air, but some kind of compressed gas. Take a second look when you buy this stuff: a lot of it is Freon or some other chlorinated fluorocarbon (CFC), which enlarges the hole in the ozone layer. Rather than using one of these, choose one of the "ozone-friendly" alternatives, such as the one marketed by Chemtronics.

This should be obvious, but when you blow dust off boards, be aware of where it is going. If you can, have the vacuum cleaner nearby, or take the board to another area; then you'll have better luck. *Please* don't hold the board over the PC's chassis and blow off the dust with compressed air—all it does is move the dust, not *remove* the dust.

The second evil is that dust can clog spaces, such as:

▶ The air intake area to your power supply or hard disk

▶ The space between the floppy disk drive head and the disk

To combat the floppy drive problem, some manufacturers offer a floppy dust cover that you put in place when the machine is turned off. The sad part of this is that you really need the cover when the machine is on. CRT (cathode ray tube) displays have an unintended, unexpected, unpleasant, and unavoidable side effect—they attract dust. Turn your monitor on, and all the dust in the area drops everything (what would dust particles drop, I wonder?) and heads straight for the display. Some of the particles get side-tracked and end up in the floppy drives.

One place that creates and collects paper dust is, of course, the printer. Periodically, vacuum or blow out your printer, *away* from the computer (remember, dust goes somewhere when blown away).

By the way, another fertile source of dust is ash particles. Most of us don't burn things indoors, *unless* we are smokers. If you smoke, fine: just don't do it near the computer. Years ago, I ran across a study by the U.S. Government Occupation Safety and Hazard Administration (OSHA), which estimated that smoke at a computer workstation cuts the computer's life by 40 percent. That's $1200 on a $3000 workstation. (Alas, I saw that back in 1985 and didn't note the information in detail—I wish I had!—so I can't cite the particular study.)

MAGNETISM

Magnets—both the permanent and electromagnetic type—can cause permanent loss of data on hard or floppy disks. Most often, the magnetism found in an office environment is produced by electric motors and electromagnets. A commonly overlooked electromagnet is the one in phones that ring using a real bell (not common these days). The clapper is forced against the bell (or buzzer, if the phone has one of those) in the phone by powering an electromagnet. If you absent-mindedly put such a phone on top of a stack of floppy disks, and the phone rings, you will probably have unrecoverable data errors on at least the top one.

Don't think you have magnets around? How about:

▶ Magnets to put notes on a file cabinet

▶ A paper clip holder with a magnet

▶ A word-processing copy stand with a magnetic clip

▶ A magnetic screw extractor

Another source of magnetism is, believe it or not, a CRT. I have seen disk drives refuse to function because they were situated inches from a CRT. X-ray machines in airports similarly produce some magnetism, although there is some controversy here. Some folks say, "Don't run floppies through the X-ray—walk them through." Others say the X-ray is OK, but the metal detector zaps floppies. Some people claim to have been burned at both. Personally, I walk through an average of three to four metal detectors per week carrying 3.5-inch floppy disks and have never (knock wood) had a problem. My laptops have been through X-ray machines everywhere, and I've never lost a byte on the hard disk because of it.

Airport metal detectors should be sufficiently gentle for floppies. Magnetism is measured in a unit called *gauss*. Metal detectors *in the United States* (notice the emphasis) emit far less gauss than that necessary to affect disks. I'm not sure about Canada and Europe, but I notice that the fillings in my teeth seem to set off the metal detectors in the Ottawa airport.

What about preventive maintenance? For starters, get a phone with a ringer that is not a real bell, to minimize the chance of erasing data inadvertently. Another large source of magnetism is the motor in a printer—generally, it is not shielded (the motors on the drives don't produce very much magnetism, in case you're wondering).

Do you (or someone that you assist) work in a word-processing pool? Many word processors (the people kind, not the machine kind) use a copy stand that consists of a flexible metal arm and a magnet. The magnet holds the copy to be typed on the metal arm. The arm can sit right in front of the operator's face so that he or she can easily type the copy.

The problem arises when it's time to change the copy. I watched a word-processing operator remove the magnet (so as to change the copy) and slap the magnet on the side of the computer. It really made perfect sense—the case was steel and held the magnet in a place that was easy to access. The only bad part of the whole operation was that the hard disk on that particular PC chassis was mounted on the extreme right side of the case, right next to the magnet. You can start to see why I hate magnets.... A few years ago, I was a keynote speaker at a conference in San Antonio, next to the Alamo. As part of the "thank you" package that the conference organizers put together, we speakers got a refrigerator magnet in the shape of the Alamo. After almost placing my wallet (with my credit cards in it) on the magnet, almost laying demonstration floppies that I'd gotten at the conference on it, and almost storing the Alamo magnet in my laptop case (you know, next to the laptop's hard disk and any floppies that I had in the case), I finally gave up and threw the magnet away before I had a chance to *really* do some damage.

Oh, and by the way, *speakers* have magnets in them. Years ago, a friend purchased a home entertainment system: a VCR, a stereo, and some monster speakers. That's when I noticed that he had stacked his videotapes on top of the speakers. I almost didn't have the heart to tell him, but I eventually advised him that his videos were history—and, sad to say, they *were*. Today's multimedia PCs all have speakers that claim to have shielded magnets, but I've got a Sony woofer/satellite speaker system that makes my monitor's image get wobbly when I put the speakers too near the monitor. No matter what the manual says, I think I'll just keep the floppies away from there.

My advice is to go on an antimagnet crusade. Magnets near magnetic media are disasters waiting to happen.

A sad story: a large government agency's data center bought a handheld magnetic bulk floppy eraser. (I'm not sure why—they weren't a secret shop and thus did not have the need.) The PC expert in the shop tested it on a few junk floppies and then turned it off and didn't think about it. The next day, he remembered that he had left it on top of a plastic floppy file drawer. This meant that the eraser, even though turned off, was about an inch from the top of the floppies. He spent the next day testing each of the floppies, one by one. Most were dead. They got rid of the bulk eraser. I'm not sure what they did with the PC expert.

STRAY ELECTROMAGNETISM

Stray electromagnetism can cause problems for your PC and, in particular, for your network. Here, I'm just referring to any electromagnetism that you don't want. It comes in several varieties.

- ▶ Radiated *electromagnetic interference* (*EMI*)
- ▶ Power noise and interruptions
- ▶ *Electrostatic discharge* (*ESD*)—static electricity

Electromagnetic Interference

EMI is caused when electromagnetism is radiated or conducted somewhere that we don't want it to be. I discuss two common types—crosstalk and RFI—in the next two sections.

Crosstalk

When two wires are physically close to each other, they can transmit interference between themselves, and this interference is called *crosstalk*. I'm not talking about short circuits here: the insulation can be completely intact. The problem is that the interfering wire contains electronic pulses. Electronic pulses produce magnetic fields as a side effect. The wire being interfered with is touched or crossed by the magnetic fields. Magnetic fields crossing or touching a wire produce electronic pulses as a side effect. (Nature is, unfortunately, amazingly symmetrical at times like this.) The electronic pulses created in the second wire are faint copies of the pulses (the signal) from the first wire. These pulses interfere with the signal that we're trying to send on the second wire.

Crosstalk is not really a problem when applied to power lines, although I have heard of cases in which the alternating current in power lines creates a hum on a communications line through crosstalk. The larger worry is when bundles of wires are stored in close quarters, and the wires are data cables.

There are five solutions to crosstalk:

▶ Move the wires farther apart (not always feasible).

▶ Use twisted-pair cable (varying the number of twists reduces crosstalk).

▶ Use shielded cable (the shield reduces crosstalk—don't even think of running ribbon cables for distances more than six feet).

▶ Use fiber-optic cable—it's not electromagnetic, it's photonic. (Is that a great word, or what? It means that light instead of electricity is used to transmit data, so there's no crosstalk.)

▶ Don't run cables over fluorescent lights. The lights are noise emitters.

I once helped troubleshoot a network that had been installed in a classroom. The contractor had run the wires through the ceiling, but the network seemed to not work. (Ever notice how often the words "network" and "not work" end up in the same sentence? A Russian friend calls them "nyetworks.") I pushed aside the ceiling tiles and found that the cable installer had saved himself some time and money by foregoing cable trays, instead wrapping the cables around the occasional fluorescent lamp. So, on a hunch, I said to the people that I was working with, "Start the network up again," and I turned off the lights. Sure enough, it worked.

Radio Frequency Interference

Radio Frequency Interference (*RFI*) is high-frequency (10kHz radiation). It's a bad thing for computer communications. Sources are:

- ▶ High-speed digital circuits, like the ones in your computer

- ▶ Nearby radio sources

- ▶ Cordless telephones

- ▶ Keyboards

- ▶ Power-line intercoms (intercoms that use the power line's 60Hz as the carrier wave)

- ▶ Motors

Worse yet, your PC can be a *source* of RFI. If this happens, the FCC police come to your place of business and take your PC away. (Well, not really. But they *will* fine you.)

RFI is bad because it can interfere with high-speed digital circuits. Your computer is composed of digital circuits. RFI can seem sinister because it seems to come and go mysteriously. Like all noise, it is an unwanted signal. How would we go about receiving a *wanted* RF signal? Simple—construct an antenna. Suppose we want to receive a signal of a given frequency? We design an antenna of a particular length. (Basically, the best length is one quarter of the wavelength. A 30-meter wavelength is best picked up by a 7.5-meter antenna. But it's not important that you know that—to learn more about it, pick up an amateur radio book.) Now suppose there is some kind of RFI floating around. We're safe as long as we can't receive it. But suppose the computer is connected to the printer with a cable that, through bad luck, happens to be the correct length to receive that RFI? The result: printer gremlins. Fortunately, the answer is simple: shorten or lengthen the cable.

Electric motors are common RFI-producing culprits. I recently saw a workstation in Washington where the operator had put an electric fan (to cool *herself*, not the workstation) on top of the workstation. When the fan was on, it warped the top of the CRT's image slightly. Electric can openers, hair dryers, electric razors, electric pencil sharpeners, and printers are candidates. Sometimes it's hard to determine whether the device is messing up the PC simply by feeding back noise onto the power line or whether it is troubling the PC with RFI. The answer either way is to put the devices on separate power lines.

Your PC also *emits* RFI, which can impair the functioning of other PCs, televisions, and various sensitive pieces of equipment. By law, a desktop computer cannot be sold unless it meets "Class B" specifications. The FCC requires that a device 3 meters from the PC must receive no more than the RFI shown in Table 10.1.

TABLE 10.1: Permissible RF Output (FCC Class B Specification)

FREQUENCY	MAXIMUM FIELD STRENGTH (MICROVOLTS/METER)
30–88MHz	100
89–216MHz	150
217–1000MHz	200

RFI became an issue with personal computers when the PC came out because IBM had shielded its PC line and sought to make life a little tougher on the clonemakers. By pushing the FCC to get tough on PCs, IBM had a bit of a jump on the market. Unfortunately, getting Class B certification isn't that hard, and just about every PC qualifies these days: clonemakers now say that their machines are "FCC Class B Certified." This has caused the reverse of IBM's original intent, because the FCC certification seems a mark of legitimacy. In reality, FCC certification is not a measure of good design, quality components, or compatibility; it just means that the equipment doesn't produce excessive amounts of electromagnetic interference.

You protect your PC from the devices around it and you protect the devices from your PC in the same way. If the PC doesn't leak RFI, it's less likely to pick up any stray RFI in the area. Any holes in the case provide entry/exit points. Use the brackets that come with the machine to plug any unused expansion slots. To prevent unplanned air circulation paths, it is also a good idea to plug unused expansion slots. Ensure that the case fits together snugly and correctly. If the case includes cutouts for interface connectors, find plates to cover the cutouts or simply use metal tape.

A simple AM radio can be used to monitor RFI field strength. A portable radio is ideal, because it has light headphones and a small enough enclosure to allow fairly local signal strength monitoring. A cheap model is best—you don't want sophisticated noise filtering. Tune it to an area of the dial as far as possible from a strong station. Lower frequencies seem to work best. You'll hear the various devices produce noises. I first noticed these noises when working ages ago on a clone computer with an XT motherboard, a composite monitor, an external hard disk, and a two-drive external Bernoulli box. The quietest part of the system was the PC: the hard disk screamed and buzzed, the Bernoulli made low frequency eggbeater-like sounds, and the monitor produced a fairly pure and relatively loud tone.

The PC sounded different, depending on what it was doing. When I typed, I heard a machine-gun–like sound. When I asked for a text search, the fairly regular search made a "dee-dee-dee" sound. It's kind of fun (okay, I guess I don't get out much), and you might pop the top on your system and do a little "radio astronomy" on it.

I've also used the radio in a number of other ways. Once, I received a new motherboard, a 486 that I was going to use to upgrade a 286 system. I installed it, and nothing happened. No beeps, no blinking cursor, nothing but the fan. So I removed the motherboard and placed it on a cardboard box (no electrical short fears with a cardboard box). Then I placed a power supply next to it, plugged in the P8/P9 connectors, and powered up. I ran the radio over the motherboard and got no response, just a constant hum. Placing the radio right over the CPU got nothing. I reasoned that what I was hearing was just the clock circuit. I felt even more certain of my guess when I noticed that the CPU had been inserted backward into its socket. One dead motherboard, back to the manufacturer.

Power Noise

Your wall socket is a source of lots of problems. They basically fall into these four categories:

- ▶ Overvoltage and undervoltage
- ▶ No voltage at all—a power blackout
- ▶ Transients—spikes and surges
- ▶ User-induced power-up power surges

In this section, we'll look at this fourth category. In the process, I'll have to weigh in on The Great PC Power Switch Debate.

Leave Your Machines On 24 Hours a Day

What user-induced power surges, you say? Simple: every time you turn on an electrical device, you get a power surge through it. Electrical devices receive some of the greatest stresses when they are turned on or turned off. When do light bulbs burn out? Think about it—they generally burn out when you first turn them on or off. One study showed that when a device is first turned on, it draws as much as four to six times its normal power for less than one second. (This phenomenon is called *inrush current* in the literature. I found this bit of information on page 27 of *Computer Electric Power Requirements* by Mark Waller, published by Sams in 1987.) For that brief time, your PC may be pulling 600 to 900 watts—not a prescription for a long PC life.

The answer? Leave your PCs on 24 hours a day, seven days a week. We've done it at my company for years. You can turn the monitor off if you want, and also turn off the printer.

What? You're still not convinced? I know, it seems nonintuitive—most people react that way. But it really does make sense. First of all, consider the things that you keep on all the time, such as:

▶ Digital clocks, which obviously run continuously, incorporate some of the same digital technology as microcomputers, and they're pretty reliable.

▶ Calculators—I've seen accountants with calculators that are on all the time.

▶ Mainframes, minis, and your phone PBX never go off.

▶ TVs (part of the TV is powered up all the time so that it can "warm up" instantly, unlike older sets).

▶ Thermostats—the temperature-regulating device in your home or business is a circuit that works all the time.

Most of the things that I just named are some of the most reliable, never-think-about-them devices that you work with.

In addition to the things I've already said, consider the hard disk. All disks incorporate a motor to spin them at high speeds (depending on the drive, they may spin at speeds ranging from 3,600 to 10,000rpm). You know from real life that it's a lot harder to get something moving than it is to keep it moving. (Ever push a car?) The cost, then, of turning hard disk motors on and off is that sometimes they just won't be able to get started.

For example, back in 1984 I bought my first hard disk, an external 32MB drive. It cost $929, and although it's dead and buried now, for years I was loathe to stop using it, because nine hundred bucks is a lot of money. For a long time, I kept it attached to a server and constantly running. This illustrates the don't-turn-it-off point of view. The drive required a "jumpstart" when it was turned off overnight: if the thing didn't want to work, we just removed it from the system, took off the hard disk's circuit board to expose the motor, and gave the motor a spin. After a couple of spins, we reassembled it, and it would start up fine. (No, I didn't put anything important on it, but it was a great demonstration tool. And it kept data just fine.)

Here's the point: as long as we didn't turn the system off, the hard drive worked quite well, at least as well as old 32MB hard drives work. This applies to hard disks in general, and in fact to anything with a motor. Yes, the motor's life is shortened when continuously on, but even then the expected life of the motor is beyond the reasonable life of a hard disk.

Leaving your computer on all the time heads off thermal shock, which is yet another reason to leave it on. Machines should never be power cycled quickly. I've seen people fry their power supplies by turning their computers on and off several times in a 30-second period "to clear problems" and end up creating bigger problems.

A final word of caution. Leaving the machine on all the time is a good idea only if:

▶ Your machine is cooled adequately. If your machine is 100 degrees inside when the room is 70 degrees, it'll overheat when the room goes to 90 degrees on summer weekends when the building management turns off the cooling in your building. Make sure your machine has a good enough fan to handle higher temperatures.

▶ You have adequate surge protection. Actually, you should not run the machine at all unless you have adequate surge protection.

▶ You have fairly reliable power. If you lose power three times a week, there's no point in leaving the machines on all the time—the power company is turning them off and on for you. Even worse, the power just after a power outage is noise-filled.

Before moving on, let's take a quick peek at some other kinds of power problems.

Transients

A *transient* is any brief change in power that doesn't repeat itself. It can be an undervoltage or an overvoltage. Sags (momentary undervoltage) and surges (momentary overvoltage) are transients. Being brief, the transient may be of a high enough frequency that it slips right past the protective capacitors in your power supply and punches holes in your chips. (No, they're not holes you can see, at least not without some very good equipment.) Transients have a cumulative effect—the first 100 may do nothing. Eventually, however, enough chickens come home to roost that your machine decides, one day, to go on vacation. (You might say that if enough chickens come home to roost, the machine "buys the farm." Permanently.)

Overvoltage

You have an *overvoltage* condition when you get more than the rated voltage for a period of greater than 2.5 seconds. Such a voltage measurement is done as a moving average over several seconds.

Chronic overvoltage is just as bad for your system as transient overvoltage: the chips can fail as a result of it.

Undervoltage

Summer in much of the country means air conditioners are running full blast, and the power company is working feverishly to meet the power demands that they bring. Sometimes it can't meet the full needs, however, so it announces a reduction in voltage called a *brownout*.

Brownouts are bad for large motors, like the ones you'd find in a compressor for refrigeration. Brownouts make your TV screen look shrunken, and they confuse power supplies. A power supply tries to provide continuous power to the PC. Power equals voltage times current. If the voltage drops and you want constant power, what do you do? Simple: draw more current. But drawing more current through a given conductor heats up the conductor. The power supply and the chips get hot and may overheat.

Surge protectors can't help you here. A power conditioner can—it uses a transformer to compensate for the sagging voltage.

Electrostatic Discharge

ESD—or, as you probably know it, *static electricity*—is annoyingly familiar to anyone who has lived through a winter indoors. The air is very dry (winter and forced hot-air ducts bring relative humidity to about 20 percent in my house, for example) and is an excellent insulator. You build up a static charge and keep it (until you touch something like a metal doorknob—or much worse, your computer). On the other hand, in the summer, when relative humidity can be close to 100 percent (until 1998 I lived in a suburb of Washington, D.C., a city built over a swamp), you build up static charges also, but they leak away quickly due to the humidity of the air. Skin resistance also has a lot to do with dissipating charges. The resistance of your skin can be as little as 1,000 ohms when wet and 500,000 ohms when dry. (This fun fact is courtesy of Jearl Walker's *Flying Circus of Physics*, published by John Wiley in 1977.)

You know how static electricity is built up. Static can damage chips if it creates a charge of 200 volts or more. If a static discharge is sufficient for the average person to notice it, it is at least 2,000 volts.

Scuffing across a shag rug in February can build up 50,000 volts. This is an electron "debt" that must be paid. The next metal item you touch (metal gives up electrons easily) pays the debt with an electric shock. If it's 50,000 volts, why doesn't it electrocute you when you touch the metal? Simple, the amperage (which is the volume of electricity) is tiny. This is because even though the voltage is high, the resistance is up in the millions of ohms, and 50,000 volts divided by millions of ohms is a tiny amount of current. (As my physics professor used to tell us, "Twinkle, twinkle, little star; power equals I squared R." And people say physics is dull.) Different materials generate more or less static. Many people think that certain materials are static-prone and that others are not. As it turns out, materials have a triboelectric value. Two materials rubbed together will generate static in direct proportion to how far apart their triboelectric values are.

Some common materials, in order of their triboelectric values, are

- ► Air
- ► Human skin
- ► Asbestos
- ► Rabbit fur
- ► Glass
- ► Human hair
- ► Nylon
- ► Wool
- ► Fur
- ► Lead
- ► Silk
- ► Aluminum
- ► Paper
- ► Cotton

Part ii

- ▶ Steel wool

- ▶ Hard rubber

- ▶ Nickel and copper

- ▶ Brass and silver

- ▶ Gold and platinum

- ▶ Acetate and rayon

- ▶ Polyester

- ▶ Polyurethane

- ▶ Polyvinyl

- ▶ Chloride

- ▶ Silicon

- ▶ Teflon

Once an item is charged, the voltage potential between it and another object is proportional to the distance between it and the other item. For instance, suppose I charge a glass rod with a cotton cloth. The glass will attract things below it on this list, like paper, but will attract more strongly things listed below paper.

Why does static damage PC components? The chips that largely constitute circuit boards are devices that can be damaged by high voltage, even if at low current. The two most common families of chips are CMOS (Complementary Metal Oxide Semiconductor) chips—which include NMOS (Negative Metal Oxide Semiconductor), PMOS (Positive Metal Oxide Semiconductor), and an assortment of newer devices that seem to appear on an almost daily basis—and TTL (Transistor-Transistor Logic) chips. TTLs are an older family. TTLs are faster-switching chips—so potentially faster chips (memories, CPUs, and such) could be designed with TTL. Ah, but TTL has a fatal flaw: it draws a lot of power. TTL chips need much more electricity than CMOS chips, so they create more heat, and so, while fast TTL CPUs could be constructed, CPUs are tough because densely packed TTLs produce so much heat that they would destroy themselves. One common family of TTL chips has ID numbers starting with 74, as in 7400, 7446, 74LS128, and the like. Actually, the LS in the middle of the ID means it is a variant on TTL called Low power Schottky, hence the LS.

CPUs and memories are generally CMOS chips. CMOS has a lower theoretical maximum speed, but it runs on a lot less power. Sadly, they are also more subject to static electricity damage. TTL chips can withstand considerably more static electricity than CMOS chips. By the way, CPUs and memories are all CMOS.

Even if static doesn't destroy a chip, it can shorten its life. Static is, then, something to be avoided if possible. Another effect occurs when the static is discharged. When the fat blue spark jumps from your finger to the door-knob, a small electromagnetic pulse (EMP) is created. This isn't too good for chips either. (It's the thing you've heard about that could cause a single nuclear explosion to destroy every computer in the country, except a lot smaller.) The way I get rid of my static is to discharge the static buildup on something metal that is not the computer's case. A metal desk or table leg is good.

For your business, however, you may want something a trifle more automatic. The options are

- ▶ Raise the humidity with a humidifier (evaporative, not ultra-sonic—ultrasonic creates dust).

- ▶ Raise the humidity with plants or perhaps an aquarium.

- ▶ Install static-free carpet.

- ▶ Put antistatic "touch me" mats under the PCs.

- ▶ Make your own antistatic spray (see below).

From the point of view of comfort, I recommend the first option strongly. Your employees don't feel dried-out, and the static problem disappears. If you raise humidity to just 50 percent, the problem will go away.

You can make inexpensive, homemade antistatic spray. Just get a spray pump bottle and put about an inch of fabric softener in it. Fill it the rest of the way with water, shake it well, and you've got a spray for your carpets to reduce static. Just spritz it on the rug, and the rug will smell nice, and everyone will know that you've been busy. (I hear you asking, "How long does it last?" Don't worry, you'll know.)

In a similar vein, a person from a temporary services agency once told me that they tell their word-processing operators to put a sheet of Bounce under the keyboard to reduce static. Although this may make the area smell nice, it will have no effect on static around the computer.

Technicians who must work with semiconductors all the time use a ground strap to minimize ESD. The idea with a ground strap is that you never create a spark—and therefore EMP—because you've always got a nice ground connection that's draining off your charges. A good ground strap is an elastic wristband with a metal plate built into it to provide a good electrical connection, attached to a wire with an alligator clip. You put the clip on something grounded—the power supply case is the most common place—and put the strap around your wrist. As you're connected to a ground, you continuously drain off your charges. A resistor in the ground strap slows down the discharge process a bit (from a microsecond to a few milliseconds), so you don't end up with one of the dangerous sparks that we've discussed before. If you do a lot of board work in a dry place, ground straps are essential. Several Silicon Valley defense-contracting firms have a policy of firing employees for not wearing their ESD wrist straps when working on high tech equipment such as satellites and military equipment.

When you must handle electronic components, take these precautions:

▶ Get an antistatic strap.

▶ Reduce the amount of static that you transfer to a chip with a ground strap, or remember the high-tech equivalent of knocking wood—touch unpainted metal periodically. One member of my staff has suggested handling chips only while naked on a wooden floor. While this might be entertaining to some of the staff, it would not, unfortunately, prevent static charges from building up, since on a very dry day, even the movement of your hair can build up a charge.

▶ Get an antistatic mat. They're cheap.

▶ Don't handle components in areas having high static potential. For example, avoid carpets unless they are antistatic or in high humidity environments. Don't wear an acrylic sweater when changing chips. Get leather-soled shoes. If your work environment allows it, you can really avoid static by removing your shoes and socks.

▶ Don't handle chips any more than is necessary. If you don't touch them, you won't hurt them.

▶ Use antistatic protective tubes and bags to transport and store chips.

▶ If possible, pick up components by their bodies. Don't touch the pins any more than necessary.

▶ Have I mentioned yet that you should have an antistatic strap and use an antistatic mat?

Use the proper precautions, and your PC won't get a big "charge" out of being touched by you.

AVOIDING WATER AND LIQUIDS

Water is an easy hazard to detect and avoid. You don't need any sophisticated detection devices. Shielding is unnecessary—you just keep the computer away from water.

Water and liquids are introduced into a computer system in one of several ways:

▶ Operator spills

▶ Leaks

▶ Flooding

Spills generally threaten the keyboard. One remedy—the one recommended by every article and book I've ever read on maintenance—is to forbid liquids near the computer. In most shops, this is unrealistic. Some people use clear flexible plastic covers on the keyboard, kind of like what Burger King uses on their cash registers. They've got normal cash registers, but they have a plastic skin over the keys that allows the user to spill "special sauce" all over the keyboard without harming it. Use the plastic covers, and they can just hose down the keyboard. (Just kidding.) With one of these keyboard "skins," you might say that you can "practice safe typing."

SafeSkin is offered by Merritt Computer Products in Dallas. Their address is listed in Appendix A. They offer versions for the various odd keyboards in the PC world.

A similar disaster, flooding, sometimes occurs. Don't assume that flooded components are destroyed components. Disassemble the computer, and clean the boards by cleaning the contacts and edge connectors. You can buy connector cleaner fluids, or some people use a hard white artist's eraser—do not use pencil erasers! (A Texas Instruments study showed that they contain acids that do more harm than good to connectors.) Blow out crevices with compressed air. (And if you do disassemble, clean, dry, and reassemble your computer, and then find that it works, write the manufacturer a letter; they might put your face in an advertisement.)

Avoid floods by thinking ahead. Don't store any electrical devices directly on the floor; they'll be damaged when the floor is cleaned. Generally, flooding indoors is under six inches. Be aware of flooding from improper roofing; when installing PCs, don't put one in directly under the suspicious stain on the ceiling. ("Oh, that—it was fixed two years ago. No problem now.")

Corrosion

Liquids (and gases) can accelerate corrosion of PCs and PC components. Corrosive agents include:

▶ Salt sweat in skin oils

▶ Water

▶ Airborne sulfuric acid, salt spray, and carbonic acid

Your fear here is not that the PC will fall away to rust; the largest problem that corrosion causes is oxidation of circuit contacts. When a device's connector becomes oxidized, it doesn't conduct as well, and so the device does not function or—worse—malfunctions sporadically. Salt in sweat can do this, so be careful when handling circuit boards; don't touch edge connectors unless you have to. This is why some firms advertise that they use gold edge connectors; gold is resistant to corrosion.

You don't believe that you have detectable traces of finger oils? Try this simple experiment. Pour a glass of soda or beer into a very clean glass—preferably a plastic cup that has never been used before. There will be a noticeable "head" on the drink. (Diet soda seems particularly fizzy.) Now put your finger into the center of the head, just for a second. The head will rapidly dissolve, because the oils damage the surface tension required to support the head. It's the quickest way to eliminate a large head so you can pour a larger glass of beer. Or you could try buying a nice new 20-inch color computer monitor and see how many of your colleagues fail to understand that it is not a touch-screen device. You will end up with numerous thick, oily smudge marks on your monitor that are very visible and annoying when a dark background is displayed on it.

Carbonated liquids include carbonic acid, and coffee and tea contain tannic acids. The sugar in soda is eaten by bacteria that leave behind conductive excrement—like hiring some germs to put new traces on your circuit board. Generally, try to be very careful with drinks around computers.

Don't forget cleaning fluids. Be careful with that window cleaner that you're using to keep the display clean. If your PC is on a pedestal on the floor, and the floor is mopped each day, some of the mopping liquid gets into the PC. Cleaning fluids are very corrosive.

You can clean edge connectors with either hard white erasers (remember, don't use the pink erasers—they're acidic!) or connector cleaner products.

MAKING THE ENVIRONMENT "PC FRIENDLY"

Let's sum up what we've seen in this chapter. Protect your PC by doing the following:

- ▶ Check power considerations:
    - ▶ No heating elements (Mr. Coffee, portable heaters) in the same outlet as a PC
    - ▶ No large electric motors (refrigerators, air conditioners) on the same line as the PC
    - ▶ Some kind of power noise protection
- ▶ Check temperature ranges:
    - ▶ Maximum 110 degrees F (43 degrees C)
    - ▶ Minimum 65 degrees F (18 degrees C)

The minimum temperature can actually be considerably lower, as long as the computer remains *on* all the time.

- ▶ Prevent dust buildup—you can buy (from PC Power and Cooling) power supplies with a filtered fan that suck air in through the *back* rather than the usual approach of pulling it in through the front.
- ▶ Make sure there isn't a vibration source like an impact printer on the same table as the hard disk.
- ▶ Make sure you're familiar with or (if you're a support person) teach your users about:
    - ▶ Leaving the machines on all the time
    - ▶ Keeping cables screwed in and out of the way
    - ▶ Basic "don't do this" things in DOS, like formatting the hard disk
- ▶ Protect against static electricity.

WHAT'S NEXT?

Now that Mark Minasi has shown you how to protect your computer hardware against the most common environmental hazards, in the next chapter Ben Ezzell teaches you how to install memory in your computer and how to determine how much memory is required to best suit your needs.

Part ii

Chapter 11

INSTALLING MEMORY (RAM)

by Ben Ezzell

Random Access Memory, or RAM for short, is part of the engine that runs your computer. Although advertisements and sales pitches place a large emphasis on CPU speed, touting the clock speed of the central processing unit in the same manner that car dealers wax rapturous about raw horsepower, the amount of RAM in your computer is often more important than the processor type and clock speed.

The amount of RAM in your computer is something like the road on which you drive your car. A larger engine may allow your car to go faster, but if the only road you're permitted to drive on is your driveway, you can't go very fast—a driveway just doesn't give you any room to build up speed. In the case of your computer, a faster or more advanced CPU may do things faster—but without memory, your "engine" is limited in its performance by a lack of space in which to run.

In brief, both your CPU and your available memory determine how well your computer is going to work and how fast it will work. Of the two, a slow CPU with sufficient memory will generally outperform a fast CPU with limited memory.

One advantage of this relationship between CPU and memory is that you can add memory to your computer quickly, simply, and (nowadays) without much cost. In fact, adding more memory is not only the least expensive upgrade you can make, it's also the most important in terms of performance.

How Much Memory Is Enough?

In the "good old days"—back when DOS was the standard operating system—the amount of memory in your computer was less critical. And, in the very early days, when PCs were first being introduced, computers were commonly sold with a grandiose 16KB (that's kilobytes, not megabytes) of memory and with the capability of upgrading to a whopping total of 48 or, sometimes, 56KB or 64KB. At the time, memory was expensive—very expensive.

As PCs began to be popular and MS-DOS took its place as the pre-eminent operating system in the market, an arbitrary and badly chosen upper limit for memory was set at 640KB, with the addresses above the 640KB limit reserved for the system video and for other system processes.

Very early on, a mere 640KB proved to be very constricting. Applications running under DOS simply could not—that is, were not permitted to—reach memory addresses above the 640KB limit. The arbitrary limit was enforced by the structure of DOS itself as well as by the address structures permitted for applications executing under DOS.

NOTE

The 640KB limitation was set by a young computer entrepreneur who was quite satisfied that 640KB of memory were more than adequate to satisfy anyone's requirements. Of course, the entrepreneur in question was one Bill Gates, and the segment:offset addressing schema that resulted remained an industry bottleneck for years, even as prices for RAM chips dropped and memory requirements rose, both quite sharply.

To address the unfortunate limitations built into DOS, two methods of accessing and using memory beyond the 640KB limit were developed:

▶ XMS (Extended Memory Specification)

▶ EMS (Enhanced Memory Specification)

These methods were supported by a variety of utilities to allow applications to have access to physical memory above the 1MB address point.

Today DOS is simply a historic relic—to the regret of very few, if any, computer users—and virtually all users have moved to more advanced operating systems, with the Windows operating systems dominating the market. At the same time, even the most basic computer sold today is provided with a minimum of 16MB of RAM memory—approximately 1,000 times as much as was supplied with the earliest PCs.

Although Microsoft has made varying claims about the minimum amount of memory that various versions of its operating systems need in order to function correctly, the minimums stated have always been just that: bare minimums with which a specific version of Windows will—however poorly—function. To be more specific, the accepted definition of "minimum configuration" for a graphical operating system (such as Windows) is the smallest amount of memory that will allow the operating system to handle all the system's advanced graphical tasks and to run one or two typical applications at the same time without performance suffering badly.

With Windows 3.x, for example, the minimum requirement was 4MB of RAM, which was a major jump from the 640KB expected under DOS. As I said, however, this 4MB requirement was a minimum; by adding another 4MB to bring the system up to 8MB, performance was greatly enhanced.

Windows 3.x was not an operating system in the true sense; it ran on top of DOS and was subject to the limitations imposed by DOS, including the limitation that it did not have true access to memory beyond 640KB. To get around the 640KB limitation, Windows 3.x could be enhanced by

Part ii

the appropriate installation of EMS/XMS memory drivers, such as Quarterdeck's QEMM (Quarterdeck Extended Memory Manager).

The first operating system that really could address memory directly without using block-swapping memory drivers was OS/2 (way back in 1989 and thus predating Windows 3, which originally came out in 1990). It did not operate on top of DOS and was not subject to the same memory limitations.

NOTE

Despite the fact that OS/2 was originally a joint project between Microsoft and IBM, the popularity of the operating system was limited because it required more memory (at a time when memory was expensive) as well as more-advanced CPUs than average users felt they could afford.

In the Microsoft world, it was not until the introduction of Windows NT Workstation (version 3.1, released in 1992) that the 640KB limit was finally left behind. Windows NT Workstation was a true operating system: it did not require DOS. It did, however, need more memory than was required by Windows 3.0; like Windows 3.1, Windows NT Workstation also benefited from more powerful (faster) CPUs.

Windows NT expected a minimum of 16MB of RAM but benefited from larger amounts. Because both memory and advanced CPUs were still relatively expensive, Windows NT Workstation did not become popular with the average user and, instead, was adopted primarily in corporate and research environments where cost was less important than speed and power.

For the average user, then, the 640KB barrier—however it may have been masked by Windows 3.x—did not vanish until the introduction of Windows 95. Even though Windows 95 (appearing, of course, in 1995) still contained 16-bit code for backward compatibility to run DOS and Windows 3.x applications, it was a true operating system and was thus independent of the structural limitations of DOS.

Windows 95 was billed as requiring a minimum of 8MB of RAM. (Actually, Microsoft claimed that Windows 95 *could* run in 4MB of RAM, a fact that was proved by several demos, but they didn't recommend it. For one thing, on 4MB it "ran" in the same sense that a tortoise "runs.")

Windows 95 was introduced at a time when memory chips were relatively inexpensive (compared with when Windows 3.x was first available), so installing 8MB in a computer was not a financial strain, and at the time, units were commonly being sold with 16MB standard. For advanced users—particularly those working with video or with large amounts of complex data—upgrades to 32MB were more than helpful, providing significant improvements in performance.

With the introduction of Windows 98, the bar was raised again, with a minimum requirement of 16MB. As usual, a more realistic configuration would have 32MB; advanced users with complex requirements may well want to install 64 or 128MB—or even more.

NOTE

Claims have been made for running Windows 98 under 12MB of RAM, but given today's prices and SIMM (single inline memory module) configurations, you may as well stick with a minimum of 16MB.

Windows 98 SE was the newest Windows operating system before the introduction of Windows 2000 Professional in the spring of 2000. As you can see in Table 11.1, Windows 98 SE requires a minimum of 24MB of RAM. I can tell you from personal experience that 24MB is no way near enough. I'm running Windows 98 SE on two computers; one has 48MB of RAM, and the other has 64MB. There's no contest—64MB is much to be preferred.

On the machine that has 64MB, I dual-boot Windows 98 SE and Windows 2000 Professional. As you can see in Table 11.1, 64MB is the minimum amount of RAM that Microsoft recommends. In this case, the minimum gives you a workable system, but 128MB would be much, much better. The bottom line is that you want as much memory as your computer can handle and as you can afford.

TABLE 11.1: Operating System Memory Requirements

OPERATING SYSTEM	MINIMUM	REALISTIC	ADVANCED USERS
Windows 3.x	4MB	8MB	n/a
Windows 95	8MB	16MB	32MB
Windows 98	16MB	32MB	64/128MB
Windows 98 SE	24MB	48MB	64/128MB
Windows NT 4 Workstation	16MB	64MB	128/256MB
Windows 2000 Professional	64MB	128MB	192/256MB

Windows Swap Files

Windows uses a mechanism called a *Windows swap file* to extend the amount of RAM available for executed applications. A swap file is a file on the hard drive that is managed as if it were an extension of the system RAM, and the operating system uses it to store data that is not immediately required.

NOTE

OS/2, Linux, and other operating systems also use swap files in a similar fashion and for the same reasons.

When Windows needs more memory than is physically available, such as for spooling a large print job or for many other purposes, Windows *swaps* some part of the data from active RAM to the swap file, freeing RAM for more important uses. This is a background process that is happening all the time you are working; it doesn't require your attention or any special provisions by the applications being executed.

In effect, even if a computer has only 16MB of RAM, Windows can still attempt to use much more memory by treating a part of the hard drive as a special-purpose file that functions like (emulates) a larger block of RAM.

The downside of using a swap file is simple: transferring and retrieving data from this "virtual" memory—that is, the swap file on the hard drive—is labor intensive, and it is slower than accessing data that is located in physical RAM (active memory). Windows optimizes this process by swapping elements out of memory on the basis of use—that is, sending less recently used material to the swap file in preference to frequently or recently used data.

The big advantage of having a large amount of RAM (active memory) is that Windows will only resort to the swap file when the active memory is filled (or is about to be filled).

RAM versus Hard Drives

Partially because the hard drive (swap file) is used as an extension of RAM memory, users sometimes become confused about the difference between RAM and disk memory. Although a large hard drive allows you to store a great many applications and data files, the size of the hard drive has nothing to do with system performance (other than giving you some place in which to create your swap file) and is not a replacement for RAM.

How Much Memory Is Installed?

Before you run out and buy more memory for your computer, take this simple first step: find out how much memory you have installed already.

Although there is no "memory gauge" on the front of your computer, a memory test is performed every time you power up (that is, boot or reboot) your computer. The memory test is commonly identified by the BIOS (basic input/output system)—not by the operating system—as part of the POST (power-on self test)—and its report may look something like this:

```
Memory Test: 65536K OK
```

NOTE

The BIOS is a set of instructions stored in ROM that runs tests of various kinds when you first turn on the computer.

This particular reading is rather easy to miss because, commonly, it goes by so fast that you don't really have time to see it unless you are looking for it. The length of time the report appears on screen depends on the BIOS settings and the CPU speed.

You can, however, check your system to determine the amount of memory installed in several other ways. The easiest way is to right-click My Computer on the Desktop, which opens the System Properties dialog box at the General tab. As shown in Figure 11.1, the General tab displays the amount of installed RAM at the bottom of the screen.

You can also get information about installed RAM from the MS-DOS Prompt window. In Windows 98 SE, follow these steps:

1. Choose Start ➤ Programs ➤ MS-DOS Prompt to open the MS-DOS Prompt window.

2. At the prompt, type **mem.**

You'll see something similar to the screen shown in Figure 11.2.

As you can see, the Mem utility is reporting memory as though the old DOS 640KB limits were still relevant and reports the bulk of the memory available as XMS memory (see the Total column), while the real total is the sum of the Conventional, Reserved, and XMS memory.

NOTE

Under Windows 95/98/98 SE/NT, the distinctions between Conventional, Reserved, and XMS memory really no longer exist or apply.

Part ii

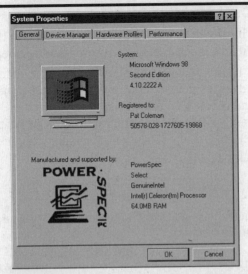

FIGURE 11.1: Open the System Properties dialog box to find out how much RAM is installed in your computer.

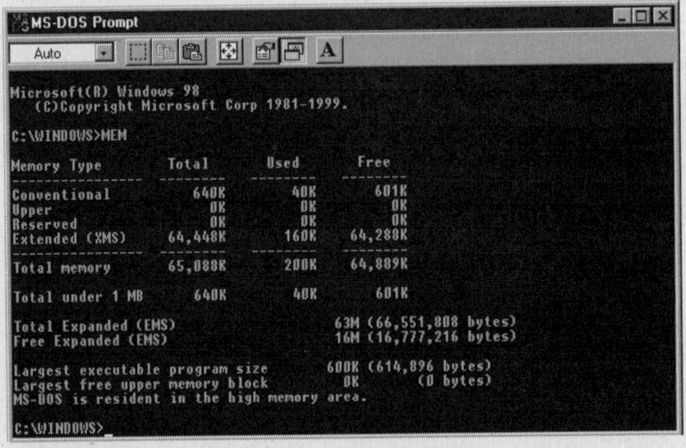

FIGURE 11.2: Using the DOS Mem utility

Yet another way to check system memory is to open the Systems Properties dialog box and click the Performance tab, as shown in Figure 11.3. Here the system memory is reported as 64.0MB of RAM, without any obsolete references to Conventional, Reserved, or XMS memory settings.

From the Performance tab, you can also check to see how virtual memory (the swap file) is being managed and change these settings if you want. Click the Virtual Memory button to open the Virtual Memory dialog box, which is shown in Figure 11.4.

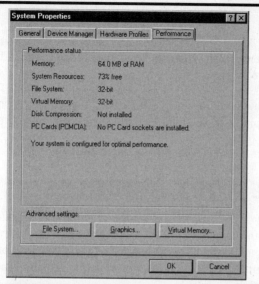

FIGURE 11.3: Using the Performance tab to check system memory

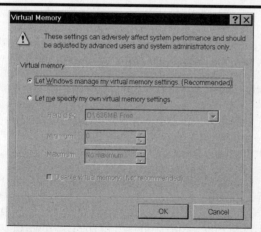

FIGURE 11.4: Virtual memory settings

With rare exceptions, the optimum choice for managing virtual memory is to allow Windows to handle virtual memory. If necessary, however, you can specify which physical or logical drive to use for the swap file, and you can specify a minimum and a maximum size for the swap file. In addition, you can disable virtual memory entirely.

WARNING

Disabling virtual memory is not recommended, because selecting this option will have adverse effects on system performance and may even cause the system to hang or crash.

Once you know how much memory is installed in your system and have decided to add memory, the next step is to determine what type of memory your system uses.

TYPES OF MEMORY MODULES

Simply walking into your neighborhood computer store or office supply store (or contacting an Internet supplier) and buying more memory is not appropriate. Before buying memory, you need to know what kind of memory chips your computer uses and you also need to decide what kind of memory to upgrade with.

TIP

If you are using a portable or laptop computer, your options may be further limited by which memory upgrades the computer will accept and even whether there is space in the portable to add more memory. For portable or laptop computers, you should contact the manufacturer or consult a reliable computer shop/technician.

Computer memory comes in a variety of configurations, as described by such factors as packaging, speed, and type.

Memory Packaging

In the early days of PCs, memory was purchased as "DIP chips." DIP was shorthand for Dual-Inline Pins, which referred to the two rows of pins that protruded from opposite sides of the chip package and bent down to plug into a DIP socket.

Today, instead of installing individual chips, you add to the main memory in most computers by installing *package* chips; more than one chip is mounted on a SIMM or DIMM (dual inline memory module). I'll discuss how you identify the type of package you have or need later in this section.

Packaging details are only one consideration, however.

Memory Speed

A second consideration is speed. There are actually two considerations here. First, memory speed is not the same as the CPU speed. For one thing, it is measured in *nanoseconds* (abbreviated *ns*), and the smaller the number, the faster the memory—for example, a 50ns chip is faster than a 70ns chip. Compare that with the speeds you typically see for CPUs; in this case, the higher the number, the faster the processor: 300MHz (megahertz) is definitely faster than 166MHz.

NOTE

The numeric readout on the front of many computers is indicating the CPU speed, not the memory speed. (Actually, the speed indicated may or may not bear any relationship to the actual CPU speed.)

The second consideration when it comes to memory speed is whether you plan to mix speeds. On the one hand, slower memory chips can be installed as additions to faster chips in a computer, but your computer will then treat *all* of your memory as though it were *all* rated at the slower speed. On the other hand, you should avoid installing chips that are faster than the computer is rated to use (the computer motherboard, that is).

NOTE

The motherboard is sometimes referred to as the mainboard.

To determine the memory speed supported by the computer, refer to the documentation for your computer. Specifically, refer to the documentation for the computer's motherboard, which should tell you what type of memory is required, what packaging (module type) is used, and what memory speed is supported.

Memory Blocks

Computer memory is installed in blocks. Normally, the computer motherboard will have four sockets for memory packages. Commonly two of these will be used when the computer is manufactured, leaving two slots (sockets) open for memory expansion.

Therefore, if you want to add 16MB of memory to the existing memory, you would want to buy two 8MB modules, installing one in each of the two open sockets.

If there are no open sockets for memory, you may need to remove existing modules and replace them with larger capacity modules. Your computer motherboard documentation should also tell you whether you must replace/upgrade memory modules in pairs only or whether single memory modules can be installed.

Memory Types

Two principal types of RAM are in use: DRAM (dynamic RAM) and SRAM (static RAM), but these exist in a number of variations, each with different characteristics.

DRAM Dynamic Random Access Memory is both the most common and the cheapest type of memory chip, but it is also the slowest. DRAM consists of capacitors that store individual bits (1s and 0s) of data. The capacitors hold a charge only for a brief period—milliseconds, actually—and must be continually refreshed to maintain the data; hence, these are termed dynamic RAM. DRAM chips constitute the bulk of the memory used in computers and are found in both low-cost SIMMs and DIMMs.

SRAM Static Random Access Memory chips consist of banks of transistors that do not need to be refreshed and are roughly four times faster than DRAM memory. In general, SRAM chips are also larger than other types of memory and are commonly used only in some of the more specialized memory requirements in a computer, such as pipelined burst or synchronous cache memory where speed is at a premium.

EDO RAM Extended Data Out Random Access Memory is the fastest memory because EDO RAM can read and write data from different locations at the same time. EDO RAM is faster than DRAM, speeding memory performance by as much as 40 percent, but is effective only up to bus speeds of 66MHz; today's CPUs commonly operate at much higher speeds.

FP Mode DRAM Fast Page-Mode DRAM is similar to EDO RAM but uses a different access mode, with random page access speeds of less than 30MHz—much slower than the bus speed. To compensate for this discrepancy, DRAM manufacturers use a RAM cache as a bridge between slow memory and faster CPUs.

SDRAM   Synchronous Dynamic RAM (also called PC-100 RAM) is faster than EDO RAM; it handles bus speeds up to 100MHz, but it's also more expensive. SDRAM is synchronized with the system clock; that is, it runs at the CPU's speed.

Sync SRAM   Synchronous burst SRAM, like SDRAM, is also synchronized with the system clock, making it faster than the Async SRAM commonly used in L2 caches.

PB SRAM   Pipeline Burst SRAM uses pipelining to collect data requests, which are executed as a burst on a nearly instantaneous basis. PB SRAM is designed to work at bus speeds higher than 75MHz; it is a major component in Pentium systems.

ECCDRAM   Error Correcting Circuit DRAM; not in wide usage.

VRAM   Video Random Access Memory is used on video cards. VRAM is similar to DRAM but has two ports to increase access speeds. One port is used to read VRAM contents to constantly update the display, and the second port is used to write changes to the display data. The combination significantly increases video performance, as well as reducing the load on the CPU. Adding additional video memory allows your computer to support higher screen resolutions and higher color resolutions and improves system performance by making it easier (faster) to create images on the screen.

When upgrading system RAM, you *must* use the same type of memory modules. For example, if your computer uses DRAM modules, you can only add additional DRAM modules; you cannot change to EDO RAM or SRAM. The reason is simple: the circuits on the motherboard do not support other types of memory and may be damaged or may fail to operate if you try to force the issue.

In some cases, particularly with newer motherboards, more than one type of memory may be supported, and sockets may be provided for different types of modules. Always refer to the documentation for your computer motherboard to determine which module types are supported. (Actually, these types of boards are rare and are typically provided for specialty purposes only. You will find few vendors willing to deal in these types of boards and few people who will need them.)

NOTE

Chips known as Parity RAM chips included an extra bit for every byte (eight bits) of memory; the extra bit was used to verify the data during use. Although parity memory was common in early computers, RAM has been greatly improved since the first computers, and the parity bit is no longer required. Parity RAM is now difficult to find and is not necessary for contemporary machines.

SIMM and DIMM Memory Sockets

Although DIP chips are still manufactured, most of us are not expected to work with them individually. They are awkward to install and even harder to remove without inflicting damage; they also occupy unacceptable amounts of valuable board space. Today, instead of expecting users and administrators to install chips individually, the chipmakers install (package) the DIPs in modules that are small strips of phenolytic board (circuit board) with etched traces leading to contacts along the side. The person installing the memory merely has to hold the board along the edges that don't have the contacts (in other words, please don't touch the contacts), and slip it into the memory socket in such a way as to align the board's connectors with the socket's connectors. Typical individual modules may include anywhere from three to nine DIP chips.

SIMM Modules

Single { } in line memory module
Double { }

The first modular memory package introduced was the SIMM, which held a single row of chips soldered to one side of a narrow circuit board with contacts on one edge that is inserted in a socket. SIMMs may also come with chips installed on both sides, and they come in three varieties: 30-pin, 72-pin, and 168-pin designs.

The 30-pin SIMMs are commonly found on older computers, and the 72-pin SIMMs are used with newer motherboards. The 168-pin design is usually reserved for the newer DIMM design (described in the next section).

To install a SIMM module (see Figure 11.5), hold it at an angle (approximately 45 degrees), and slip it into the socket. One end of the SIMM has a hole matching a pin in the socket holder, a notch in one end of the board at the end of the row of contacts, and an offset notch near the center (see Figure 11.6). The SIMM can be installed in only one way, and the hole and notches are designed to ensure that the module is installed correctly.

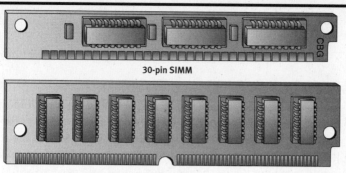

30-pin SIMM

72-pin SIMM

FIGURE 11.5: Single and double-sided SIMMs

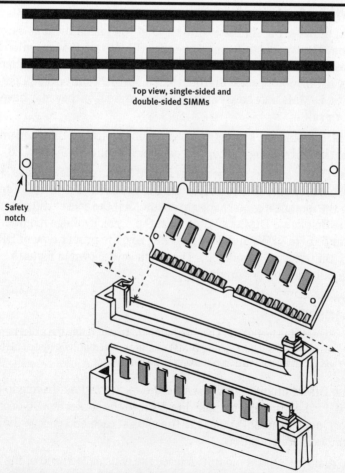

Top view, single-sided and
double-sided SIMMs

Safety
notch

FIGURE 11.6: Installing a SIMM module

WARNING

Never *force* a SIMM into the socket!

The SIMM module should seat in the socket without force. Once the module is seated at an angle, hold the module down in the socket, and tilt it back until the clips at each end of the socket snap into position.

To remove a SIMM module, release the clips at each end of the socket—by pulling both of them gently outward, away from the module—allowing the module to tilt out. Once the module is tilted, you can easily lift it free from the socket.

DIMM Modules

DIMM modules are similar to SIMMs, and you install them in the same fashion. The two big differences are that DIMMs are thicker, with chips stacked to provide more memory per module; and that DIMMs commonly use a 168-pin socket rather than a 30- or 72-pin socket. Like SIMMs, DIMMs may have chips on only one side, or they may have them on both sides.

All DIMM modules have two notches, one near the center and one near one of the ends, along the contact edge (see Figures 11.7 and 11.8).

The DIMM sockets on the motherboard have a couple of "keys" (precisely positioned nubs) corresponding to precisely positioned notches along the module's contact edge to ensure that the socket will only accept, for the first key, a DIMM module with the correct voltage requirements (either 5.0V or 3.3V) and, for the other key, the proper type of DRAM (RFU, Buffered, or Unbuffered). The notch keys shown in Figure 11.8 are for an unbuffered 3.3V module.

NOTE

Refer to the manual for your motherboard to determine the exact parameters required before purchasing DIMM modules. Attempting a match merely from visual characteristics is not likely to be correct.

The DIMM module should seat in the socket without having to be forced, by inserting the module directly into the socket at a 90-degree angle. Once the module is seated, the clips at each end engage the module and hold it in position.

To remove a DIMM module, release the clips at each end of the socket by pulling both of them gently outward, away from the module.

WARNING

Although many motherboards manufactured before 1997 provide sockets for both SIMMs and DIMMs, different voltages are required for each type; thus, mixed usage is *not* supported.

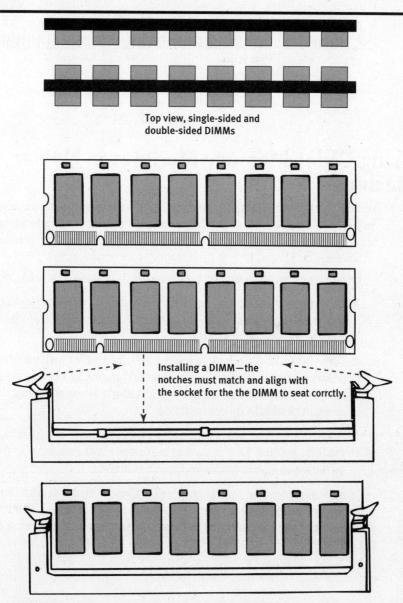

Top view, single-sided and double-sided DIMMs

Installing a DIMM—the notches must match and align with the socket for the the DIMM to seat corrctly.

FIGURE 11.7: Dual inline memory modules (DIMM)

Part ii

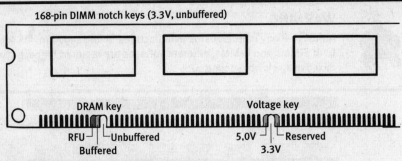

FIGURE 11.8: 168-pin DIMM notch keys

Using Older Memory Modules in Newer Machines

You can install older memory modules such as 30-pin SIMMs in newer motherboards that have only 72-pin sockets by using a module adapter. Module adapters are inexpensive and provide four or eight 30-pin sockets on an extended board with a 72-pin connector on the side.

Before using an adapter, however, you need to consider the following:

▶ Memory is cheap today, and it may actually be more practical to buy new memory using 72-pin SIMM or 168-pin DIMM modules than to reuse older memory.

▶ Some 30-to-72-pin adapters may physically conflict with installed conventional modules. Some adapters are made extra wide in order to position the adapter sockets above the area where the conventional SIMMs are installed.

▶ Some companies will accept older 30-pin memory modules as a trade-in against 72-pin packages, or they will remount 30-pin packages as 72-pin packages for a nominal fee.

In any case, consider the economics first before deciding whether to replace or reuse existing memory, but also plan ahead. Think about what your memory requirements are today and what they might be six months in the future.

Planning Memory Requirements

Although memory is probably the cheapest and most effective computer upgrade, the slots where memory can be installed on your motherboard are limited. Because of this, simply adding memory today and then having to replace it in a few months because you need more memory can be expensive. For this reason, it pays to think about what your future memory requirements will be and how you might upgrade for the future.

Table 11.2 summarizes the memory demands for a variety of common applications and activities being performed on one of today's PCs running Windows 95, 98, or 98 SE.

TABLE 11.2: RAM Requirements for Optimal Operation on a Typical Windows 95/98/98 SE Machine

APPLICATIONS AND USE	MIN	MAX
Light use of word processing, e-mail, database. Not more than one or two applications open at a time.	16MB	24MB
Medium use of word processing, e-mail, fax, communications, spreadsheets, business graphics, database. Not more than one or two applications open at a time.	24MB	32MB
Number crunching with spreadsheets, accounting software. Not more than one or two applications open at a time.	32MB	48MB
Heavy number crunching, spreadsheets, statistical applications, large databases. Commonly three or more applications open at a time.	48MB	64MB
Page layout, light illustration/ graphics; also application development using most compilers. Commonly not more than one or two applications open at a time.	64MB	96MB
Medium illustration/graphics, including photo editing, extensive presentation software, font packages, multimedia. Commonly three or more applications open at one time.	96MB	128MB
Power users, heavy graphics editing, developers with complex compiler packages. Commonly with multiple applications open at any time.	128MB	256MB

The requirements in Table 11.2 are optimums, not minimums, for the different types of usage, and virtually all the categories of applications will run using less memory than specified.

Part ii

Sources

Where you buy memory and where you get the best price is always an open question. Once you know the type and size of modules needed, a variety of Internet search services can provide you with sources, and you can compare prices.

What you should be considering, however, is the reliability of the source. Paying a dollar or two more to a reliable dealer can save you a whole lot of dollars later. Sometimes memory goes bad. Sometimes you may be wrong about what kind you needed. Sometimes a mistake can be made by the supplier. Dealing with someone you know—and someone who can guarantee quality—is the real economy.

Also, most reputable dealers will have a means for testing memory modules, so ask for the modules to be tested before leaving the store. This in itself can save headaches.

INSTALLATION

Installing RAM is probably the easiest upgrade you can perform on your computer. Installing memory can take 10 minutes or less and can make even a slow computer perform much better.

> **NOTE**
> RAM memory is the highway your computer CPU runs on!

The more memory in your computer, the less time the system needs to spend swapping data into and out of the Windows swap file, and the faster the CPU can work.

In actual fact, it will probably take you longer to learn the terminology and to research what type of memory your computer uses than it will to actually install the memory.

Static Electricity—IMPORTANT!

Before you touch anything inside the computer and before handling parts for installation, you should make absolutely sure that you have discharged your static electricity. If you do not, even a small static charge—one that you do not even notice—can permanently damage computer components.

WARNING

Always unplug your computer before installing any components. Although voltages inside the computer are too low to harm you (or to even notice), they are plenty strong enough to damage the tiny electronic components! Never install or remove components while the computer is powered up or plugged in!

A static charge can be produced by a variety of circumstances: walking across a carpeted floor, sliding across a fabric seat cushion, wearing the kind of fabric that generates static charges easily merely from the act of walking (as your trouser legs brush against each other), touching the TV, and so on. All these and others can cause static buildup, especially in a dry environment.

Guarding against static is simple: after sitting down but before you reach for those memory chips or the card you're about to install, reach out and ground yourself by opening the computer case and touching the metal frame inside the computer. Do this before you touch any component inside or outside the computer.

Alternatively, you can buy a grounding strap at any electronic supply store or Radio Shack. The strap attaches by one end to your wrist, usually with a Velcro strap. A coiled wire attached to the strap has a clip on the other end. Once the clip is attached to the chassis of the computer, you are grounded, and any static charge is equalized.

NOTE

Grounding is not required during normal usage. Only while working with electronic components.

Opening the Computer

Obviously, the first step to adding memory to your computer is opening the computer. You've probably done this before, as you needed to open the computer simply to determine what type of module is required and how much space—that is, what open slots—you have available.

The procedure in this section is for desktop computers made by what we used to call "clone" manufacturers, who all followed more or less standard equipment designs. If you have a portable or laptop computer, the designs vary tremendously, and the following instructions may only apply in part.

Part ii

NOTE

If you are upgrading a portable or laptop computer, you *must* refer to the manual for the laptop for instructions. The locations, types, and methods of access vary greatly from one brand to another and from one model to another. If you are in doubt, consult a qualified computer technician for assistance.

Before doing anything, close all open programs, shut down your computer, and then turn off the computer.

Next (and this is where the portable/laptop instructions probably begin to differ from the instructions for a desktop machine), slide the computer out and disconnect the cables from the back. Pay attention to which cables are connected where, and if you are not familiar with the cabling, make notes or draw yourself a diagram. This can save you a lot of trouble later.

And be sure to unplug the power cord from the computer. This will ensure that the computer is not left powered on and that it is not accidentally powered up during installation or examination.

WARNING

Having the power on while removing or installing modules or cards can result in serious damage both to the items being installed or removed and to the computer as a whole!

Now you are ready to open the case. Some computers allow the case to be removed or opened by simply pinching a tab, lifting a lever, or turning one or two knurl nuts, but most require removing anywhere from two to six screws.

If you must remove screws, these are commonly Phillips screws or may also have hex heads. Do not remove any screws holding the power supply (near the computer's fan and electrical power connector) or ports, all of which are found on the rear of the machine. The screws holding the case in place are along the sides and are visibly anchoring the metal shell to the rear of the frame. (See Figure 11.9.)

Once the screws have been removed, you should be able to remove the outer case by sliding it back (or forward in some cases). In many cases, it may be necessary to lift the back of the case to disengage a lip that interlocks with the front and side panels.

Again, before touching anything inside, ground yourself to the metal frame to discharge any static electricity.

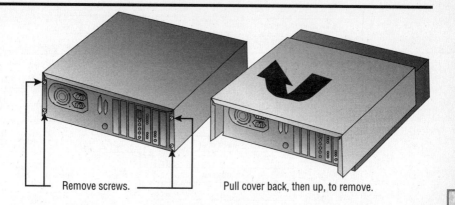

Remove screws.   Pull cover back, then up, to remove.

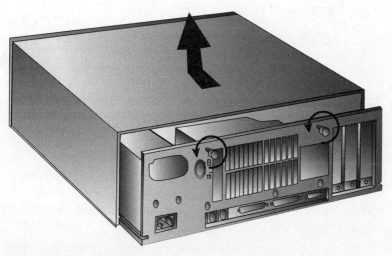

FIGURE 11.9: Removing the computer case

Locating the Memory Sockets

The RAM memory modules and sockets can be located in several places inside the computer. The manual for your computer's motherboard should have a diagram showing the placement and location of the sockets and other principle components (see Figure 11.10). Even without the diagram, however, these sockets are usually easily identified.

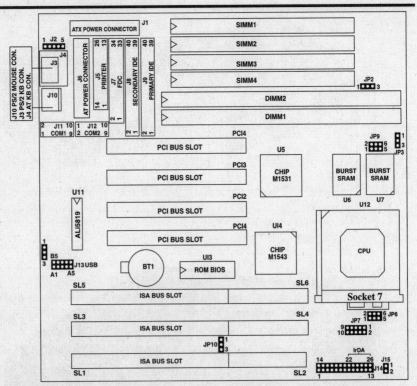

FIGURE 11.10: A typical motherboard layout diagram

Looking at the motherboard from the front, the SIMM sockets are usually on the far right of the board and may be located to the rear or farther forward toward the front. Also, some manufacturers place the SIMM sockets at the front left of the motherboard.

If both SIMM and DIMM sockets are provided, they are normally next to each other with a bank of four SIMM sockets and two DIMM sockets.

In some cases, particularly for SIMMs at the right rear, cables may be covering the area, making access difficult. Therefore, it may be necessary to unplug one or more cables before adding or removing memory modules. Read through the following subsections to see if any of these apply to your situation.

NOTE

Once you determine which type of socket your computer uses (30- or 72-pin SIMM, or 168-pin DIMM) and whether you have free sockets in which to install additional memory, and once you have cleared the access to the memory sockets, you can proceed to the sections "Is Space Available?" and "Adding New Memory," later in this chapter.

TIP

The instructions in this and the following sections are very detailed in order to cover a variety of situations and configurations found on different motherboards. These are not intended to scare you or to dissuade you from installing memory upgrades, only to provide a full and complete description of the various problems that you might encounter and how to handle them without damaging your computer.

Dismounting the Power Supply

Although it is a rare situation, in some configurations you may have to remove the power supply—the large rectangular box mounted at the top or right rear of the chassis—to gain access to the SIMM sockets.

The power supply commonly has a large number of wire bundles— most are colored white, red, yellow, orange, blue, and black—with a larger black electrical cord leading to the power switch on the front of the case.

You can dismount the power supply by removing four screws on the rear and swinging the power supply box out of the way, commonly without needing to disconnect any power leads from the motherboard or from other units within the case.

If you do need—in extreme cases—to remove power connections, you may be faced with two different types of power connectors: the AT connector or the ATX connector.

NOTE

Some newer motherboards—such as the one illustrated—may have both the AT and ATX connectors present but will use only the one set matching the enclosure's power supply.

The AT Power Connector   The AT power connector is the most common and is found on all older motherboards. It consists of two plugs usually at the rear of the motherboard. The two side-by-side plugs constituting the AT power connector can be pulled straight up—*gently*—until they catch. The plugs are then tilted—again, *gently*—about 45 degrees to disengage the keys (protruding plastic tabs) along one side from the locking strip.

Notice the two black wires, one on each plug, in the center. When the AT power connector is reinstalled, you must place the plugs with the black wire to the center and the keys against the arresting strip. Tilt the plug at a 45-degree angle to engage the keys with the arresting strip, bring the plug back to the upright position, and—*without force*—slide the plug down over the pins, as shown in Figure 11.11.

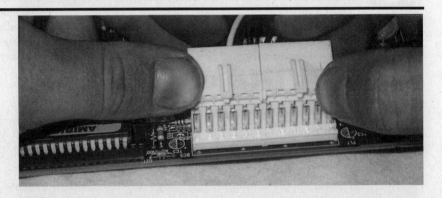

FIGURE 11.11: AT power connectors

Each AT connector has five wires and connects to five pins. Be sure that the connectors are not misaligned and that they are correctly in place with the two black wires side by side in the center. Do not apply power until you have checked all plugs and connections.

WARNING

Never force any connector of any kind to fit into a socket! Connectors in computers are "keyed" by shape or by type so that they can only be installed easily one way. Forcing a connector into a socket usually means that the connector is not aligned correctly or is not the correct connector for that socket. *Forcing incorrect connections can and will seriously damage your computer.*

The ATX Power Connector   The ATX power connector is for the newest ATX enclosures and is used primarily (but not exclusively) with Pentium II motherboards using the Slot 1 design. Unlike the AT power connectors, the ATX connector has two rows of pins and can only be installed one way.

Other Power Connectors   Other connectors from the power supply go to your floppy drive, hard drive(s), CD-ROM drive(s), and, often, to a cooling fan attached to the CPU. These can all be disconnected by firmly grasping the white plastic shell—do not ever pull on the wires—and pulling the plug straight out. Some of these plugs may be rather tight. This type of connector is often difficult to disconnect (and connect) and should be disconnected only if absolutely necessary.

Notice that these plugs have two beveled corners and that the sockets where they are mounted also have beveled corners. These permit the plugs to be inserted in the sockets in only one way. Although they are tight, they will go in or come out without the use of excessive force.

Another type of power plug in use is a smaller, rectangular plug that commonly connects to the floppy drive only (see Figure 11.12). This plug has keys—those protruding plastic tabs—along one side that slide together with the plastic mounting on the unit. Again, be sure the plug is inserted correctly and do not force the plug to go in if it is not a smooth fit. This type of plug is easy to remove and install without force.

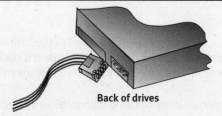

Back of drives

FIGURE 11.12:   A small 12V/5V power plug for 3.5-inch drives

Removing Ribbon Cable Connectors

The motherboard on a newer computer or a plug-in board on older computers will have several (as many as six or more) gray ribbon cables connecting to the floppy drive, to one or more hard drives, to one or more CD-ROM drives, and to the parallel and serial port connectors on the back plate of the chassis.

NOTE

The newest Slot 1 motherboards for the Pentium II have the serial and parallel ports permanently mounted at the rear of the board and do not have cables or connectors for these ports.

On newer systems, all these ribbon cables are connected to the motherboard. On older systems, they may be connected to two or more plug-in boards or some combination of both.

Usually there's enough slack in the cables to permit you to move them around to get at what's behind or underneath them. In some cases, however, they may be so much in the way when you're trying to reach the SIMM sockets that they require removal.

Before removing any flat ribbon cables, please note that each of these cables—even though they are different widths—has a marked stripe on one side. This is important! You need to remember which end of the connector connects to the color-coded edge of the cable. Fortunately, each flat ribbon cable carries some indication along one side or edge to make it easy to keep track of which side is which, and, commonly, there will also be a small number 1 (or possibly only a dot) on the motherboard next to the end of the socket where the marked end of the cable belongs. However, the only way this "mating" is helpful is if both of those features are actually present and visible. It will save you a lot of neck craning and eyestrain if you simply write down the correspondences (along the lines of "red edge to right side") before you disconnect the cable.

TIP

For rainbow (that is, multicolor) ribbon cables, the marker is a black wire with a brown wire immediately next to it. For gray ribbon cables, the marker is commonly a red or black stripe along one side but may be any type of continuous marking.

If it is necessary to remove one or more of these ribbon cables for access, mark the cables as you remove them. Each connector should have a label on the motherboard—such as J9, J10, J11, and so on—to identify the cable. Using a piece of tape or a marker, mark the cable with the same identifier.

Look at the connectors on the motherboard. Each is a double row of pins and may or may not be surrounded by a plastic shell outlining the connector.

If the connector has a shell, this will make it easier to align and replace the plug and may, as well, have a slot on one side at the center to accept a matching key on the plug on the ribbon cable.

If the connector does not have a shell, be careful replacing the plug to be sure that both rows of pins are mated and that the plug is not off to one end or the other. Also be sure that no pins are bent or tilted. And as before, let me repeat: *do not force the connection!*

Finally, the marked side of the ribbon cable must be replaced with the same alignment—corresponding to the mark or number 1 on the motherboard—that it had when it was removed.

Motherboard/Daughterboard Combinations   Some computer manufacturers—including Compaq, Hewlett-Packard, Packard Bell, and Dell—use a motherboard/daughterboard design in which the motherboard (mainboard) has a special connector along one side that mounts the daughterboard at a right angle. In turn, the daughterboard provides mounting slots for multiple plug-in cards.

Depending on the configuration, it may be necessary to remove the plug-in boards or even the daughterboard to gain access to the SIMM sockets. Fortunately, removing cards is as simple as gently rocking them back and forth (front to back, that is; not side to side!) along the connecting edge until they can slip straight out of the socket.

 NOTE

Although this may sound like a bad joke, there have been reports of individuals who have used silicon sealant to "protect" card connections and have sealed cards into their slots. DON'T DO THIS! Others have used solvent or cleaners (such as Windex) to remove dust and dirt, and some people have reportedly even gone a step further and sprayed lubricants, such as WD-40, all over the insides of their computers (and sometimes opening their hard drives to lubricate the interiors)! Again: don't do this either. Since any of these products—sealants, cleaners, or lubricants—can produce serious and detrimental results, never attempt to add anything other than an actual computer component to the inside of your computer.

Is Space Available?

If you find the SIMM sockets in your system (see Figure 11.13) but no modules are installed, the computer was hardwired by the manufacturer with a small amount of memory on the motherboard. In this case, consult the manufacturer's manual to determine what type of memory is required and what module configurations are accepted.

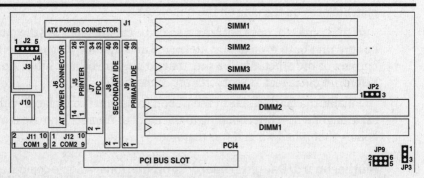

FIGURE 11.13:   72-pin SIMM and 168-pin DIMM sockets

More often than discovering that there are no modules whatsoever, you will find your SIMM (or DIMM) sockets but discover that there are no empty sockets. This does not mean that you cannot upgrade your computer, only that you will need to remove some of the existing modules to replace them with modules with a higher capacity.

Before you blithely set about doing so, take note of this important fact: many computers require memory modules to be installed as pairs, using two sockets at a time with modules with the same capacity in each. In this situation, the four SIMM connectors commonly consist of two *banks* of memory and are identified as bank 0 and bank 1.

NOTE

Configurations vary, so a bank of memory may consist of one socket, two sockets, or even four sockets. Consult your computer motherboard's documentation for details.

Alternately, if DIMM sockets are present, the two DIMM sockets may be identified as bank 0 and bank 1 while the pairs of SIMM sockets are identified as bank 2 and bank 3.

WARNING

When a computer requires a two-socket bank but only one socket has SIMMs installed, or when there are two sockets but the SIMMs are mismatched, the computer may fail to boot or may report an error during the POST (power-on self test).

Shortcuts

If you have never upgraded your 486 computer—that is, the configuration remains as it was supplied by the manufacturer—you can assume that older 486s will have a four-socket bank for 30-pin SIMMs with two SIMMs installed. For a late model 486, a four-socket bank for 72-pin SIMMs will have one module installed. For Pentium systems, the common configuration is four 72-pin sockets with two modules installed.

Thus, if your computer reports 16MB of RAM, you could expect to find either two 8MB SIMMs or one 16MB SIMM installed.

If you have upgraded memory previously but don't remember, you will likely find that the SIMM sockets are filled and that you will need to replace one (or probably two) of the existing modules with higher-capacity modules.

Before You Buy

You should know four things before buying memory for your computer: how much memory you need, the memory access speed, the memory type, and the contact type.

How Much Memory?

Let's assume that you have a computer with 24MB of RAM installed and you want to upgrade to 32MB. Well, the immediate assumption would be that you need to add 8MB, right?

The immediate assumption, however, is not necessarily the right one.

First, because you have 24MB installed, you probably have two 8MB SIMMs and two 4MB SIMMs with all four slots filled. Therefore, you're going to remove the two 4MB SIMMs to make room for additional memory.

Second, now that you've decided that you need 16MB—instead of only 8MB—are you going to go out and buy a single 16MB module?

Well, the answer is "no" again simply because the system will probably work better if you buy two new 8MB modules rather than a single 16MB module. Remember, a lot of boards require memory in full banks, and even those that don't require this may still work better using paired modules by supporting interleaving.

Now, what about later? Are you going to find yourself needing more memory later? And will you—six months from now—be pulling the 8MB SIMMs to replace them with 16s?

If this appears even likely, why not simply install two 16MB SIMMs now and bring the system up to 48MB? Then, later, if you do need more memory, you can replace the remaining 8MB modules to go from 48MB to 64MB.

Remember, the dealer may be willing to offer you a trade-in on the old memory, or you may know someone who could use it. And memory is cheap—why be stingy in the short run and waste money in the long run?

Memory Access Speed

Okay, maybe you can't find the manual for the motherboard, but you still need to know what access speed is required. To find out, you can remove one of the existing SIMMs and read the label on the chips. On one side of the chip, there should be a series of characters followed by a dash and a number. That number is the chip's access speed. This may be a 2-digit number (such as 60, 70, 80) or a single digit (such as 6, 7, 8)—either of which means essentially the same thing, for example, a 6 or a 60 identifies a 60ns access speed.

EDO, Non-EDO, or Other

This consideration applies primarily to Pentium-based (or equivalent) computers in which EDO chips are used to provide faster operations between the memory and the CPU. EDO chips can be used in non-EDO computers without any problems.

However, the converse is not acceptable: placing non-EDO RAM in an EDO system may result in the computer not booting. Alternately, if it does boot, the computer operates more slowly than if the proper EDO chips were used.

Many of the newer computer motherboards support multiple types of chips. My own, as an example, accepts DRAM, EDO RAM, or FP Mode DRAM using either 72-pin SIMM or 168-pin DIMM modules (but not both). If there is a question, the best way to find out is—as before—by referring to the manual for your motherboard or asking a knowledgeable technician.

Contact Types: Tin or Gold

The fourth item is the type of contacts used in the SIMM or DIMM sockets. These may be either tin or gold, with the higher-end systems using gold contacts, of course. Ideally, the modules you install should have matching metals to prevent deterioration of the contacts. This particular information is not commonly found in your motherboard manual, but a strong flashlight should tell you if the contacts in the socket are tin (a silver color) or gold.

Adding New Memory

Okay, you've purchased new memory modules and you're ready to install them.

1. The modules were shipped or supplied to you in an antistatic plastic bag or wrapping. This is a plastic that contains embedded carbon particles—which are conductive—and which prevent a static buildup or static charge from damaging the chips on the modules. Do not remove the modules from the protective enclosure and toss them around, drop them in your pocket, or carry them around unwrapped.

NOTE
Leave the computer modules in their protective wrapping until you are ready to install them!

2. After disconnecting the computer and opening the case—as described previously—ground yourself by touching the metal chassis or by connecting the ground strap. (See Figure 11.14.)

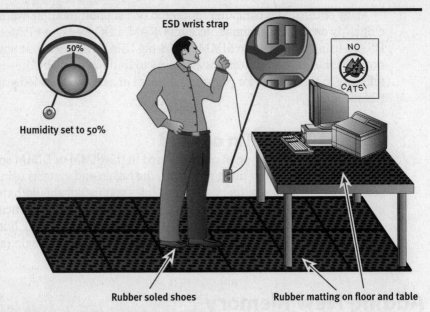

Humidity set to 50%

ESD wrist strap

NO CATS!

Rubber soled shoes

Rubber matting on floor and table

FIGURE 11.14: A static-free environment

3. If you are removing memory modules to make space for new modules, place the old modules in the same protective wrapping or, temporarily, lay them on a grounded metal surface—such as the power supply case. But be sure to place them in a protective wrapping before you finish.

4. Remove the new module(s) from the protective wrappings. Hold the modules by the edges, and be careful not to touch the metallic contacts.

5. Identify the notched end of the module and the hole matching the pin on the locking post. Fit the module into the socket at a 45-degree angle for a SIMM module or at a 90-degree angle for a DIMM module.

6. Seat the module with gentle pressure, and then lift to bring the module upright. The module should snap into position solidly with two clips, one at each end, holding the module in the upright position.

7. Both ends of the module should be the same height and neither end of the module should give under gentle pressure.

8. If the module does not appear to be seated correctly, release the end clips—if necessary—and try to reseat the module.

WARNING

Do not, under any circumstances, attempt to force a fit. Investigate the possibilities that you've either tried to insert the module incorrectly or have the wrong sort of module. If nothing seems wrong other than the fit, return the module for another one to see if it makes any difference (and take advantage of the dealer's expertise at the same time by asking for advice).

9. Once the module(s) are in place, replace any other components that had to be removed, reconnect any cables that were removed for access, and double-check all alignments, connections, and installations.

10. Turn on the machine (before replacing the cover) to ensure that the installed memory is recognized and functioning correctly.

   ▶ During the boot POST, the BIOS may report an error. The wording of the error depends on the BIOS installed, but should offer on-screen instructions. The reason for the message—if one appears—is simply that the system has recognized a change but needs to update the system configuration accordingly.

   ▶ Most newer systems will recognize the change, update the system settings automatically, and may or may not issue a warning message.

11. If the computer fails to reboot or if the change in memory is not recognized, shut down the computer, remove the newly installed modules, and carefully go back over the checklist to ensure that you have the appropriate memory module types.

12. If this does not identify a problem, try to reinstall and reseat each of the modules following the preceding steps. If this still does not resolve the problem, seek technical assistance from a trusted computer store or dealer.

Part ii

Success!

In most cases, you should be able to install or upgrade your computer memory without any particular problems. This is a simple process and should take much less time than it has taken for you to read through this chapter (even if you are a speed reader). And, once it's done, you should find that your applications run faster and more efficiently and that overall performance is visibly improved.

And—please don't dislocate your shoulder doing so—you can give yourself a well-earned pat on the back.

WHAT'S NEXT?

Now that you've done the hardest part of adding memory to your computer—that is, now that you've read about all the varieties and concerns that might affect your particular configuration—you should feel confident about trying it for yourself. Once you have more memory, of course, your machine should zip along so much better than before that you'll start wondering why you don't just add a few higher-level applications and gizmos (peripherals) while you're at it. In the next chapter, written by Ben Ezzell especially for this book, you'll learn how to add a new or replacement hard drive to provide storage space for those flashier applications, and you'll be introduced to the basics of adding cards for those new and improved gizmos.

Chapter 12

INSTALLING HARD DRIVES AND CARDS

by Ben Ezzell

O ther than installing memory (see Chapter 11), the most common computer upgrades involve either installing a new hard drive or installing some type of peripheral card, such as a new video card, a sound card, or a network card. (Granted, calling these "peripheral"—rather than "integral"—in the face of their importance to the operations of the computer does sound rather specious, but, technically, anything that is not directly involved in supporting the CPU is termed peripheral.) In this chapter, I'll discuss both topics, beginning with hard drives, CD-ROM drives, and devices that connect through SCSI (Small Computer Systems Interface) or IDE (Integrated Drive Electronics) ports. Then, under cards—peripherals—we will look at how to install a new device, how Plug and Play functions, and how to resolve device conflicts.

Installing a New Hard Drive

One of the simpler upgrades for your system is to install an additional hard drive or replace an existing hard drive. Although this is done occasionally because of the failure of the existing hard drive, the more common reason is simply the need for increased storage capacity.

In the early days, a hard drive for a desktop computer was probably a 40MB drive. If you were really out there in the extremes, you might have had an 80MB drive. At one time, however, an 80MB unit was the largest capacity manufactured, and it was a full-height 5.25-inch format. That is, the unit was 6 inches wide and 3.5 inches high and occupied the same space as a 5.25-inch diskette drive.

Today, the standard format for a hard drive is what is called a 3.5-inch format, meaning that it occupies the same bay size as a 3.5-inch floppy drive—approximately 4 inches wide and 1 inch tall.

At the same time, the thought of a mere 80MB drive would be laughable, with common capacities for hard drives beginning above the gigabyte range and easily running in excess of 8GB—a hundred times larger than those available less than a decade ago.

In short, the physical size of your hard drive is pretty well standardized—portable and laptop drives excepted—but you do have a wide choice of capacities. Of course, in a hard drive, capacity is all that's important anyway, isn't it?

Selecting a Hard Drive

Practically speaking, few criteria are involved in selecting a hard drive. Unless you have very unusual requirements, the selection process can normally center around five factors: IDE/EIDE (Integrated Drive Electronics/ Enhanced IDE) or SCSI, drive capacity, price, speed, and reliability, and usually in that order.

Types of Drives: SCSI vs. IDE

Although several types of hard drive interfaces have been used in the past, today there are essentially two types: SCSI and IDE/EIDE. Figuring out which of these two interfaces you are using is a relatively simple task. For one thing, if you bought your computer recently—that is, in the past two or three years—you probably have an IDE/EIDE interface instead of a SCSI.

The simplest way to determine whether you have a SCSI controller installed is to watch the computer screen during power up. Following the power-on self-test (POST), the system will report on the hardware configuration, listing the processor type, memory, and the primary installed devices. A typical system configuration report is shown below, but the format of the display (and the contents) on your system may vary.

```
+------------------------------------------------+
_ CPU Type      : IDT WinChip C6  Base Memory    :  640K    _
_ Co-Processor  : Installed       Extended Memory :  64512K  _
_ CPU Clock     : 200MHz          Cache Memory    :  512K   _
 ----------------------------------------------_
_ Diskette Drive A : 1.44M, 3.5 in.    Display Type  : EGA/
VGA  _
_ Diskette Drive B : None             Serial Port(s) : 3F8 2F8  _
_ Pri. Master Disk : LBA ,Mode 4, 3166MB Parallel Port(s) :
378  _
_ Pri. Slave Disk : LBA ,UDMA 2, 5250MB Cache L2 Type   :
Pipe-Burst _
_ Sec. Master Disk : CDROM,Mode 3    SDRAM at Rows   :
None   _
_ Sec. Slave Disk : CDROM,Mode 3     DRAM at Rows    : 4 6   _
_ Power Management : Disabled       Fast-Page at Rows :
None   _
+------------------------------------------------+
```

```
PCI device listing......
```

Bus No.	Device No.	Func No.	Vendor ID	Device ID	Device Class	IRQ
0	5	0	1023	9660	Display Controller	9
0	6	0	1011	0014	Network Controller	5
0	11	0	10B9	5229	IDE Controller	14
0	15	0	10B9	5237	Serial Bus Controller	11

In this example, the system is reporting that we have two IDE controllers (Pri. and Sec.) with two hard drives on the primary controller and two CD-ROMs on the secondary controller. Note that the controller is not explicitly identified as an IDE/EIDE device, but since it is not identified as a SCSI device, IDE/EIDE is inferred.

TIP

If you have trouble reading the system configuration report display (since it may go past quite quickly), press the Pause/Break key to freeze the screen.

If a SCSI controller were present here, a separate sequence of messages would identify the controller and, as the controller searched through the possible device IDs, any attached SCSI devices. Note, however, that the simple presence of a SCSI controller does not mean that the system drives are SCSI since a SCSI controller is often used for scanners or other peripheral devices while the system hard drive(s) remains IDE.

A second and perhaps more convenient method of identifying the drive type under Windows 95/98/98 SE/NT is to simply query the system itself. Right-click the My Computer icon on the Desktop to open the System Properties dialog box, and click the Device Manager tab (see Figure 12.1). Here I scrolled down to find Hard Disk Controllers, clicked the plus sign that precedes it, and then double-clicked the Standard item to open the dialog box for that controller.

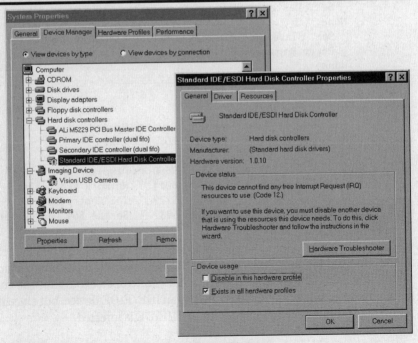

FIGURE 12.1: The System Properties Device Manager

In Figure 12.1, the Device Manager tab shows the disk drives, and the dialog box for the selected controller (which is on the right) shows the hard disk controllers. In this system, a SCSI controller is installed—an Adaptec SCSI Controller—but the only hard drives shown are identified as IDE drives. In this case, the SCSI controller is used for a scanner but does not—at present—support any hard drive devices.

Of course, since a SCSI controller is present, it would be possible and practical to add a SCSI hard drive (or multiple drives) if desired. You should be aware, of course, that SCSI hard drives do tend to be more expensive than IDE drives of the same size. On the other hand, if your circumstances demand access to large quantities of data very rapidly, installing a SCSI drive can easily offset the difference in cost.

Once you identify the controller type, installation is essentially the same for both IDE/EIDE and SCSI drives. Where appropriate, differences and special requirements are noted in the following instructions.

IDE/EIDE The IDE standard (shorthand for Integrated Drive Electronics, and identifying an interface for connecting hard drives to a computer) has been replaced today by the EIDE standard, which is faster than IDE, allows more memory, and can connect as many as four physical drives (two on each EIDE port such as hard drives, tape drives, and CD-ROM drives) to the computer.

NOTE

A physical hard drive can be partitioned into multiple "logical" drives, each identified by a separate drive letter. The controller, whether IDE or SCSI, is only concerned with the physical device and is not affected by the partitioning.

Most motherboards sold today include primary and secondary IDE/EIDE ports directly on the motherboard (see Figure 12.2), eliminating what used to be a need in older systems for separate hard-disk controller cards. Each connector can support two devices, which may be either hard drives or CD-ROM drives.

However, because many manufacturers offer on-board SCSI controllers, you should always check your motherboard manual or your existing drive to determine whether you are using an IDE/EIDE or SCSI controller.

Part ii

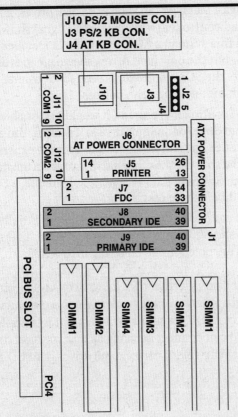

FIGURE 12.2: Primary and secondary EIDE connectors

SCSI   SCSI (pronounced "scuzzy") originated as a high-speed interface used to connect such devices as hard drives, CD-ROM drives, floppy drives, tape drives, scanners, and printers to the computer. Originally developed by Shugart Associates (now Seagate Technologies), a single SCSI port was able to connect seven other devices, each of which was identified by a number from 0 through 7 (the SCSI port itself also requires an identifier) that is set by a manual dip switch on each device.

Newer versions of the SCSI standard—called SCSI-2 (a.k.a., Fast SCSI or Fast-Wide SCSI) and SCSI-3 (a.k.a. Ultra SCSI)—can connect as many as 15 devices (identified as 0 through 15), have higher transfer rates, and support longer cable runs between the computer and the device.

Although a variety of manufacturers, including Asus, Intel, Shuttle, and Supermicro, provide motherboards with on-board Ultra Wide SCSI adapters, other SCSI-equipped systems use plug-in cards (such as Adaptec's) to provide the SCSI port and include an external Centronics adapter at the back of the card.

Using the SCSI interface, multiple devices can be "daisy-chained" by cabling from one device to the next, but the standard also required null-terminators on the last device on the cable. Later versions of SCSI controllers, however, support smart-termination devices, relieving you of the necessity of plugging in external terminators or adding terminator strips to (or removing them from) the devices.

NOTE

Not all new SCSI devices are smart-terminated, and many still require physical terminators to function correctly.

The SCSI standard has been largely replaced by the EIDE standard, in part because the IDE interface is cheaper to manufacture, but SCSI interfaces are still in use—including motherboards with built-in SCSI controllers—and SCSI hard drives continue to be manufactured.

In situations where drive access speed is considered critical, SCSI is often preferred to IDE because of higher data transfer rates. This latter consideration, however, is unlikely to affect most users.

Capacity

As a general rule, most people want the largest hard drive they can afford. There's good reason for this. Given the continuing bloat as new versions of applications are introduced and the fact that creeping "featurism" (the adding of more and more features) is not a trend likely to be reversed in the foreseeable future, it only makes sense to buy the largest-capacity drive available without placing an undue strain on your budget.

Or, in brief, go ahead and buy the biggest you can afford—because you *will* need it sooner or later.

The good news in all this is that prices for hard drives, like prices for memory, are following a steep downward trend. And it is a trend that shows no signs of being halted.

At the time this material is being written, hard drives are running somewhere in the range of 2¢ to 4¢ per megabyte—that is around $30 per gigabyte for multi-gigabyte drives. But, by the time this book is published, the price cited here may well be on the high side.

Price

Since price is simply a matter of your pocketbook, there isn't much to say about this criterion except to suggest that you can expect to pay something over $100 for a hard drive but probably less than $200. Exactly how much depends on what size capacity you choose.

But, because prices can vary widely for the same hard drive—yes, for the same model, capacity, and manufacturer—it can pay to shop around. One good place to start shopping and making price comparisons is, of course, the World Wide Web. Try out www.search.com or www.shopper.com (both are CNET sites) or www.ComputerShopper.com, a ZDNet offering.

On the Web, a quick request for hard drive prices revealed 6.5GB (which is a medium-capacity) drives at prices ranging from $113.77 up to $239.95 (1.8¢/MB to 3.7¢/MB). The variations were simply the prices quoted for the same unit by different suppliers.

At the same time, a smaller 3.2GB drive was also available at similar prices, which meant the lowest-priced smaller drives were starting at the high end of the larger drive's cost-per-megabyte range—and the highest-priced smaller drives came to *twice* the per-megabyte cost of the larger drives!

Checking on the largest-capacity drives offered—in the 9 and 10GB range—I found prices beginning at 7¢/MB and running as high as 9¢/MB, making these considerably more expensive than the mid-capacity units.

Thus, if a really large-capacity system is required, your best price break may be to buy two mid-capacity units rather than pursue the largest-capacity unit available.

Speed

Hard drive speeds are commonly rated by two criteria: transfer rate and access or seek time performance.

Transfer rates—the rate at which data is read from or written to the hard drive—are commonly specified as a range such as 4.6 to 8.1 megabits per second.

Access or seek time performance is the time required for the drive heads to find a particular location on the drive. Because some tracks are faster to reach than others, the values quoted are average seek times for the drive. Seek times are given in milliseconds (ms) and should be less than 14ms for a good drive.

Except in rare, application-critical circumstances, neither of these factors are particularly important, and speed information is not commonly available when you are querying prices for hard drives. If this information is important to you, the best sources are to check the manufacturer's home pages for details.

Reliability

Unfortunately, reliability is usually the last factor people consider when buying a hard drive. Fortunately, reliability has become far less of a problem than it was in earlier years, simply because all hard drives have become much more reliable.

If you have questions about the reliability of a drive, the best way to find out is to ask others what types of drives they prefer and why.

If you're a novice and you ask other novices, you're probably going to get a blank look in response. But power-users and technicians tend to have very firm preferences based on experience with a variety of drives.

Overall, almost all drives manufactured today tend to be very reliable *as long as they are not actively mistreated.*

WARNING

Do not—under any circumstances—open a hard drive case or attempt to modify the hard drive in any way, shape, or fashion!

If you really want to see what is inside, ask your local computer store. They will probably have a junked unit—with the case off—that you can look at. Removing the case from any hard drive will not only invalidate the warranty but will also cause the drive to self-destruct in a very short time...often as fast as a few minutes after you try to use it again, and sometimes within seconds of turning it on.

Removable Drives

Removable drives allow a hard drive to be physically removed from a system—without opening the case—and replaced by another hard drive or allow a hard drive to be carried from one location to another. This is accomplished by installing the drive in a cartridge that plugs into a drive bay. Mounting kits are available for both EIDE and SCSI devices.

Part ii

Swapping hard drives can have several benefits. A removable drive allows the information on the drive to be conveniently carried from one machine to another. Removing one drive and replacing it with another can allow a different operating system to be booted or can allow a single machine to be shared—with perfect privacy—between different users.

However, the problems with drive swapping are several.

WARNING
Both EIDE and SCSI drives must only be swapped when the system is powered down. Hot-swapping is supported only by a few, specialized devices.

Any time an EIDE drive is removed or added, the system BIOS must be updated with information about the changed drive. (One exception: if one drive is removed and replaced with a physically identical drive—that is, with a drive that has the same model number and manufacturer, not the same files and folders—the update is not required.) Setting the system BIOS is discussed later in this chapter.

NOTE
There are also solutions that support hot-swapping for both EIDE and SCSI drives. If hot-swapping is needed, consult your local computer dealer for supporting software.

If you add, remove, or swap a SCSI drive, no BIOS information is required, and no update is necessary. This is one reason for the popularity of SCSI devices. Although no BIOS changes are required, a terminator for the data line may still be necessary.

Older Hard Drives

Installing a new hard drive does not automatically mean that you need to replace your existing drive. If you are using SCSI drives, you can have as many as seven hard drives (and/or CD-ROM drives, scanners, printers, or other devices) connected. Using EIDE, the limit is four devices; like SCSI, these may be any mixture of hard drives or CD-ROMs.

Thus, if you have a computer with an EIDE interface, a single hard drive, and a single CD-ROM drive but you need more capacity, you are already in a position to add two additional hard drives...without replacing your existing drive and without losing the information on the existing drive.

Alternately, if you have all available slots in use already, you will—rather obviously—need to remove a device before adding a new, larger one. Likewise, if all controller positions are in use, some device will need to be removed before a new unit can be installed.

IDE/EIDE Controllers

Each EIDE controller—that is, each controller plug on the motherboard—can manage two physical devices. These may be two individual hard drives, one hard drive and one CD-ROM drive, or two CD-ROM drives. Today's motherboards provide two EIDE controllers, which support a maximum of four devices in any combination.

Each of the EIDE controller connectors accepts a rectangular 40-pin connector to a ribbon cable. The ribbon cable should have two additional 40-pin connectors to attach to the two devices to be supported. Deciding which connector should be attached to which drive and which connector should be attached to the motherboard is purely a matter of convenience, believe it or not—the order of the connections is actually irrelevant. However, what *is* relevant is that you must do something to let the computer know which device is which.

When connecting two devices—of any type—to any IDE/EIDE controller, one device must be identified as the master (or primary) device and the other as the slave (or secondary) device, as described next.

Master/Slave Drives (IDE/EIDE Only)

When a single hard drive (or CD-ROM drive) is connected to an IDE/EIDE controller, the drive is always the master or primary drive, and the units are shipped from the factory with jumpers—small connectors (approximately a quarter-inch each) across two pins somewhere on the hard drive—identifying them as such (that is, as master units).

When two units are installed on the same controller—that is, are connected to the same cable—one must be identified as the master and the other as the slave. This also determines the order in which the drives are recognized and the drive letters are assigned when the system boots, with the master drive being recognized first and receiving the lower drive letter (see the later section "Partition and Drive Letter Assignments").

Normally, a jumper must be removed in order to identify the unit as a slave or secondary unit. You will need to consult the documentation supplied with the hard drive—the documentation is usually no more than a single page—to determine which jumper is used for this purpose. Table 12.1 and the illustration in Figure 12.3 are taken from a Maxtor 7000AP/A series hard drive, but other drives are generally similar (the location of the jumpers and the identifying numbers will vary on different makes).

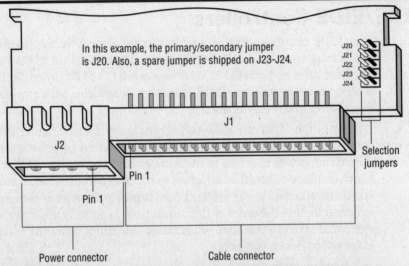

In this example, the primary/secondary jumper is J20. Also, a spare jumper is shipped on J23-J24.

J20
J21
J22
J23
J24

J1

J2

Selection jumpers

Pin 1

Pin 1

Power connector

Cable connector

FIGURE 12.3: Power, controller, and selection jumpers on a typical hard drive

TABLE 12.1: Typical Primary/Secondary Jumper Options

PRIMARY/SECONDARY DRIVE OPTION	J20 INSTALLED?
Only drive in a single-drive system	Installed
Primary drive in a dual-drive system	Installed
Secondary drive in a dual-drive system	Removed

TIP

When removing a jumper, do not discard it. Instead, place the jumper over one pin leaving the second pin in the pair free. In this way, the jumper can be restored at a later time if necessary.

Primary and Secondary IDE Controllers

On today's motherboards that use IDE/EIDE controllers, two controller ports are commonly supplied. On older systems, on which the hard drive (IDE) controller is on an add-in card, the controller card may also supply both a primary and secondary controller. To identify the primary and secondary controllers, simply look for the labeling on the motherboard or the controller card.

Ideally, the drive you want to boot from should be connected to the primary controller, and CD-ROM drives are generally placed on the secondary controller.

If, however, you are expecting to do a great deal of data transfer from one physical drive to another, placing each of the physical drives on separate controllers can increase the transfer rate. This is only required, however, in specialized circumstances such as maintaining mirrored drives.

Partition and Drive Letter Assignments

A physical hard drive can be divided into multiple "logical drives." This process is known as *partitioning* the drives. To the system, each of the logical drives appears as a separate hard drive and is assigned a separate drive letter. In this section, we'll look at how the computer recognizes and identifies multiple drives, whether physical or logical. (For more information on how to create logical drives, see the "Partitioning and Formatting" section later in the chapter.)

When multiple physical drives and CD-ROMs are installed on IDE/EIDE controllers, a few rules govern how drive letters will be assigned to those physical drives and to any logical drives they contain. To begin with, the primary physical drive on the primary controller is always assigned the drive letter C. (Drives A and B are reserved for floppy drives.)

If any of the drives have logical partitions, the first drive letter (C) is assigned to the primary *partition* on the primary drive, and the next drive letter (D) is assigned to the primary partition on the secondary drive. The logical partitions are then assigned drive letters in sequence, beginning with the logical drives on the primary drive.

NOTE

Drive letter assignments are limited to the 26 letters of the English alphabet, with the designations A and B reserved for floppy drives only.

If three or more physical drives are installed using both the primary and secondary controllers, the first three drive letters are assigned to, respectively:

1. The primary partition on the primary drive on the primary controller

2. The primary partition on the secondary drive on the primary controller

3. The primary partition on the primary drive on the secondary controller

As before, the logical partitions are then assigned drive letters in sequence, beginning with the logical drives on the primary drive.

Table 12.2 shows an example using three physical hard drives that have been partitioned into several logical drives and a single CD-ROM drive that supports four CDs (that is, a CD changer).

NOTE

Drive letters are assigned to CD-ROM drives after all hard drives have been assigned.

TABLE 12.2: Hard Drive Partitions

Drive Letter	Primary Hard Drive on Primary Controller	Secondary Hard Drive on Primary Controller	Primary Hard Drive on Secondary Controller	CD-ROM Drive on Secondary Controller
C	Primary partition			
D		Primary partition		
E			Primary partition	
F	1st logical partition			
G	2nd logical partition			
H		1st logical partition		
I		2nd logical partition		
J			1st logical partition	
K			2nd logical partition	

TABLE 12.2 continued: Hard Drive Partitions

Drive Letter	Primary Hard Drive on Primary Controller	Secondary Hard Drive on Primary Controller	Primary Hard Drive on Secondary Controller	CD-ROM Drive on Secondary Controller
L			3rd logical partition	
M				1st CD-ROM
N				2nd CD-ROM
O				3rd CD-ROM
P				4th CD-ROM

Part ii

Installation

Installing a new drive is extremely simple. Once you have selected a hard drive, installation consists of mounting the unit inside the computer, connecting the data cable and the power cable, and, for IDE/EIDE drives, configuring the BIOS to recognize the new drive. Once a new drive has been installed, it still needs to be formatted and, optionally, partitioned before it can be used.

Opening the Computer

Obviously, the first step to adding a hard drive to your computer is opening the computer for access. To do this, follow the procedures outlined in Chapter 11 in the section "Opening the Computer."

Drive Bays

Once the computer is open, a visual examination will tell you what space is available for physically mounting a hard drive. Most computer cases provide an assortment of places where a drive can be mounted. Most cases have two or three 5.25-inch half-height bays (used for CDs) and two 3.5-inch bays (for diskette, ZIP, and Jaz drives), but will also have space for two to four 3.5-inch form hard drives. The latter may be below the 3.5-inch bays, on the side of the power supply supports, or tucked almost anywhere within the case. If only 5.25-inch bays are available, mounting trays can be used to locate a 3.5-inch form hard drive in a larger bay. The only real crite-rion is that the drive be mounted securely and in a position where it will not interfere with the other hardware, cards, and so on.

TIP

Because hard drives do generate some heat, it can be advantageous to leave some space for air circulation between drive units when possible.

Once you have selected a mounting position for the new drive, the drive can be mounted in either a vertical or horizontal position and should be secured in place with 6/32 by .25-inch screws. Do not use screws longer than .25 inch since longer screws could, potentially, damage the hard drive.

WARNING

Although hard drives can be mounted either vertically or horizontally, they should not be mounted at any other angle. Incorrect mounting places a strain on the disk bearings and shortens the life of the drive.

Cables and Connectors

Once the drive is mounted, connect a 40-pin ribbon connector, ensuring that the marked side of the ribbon—which identifies pin 1—is next to the power connector. Most hard drive connectors have a surrounding shell with a slot matching a key on the connecting plug. However, the shell is not universal, and not all plugs have the corresponding key.

Some cables also have one pin position plugged and expect the corre-sponding connection on the hard drive to have a pin missing at the same position. Again, this is not universal.

In any case, if the ribbon connector is not installed correctly, the drive will not function.

The ribbon connector should never be forced. If the connector does not slide on smoothly, check for bent pins, incorrect alignment, or other errors.

WARNING

Never force a connection! If a plug does not connect smoothly, this is usually because there is a problem that should be corrected.

Power Connectors   Last, connect a power cord to the hard drive. The connectors for the power cords, unlike most other connectors, do take a moderate amount of pressure to connect but still should not be forced. These connectors are rectangular with four pins and two beveled corners so that the plugs can only be connected in one way. Ensure that they are inserted correctly and seated firmly.

If you do not have a free power connector, a Y-adapter can be used. A Y-adapter has a single female connector to join to an existing power cord and two male connectors on 3- or 4-inch lengths of wire. Remove a connector from one of the drives already installed, install the Y-adapter, and reconnect the original drive and the new drive.

Now you are ready to turn on the computer.

Updating the BIOS (for IDE/EIDE Only)

After installing a new IDE/EIDE drive, the first time the computer is powered up, the system BIOS must be updated to recognize the new drive or the changed drive. As you power up the system, you will have to hold down a key to trigger the CMOS Setup utility that allows you to set values for the system BIOS.

NOTE
Most BIOS configurations respond to the Delete key, but some expect a function key or some combination of keys. A prompt on the screen should inform you which key or combination is required.

Exactly what the CMOS Setup will look like depends on which BIOS is installed on your machine, but all BIOS versions will have features similar to those described here for an Award BIOS.

Because today's hard drives are able to "describe" themselves, the simplest place to start is with the IDE HDD AUTO DETECTION option (HDD here refers to Hard Disk Drive). After you select auto detection, the BIOS will step through the primary and secondary IDE controllers, auto-detecting master and slave drives for each. As each drive is detected, you will be prompted to save the information found.

NOTE
CD-ROM drives, although managed by the IDE/EIDE controller, are not detected by the IDE HDD AUTO DETECTION mechanism. In any case, however, CD-ROM drives do not require the type of drive parameter settings used by hard drives.

After the IDE HDD AUTO DETECTION option has finished, you can go to the STANDARD CMOS SETUP option to see the results returned by the auto detection feature. A typical setup with two hard drives on the primary controller and two CD-ROM drives on the secondary controller might report something like this:

HARD DISKS	TYPE	SIZE	CYLS	HEAD	PRECMP	LANDZ	SCTR	MODE
Primary Master:	USER	3166	767	128	0	6135	63	LBA
Primary Slave:	USER	5248	638	255	0	10849	63	LBA
Secondary Master:	AUTO	0	0	0	0	0	0	AUTO
Secondary Slave:	AUTO	0	0	0	0	0	0	AUTO

NOTE

In the past, the BIOS would contain a list of common drive settings, which you could select from the list. Today, it is impractical to list all drive types as predefined parameter lists, and virtually all drives will be identified as USER, meaning *"user defined."*

In this report, the first (master) hard drive is a 3.1GB drive, and the secondary drive is 5.2GB. Although one drive reports 128 heads and the other reports 255, neither drive actually has this many physical heads (both have 16 physical heads). Instead, the figures are a compromise between what the BIOS and the system can accept and arguments that will allow the drive to function correctly.

If at all possible, use the auto detection feature to set up your new drive. If this does not work for any reason, refer to the documentation supplied with the drive to find the appropriate settings, and enter the values for CYLS (cylinders), HEAD (heads), and SCTR (sectors) yourself. The drive sizes will be calculated automatically from this information.

NOTE

The PRECMP (pre-compensation) and LANDZ (landing zone) settings are not needed by today's drives but might be supplied anyway by auto detection.

Partitioning and Formatting

After installation, but before a drive can be used, the drive must be prepared for operation. You begin by using the fdisk utility, which prepares a new hard drive by creating a primary, bootable partition and which can also be used to create secondary, logical partitions.

TIP

If you are installing a new drive that will be the boot drive or that will be the only drive on the computer, before installation you will need to have a bootable floppy disk that should also contain fdisk.exe, format.com, and, optionally, sys.com. Remember, the primary drive will *not* be bootable until it has been prepared for use by partitioning, formatting, and copying the system files to the hard drive.

Although you can use fdisk to create logical partitions, PowerQuest's Partition Magic (which is discussed in the following sections) offers much more powerful features and allows you to create partitions and resize existing partitions without losing or destroying existing data files.

To start fdisk, choose Start ➤ Run, and type **fdisk.** The Windows 98/98 SE version of fdisk (which is also available with Windows 95 version B) will begin with a warning:

```
Your computer has a disk larger than 512 MB. This version of
Windows includes improved support for larger disks, resulting
in more efficient use of disk space on large drives, and
allowing disks over 2 GB to be formatted as a single drive.
IMPORTANT: if you enable large disk support and create any
new drives on this disk, you will not be able to access the
new drive(s) using other operating systems, including some
versions of Windows 95 and Windows NT, as well as earlier
versions of Windows and MS-DOS. In addition, disk utilities
will not be able to work with this disk. If you need to
access this disk with other operating systems or older disk
utilities, do not enable large drive support.
Do you wish to enable large disk support <Y/N>........? [Y]
```

NOTE

Windows 95 version B was an upgrade to the original release of Windows 95. This revision has been available online from Microsoft, but was also installed by OEMs (original equipment manufacturers) and dealers on many computers prior to the release of Windows 98.

The "large disk support" referred to, of course, is the FAT32 file system. FAT32 has the advantage over conventional FAT (FAT16) of supporting smaller cluster sizes on large drives and, therefore, has more efficient storage.

In any case, once you enter fdisk, you'll see the screen displayed in Figure 12.4, which has five options.

Part ii

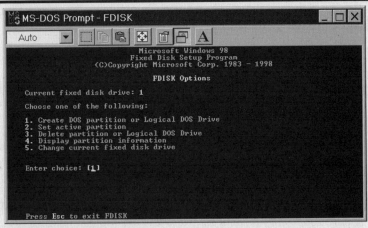

FIGURE 12.4:   FDISK options

At the top, notice that the current fixed disk drive is identified as disk number 1. If you have only one hard drive (fixed disk), proceed with step 2. However, if you have more than one physical hard drive—that is, you have just installed a second or third drive—the first task is to make sure that you are operating on the correct physical drive. Follow these steps:

1. Select option 4 to display partition information for the selected drive. Figure 12.5 shows a fixed disk that contains two partitions: an active primary DOS (PRI DOS) partition and an extended DOS (EXT DOS) partition. The primary partition is also identified as a FAT16 volume.

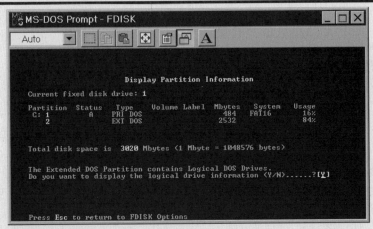

FIGURE 12.5:   Partition information

The extended DOS partition is also identified as containing logical drives, and the logical drive information is shown in Figure 12.6.

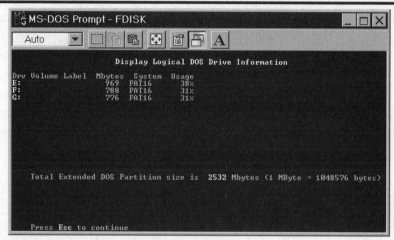

FIGURE 12.6: Logical DOS drive information

Here the extended DOS partition has been divided into three logical drives identified as E through G, and each one is also a FAT16 drive format.

NOTE

If I had selected a new, unformatted drive with no primary partitions, the display would report that no partitions existed, and I would press Escape to leave this screen and return to the options shown in Figure 12.4.

2. Option 5 allows you to select a new physical drive. Remember, you want to operate on the newly installed drive—not on an existing physical drive that already contains files and data—for the simple reason that fdisk's operations will destroy any existing information. Once you identify the correct physical drive, proceed with step 3.

3. Select option 1 to create a partition on the new drive. If you do not want to create logical partitions at this time, use 100 percent of the available space for the primary partition. Alternately, if you want one or more drives in addition to the

primary partition, specify the amount of space to use for the primary partition either in megabytes (MB) or as a percentage of the total.

4. After creating a primary partition, select option 2 to make the primary partition active if this drive will be your boot drive. If this is a second physical hard drive—that is, if you're not planning to boot from it—the primary partition should *not* be made active.

5. If you want to create one or more logical partitions, return to option 1 to select the option for creating a logical drive, using the remaining space free on the fixed disk or specifying a part of the space to be used for the logical drive.

6. Repeat step 5 to create additional logical drives if desired.Once you finish creating a primary partition and, optionally, logical partitions, exit fdisk by pressing Escape.

Before the primary partition or any logical partitions can be used, they also must be formatted using `format.com`. From the DOS prompt—or from an MS-DOS window—enter **FORMAT *X*:** where you replace the X with the drive designation identifying the partition to be formatted. If this is the primary partition on your boot drive, enter the command as **FORMAT C: /s**. This copies the system files to the drive when the format operation is complete, making the drive bootable. Other drives—primary or logical—do not need to be made bootable.

If you attempt to format a drive that has already been formatted and contains information, you will be prompted and reminded that the requested operation will destroy existing files. This is a good indication that you entered the wrong drive designation and that you should go back to fdisk, select option 4 to display partition information, and make a note of the drive identifier for each of the newly created drives.

NOTE
You must also be sure to format all logical drives as well as your primary partition.

Partition and Format Utilities

Although you can use the fdisk utility to create partitions, it is an awkward tool. The existing drive contents are destroyed before a partition can be changed, and a separate format operation is required after changing or creating any partition. In contrast, several third-party products make changing partitions almost a snap—whether resizing a partition or adding a new partition. Based on my experience with several of these utility programs, Partition Magic from PowerQuest is by far the best utility for the task.

PowerQuest's Partition Magic   Partition Magic is an all-in-one utility that allows you to resize or move existing partitions; create, format, and activate new partitions; select or change drive formats; and change cluster sizes. Further, you can do all this *without* erasing existing data files from any drive.

Partition Magic version 5 is the latest release, and you can obtain it by going to www.partitionmagic.com. Its most valuable features include the following:

- ▶ Wizards that guide you step by step through each task.

- ▶ Previews that show you the effects of partitioning your drive before actually making the changes you've selected.

- ▶ Support for hard drives larger than 20MB.

The ability to convert between file systems without losing data, including FAT to FAT32, NTFS, HPFS, FAT32 to FAT, NTFS to FAT, and NTFS to FAT32. In addition, you can use Partition Magic to convert a primary drive to a logical drive and vice-versa.

In a nutshell, however, it's ease of use that makes Partition Magic such an attractive alternative, and you can use it with DOS, Windows 95/98/98 SE, Windows NT, and Windows 2000.

16-Bit vs. 32-Bit Drive Formats

Several drive formats have been introduced over the years, but all function by dividing a drive—whether a floppy disk, hard drive, or logical drive—into clusters for addressing. Each file written to a drive is written to one or more clusters, using however many clusters are required to contain the file.

The downside to clusters is that any file—regardless of size—always occupies some integral number of clusters. That is, if a file is only 10 bytes in size but the cluster size is, for example, 2 kilobytes, then the 10 bytes are still using 2 kilobytes—2,048 bytes!—of storage on the drive. Likewise, if the file were 2,058 bytes (that is, 2KB + 10 bytes), the file would occupy two clusters (thus, 4KB, or 4,096 bytes of space).

The problem becomes incrementally worse as the size of the physical or logical drive increases, because the cluster size increases as well. Let's see why and how this happens.

First, the number of possible clusters is limited by the address size of the disk format. For example, the first widespread PC disk format (practically speaking, that is; we're ignoring several that are no longer in use) was the *FAT* or *FAT16* file system, which uses 16-bit cluster addresses to identify where files are located within a drive (FAT being an acronym for File Allocation Table). The problem inherent in the FAT system is that 16 bits only affords you a maximum of 65,535 addresses. Thus, no more than that same number of clusters can be created on an individual drive, because there would be no way to keep track of more than that many— and that is *regardless* of the drive size!

The way that manufacturers traditionally got around this FAT restriction was to increase the size of the clusters. A large number of bigger clusters can provide a lot more storage space than the same number of small clusters; the tradeoff, as mentioned earlier, is that a great many of those big clusters may be wasting space. For example, reconsider the exercise we performed earlier: on a drive that's between 256MB and 511MB, if you have a file that's only 10 bytes in size, that file is going to take up 8 kilobytes! (The cluster sizes for drives of different sizes are given a little later in this section.)

NOTE
Although some programs such as Partition Magic will allow you to select a cluster size for a drive, this is not normally necessary. When you elect to use a FAT16 format for a drive, the cluster size is set automatically to a supported size. Likewise, if you convert a FAT16 to a FAT32 drive, the cluster size is adjusted appropriately.

As you would expect, 32 bits can provide far more addresses than 16 bits can. Thus, a 32-bit system can keep track of a huge number (2^{32} or 4,294,967,296) of clusters. This, in turn, provides for corresponding reductions in cluster sizes, because with that many more clusters available, you can squeeze more of them into the space available, reducing their individual sizes and at the same time reducing the amount of space that any one of them might otherwise be wasting. (And a lot of them were wasting space under the other system!)

With the introduction of the OS/2 operating system, the HPFS file system (High Performance File System) offered the first 32-bit file allocation system. The problem with HPFS drives, however, is that they are not recognized by operating systems other than OS/2. Similarly, Windows NT also introduced a new 32-bit file allocation system—NTFS—which also provided file access security as well as improved error recovery and other important features. Again, the problem with NTFS drives is simply that these are not recognized by any operating system except Windows NT and Windows 2000.

When Windows 95 was first introduced, the FAT (FAT16) file system was still the default and the only file allocation system supported. Later, with Windows 95 B, a new file system called *FAT32* was introduced, using, as the name implies, 32-bit allocation tables.

The FAT32 file system introduced with Windows 95 B continues to be supported under Windows 98 and 98 SE, but it also has the limitation of not being recognized by Windows NT, OS/2, or Linux. Windows 2000 does use and recognize the FAT32 system as well as both NTFS and FAT16, but, to date, FAT16 remains the only universally recognized disk/drive format for PCs.

Cluster Sizes

The importance of a FAT32 (or any 32-bit) drive format compared with FAT16 is shown in Table 12.3.

TABLE 12.3: A Comparison of Cluster Sizes under FAT16 and FAT32

PARTITION SIZE	FAT16 CLUSTER SIZES	FAT32 CLUSTER SIZES
0–31MB	512 bytes	N/A
32–63MB	1KB	512 bytes
64–127MB	2KB	512 bytes
128–255MB	4KB	512 bytes
256–511MB	8KB	1KB
512MB–1GB	16KB	2KB
1–2GB	32KB	4KB
2–8GB	N/A	4KB
8–16GB	N/A	8KB
16–32GB	N/A	16KB
32GB–2TB (terabytes)	N/A	32KB

Remember, the smaller the cluster size, the less space is wasted on the drive. Converting from the FAT16 to FAT32 format can recover anywhere from 15 to 30 percent of the drive capacity overall.

In Windows 98 SE, you can use the Drive Converter to convert a drive from FAT16 to FAT32. (Choose Start ➢ Programs ➢ Accessories ➢ System Tools ➢ Drive Converter (32). After you run Drive Converter, you'll need to run Disk Defragmenter, which takes a while but is well worth the time. When I recently converted a hard disk to FAT32, I gained almost 50 percent more space on the disk.

Installing Peripheral Cards

As I mentioned earlier, calling these items "peripheral" rather than "integral" in the face of their importance to the operations of the computer does sound rather specious, but, technically, anything that is not directly involved in supporting the CPU is termed peripheral.

In general, installing a new peripheral card in your computer is a routine operation—after you have the new card, you open the computer case, insert the card in a card slot, close up the computer, and turn it on, right?

Well, it's almost that simple. Of course, you may need to install drivers after installing the card, but the steps listed above are, essentially, the basic requirements.

But, first thing, before you buy a peripheral card, you should know two pieces of information:

▶ Do you have an open slot in the computer where the card can be installed?

▶ What kind of slot is it?

Let's start with the more complicated one first.

Four Types of Card Slots

Computer motherboards can have as many as four types of card slots, each accepting a different board configuration. The four types of card slots are:

▶ AGP (Accelerated Graphics Port)

▶ ISA (Industry Standard Architecture)

▶ PCI (Peripheral Component Interconnect)

▶ VESA (Video Electronics Standards Association)

Of these, the last-named (VESA) is fairly archaic, though it can be found on some legacy PCs.

NOTE

Many common motherboard configurations today provide three ISA slots and four PCI slots, and some provide three ISA, three PCI, and one AGP slot.

Accelerated Graphics Port   AGP slots are found on most new Pentium (II and III) motherboards and are used exclusively for high-performance video cards. These are usually provided together with a combination of ISA and PCI slots to support other types of peripherals.

ISA Bus Slots   ISA bus slots are the most common type of peripheral card slot and will be found on virtually all computer motherboards. ISA slots are easily identified since these are the longest slots on standard boards; they consist of two unequal sections positioned end to end, with the longer of the two sections to the rear of the motherboard. Also, for an ISA slot, the connections in both sections are the same size and have the same spacing (compare to VESA slots, later in this section).

Although all types of peripheral cards, including video, are available to fit ISA slots, some older, 16-bit cards might only use a portion of the slot, commonly the longer section to the rear of the motherboard.

PCI Bus Slots   PCI slots are easily identified because the slots are shorter than an IDE slot; also, they consist of only a single connector. These slots have smaller contacts with closer spacing. PCI slots are today's most popular standard for video cards, but are also widely used for network cards and some other peripherals.

VESA Bus Slots   VESA slots were an interim design, originally intended to replace ISA slots, offering a wider data path and consisting of two unequal socket sections that differ in both contact size and spacing. The first section of the socket—toward the rear of the board—was the same as an ISA slot, but the second section, toward the center of the board, commonly used a different color of plastic mount and had much tighter spacing in the contacts. Today, peripheral cards for VESA slots are not readily available. However, motherboards requiring VESA cards can be easily and inexpensively upgraded to newer systems using ISA/PCI slots.

Part II

Installing a Card

WARNING

Do not—*ever*—install a card or any other device while the computer is turned on!

To install a card, begin by shutting down the computer and removing or opening the computer case (the instructions for doing so are given in Chapter 11). Your new computer card should be enclosed in a static-proof envelope or wrapping. Before removing the card from the wrapping, refer to the section "Static Electricity—IMPORTANT!" in Chapter 11 for instructions on preventing damage from static electricity.

Although cards do vary widely in their susceptibility to damage from static charges, all cards should be treated as though they were potentially vulnerable.

To install the card, follow these steps:

1. Select the slot where the card will be installed.

WARNING

Some longer cards may extend the full length of the motherboard. This can be a bad thing, because when you go to install the card you discover that it will extend into some part of the space that is already occupied by the CPU (Socket 7 types). In general, fans and heat sinks on the CPU do not allow vertical clearance for longer cards to be seated above them, and such cards should be placed in a slot that does not conflict with the CPU.

2. If necessary, remove the corresponding slot cover from the rear of the case. In some cases, the slot covers are shiny metal "blanks" covering the slot's window through the back of the case and are mounted with a single screw; other cases have punch-out plastic blanks that can be broken loose and discarded. If you're replacing a card that was already sitting in this slot position, there will be no blank cover to remove.

3. Be sure that the card's connector edge matches the connectors for the card slot. A simple visual examination should be sufficient to determine that the length and spacing correspond.

WARNING

Try not to handle the bare connectors on the board edge. Oils and acids from your skin can cause corrosion and may result in eventual failure.

4. Insert the card into the slot. The rear edge of the card has a 4- to 5-inch metal flange—which might or might not contain external connectors—that resembles the metal piece that covers blank slots (as described in step 2). This flange will be used to fasten the card to the rear of the case. Be sure that this metal plate and any connectors slide freely into the opening in the rear of the case. Ensure that the card seats in the connector evenly. Press firmly into place (but don't apply enough force to crack the motherboard underneath!).

5. Use one screw to anchor the metal flange to the bracket at the rear of the computer case.

6. Close the computer case, and attach any external connectors required by the new card before powering up the computer.

In most situations, you'll now have to tell your system somehow just what it is that you've installed and how you expect to use it. That's the topic of the next section.

Configuring Peripherals

Unfortunately, physically installing a peripheral card is only half the task, because in most cases, you will also need to install a driver or configure the peripheral in some fashion or another.

The first thing to do after installing a peripheral is to turn the machine on to see if the new device works, because this is the point at which you will discover whether the device—and your system—are Plug-and-Play compatible.

NOTE

Some peripheral cards may have custom installation software or may be supplied with special drivers. Always begin by reading the installation instructions supplied with the device.

Plug and Play (PnP)

Plug and Play—or, as disappointed users sometimes refer to it, Plug and *Pray*—is a standard methodology that is intended to allow peripheral

Part ii

devices to communicate with the system, to inform the system which drivers are needed, and to allow the system to configure the device for operating compatibly with all other devices installed. Although the intention is laudable, the reality sometimes falls short of the idea.

In actual fact, Plug and Play does work and, for the most part, works well. The problem with Plug and Play is that it depends on three items: the operating system, the motherboard, and the devices that are installed on your system:

▶ As for the operating system, although both Windows 95 and Windows 98/98 SE provide support for Plug and Play, one of the biggest advantages provided by Windows 98 was its improved support for Plug and Play.

NOTE
DOS and NetWare do not support Plug-and-Play operations.

▶   The motherboard in your computer is also partially responsible, because the BIOS must recognize and support Plug-and-Play functions before the operating system can query devices on boot.

▶ Finally, the other devices themselves must also be Plug-and-Play compatible, because they must be able to recognize a query, respond with information about their requirements, and accept configuration instructions.

Because Plug and Play depends on trilateral support, failure of a device to be recognized cannot be blamed entirely on any single element.

Assuming that your system (and BIOS) are Plug-and-Play compatible and that your newly installed peripheral is also Plug-and-Play aware, you can expect to see a message saying that the system has recognized new hardware and is installing it when you reboot Windows 95/98/98 SE.

At this point, you may be prompted to insert the Windows installation CD—for drivers—or you may need to use a diskette or CD supplied with the device.

In any case, you should begin by reading the documentation supplied with the device or by looking for ReadMe.txt files on the accompanying CD or diskette.

If you are unable to install a driver or if the drivers supplied do not work correctly, a common alternative is to check on the Internet for the manufacturer's Web site to see if new or updated drivers are available.

Non–Plug-and-Play and Custom Configurations

If it turns out that your system isn't quite up to Plug and Play, or that you didn't install a Plug-and-Play–compliant component, you'll have to configure the peripheral yourself. Sometimes, even for the best systems, Plug-and-Play installation fails, and custom configuration is needed. Fortunately, both situations are becoming increasingly rare, but such occasions do arise.

If this is the case—or if you are simply curious about your system configuration—Windows 95 and 98/98 SE provide a simple utility offering extensive and detailed system information as well as the opportunity, when necessary, to change or adjust configurations.

Access to System Information   To access system information, right-click the My Computer icon on your Desktop, and select Properties from the shortcut menu to open the System Properties dialog box, and then click the Device Manager tab, which is shown in Figure 12.7.

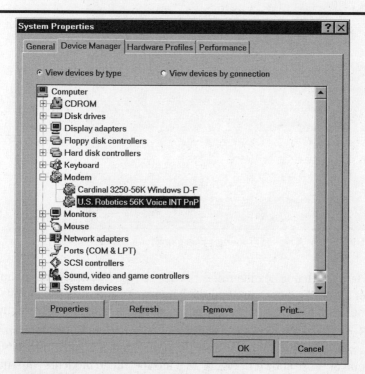

FIGURE 12.7:   The System Properties dialog box

The Device Manager tab shows devices in a tree view arranged by type. If any device was incorrectly installed or was not recognized, a "bang" icon—a yellow exclamation mark—appears next to the device's icon.

In this example, the Modem branch has been expanded to show that two modems are installed on this system: the first a Cardinal 56K and a second (highlighted) from U.S. Robotics.

Clicking the Properties button—or double-clicking an item—displays the Properties dialog box for the selected device, as shown in Figure 12.8.

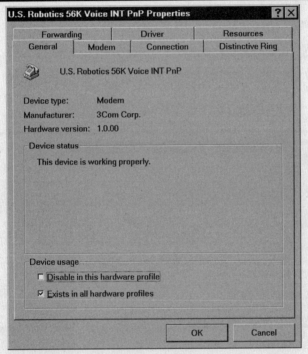

FIGURE 12.8: A typical Properties dialog box for a device

Here the dialog box identifies the device type (Modem), the manufacturer (3Com Corporation), and the hardware version (1.0.00) for this model, as well as informing us that the device is functioning correctly.

Several other tabs provide additional information. Which tabs appear and which types of information are supplied depend on the device type—several of those shown in Figure 12.8 are specific to modems—but, in general, there will be at least a tab for Driver and one for Resources.

The Driver tab supplies information about the software driver(s) installed for this device and provides options for updating them.

The Resources tab (see Figure 12.9) is the key to customizing an installation and shows the current resource usage for the device—that is, the I/O addresses and the IRQ used by the device.

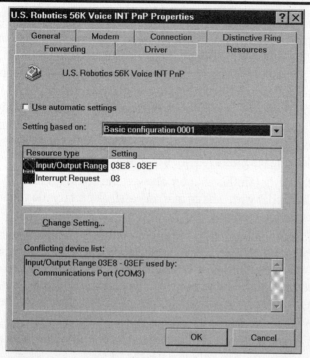

Part ii

FIGURE 12.9:   Resource usage

In this example, I've changed the configuration deliberately to report a conflict with another device, COM3. Normally, by selecting the Use Automatic Settings option, the operating system would be allowed to resolve conflicts between devices, and, by the time you looked at it, no problems would be reported.

When this is not the case—that is, if the Conflicting Device List does show a problem—you can turn off the automatic settings and then select from a drop-down list of basic configurations.

The list will show four (or more) basic configurations. Stepping through the configurations will show the settings for each and report (as shown) any conflicts found for those settings.

Also, if the conflict cannot be resolved using any of the basic configurations provided, highlight the I/O or IRQ settings, and click the Change Setting button to adjust the values.

NOTE

Depending on the device and the driver, the system may or may not allow configuration settings to be changed. Not all devices can be customized.

IRQ (Interrupt) Settings   Although earlier systems supported only 8 Interrupt Request values (IRQs), today's systems support 16 IRQs, numbered 0 through 15. Many of these—that is, motherboard components and elements—are required by the system, and frequently you'll find that not enough IRQs are free for the peripherals you want to add. In particular, some of the more advanced video cards and sound cards—each requiring multiple interrupts or multiple address resources—have been cited as IRQ hogs in not leaving resources free for other required peripherals.

Figure 12.1, earlier in this chapter, showed the Standard IDE/ESDI Hard Disk Controller with a bang marker—a black exclamation mark on a yellow background—indicating that the device is not functional.

Either clicking the Properties button or double-clicking the item displays the Properties dialog box for the device with an explanation of the problem—in this case, the device is disabled because there is no free Interrupt Request (IRQ) that can be assigned. In other cases (but more rarely), the problem might occur when two devices are attempting to use the same I/O addresses.

In general, most hardware devices are generally only able to use specific interrupts or certain memory ranges for I/O.

In the Properties dialog box for the device, click the Hardware Troubleshooter button to step through a series of checks that include a list of which interrupts the device can recognize. You will also have an option to disable some other devices—generally devices that the system considers optional—to try to free an interrupt for use by the selected device.

Unfortunately, the choices may not be items *you* consider optional, and, even when they are, disabling them may not necessarily free a usable interrupt to the device you are attempting to enable.

In some cases, what you can do—by examining the tabs in the Properties dialog boxes for other devices—is to find another device that is currently using an interrupt or other resource that is acceptable to the desired device. Once you locate such a device, you are then faced with two options.

First, it may be possible to change the configuration for the conflicting device in order to free an interrupt or to use different memory addresses if this is where the conflict occurs, thus freeing resources for use by the desired device.

If that approach is not possible, however, your only remaining recourse may be to disable another device—by selecting the Disable In This Hardware Profile check box—to free resources for the desired device.

The drawbacks, of course, are that you are generally not willing to give up one device in order to use another or that disabling certain devices may cause system problems.

If you are encountering problems in this area, your best recourse may be simply to consult a qualified professional for advice and suggestions. In the future, however, new standards should alleviate many of these dependencies on highly limited resources. For further solutions, see the section "Universal Serial Bus and IEEE 1394" following this section.

Memory Address Settings   Memory address settings are port addresses used to communicate with the peripheral device. Refer to your device documentation before attempting to change address settings, because not all devices will be compatible with all settings. For further solutions, see the following section.

Universal Serial Bus (USB) and IEEE 1394 (FireWire)

Because of legacy problems encountered in installing peripherals—most notably the lack of sufficient IRQs to handle all the devices that today's computers may be asked to employ—two standards for peripheral support were developed:

▶ Universal Serial Bus (USB)

▶ IEEE 1394 devices (FireWire devices)

Windows 98 and 98 SE support both of them. (Windows 95 offers limited support as well.)

TIP

Older motherboards may not support USB and FireWire and therefore may require hardware upgrades. Newer motherboards, however, are relatively inexpensive if you simply transfer your old CPU to the new board.

The USB standard allows multiple devices to be attached to a computer without needing free interrupts (IRQs), without requiring adapter cards, and, in most instances, without removing the case! Further, USB devices can be connected—and disconnected—even when the computer is turned on. When a new USB device is connected, the USB-aware system automatically recognizes the device and enables it without requiring rebooting. Likewise, when a USB device is disconnected from the system, no reconfiguration, reboot, or power-down is required. USB devices include scanners, cameras, mice, keyboards, external CD-ROM devices, printers, and the keyboard.

FireWire is similar in purpose to USB, but differs in the types of devices it is intended for. Like USB, FireWire does not require adapter cards or IRQs; unlike USB, FireWire is designed principally for devices needing higher bandwidth, such as digital video cameras and storage devices.

In this chapter, we've covered most of the essentials for installing hard drives and device cards. This does not, however, mean that you may not find yourself needing further technical advice. Unfortunately, computers are sufficiently complex so that there are few simple answers that will cover all contingencies. I certainly hope that the information here will assist you in most situations and that those occasions when you require further technical assistance will be few.

WHAT'S NEXT?

In Part III, we are going to take a look at the Microsoft Office 2000 suite of programs and at two of the applications that are included: Word and Excel. In Chapter 13, we'll give you some tips for getting started and using all the Office applications, and then in the next two chapters, we'll take you step by step through Word and Excel basics.

PART iii

OFFICE BASICS

Chapter 13

WORKING IN OFFICE 2000

Today's software tools provide many challenges, but they also provide even greater opportunities to show off your skills, impress your boss and your customers, and earn the respect—and envy—of your co-workers. Microsoft Office 2000 is a toolkit jam-packed with powerful tools. Whether you work for a multinational corporation or run your own small business, Office 2000's top-of-the-line tools will help you upgrade your existing skills so you can work smarter and more efficiently. With Office 2000 you can manage your busy calendar, track important contacts, make sound financial projections, produce impressive proposals, create dynamite presentations, and establish and maintain a sensational presence on the World Wide Web.

Adapted from *Office 2000: No Experienced Required*
by Gini Courter and Annette Marquis
ISBN 0-7821-2293-0   742 pages $24.99

This chapter will familiarize you with the shared features in Office 2000. If you've used Office 95 or Office 97, a lot of this will be old territory, but you should still quickly work through the chapter, particularly to see the new and enhanced features in Office 2000. You're sure to pick up one or two new concepts that you'll use over and over.

MASTERING OFFICE

Microsoft's Office 2000 Suite comes in four flavors:

- ▶ Standard
- ▶ Small Business
- ▶ Professional
- ▶ Premium

The Standard Suite includes Word, Excel, Outlook, and PowerPoint. The Small Business Suite includes Word, Excel, Outlook, Publisher, and Small Business Tools. The Professional Suite includes the programs in the Small Business Suite plus Access and PowerPoint. The Premium Suite includes the programs in the Professional Suite plus FrontPage and PhotoDraw.

In this part of the book, we'll first look at some features and operations common to all Office applications, and then we'll devote a chapter each to Word and Excel.

If you have worked with prior releases of Office, you'll just need to learn some new and improved techniques for the Office 2000 version. Office 2000 programs support better integration than ever before: between applications, between yourself and other users, and with the Internet and intranets.

Office 2000 also includes a number of smaller tools:

Microsoft Graph   A program to create line, bar, and pie charts for use in Office applications

WordArt   A text-graphics program

The Clip Gallery   An archive of clip art, sounds, and video

All the applications include the Office Assistant, an active Help feature that offers timesaving advice to help you work more efficiently.

EXPLORING COMMON FEATURES IN OFFICE

One of the best things about Office 2000 software is that each application has several useful features in common. If you want to save a letter in Word, a database in Access, or a spreadsheet in Excel, the Save button not only looks the same, but you can locate it in approximately the same place. This section explores some of Office's universal, commonly used features to give you a general introduction.

Launching the Shortcut Bar and New Office Documents

Typical of Windows applications, you have more than one way to get the job done. You can start using Office 2000 three ways: clicking a New Document button on the Office Shortcut Bar, using the Start menu to open a New Office Document, or navigating through the Programs menu to open the actual Office application. The Microsoft Office Shortcut Bar does not automatically appear the first time you use Office 2000 after installation. To open it, click the Start button and choose Programs ➤ Microsoft Office Tools ➤ Microsoft Office Shortcut Bar. You'll be asked if you want it to open automatically when you launch Windows, and then the Shortcut Bar will appear in its default vertical position along the right side of the screen. The Shortcut Bar shown here has been resized to a horizontal position:

NOTE

The Office Shortcut Bar opens vertically by default. You can click and drag it against any edge of the screen, or you can drag it out to make it a free-floating palette.

The Shortcut Bar is, obviously, the easiest way to launch any of the Office 2000 applications, and it even has a button for Publisher. If you elect not to show the Shortcut Bar on your Desktop, try one of these other

Part iii

two ways to open a new document or an Office application. Click the Windows Start button to open the Start menu:

Choose New Office Document or Open Office Document from the top of the Start menu. For brand-new, blank documents, Office 2000 presents you with a host of choices via the New Office Document dialog box—everything from memos and legal briefs to spreadsheets and Web pages are represented there. If you prefer to launch the application and then open a document, choose Programs from the Start menu. The Office 2000 programs appear as individual choices on the Programs menu. Click any program to launch it.

Using the Office 2000 Interface

The Office 2000 applications share a common user interface. This means, for example, that once you're familiar with the *application window* in Excel (see Figure 13.1), getting around in the application window in Word will be a piece of cake. Likewise, you'll notice a lot of other similarities between the applications. Working in Windows applications is like déjà vu; you will see certain features and tools again and again.

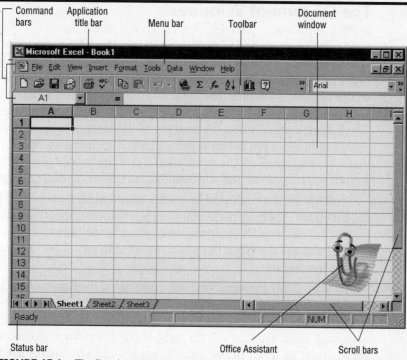

Command bars   Application title bar   Menu bar   Toolbar   Document window

Status bar   Office Assistant   Scroll bars

FIGURE 13.1: The Excel application window

At the top of each application window is a *title bar* that contains three buttons: Minimize, Maximize or Restore, and Close. Use these buttons to change the size of your window or to close the window itself. When you're working in an application, you'll usually want to maximize it. Before you switch to something else, minimizing the first application will free up system resources, making more memory available to the active application. When a window is maximized, the Restore button is displayed; when it is restored, the Maximize button is displayed.

Even with the application window maximized, the Windows Taskbar shows all open applications, so you can easily switch between open Office 2000 applications by clicking an application's Taskbar button. Clicking the Close button on the title bar closes the application, returning you to the Windows Desktop or to another open application.

Part iii

The Document Window

In each application, your work area is known as the *document window*. Here you're surrounded by the tools you need to get the job done: *scroll bars* to move the display, a status bar to keep you informed of an operation's progress, and the *command bars* at the top of the screen to access all the program's features. You'll use two types of command bars: menu bars and toolbars. The menu bar organizes the features into categories: File, Edit, Help, and so on. Clicking any of the categories opens a list of related features for you to choose from. Many of the menu bar options open dialog boxes that allow you to set several options at once related to the feature you choose—all the print options, all the font settings, and so on.

Toolbars are the command bars with graphical buttons located below the menu bar. Toolbars make many of the most commonly used features only one click away. Use toolbars when you want a shortcut to a common feature, and use the menu bar when you want to see *all* the options related to a feature.

In Office 2000, Personal toolbars, comprising the Standard and Formatting toolbars of previous versions, share one row to conserve space in the document window. If a toolbar button you want to use is not available, click the down arrow to the right of either toolbar, and choose the button from the list. This button will replace a less frequently used button from your toolbar.

Office 2000 menus are also personalized to the features you use most commonly. If a drop-down menu has more than a handful of commands, Microsoft has "folded" up less commonly used features. When you see a set of small, double arrows at the bottom of a drop-down menu, select them to reveal all the menu commands, or wait a few seconds, and the menu will "unfold"—you don't even need to click the mouse (see Figure 13.2).

NOTE

If the Personal toolbars option does not suit you, you can display full menus and view the complete Standard and Formatting toolbars on separate rows by choosing View ➢ Toolbars ➢ Customize and clearing the first three check boxes on the Options tab.

FIGURE 13.2:   The Word Edit menu with all the available commands showing

Accessing Commands

If toolbars and menu bars aren't enough, you can execute commands from one of the many context-sensitive shortcut menus or by using shortcut keys. For example, to copy selected text in any application, you can:

▶ Click the Copy button on the Standard toolbar.

▶ Choose Edit ➣ Copy from the menu bar.

▶ Right-click the selected text; then choose Copy from the free-floating shortcut menu.

▶ Hold Ctrl and press C.

Part iii

Notice that the Copy button and the keyboard shortcut are both shown on the Copy menu selection, so you can use the menu bar to help you identify quicker ways to access features you commonly use. *ToolTips* provide additional help with commands. If you're uncertain which toolbar button to use, point to the button and hover for a moment; a ToolTip will appear, showing the button's name.

The Office Assistant

The *Office Assistant* is Microsoft's social help interface for Office 2000. The Office Assistant (see Figure 13.3) crosses all applications and provides help for specific features of each application. You can choose from several Assistants by selecting Choose Assistant from the shortcut menu. Each has its own "personality," including Rocky the power puppy, Mother Nature symbolized as a globe, and an animated Genius with a definite resemblance to Albert Einstein.

FIGURE 13.3: Office Assistant Clippit offering help

The new, improved Office Assistant is free to move around within the application window and displays tips that guide you to better ways to complete a task. The Assistant will offer help the first time you work with a feature or if you have difficulty with a task. Sometimes the offer is subtle—Clippit will blink, Rocky wags his tail, or the Genius produces a light bulb. Sometimes the Assistant can be entertaining; in Office 2000 the Assistant icon changes shape during certain basic tasks like saving or running SpellCheck. Offers of help can also be a bit more direct. If, for example, you open a Wizard, the Office Assistant pops up to ask if you'd like help with the feature.

After you've worked with Office 2000 for a few days, you might decide that you'd like a little less help from your eager Assistant. To change the Assistant's options, click the Assistant's Options button to open the

Office Assistant dialog box. Click the Options tab to display the Options page, shown in Figure 13.4.

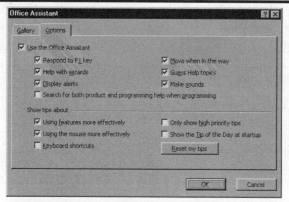

FIGURE 13.4: The Office Assistant dialog box

The Office Assistant is shared by all the Office 2000 programs. Any options you change affect the Assistant in all the Office programs, so if you need an increased level of assistance with Excel, you get the same increased level of assistance with Word.

When you're ready to go it alone, you can close the Assistant window to return it to the Standard toolbar. If you start to get lonely, just click the Office Assistant button to invite the Assistant back into your office.

TIP

For help with any dialog box in Office 2000, click the dialog box Help button (with the question mark), and then click the dialog box control you want help with.

WORKING WITH FILES

One of the great things about Office 2000 is that the dialog boxes used for common file functions are similar in all the applications. In this section, we'll look at the common features of the dialog boxes.

Creating Something New

You can easily create new documents from the Windows Start menu. Selecting New Office Document opens the New Office Document dialog

Part iii

box, shown in Figure 13.5. Each tab contains *templates* for a number of similar documents. Some of the templates (for example, the Fax templates) include text, graphics, or other content. Blank document templates for all the applications—a blank template for an Access database, Word document, Excel worksheet, and PowerPoint presentation—are found on the General page of the New Office Document dialog box.

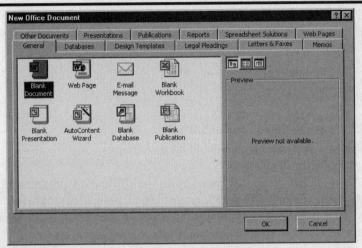

FIGURE 13.5:   The New Office Document dialog box

To open an application, simply double-click any document in the dialog box. If you're already in an application, you have two ways to create a new document.

 Click the New button on the Standard toolbar to open a new, blank document in the active application. If you want a new template instead of a blank document, choose File ➢ New from the menu bar to open the New dialog box with templates appropriate for the active application.

Saving a File

 When you're finished working with a document or have completed a sizable amount of work and want to store it before continuing, choose File ➢ Save from the menu bar, or click the Save button on the Standard toolbar to open the Save As dialog box, shown in Figure 13.6.

The dialog box opens to your default *folder* (directory), but clicking in the Save In text box opens a drop-down list of accessible drives, as shown in Figure 13.7. Select a drive to display the folders on the drive in the pane below the list.

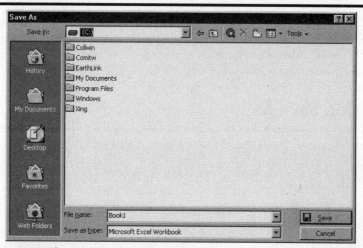

FIGURE 13.6: The Excel Save As dialog box

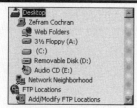

FIGURE 13.7: Save In drop-down list

Double-clicking any folder opens it so that you can view the files and folders it contains. When you have located the proper drive and folder, enter a filename in the File Name text box at the bottom of the dialog box. With Windows 95/98/98 SE, filenames can be a maximum of 255 characters, use uppercase and lowercase letters, and contain spaces. They can't contain punctuation other than underscores, hyphens, and exclamation points. And unlike filenames on the Macintosh, they are not case-sensitive: *MY FILE* and *My File* are the same filename. Make sure the name of the current drive or folder appears in the Save In text box, and then click the Save button to save the file.

WARNING

All the Office 2000 program dialog boxes locate documents based on a file *extension*—the three characters following a period in a filename. For example, Word documents have the .doc extension. Don't create your own extensions or change the extensions of existing documents. If you do, the Office 2000 applications will have trouble finding your files—and that means so will you!

Using Save As

After you've saved a file once, clicking Save saves the file without opening the dialog box. If you want to save a previously saved file with a new name or save it in another location, choose File ➢ Save As from the menu bar to open the Save As dialog box. The Save As feature is particularly useful if you are using an existing document to create a new document and you want to keep both the original *and* the revised document.

If you share files with people using other programs or older versions of Office programs, they may not be able to open your Office 2000 files. You can, however, save your file in a format they can open. In the Save As dialog box, scroll through the Save As Type drop-down list, and select an appropriate file format. The Save As Type drop-down list from Word is shown in Figure 13.8.

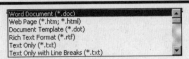

FIGURE 13.8: Save As Type drop-down list

Closing a File

To remove a document from the document window, choose File ➢ Close. If you close a document that has been changed since it was last saved, you will be prompted to save your changes.

Sending Files Using E-Mail

Every Office 2000 application—Word, Excel, PowerPoint, Outlook, Access, and Publisher—has two new standard features to help you send files via e-mail. You can either send your file as an e-mail message, or you can attach it to an existing e-mail message, by simply choosing one File menu option.

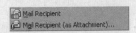

To send a document as an e-mail message, open it in the appropriate Office application, and choose File ➢ Send To ➢ Mail Recipient. A space appears at the top of the document where you can fill in the e-mail address(es) and send it on its way.

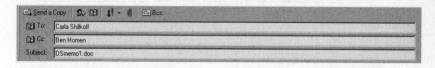

If you prefer to send the document as an attachment, choose File ➢ Send To ➢ Mail Recipient (As Attachment). A separate e-mail window appears, showing the document as an icon in a window at the bottom, with space for you to type a message before you send it out.

Opening an Existing File

You can open an existing Office 2000 document in three ways. If the document was created recently, click the Windows Start button and open the Documents menu. If the document appears there, you're in luck—you can open it directly from the menu.

If the document doesn't appear on the Documents menu, choose Open Office Document from the Start menu, and Office opens an Open Office Document dialog box. Use the Look In drop-down list to locate the folder that contains the file.

If you're already working in PowerPoint, for example, and want to open an existing presentation, click the Open button on the Standard toolbar to open the Open dialog box, shown in Figure 13.9.

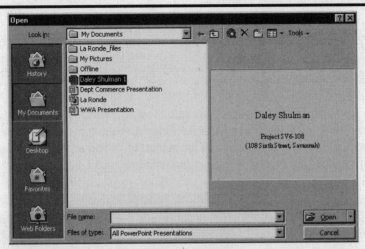

FIGURE 13.9: PowerPoint's Open dialog box

This Open dialog box is just like the Open Office Document dialog box, but it is filtered to show only PowerPoint files. Use the Look In drop-down list to locate the proper folder and file.

Converting Files from Other Formats

Office 2000 applications will open files created in other applications and earlier versions of Office. However, Access and Publisher use different file formats those used in previous versions, so the application has to create a converted copy of the file before it can be opened. For instance, Access 2000 will open a database created in Access 2 or Access 97, but it tells you to convert the database, as shown in Figure 13.10. If you choose not to convert the database, you won't be able to change the database's structure, but you will still be able to use the database.

NOTE

Word, Excel, and PowerPoint documents created in Office 2000 do need to be converted before they can be opened in Office 97. You may lose a little special formatting that is only available in Office 2000, but you will still be able to work with the Office 2000 document using Office 97.

FIGURE 13.10: The Access conversion prompt

Print Preview and Printing

Every Office 2000 application except PowerPoint and Publisher allows you to preview a document before printing. Click the Print Preview button on the Standard toolbar to open the preview window. The preview windows themselves vary in each application.

To print a document, choose File ≻ Print from the menu bar to open the Print dialog box, shown in Figure 13.11. Although each application's Print dialog box is slightly different, all allow you to select a printer, choose the number of copies, and specify what should be printed. Clicking the Options button at the bottom of the dialog box opens a dialog box in which you select print quality and other settings.

To immediately send a document to the printer using the default print options (and without opening a dialog box), click the Print button on the Standard toolbar. This can be convenient in most of the applications, but is problematic in PowerPoint, where the default print settings are full-page pictures of each slide in a presentation. What a way to tie up a printer!

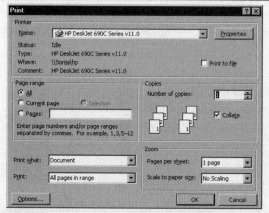

FIGURE 13.11: Word's Print dialog box

Part iii

Editing in Office 2000

Many editing features are shared among Office 2000 applications. Each application may have a quicker or easier way of editing in particular circumstances, but in this section, you'll learn those features that work no matter where you are or what you're doing.

The Insertion Point

The insertion point is the flashing vertical bar that shows where the next character you type will appear. You'll see the blinking insertion point, shown in Figure 13.12, as soon as you open a document or form. The only exception is Excel, in which the insertion point appears after you begin typing.

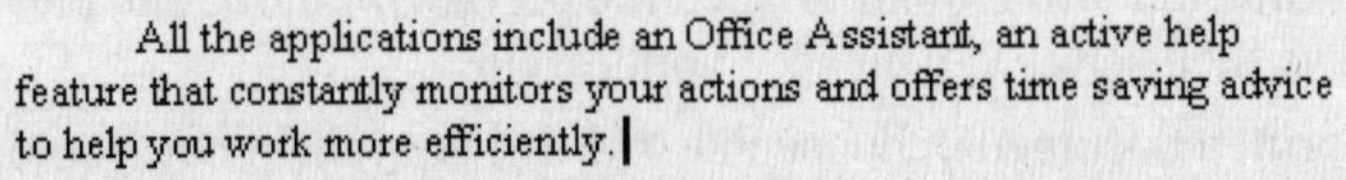

All the applications include an Office Assistant, an active help feature that constantly monitors your actions and offers time saving advice to help you work more efficiently.|

FIGURE 13.12:   The insertion point moves to the right as new text is added.

When you move the mouse pointer into an area where you can enter or edit text, the pointer changes to an I-beam. To edit existing text, move the insertion point by moving the I-beam to the text you want to edit. Click, and the insertion point will jump to the new position. You can then type new text or delete existing text at the insertion point.

Correcting Mistakes

Helping you to correct mistakes is one of the many things Office 2000 does exceptionally well. In its simplest form, Office will let you erase existing text manually. At its most powerful, Office can automatically correct the words you most commonly misspell.

Backspace and Delete

Most people are familiar with using the Backspace and Delete keys on the keyboard to delete text, but you're not alone if you confuse when to use which one:

▶ Backspace (represented by a left-pointing arrow on the keyboard) erases one character to the *left* of the insertion point.

▶ Delete erases one character to the *right* of the insertion point.

Use whichever is more convenient, based on where your insertion point is.

Undo and Redo

 Office 2000 is exceptionally forgiving. The Undo button on the Standard toolbar lets you reverse an action or a whole series of actions you have taken. The Undo button will dim when you have reached the last action you can undo. Click the drop-down arrow next to the Undo button and scroll down the history to reverse multiple actions in one step:

If you change your mind again, clicking the Redo button reverses the last Undo. In Office 2000, you can use the Undo and Redo histories to reverse multiple actions in all the applications. Each application, though, has its own rules about how far you can undo.

Overtype and Insert Modes

The default editing mode in Office 2000 is Insert: if you enter new text in the middle of existing text, the original text will move to the right to accommodate it. Overtype mode replaces existing text with the newly entered text. To toggle between Insert and Overtype modes, press the Insert key on the keyboard.

A Quick Look at Spelling

No matter how many spelling tests you may have failed in elementary school, you can still produce documents that are free of spelling errors. The Spelling feature is available in all Office 2000 applications, including e-mail created in Outlook. Word and PowerPoint will flag misspelled words as you type by placing a wavy red line underneath possible misspellings.

mispelled

All you have to do is right-click a flagged word to open the Spell It pop-up menu, which lists suggestions for the proper spelling. Click the correct spelling, choose to ignore the word, or have Office add the spelling to your custom dictionary—a good idea with names you use a lot. That way Spell It won't flag the name the next time you use it.

In the other applications, you'll have to ask Office to check your spelling by clicking the Spelling button on the Standard toolbar. Office reviews your document, flags possible misspelled words, and opens the Spelling and Grammar dialog box:

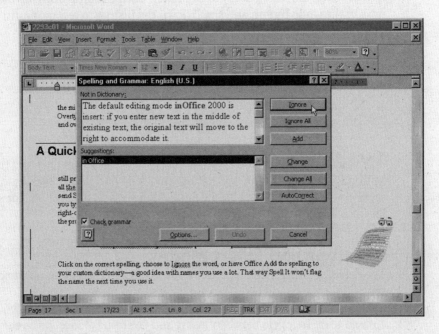

The Spelling and Grammar dialog box gives you all the same options as the Spell It pop-up menu and a few additional ones. Here you can choose to Ignore All occurrences of the word or to Change All occurrences to the correct spelling. You can also enter the correct spelling. All the Office applications share a custom dictionary, so words you add in one application aren't flagged in others.

Automatic Fixes for Common Errors

Most Office 2000 applications access a shared feature called AutoCorrect. With AutoCorrect you can build your own list of common misspellings. When Office encounters one of those words, it automatically fixes it for you. Some words, such as "adn" and "teh," are already in the list. As you correct misspelled words, you can add them to the AutoCorrect list.

AutoCorrect is one of the options in both the Spell It pop-up menu and the Spelling and Grammar dialog box. You can also access it by choosing Tools ➤ AutoCorrect.

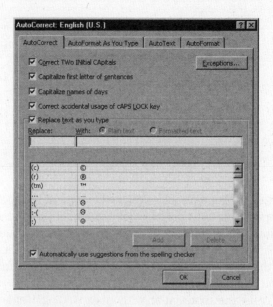

Once you add a word to the AutoCorrect list, you never have to worry about correcting the spelling error again. Also, AutoCorrect can recognize and replace common combinations of symbols such as the copyright symbol (c) and the "smilicon :)" now popular online. A couple of words of caution, though:

▶ Be sure to verify you are adding a correctly spelled word to the AutoCorrect list.

▶ Don't add words that mean something else when you spell them differently. For example, if you commonly reverse the "r" and the "o" in "from," don't add this error to the AutoCorrect list, or every time you want to type "form" AutoCorrect will automatically change the word to "from."

AutoCorrect also gives you a number of options that you can leave on or turn off based on your personal preferences, such as correcting two initial capitals and capitalizing the names of days. Choose Tools ➤ AutoCorrect to open the AutoCorrect dialog box. If you want to turn AutoCorrect off entirely, click to remove the check mark in front of Replace Text As You Type. The Exceptions button provides you with two options. You can

Part iii

add abbreviations that you type regularly, so that AutoCorrect doesn't automatically capitalize the next word. You can also add words that require two initial caps, so it doesn't automatically change them.

Although AutoCorrect is designed to prevent typing and spelling errors, it is also valuable as a shortcut tool. You can enter words that you type regularly into your AutoCorrect list to save yourself time and keystrokes—long company names, for example, or legal or medical terminology. Just enter a code that you will recognize, such as USA, and AutoCorrect will expand it for you into United States of America. However, if you think you will ever want to use the abbreviation without expanding it, enter a slash (/) or some other character in front of the abbreviation (/USA). You can then choose whether to have AutoCorrect supply the long form (by typing **/USA**) or use the abbreviation (by typing **USA** without the slash).

SELECTING, MOVING, AND COPYING

Whether you are correcting mistakes or shuffling your whole document around, the first step is knowing how to select text. Once text is selected, it can be moved, copied, deleted, aligned, or resized.

Selecting Text

Each application has its own shortcuts to selecting. However, no matter where you are, you can always drag to select—even in a dialog box. To select by dragging, move the insertion point to the beginning or the end of the desired text string, hold down the mouse button, and move in the desired direction. Selected text changes to reverse video—the opposite color from the rest of the text. To unselect text, click anywhere in the document.

WARNING

Selected text is automatically deleted if you press any key on the keyboard. If you accidentally delete text in a document, click Undo. Undo won't work in dialog boxes.

Moving and Copying Text

Now that you can select text, you can move and copy text in any of the Office applications; for example, you would move text to rearrange sentences in a Word document or topics in a PowerPoint presentation. When you *move* a selection, the original is deleted and placed in the new location. *Copying* text leaves the original in place and creates a copy in the new location.

You can move text by cutting it from its current location and pasting it in a new location. When you cut a block of text, it is deleted from your document and copied to the *Clipboard*. Copying text moves a copy of the text to the Clipboard without deleting the original. The Clipboard is part of the computer's memory set aside and managed by Windows. The Clipboard can hold only one piece of information at a time, but that piece of information can be text, a graphic, or even a video clip.

Follow these steps to move or copy text:

1. Select the text you want to move or copy.

  2. Click the Cut or Copy button on the Standard toolbar.

3. Move the insertion point to where you want the text to appear.

 4. Click the Paste button.

All the moving and copying techniques work with pictures or other objects just as they do with text.

TIP

Cut, Copy, and Paste are standard Windows functions, and as a result, they have corresponding shortcut keys that you can use even if menu and toolbar options are not available. Select the text or object and press Ctrl+X to cut, Ctrl+C to copy, or Ctrl+V to paste.

Part iii

Pasting Multiple Items

A new feature of Office 2000 is Collect and Paste, which lets you copy a maximum of 12 items and save them to a temporary Clipboard where you can select and paste them all at once. This makes it easier to move several items from one place to another, without forcing you to scroll up and down or split the screen.

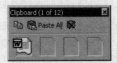

To select items for collecting and pasting, choose your items in order by pressing Edit ➤ Copy or Edit ➤ Cut, and the Clipboard toolbar appears. After you move to the new location in the document where you want to paste the items, insert them one by one by clicking them and clicking the Paste button, or clicking the Paste All button on the Clipboard toolbar.

ADDING PIZZAZZ

One of the primary benefits of using Windows applications is the ease with which you can give your documents a professional appearance. The right combination of fonts, font styles, sizes, and attributes can make your words or numbers jump right off the page.

Fonts and Font Styles

Selecting the right font can be the difference between a professional-looking document and an amateur effort that's tedious to read. Fonts are managed by Windows, which means that a font available in one application is available in all Windows applications. You can access fonts and many of their font attributes right from the Formatting toolbar. Word's Formatting toolbar is shown in Figure 13.13.

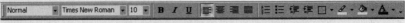

FIGURE 13.13: Word's Formatting toolbar

To change the font, click the drop-down arrow next to the font name. Either Times New Roman or Arial is the default font, depending on the application. All Windows True Type fonts (designated by the TT in front of them) are scaleable, which means that you can make them any size by entering the desired size in the Font Size text box. Of course, you can also select from the sizes in the drop-down list.

To turn on Bold, Italics, or Underline, click the corresponding button on the toolbar. Remember that you must select existing text before you can change the font or font style.

For all of the available font options, choose Format ➤ Font, or in Excel choose Format ➤ Cells, and click the Font tab to open the Font dialog box:

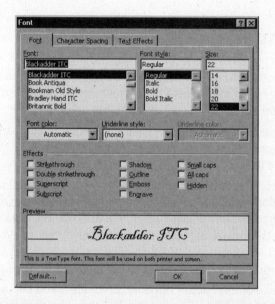

Here you can see what the fonts look like in the Preview window. You can also choose from several underline options, although the options that are available depend on the application. For example, you can choose a Wave underline style in Word and a Double Accounting underline style in Excel. You can also apply a number of different effects to your text such as Strikethrough, Superscript, and Subscript. Word and PowerPoint also have effects such as Shadow and Emboss.

With all the color printers around today, being able to add colors to text is an important feature. Font Color is available from most toolbars as well as from the Font dialog box. There are also many new fancy, decorative fonts available in Office 2000, a few of which are shown in Figure 13.14.

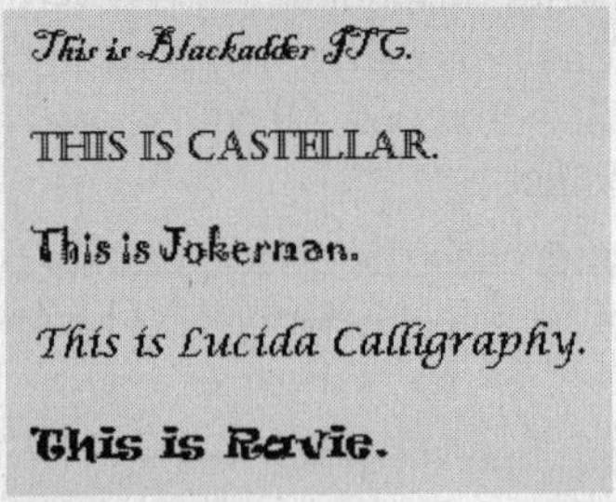

This is Blackadder ITC.

THIS IS CASTELLAR.

This is Jokerman.

This is Lucida Calligraphy.

This is Ravie.

FIGURE 13.14: Some new decorative fonts shown in Word

Copying Existing Formats

Once you have formatted text just the way you like it, there is no need to re-create it for other text that you want formatted the same way. You can easily copy that format to other text in your document using the Format Painter.

 Select the text with the format you want to copy, and click the Format Painter button on the Standard toolbar. Your mouse pointer changes shape to an I-beam with a paintbrush next to it.

 Drag the Format Painter I-beam over some existing text, and it will be reformatted to look just like the text you copied. Once you've applied the format, the Format Painter will turn off automatically. If you need to copy the formatting more than once, select the text you want to copy and double-click (instead of single-clicking) the Format Painter button. When you are finished, click the Format Painter button again to turn it off.

The Format Painter not only copies fonts and font attributes but other formatting such as line spacing, bullets and numbering, borders and shading, and indents.

WHAT'S NEXT?

Now that you have an overview of Office tools and operations, you're ready to work with some specific applications. In the next chapter, Guy Hart-Davis will help you get started with Word, the word-processing program that is part of Office 2000.

Chapter 14

CREATING SIMPLE WORD DOCUMENTS

In this chapter, we'll look at how to work with Word documents. You'll create a new Word document and save it to disk. After that, I'll discuss how to close a document you've been working on and how to reopen that document or open another document. Along the way, I'll discuss the most common things you'll want to do in documents you create: enter text in them, undo mistakes you've made, and insert information such as dates or special characters.

WORD 2000
NO EXPERIENCE REQUIRED

Adapted from *Word 2000: No Experience Required*
by Guy Hart-Davis
0-7821-2400-3   448 pages $19.99

CREATING A NEW DOCUMENT

When you run Word, it opens a new blank document and names it Document1.

 To create a new document based on the default template (Blank Document), click the New Blank Document button on the Standard toolbar or press Ctrl+N. Word will open a new document named Documentx (Document2, Document3, and so on).

At other times, you'll probably want to create a new document based on a template that already contains some text or that provides a different look and feel than the default template. A *template* is the skeleton upon which a document is based. To create a new document based on a different template:

1. Choose File ➤ New. Word will display the New dialog box (see Figure 14.1).

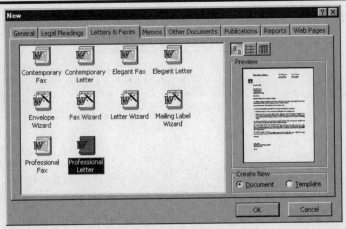

FIGURE 14.1: To create a new document based on a template other than Blank Document, choose File ➤ New, and select the template in the New dialog box.

2. In the Create New group box at the lower-right corner of the New dialog box, make sure that the Document option button is selected rather than the Template option button. (You use the Template option button for creating a new template.)

3. In the New dialog box, choose the tab that contains the type of document you want to create: General, Legal Pleadings,

Letters & Faxes, Memos, Other Documents, Publications, Reports, or Web Pages.

▶ If you didn't install all the templates that Word offers, you may not see all these tabs in the New dialog box. Then again, if you or someone else has created more templates in another folder, you may see more tabs than those listed here.

▶ To see a preview of a template in the tab you chose, click a template. The preview will appear in the box on the right side of the New dialog box.

NOTE

A *template* is a special type of document that you use to produce documents that share the same look or contents. Templates can contain styles, AutoText entries, toolbars, and macros. By basing a document on a different template, you can change its styles instantly, change its look completely, and virtually typeset it differently, in seconds. (Word calls this "attaching" a template to a document.) Take a look at the Preview box as you click some of the templates to get an idea of what is available.

▶ You can choose from three views of the templates available by clicking any of the three buttons above the Preview box. The leftmost button gives the Large Icons view; the second gives the List view; and the third gives the Details view.

TIP

Details view offers the most information of the three views, and you can sort the templates by name, size, type, or date last modified by clicking the buttons at the top of the columns.

4. To start a document based on the template you chose, double-click the icon or listing for the template, or click it once and then click the OK button.

WORKING WITH TEXT

As in most word-processing applications, Word's basic unit is the paragraph. These aren't paragraphs as people generally understand them: a paragraph in Word consists of a paragraph mark (made by pressing the

Enter key) and any text (or graphic) between it and the previous paragraph mark (or the beginning of the document). In other words, a paragraph consists of anything (text, a graphic, space, or even nothing at all) that appears between two paragraph marks, up to and including the second paragraph mark. Strange as it seems, a paragraph mark with nothing between it and the previous paragraph mark is considered a full paragraph. You can treat each paragraph as a unit for formatting with styles or for moving and copying.

Each blank document you create contains one paragraph, which is located at the start of the document. You can add as many paragraphs to a document as you need.

TIP

If you don't see paragraph marks on your screen, click the ¶ button on the Standard toolbar. This is the Show/Hide ¶ button, and it toggles the display of spaces, tabs, paragraph marks, and the like. Some people find it easier to work with these marks displayed; others find them distracting. You can also display and hide these marks by pressing Ctrl+Shift+8.

Entering Text

To enter text into your document, position the insertion point where you want the text to appear and type. Word will automatically wrap text as it reaches the end of a line, so you don't need to press the Enter key when you get there. Press the Enter key when you need to start a new paragraph.

NOTE

If you're working in Normal view, Word will adjust the display of the text to suit the screen and window size, rather than display the text as it will appear when you print it. For precise layout, you'll need to work in Print Layout view (View ➢ Print Layout) rather than Normal view.

If you want to move to a new line without starting a new paragraph— for example, so there is no extra space between lines—press Shift+Enter to start a new line within the same paragraph.

As you reach the end of a page, Word will automatically break text onto the next page. If you want, you can start a new page at any point by inserting a page break. To do so, press Ctrl+Enter.

In Print Layout view, Web Layout view, and Print Preview, Word 2000 provides a feature called Click and Type that enables you to double-click where you want to enter text on the page. Word automatically enters any blank paragraphs and tabs required to position the insertion point where you double-clicked and changes the alignment of the paragraph if necessary. (If there are already superfluous blank paragraphs or tabs beyond where you double-clicked, Word removes them automatically.) For example, to create a centered heading one-third of the way down the fresh page in a new blank document, double-click one-third of the way down the page and in the middle of the line. Word will place the insertion point there, add blank paragraphs from the top of the page to the line of the heading, and apply center alignment. You can then create a right-aligned paragraph at the bottom of the page by double-clicking at the right margin toward the bottom of the page.

The mouse pointer displays the type of alignment that Click and Type will implement if you double-click in that area: centering around the horizontal middle of the page, right alignment near to the right margin, and left alignment everywhere else.

Insert and Overtype Modes

Word offers two *modes* (methods of behavior) for adding text to your documents: Insert mode and Overtype mode. In *Insert mode* (the default mode), characters you type are inserted into the text at the insertion point, pushing along any characters to the right of the insertion point. If you want to type over existing text in Insert mode, select the text using either the mouse or the keyboard (see a later section for instructions on selecting text), and type the text you want to insert in its place. In Insert mode, the OVR indicator on the status bar is dimmed.

`OVR` In *Overtype mode*, any character you type replaces the character (if any) to the immediate right of the insertion point. When Word is in Overtype mode, the OVR indicator on the status bar is active (darkened).

To toggle between Insert mode and Overtype mode, double-click the OVR indicator on the status bar or press the Insert key. Alternatively, choose Tools ➤ Options to display the Options dialog box, click the Edit tab to display it, select the Overtype Mode check box, and click the OK button.

Moving the Insertion Point

In Word, you can move the insertion point using the mouse, the keyboard, or a combination of the two. In most situations, you can use whichever means you prefer, though you will probably find the mouse easier for some operations and the keyboard easier for others.

Part iii

Using the Mouse

To position the insertion point using the mouse, simply move the insertion point to where you want it, and click.

Use the vertical scroll bar to move up and down through your document (or, if you have an IntelliMouse or other scrolling mouse, use the mouse's roller). When you scroll with the scroll bar (the thumb) in a multipage document, Word will display a small box next to the scroll bar showing which page and heading you're scrolling past. Use the horizontal scroll bar to move from side to side as necessary.

TIP

If you often need to scroll horizontally in Normal view to see the full width of your documents, turn on Word's Wrap To Window option, which makes the text fit into the current window size, regardless of width. To turn on Wrap To Window, choose Tools ➤ Options, click the View tab, and select the Wrap To Window check box. Click the OK button to close the Options dialog box.

Click the Next Page and Previous Page buttons at the foot of the vertical scroll bar to move to the next page and previous page. Make sure that these buttons are black, which indicates that Word is browsing by pages. If they're blue, Word is browsing by a different item, such as sections or comments; clicking the buttons while they are blue will take you to the next (or previous) section or comment in the document. To reset Word to browse by pages, click the Object Browser button between the Next and Previous buttons and choose the Browse By Page button in the Object Browser list, as shown here.

NOTE

The Object Browser is a feature introduced in Word 97 that allows you to choose which type of item you want to navigate to in the document. You can move to the previous or next field, endnote, footnote, comment, section, page, Go To item, Find item, edit, heading, graphic, or table. This provides a way of moving quickly from one instance of an item to the next or previous instance. For example, if you need to check each table in a document, choose Table from the Object Browser list, and then use the Previous and Next buttons to navigate from table to table.

Using Keyboard Shortcuts

Word offers a number of keystroke combinations to move the insertion point swiftly through the document without removing your hands from the keyboard. Besides the left arrow (←) to move left one character, right arrow (→) to move right one character, up arrow (↑) to move up one line, and down arrow (↓) to move down one line, you can use the following:

Keystroke	Action
Ctrl+→	One word to the right
Ctrl+←	One word to the left
Ctrl+↑	To the beginning of the current paragraph or (if the insertion point is at the beginning of a paragraph) to the beginning of the previous paragraph
Ctrl+↓	To the beginning of the next paragraph
End	To the end of the current line
Ctrl+End	To the end of the document
Home	To the start of the current line
Ctrl+Home	To the start of the document
PageUp	Up one screen's worth of text
PageDown	Down one screen's worth of text
Ctrl+PageUp	To the first character on the current screen
Ctrl+PageDown	To the last character on the current screen

TIP

You can quickly move to the last three places you edited in a document by pressing Shift+F5 (Go Back) once, twice, or three times. This is especially useful when you open a document and need to return to the point at which you were last working.

Selecting Text

Word offers a number of ways to select text: you can use the keyboard, the mouse, or the two in combination. You'll find that some ways of selecting text work better than others with certain equipment; experiment to find which are the fastest and most comfortable methods for you.

Selected text appears highlighted in reverse video—for example, if your normal text is black on a white background, selected text will be white on a black background.

Selecting Text with the Mouse

The simplest way to select text with the mouse is to position the insertion point at the beginning or end of the block you want to select and then click and drag to the end or beginning of the block.

TIP

Word offers an automatic word-selection feature to help you select whole words more quickly with the mouse. When this feature is switched on, as soon as you drag the mouse pointer from one word to the next, Word will select the whole of the first word and the whole of the second; when the mouse pointer reaches the third, it selects that too, and so on. To temporarily override automatic word selection, hold down the Alt key before you click and drag. To turn off automatic word selection, choose Tools ➤ Options to display the Options dialog box. Click the Edit tab to bring it to the front of the dialog box, and clear the When Selecting, Automatically Select Entire Word check box. Then click the OK button. To turn automatic word selection on, select the When Selecting, Automatically Select Entire Word check box.

You can also select text with multiple clicks:

▶ Double-click in a word to select it.

▶ Triple-click in a paragraph to select it.

▶ Ctrl+click in a sentence to select it.

In the *selection bar* on the left side of the screen (where the insertion point turns from an I-beam to an arrow pointing up and to the right), you can click to select text as follows:

▶ Click once to select the line the arrow is pointing at.

▶ Double-click to select the paragraph the arrow is pointing at.

▶ Triple-click (or Ctrl+click once) to select the entire document.

Selecting Text with the Keyboard

To select text with the keyboard, hold down the Shift key and move the insertion point by using the keyboard shortcuts listed in the section titled "Using Keyboard Shortcuts" earlier in this chapter.

SELECTING TEXT WITH THE EXTEND SELECTION FEATURE

You can also select text by using Word's Extend Selection feature, though for most uses it's slow and clumsy. Press the F8 key once to enter Extend Selection mode; you'll see EXT appear undimmed on the status bar. Press F8 a second time to select the current word, a third time to select the current sentence, a fourth time to select the current paragraph, and a fifth time to select the whole document. Then press the Escape key to turn off Extend Selection mode.

Extend Selection also works with other keys on the keyboard: To select a sentence, press F8 at the beginning of the sentence, and then press the punctuation mark that appears at the end of the sentence. To select some text, position the insertion point at the beginning of that text, press F8, and then press the letter up to which you want to select. If there is another instance of the letter before the one you want to select, press the letter again.

To select a paragraph, place the insertion point at the start of the paragraph, press F8, and then press the Enter key.

Selecting Text with the Mouse and Keyboard

Word also offers ways to select text using the mouse and keyboard together. These techniques are well worth trying, as you can quickly select awkward blocks of text—for example, if you want to select a few sentences from a paragraph or to select columns of characters.

To select a block of text using the mouse and the keyboard, position the insertion point at the start (or end) of a block and click. Then move the insertion point to the end (or start) of the block—scroll if necessary with the mouse roller or the scroll bar, but don't use the keyboard—hold down the Shift key, and then click again.

To select columns of characters, hold down the Alt key, and click and drag from one end of the block to the other (see Figure 14.2). This technique can be very useful for getting rid of extra spaces or tabs used to align text.

NOTE

Selecting text in a table works a little differently from selecting regular text. Play around a little to get comfortable with tables.

Part iii

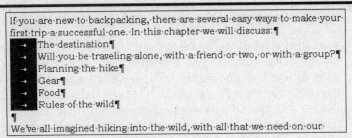

If·you·are·new·to·backpacking,·there·are·several·easy·ways·to·make·your·
first·trip·a·successful·one.·In·this·chapter·we·will·discuss:¶
→   The·destination¶
→   Will·you·be·traveling·alone,·with·a·friend·or·two,·or·with·a·group?¶
→   Planning·the·hike¶
→   Gear¶
→   Food¶
→   Rules·of·the·wild¶
¶
We've·all·imagined·hiking·into·the·wild,·with·all·that·we·need·on·our·

FIGURE 14.2:   To select columns of characters without selecting whole lines, hold down the Alt key and drag through the block.

Deleting Text

Word lets you delete text swiftly and easily:

▶ To delete a block of text, simply select it, and press the Delete key.

▶ To delete the character to the left of the insertion point, press the Backspace key.

▶ To delete the character to the right of the insertion point, press the Delete key.

▶ To delete the word to the right of the insertion point, press Ctrl+Delete. This actually deletes from the insertion point to the beginning of the next word (or the end of the line, if the current word is the last one in the line); so if the insertion point is in a word when you press Ctrl+Delete, you won't delete the whole word.

▶ To delete the word to the left of the insertion point, press Ctrl+Backspace. Again, if the insertion point isn't at the end of the word, only the part of the word to the left of the insertion point will be deleted.

TIP

You can also delete selected text by choosing Edit ➤ Clear or by right-clicking in the selection and choosing Cut from the shortcut menu that appears. (Some shortcut menus—which are different for different elements of Word documents—don't have a Cut command.)

Cutting, Pasting, and Moving Text

You can easily copy and move text (and graphics) around your document either by using the Cut, Copy, and Paste commands or by using

Word's drag-and-drop feature, which lets you copy or move text using your mouse.

The Office 2000 applications improve on previous versions by having their own Clipboard, which can contain a maximum of 12 copied or cut items, rather than relying on the Windows Clipboard, which can contain only one text item and one graphical item at a time. This Office Clipboard is implemented as a toolbar, and its contents are available to each of the Office applications. As shown in Figure 14.3, the Office Clipboard uses icons to indicate the type of information each of the 12 storage containers holds: a Word document icon for text from a Word document, an Excel spreadsheet icon to indicate cells from a spreadsheet, an Excel chart icon to indicate a chart, a PowerPoint slide icon to indicate a slide from a presentation, and so on.

FIGURE 14.3: The Office Clipboard can contain a maximum of 12 items of different types. To see a simplified version of the contents of an item on the Clipboard, move the mouse pointer over it so that a ToolTip appears.

As you cut or copy items, they are added to the Office Clipboard until it contains 12 items. When you cut or copy a thirteenth item, Word or the Office Assistant will warn you that copying this item will drop the first item from the Clipboard. Choose OK or Cancel.

You can paste any individual item from the Clipboard to the current position of the insertion point by clicking it. Alternatively, you can paste all the items from the Clipboard by clicking the Paste All button on the Clipboard's toolbar. The Paste All command is useful for gathering a number of items in sequence—for example, you might want to cull a dozen headings or paragraphs from a report to create a summary.

When the Clipboard is full or nearing full, you can remove all the items from the Clipboard by clicking the Clear Clipboard button on the Clipboard's toolbar.

The most recent text item or graphical item on the Office Clipboard is also placed on the Windows Clipboard, so you can transfer information to and from non-Office programs. Likewise, the current text or graphical item on the Windows Clipboard is also placed on the Office Clipboard.

 Cut   The Cut command removes the selected text (or graphics) from the Word document and places it on the Office Clipboard and Windows Clipboard. From there, you can paste it into another part of the document, into another document, or into another application. To cut the current selection, click the Cut button, right-click and choose Cut from the shortcut menu, choose Edit ➤ Cut, or press Ctrl+X.

 Copy   The Copy command copies the selected text (or graphics) to the Office Clipboard and the Windows Clipboard. From there, you can paste it into another part of the document, into another document, or into another application. To copy the current selection, click the Copy button, right-click and choose Copy from the shortcut menu, choose Edit ➤ Copy, or press Ctrl+C.

 Paste   The Paste command pastes a copy of the Windows Clipboard's contents into your Word document at the insertion point. To paste the contents of the Windows Clipboard, right-click and choose Paste from the shortcut menu, click the Paste button, choose Edit ➤ Paste, or press Ctrl+V.

USING UNDO AND REDO

Word provides an Undo feature that can undo one or more of the last actions that you've taken, and Word provides a Redo feature that can redo anything that you've just chosen to undo.

 To undo the last action you've taken, click the Undo button on the Standard toolbar, press Ctrl+Z, or choose Edit ➤ Undo. To undo more than one action, click the arrow to the right of the Undo button and choose the number of actions to undo from the drop-down list, as shown here.

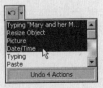

 To redo a single action, click the Redo button on the Standard toolbar, press Ctrl+Y, or choose Edit ➤ Redo. (Often, the Redo button is on the part of the Standard toolbar that is covered by the Formatting toolbar.) To redo more than one action, click the arrow to the right of the Redo button and choose the number of actions to redo from the drop-down list.

When there is no action that can be undone, the Undo button will be dimmed and unavailable. When there is no undone action that can be redone, the Redo button will be dimmed and unavailable.

WARNING

There are a few actions that Word *can't* undo, including File ➣ Save, File ➣ Close, and a number of others. If you find yourself needing to undo an action that Word says it cannot undo, you may need to resort to closing the document without saving changes to it. You will lose all changes made since the last time you saved it — but if you've done something truly horrible to the document, this sacrifice may be worthwhile. (This is another argument for saving your documents frequently, preferably after just enough reflection to be sure you haven't ruined them.)

INSERTING A DATE

To insert a date in a document:

1. Position the insertion point where you want the date to appear. (If necessary, use the Click and Type feature to position the insertion point.)

2. Choose Insert ➣ Date And Time to display the Date And Time dialog box (see Figure 14.4).

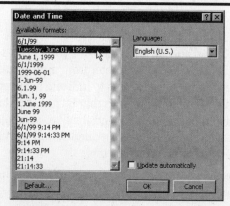

FIGURE 14.4: Use the Date And Time dialog box to quickly insert a date in a document.

3. In the Available Formats list box, choose the date format that you want to use.

   ▶ The Language drop-down list box will show the language you're currently working in. You can choose another language—for example, *English (Australian)* instead of *English (US)*—to see the date formats available for that language.

   ▶ If you want to make the date format in the Available Formats list box the default date format, click the Default button, and then choose the Yes button in the confirmation dialog box that appears. Word will then select that date format automatically every time you display the Date And Time dialog box.

4. If you want the date to be updated every time the document is opened, select the Update Automatically check box. This is useful for documents such as reports, which you often want to bear the date (and perhaps the time) on which they were printed, not the date on which they were created. For documents such as business letters and memos, on the other hand, you usually will want to make sure this check box is cleared, so that the date you insert remains the same no matter when you open or print the document.

5. Click the OK button to insert the date in your document.

INSERTING SYMBOLS AND SPECIAL CHARACTERS

Word offers enough symbols and special characters for you to typeset almost any document. Symbols can be any character from multiplication or division signs to the fancy ➤ arrow Sybex uses to indicate menu commands. Special characters are a subset of symbols that include em dashes (—) and en dashes (–), trademark symbols (™), and the like—symbols that Microsoft thinks you might want to insert more frequently and with less effort than the symbols relegated to the Symbols tab.

To insert a symbol or special character at the insertion point or in place of the current selection:

1. Choose Insert ➤ Symbol to display the Symbol dialog box (see Figure 14.5).

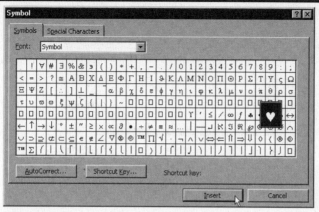

FIGURE 14.5: In the Symbol dialog box, choose the symbol or special character to insert, and then click the Insert button.

2. To insert a symbol, click the Symbols tab to bring it to the front of the dialog box (if it isn't already there) and then choose the symbol to insert from the box.

   ▸ Use the Font drop-down list to pick the font you want to see in the dialog box. For some fonts, a Subset drop-down list will appear to the right of the Font drop-down list; you can also choose a different subset of the font from this drop-down list.

   ▸ To enlarge a character so you can see it more clearly, click it once. An enlarged version of it will pop out at you. You can then move the zoom box around the Symbol dialog box by using the arrow keys or by clicking it and dragging with the mouse.

NOTE

Word will display a shortcut key for the symbol (if there is one) to the right of the Shortcut Key button. If you're often inserting a particular symbol, you can use the shortcut key instead—or you can create a shortcut key of your own. You can also create an AutoCorrect entry, which can be a handy way of inserting symbols in text.

3. To insert a special character, click the Special Characters tab to bring it to the front (unless it's already there). Choose the character to insert from the list box (see Figure 14.6).

Part iii

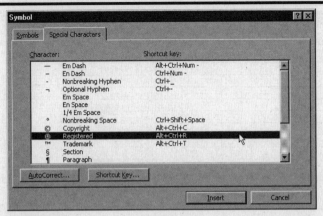

FIGURE 14.6: Choose a special character from the Special Characters tab of the Symbol dialog box, and then click the Insert button.

4. To insert the symbol or special character, click the Insert button. Word will insert the character, and the Cancel button will change to a Close button.

TIP
You can also insert a symbol or a special character by double-clicking it.

5. To insert more symbols or special characters, repeat steps 2 through 4.

6. Click the Close button to close the Symbol dialog box.

If you find yourself inserting a particular symbol or special character frequently, you can create a shortcut key combination for placing it more quickly. As you can see in the Symbol dialog box, many of the symbols and special characters already have shortcut keys assigned, but you can replace these with more convenient keyboard shortcuts of your own if you prefer.

SAVING A WORD DOCUMENT

The first time you save a Word document, you assign it a name and choose the folder in which to save it. Thereafter, when you save the document, Word uses that name and folder and does not prompt you for changes to them—unless you decide to save the file under a different name or in a different folder, in which case you need to use the File ➢ Save As command rather than File ➢ Save. I'll discuss this in a moment.

TIP

You can also save different versions of the same document in the same file.

Saving a Document for the First Time

To save a Word document for the first time:

1. Click the Save button, or choose File ➢ Save. Word will display the Save As dialog box (see Figure 14.7).

NOTE

In dialog boxes that show filenames, you'll see file extensions (for example, .doc at the end of a Word filename) only if you chose to see them in Windows Explorer. To display extensions in Explorer, choose View ➢ Options and clear the Hide MS-DOS File Extensions For File Types That Are Registered check box on the View tab of the Options dialog box or the Folder Options dialog box (these vary among Windows 95, Windows 98/98 SE, NT Workstation 4, and Windows 2000). Then click the OK button.

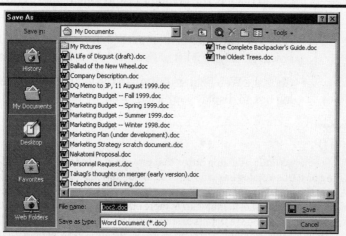

FIGURE 14.7: In the Save As dialog box, choose the folder in which to save your file, and then enter a name for the file.

2. In the Save In box at the top of the Save As dialog box, choose the folder in which to save the document.

   ▶ Click the drop-down list button to the right of the Save In drop-down list to display the drop-down list of computers, folders, and locations accessible from your computer.

- ▶ Click the Up One Level button (or press the Backspace key with the focus on the folder list) to move up one level of folders, or double-click a folder to open it and display its contents.

- ▶ Click the Back button (the button with the blue arrow pointing to the left) to move to the folder you were in previously. This button works like the Back button in Internet Explorer (or any other Web browser). When you display the ToolTip for this button, it will show the name of the folder to which clicking the button will take you.

- ▶ Click the History button in the left panel of the dialog box to display the list of documents and folders you've worked with recently. (This list of documents is stored as links in the \Office\Recent\ folder.)

- ▶ Click the My Documents button in the left panel of the dialog box to display the \My Documents\ folder.

- ▶ Click the Desktop button in the left panel of the dialog box to display the computers and folders on your computer's desktop.

- ▶ Click the Favorites button in the left panel of the dialog box to display your list of Favorite folders and documents.

- ▶ Click the Web Folders button in the left panel of the dialog box to display your list of Web folders.

TIP

Like many Windows dialog boxes that provide access to files, Word's Save dialog box, Open dialog box, and others provide various ways in which to view and sort the files. The default view, shown in Figure 14.7, is List view, which shows an unadorned list of filenames. For more information, click the View drop-down list button and choose Details to show the Details view, which shows the Name, Size, Type (for example, Microsoft Word Document), and Modified (that is, last-modified) date for each file. You can also choose View ➢ Properties to show a panel of properties on the right side of the dialog box or View ➢ Preview to display a preview panel on the right side of the dialog box. To sort the files, choose View ➢ Arrange Icons and then By Name, By Type, By Size, or By Date, as appropriate, from the submenu. In Details view, you can click the column headings to sort the files for that column: click once for ascending sort order, and click again to reverse the order.

3. In the File Name text box, enter a name for your file.

   ▶ With the Windows 95, Windows 98/98 SE, Windows NT, and Windows 2000 capacity for long filenames, you can enter a thorough and descriptive name—up to 255 characters, including the path to the file (that is, the name of the folder or folders in which to save the file).

   ▶ You can't use the following characters in filenames (if you do try to use one of these, Word will advise you of the problem):

Colon	:
Backslash	\
Forward slash	/
Greater-than sign	>
Less-than sign	<
Asterisk	*
Question mark	?
Double quotation mark	"
Pipe symbol	|

4. Click the Save button to save the file.

TIP

To save all open documents at once, hold down one of the Shift keys on your keyboard, and then, with your mouse, choose File ➢ Save All. Word will save each document that contains unsaved changes, prompting you for filenames for any document that has never been saved. If you have made changes to any of the templates on which the documents are based, Word will prompt you to save the template as well.

5. If Word displays a Properties dialog box for the document (see Figure 14.8), you can enter identifying information on the Summary tab.

   ▶ In the Title box, Word displays the first paragraph of the document (or a section of it, if it's long). You'll often want to change this.

   ▶ In the Subject box, describe the subject of the document, and enter any keywords that will help you remember the document in the Keywords box.

► In the Author and Company boxes, Word displays the username from the User Information tab of the Options dialog box.

► Fill in other boxes as desired, and then click OK to close the Properties dialog box and save the file.

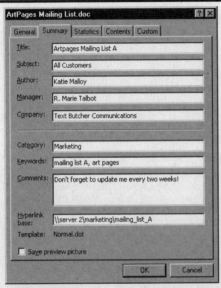

FIGURE 14.8: You can enter identifying information in the Properties dialog box.

NOTE

Whether the Properties dialog box appears depends on the Prompt For Document Properties setting on the Save tab of the Options dialog box. To have Word automatically prompt you for summary information, choose Tools ➢ Options, click the Save tab, select the Prompt For Document Properties check box, and click OK.

Saving a Document Again

To save a document that you've saved before, click the Save button, choose File ➢ Save, or press Ctrl+S (the shortcut for Save). Word will save the document without consulting you about the location or filename.

Saving a Document under Another Name

One of the easiest ways to make a copy of a Word document is to open it and save it under a different name. This technique can be particularly useful if you've made changes to the document but don't want to replace the original document—for example, if you think you might need to revert to the original document and you've forgotten to make a backup before making your changes. The Save As command can also be useful for copying a document to a different folder or drive—for example, if you want to copy a document to a floppy drive or to a network drive.

To save a document under a different name or to a different folder:

1. Choose File ➢ Save As to display the Save As dialog box.

2. Enter a different name for the document in the File Name box or choose a different folder in the Save In area.

3. Click the Save button to save the document.

If the folder you chose already contains a document of the same name, Word will ask whether you want to overwrite it. Choose Yes or No. If you choose No, Word will return you to the Save As dialog box so that you can choose a different name or different folder.

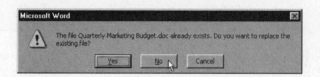

Part iii

SAVING A WORD DOCUMENT IN A DIFFERENT FORMAT

Word lets you save documents in formats (file types) other than Word—for example, the file formats of other word processors. To save a file in a different format, you need to have Word's converter file for that format installed on your computer. If you don't, Word will prompt you to install the converter. Choose the Yes button, and the Windows installer will install the converter in question and notify you when it has finished doing so.

To save an existing file in a different format:

1. Choose File ➢ Save As. Word will display the Save As dialog box.

2. Scroll down the Save As Type drop-down list and choose the file type you want to save the current document as.

3. If you want, enter a different filename for the file.

4. Click the Save button or press Enter.

NOTE

If you haven't saved the file before, you can choose File ➢ Save instead of File ➢ Save As to open the Save As dialog box. You'll also need to specify a name for the document.

CLOSING A DOCUMENT

To close the current document, choose File ➢ Close, press Ctrl+F4, or click the Close button on the document window. If the document contains unsaved changes, Word will prompt you to save them and will close the document when you're finished.

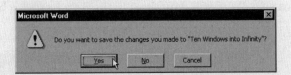

If the document has been saved before and if there are no new changes, Word will simply close the document. If you've created a new document but never changed it or saved it, Word will close it without prompting you to save it.

TIP

To close all open documents at once, hold down one of the Shift keys on your keyboard, then, with your mouse, choose File ➢ Close All. (Interestingly enough, the Close All choice appears on the File menu even when you have only one file open in Word.)

OPENING A WORD DOCUMENT

To open a Word document:

1. Click the Open button on the Standard toolbar, choose File ➢ Open, or press Ctrl+O. Word will display the Open dialog box

(see Figure 14.9). The Open dialog box provides several methods of navigating to the folder and file you want to open.

2. If you're already in the right folder, proceed to step 3. If not, use the techniques described for the Save As dialog box in the section titled "Saving a Document for the First Time" to navigate to the folder holding the document you want to open. You'll notice that the Open dialog box has a Look In drop-down list rather than a Save In drop-down list, but otherwise everything works the same.

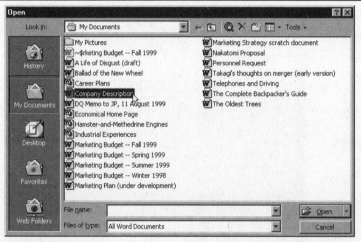

FIGURE 14.9: In the Open dialog box, use the Look In box to navigate to the folder that contains the document you want to open, then highlight the document and click the Open button.

Part iii

3. Choose the document to open, then click the Open button.

TIP

To open several documents at once, click the first one in the Open dialog box to select it. Then, to select contiguous documents, hold down Shift and click the last document in the sequence to select it and all the ones between it and the first document. Then click the Open button. To select noncontiguous documents, hold down Ctrl and click each document you want to open and then click the Open button. (You can also combine the two methods of selection: First use Shift+click to select a sequence of documents, then use Ctrl+click to select others. To deselect documents within the range you have selected, use Ctrl+click.)

Opening Word Documents Using Windows Techniques

Windows 95, Windows 98/98 SE, Windows NT 4, and Windows 2000 offer several ways to open a Word document quickly. If you've used the document recently, pop up the Start menu, choose Documents, and choose the document from the list of the 15 most recently used files (as shown here). If Word is already open, Windows will just open the document for you; if Word isn't open, Windows will open Word and the document at the same time.

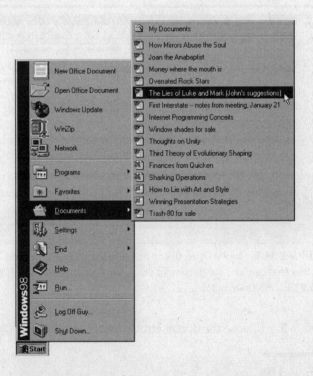

In Windows 98 SE, the Documents menu also provides a shortcut to the \My Documents\ folder, the default location for storing your documents. In Windows NT 4 with Internet Explorer 4 or Internet Explorer 5 installed, the Documents menu provides a shortcut to the \Personal\ folder, the default location for storing your documents in NT. Click the My Documents shortcut or the Personal shortcut to display that folder in an Explorer window, from which you can launch a document by double-clicking.

If you need to open a Word document frequently but can't be sure that it will always be among your 15-most-wanted files on the Start menu's Documents menu, you can create an icon for it on the Desktop. To do so, either right-click the Desktop, choose New ➤ Shortcut, and then Browse for the document in the Create Shortcut dialog box; or, more simply, open an Explorer window, find the Word document you want to keep handy, and right-drag it to the Desktop. Windows will invite you to create a shortcut to the document; go right ahead.

TIP

To quickly open one of the documents you worked on most recently from inside Word, pull down the File menu and choose one of the most recently used documents listed at the bottom of the menu. (By default, Word lists four files, but you can change this by using Tools ➤ Options, selecting the General tab, and changing the number in the Entries box for the Recently Used File List. Alternatively, you can turn off the display of recently used documents by clearing the Recently Used File List check box.

To keep a document in an even more handy place than the Desktop, you can create a shortcut for it on a Quick Launch toolbar if you're using the Active Desktop. To do so, open an Explorer window, find the document, right-drag it to the Quick Launch toolbar in question, and choose Create Shortcut Here from the resulting context menu. You'll then be able to launch the document (and Word, if it isn't already running) by clicking the icon on the Quick Launch toolbar.

Finding Word Documents

The Open dialog box also lets you quickly search your computer for documents that contain a certain word or phrase that matches a certain description. This can be useful when you need to find a document whose name or location you've forgotten but whose contents you can remember.

To search for a document:

1. Choose File ➤ Open or click the Open button on the Standard toolbar to display the Open dialog box.

2. If you know which folder the document is in, navigate to that folder in the Open dialog box.

3. Make sure the Files Of Type drop-down list at the bottom of the Open dialog box is showing the type or types of files you

want to search for. If you're searching for Word documents, templates, or Web pages, you'll probably want the All Word Documents choice.

4. Click the Tools button (located toward the upper-right corner of the Open dialog box) and choose Find from the drop-down menu, or press Ctrl+F, to display the Find dialog box (see Figure 14.10). The Find Files That Match These Criteria list box will display what Word is currently set to search for. For example, if you chose All Word Documents in the previous step, the Find Files That Match These Criteria list box will display *Files of type is All Word Documents*.

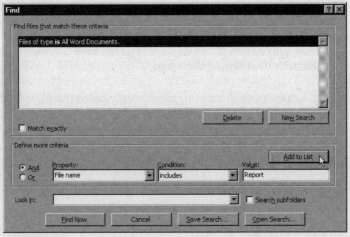

FIGURE 14.10: Use the Find dialog box to locate a document by name, by part of its name, by a word or phrase it contains, or by its properties.

5. In the Define More Criteria group box, choose a criterion on which to search:

   ▶ To refine a search, make sure the And option button is selected. (Use the Or option button to search for files that meet either of two criteria.)

   ▶ In the Property drop-down list, choose the property of the file for which you want to specify information. The default is File Name, which you use to search for a file by its name. You can also choose other properties such as Author, Company, Comments, Keywords, Last Modified,

Subject, Title, and other document properties. These correspond to the information that Word displays on the five tabs of the Properties dialog box. As an example, say you want to search for Word documents whose names include the word *Report*. You would choose File Name in the Property drop-down list.

▶ In the Condition drop-down list, choose a suitable condition for the property you chose. The options in the Condition drop-down list vary depending on the property: for text properties such as File Name or Author, the list contains options such as Includes, Begins With, and Ends With, while for temporal properties such as Last Modified, you'll see choices such as Yesterday, Today, Last Month, and so on. In our example search, you would choose Includes in the Condition drop-down list.

▶ In the Value text box, enter the information with which to compare the property. The Value text box will be dimmed and unavailable for temporal conditions and some other conditions. In our example search, you would enter **Report** in the Value text box.

▶ Click the Add To List button to add the criterion to the list of criteria. The Find Files That Match These Criteria list box will change to reflect the criterion you specified. In our example, it will now read *File name includes Report. Files of type is All Word Documents.*

TIP

One of the most useful properties to use in a search is the Text Or Property property, which enables you to search for a document by one or more of the words in it. With the Text Or Property property, you can specify Includes Words, Includes Phrase, or Includes Near Each Other in the Condition drop-down list. For example, if you need to locate all documents with the words *Khyber Pass* in them, you would choose Text Or Property in the Property drop-down list and Includes Phrase in the Condition drop-down list, then enter **Khyber Pass** in the Value text box.

6. If necessary, add further criteria by repeating step 5.

7. In the Look In drop-down list, make sure that an appropriate folder or drive is selected. (The Look In drop-down list will

Part iii

show the folder you chose in step 2.) To change the drive, click the drop-down list button and choose the drive from the resulting list.

8. Select the Search Subfolders check box if you want the search to include subfolders of the folder or drive you chose. Unless you're sure of the folder that contains the document, it's usually a good idea to select this check box.

9. If you think you'll want to save this set of search criteria, click the Save Search button to display the Save Search dialog box. Enter a name for the search criteria in the Name For This Search text box and click the OK button.

10. Click the Find Now button to search for files that match the criteria you specified. Word will display the files it finds in the Open dialog box. Choose the file you want and click the Open button to open it.

To use a saved search, display the Find dialog box as described above, then click the Open Search button to display the Open Search dialog box. Select the search you want to use and click the Open button to open it. You can then add search criteria if necessary, or click the Find Now button to run the search.

OPENING A NON-WORD DOCUMENT

Word can open files saved in a number of other formats, from plain-text ASCII files to spreadsheets (for example, Lotus 1-2-3) to calendar and address books. To open a file saved in a format other than Word, you need to have the appropriate converter file installed on your computer so that Word can read the file. Generally speaking, the easiest way to tell if you have the right converter installed for a particular file format is to try to open the file; if Word cannot open it, it will prompt you to install the converter. Choose the Yes button. The Windows Installer will install the converter and will notify you when it has finished doing so.

To open a document saved in a format other than Word:

1. Select File ➤ Open to display the Open dialog box.

2. Choose the folder containing the document you want to open.

3. Click the drop-down list button on the Files Of Type list box at the bottom-left corner of the Open dialog box. From the

list, select the type of file that you want to open. If Word doesn't list the file that you want to open, choose All Files (*.*) from the drop-down list to display all the files in the folder.

4. Choose the file in the main window of the Open dialog box, then click the Open button or press Enter to open the file.

WHAT'S NEXT?

OK, so you've mastered basic Word tasks, you can cut, copy, and paste like a pro, and you're opening and closing documents all over the place. Next we'll take a look at Excel basics—entering data in a worksheet and creating workbooks.

Chapter 15

UNDERSTANDING AND ENTERING DATA IN EXCEL

Microsoft Excel is a spreadsheet program, the electronic version of the green, lined sheets of paper that people used in the "olden days" to create budgets, track accounts payable and receivable, monitor inventory, and so on. In Excel, a document is called a *workbook*, which is the basic file in Excel, and each workbook can contain multiple pages, which are called *worksheets*. In this chapter, you'll find out how to enter various types of data in a worksheet.

Adapted from *Excel 2000: No Experience Required*
by Gene Weisskopf
ISBN 0-7821-2374-0   423 pages $19.99

UNDERSTANDING THE DIFFERENCE BETWEEN VALUES AND TEXT

In general, Excel accepts two types of data: values and text. As a rule, if an entry you make is not a value, Excel treats it as text.

Values: Numbers, Formulas, and Dates

A value is any datum that has significance beyond the characters you type, such as a numeric value. Excel aligns most values, such as numbers and dates, with the right side of their cells. To see how Excel displays values, you can enter the following values in a new worksheet:

Numbers   Enter **14.5** in cell A1. This is a numeric value that you can include in a formula.

Formulas   Enter the formula **=22+A1** in cell A2. The result will be 36.5.

Dates   Enter the formula **=A4** in cell B4. Now enter **12/31/99** in cell A4. The display will show 12/31/99, but look at the result of the formula in B4—36525. The appearance of cell A4 didn't fool the formula in B4. The result shows that an underlying number represents the date in A4. The "Entering Dates and Times" section, later in this chapter, explains how Excel handles dates.

TIP

The way Excel formats dates, times, and currency depends on the Regional Settings, which you'll find in Windows Control Panel.

Delete the formula in B4, and the worksheet you just created should look like the one shown here.

	A	B
1	14.5	
2	36.5	
3	This is a value	
4	12/31/99	
5		

Only certain characters are allowed when you are creating a value, as discussed in the section "Entering Numbers" later in this chapter. Entering text is a lot simpler, because there are really no rules to follow.

Text: Anything That Is Not a Value

Excel checks each entry you make and determines its type. If it is not a value, it is text—whether you intended that or not! Excel aligns text entries with the left side of their cell. To see how Excel displays text entries, you can enter the following in a worksheet:

Plain text   In cell C1, enter **This is cell C1**. In C2, enter **123 Main St.** Both of these are text entries, even though they include numeric characters. You can tell that Excel does not consider an entry numeric in a couple of ways. If Excel left-justifies an entry in its cell, it's likely a text entry. If you include the cell address in a formula in another cell, such as **=C3+1** in the above example, watch what happens. The result #VALUE! indicates that Excel cannot find a valid result because you can't add text (C3) and numbers.

Invalid formulas   Enter **22+A1** in cell C3. Because the equals sign is missing, Excel takes this entry as plain text even though it looks like a formula.

Invalid dates   Enter **12/42/99** in cell C4. Excel knows that December 42, 1999, is an invalid date and enters it as text. Notice how the "date" is left-justified in its cell.

Now your worksheet should look like this:

	A	B	C	D	E
1			This is cell C1		
2			123 Main St.		
3			22+A1		
4			12/42/99		
5					

ENTERING TEXT

Text entries might include column and row headings (Jan, Feb, Mar, Widget 1, Widget 2, and so on); report titles (Expense List for Analytical Dept.); cell identifiers (principal, interest, term); and small paragraphs of descriptive text.

Forcing an Entry to Be Text

If the text you are entering can be taken as a value, Excel will treat it that way. For example, suppose you're entering three cell identifiers that include a person's name and a year: **Mark 00**, **Fred 00**, and **Jan 00**. The first two will be taken as text, but Excel will take the third as the date January 1, 2000, and treat it as such.

You can force Excel to take an entry as text by preceding the entry with an apostrophe, such as **'Jan 00**.

Making Long Text Entries

A cell can hold more characters than you will ever want to enter, but the default column width in Excel is only about eight characters (in the standard, default font size).

A text entry that is longer than its column is wide will overhang its cell and appear to extend outside the cell. But it only does so on the display—it's still contained within its cell.

There's nothing wrong with this overhanging text, and you will frequently make entries that overhang. But you need to watch one thing: an entry in a cell next to the long text will cut it off at that cell, so the extended entry no longer overhangs. The worksheet shown here has the same long text entry in cells A1 and A3. But there's also an entry in B3, which truncates the text in A3.

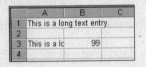

If a long text entry is "trapped" by adjacent entries and cannot overhang its cell, you can fit it within its cell in two ways:

▶ Use a smaller font.

▶ Widen its column.

Another nifty way to handle a long entry is to force it to appear on two or more lines within the same cell. Follow these steps:

1. Click in an empty cell.

2. Type some text.

3. Hold down Alt and press Enter.

4. Type some more text.

Notice that all text is inside the cell and that the row height changes to accommodate additional lines.

NOTE

If you select a range of cells to print, any overhanging text that extends outside that range will not appear on the printout if you print with the Selection option. Be sure either to include all columns over which the text extends or to print with the Active Sheets option, which will print anything that appears on all selected worksheets.

ENTERING NUMBERS

You have to pay a bit more attention when you're entering numbers and other values. If you don't, you might end up making a text entry that happens to *look* like the value you intended, and you might not catch the problem.

For example, if you mix text characters within a number, you will usually end up with a text entry. If you enter **125 lbs**, Excel treats the entry as text. Labels (such as lbs, dollars, and so on) must not be in the same cell as a numeric value if you intend to perform calculations based on the value. Put labels in an adjacent cell or in the column or row heading.

Including Formatting Characters

You can include some nonnumeric characters in a number. If you preface a number with a currency symbol, such as $, or include a thousands separator, such as a comma, Excel knows what to do with those characters and treats the entry as a number. It applies the appropriate numeric format to the cell to make it look the way you entered it. To see how this works, enter **$1,234** in a cell, and then compare the display of that cell with what's actually in it by clicking the cell to make it active and then looking at the Formula bar.

If you append a percent sign (%) to a number, Excel divides the number by 100, making it a percentage, and applies a numeric format to it so that it looks like a percentage. For example, enter **15.8%** in a cell and then write a formula in another cell that multiplies a number by the cell that contains the 15.8%. In this case, Excel leaves the percent sign in the cell; as long as it is there, the number that precedes it will be handled as a percentage.

Entering Large Numbers

Unlike a long text entry, a numeric entry (whether a number or the result of a formula) must fit within the width of its cell; it will *not* overhang the cell. Instead, Excel will accommodate a number that is too long for the cell width by expanding the width of the column (up to a maximum width of about 12 characters), as long as the column width has not already been adjusted. Otherwise, Excel will display the number in a numeric format style that makes it fit within the current width of the cell.

For example, on a new worksheet, enter the number **1234567890** in cell A1, and you'll see that Excel widens column A so that the entire number is displayed. Now see how Excel displays the number when it cannot widen the column:

1. In the column heading, point to the dividing line between columns A and B so that the pointer changes to a double-headed arrow.

2. Drag the column edge to the left just a character or two to shrink column A.

3. Release the mouse button, and you'll see that Excel must now change the way the number is displayed in order to fit it within the new width of the column.

If Excel is using its typical default font size, the number should be displayed as 1.23E+09 (if it's not, try adjusting the column width until it is). Excel chose the Scientific format to display this number, which allowed it to "fit" within its column width.

NOTE

If you apply a specific format to a cell, Excel will *not* change it to a different format when the number is too large to fit within its cell.

Try making column A a lot narrower, leaving it only a few characters wide. You'll see that when a column is too narrow to display a number, Excel displays only pound signs instead of the number.

At this point, you can widen the column to display the number as you entered it or apply a smaller font to the cell.

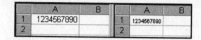

ENTERING FORMULAS AND TEXT VALUES

The data in a formula can consist of numbers, text values, functions, or cell addresses that you combine with arithmetical operators. The operators include the usual + and −, with the asterisk (*) for multiplication and the forward slash (/) for division.

Excel calculates the formula as soon as you enter it and displays the result on the screen.

NOTE

A formula *must* begin with an equals sign (=) for Excel to recognize it as such. Otherwise, your "formula" will be taken as plain text, with no resulting value. You can preface a formula with + or −, but Excel will add an = to the beginning of the formula anyway.

A text value, or text string, is really a formula that produces a text value for a result. You can do some slick tricks when you start combining text values within formulas; the process is called *concatenation*.

To create a simple text value, enclose it in quotation marks and treat it as a formula:

```
="This is a text value"
```

To concatenate this with other text, use the ampersand (&):

```
="This is a text value "&"and so is this."
```

The result of this formula is the sentence:

```
This is a text value and so is this.
```

If you enter your name in cell A1, either as plain text or as a text value, this formula would make sense:

```
="My name is "&A1
```

Give it a try. Note that the cell reference is not enclosed in quotes, because it is the contents of that cell that you are referencing.

Part iii

ENTERING DATES AND TIMES

You can enter dates or times in any style that suits you, such as:

```
2000, 31st of December
```

However, you will usually want to enter them in a style Excel recognizes so that you can:

▶ Perform date or time arithmetic, such as subtracting one date from another to determine the number of days between them.

▶ Sort a range of cells based on their dates in one of the columns.

▶ Find all records in a database that have a date greater than a specified date.

▶ Fill a column with dates that are one week apart.

TIP

Pressing Ctrl+; (semicolon) enters the current date, and pressing Ctrl+: (colon) enters the current time. These are especially handy because, unlike the NOW() function (which updates to the current date and time whenever the file is opened), the date and time are static and never change when entered this way.

Entering Dates and Times That Excel Recognizes

The easiest way to enter a date or a time is to use a style that Excel recognizes. For the date December 31, 1999, and the time 3:30 P.M., this small worksheet shows the valid styles (although other styles are understood, they are converted to one of the styles shown here). When you don't include the day, Excel assumes the first of the month; when you don't include the year, Excel assumes the current year.

	A	B	C
1	12/31/99	31-Dec-99	
2	31-Dec	3:30 PM	
3	Dec-99	15:30	
4			
5			
6			

Remember, when you're entering a date or time, do *not* preface it with an equals sign; Excel will assume that you are entering a formula, such as 12 divided by 31 divided by 99.

NOTE

The date and time styles that Excel recognizes are determined in part by the choices you make in Control Panel's Regional Settings tool under the Date and Time tabs.

When you enter dates or times in an "approved" style, Excel actually performs a shortcut that lets you avoid several steps, as discussed next.

Understanding Excel's System of Chronology

Excel represents dates with whole numbers and times with fractions. It begins with the date January 1, 1900, and refers to it as a 1. January 2 of that year is a 2, and so on. Therefore, January 1, 1901, is 367 (or 367 days after January 1, 1900), January 1, 1950, is 18,264, and January 1, 2000 is 36,526. This makes it easier for Excel to use dates in calculations. You can calculate the number of days an employee has worked, calculate vacation time, amortize a loan, and more.

A time in Excel is calculated as a fraction of 24 hours; so midnight is 0.0, 6:00 am is 0.25, noon is 0.50, and 11:59 P.M. is something like 0.999. So January 1, 2000, 6:00 P.M. is represented as 36,526.75. Just remember that the time fraction is letting you know how much of the day has passed (noon is .50 or half way through the 24-hour day). Calculating date and time numbers is simple enough—if you're a computer! Excel includes a variety of functions for calculating the correct number for a date or time. For example, you can use =DATE(99,12,31) to enter that date or =NOW() to enter the current date and time.

It's easy to see how you can perform date arithmetic when numbers represent the dates. To calculate the date that is one day after December 31, 1999, simply add 1 to it, producing the number 36526. The second trick is to make that number appear as a date.

Applying a Date or Time Format

When you enter the date 12/31/99 into a cell, Excel actually does two things:

- ▶ Keeps track of the date's number, 36525.

- ▶ Applies a numeric format to the cell to make it look like a date.

Part iii

To select the date or time format you want, follow these steps:

1. Choose Format ➤ Cells to open the Format Cells dialog box, as shown in Figure 15.1.

2. Click the Number tab.

3. Choose Date or choose Time in the Category list.

4. Select a format from the Type list.

5. Click OK.

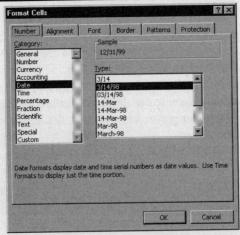

FIGURE 15.1:   Applying a date format via the Format Cells dialog box

To view all the tabs in the Format Cells dialog box, Excel must be in Ready mode (in other words, you can't be editing the cell). You'll find a variety of date and time formats, and you're free to design your own custom formats too.

USING AUTOFILL AND CUSTOM LISTS

Excel includes a variety of tools for helping you enter data. The first one I'll discuss is AutoFill, which can enter a sequence of data at the touch of a button.

Actually, that should be at the touch of your mouse. You create an Auto-Fill sequence by dragging the *fill handle* over the cells you want to fill. The fill handle is the small black box in the lower-right corner of either the active cell or the selected cells. When you point to it, the mouse pointer changes to crosshairs.

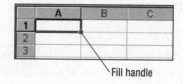

Fill handle

NOTE

If you don't see a fill handle, choose Tools ➤ Options to open the Options dialog box, click the Edit tab, and then click the Allow Cell Drag And Drop check box. Click OK, and you're ready to go.

AutoFill creates cell entries in a selected range based either on the "seed" entry in the first cell of that range or on the first and any consecutive filled cells. For example:

▶ Placing a 1 in the first cell of the selected range and placing a 3 in the next cell produces 5, 7, 9, and so on in the following cells of the selected range. Placing a 1 in the first cell and a 5 in the next cell produces 9, 13, 17, and so on.

▶ The text seed entry Widget 1 produces Widget 2, Widget 3, and so on.

▶ The seed entry Jan produces Feb, Mar, and so on.

▶ The seed entry Qtr 1 produces Qtr 2, Qtr 3, Qtr 4, Qtr 1, and so on, and the seed entry Qtr 1 and the next entry Qtr 3 produce Qtr 1, Qtr 3, Qtr 1, and so on.

Excel comes with several ready-made AutoFill custom lists, such as the days of the week and the months of the year. It's easy to create your own as well, as you'll see in the section "Working with Custom Lists" later in this chapter.

Filling a Range from One or More Seed Values

AutoFill can create a sequence from just about any numeric entry or text entry that has a numeric prefix or suffix. To see how this works, click the

New button on the Standard toolbar to open a blank worksheet, and follow these steps:

1. Enter **Week 1** in cell A1.

2. Select cell A1 if it isn't already selected.

3. Point to the fill handle in the lower-right corner of the cell; the mouse pointer will change to crosshairs.

4. Drag the fill handle straight down to select as many rows as you want to fill. A small window appears by the mouse pointer and displays the exact cell entry that will be created if you stop dragging.

5. Release the mouse button, and Excel completes the sequence.

These steps produced the sequence Week 1, Week 2, and so on. Let's try a few more. Make the following seed entries in the same worksheet in the cells indicated:

B1	**Qtr 1**
C1	**1st Quarter**
D1	**1/1/00**
E1	**Jan-00**

Now repeat steps 2 through 5 for each of the cells B1 through E1. Your worksheet should look like the worksheet in Figure 15.2.

	A	B	C	D	E	F
1	Week 1	Qtr 1	1st Quarter	1/1/00	Jan-00	
2	Week 2	Qtr 2	2nd Quarter	1/2/00	Feb-00	
3	Week 3	Qtr 3	3rd Quarter	1/3/00	Mar-00	
4	Week 4	Qtr 4	4th Quarter	1/4/00	Apr-00	
5	Week 5	Qtr 1	1st Quarter	1/5/00	May-00	
6	Week 6	Qtr 2	2nd Quarter	1/6/00	Jun-00	
7	Week 7	Qtr 3	3rd Quarter	1/7/00	Jul-00	
8	Week 8	Qtr 4	4th Quarter	1/8/00	Aug-00	
9	Week 9	Qtr 1	1st Quarter	1/9/00	Sep-00	
10						

FIGURE 15.2: AutoFill lets you create a sequence based on a seed entry that contains a number.

TIP

The sequences based on quarters, such as Qtr 1, rely on AutoFill's ability to recognize that a year contains four quarters.

Now try a multiple seed AutoFill, in which you use your seed entries to determine the increments of the sequence. Make the following entries on a blank worksheet (you can use Sheet2 in the current workbook). This time we'll fill across the rows:

A1	**1**
B1	**3**
A2	**1/1/99**
B2	**1/8/99**
A3	**Jan-99**
B3	**Jan-00**

Now select all the seed entries, A1:B3, and drag the fill handle for that range across the worksheet to column H. Release the mouse button, and your worksheet should look like the worksheet in Figure 15.3.

NOTE

Regardless of how you enter Jan 99 or Jan 00, Excel inserts a hyphen between the month and the year.

	A	B	C	D	E	F	G	H	I	J	K	L
1	1	3	5	7	9	11	13	15				
2	1/1/99	1/8/99	1/15/99	1/22/99	1/29/99	2/5/99	2/12/99	2/19/99				
3	Jan-99	Jan-00	Jan-01	Jan-02	Jan-03	Jan-04	Jan-05	Jan-06				
4												

FIGURE 15.3: When you enter incremental seed entries, AutoFill continues the sequence.

Using AutoFill to Create a Series

You can create any kind of series you can think of using the AutoFill feature. To see just one example, follow these steps:

1. Click the New button on the Standard toolbar to open a blank workbook.

2. Type **3/31/99** in cell A1 and press Enter.

3. Type **6/30/99** in cell A2 and press Enter.

4. Drag the mouse over both cells to select them.

5. Drag the fill handle down several rows and release the mouse button to create the series.

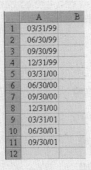

	A	B
1	03/31/99	
2	06/30/99	
3	09/30/99	
4	12/31/99	
5	03/31/00	
6	06/30/00	
7	09/30/00	
8	12/31/00	
9	03/31/01	
10	06/30/01	
11	09/30/01	
12		

You can also create a series in multiple columns or rows by placing a seed entry in two or more cells. To do so, follow these steps:

1. Type **1-99** in cell C1, **1-00** in cell D1, and **01-2001** in cell E1.

WARNING

If you do not enter the full year for 2001, Excel assumes that 1-01 is January 1 of the current year.

2. Drag the fill handle for cell C1 down one cell to create Feb-99 and repeat for the remaining seed entries.

3. Select the cells C1 to E2 and then drag the fill handle down to create all three series simultaneously.

C	D	E
Jan-99	Jan-00	Jan-01
Feb-99	Feb-00	Feb-01
Mar-99	Mar-00	Mar-01
Apr-99	Apr-00	Apr-01
May-99	May-00	May-01
Jun-99	Jun-00	Jun-01
Jul-99	Jul-00	Jul-01
Aug-99	Aug-00	Aug-01
Sep-99	Sep-00	Sep-01
Oct-99	Oct-00	Oct-01
Nov-99	Nov-00	Nov-01
Dec-99	Dec-00	Dec-01

NOTE

Excel automatically formats the month and year to an alphanumeric format. If you want the dates to appear numerically, select that format in the Format Cells dialog box.

Using Other AutoFill Tricks

Dragging the AutoFill handle lets you perform some other tasks as well.

▶ To create a multiple seed sequence in decreasing values, select the seed values and drag up or to the left, but *past the beginning of the selection* to avoid erasing the cells. For instance, if cells A12:A13 contain the numbers 1 and 2, you can select those cells and drag the fill handle up to A1 to create a decreasing sequence to −10.

▶ To erase a range of cells, select a range and drag the fill handle *inside* the range; when you release the mouse button, the cells are erased. For example, create a series in cells A1:B10. With the series still selected, drag the fill handle up to row 6. Release the mouse button, and the cells in A6:B10 will be erased.

▶ To insert cells, hold down the Shift key while you drag the fill handle.

▶ To display a shortcut menu of choices, drag the fill handle while holding down the right mouse button, and then release the button.

Working with Custom Lists

The second way that AutoFill can create a sequence is from existing lists of data. Several lists are built into Excel. To display two of those lists, follow these steps:

1. In cells A1:D1 of a blank worksheet, enter **Jan**, **January**, **Mon**, and **Monday**.

2. Select those cells.

3. Drag the fill handle down a dozen or so rows and release the mouse button.

Now you know that the days of the week and the months of the year are ready-made lists.

Excel makes it easy for you to create your own lists, which can consist of just about anything—the names of the planets of our solar system, inventory items, the departments of your company, and so on. To create a custom list, follow these steps:

1. Choose Tools ➤ Options to open the Options dialog box, shown in Figure 15.4.

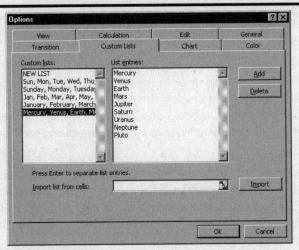

FIGURE 15.4: The Custom Lists tab in the Options dialog box contains the sequences for the AutoFill feature.

2. Click the Custom Lists tab.

3. Select NEW LIST in the Custom Lists window.

4. In the List Entries window, enter your custom list items (such as the names of the planets in our solar system, as shown in Figure 15.4). Press Enter after typing each item.

5. When you're finished, click Add, and then click OK.

When you want to use this new list, enter one of the items from your list in the worksheet, and use that item as a seed value to fill the cells in an adjacent row or column. AutoFill will find the item in one of its lists and continue the sequence based on that list.

Adding a Custom List to AutoFill from the Worksheet

If the sequence you want to create is already in the worksheet, you can import it into Custom Lists. Follow these steps:

1. Highlight the list by dragging the mouse over the items.

2. Click Tools ➢ Options to open the Options dialog box.

3. Click the Custom Lists tab.

4. Click the Import button to add the list.

5. Click OK.

You can also import worksheet elements without first selecting the list. Follow these steps:

1. Click Tools ➤ Options to open the Options dialog box.

2. Click the Custom Lists tab.

3. Click the Collapse Dialog button in the Import List From Cells text box to open the Options - Import List From Cells dialog box in the worksheet.

                                                 Collapse Dialog button

4. Select the list elements in the worksheet, and then click the Collapse Dialog button again to return to the Options dialog box.

5. Click the Import button to add the list, and then click the OK button to return to the worksheet.

FILLING A RANGE WITH A SERIES

You can fill a selected range with a series of numbers or dates (which we know are actually just formatted numbers) by choosing Edit ➤ Fill and then choosing Down, Right, Up, or Left to copy the first entry in the selected range to the other cells in the selection.

You have still another way to fill a range with a series. Choose Edit ➤ Fill ➤ Series to open the Series dialog box (see Figure 15.5), which offers some useful options and both complements and extends the AutoFill feature discussed in the previous section.

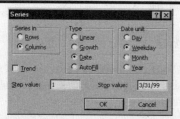

FIGURE 15.5: Use the Series dialog box to fill a range of cells with a variety of series.

Part iii

Using the Series dialog box, you can create a series based on the following:

▶ The value in the first cell of the selected range that you want to fill serves as the starting value for the series.

▶ The Step Value is the amount by which each cell in the series will be incremented (or decremented if you enter a negative number) from the cell before it.

▶ The Stop Value is the highest value (or lowest if decrementing) you want the series to attain.

The other choices in the Series dialog box let you define the type of series that will be created. Series In determines whether the fill will proceed by rows or columns. The Type options let you specify the type of series to create:

Linear   The step value is added to (or subtracted from) one cell to fill the next cell.

Growth   A cell is multiplied by the step value to fill the next cell.

Date   The cells are filled by dates, based on your choice in the Date Unit options.

AutoFill   The range of cells is filled following the same rules as the AutoFill feature, discussed in the previous section.

NOTE
If you first select a range of data, you can use the Trend option in the Series dialog box to replace that data with data that will produce either a linear or best-fitted curve, depending on whether you selected the Linear or Growth fill types. If you don't want to overwrite your data, copy it to another range, and use that data for the Series command.

ENTERING DATA WITH AUTOCOMPLETE AND PICK LIST

Excel's AutoComplete and Pick List features are wonderful tools for entering repetitive data quickly and consistently. The best way to understand these tools is to use them in a short example.

Letting AutoComplete Do Your Typing

First, we need to create a column of sample data. For this example, we'll use the months of the year. Follow these steps:

1. In cell A1, enter **January**.

2. Select A1, drag the fill handle down to A12, and release the mouse button to let AutoFill create the months of the year in cells A1:A12.

Now you have a column of data. In the real world, your data might be a customer list that fills hundreds or thousands of rows, with many of the entries being repeated throughout, such as cities, states, product names, and so on. Let's continue entering new data and repeating existing entries in the column.

3. Select the first blank cell beneath the data, which in this case is A13.

4. Enter **February**, but type slowly and watch the cell as you do.

As soon as you type the F, the AutoComplete feature looks in the column above, sees that only one entry begins with the letter *F*, and completes your entry for you. At this point, you have four options:

▸ Accept this suggested entry by pressing Enter or selecting the next cell.

▸ Continue typing slowly and see if AutoComplete finds another matching entry based on the additional characters you type.

▸ Continue typing to complete the entry, ignoring the AutoComplete suggestion.

▸ Press F2 for edit mode, and revise the AutoComplete suggestion to create a new entry.

5. Complete this cell entry and move down to A14.

6. Watch the cell and type **J**. No AutoComplete suggestion is made, because several entries in the cells above begin with that letter.

7. Type **u**; still no suggestion.

8. Type **n**, and now Excel suggests the only entry to match those letters—June.

You can accept this entry, knowing that it is spelled exactly like the earlier entry in the column, including the case of the letters.

Selecting Data from a List

Another way to enter data in a cell without typing it is to select it from a list that is built from the cells above it. You can display the list in two ways:

▶ Right-click the cell, and choose Pick From List from the shortcut menu.

▶ Press Alt+down arrow.

Excel alphabetizes the Pick List entries so that it is easy to find the one you want.

Here are a few rules to keep in mind when you are ready to use the AutoComplete and Pick List features:

▶ AutoComplete and Pick List look only at the column above or below and therefore won't be of any help when you're entering data across rows. There can be no blank cells between the active cell and the data above.

▶ AutoComplete and Pick List work only for text entries, not for numbers (including dates) or formulas.

To disable these features (they might slow to a crawl if you have thousands of unique entries in a column), follow these steps:

1. Choose Tools ➢ Options to open the Options dialog box.

2. Click the Edit tab.

3. Clear the Enable AutoComplete For Cell Values check box.

4. Click OK.

KEEPING YOUR SPELLING ACCURATE

With Excel's spell-checking capabilities, the spelling in your worksheets can be just as accurate as the spelling in your word-processing documents. In fact, when you're using the Microsoft Office 2000 suite, Excel and the other Office applications all share the same spelling dictionaries.

You can correct misspelled words in Excel in two ways:

▶ Choose Tools ➤ Spelling to find errors anywhere in the active workbook.

▶ Let the AutoCorrect feature automatically correct common typing errors as you make them.

Checking Spelling in the Workbook

Before you begin spell checking, you can select the part of your workbook that you want to check:

▶ Select only a single cell if you want Excel to spell check the entire active sheet, including all text cell entries, cell comments, embedded text or drawn objects, and charts.

▶ Select multiple sheets to spell check them all (click the first sheet's tab, hold down Shift, and then click the last sheet's tab).

▶ Select cells or objects first, if you want Excel to spell check only those elements.

If you run spell check while you are editing the text in a cell or object, Excel checks only that text.

 To begin spell checking, choose Tools ➤ Spelling, click the Spelling button on the Standard toolbar, or press F7. If no suspected misspellings are found, Excel displays a dialog box reporting that the spell checking is finished.

If Excel finds a misspelled word (or rather, a word that is not in the spell checker's dictionary), Excel display the Spelling dialog box (see Figure 15.6).

Part iii

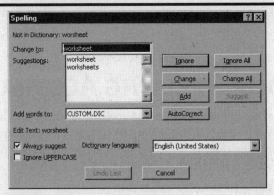

FIGURE 15.6: The Spelling dialog box displays a suspected misspelled word and offers a list of suggested replacements.

NOTE

When you have not selected any cells or objects, the spell checker proceeds row by row from the current cell to the end of the sheet and will continue from the beginning of the sheet at your request.

If the Word Is Spelled Correctly

The spell checker flags many words that are actually correct, especially names or uncommon technical or medical terms. When the suspect word is correct, you can do any of the following:

▶ Click Ignore to bypass this word and continue spell checking; if the suspect word appears again, Excel flags it again.

▶ Click Ignore All to bypass all occurrences of the suspect word during this spell-checking session.

▶ Click Add to add this word to the dictionary (by default, this is the `custom.dic` dictionary file). In the future, Excel will recognize that the word is spelled correctly.

If the Word Is Misspelled

If the word in question is incorrect, you can either type the correct spelling in the Change To field or select a word in the Suggestions list. You then have several options:

▶ Click Suggest to display a list of suggestions for that word.

▶ Click Change to replace the misspelled word with the word in the Change To field.

▶ Click Change All to correct all occurrences of the misspelled word.

▶ Click AutoCorrect to add this word to the AutoCorrect list. In the future, AutoCorrect will automatically replace the misspelled word with the correct word.

Letting AutoCorrect Fix Errors As They Occur

The AutoCorrect feature in Excel is also found in the other Microsoft Office 2000 applications. It watches as you type and automatically replaces a word it finds in its built-in list with an alternate. The list of words (which is shared by other Office applications) can include:

▶ Commonly misspelled words, such as "adn" for "and" and "teh" for "the."

▶ Abbreviations for words that you enter frequently so that, for example, when you type **wdc**, AutoCorrect replaces it with "Washington, D.C."

To turn this feature on and off and access its list of words, choose Tools ➢ AutoCorrect to open the AutoCorrect dialog box, shown in Figure 15.7.

Before you try this feature, choose Tools ➢ AutoCorrect to verify that AutoCorrect is enabled—the Replace Text As You Type check box should be checked. Choose OK or press Enter to close the AutoCorrect dialog box.

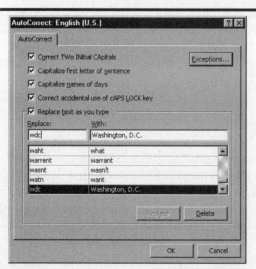

FIGURE 15.7: The AutoCorrect dialog box lets you turn the feature on or off and add to or revise its list of words.

Part iii

To see what AutoCorrect can do, click a cell and type the sentence below exactly as it is spelled. Watch the results on the screen as you do:

```
Teh poeple saw the sohw at tje cafe.
```

While you type merrily away, AutoCorrect silently picks up after you. Not bad, wouldn't you say?

To add an abbreviation to the list to speed your typing, follow these steps:

1. Choose Tools ➤ AutoCorrect to open the AutoCorrect dialog box.

2. Type the abbreviation in the Replace field.

3. Type what the abbreviation stands for in the With field, and then click Add. You'll see both entries appear in the list.

4. Click OK.

5. Return to the worksheet and type the abbreviation you just added. Press the spacebar or press Enter, and watch how quickly AutoCorrect replaces your abbreviation with its spelled-out equivalent.

The AutoCorrect dialog box has several nifty options. For example, check the Correct TWo INitial CApitals check box, and if you type **SPokane**, Excel changes it to Spokane.

Because there are no absolutely fixed rules of capitalization, you can create a list of words or abbreviations whose capitalization style will be ignored by AutoCorrect. In the AutoCorrect dialog box, click Exceptions to open the AutoCorrect Exceptions dialog box, and enter your terms in the Don't Correct field.

WHAT'S NEXT?

This chapter completes our tour of the Office 2000 Suite and two of its applications. Now it's time to turn to the Internet, that network of networks you can use to buy drugstore items, trade stocks, research your family tree, and just about anything else you can think of. We'll start with an overview of the basics, written by Christian Crumlish.

PART IV
THE INTERNET

Chapter 16

UNDERSTANDING INTERNET AND WORLD WIDE WEB BASICS

These days the Internet seems to be everywhere. Web addresses appear on television ads and billboards. There are TV shows and magazines devoted to the Internet. And virtually every new computer program that comes out has some Internet features. With the arrival of Windows 98 and now Windows 98 Second Edition, your computer Desktop can connect you just as easily to Internet resources as it does to the files on your hard drive.

Adapted from *The Internet: No Experience Required*
by Christian Crumlish
ISBN 0-7821-2168-3   528 pages $24.99

I know, you're raring to go. You want to start sending and receiving e-mail, browsing the Web, and exploring the global library of fun stuff out on the Internet. Well, I don't want to hold you back. Feel free to skip to Chapter 18, and start right in on e-mail (or even jump to Chapter 19 to start messing around with the World Wide Web). However, if you're not clear on what the Net actually is, how you get access to it, and what you can do once you're there, you'll want to peruse this chapter first.

Notice that I just used the word *Net* and not *Internet*. For the most part, the words are synonymous, although some people will use the word Net to refer to just about any aspect of the global internetworking of computers.

INTRODUCING THE INTERNET

Everybody talks about the Internet and the World Wide Web these days, but most people don't really know what the Internet is or what the differences are between the Internet and the Web. One reason for this is that how the Internet looks depends on how you come across it and what you do with it. Another reason is that everyone talks about it as if it's actually a network, like a local network in someone's office or even a large global network like CompuServe. Fact is, it's something different. A beast unto itself. The Internet is really a way for computers to communicate.

As long as a computer or a small network can "speak" the Internet lingo (or *protocols*, to be extra formal about it) to other machines, it's "on the Internet." Of course, the computer also needs a modem or a network connection and other hardware to make contact too. Regardless of the hardware needs, if the Internet were a language, it wouldn't be French or Farsi or Tagalog or even English. It would be Esperanto.

Having said that, I might backtrack and allow that there's nothing wrong with thinking of the Internet as if it were a single network unto itself. It certainly behaves like one in a lot of important ways. But this can be misleading. No one "owns" the Internet. No one even really runs it. And no one can turn it off.

Communicating through E-Mail or Discussion Groups

In addition to being a network of interconnected computers, the Internet is also a collection of tools and devices for communicating and storing information in a retrievable form.

Take e-mail, for example. If you work in an office with a local area net-work, chances are you have an e-mail account and can communicate with people in your office by sending them messages through the company's internal system. (See Chapter 18 for an in-depth discussion of all the ins and outs of e-mail.) This is not the Internet.

Similarly, if you have an account at America Online and you send a message to someone else at AOL, you're still not using the Internet. But, if your office network has a *gateway* to the Internet, and you send e-mail to someone who does not work at your office, you are sending mail over the Internet. Likewise, if you send a message from your AOL account to someone at CompuServe or elsewhere, again you are sending messages over the Internet (see Figure 16.1).

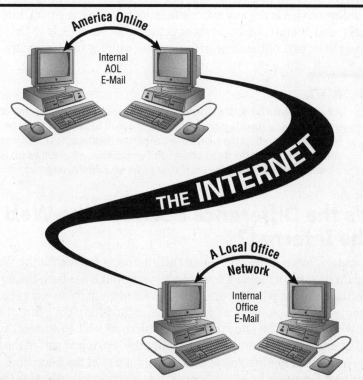

FIGURE 16.1: The Internet carries e-mail from one network to another.

NOTE

A *gateway* is a computer or the program running on it that transfers files (or e-mail messages or commands) from one network to another.

Part iv

But from your point of view, the Internet is not just a collection of networks all talking to one another. A single computer can also participate in the Internet by connecting to a network or service provider that's connected to the Internet. And although the local office network I described and the big commercial online services are not themselves the Internet, they can and often do provide access through their gateways to the Internet. (I cover online services later in this chapter, in the "Cruising the Net at Home" section.)

All this can be confusing to first-time Internet users (universally referred to as *newbies*). Say you have an AOL account and you join one of the *discussion groups* (bulletin boards) there. It may not be obvious to you right away whether you're talking in an internal venue—one only accessible to AOL members—or in a public Internet newsgroup. One of the benefits of an online service is the way various functions, including e-mail, Internet access, and online content, are brought together seamlessly so that they appear to be part of the same little program running on your computer.

NOTE

A *bulletin board* is a public discussion area where people can post messages— without sending them to anyone's individual e-mail address—that can be viewed by anyone who enters the area. Other people can then reply to posted messages, and ongoing discussions can ensue. On CompuServe, a bulletin board is called a *forum*. On the Internet, the equivalent areas are called *newsgroups*.

What's the Difference between the Web and the Internet?

Nowadays, most of the hype about the Internet is focused on the World Wide Web. It has existed for less than 10 years, but it has been the fastest-growing and most popular part of the Net for many of those years (except, perhaps, for the voluminous flow of e-mail around the globe). But what is the Web, and is it the same thing as the Internet? Well, to answer the second question first: yes and no. Technically, the *Web* is just part of the Internet—or, more properly, a way of getting around part of the Internet. But it's a big part, because a lot of the Internet that's not (strictly speaking) *part of* the Web can still be reached with a Web browser.

So the Web, on one level, is an *interface*. A window onto the Net. A way of getting to where you're going. Its appeal derives from three benefits:

▶ It disguises the gobbledygook that passes for Internet addresses and commands. (See "Getting on the Internet" later in this chapter.)

▶ It wraps up most of the different features of the Internet into a single interface used by Web applications.

▶ It allows you to see pictures and even hear sounds or watch movies (if your computer can hack it), along with your helpings of text.

TIP

To play sounds, your computer needs a sound card and speakers and, before the release of Windows 98 SE, some kind of software (such as Microsoft Sound Recorder for Windows). To play movies, your computer needs a lot memory (or else the movies will look herky-jerky) and, before the release of Windows 98 SE, some kind of software (such as Media Player or QuickTime). Now, however, you no longer need more than one player on your PC. Windows 98 SE includes the Windows Media Player, with which you can play sounds, movies, and mixed-media files.

It helps to know a little bit about the history of the Net to understand why these three features of the Web have spurred the Internet boom. First of all, before the Web existed, doing anything beyond simple e-mailing (and even that could be difficult, depending on your type of access) used to require knowing weird Unix commands and understanding the Internet's system for numbering and naming all the computers connected to it. If you've ever wrestled with DOS and lost, you can appreciate the effort required to surmount this type of barrier.

Imagine it's 1991 and you've gotten yourself an Internet account, solved the problems of logging in with a communications program to a Unix computer somewhere out there, and mastered the Unix programs needed to send and receive e-mail, read newsgroups, download files, and so on. You'd still be looking at lots of plain text, screens and screens of words. No pictures. Well, if you were dying for pictures, you could download enormous text files that had begun their lives as pictures and then were encoded as plain text so that they could be squeezed through the text-only pipelines that constituted the Net. Next you'd have to decode the files, download them onto your PC, and then run some special program to look at them. Not quite as easy as flipping through a magazine.

The Web uses a coding method called *hypertext* to disguise the actual commands and addresses you use to navigate the Net. Instead of these commands and addresses, what you see in your *Web browser* (the program you use to travel the Web) is plain English keywords highlighted in some way. Simply click the keywords, and your browser program talks the

Internet talk, negotiates the transaction with the computer at the other end, and brings the picture, text, program, or activity you desire onto your computer screen. This is how all computer functions should work (and probably how they will work one day).

Early Unix-based Web browsers, such as Www (developed at CERN, the European particle physics laboratory where the Web was invented) and Lynx (developed at the University of Kansas), were not especially attractive to look at, but they did offer the "one-step" technique for jumping to a specific location on the Net or for downloading a file or a piece of software.

The next advance on the Web was the development of graphical Web browsers that could run on a desktop PC (or Macintosh), permitting the user to employ the familiar point-and-click techniques of other software and incorporating text formatting and graphics into the browser screen. The first program of this type was NCSA Mosaic, which was developed at the National Center for Supercomputer Applications and distributed for free.

Furthermore, the various Web browsers can more or less substitute for a plethora of little specialty programs (such as Gopher clients, newsreaders, FTP programs, and so on) that you had to assemble and set up yourself "in the old days." The browsers all have their own little idiosyncrasies, but they're still remarkably uniform and consistent compared with the maze of different programs and rules you had to work your way through just a few years ago. These days, the two most popular browsers are Netscape Navigator, shown in Figure 16.2 (which is now part of Communicator, Netscape's all-purpose network client program) and Microsoft Internet Explorer. (For information on both these browsers, see Chapters 19 and 20.)

NOTE

"Just a few years ago" is the old days on the Internet. Changes happen so rapidly in the online world that time on the Internet is like "dog years"—something like seven years go by for each one in the real world.

The Web has made it possible for browsers to display pictures right in the midst of text, without your having to know how to decode files. A picture's worth a lot of words, and pictures look better in newspaper articles and on TV than scads of typewritten text. So this final ingredient made the Web seem both accessible and interesting to people who would never in a million years care to learn what a Unix "regular expression" is.

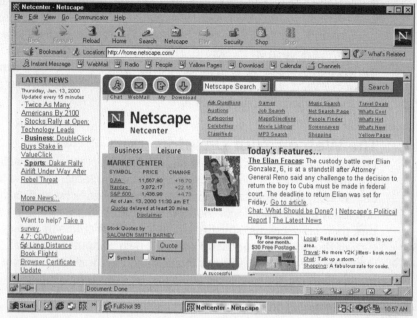

FIGURE 16.2:   Netscape Navigator is a popular World Wide Web browser program.

I have tried to answer the question that heads up this section: What's the difference between the Web and the Internet? Technically the Web and the Internet are not exactly the same, but for all intents and purposes they have a lot in common. Web browsers are the must-have programs that have made the Internet what it is today.

NOTE

You can use the Internet and the Web to find new friends and uncover fun facts and interesting Web sites. Individuals and groups all over the planet have gotten together on the Internet to explore mutual interests. Environmental and political causes, pets, sports, leisure activities, the arts, and the sciences are just some of the popular topics continually updated on the Internet.

Discovering What's New on the Net

These days, the latest Internet developments are mostly being driven by the access tools. Browser makers Netscape and Microsoft are each trying to

Part iv

develop all-in-one solutions that make their own products the "platform" for everything you do on the Net. New companies are offering free Internet accounts with a Web-based e-mail interface. The catch? You have to keep the ad window open on the screen. There are even Internet solutions that don't require you to have a computer, such as WebTV (your TV plus a modem plus a keyboard plus a remote), or a modem, such as DirectPC (your computer plus a special satellite hook up).

The Web on Your Desktop

From the user's point of view, the biggest changes planned for day-to-day Internet and World Wide Web use are in the way Internet access is being built directly into computer operating-system desktops (as well as directly into many new applications). Both Netscape and Microsoft are trying to turn their browsers into substitute desktops, more or less merging your view of the Internet (out there) and your own computer (in here). The integration of Windows 98 with Internet Explorer was an ambitious step in this direction.

NOTE

The Internet has also become a great source of career information. Companies list jobs and freelance opportunities. You can research companies on the Internet and train yourself on a variety of topics that might come up in an interview. You can find business contacts and develop new ones through Internet e-mail, conferencing, and forums on particular subjects.

News Beamed onto Your Screen

Entrypoint is a program that places a toolbar (see Figure 16.3) on the screen with buttons that you can click for instant access to the latest headlines, stock quotes, sports news, financial information, weather, travel information, and more. You can personalize the type of information you want to receive in all sorts of ways.

To download Entrypoint for free, go to www.entrypoint.com.

FIGURE 16.3: Entrypoint gives you instant access to Desktop news.

Applications with Internet Features

The growth of the Internet, coupled with the advent of smaller, local, company or organization intranets running on Internet principles, has led users to expect their everyday business software to help them deal with retrieving remote documents, collaborate with colleagues over network links, and save or publish documents to Web and intranet servers. To meet this demand, software publishers are adding Internet features to their programs left and right. You can expect your next upgrade of various programs to include the ability to transfer files (open them from and save them to remote computers) and probably to create documents and reports in HTML (hypertext Web format) as well.

NOTE

Knowing how to use Internet features in common business applications is a great job skill, even if you don't work in a high-technology field. All kinds of companies are depending more on the Internet and the World Wide Web to find information and promote and sell their services and products. Companies and organizations are also developing in-house intranets to store policies, manuals, and other information. Having knowledge of the Internet is certainly a big plus in today's competitive job market.

GETTING ON THE INTERNET

So what exactly does it mean to be "on the Internet"? Generally, if someone asks you, "Are you on the Net?" it means something like, "Do you have an Internet e-mail address?" That is, do you have e-mail and can your e-mail account be reached over the Internet? With the popularity of the Web being what it is, another common interpretation of what it means to be on the Net is, "Do you have the ability to browse the World Wide Web?" Often these two features—Internet e-mail and Web access—go hand in hand, but not always. We're also getting to a time when being on the Internet will entail having your own home page, your own "place" on the Web where information about you is stored and where you can be found.

Cruising the Net at Work

More and more companies these days (as well as schools and other organizations) are installing internal networks and relying on e-mail as one of the ways to share information. E-mail messages replace interoffice memos, at least for some types of announcements, questions, and scheduling purposes. The logical next step for most of these organizations is to connect their internal network to the Internet through a gateway. When this happens, you may suddenly be on the Net. This doesn't mean that anything will necessarily change on your desktop. You'll probably still use the same e-mail program and still send and receive mail within your office in the same way you always have.

WARNING

Some companies run Internet-usage monitoring programs that tell them how long employees have been using the Internet and what type of sites they are visiting. Use good judgment when you surf the Internet at work, and try to explore only those sites that have potentially important work-related information.

What will change at this point is that you'll be able to send e-mail to people on the Internet outside your office, as long as you type the right kind of Internet address. (Generally, this means adding @ and then a series of words separated by periods to the user name portion of an address, but I'll explain more about addresses in "The Anatomy of an Internet Address" later in this chapter.) Likewise, people out there in the great beyond will be able to send e-mail to you as well.

Depending on the type of Internet connection your company has, e-mail may be all you get. Then again, it might also be possible for you to run a Web browser on your computer and visit Internet sites while sitting at your desk. Of course, your company will only want you to do this if it's relevant to your job, but it works the same way whether you're researching a product your company uses or reading cartoons at the Dilbert site.

NOTE

Your ability to find information on the Internet that your company needs will become a highly prized career asset, especially as more and more organizations contribute to the growth of the Internet.

Cruising the Net at Home

If you're interested in exploring the Internet as a form of entertainment or for personal communication, a work account is not really the way to do it. (An account minimally consists of a user name and an e-mail Inbox; it may also provide storage space on a computer or access to a Web server.) You'll need your own personal account to really explore the Internet on your own time, without looking over your shoulder to make sure nobody's watching.

NOTE

If your office is quite sophisticated, you may actually be able to dial into a company network from home via a modem to check your e-mail messages.

Your best bet is to sign up for an account from a commercial online service or a direct-access Internet Service Provider. What's the difference between those two choices? Well, an *online service* (such as CompuServe, America Online, Prodigy, Microsoft Network, and so on) is first and foremost a private, proprietary network, offering its own content and access to other network members, generally combined with Internet access. An *Internet Service Provider* (*ISP*) offers only access to the Internet and no proprietary content (or only very limited local information and discussion groups). Figure 16.4 illustrates this distinction.

If you just want to get your feet wet before plunging wholeheartedly into the Net, I recommend signing up for a free trial account at one of the online services. If you like what the Internet has to offer, then switch to a direct-access ISP. ISPs don't try to compete with the Internet by offering their own content and sponsors. Instead, they function as a gateway, getting you onto the Internet and letting you go wherever you want.

An ISP account generally includes, along with an e-mail address and access to the Internet, storage space on a computer somewhere on the Net. You are usually billed monthly, and depending on the provider, there may be a surcharge based on the amount of time you spent connected that month or the amount of space you used on their hard drive.

But how do you use an account? Well, you need a computer with a modem, and you need software that knows how to use that modem to call up (dial up) your provider and allows you to log in to your account. Fortunately, most modems come with their own software.

Your ISP will take care of all the technical details for you and will probably supply you with a setup disc and easy-to-use software for connecting to the Internet. (For more information about ISPs, see Chapter 17.)

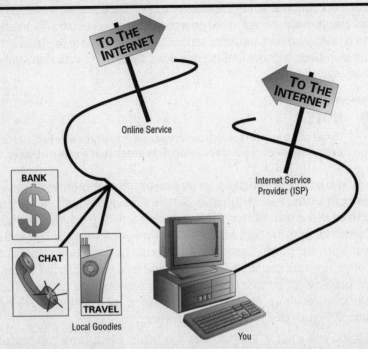

FIGURE 16.4: Online services connect you to the Internet but encourage you to explore their own offerings, whereas ISPs just connect you to the Internet and let you fend for yourself.

WARNING

By the way, the speed of your modem—and that of the modem at the other end of the dial-up line, that is, your provider's modem—determines the speed of your Internet connection, and even the fastest modems these days are still slower than a direct network connection to the Net, such as you might enjoy at your office.

The Anatomy of an Internet Address

One of the confusing things to Internet newbies is that the word "address" is used to mean at least three different things on the Internet. The most basic meaning—but the one used least often—is the name of a computer, also called a *host* or *site*, on the Internet in the form something.something.something. (To really use the lingo properly, you have to pronounce the periods as "dot"—you'll get used to it, and it saves a lot of time over the long haul.) For example, I publish a magazine (or 'zine) on the Internet called *Enterzone*; it's stored on a machine at Vassar that is part of the American Arts and Letters Network. The address of that machine is

```
ezone.org
```

Reading from right to left, you first have the *domain*, `org`, which stands for (nonprofit) organization. Next you sometimes have a *subdomain*. Finally, you have the *hostname*, `ezone`, which is the name (or a name) of the specific computer the magazine is stored on.

Another type of address is an e-mail address. An e-mail address consists of a *user name* (also called a *login*, a *log-on name*, a *userID*, an *account name*, and so on), followed by an at sign (@) and then an Internet address of the type just described. So, for example, say you want to send mail to me in my capacity as editor of Enterzone. You could address that e-mail message to a special user name created for that job (it will stay the same even if someone else takes over in the future):

```
editor@ezone.org
```

The third type of address is the kind you see everywhere these days, on billboards, on TV commercials, in the newspaper, and so on—a Web address, also called a *URL* (*Uniform Resource Locator*). The Web address of that magazine I told you about is

```
http://www.ezone.org/ez
```

TIP

You can leave out the www. portion of the address when using certain Web browsers. Some Internet addresses use the http:// designation, but leave out the www. portion, so try both ways if you have difficulty getting through.

Fortunately, you often can avoid typing in Web addresses yourself and can zip around the Web just by clicking preestablished *links*. Links are highlighted words or images that, when clicked or selected, take you directly to a new document, another part of the current document, or some other type of file entirely.

NOTE

The most common domain names on the Internet are .com, a commercial organization; .edu, an educational institution; .gov, a branch of the U.S. government; .int, an international treaty organization; .mil, a branch of the U.S. military; .net, a network provider; and .org, a nonprofit organization.

USING THE NET WITH OTHER PLATFORMS

Of course, Windows 98 SE and Internet Explorer 5 integrate the Web and your computer desktop more closely than any previous software. But if you sometimes work with other platforms, such as the Macintosh or Unix, you'll be glad to know that the Internet makes some of the seemingly important distinctions between types of computers a lot less important. The information out on the Internet, the public discussion areas, and the World Wide Web look and act more or less the same, no matter what kind of computer you use. In fact, the Web is quickly becoming a sort of universal computer platform now that certain types of programs and services are being designed to run on the Web, rather than to run on one specific type of computer.

Part of the elegance of the Internet is that much of the heavy-duty processing power and storage of large programs and dense information takes place "out there," and not on your computer. Your computer—whether it's a PC, a Mac, or a Unix workstation—becomes just a convenient beanstalk to climb up to the land of the Internet giants. You'll sometimes hear this common structure of Internet facilities referred to as *client-server* (sorry for the jargon). In this scenario, you are the client (or your computer or the program running on it is), and the information source, or World Wide Web site, or mail-handling program is the server. Servers are centralized repositories of information or specialized handlers of certain kinds of traffic. All a client has to do is connect to the right server and a wealth of goodies are within your reach, without your having to overload your machine. This is a major reason that it doesn't matter what kind of computer you prefer.

WHAT YOU CAN DO ON THE NET

I've touched on the most popular facilities on the Internet—e-mail and the World Wide Web—but I'll run down some of the other useful features.

Search Services   Once you start exploring the Web, you might get tired of its disorganization (imagine a library in which every card-carrying member worked part-time as a librarian for one of the shelves, and each micro-librarian used their own system for organizing their section) or of not knowing for sure where anything is on the Internet. Fortunately, a lot of useful *search services* (also known as *search engines* or *search tools*) are available on the Net. A *search service* is a program or a Web page that enables you to search an Internet site (or the entire Internet) for a specific word or words. Figure 16.5 shows the Customize Search Settings dialog box in Internet Explorer. Using this dialog box, you can specify what to search for and which search service or services to use. You'll find all the details in Chapter 19.

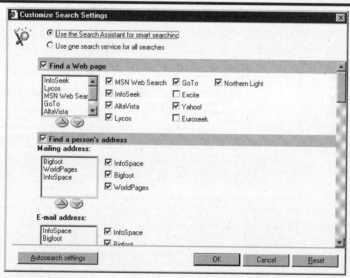

FIGURE 16.5: In Internet Explorer, you can search a single search service or several at once.

Usenet   For many Internet users, the first step beyond e-mail and the Web is into the Internet's sometimes loosely organized system of public message boards called *Usenet* (or simply News). Here you'll find discussion groups (known as "newsgroups") on just about any area of interest imaginable. People "post" messages expressing opinions on topics related to the group or looking for information; other people reply with their own opinions or the requested information.

Usenet has a highly evolved subculture and a set of rules for good behavior known as "Netiquette." For example, if a newsgroup provides a FAQ (answers to Frequently Asked Questions), it's good Netiquette to read the FAQ before asking the whole group your question; someone may have

Part iv

already answered it. A good way to get started with newsgroups is to "lurk"—to read discussions without participating. Both Internet Explorer and Netscape Navigator provide access to News, directly and through search engines.

Figure 16.6 shows a newsgroup posting in response to a question about which is the best search engine.

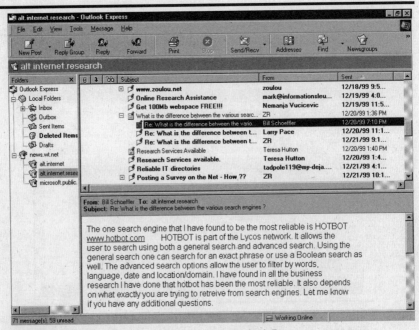

FIGURE 16.6: A newsgroup posting open in Outlook Express

WARNING

You can and will find anything about anything in newsgroups, which are not censored. When I run across offensive material, I just get it off my screen ASAP.

Chat   If you prefer the idea of communicating with people "live" rather than posting messages and waiting for people to reply later, you'll want to know about the various chat facilities available on the Internet—particularly *IRC (Internet Relay Chat)*. Briefly, if you're connected to another user via Chat, you can type messages back and forth. Each of you will see the other's response right away. It's like a telephone call, on your computer screen. And more than two people can participate, in conferences known as "chat rooms." A Chat program is part of Netscape Communicator, the larger suite that includes Navigator; Internet Explorer's NetMeeting tool also includes a Chat feature. In addition, you'll find chat rooms on a lot of Internet sites. Figure 16.7 shows a computers chat room on Yahoo!

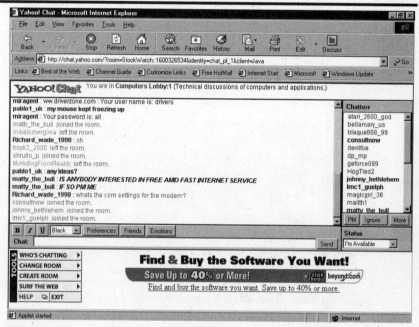

FIGURE 16.7: Lots of people spend lots of time in chat rooms these days.

FTP   The File Transfer Protocol is one of the Internet's oldest and most reliable tools for exchanging ("uploading" and "downloading") files of any kind. FTP servers (known as "hosts") can make files available to specific users (who must provide a password) or to anyone (a technique called "anonymous FTP"); for example, software companies often provide updates or demonstration versions of their products for downloading via anonymous FTP. With both Internet Explorer and Netscape Navigator you can connect to FTP sites, either by clicking links to them in some Web pages or by typing the server's URL in the browser's Address or Location field.

Figure 16.8 shows a list of FTP sites I found by searching on the term *Internet.*

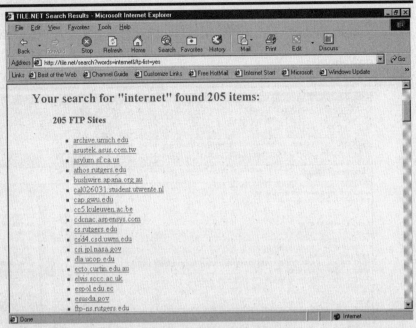

FIGURE 16.8:   To open one of these sites, click its address.

Building Your Own Web Page   Finally, if you want to join the ranks of people with their own home pages on the Web—to create a "presence" on the Net or publicize your favorite Internet sites—you can build your own Web page. Figure 16.9 shows the home page of some friends of mine. They use it to communicate their news to friends and family.

TIP

If you're interested in learning how to create Web pages, check out the following excellent books, all available from Sybex: *web by design: The Complete Guide*, Molly E. Holzschlag, 1998 (0-7821-2201-9); *Effective Web Design: Master the Essentials*, Ann Navarro and Tabinda Khan, 1998 (0-7821-2278-7); *Instant Web Pages!*, Peter Weverka, 2000 (0-7821-2750-9).

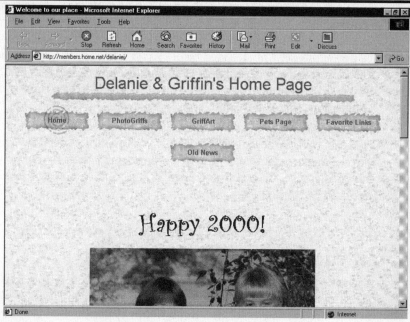

FIGURE 16.9: A personal home page

Downloading Files from the Internet

Another aspect of the Internet that you will especially enjoy is the ability to download files from a vast selection of sample applications, digital art and music, and many other offerings. Software companies promote their new products by maintaining sites where their customers can obtain samples, updates, and related information. Entertainment conglomerates supply sound and video files for movies, bands, and video games. Some organizations just collect information relevant to their interests, such as schedules of upcoming activities, databases of similar organizations, and the like.

WARNING

Before you attempt to access files from the Internet, you should protect your computer (or your company's network) with antivirus software. Computers downloading Internet files are a major point of entry for computer viruses. Chapter 8 contains detailed information about viruses and antivirus software.

Part iv

The files obtained from the Internet can be quite large, so they often arrive compressed to a smaller size, and they may also be coded for protection against unauthorized use or modifications. These files have to be decompressed and decoded before you can use them. Compression-decompression software and decoding applications are readily available, both as free Internet downloads (called *freeware*) and as commercial applications that you pay for.

Many Internet users are concerned about their privacy while using the Net, especially if they are filling out forms or making purchases with credit cards. Programming geniuses have given us applications that try to protect our good credit and our privacy. Some of these efforts are even given away free on the Internet.

Using Web Sites to Gather Information about the Internet and the Web

You can visit the Internet itself to find details about its history, policies, and users. Use the Web sites listed below as the starting point for a journey through various interpretations of how to use the Internet, how it evolved, and how it should be regulated. These sites all contain links to even more sites that will take you surfing farther afield in your quest for knowledge about the Web.

Internet Society `http://info.isoc.org` A site that includes Internet history and statistics, as well as links to other technical organizations dealing with the Web and communication in general.

Electronic Frontier Foundation `http://www.eff.org` A mainly civil-rights–oriented site with many pages on free speech, privacy, and policy.

World Wide Web Consortium `http://www.w3.org` A site hosted by MIT, with support from the European Union, and DARPA (the defense agency that developed the Internet). This site has everything from very technical and lengthy documents to press releases and policy statements.

WHAT'S NEXT?

You now have an overview of what the Internet is and what you can do with it, but before you can use a browser or send e-mail, you must be connected to the Internet. In the next chapter, Robert Cowart tells you about the types of connections, how to choose an ISP, how to configure a Dial-Up Networking connection, and how to share an Internet connection on a network.

Chapter 17

CONNECTING TO THE INTERNET

Before you can use Internet Explorer (or any other Internet application program), you must connect your own computer to the Internet. In this chapter, you will find information about choosing an Internet Service Provider (ISP); making the connection through a modem, a local area network (LAN), or other link; and installing and configuring your system for a TCP/IP (Transmission Control Protocol/Internet Protocol) connection.

Adapted from *Mastering Windows 98 Second Edition* by Robert Cowart
ISBN 0-7821-2618-9   893 pages $39.99

One of the most fascinating features in Windows 98 Second Edition is Internet Connection Sharing (ICS). This allows networked computers to share a single modem connection to the Internet. Although most business network users have been doing this with proxy-server software for a while, ICS makes it that much easier, especially for the growing number of home networks.

NOTE

TCP/IP is the networking software (protocol) that allows many different kinds of computers to interact with one another regardless of type and operating system. First debuted in 1978 for use on the ARPAnet (the predecessor of the Internet), TCP/IP remains the most widely used network protocol software today, and it forms the basis of the Internet. It is not owned by any one agency or company.

WHAT KIND OF CONNECTION?

Choosing a way to connect your computer to the Internet is a trade-off between performance and cost; more money gets you a faster link between your own system and the backbone. (Just like in the human body, the Internet's backbone forms the core high-speed communications channel on which the Internet is built.) Although the difference between file transfers through a modem and a high-speed link can be dramatic, the cost of improved performance may not always be justified. For most home users and many small businesses, a dial-up telephone line and a 33.6Kbps (kilobits per second) or 56Kbps modem is still the most cost-effective choice.

If it's available in your area, you might want to consider ISDN (Integrated Services Digital Network) as an alternative to conventional POTS (Plain Old Telephone Service) lines. ISDN is more expensive and complicated to install and configure, but once it's in place, it offers substantially faster network connections. Your ISP can tell you if ISDN service is available and explain how to order the lines and obtain the necessary interface equipment.

In a larger business, many users can share the same link to the Internet, so a connection with more bandwidth is probably a better approach. Many users can share a single high-speed connection through a LAN, so the cost per user may not be significantly greater than that of a second telephone line.

If your PC is already connected to a LAN, you should ask your network administrator or help desk about setting up an Internet account; it's likely that some kind of connection in already in place. If you have just set up a small network in your home or office, you can use ICS to make sharing a connection easier.

As with most decisions related to data communications, the simple answer to "What kind of connection should I use?" is "The fastest that you can afford." With the drastic increase in the number of Internet users, and growing awareness of how aggravating a slow connection can be, alternatives are beginning to crop up. A variety of higher-speed access vendors have appeared in recent months. Cable modems that use existing cable-TV service wires, digital satellite dish systems, and new telephone-system technologies such as ADSL (Asymmetrical Digital Subscriber Line) are among the most promising. Table 17.1 lists several types of connections and the speed(s) you can expect from each. The prices are in flux, obviously. Also, don't forget that hardware equipment is needed for all of these solutions. You can buy an analog modem for about $50, but some of the other solutions will cost you thousands for your hardware. Some of these solutions, such as satellite hookup, do not include the ISP costs, either. ISPs supply only the hookup to their systems, one stop short of the Internet.

TABLE 17.1: Popular Means for Connection to the Internet

TECHNOLOGY	SPEED / NOTES	SPEED*	TYPICAL COST
Standard 28.8Kbps–56Kbps dial-up service over standard POTS lines	8.8Kbps–33.6Kbps or so. Rarely is 56Kbps achieved due to noise on phone lines.	1x	$20/month + telephone connect charges
ISDN	56Kbps–128Kpbs	2x–4x	$20–$50/month + connect time (typically 1 cent/minute)
Satellite	Varies, typically 400Kbps, some as high as 27Mbps	8x–900x	$20/month + ISP charges
T-3	45Mbps	1,500x	$32,000/month
T-1	1.54Mbps	50x	$3,300/month
Frame relay	Available in 64Kbps increments, up to 1.5Mbps	Up to 50x	$200–$500/month depending on speed

Part iv

TABLE 17.1 continued: Popular Means for Connection to the Internet

TECHNOLOGY	SPEED / NOTES	SPEED*	TYPICAL COST
xDSL—includes ADSL, IDSL (ISDN Digital Subscriber Line), SDSL (Single-Line Digital Subscriber Line), HDSL (High-bit-rate Digital Subscriber Line), VDSL (Very High Speed Digital Subscriber Line), RADSL (Rate Adaptive Digital Subscriber Line)	Asymmetrical Digital Subscriber Line (ADSL) can deliver up to 8Mbps over the 750 million ordinary existing "twisted pair" phone connections on earth. Actual speed offerings of these technologies range from 1.5Mbps to as high as 60Mbps on VDSL.	50x–2000x	$75/month (128Kbps), $250/month (768Kbps) + ISP service
Cable modem, using existing TV cable systems	10Mbps maximum. In reality probably about 1.5Mbps with typical number of users. Some systems offer only 500Kbps. Most systems require separate phone line for uplink since they only *receive* data over the cable. Others are bi-directional.	50x	$40/month

*Relative to 28.8 modem (approximately)

TIP

For a good source of information on high-speed Internet connections, and the inside scoop, check this site: `http://www.teleport.com/~samc/cable1.html`. It's extremely complete.

Now come back down to Earth for a moment, and stop daydreaming about how fast your connection to the Internet *could* be. For the time being, it will probably be either 56Kbps using one of the three 56Kbps standard modem types (but you'll probably only get about 33Kbps maximum connect speed) or 128Kbps using ISDN. But I expect that a combination of ISDN, ADSL, and cable modems will dominate the market for high-speed seekers soon. Even then, good old POTS line dial-ups will continue to be popular since they work on virtually any phone line and accounts are cheap.

However, the telcos (that's short for telephone companies) have a vested interest in stopping people from tying up phone lines with modems all day, since the telephone system was designed for relatively short-term

Integrated Services Digital Network

connections and works most economically that way. ADSL is a terrific solution for delivery of data and even video, since it uses the existing phone wires (no cable wiring necessary), *and it doesn't tie them up for other uses.* What, you say? That's right, you can pick up the regular old phone and make calls while your computer stays online downloading Web pages at T-1 speeds. This is because the Internet data is carried inside a high-frequency carrier signal that rides on top of the phone lines regardless of whether low-frequency voice calls are going on.

With that background, let's get down to the job of getting your modem hooked up and maybe even getting you online. *PPP - Point to Point Protocol*

TCP/IP Transmission Control protocol / Internet Protocol

CHOOSING A SERVICE PROVIDER

As you know, the Internet is the result of connecting many networks to one another. You can connect your own computer to the Internet by obtaining an account on one of those interconnected networks.

Several kinds of businesses offer Internet connections, including large companies with access points in many cities, smaller local or regional ISPs, and online information services that provide TCP/IP connections to the Internet along with their own proprietary information sources. You can use popular programs such as Internet Explorer with a connection through any of these services.

When you order your account, you should request a PPP connection to the Internet. PPP is a standard type of TCP/IP connection, which any ISP should be able to supply.

The Information Superhighway version of a New Age gas station, ISPs are popping up all over the country (and all over the world, for that matter). And like long-distance telephone companies, they offer myriad service options. If you're not among the savvy, you may get snowed into using an ISP that doesn't really meet your needs. As with long-distance telephone providers, you'll find that calculating the bottom line isn't that easy. It really depends on what you are looking for. Here are some questions to ask yourself (and any potential ISP):

- ▶ Does the ISP provide you with an e-mail account? It should.

- ▶ Can you have multiple e-mail accounts (for family members or employees)? If so, how many?

- ▶ Do they offer 56Kbps support? If so, which format? It should match your modem.

▶ Will they let you create your own *domain name*? For example, I wanted the e-mail address bob@cowart.com rather than something cryptic like bobcow@ic.netcim.net. Sometimes creating your own domain name costs extra, but it gives your correspondents an easier address to remember. You can decide if it's worth it.

▶ Does the ISP provide you with a news account so you can interact with Internet *newsgroups*? It should, and it shouldn't restrict which newsgroups you'll have access to unless you are trying to prevent your kids from seeing "dirty" messages or pictures.

▶ Do you want your own Web page available to other people surfing the Net? If so, does the ISP provide online storage room for it? How many "hits" per day can they handle, in case your page becomes popular? How much storage do you get in the deal? Do you want them to create the Web page for you?

▶ What is the charge for connect time? Some ISPs offer unlimited usage per day. Others charge by the hour and/or have a limit on continuous connect time.

▶ Do they have a local (that is, free) phone number? If not, calculate the charges. It may be cheaper to use an ISP that charges more per month if there are no phone company toll charges to connect.

▶ Do they have many points of presence or an 800 number you can use to call into when you are on the road?

▶ Do they have too much user traffic to really provide reasonable service? Ask others who use the service before signing up. This has been a major problem with some ISPs, even biggies like AOL. Smaller providers often supply faster connections. Remember that even if you can connect without a busy signal, the weakest link in the system will determine the speed at which you'll get data from the Net. Often that link is the ISP's internal LAN that connects their in-house computers. It's hard to know how efficient the ISP really is. Best to ask someone who's using it.

▶ Are they compatible with the programs you want to use? Can you use Internet Explorer or Netscape Navigator? Which newsgroup and mail programs are supported?

TIP

If you have access to the Web, try checking the page http://www.thelist.com/. You'll learn a lot about comparative pricing and features of today's ISPs, along with links to their pages for opening an account. Another good site is http://www.boardwatch.com/.

Using a National ISP

The greatest advantage of using a national or international ISP is that you can probably find a local dial-in telephone number in most major cities. If you want to send and receive e-mail or use other Internet services while you travel, this can be extremely important.

The disadvantage of working with a large company is that it may not be able to provide the same kind of personal service that you can get from a smaller, local business. If you must call halfway across the continent and wait 20 minutes on hold for technical support (especially if it's not a toll-free number), you should look for a different ISP.

Many large ISPs can give you free software that automatically configures your computer and sets up a new account. Even if they don't include Internet Explorer in their packages, you should be able to use some version of the program along with the application programs they do supply.

You can obtain information about Internet access accounts from the national service providers listed in Table 17.2.

Many local telephone companies and more than a few cable TV companies are also planning to offer Internet access to their subscribers. If it's available in your area, you should be able to obtain information about these services from the business office that handles your telephone or television service. In San Jose, California, a local UHF TV station is using TV broadcasting technology to deliver high-speed Internet service, for example.

TABLE 17.2: National Internet Service Providers

ISP	PHONE NUMBER	WEB ADDRESS
AT&T WorldNet	1-800-288-3199	http://www.att.net
MCI WorldCom	1-800-444-3333	http://www.wcom.com/
PSInet	1-800-395-1056	http://www.psi.net/

Part iv

TABLE 17.2 continued: National Internet Service Providers

ISP	PHONE NUMBER	WEB ADDRESS
MindSpring	1-888-MSPRING (1-888-677-7464)	http://www.mindspring.net/
EarthLink Sprint	1-888-EARTHLINK (1-888-327-8454)	http://www.earthlink.com/
Concentric Networks	1-800-939-4262	http://www.concentric.com/

Using a Local ISP

The big national and regional services aren't your only choice. In most U.S. cities, smaller local service providers also offer access to the Internet.

If you can find a good local ISP, it might be your best choice. A local company may be more responsive to your particular needs and more willing to help you get through the inevitable configuration problems than a larger national operation. Equally important, reaching the technical support center is more likely to be a local telephone call. Furthermore, in some rural areas you might find that a local ISP is the only Internet service with a local dial-up number, making it your only option for avoiding long distance charges while you are online.

But, unfortunately, the Internet access business has attracted a tremendous number of entrepreneurs who are in it for the quick dollar—some local ISPs are really terrible. If they don't have enough modems to handle the demand, or if they don't have a high-capacity connection to an Internet backbone, or if they don't know how to keep their equipment and servers working properly, you'll get frequent busy signals, slow downloads, dropped lines, and unexpected downtime rather than consistently reliable service. And there's no excuse for unhelpful technical support people or endless time on hold. If a deal seems too good to be true, there's probably a reason.

To learn about the reputations of local ISPs, ask friends and colleagues who have been using the Internet for a while. If there's a local computer user magazine, look for schedules of user group meetings where you can find people with experience using the local ISPs. If you can't get a recommendation from any of those sources, look back at the previous Tip regarding lists of ISPs on the Web (assuming you already have Web access, which I realize is sort of a catch—22).

TIP

No matter which service you choose, wait a month or two before you print your e-mail address on business cards and letterhead. If the first ISP you try doesn't give you the service you expect, take your business someplace else.

Connecting through an Online Service

One of the welcome additions to later versions of Windows 95 has continued into Windows 98 SE. It's the inclusion of easy sign-up software for the major information services in the United States. Evidently this was done in reaction to complaints that Microsoft Corp. was gaining unfair advantage by bundling software for their own service, The Microsoft Network. The services included are America Online, CompuServe, AT&T Worldnet, and Prodigy Internet. Any one of these services will get you connected to the Internet, using a "name brand" so to speak.

With the exception of Worldnet, which offers little more than a standard ISP connection, these services not only get you connected to the Internet—they sell you *content* too. Content providers such as CompuServe have been around for years now (I think I signed up with them about 10 years ago, before the Internet was used by anyone except universities and government agencies). In essence, these outfits are their own isolated mini Internet, with e-mail, bulletin boards, chat groups, and so forth. They typically provide you with special software that makes the whole process of working online simpler than using the more generic software tools designed for e-mail, newsgroups, and the Web. The proprietary information content supplied on services such as AOL and CompuServe is also a bit more supervised than what is available on the Internet at large. On the other hand, you're often somewhat crippled, since you may not be able to use the latest Web browsers.

In addition to supplying their own content, all the major services such as AOL now will connect you through to the Internet, so you can use the Web, newsgroups, and Internet mail. I'd want to use a generic ISP such as Netcom, myself, since I want to be allowed the choice of Web browser I use (Netscape Navigator, Internet Explorer, NeoPlanet, and so on) and which mail reader (Eudora, Netscape Messenger, Outlook, Pegasus Mail, and so on). Services such as AOL and CompuServe don't give you a big choice there. But if a service lets you use the latest versions of Internet Explorer or Netscape Navigator for Web browsing, and the mail program they give you is decent (has folders to organize your mail, has a decent editor, and displays or deals reasonably with attachments such as gif and jpg pictures), then go for it, especially if they make it easy to get hooked up.

Be careful, though. Generally speaking the most expensive way to connect to the Internet has been through one of these national providers. I used to pay $6/hour to be connected to CompuServe, for example. And that amounted to a monthly bill far and away more expensive than the $19 I pay to Netcom now to get unlimited hours on the Internet. AOL and CompuServe are now keeping up with the Joneses (or down, rather) and offering flat rates for unlimited access. Read the fine print to see just what you *do* get for the bucks you spend. Also check the access numbers to see that you won't be paying additional hourly phone connect charges. Then choose.

NOTE

By selecting an online service provider listed in the Online Services folder (not the MSN icon), you will be establishing an account with that online service provider and not with Microsoft Corporation. Therefore, your payment will be due to the online service provider. The online service provider you select will provide you with specific payment instructions.

If you decide to select one of the online service providers listed in the Online Services folder, just click the icon for that online service provider; this will begin setting up your computer for access with that provider. Here's how:

1. Clear the Desktop by clicking the Desktop icon in the Quick Launch bar at the bottom of the screen or by any other method.

2. Look for a folder called Online Services and open it.

3. Run the icon of the service you want to check out. A "splash" screen about the product will appear, or you'll be prompted to insert your Windows CD-ROM, or take some other action, depending on the service. You should ensure your modem is on and connected to the telephone line, since a phone call will be made to sign you up. You'll need a credit card number, too, so get that ready.

4. Once signed up, you'll see instructions about what your services will include, how to proceed, and how to connect with the Internet.

WARNING

There may be specific instructions for how to run their software with Windows 98 SE. Be sure to carefully answer any questions or read relevant instructions about the operating system you are using. For example, AOL has different versions of its software for Windows 3.11 than for Windows 95 or 98/98 SE. Read carefully.

GETTING DIRECTLY ON THE INTERNET—FINDING A LOCAL ISP

Suppose you don't want to use one of the big content providers such as AOL, CompuServe, or AT&T, and you just want onto the Internet. Then what? As you probably know, there are thousands of smaller ISPs out there in the world, especially in the United States. These are the folks that don't supply "content" as AOL and CompuServe do, but that's OK. Maybe all you want is to get onto the Internet, not join clubs on AOL. So why pay for AOL or CompuServe features you don't need or be limited by their regulations or, in some cases, censorship of the material they'll provide you? Or be limited by the types of Web browser or mail or news readers they support?

These are some of the reasons that many folks get directly onto the Internet via a local or even a national ISP. As I've mentioned, I, for one, use Netcom, probably the nation's largest ISP. They have dial-up numbers almost everywhere in the country, which is great. I can travel and still plug in my laptop, make a local call, and get my mail. For my ISDN line, I use a different provider, called Verio, in Berkeley, California. They are only local, but it's affordable ISDN service.

So, if you've decided that you can get cheaper or better service through a generic ISP, Microsoft has made it easy to get connected to the Internet via a little Wizard called Get On The Internet. Normally you'd have to find out on your own who your local ISPs are, and call them or otherwise contact them to get signed up for service. This can be a hassle. Depending on where you live, some local newspapers or computer rags sometimes list all the ISPs in the area. (This is true here in the San Francisco Bay Area where I can find a huge chart of all the local ISPs in the *Computer Currents* magazine.) Microsoft decided to make this process easier by providing a Web page that lists ISPs around the country.

Part iv

So, how do you get connected to an ISP? It's easy. In fact, if you don't have some dial-up connections to the Internet already, and you've tried running Outlook Express or Internet Explorer, you've probably already seen the Get Connected dialog box that has been insistently trying to sign you up with an ISP.

TIP

Have your Windows 98 SE Setup CD handy. The Wizard may need to install some Windows 98 SE files in order to set up your Internet connection.

1. Click Start ➢ Programs ➢ Accessories ➢ Internet Tools ➢ Internet Connection Wizard.

2. You'll see the Internet Connection Wizard dialog box shown in Figure 17.1. Choose which kind of setup you want. Referring to the figure, the choices, in order, do the following:

   ▶ Show you a list of ISPs and help get you signed up with them.

   ▶ Set up the computer for use with your current ISP account, assuming you have one.

   ▶ Set up a connection manually, or set up a connection via a LAN.

FIGURE 17.1: Running the Internet Connection Wizard

3. Click Next. You may be asked which modem you want to use. Then it will try to dial your modem and call a toll-free number that accesses the Microsoft Internet Referral Service. If you are having trouble connecting, click Help in the dialog box and this will run the Internet Connection Wizard Help with troubleshooting tips.

4. When you finally connect to the service, the Wizard displays a list of ISPs with some facts about each. If you chose the "Sign up for a new account" option back in the first dialog box, you'll see a list similar to that shown in Figure 17.2. Since they will undoubtedly be modified from time to time, I won't try to second guess what the remote instructions will say when you read them. However, you will probably have to provide information such as your address and credit card number. Just follow the instructions you find there. A phone number is usually listed for each service if you don't feel comfortable signing up using this Wizard. If you want to quit the whole shebang and sign up later, click Cancel at the bottom of the page.

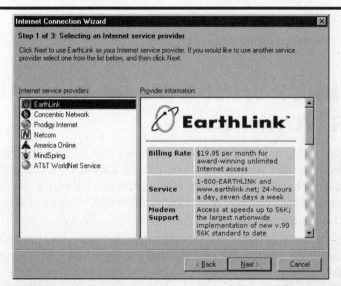

FIGURE 17.2: Typical ISP display resulting from using the Internet Connection Wizard

Part iv

It's likely that you'll see the more national ISPs and information services listed here. No big surprise, I guess. It probably takes some doing to get on the Microsoft list. As I said earlier, you might have to sleuth around to find the smaller fry ISPs in your local area. If you don't want to go with one of the ISPs listed in the Microsoft Internet Referral Service, you will have to go back to the first screen of the Wizard and choose the second or third option. Contact the ISP you want to sign up with the "old-fashioned" way (in other words, call them on the phone). They should provide you with the following pieces of information to help you get your account set up in Windows:

▶ A phone number to use for your Internet connection

▶ Your *user name* (might also be called *User ID* or *Login name*)

▶ A dial-up password

Additionally, if your account includes mail service, you obtain the following information:

▶ Your e-mail address

▶ Incoming mail server type (POP3, IMAP, or HTTP) and address

▶ Outgoing mail server (SMTP) address

▶ Mail account login name and password

SETTING UP WINDOWS 98 SE DIAL-UP NETWORKING

The premium ISPs that show up when you run the Connection Wizard create ready-to-roll Dial-Up Networking profiles for you. By the time you're through entering all your identification and billing information, and clicking on some buttons, all the dirty work that previous versions of Windows required is done automatically.

But what if you're using a little backwoods ISP? Then you have a little more work to do. As a rule, simply ask the ISP for some printed material about how to set up your Dial-Up Networking connection to work with their service. They undoubtedly have printed matter about this or can walk you through the necessary steps over the phone. There are several hairy dialog boxes you get to via the Dial-Up Networking (DUN) folder (My Computer ➤ Dial-Up Networking) and via Control Panel ➤ Network.

Creating a new profile is not difficult, but it's a little more complicated than simply clicking an option in the Internet Connection Wizard. Here are the basics, just so you know what you're talking about when you do contact the ISP, or if you have the info already and want to get set up to configure a Dial-Up Networking connection profile. You must complete two separate procedures: load the software and create a connection profile.

Loading the Software

If you didn't load Dial-Up Networking when you installed Windows 98 SE, you must add it before you can connect to the Internet. Follow these steps to add the software:

1. Open Control Panel.

2. Click Add/Remove Programs to open the Add/Remove Programs Properties dialog box.

3. Click the Windows Setup tab.

4. Select the Communications item from the Components list, and click the Details button to open the Communications dialog box.

5. Make sure there's a check mark next to the Dial-Up Networking component, and click the OK button.

6. When you see a message instructing you to insert software disks, follow the instructions on the screen.

7. When the software has been loaded, restart the computer.

8. Control Panel should still be open. Click the Network icon to open the Network dialog box.

9. Click the Add button to display the Select Network Component Type dialog box, shown in Figure 17.3.

10. Select Protocol in the list of component types, and click the Add button to open the Select Network Protocol dialog box.

11. Select Microsoft from the list of manufacturers, and select TCP/IP in the list of network protocols. Click the OK button.

12. You should see TCP/IP in the list of network components. Click the OK button to close the dialog box.

Part iv

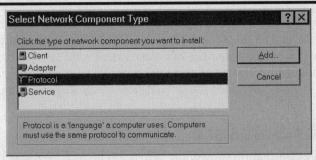

FIGURE 17.3: Use the Select Network Component Type dialog box to set up Dial-Up Networking.

Creating a Connection Profile

Once you've added support for TCP/IP networking, you're ready to set up one or more connection profiles. Follow these steps to create a profile:

1. Start Dial-Up Networking from the My Computer folder, or choose Start ➤ Programs ➤ Accessories ➤ Communications ➤ Dial-Up Networking.

2. Double-click Make New Connection to open the Make New Connection dialog box.

3. The name of the computer you will dial is also the name that will identify the icon for this connection profile in the Dial-Up Networking folder. Therefore, you should use the name of your ISP as the name for this profile. If you have separate profiles for telephone numbers in different cities, include the city name as well. For example, if you use EarthLink as your access provider, you might want to create profiles called EarthLink Chicago and EarthLink Boston.

4. Click the Next button to move to the next screen, and type the telephone number for your ISP's PPP access. Click Next again.

5. Click the Finish button to complete your work with the Wizard.

6. You will see a new icon in the Dial-Up Networking window. Right-click this icon, and select the Properties command to open a dialog box for this connection.

7. Click the Server Types tab to bring it to the front, as shown in Figure 17.4.

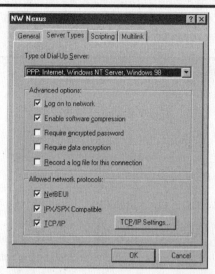

FIGURE 17.4: Use the Server Types tab to set up a PPP connection.

8. Choose the PPP option in the drop-down list of dial-up server types.

9. Make sure there are check marks next to these options:

   ▶ Log On To Network.

   ▶ Enable Software Compression.

   ▶ TCP/IP (You can turn off NetBEUI and IPX/SPX Compatible if you are only connecting to the Internet. Those are used for networking with IBM PCs running Novell and Microsoft networking protocols on a LAN.)

10. Click the TCP/IP Settings button to open the TCP/IP Settings dialog box.

11. Ask your ISP how to fill in this dialog box. You will probably use a Server Assigned IP Address and specific DNS addresses, but your ISP can give you the exact information you need. *This is an important step!*

12. Click the OK buttons to close all the open dialog boxes.

Part iv

To confirm that you have set up the connection profile properly, turn on your modem, and double-click the new connection icon. When the Connect To dialog box, shown in Figure 17.5, appears, type your user ID and password, and click the Connect button. Your computer should place a call to the ISP and connect your system to the Internet.

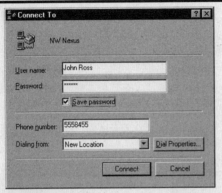

FIGURE 17.5:   The Connect To dialog box shows the name and telephone number of your ISP.

If you have accounts with more than one ISP, or if you carry the same computer to different cities, you can create separate connection profiles for each ISP or each telephone number. If you aren't worried about other people using your computer to connect to your ISP, place a check mark next to the Save Password option.

CHANGING THE DEFAULT CONNECTION

When setup is complete, you will have a Dial-Up Networking connection profile for each of your ISPs. Internet Explorer and other Winsock-compliant or Internet-dependent programs will use the current default to connect your computer to the Internet whenever you start the programs. But what if you have several connections and want to declare which one will be the default that Windows should use?

To change the default, follow these steps:

1. Open Control Panel, and click the Internet Options applet to open the Internet Properties dialog box.

2. Click the Connections tab (see Figure 17.6).

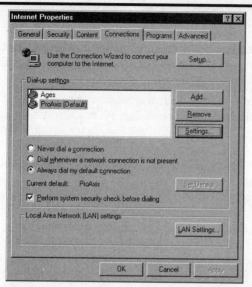

FIGURE 17.6: Use the Connections tab to change the default connection profile.

3. In the list of dial-up connections, choose the one that you want as the default and click Set Default.

4. Click OK to close the dialog box, and then close Control Panel.

TELLING INTERNET PROGRAMS NOT TO DIAL THE PHONE!

Notice in Figure 17.6 that you can choose to connect via the local area network rather than by a modem. This is intended for workstations connected to a local area network running the TCP/IP protocol and which has a connection to the Internet via a router, ICS, or some other approach such as Microsoft Small Business Server or Windows 2000 Server. But you can use this setting to your advantage, even if you've just got a lowly stand-alone computer.

Here's why: It can be annoying when you open your mail program or Internet Explorer or Netscape Navigator and suddenly the phone is being dialed by Windows in hopes of making life easy for you by connecting automatically to the Internet to carry out your wishes. Maybe you're on the phone already, talking to someone, and don't want your modem blasting into your ear. Or you want to ensure that

CONTINUED ➡

if you're not home, but you've left your computer on, that your e-mail program doesn't cause Windows to dial the phone and stay online accidentally, racking up connect-time charges.

If you choose Never Dial A Connection in the dialog box in Figure 17.6, running Internet Explorer or Outlook Express or Netscape Navigator will not run the phone dialer to try to log you on. Actually, nothing will happen except that you'll most likely eventually get an error message from your program saying a connection couldn't be made. Make your connection to the Net manually, by running the DUN profile from My Computer ➢ Dial-Up Networking. Once connected, you can run your Internet programs without having them try to dial the phone. In fact, what I do is tell any Internet programs (that is, Winsock-compatible programs) that they are not to bother connecting to the Internet except through the LAN. (How you do this depends on the program. Some have no settings and rely on the default setting explained earlier.)

Anyway, this arrangement can give you much more flexibility. For example, when I want to connect to the Internet, I run the DUN profile for the connection I want at the time. Sometimes I want a fast connection, so I dial up with my ISDN connection. Other times I want to be on all day with minimal cost, so I use my analog Netcom connection ($19.95/month unlimited connect time). The programs I'm using don't know how the connection was made. All they know is that the TCP/IP connection to the Internet is active. As long as the little connection icon appears down on the Taskbar's right edge:

all popular Winsock Internet programs such as Netscape Navigator, Eudora, Pegasus Mail, Internet Explorer, WS_FTP, and so on should work fine. When it's time to get off the connection, I have to do that manually, too (or face the consequences). I double-click the little connection icon to open the Connected To dialog box:

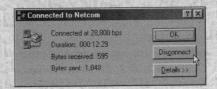

and click Disconnect.

SHARING YOUR INTERNET CONNECTION WITH NETWORKED COMPUTERS

Personal computers in the home are nothing new. The relatively mature PC market—combined with remarkable price drops on new computers in recent years—means that many homes now have multiple PCs. These multi-PC owners are now seeking to create their own networks to connect all those computers. The online news source CNET (www.cnet.com) projects that the home networking market will grow from an expected $230 million in 1999 to $1.4 billion by 2003.

Microsoft is doing its best to keep pace with the growing home network market, and Windows 98 SE includes a number of useful tools to make networking worthwhile. As I said earlier, perhaps the most interesting new feature is Internet Connection Sharing (ICS), which allows computers on your home network to share a single Internet connection. This means that two or more computers can access the online world using only a single phone line and modem.

Admittedly, this kind of sharing is nothing new. Networked computers have been able to share Internet access over the network for years using third-party proxy server software. The proxy server is usually set up on the network server, and workstations go online through that central connection. Because ICS is incorporated into Windows 98 SE, the whole process is far simpler. Installing ICS is no more complicated than installing any number of other Windows components, such as WebTV or Desktop Themes.

NOTE

ICS can put a real strain on your modem connection, especially if more than one computer is trying to access the Internet simultaneously. As a general rule, assume that each Internet user will require 28.8Kbps worth of bandwidth. Thus, if you have two computers sharing the connection, it should be capable of 56Kbps transfer rates. With three or more computers on ICS, your best bet is to upgrade to an ISDN or DSL connection. Otherwise, you may find that even relatively simple actions such as downloading e-mail or viewing a Web page is maddeningly slow, if not impossible.

Part iv

Setting Up Internet Connection Sharing (ICS)

For now, I'll assume that you already have your network up and running. If not, see Chapter 23 to learn how to get your PCs networked. Once your network is up and running, decide which computer will be used to facilitate the Internet connection. This will be called your Connection Sharing computer.

Next, make sure that the modem and Dial-Up Networking connection in your Connection Sharing computer is installed and ready. Beginning on the Connection Sharing computer, place your Windows 98 SE CD into the drive and follow these steps:

1. Run Control Panel, and open the Add/Remove Programs applet.

2. Click the Windows Setup tab to bring it to the front. Choose Internet Tools, and click Details.

3. Place a check mark next to Internet Connection Sharing and click OK twice.

NOTE

If you do not have the Internet Connection Sharing option available in your Internet Tools list, you probably don't have the Second Edition of Windows 98. Double-check the documentation that came with your Windows 98 CD to make sure that it is the Second Edition and that it includes ICS.

4. The Internet Connection Sharing Wizard begins. Click Next to begin the setup process. You will first be asked to create a Client Disk to be used when setting up ICS on the other computers on your network. Follow the instructions on screen to create the disk.

5. When you are done creating the Client Disk, click Finish to complete installation. You will be prompted to restart the computer.

6. After the computer is restarted, open Control Panel again, and click Internet Options to open the Internet Properties dialog box. Click the Connections tab, and then click Sharing, as shown in Figure 17.7.

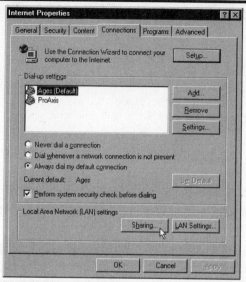

FIGURE 17.7:   Click Sharing on the Connections tab to configure your Connection Sharing computer.

7. In the Internet Connection Sharing dialog box, make sure there is a check mark next to Enable Internet Connection Sharing. Also check that your dial-up adapter is listed under Connect To The Internet Using and that your correct network adapter appears at the bottom. Click OK to exit all the dialog boxes.

Now that your Connection Sharing computer is configured, you need to set up the other computers on your network to utilize the shared connection. Take the Client Disk you created in step 4 with you and perform the following:

1. Insert the Client Disk into the floppy drive.

2. Choose Start ➤ Run to open the Run dialog box, and in the Open box, type **a:\icsclset.exe**.

3. Click OK to open the Browser Connection Setup Wizard, and then click Next. The Wizard warns you that it is about to check—and change—the settings in the Web browser, as shown in Figure 17.8. Click Next to proceed.

4. Click Finish in the last Wizard screen.

Part iv

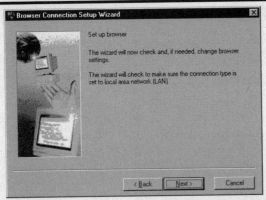

FIGURE 17.8: The Browser Connection Setup Wizard will set up your browser to access the Internet over your LAN instead of a dial-up connection.

The Wizard changes the connection setting in your browser so that it looks for an Internet connection over the LAN instead of a dial-up. If the client computer has Internet Explorer 5, you can view this change by opening Control Panel and launching the Internet Options applet. On the Connections tab, you will see that Never Dial A Connection has been selected, as shown in Figure 17.9. This is important to note, especially if the client is a computer you plan to remove from the network periodically (such as a laptop). In this case, I recommend you choose Dial Whenever A Network Connection Is Not Present instead.

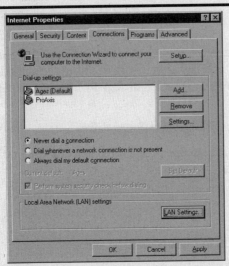

FIGURE 17.9: If the client computer is a laptop or will be removed from the network periodically, consider changing the settings in this dialog box.

WHAT'S NEXT?

Now that you have your Internet connection set up, it's time to take a look at the most-used Internet application—e-mail. In the next chapter, Christian Crumlish gives you an overview and then gives step-by-step instructions for using Outlook Express and Netscape Messenger.

Chapter 18

COMMUNICATING WITH E-MAIL

This is the real stuff. The reason you're on the Net. E-mail! Instant (more or less) communication with people all over the globe. Once you can send and receive e-mail, you're wired.

When you get used to sending e-mail, you'll find that it's as useful a form of communication as the telephone, and it doesn't require the other person to drop whatever they're doing to answer your call. You can include a huge amount of specific information, and the person you sent mail to can reply in full in their own good time. And unlike the telephone, with e-mail you can write your message and edit it before you send it.

· ·

Adapted from *The Internet: No Experience Required*
by Christian Crumlish
ISBN 0-7821-2168-3   528 pages $24.99

E-mail is the lifeblood of the Internet. Daily, millions of written messages course through the wires, enabling people all over the planet to communicate in seconds. One reason for the widespread use of the Internet as the international computer network is that it's a flexible enough system to allow just about any type of computer or network to participate. Of course, this chapter assumes you're using a PC with Windows 98 SE and either the Outlook Express program that's bundled with Internet Explorer or the Netscape Messenger program included in the Netscape Communicator suite. But it's important to remember that e-mail programs basically do the same things.

I'll start off by explaining the most common activities associated with e-mail, the kinds of things you'll want to know how to do no matter what program you have. I'll use generic terminology in this part of the lesson, such as Inbox and Outbox, even if some specific programs use different terms for the same ideas. Focus on the concepts and the standard features, not what they're called in one program or another. Then, I'll cover specific commands and tips for the e-mail programs you're most likely to use.

NOTE

Christian Crumlish wrote *The Internet: No Experience Required* for all new Internet users, no matter what operating system and software they are using, not just for Windows 98 SE users working with Internet Explorer or Netscape Communicator. In particular, its e-mail chapters include extensive coverage of other e-mail programs that we've omitted in adapting this material for *PC Complete*. If you have access to a Macintosh or Unix system, or if you have a mailer such as Eudora or Pegasus, you may want to consult *The Internet: No Experience Required* for details.

E-MAIL BASICS

These are the things that you will do most often with e-mail:

- ▶ Run the mail program
- ▶ Send mail
- ▶ Read incoming mail
- ▶ Reply to mail

▶ Delete mail

▶ Exit the mail program

In the second half of this chapter, I'll show you some additional e-mail tricks you might find useful, such as how to forward mail and create an electronic address book.

Running an E-Mail Program

You start most e-mail programs the way you do any program, usually by double-clicking an icon or by choosing a program name from a menu (the Programs menu in Windows 98 SE). If your Internet connection is not already up and running, your e-mail program may be able to start that process for you.

Your e-mail program will start and show you either the contents of your Inbox (the mailbox where your new messages arrive) or a list of all your mailboxes (in which case you'll want to open the Inbox).

NOTE

There are some new free Internet accounts (such as Hotmail and Juno.com) that offer Web-based e-mail access. The accounts are paid for by advertising you have to keep on your screen while you're connected. To find out more about them, go to http://www.hotmail.com or http://www.juno.com in your Internet browser.

In addition to an Inbox where just-arrived messages appear, you'll automatically have an Outbox in which copies of your outgoing messages can be saved (some programs will do this automatically), and you'll usually have a deleted-messages or Trash folder where discarded messages are held until they are completely purged.

Mailbox folders generally list just the sender's name and the subject line of the message (and probably its date as well). When you double-click a message in any of your mailbox folders, the message opens in a window of its own.

Sending Mail

All mail programs have a New Message or Compose E-Mail command, often located on a message menu, and they usually have a keyboard shortcut for the command as well, such as Ctrl+M for New Message. When you start a new message, your program will open a new window. Figure 18.1 shows a new message window in Outlook Express.

TIP

You can also save addresses and then select them from an address book or list of names rather than type them in directly. See "Managing an Address Book" later in this chapter for more on this.

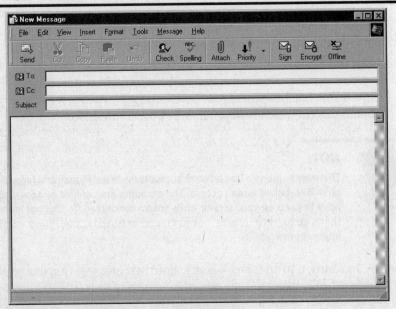

FIGURE 18.1: A blank New Message window

Type the address of the person to whom you want to send the mail. The person's address must be in the form username@address.domain, where username is the person's identifier (the name they log in with); address is the identifier of the person's network or machine on the network (the address might consist of several words—the host and subdomain—separated by dots); and domain is the short code at the end indicating whether the address is a business (.com), a nonprofit (.org), a university (.edu), a branch of the government (.gov), a part of the military (.mil), and so on. (Some e-mail programs require special text before or after the Internet e-mail address.)

By the way, all the rules just mentioned apply only to sending mail over the Internet. Generally, if you're sending mail to someone on your own network (or another member of your online service or a subscriber of your service provider), you only have to specify the username, not any of the Internet information.

TIP

The easiest way to send mail to someone is to reply to mail that they've sent you. If you're not sure exactly how to form someone's e-mail address, ask them to send you some mail and then simply reply to it. That's what I always do.

One of my addresses is `xian@netcom.com` (you pronounce the "@" as "at," and the "." as "dot"). I log in as "xian," my service provider is Netcom, and Netcom is a commercial business.

Sending Mail to People on Other Networks

Many people have Internet addresses even though they are not, strictly speaking, on the Internet. Most other networks have gateways that send mail to and from the Internet. If you want to send mail to someone on another network, you'll need to know their identifier on that network and how their network address appears in Internet form. Here are examples of the most common Internet addresses:

Network	User name	Internet Address
America Online	Beebles	`beebles@aol.com`
AT&T Mail	Beebles	`beebles@attmail.com`
CompuServe	Beebles	`beebles@cs.com`
MCI Mail	555-7777	`555-7777@mcimail.com`
Microsoft Network	Beebles	`beebles@msn.com`
Prodigy	Beebles	`beebles@prodigy.com`

To compose and send a message, follow these steps:

1. After entering the recipient's address in the Address box, press Tab and then type a subject in the Subject box (keep it short). This will be the first thing the recipient of your mail sees.

TIP

The subject you type in the subject line should be fairly short, but should be a good description of the contents of your message. Good subject lines can help recipients categorize their mail and respond more quickly to your messages.

2. If you want to send a copy of the e-mail message to more than one recipient, you can either:

    ▶ Type that person's address on the Cc line.

    ▶ Type multiple addresses in either the To or Cc line, separating each address by a comma or a semicolon. In some e-mail programs, the addresses may appear on separate lines.

TIP

In both Internet Explorer and Netscape Messenger, you can press Tab to jump from box to box or from area to area when filling in an address and subject. You can also just click directly in the area you want to jump to.

3. Press Tab until the insertion point jumps into the blank message area.

4. Type your message, and when you are done, send the message or add it to a *queue*, a list of outgoing messages to be sent all at once. Click the Send button, or choose File ➤ Send Message. Figure 18.2 shows a short e-mail message.

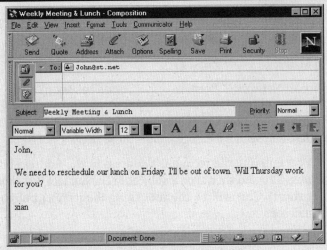

FIGURE 18.2: A short e-mail message to a friend

TIP

Both Outlook Express and Netscape Messenger can word-wrap your message, so you only have to press Enter when you want to start a new paragraph. I recommend leaving a blank line between paragraphs, to make them easier to read.

You can also filter messages, which is the same thing as sorting them according to some criteria as they come into your Inbox. The post office sorts mail according to zip code, and you can use your e-mail program to automatically sort messages according to who sent them, the subject, the date they were sent or received, or any other category that is useful to you from an organizational standpoint. And you can flag messages according to the urgency of the response needed or other priorities. These options provide you with powerful organizational tools and transform your messages into valuable records that can be filed and retrieved for later reference. See "Filtering Messages As They Come In" later in this chapter for more on message filters.

Reading Mail

Whenever I connect to the Net, the first thing I do is check my e-mail. It's like checking your mailbox when you get home, except the contents are generally more interesting—and usually don't contain bills! Some mail programs (including Outlook Express and Netscape Messenger) combine the process of sending queued messages with checking for new mail. Most also check for new mail when you first start them.

Unread (usually new) mail appears with some indicator that it's new, such as the Subject line in bold or a bullet or check mark next to the new messages. This is supposed to help you pick out the messages you haven't read yet, so you don't miss any.

Here are the steps for reading an e-mail message:

1. Open your e-mail program by double-clicking its shortcut icon or selecting it from the Start menu. By default, both Outlook Express and Netscape Messenger begin by displaying your Inbox contents automatically.

2. To view the contents of a mail message, highlight it in the Inbox window and press Enter (or double-click it). Figure 18.3 shows an incoming message in Outlook Express.

Part iv

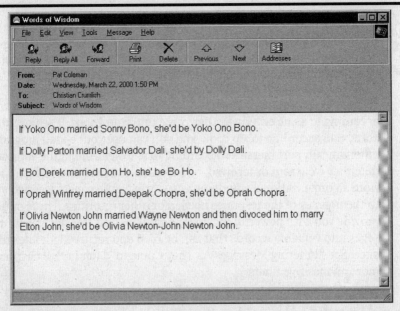

FIGURE 18.3: Here's an e-mail message I received.

3. If the message continues beyond the bottom of the window, use the scroll bar to see the next screenful.

4. After reading the message, you can close or reply to the message.

TIP

I keep my mail around until I've replied to it. I could save it to a mailbox (as I'll explain later in this chapter), but then I might forget about it. When my Inbox gets too cluttered, I bite the bullet and reply to mail I've been putting off, and then I delete most of it.

Replying to Mail

Both Outlook Express and Netscape Messenger offer menu options and toolbar buttons for replying to messages you've received. When you reply to an e-mail message, your new message is automatically addressed back to the sender, and you can easily quote the message you received.

TIP

If you start to reply by mistake, just close the message window and don't save the reply if prompted.

To reply to an e-mail message, follow these steps:

1. Highlight the received message in the Inbox or open the message, and then click the Reply (or Reply To Author) command.

2. Your program will create a new message automatically addressed to the sender of the message you're replying to. In Netscape Messenger, you can click the Quote button to include the original message. In Outlook Express, you'll need to choose Tools ➢ Options and, in the Send tab, click Include Message In Reply.

TIP

Any Web addresses mentioned in e-mail messages to you can function as clickable links in Netscape Messenger and Outlook Express. To use these links, click the highlighted address, which will probably be underlined or depicted in a different color, such as blue. You will be transported to the Web site using that address. Outlook Express users can also add Web shortcuts as file attachments. Just click the Web icon to head for that site.

3. Sometimes, you'll want to reply to everyone who was sent a copy of the original message. Select Reply To All or a similar command to send your reply to everyone.

4. Tab to the subject line and type a new subject if the old one isn't very meaningful anymore. (People often fail to change the subject line of messages, even when the conversation has evolved onto a new topic.)

5. Add other recipients if necessary, or tab your way into the message area to type your reply, and then choose the Send (or Queue) command when you are done.

TIP

E-mail tends to take on a life of its own, with people forwarding you messages from other people asking for help, information, you name it. Sometimes people send you long chains of related messages, often called *threads*. To avoid confusion when replying to a message forwarded to you, or when replying to many recipients, direct the mail program to "retain the original text," or however the command is worded, so that people reading the message will know what you are talking about and will know the history of the issue. However, if the thread starts getting too long, try to abbreviate it as described below in the "Using Proper E-Mail Netiquette" section.

Deleting Mail

If you have read a piece of mail and you're positive that you have no need to save it, you should delete it so that it doesn't clutter up your Inbox (and waste precious hard-disk storage space). To delete a message, highlight it and press Delete (or click the Delete button).

Using Proper E-Mail Netiquette

Like any social system, the Internet has evolved to the point where its users observe a variety of informal rules for interacting politely. Collectively, these rules are known as *Netiquette,* and most of them can be inferred through the application of some common sense to various social situations.

For example, it's generally not considered good manners to misquote what someone said when talking to someone else, to take their words out of context, or to repeat something that was told to you in confidence (though the media and gossips often commit such acts!). Think of e-mail as a kind of online conversation. If people send you messages containing sensitive material, don't forward them on to others without the author's permission.

If you retain only part of the original text of messages in your replies (to keep the replies from becoming too long), be sure it is not misleadingly taken out of its full context (and likely to be misinterpreted). And please do not intersperse your own comments with the retained pieces of other people's messages so that it's not clear to the recipients who wrote what.

Keep Your Messages Brief and Tactful

When you write messages to business associates and colleagues, stick to the point and be informative. Break up large blocks of text into smaller paragraphs. Reread your messages and run a spell check before sending them—this will give you a chance to minimize mistakes, fix poorly organized sentences, and reconsider bad word choices.

If you are writing to friends (or potential friends in newsgroups or chat rooms), you can relax a little more, but still hold back on anything that could be considered offensive, even if you think it's funny and you are sure that your friends will, too. Seemingly innocuous statements in spoken conversation can take on a whole new meaning when written down. Figures of speech, jokes, and your own private way of referring to situations or people seem a lot more serious when viewed in writing.

WARNING

The old adage about never saying or putting anything in writing that you would not want to see in a headline the next day applies to e-mail and the Internet. Now you also have to worry about your words appearing on someone's Web page or showing up when someone searches the Web, a chat service, or a newsgroup. Journalists search the Web for juicy opinions every day. There's no law preventing potential employers from checking you out on the Web and uncovering some embarrassing thing you wrote or posted years ago.

When replying to messages, try to minimize the amount of quoted text that you keep in your return message. Leave enough so it's clear what you're replying to (people don't always remember exactly what they wrote to you). However, as mentioned at the beginning of this section, don't send abbreviated message bits attributed to other people that could be taken out of context. Just use your good common sense!

Don't Fly off the Handle

E-mail is a notoriously volatile medium. Because it is so easy to write out a reply and send it in the heat of the moment, and because text lacks many of the nuances of face-to-face communication—the expression and body cues that add emphasis, the tones of voice that indicate joking instead of insult, and so on—it has become a matter of course for many people to dash off ill-considered replies to perceived insults and therefore to fan the flames of invective.

This Internet habit, called *flaming*, is widespread, and you will no doubt encounter it on one end or the other. All I can suggest is that you try to restrain yourself when you feel the urge to fly off the handle. (And I have discovered that apologies work wonders when people have misunderstood a friendly gibe or have mistaken sarcasm for idiocy.)

TIP

If you are the sort to flare up in an angry response, or if you find yourself getting emotional or agitated while composing a response to a message that upsets you, save your message as a draft rather than sending it right away. You can review the draft message later when you have calmed down, and you can decide then whether you want to send it, or you can send the draft to a disinterested third party and ask them if it is too harsh before you send it out.

Exiting an E-Mail Program

When you are finished sending, reading, and replying to mail, you can quit your program or leave it running to check your mail at regular intervals. You can quit Outlook Express or Netscape Messenger by selecting File ➤ Exit or by clicking the Close button.

TRYING OUT MICROSOFT OUTLOOK EXPRESS AND NETSCAPE MESSENGER

Well, now you know the basic e-mail moves no matter which program you're using. In the following sections, I'll detail the specific commands for our two e-mail programs. The second half of this chapter covers some of e-mail's more interesting possibilities. Jump to Chapter 19 if you're impatient to get onto the World Wide Web.

Microsoft Outlook Express

Outlook Express is an Internet standards-based e-mail and news reader you can use to access Internet e-mail and news accounts. In this section, we'll look at how to use Outlook Express Mail.

You can open Outlook Express by selecting Start ➤ Programs ➤ Outlook Express or by clicking the miniature Launch Outlook Express icon in the Quick Launch toolbar to the immediate right of the Start button.

NOTE

You'll start off in a window showing two panes. The pane on the left shows the various features of the program that are available, with your Inbox first and foremost. The pane on the right shows you the contents of your Inbox (but you can click any other folder, and Outlook Express will show its contents below). Outlook Express has a big Preview pane that shows you the contents of the highlighted message. You can turn this Preview on or off and change its appearance and location by choosing View ➢ Layout.

Here's how to create a new Outlook Express e-mail message:

1. Click the New Mail button to open the New Message window.

2. Type an address and press Tab to get down to the Subject box where you can type a subject.

3. Tab down to the message area, and type your message. Click the Send button. If you are accumulating messages to send in bulk, choose File ➢ Send Later, and then click the Send/Recv button in the main Outlook Express window when you are ready to send them all.

To read a message in your Inbox, just double-click its subject line. The message will appear in its own window. To reply to the message, select Reply or Reply All. Outlook Express will supply the recipient's address. Proceed as if you were sending a new message.

To delete a message, just highlight it, and click the Delete button or press the Delete key on your keyboard. The message will be moved to the Deleted Items folder until you specifically open that folder and delete its contents.

TIP

To undelete a message, open the Deleted Items folder and select the message you want to restore. Then choose Edit ➢ Move To Folder, choose the Inbox folder from the Move dialog box that appears, and click OK.

Netscape Messenger

Netscape Communicator sports a full-featured mail program called Netscape Messenger.

Part iv

NOTE
You'll learn more about Netscape Communicator's Web capabilities in Chapter 20.

Using Netscape Messenger for e-mail is a lot like using Outlook Express and many other mail programs. Here's how to create and send an e-mail message:

1. Choose File ➤ New ➤ Message, choose Message ➤ New Message, or click the New Message button to open the Composition window.

2. Type an address in the To box. Press Tab and type a subject.

3. Press Tab again to enter the message area and type your message (see Figure 18.4).

4. When you're done, click the Send button.

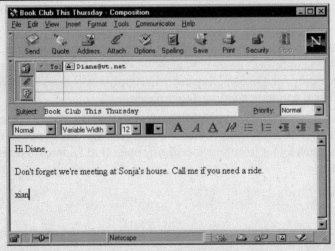

FIGURE 18.4: The Netscape Messenger window with a message ready to be sent

If you receive mail while working in Netscape (the little envelope in the lower-right corner of the Netscape window will alert you), choose Window ➤ Inbox. (The first time you do this, Netscape may require you to enter your password.) Remember that any Web addresses mentioned in Netscape Messenger e-mail messages you receive will function as clickable links. That means when you finish reading, all you have to do is click a highlighted word to go to that Web page and start surfing. For more information on the Web, see Chapter 19.

Here are some other Netscape Messenger commands you will find useful:

▶ To reply to a message, click the Reply button, or choose Message ➤ Reply.

▶ To delete a message, just highlight it and click the Delete button. Netscape will move the message to the Trash folder.

▶ To undelete a message, select the Trash folder in the drop-down folder list, select the message, and then drag the message to Inbox.

USING E-MAIL MORE EFFECTIVELY

Now that you've learned the essentials of sending and receiving e-mail, we'll use the rest of this chapter to look at somewhat more advanced techniques that can help to streamline your work with either Outlook Express or Netscape Messenger.

Sending Mail to More Than One Person

Sometimes you'll want to send a message to more than one recipient. You can do this in one of several ways. Both Outlook Express and Netscape Messenger (as well as most other programs) allow you to list multiple recipients in the To line, usually separated by commas (some programs require that you use a different character, such as a semicolon, to separate addresses). Most programs also have a Cc line. As with traditional paper office memos, the Cc line in an e-mail message is for people who should receive a copy of the message, but who are not the primary recipients.

NOTE

When you reply to a message, your reply will be sent only to the person in the To line if you select the option. If you select Reply To All, your reply will be sent to everyone in the Cc list as well.

Some programs also offer a Bcc line, which lets you list one or more people to receive blind copies of that message. This means that the primary (and Cc) recipients will not see the names of people receiving blind copies.

Part iv

WARNING

You can typically include as many names on the Cc line as you want, but some mail servers will "choke" on a message if its headers are too long.

Sending Files via E-Mail

It sounds too good to be true. Just "attach" a file to an e-mail message, and it zips across the globe to your recipient, without having to be put on a disk and sent by mail or courier. Naturally, it's not that simple. Some files are just too big to send this way (anything close to a megabyte is probably too big). Let's start with what an attachment really is.

NOTE

Each Internet Service Provider is a little different, so you can experiment with the size of files you can send. Some services limit the size of files you may attach to messages, while others will take anything, but the transmission may become extremely slow. You can compress files to make them smaller, and you can send each file in a group of files in separate messages to keep the size small.

Attaching Files to E-Mail Messages in Outlook Express

An *attachment* is a data file, in any form, that your program will send along with your e-mail message—it could be a word-processing file, a picture, a spreadsheet, or any other kind of file. In Outlook Express, use one of these options to attach files to your messages:

▶ Use Explorer or My Computer to open the window the file is in, click the file, and drag it into the new message window.

▶ Choose Insert ➤ File Attachment, and choose the file you want from the Insert Attachment dialog box that appears, and then click OK. Figure 18.5 shows an attached file in an Outlook Express message. Your recipient can double-click the icon next to the filename on the Attach line to open the attached file.

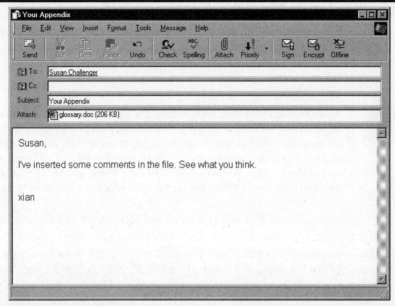

FIGURE 18.5: Outlook Express inserts an icon and the filename of the attachment on the Attach line.

Attaching Files to Netscape Messenger E-Mail

Netscape Messenger's provisions for attaching files to e-mail are quite simple. You can also attach Web page links to your messages with these commands:

1. Choose Message ➤ New Message to open the Composition window.

2. Address your message, and type your message in the message body. To attach a file to the message, click the Attach button.

3. Choose File (you can also attach Web pages, among other things).

4. In the Enter File To Attach dialog box, choose the file you want to send, and then click Open.

5. Click the Save button or the Send button to save a draft or send your message on its way.

Forwarding Mail to Someone Else

If someone sends you an e-mail message and you'd like to send a copy of it to someone else, most mail programs let you select a Forward command.

WARNING

Never send mail to a third party without the express permission of the original sender. Also, be sure to use a *reply separator*, such as a solid horizontal line, between all of the forwarded e-mail messages to delineate where one person's response ends and another begins (most e-mail programs add reply separators automatically). This will avoid confusion about who wrote what and will avoid uncomfortable situations for both you and those who send you e-mail.

In both Outlook Express and Netscape Messenger, the Forward command is on the same menu or toolbar as the Reply command, and it works in almost the same way. The difference is that your mail program won't insert the original sender's e-mail address into the To line. Instead, the To line will be blank so you can fill in the address of the person you are forwarding the message to. The original message will automatically be included in the new message, often with some characters (like the standard ">" Internet e-mail quoting character) or other formatting to distinguish it from what you yourself write.

Here's how to forward e-mail messages:

1. Open your e-mail program, and either highlight or open the message you want to forward.

2. Click the Forward icon in the toolbar of your e-mail program. A new message window will appear with the forwarded message included in the text area.

3. Enter the recipient's e-mail address on the To line and then Tab your way down to the message area.

4. Edit the message if you want, or add your own note to the beginning, perhaps explaining why you are forwarding the message.

5. Send the message as usual.

Enhancing Your E-Mail with HTML Formatting

Internet mail has long been an "unformatted" medium, with only a guarantee that basic text would be transmitted from site to site. Formatted messages typically lose their formatting as soon as they pass through an e-mail gateway. Some mail programs can understand or create formatting that conforms to the Internet's MIME standard, but again, not all programs recognize MIME, so the point of the formatting may be lost.

Now, some mail programs are more closely integrated with Web browsers, such as Netscape Messenger, part of the same Netscape Communicator suite that contains Netscape Navigator. Microsoft Outlook Express, which is installed as part of Windows 98 SE, works in tandem with Internet Explorer. These e-mail programs have become more Web-savvy: they can recognize Web addresses (URLs), hyperlinks, and now most HTML formatting. (HTML is the coding language used to create Web documents.)

WARNING

Don't rely too heavily on any "brand" of formatting to make your point, because you can't be sure your audience will see the pulsing, blinking green text or other effects you may add. Your careful selection of just the right font may also backfire when the message arrives, because some programs substitute basic fonts for less common fonts, resulting in poorly aligned text at the message's destination.

Both Outlook Express and Netscape Messenger also let you create messages with HTML formatting. In fact, you can compose mail messages much the same way you can Web pages, inserting images and links to pages on the Web or other Internet resources. You don't need to "know the code" either, because the software makes it as easy to add HTML formatting as it is to change font styles with your word processor.

Formatting an E-Mail Message with HTML in Outlook Express

Your messages will resemble Web pages if you use Outlook Express HTML formatting to add colorful fonts and even graphics. Just the two steps here give you this capability:

1. Choose Format ➤ Rich Text (HTML). The Formatting toolbar will appear at the top of your message.

2. Select the text to be formatted and use the buttons on the Formatting toolbar to add HTML formatting, such as bold and italic, bulleted lists, alignment (center, flush left, or flush right), and text color.

Formatting an E-Mail Message with HTML in Netscape Messenger

In Messenger, you can add any HTML formatting (or insert hyperlinks or even graphic images) to your message using the convenient toolbar in the Composition window. (Insert links and images with the Insert menu.)

Writing E-Mail with Your Word Processor

If you're more comfortable writing in a word-processing program than you are writing in your e-mail program, you can write your message there, copy it using the Copy command, and then switch to your e-mail program and paste it into a new message window.

One problem with putting word-processed text into e-mail messages is that some e-mail programs substitute special characters for apostrophes and quotation marks. If they are not correctly interpreted by the receiving program, these special characters come out as garbage characters that make your mail harder to read. Also, there are sometimes problems with line breaks, either with lines being too long or with extraneous characters (weird stuff, such as ^M or =20) appearing at the end of each line.

Here's how to copy a message from your word processor to your e-mail:

1. In your word processor, create your message. When you are done, save it as a text file. (Figure 18.6 shows a text file I created in Microsoft Word 2000.)

2. Close the file and open it again to ensure that none of the special (nontext) characters are still in the file. Look for odd characters that you would not see on a standard keyboard and delete them.

3. Select the entire document and copy it (Ctrl+C in Windows programs).

4. Then switch to your e-mail program.

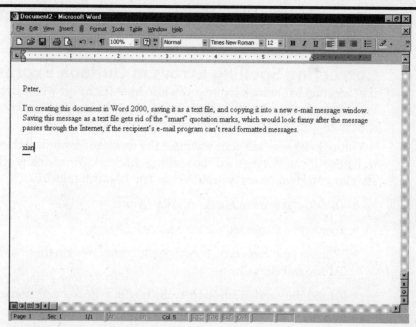

Peter,

I'm creating this document in Word 2000, saving it as a text file, and copying it into a new e-mail message window. Saving this message as a text file gets rid of the "smart" quotation marks, which would look funny after the message passes through the Internet, if the recipient's e-mail program can't read formatted messages.

xian

FIGURE 18.6: I created this file in Word 2000. Now I'm going to save it as a text file.

5. Create a new message as usual, go to the message area, and paste the text you copied (Ctrl+V).

6. The text will appear in the e-mail program as if you had typed it there.

TIP

If you're using Word 2000, you have an even easier way to send a Word document as an e-mail message. Simply choose File ➢ Send To ➢ Mail Recipient.

Checking Your Spelling

Most e-mail programs now offer spell checking (so the traditional excuses for sloppily edited e-mail messages are vanishing fast!), but the specific techniques vary from program to program (as you might expect). It's a good idea to check the spelling in a message before sending it, especially if the message is long, formal, or for some business purpose.

If you write your messages ahead of time using a word-processing program, you can use your word processor's spelling checker to check the message. You may find this easier than working with two different spelling checkers.

Correcting Spelling Errors in Outlook Express

If in addition to Outlook Express you also have Microsoft Word, Excel, or PowerPoint installed, in the Outlook Express New Message window, you can choose Tools ➢ Spelling to check the spelling of a message.

Outlook Express will start scanning the message for words it doesn't recognize. If you've ever used the spelling checker in Word or any other standard word processor, you should be familiar with this drill:

- ► To skip the word in question, click Ignore.

- ► To accept a suggested correction, click Change.

- ► To make your own correction, type the correct word in the Change To box and click Change.

- ► To add the word in question to the spelling checker's dictionary, click Add.

Spell Checking in Netscape Messenger

To check the spelling of your e-mail message in Netscape Messenger, choose Tools ➢ Check Spelling in the Composition window.

Attaching a Signature

On the Internet, it's traditional to include a short *signature* at the end of each message. An e-mail signature is a few lines of text, usually including your name, sometimes your postal (*snail mail*) address, and perhaps your e-mail address. If you are including a signature in a business message, you might want to include phone and fax numbers, and maybe the company Web page address. Many people also include quotations, jokes, gags, and so on. Signatures (also called *sig blocks*, *signature files*, *.signatures*, or *.sigs*) are a little like bumper stickers in this respect.

TIP

You can never be too careful when using company online resources, so consider adding a disclaimer to your signature block if you post to Usenet groups or mailing lists from a corporate e-mail address. The disclaimer can identify your views as solely your own and not those of the company.

Some e-mail programs do not support signature files, particularly those designed for local networks and those of some online services where signatures are less common, but many do and more are adding the feature all the time. Here's my current signature (I change it from time to time):

```
Christian Crumlish          http://www.pobox.com/~xian
Internet Systems Experts (SYX)  http://www.syx.com
Enterzone               http://ezone.org/ez
```

It includes my name, the address of my home page on the Web, the name of my company and its home page address, and the name of my online magazine with its address.

WARNING

Test your signature block with various e-mail systems to see if it still looks good at the receiving end, especially if it uses unusual fonts, has a logo or other graphic, uses tabs, or is formatted in columns. Some of these features do not translate well to other programs, where monospaced fonts may be substituted for fancier proportional fonts.

The following two sections show you how to create your own signatures in Outlook Express and Netscape Navigator.

NOTE

Some e-mail programs let you include a graphic, such as a company logo, in your signature. For example, Microsoft Word and Outlook Express both have commands you can use to import graphics files into your signature file. Just be sure to format the signature in such a way that it looks good even for those who do not have graphics support in their e-mail setup, so that the absence of the logo or graphic will not detract from the appearance of your message. Logos are an easy way to cultivate a professional presence on the Internet.

Using E-Mail Signatures in Outlook Express

Outlook Express supports signature files. These files retain your personal or professional information and add it to your messages according to your instructions. Here are the steps for creating a standard e-mail signature:

1. Choose Tools ➢ Options to open the Options dialog box, and then select the Signatures tab.

2. Click New.

3. In the Edit Signature section, Text is selected by default. Enter the text you want to use for your signature in the box. If you have already created a signature in a file, click the File button, and then either enter the filename or click Browse to locate the file.

4. Click the Add Signatures To All Outgoing Messages check box to put this signature at the end of new messages. (You can also prevent the signature from being added to messages you reply to or forward.)

5. Click OK.

Adding a Signature File to Netscape Messenger E-Mail

Messenger's signature file feature does not include much formatting support, but you can create basic signature files and add them to your messages with a minimum amount of fuss. Here are the steps for creating and adding a signature file:

1. First, use a text editor or word processor to create and save a text file containing the signature you want to have at the end of your e-mail messages.

2. Then, in Netscape Navigator, select Edit ➤ Preferences to open the Preferences dialog box. Click the plus sign next to the Mail & Newsgroups item in the Category list.

3. Click Identity in the Mail & Newsgroups list item, and type the full path and filename of your signature file in the Signature File box (or click the Choose button to find and select the file, and click OK).

4. When you're done, click OK.

TIP

If your signature exceeds the recommended four lines (this rubric is a widely accepted Netiquette standard, though many people violate it), Netscape will warn you, but all you have to do is click OK again to accept it.

Filing Your Messages

Even after you delete all the messages you've replied to or no longer need to leave lying around in your Inbox, your undeleted messages can start to pile up. When your Inbox gets too full, it's time to create new mailboxes to store those other messages.

NOTE

Your e-mail storage should conform to your general scheme of organization. I arrange mine alphabetically, chronologically, and/or by project, depending on the person involved. Think about the best system for yourself before you find your Inbox filled with 200 messages to sort. If your e-mail program allows you to save your own messages that you have sent to other people, you will also need to organize them before they accumulate and become unmanageable.

Different programs offer different commands for creating mailboxes and transferring messages into them, but the principles are more or less the same as those used for real-life filing. Don't create a new mailbox when an existing mailbox will suffice, but do file away as many messages as you can (even if you have to create a new mailbox to do so), to keep the number of messages in your Inbox manageable. When you find yourself scrolling up and down through screenfuls of message lists trying to find a particular message, you know that your Inbox has officially become disorganized.

TIP

You can also save your messages as text files or word-processing files to move them outside the e-mail program. This way you can store them with other files related to the same topic. Choose File ➤ Save As in your message window and select a text file type. Or, select the message contents, press Ctrl+C to copy it to the Clipboard, open your word processor, paste the message into a document with Ctrl+V, and then save the new file.

Creating More Message Folders in Outlook Express

As you begin to accumulate messages, replies, and copies of original messages you sent to others, you will need additional folders to store them in for easy retrieval. Fortunately, creating new message folders isn't difficult.

In Outlook Express, it's quite easy to add new message folders to your set of personal folders:

1. Choose File ➤ New ➤ Folder.

2. In the Create Folder dialog box, select a folder in which you want to create the new folder, type a name for the folder, and click OK.

Once a folder is created, moving a message into it is even easier—simply click the message and drag it to the folder (in the left pane).

Creating New Folders for Filing Netscape Messenger E-Mail

Messenger also allows you to create new folders for filing messages. Here's how you do it:

1. Select the folder in which you want the new folder to appear.

2. Choose File ➢ New Folder.

3. Type a name for the new folder in the New Folder dialog box, and then click OK.

Filing Netscape Messenger Messages in Folders

Netscape Messenger (like the rest of the Communicator suite) has a revamped menu structure that gives toolbar buttons mini-menus of their own. This means that it really is even easier and faster to file messages in Messenger than it is in other e-mail programs, because you do not have to open a folder window or use a dialog box to find the folder where you want to put the message.

1. Highlight the message to be moved.

2. Choose Message ➢ File Message.

3. Choose the destination folder from the menu that pops up (subfolders appear on submenus).

Filtering Messages As They Come In

When you start developing carpal-tunnel syndrome from "hand-filing" all your mail as it comes into your Inbox, it's time to start looking for an e-mail program with filters (called Message Rules in Outlook Express). The basic use of a filter is to recognize a type of mail, usually by one of its headers (such as who it's from, who or what mailing list it was sent to, or what it's about) and to automatically transfer it out of your Inbox and into the appropriate folder (or mailbox, depending on what your program calls it). More sophisticated filters can send automatic replies, forward mail to other recipients, perform multiple actions (such as replying and saving a message in a specific folder), and so on.

NOTE

Your e-mail filters can also be used to automatically clear the old messages out of your Inbox. Depending on what type of functionality is built into your program, you can tell the filters to delete all messages older than a certain date. Even better, some programs (including Outlook Express) allow you to automatically archive old messages in a special file that you can move to a different directory or to storage media (tape cartridges, floppies, and so on).

Setting up a filter to work usually takes just a small investment of time compared with the donkey work you save yourself from doing in the long run. Once you start relying on filters to keep your mail manageable, you'll wonder how you ever got on without them (or you'll just up and subscribe to 12 more mailing lists!).

Sorting Outlook Express Messages with Message Rules

Mail with specified text in one or more of four headers can be automatically filed in a specified folder. Follow these steps to get started setting up rules for the e-mail messages you receive. As an example, I'll set up a rule for filing all the messages from a particular person in a folder for that person.

1. Choose Tools ➤ Message Rules ➤ Mail to open the New Mail Rule dialog box:

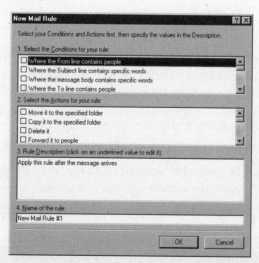

Part iv

2. In the Select The Conditions For Your rule section, click the Where The From Line Contains People check box.

3. In the Select The Actions For Your Rule section, click the Move It To The Specified Folder check box.

4. In the Rule Description section, click the Contains People hyperlink to open the Select People dialog box:

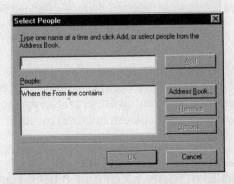

5. Type the name or select it from your address book, and click OK.

6. In the Rule Description section, click the specified hyperlink to open the Move dialog box.

7. Click New Folder to open the New Folder dialog box, enter a name for the folder, and click OK.

8. Click OK three more times.

Filtering Netscape Messenger E-Mail

Netscape Messenger's rules for filtering e-mail are quite specific. Most of the time you can use the existing rules provided by Netscape. If none of these rules are customized enough for you, you can construct unique rules for your own mail management needs.

Here's how you create a new filter for incoming messages:

1. In Netscape Messenger, choose Edit ➢ Message Filters to open the Message Filters dialog box.

2. Click the New button to open the Filter Rules dialog box.

3. In the top half of the Filter Rules dialog box, enter a name for your filter (see Figure 18.7).

4. Choose one of the nine aspects of the message to base your filter on (such as the subject, the priority, or who's on the Cc list).

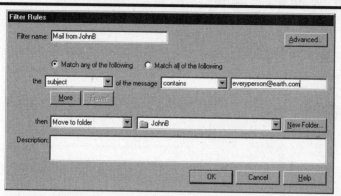

FIGURE 18.7: You can put together sophisticated filters easily with Netscape Messenger.

5. Choose one of the six comparison criteria (Contains, Doesn't Contain, Is, Isn't, Begins With, and Ends With), and then enter the text that is to be looked for or avoided in the third box.

6. Click the More button if you want to add additional criteria.

7. Below the More button, choose from six actions (usually you'll want Move To Folder—some of the instructions are more suited for discussion groups than for private e-mail), and then choose a folder (if applicable).

8. Finally, you can enter a description if you wish, and click OK.

NOTE

Netscape Messenger has no provision, as of yet, for checking mail from multiple accounts when the ISP only supports POP mail. In this instance, you can, however, have a number of User Profiles. Each profile can have a distinct e-mail address. This is very cumbersome since you have to switch profiles, but it works. If your ISP offers IMAP service, as most do, the procedure below is simple to follow.

Part iv

To check mail for multiple accounts:

1. Choose Edit ➤ Preferences ➤ Mail & Newsgroups ➤ Mail Servers (see Figure 18.8).

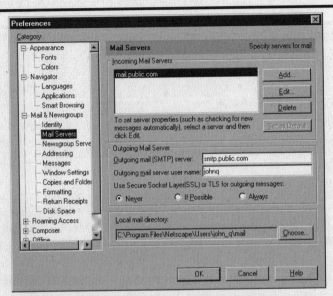

FIGURE 18.8:   The Mail Servers Preferences window

2. Click the Add button in the Incoming Mail Servers box to open the Mail Server Properties dialog box, as shown in Figure 18.9.

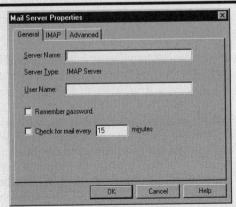

FIGURE 18.9:   The Mail Server Properties dialog box

3. Fill in your user and account information and click OK.

4. Repeat steps 1 through 3 as needed for each additional e-mail account.

Dealing with E-Mail from Several Accounts

You may find yourself with more than one e-mail account. It can happen more easily than you might think. All you need is to get a personal e-mail account and then get Internet access at work (or vice versa), and voilà! You've got multiple accounts to manage. How do you keep things straight?

There are several approaches. One is to try to keep any e-mail accounts you may have totally separate. This approach is ideal for keeping work and personal life separate or for keeping a public address and a private "back channel" for friends and emergencies.

On the other hand, some people get a personal account just to get access to an existing work account, in which case there's no reason to store the mail in separate places. Then the problem becomes how to consolidate all your mail and make sure you're not missing any of it. (A related problem is how to look at your mail when at home without deleting it from your main workspace.)

Consolidating mail from multiple accounts will make sure you get all your e-mail. You can set the secondary account (or all the accounts but one) to automatically forward mail to your primary address. However, this is not always possible. Even if it is, the methods vary from system to system, and you should check with your system administrator and ask about "automatic forwarding of e-mail."

When you want to check your work mail from your home computer, you need an e-mail application that supports remote mail connections. Microsoft Outlook 2000 has this capability (but only if your company is using Microsoft Exchange Server) and even allows you to quickly download just the message headers from your work account. Then you can select the specific messages you want to download, to minimize connection time.

Managing an Address Book

Once you start using e-mail regularly, you will probably find yourself typing a few addresses over and over or trying to remember some long and confusing ones. Fortunately, most e-mail programs enable you to create aliases (sometimes called nicknames) for these people. Aliases are shorter words that you type instead of the actual address. These lists of addresses and aliases are usually grouped together in something called an address book. Modeled on real-world address books, these windows or modules often have room for other vital information (such as street addresses and phone and fax numbers).

Some e-mail and groupware programs share a single address book with other applications on your computer, so your contact information is available to various programs.

When you type an alias or choose a name from an address book, your e-mail program inserts the correct address into the To line of your message (some programs can also insert an address into the Cc line).

You can also set up an alias for a list of addresses, so you can send mail to a group of people all at once. I've got an alias for a group of people to whom I send silly stuff I find on the Net (no one's complained yet) and another one for contributors to my online magazine.

TIP

When you make up an address book entry or alias for an e-mail address, keep it short—the whole point is to save yourself some typing—and try to make it memorable (although you can always look it up if you forget).

Using the Outlook Express Address Book

The Outlook Express address book is useful for keeping track of all the e-mail addresses of your friends and business associates. Here's how to update the address book with new names:

1. To add a name to your address book, click the Addresses button to open the Address Book dialog box, and then choose New ➤ New Contact to open the Properties dialog box.

2. Enter the person's name and e-mail address information, and then click OK.

Using address book names in Outlook Express messages is even easier than adding them:

1. To send a message to someone in your address book, create a new message as usual, but instead of typing a recipient's address, click the To button to the left of the To box to open the Select Recipients dialog box.

2. Select a name from the address book list, and click the To button.

3. Click OK to copy the address to the e-mail message.

TIP

If you want to automatically put the e-mail addresses of people you reply to in your address book, choose Tools ➢ Options, select the Send tab, and click the Automatically Put People I Reply To In My Address Book check box.

Using the Netscape Messenger Address Book

You can add names to Netscape Messenger's address book by following these steps:

1. Choose Communicator ➢ Address Book from any of the Messenger windows.

2. In the Address Book window, click the New Card button to open the New Card dialog box.

3. Enter the name, e-mail address, and nickname, and then click OK.

4. Choose File ➢ Close to close the Address Book window.

To use the addresses in your new messages, do one of the following, depending on how good your memory is:

▶ In the Composition window, type the nickname on the To line.

▶ If you don't remember the nickname you made up, click the Address button, select the name, click To, and then click OK.

FINDING INTERNET E-MAIL ADDRESSES

Because the Internet is such a large, nebulous entity, there's no single guaranteed way to find someone's e-mail address, even if you're fairly sure they have one. Still, if you're looking for an address, here are a few things you can try.

Use Search Tools on the Web

As discussed in the next chapter, Internet Explorer makes available a number of "search engines"—free services, based on the World Wide Web, that you can use to look up information. (Netscape Navigator also provides these services.) Most of them search for Web sites containing a word or phrase you specify, but some, described as "white pages," search for e-mail addresses. These services are quite easy to use. You just enter a name, optionally provide other information such as location or organization, and click a Search button. The program then reports any results it finds.

Say "Send Me E-Mail"

If you're not sure how to send mail to someone but you know they're on the Net, give them a call and ask them to send you some mail. Once their mail comes through, you should have a working return address. Copy it and save it somewhere, or make an alias for it, or just keep their mail around and reply to it when you want to send them mail (try to remember to change the subject line if appropriate, not that I ever do).

TIP

The best way to collect e-mail addresses is from people directly. Many people now have their e-mail addresses on their business cards, so you can get people's addresses this way too.

Send Mail to Postmaster@

If you know someone's domain, such as the company where they work, or you know they're on one of the online services, you can try sending mail to `postmaster@address` and asking politely for the e-mail address. Internet standards require that every network assign a real person to `postmaster@address`, someone who can handle questions and complaints. So, for example, to find someone at Pipeline, you could send mail to `postmaster@pipeline.com` and ask for the person by name.

WHAT'S NEXT?

Whew! You have just completed a very thorough examination of the e-mail capabilities of two celebrated Internet programs. Now that you're an e-mail "expert," it's time to push on and master the mysteries of the World Wide Web.

Chapter 19

WEB BROWSING WITH INTERNET EXPLORER

O bviously, the most important thing about Internet Explorer is not the program itself, but all the resources you can access using it. And, to be completely honest about it, Internet Explorer is so easy to use that you hardly need a how-to book, a manual, or even this chapter. If you know how to open any Windows 98 SE program, you know how to open Internet Explorer, and you can start browsing immediately by simply clicking links.

Adapted from *Windows 2000 Professional: In Record Time* by Peter Dyson and Pat Coleman
ISBN 0-7821-2450-X   467 pages $29.99

Thus, in this chapter we're going to move briskly through the tasks you most commonly perform with Internet Explorer. As we proceed, we'll point out some new features of version 5 and show you how to expand on what comes naturally. For example, you probably know that you can access an Internet resource by typing its URL in the Address bar. That's rather easy in the case of something such as `www.microsoft.com`, but what about `http://finance.yahoo.com/q?s=msft+brka+csco+ald+mmm+sci+lhsp+yhoo&d-v1`? In this chapter, you'll see that in Internet Explorer you have at least a half-dozen ways to access a lengthy URL such as this without ever typing it.

The good news is that as the cost of personal computers continues to drop, browsers such as Internet Explorer become easier to use and more powerful. The only bad news is that we usually don't have enough hours in the day even to skim the surface of the abundance of the Internet. You can, however, use the skills you acquire in this chapter to streamline your activities and make more efficient use of your time.

STARTING INTERNET EXPLORER

Unless you've been hiding in a cave and forgot to take along your cell phone, TV, or laptop, you've heard about the integration of Windows and Internet Explorer. Nowhere is this more apparent than in the myriad ways in which you can start Internet Explorer.

When you first start Internet Explorer after installing Windows 98 SE, you'll see the start page shown in Figure 19.1. Later in this chapter, you'll see how to specify any page you want as your start page. In the next section, we'll identify and discuss the components of the Internet Explorer interface.

From the Desktop

From the Desktop, you can start Internet Explorer in three ways:

▶ Click the Launch Internet Explorer Browser button on the Quick Launch toolbar.

▶ Double-click the Internet Explorer shortcut.

▶ Choose Start ➢ Programs ➢ Internet Explorer.

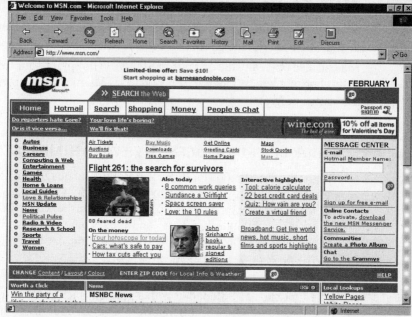

FIGURE 19.1: You can retain the page at www.msn.com as your start page or select any other page that suits your fancy or interests.

From a Hyperlink

You can also start Internet Explorer from any document in any Windows application that includes a hyperlink if Internet Explorer is your default browser. For example, if you receive an e-mail that includes a URL in the body of the message, simply click the URL to open Internet Explorer at that page. A hyperlink can be text or an image, and it is usually in a color that is different from normal text and is underlined.

NOTE

If you have only one browser, Internet Explorer, installed, it is your default browser. If you have more than one browser installed, you'll need to specify one as the default. In Internet Explorer, choose Tools ➤ Internet Options to open the Internet Options dialog box, and click the Programs tab.

Part iv

From Windows Explorer

In Windows Explorer, HTML files are indicated by the Internet Explorer icon, and when you double-click such a file, it opens in Internet Explorer.

You can also open any file on your hard drive, a floppy, or your network by choosing File ➤ Open. If it is not an HTML file, it will open in its associated program.

A LOOK BEHIND THE SCENES: VIEWING HTML PAGES

HTML is the abbreviation for HyperText Markup Language, the programming language that is used to create Web pages. HTML uses tags to tell the browser how to display the page on the screen. Tags are enclosed in angle brackets, and most come in pairs. For example, the <H1> tag defines a first-level heading, like this:

```
<H1>This is a level 1 heading.</H1>
```

An HTML file is really just a plain text file that can be created with a text editor such as Notepad or with a program such as Microsoft FrontPage. To view the HTML behind any page you open in Internet Explorer, choose View ➤ Source. The file is displayed in Notepad and looks similar to the following:

```
www.msn[1] - Notepad                                              _ 8 X
File  Edit  Format  Help

<HTML>
<HEAD>
<script language=javascript>
function mOvr(src,clrOver) { if (!src.contains(event.fromElement)) { sr
</script>
<META HTTP-EQUIV=Content-Type content="text/html; charset=iso-8859-1">

<META http-equiv=PICS-Label content='(PICS-1.1 "http://www.rsac.org/rat
<title>MSN.COM</title>
<LINK REL=STYLESHEET TYPE="text/css" HREF="/global/start_IE4_new.css">
<!-- 6/16/99 9:35:31 AM 18511 //-->
<script language="Javascript">
var userEng       = true;
var CookieAUTOREF  = "";
var qurls = new Array();qurls["sALTA"]="http://jump.altavista.digital.c
function getSearchQURL(prov) {
var url = qurls[ prov ];
return url ? url : "" ;
}
function CheckSrchFocus(){
var frm = document.searchURL.elements[1];
var sSel = frm.options[frm.selectedIndex].value;
if(sSel == "moreSrchLnk"){
var L_sURL_Text = "http://go.msn.com/npl/allinone.asp?target=http://www
frm.selectedIndex=0;
location.href = L_sURL_Text;
}else if(sSel == "div") {
frm.selectedIndex=0;
}
}
function LinkToSearchsite(){
var df=document.forms;
```

CONTINUED ➡

To return to Internet Explorer and the page displayed in the browser, click the Close button in Notepad.

If you're interested in learning more about HTML and creating Web pages, check out the following Sybex titles: *Mastering Front-Page 98* (or *Mastering FrontPage 2000*) and *Mastering HTML 4, Second Edition*.

Getting Help

You have at your fingertips several ways to get help with Internet Explorer. For starters, choose Help ➤ Contents And Index. As in Windows Help, enter a word or phrase to search for a topic. If you want to search the Web for help, click the Web Help button, and then click Support Online in the right pane. If you're connected to the Internet, you'll go to the Microsoft Product Support Services page at `http://support.microsoft.com/directory/`.

If you're new to Internet Explorer, choose Help ➤ Tour. Click any hyperlink to get information about that topic. If you're new to Internet Explorer but have used Netscape Navigator, choose Help ➤ For Netscape Users to access a list of tips and corresponding terminology.

A QUICK TOUR OF INTERNET EXPLORER

The Internet Explorer window has much in common with other Windows application windows: vertical and horizontal scrollbars display as necessary, you can size various portions of the window by clicking and dragging, and you can display a ToolTip by placing the mouse cursor over an item. In the upper-right corner are the Minimize, Restore, and Close buttons.

In this section, we'll look briefly at the components of the Internet Explorer window, and in later sections we'll look at some specific components that you can use to enrich and supplement your browsing experience. Figure 19.2 is your component roadmap.

Part iv

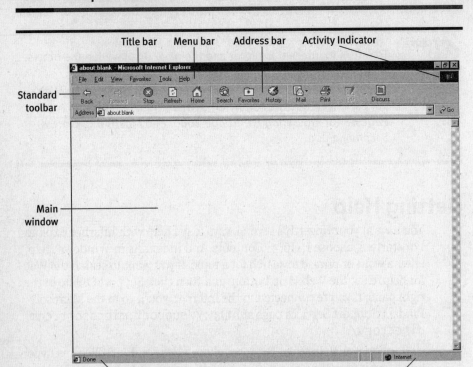

FIGURE 19.2: Many Internet Explorer window components are similar to those in other Windows applications.

Here is a general description of each component:

Title bar   Displays the name of the current Web page or other file that is displayed in the Internet Explorer window.

Menu bar   Contains a set of menus, some of which contain the same items that appear on that menu in other Windows programs.

Standard toolbar   Contains several buttons that correspond to items on the menu bar, as well as navigation buttons such as Back, Forward, and Home.

Address bar   Contains a drop-down box in which you can enter or select the resource you want to access.

Activity Indicator   Is animated when Internet Explorer is sending or receiving data.

Main window   Displays the resource—Web page, document file, image, and so on—that you most recently accessed.

Status bar   Displays information about the current state of Internet Explorer.

> ▶ When you choose a menu command, the status bar displays a description of what it does.

> ▶ When you point to a hyperlink, the status bar displays its URL.

> ▶ When you click a hyperlink to open another page, the status bar displays a series of messages related to the progress of that process.

Security zone   Displays the security zone currently active. To find out the current security zone or to change the security zone setting, choose Tools ➤ Internet Options to open the Internet Options dialog box, and click the Security tab.

MOVING AROUND THE WEB

To even begin to describe what you'll find on the Web these days is an exercise in futility. What was suspect a year ago is commonplace today, and what appears today to be well in the future may be up and running tomorrow. You can buy and sell almost any commodity, search the world's vast storehouse of information, play Blackjack, chat with somebody on another continent, witness the birth of a baby, locate a lost relative, book a cruise, scout new business opportunities—the list is indeed endless. And, as the saying goes, one thing leads to another.

The items on the Internet Explorer toolbars are your best friends in this quest, and in this section we'll take a look at their typical and not-necessarily-so-typical uses.

Going to Specific Sites

You know, of course, that you can enter a URL in the Address bar and press Enter to go to that site. You are probably also aware that you can click the down arrow at the right of the Address bar, select a URL from the list, and press Enter. (You can click Go instead of pressing Enter if you want.) And you may have noticed that on occasion when you start to type an address, it sort of finishes itself for you. That's the AutoComplete feature at work. If the address is the one you want, simply press Enter, and you're on your way to that page. If you wanted another site, just continue typing.

TIP

AutoComplete also comes to your aid in just about any other field you fill in on a Web page—stock quotes, search queries, passwords, and so on. You can often click a drop-down list and make a selection. This information is encrypted and stored on your computer and is not accessible to Web sites, so you needn't be concerned about security when you use AutoComplete.

Internet Explorer assumes that when you enter a URL in the Address bar, you want to go to a Web page or some other HTML document. Therefore, whether you enter `http://www.sybex.com` or `www.sybex.com`, you'll reach the Sybex Web site. If you want to access another type of resource, such as an FTP archive, a Telnet host, or a Gopher server, you'll need to enter the full URL, for example, `ftp://ftp.archive.edu`.

TIP

If you want to edit only part of an address that's already displayed in the Address bar, place the cursor in the Address bar, hold down Ctrl, and press the right or left arrow to jump forward or backward to the next separator character (\\\ . , ? or +).

You can also run a program from the Address bar. Simply type its path, for example, `C:\Program Files\FrontPage Express.exe`, and press Enter. To find a file using the Address bar, enter the drive letter and a colon, and press Enter. Internet Explorer opens a window similar to that shown in Figure 19.3.

In addition, you can search from the Address bar. Enter the word or phrase you want to find, and click the Search button. We'll look at searching in detail later in this chapter in the section "Finding Exactly What You Want on the Internet."

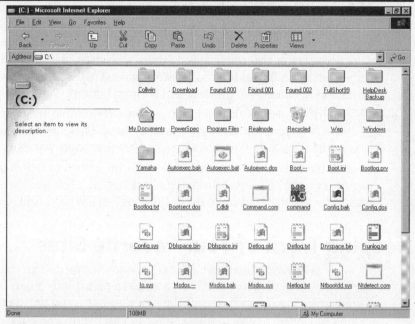

FIGURE 19.3: Finding a file with Internet Explorer

Using and Managing Links

The term *link* is short for hyperlink, which is a term, a phrase, an image, or a symbol that forms a connection with another resource that can reside on your local computer, your local network, or the Internet. You may also hear these connections referred to as hot links, hypertext links, or hypermedia. They all mean the same thing, and clicking one takes you to that resource. Links are the heart and soul of the Internet, and in the incipient days of browser development, links gave rise to ponderous discussions about the linear structure of books, film, and speech vs. the nonlinear format of the World Wide Web.

Today we seldom discuss links; we just take them for granted and click. In Internet Explorer, textual links are underlined and are usually in a different color from normal text. After you click such a link to jump to that resource and then return to the page on which the link resides, the link will be in yet another color, indicating that you've "visited" it.

To find out if an image or a symbol is a link, place the mouse pointer over it. If it's a link, the pointer becomes a hand with a pointing finger.

Moving Backward and Forward

In the past, you could easily get lost following links. You still can lose your way when you're just mindlessly surfing the Net, but Internet Explorer provides several tools that can help you retrace your steps, starting with the drop-down list in the Address bar, as we discussed in the previous section. Perhaps even handier are the Back and Forward buttons.

Click the Back button (the left-pointing arrow) to return to the page you just visited. Click the down arrow next to the Back button to select from the last four pages you visited.

Click the Forward button (the right-pointing arrow) to return to the page you visited before you clicked the Back button. Click the down arrow next to the Forward button to select from the last few pages you visited.

Keeping Track of Your Favorite Sites

As we've mentioned, Internet Explorer provides several devices you can use to prevent getting lost in cyberspace, and a particularly handy one is the Favorites bar. To open it, click the Favorites button on the Standard toolbar or choose Favorites from the menu bar. Figure 19.4 shows the screen you'll see if you click the Favorites button, and Figure 19.5 shows the Favorites menu.

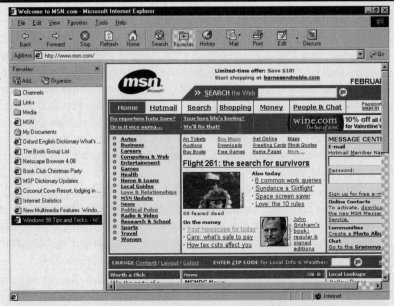

FIGURE 19.4: Click the Favorites button to open the Favorites bar.

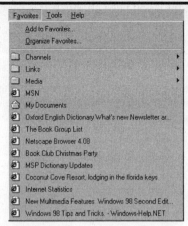

FIGURE 19.5: Choose the Favorites menu to see this drop-down list.

Adding a Site to Your Favorites List

Clicking a Favorites item takes you to that resource. Initially you'll see the following items on the Favorites menu or in the Favorites bar:

> **Links,** which opens the same list that you see on the Links toolbar. The Links toolbar is not displayed by default. To display it, choose View ➤ Toolbars ➤ Links. It contains the following:
>
> ▶ Best Of The Web
>
> ▶ Channel Guide
>
> ▶ Customize Links
>
> ▶ Free HotMail
>
> ▶ Internet Start
>
> ▶ Microsoft
>
> ▶ Windows Update
>
> ▶ Windows

> **Media,** which contains links that take you to a variety of sites such as Disney, ESPN Sports, MSNBC, and the Windows Media Showcase, a page where you can search for online audio and video.

> **MSN,** which takes you to the msn.com home page.

> **My Documents,** which opens your My Documents folder in Internet Explorer.

Part iv

You may also see a Channels folder if you used channels in a previous version of Internet Explorer.

NOTE

On some Web pages, you will see a suggestion that you "bookmark" this page. Netscape and some other Web browsers refer to a list of sites that you want to revisit as a Bookmarks list, rather than as a Favorites list.

To add a site to your Favorites list, follow these steps:

1. Go to the site you want to add.

2. Click Favorites to open the Favorites bar.

3. Click Add to open the Add Favorite dialog box:

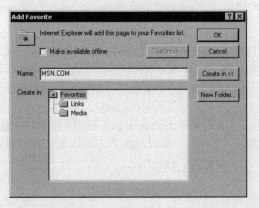

4. If you want to place this page in your top-level Favorites menu, click OK. If you want to add it to an existing folder, click Create In, select a folder, and click OK. If you want to create a new folder for this item, click New Folder, enter a name for the folder, and click OK.

5. In the Add Favorite dialog box, Internet Explorer provides a name for this Favorite site. To give the site another name in your Favorites list, replace the default name with the name you want.

6. Click OK.

   You can also add items to your Favorites list in some other ways:

   ▶ Right-click a link, and choose Add To Favorites from the shortcut menu.

▶ Right-click on the current page outside a link, and choose Add To Favorites from the shortcut menu to add that page.

▶ Drag and drop a link on a Web page to the Favorites button on the Standard toolbar.

Maintaining Your Favorites List

You'll find out soon enough that your Favorites list will grow quickly, and before too long the titles that seemed patently clear when you added the site to the list will, unfortunately, be meaningless. In addition, you may no longer really care what's happening on the Learn2.com site. To keep your list manageable, you need to do some periodic housekeeping, weeding out what you don't want and rearranging or retitling what you do keep so that it is meaningful.

Deleting a site from your Favorites list is simple: right-click it in the list, and choose Delete from the shortcut menu. You might, however, want to get in the habit of following the link before you right-click—just in case the site is more important than you remembered and you want to keep it in the list.

To move an item to another place in the list or to another folder, simply click and drag it. To create a new folder, click Organize to open the Organize Favorites dialog box, and click Create Folder.

To rename an item, right-click it and choose Rename from the shortcut menu. Type the new name and press Enter.

Returning to Where You Were

Yet another way to keep track of where you've been and to quickly revisit sites of interest is the History list. To display it, click the History button on the Standard toolbar. You'll open the History bar, which will look similar to that in Figure 19.6. Simply click a link to go to that page. Click a folder to see pages in that site that have links in the History list. To specify how many days you want to keep links in the History list, choose Tools ➤ Internet Options, and on the General tab change the number in the Days To Keep Pages In History box.

You can display the items in the History list by date, by site, by most visited, and by the order in which you visited sites today. Click the View down arrow to choose an order. If you want to search for something on the History list, click Search, enter a word or a phrase, and click Search Now.

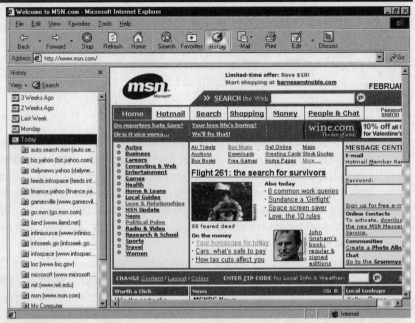

FIGURE 19.6: You can use the History bar to see where you went today and in previous days and weeks.

To delete an item from the History list, right-click it, and choose Delete from the shortcut menu. To clear the History list completely, click the Clear History button on the General tab of the Internet Options dialog box.

TIP

If you want really quick access to a Web site, create a shortcut to it on the Desktop. Right-click in an empty area of the page, and choose Create Shortcut. You'll see a message that the shortcut will be placed on your Desktop. Now all you need to do to open Internet Explorer and connect to that page is to double-click the shortcut.

Reading Mail and News and Sharing Pages

If you hear the You've Got Mail beep as you're exploring the Internet, you can quickly open your Inbox in Outlook Express by clicking the Mail button on the Standard toolbar and choosing Read Mail. To check a newsgroup, click the Mail button, and choose Read News. To compose an e-mail message, click the Mail button, and choose New Message to open the New Message window.

To send a link, follow these steps:

1. Open the page.

2. Click the Mail button, and choose Send A Link. The New Message window opens with the link in the body of the message and the site title in the Subject and Attach lines.

3. Address your message, compose your message, and click Send.

If your recipient is connected to the Internet and has a Web browser, he or she merely needs to click the link in the message to open that page.

To send the page itself, follow these same steps but choose Send Page. The current page you are viewing appears in the body of the message, as you can see in Figure 19.7.

WARNING

Before you willy-nilly include Web pages in your e-mail, be sure that your recipient's e-mail program can handle HTML messages.

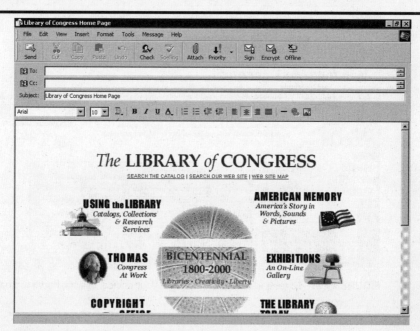

FIGURE 19.7: Sending a Web page in the body of an e-mail message

Part iv

Tuning in a Webcast

If you've used previous versions of Internet Explorer, you'll find something new on the menu when you choose View ➤ Toolbars—the Radio toolbar, which is shown in Figure 19.8. Windows Radio is a feature that gives you direct access to radio stations throughout the United States and around the world through the Internet.

To select a station, click the Radio Stations button, and choose Radio Station Guide to open the WindowsMedia.com site. Click a button to listen to a Webcast. The station's home page loads while the station is being found. To adjust the volume, move the slider on the Volume Control. To turn the radio off, click the Stop button on the Radio toolbar.

The quality of your listening experience will depend on your speakers, your system, and the speed at which you are connected. An Internet access speed of at least 56Kbps is recommended.

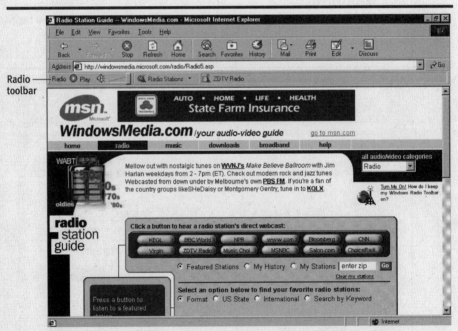

FIGURE 19.8: To tune in to music or news of your choice, use the Radio toolbar.

Saving and Printing Web Pages

If you always want to see the most current version of a Web page, you probably want to place a link to it on the Links bar or the Favorites bar. However, in some cases, you'll want to save it to your local hard drive or to a drive on your network. For example, we recently wanted easy access to a rather long U.S. government document. In this case, the document had been written and distributed over the Internet and was not going to change. It was what it was, so we saved it to our local network so that we could get to it quickly without being connected to the Internet.

Saving the Current Page

In Internet Explorer, to save the current page, follow these steps:

1. Choose File ➤ Save As to open the Save Web Page dialog box:

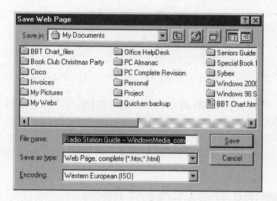

2. Select a folder in which to save the page, and in the File Name box, enter a name if you want something different from that which Internet Explorer proposes.

3. In the Save As Type drop-down box, select the format in which you want the page saved. Your choices are:

    ▶ Web Page, Complete (*.htm,*.html)

    ▶ Web Archive For Email (*.mht)

    ▶ Web Page, HTML Only (*.htm,*.html)

    ▶ Text File (*.txt)

4. Click Save.

You can also save a Web page without opening it if its link is displayed. Follow these steps:

1. Right-click the link, and choose Save Target As from the shortcut menu. You'll see a dialog box that shows you that the page is being downloaded.

2. In the Save As dialog box, select a folder, and specify a filename.

3. Click Save.

Saving Portions of a Page

You can also save only a portion of text from a Web page or an image. To save a portion of text to use in another document, select the text, and then press Ctrl+C. Open the other document, place the insertion point where you want the text, and press Ctrl+V.

To save an image, follow these steps:

1. Right-click the image, and choose Save Picture As from the shortcut menu to open the Save Picture dialog box.

2. Select a folder, a filename, and a type, and click Save.

To save an image as wallpaper, right-click the image and choose Set As Wallpaper from the shortcut menu. To specify how you want the wallpaper displayed, right-click the image on the Desktop to open the Display Properties dialog box, and select an option in the Picture Display drop-down box.

Printing the Current Page

If you want to quickly print the current page, simply click the Print button on the Standard toolbar. If, however, you want more control over what's printed and how, choose File ➤ Print to open the Print dialog box, as shown in Figure 19.9.

For the most part, this is your standard Windows Print dialog box. The difference is that you can specify how frames and links are printed. Here are the specifics:

▶ Select the As Laid Out On Screen option in the Print Frames section to print the Web page exactly as it is displayed on your screen.

▶ Select the Only The Selected Frame option to print only a frame you have previously selected. (To select a frame, click inside it in an empty space—in other words, not on a link.)

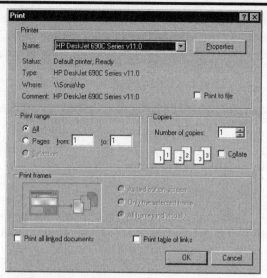

FIGURE 19.9:   The Print dialog box

▶ Select the All Frames Individually option if you want to print each frame on a separate sheet of paper.

▶ Select the Print All Linked Documents option if you want to print the pages that are linked to the current page as well. (Be sure you really want to do this; you could need lots of paper.)

▶ Select the Print Table Of Links option if you want to print a table that lists the links for the page at the end of the document.

When you have all your options selected, click the Print button on any tab to print the document.

To print the target of any link, right-click the link, and choose Print Target from the shortcut menu to open the Print dialog box.

TIP

By default, Windows does not print the background colors and background images of Web pages. First, the printed output could be illegible, and, second, unless you have a rather powerful printer, spooling and printing could be really slow. If, for whatever reason, you want or need to print the background, choose Tools ➢ Internet Options to open the Internet Options dialog box. Click the Advanced tab, scroll down to the Printing section, check the Print Background Colors And Images check box, and click OK.

Part iv

Working Offline

As we mentioned earlier in this chapter, if you want to view Web pages when you aren't connected to the Internet and their currency is not important, you can simply save them to your local hard drive. If their currency is important, you can choose to "work offline."

To make the current page available for offline viewing, follow these steps:

1. Right-click in an empty spot on the page, and choose Add To Favorites to open the Add Favorite dialog box.

2. Click the Make Available Offline check box.

3. If you want to view only certain content offline, click the Customize button to start the Offline Favorite Wizard. Follow the on-screen instructions. You can also establish a schedule for updating the page using this Wizard. Click Finish when you're done.

4. Before you close your connection to the Internet, choose Tools ➢ Synchronize to ensure that you have the most up-to-date content for the page you want to view offline.

To view pages offline, choose File ➢ Work Offline, and in the Favorites bar, select the page you want.

NOTE
In the previous version of Internet Explorer, offline viewing was called "subscribing."

FINDING EXACTLY WHAT YOU WANT ON THE INTERNET

The serendipitous experience of clicking and following hyperlinks may suffice while you're polishing off your lunch of tuna sandwich and chips or to fill the occasional lazy, rainy afternoon, but most of the time when you connect to the Internet, you have something specific in mind that you want to do or find. Regardless of what you're looking for—information about a topic, an e-mail or a mailing address, a business, a Web page, and so on—the way to find it is to use a search service. *Search service* is a relatively new term for what we referred to in the past as a search engine, a program that can search a file, a database, or the Internet for keywords and retrieve documents in which those keywords are found.

Examples of search services that you may have used include Yahoo, Excite, InfoSeek, AltaVista, and Lycos. To search with one of these services, you go to the site (for example, www.yahoo.com), optionally select a category, enter a keyword or phrase, and click Search (or some similar button). Although these search services are very efficient, you are accessing only one of them at a time.

In Internet Explorer 5, you can use the Search Assistant to search several services simultaneously. Let's do a simple search to see how this works.

Performing a Simple Search

To perform a simple search, follow these steps:

1. In Internet Explorer, click the Search button on the Standard toolbar to open the Search bar:

Part iv

TIP

If you don't see all the categories shown here, click More.

2. In the Find A Web Page Containing box, type your search terms or phrase. If you enter a phrase and want the results to contain the entire phrase, enclose it in quotation marks.

3. Click Search.

4. Scroll down the Search bar to locate a resource that seems promising, and click it to open it.

TIP

If you want to find Web pages similar to the current page, choose Tools ➢ Show Related Sites. A list of links is displayed in the Search bar.

Power Searching

In the Search bar, you can specify to search for any of the following by selecting that option:

-   ▶ A Web page
-   ▶ A person's address
-   ▶ A business
-   ▶ Previous searches
-   ▶ A map
-   ▶ A word
-   ▶ A picture
-   ▶ A word or phrase in a newsgroup

You can further refine your searches in the Customize Search Settings dialog box (click the Customize button in the Search bar), which is shown in Figure 19.10. Scroll down this dialog box to survey all your options. At the bottom of this dialog box, click Autosearch Settings to specify which search service is used when you search from the Address bar. If you want to return to the default set of search options, click the Reset button.

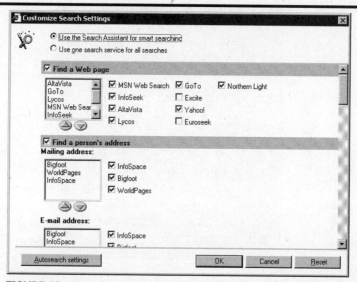

FIGURE 19.10: Refine your searches in the Customize Search Settings dialog box.

CUSTOMIZING INTERNET EXPLORER

You can personalize the way you connect to the Internet and the features of Internet Explorer in myriad ways, and to do most of this you use the Internet Options dialog box. Here we want to touch briefly on a couple of these options and also look at how you can customize toolbars.

Choosing a Start Page

As we mentioned at the beginning of this chapter, when you first install Windows 98 SE, your start page is set as www.msn.com. Until you change this setting, this is the page that will open every time you start Internet Explorer. To establish a start page of your choosing, follow these steps:

1. Open the page you want to use as your start page.

Part iv

2. Choose Tools ➢ Internet Options to open the Internet Options dialog box:

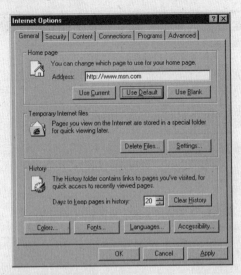

3. If necessary, click the General tab.

4. In the Home Page section, click the Use Current button.

5. Click OK.

Changing the Appearance of the Toolbars

To display or hide a toolbar, choose View ➢ Toolbars, and then select a toolbar from the submenu. To add or remove buttons from the Standard toolbar, follow these steps:

1. Right-click the toolbar, and choose Customize from the shortcut menu to open the Customize Toolbar dialog box:

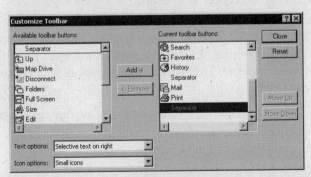

2. To add a button, select it from the pane on the left, and click Add.

3. To delete a button, select it from the pane on the right, and click Remove.

4. To specify whether or where to display button labels, click the Text Options down arrow and select from the list.

5. To specify the icon size, click the Icon Options down arrow.

6. To rearrange the order of the buttons, select a button in the pane on the right, and click Move Up or Move Down.

7. When the toolbar is to your liking, click Close.

TIP

To return to the default arrangement of the toolbar, click the Reset button in the Customize Toolbar dialog box.

To move the menu bar or a toolbar up or down, place the cursor over the left vertical bar of the bar you want to move, and drag it to a new position.

Dealing with Cookies and Temporary Internet Files

A *cookie* is a file that is stored on your computer by the server of a site that you visit. When you revisit the site, Internet Explorer sends the cookie back to the server, perhaps to identify you so that the server can present to you a customized Web page. A cookie is a simple data file that cannot "look" at your hard disk or send any other information back to the server or run other programs on your computer.

A *temporary internet file* is a copy of a Web page that you have visited. Both cookies and temporary internet files are stored in the Temporary Internet Files folder on your computer. To take a look at what's in this folder, follow these steps:

1. In Internet Explorer, choose Tools ➤ Internet Options to open the Internet Options dialog box.

2. If necessary, click the General tab, and then in the Temporary Internet Files section, click the Settings button to open the Settings dialog box.

3. Click the View Files button to open the Temporary Internet Files folder, as shown in Figure 19.11.

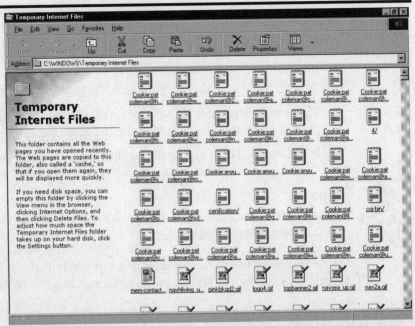

FIGURE 19.11: Cookies and temporary internet files are stored in the Temporary Internet Files folder.

4. To take a look at all the information stored for each file, select a file or move the horizontal scroll bar to the right.

When you access a Web page, Internet Explorer first checks to see if the page is in your Temporary Internet Files folder. If it is, it checks to see if the page has been updated since being stored, and if not, it loads the page from the Temporary Internet Files folder (also called the *cache*). This is obviously faster than downloading the page from the server.

If you want to save space on your local disk, however, you can empty the Temporary Internet Files folder, either manually or whenever you exit Internet Explorer. To empty the folder manually, in the General tab of the Internet Options dialog box, click Delete Files. To empty the folder automatically when you close Internet Explorer, follow these steps:

1. In the Internet Options dialog box, click the Advanced tab.

2. Scroll down to the Security section.

3. Click the Empty Temporary Internet Files Folder When Browser Is Closed check box.

4. Click OK.

WHAT'S NEXT?

Although Internet Explorer is part of Windows 98 SE and is installed when you install Windows, you can choose to use another Web browser if you want. A popular choice is Netscape Navigator, and in the next chapter Pat Coleman gives you an overview.

Chapter 20

An Alternative to Internet Explorer: Netscape Navigator

by Pat Coleman

Netscape Navigator is the Internet browser that is part of Netscape Communicator, a suite of Internet tools. Besides Navigator, these tools include an e-mail and Internet newsgroups client (Messenger), instant messaging software (AOL Instant Messenger Service, or AIM), a program for creating Web pages (Composer), and Netscape Radio. In this chapter, we'll primarily look at Navigator, but we'll also take a look at some of the other features that are available with Communicator.

NETSCAPE VS. INTERNET EXPLORER

Unless you've been under a rock somewhere, you're aware of the browser battle that raged during the last few years. While it was the only browser on the market, Netscape Navigator was given away to educational institutions. Users in these institutions developed a keen loyalty to Navigator because of its stability and ease of use for intranet and Internet purposes. Navigator helped unify the variety of operating systems in use in classrooms and administrative offices.

Navigator is still the browser of choice in many of these institutions, as well as with other organizations and individuals, but it faced an uphill struggle in the marketplace when Microsoft integrated Internet Explorer with Windows. As you will see shortly, the easiest way to obtain Netscape Navigator now is to download it with Internet Explorer.

In several ways, a browser is a browser is a browser. Clicking an underlined term on a Web page takes you to that resource; clicking the Back button takes you to the page you were previously viewing; clicking the Stop button halts the loading of a resource; and so on. But there are differences between Navigator and Internet Explorer that lead some people to prefer one or the other.

If you're reading this chapter, you are probably trying to decide whether to install Navigator, or you have it and want to know how to use it more efficiently. Obviously, I can't tell you everything you'd ever want or need to know about Navigator within these few pages, but I can get you started and point you in the direction for more information.

Let's get to it.

FINDING AND INSTALLING NETSCAPE NAVIGATOR

As I mentioned earlier, the easiest way to find and install Netscape Navigator is by using Internet Explorer, which you have if you are using Windows 98 or 98 SE. Assuming that Windows is up and running, that you have an account with an ISP (Internet Service Provider), and that you are connected to the Internet, work through the following steps to locate Netscape Navigator.

WARNING
I know from personal experience that some ISPs don't support the latest version of Navigator. Before you go to the trouble of downloading, check with your ISP.

1. From the Desktop, click the Launch Internet Explorer Browser button on the Quick Launch toolbar.

2. In the Address bar, enter the following URL:

   `http://home.netscape.com/download/index.html`

   You'll see the page shown in Figure 20.1.

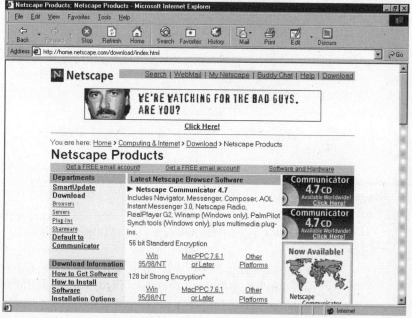

FIGURE 20.1: Select a version of Netscape to download from this page.

3. Click the version that you want to install. If you select to install the 128-bit encrypted version of the software, you'll need to accept the agreement that appears on the screen.

UNDERSTANDING ENCRYPTION

Whether you are downloading Netscape Communicator or Netscape Navigator, you can choose between Standard and Strong encryption. Encryption is the process of encoding information so that it is safe from prying eyes during transmission.

If you plan to engage in online banking or trading, you'll want to choose Strong encryption. For ordinary, everyday purposes, Standard encryption is sufficient.

Part iv

4. On the next screen, select a location from which to download, and click Download. You'll then see the File Download dialog box:

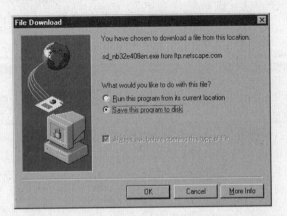

NOTE

By default, Netscape uses SmartDownload, which lets you pause the download, resume it, and surf the Web during the download process.

5. Select Save This Program To Disk, and click OK to open the Save As dialog box, as shown in Figure 20.2. By default, Netscape places the downloaded files in your Desktop folder and places an icon on the Desktop.

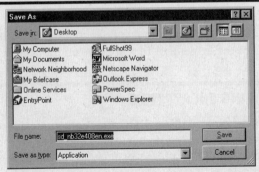

FIGURE 20.2: Select a folder in which to store the download.

6. Click Save to begin the download. Figure 20.3 shows the dialog box you'll see while the download is in progress.

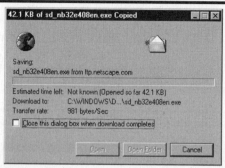

FIGURE 20.3: A download of Netscape Navigator in progress

NOTE

The time to download varies with the speed of your Internet connection. With a 56Kbps modem, I downloaded the standalone version of Navigator in about an hour. Downloading Communicator took about twice that long.

Installing Netscape Navigator

When the download is complete, you'll see the following icon on your Desktop:

Click this icon to start the installation process, and follow the on-screen instructions. When you're finished, you'll see the Netscape Navigator shortcut on the Desktop:

Part iv

Starting Netscape Navigator

To start Navigator, double-click the Netscape Navigator icon on your Desktop. You'll be asked if you want to make Navigator your default browser. Click Yes if you do; click No if you'd rather not. To avoid seeing this dialog box in the future, check the Do Not Perform This Check In The Future check box. You'll then see a page similar to that shown in Figure 20.4. You can also start Netscape by choosing Start ➤ Programs ➤ Netscape Navigator ➤ Netscape Navigator.

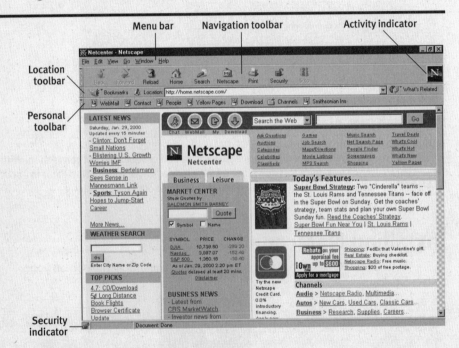

FIGURE 20.4: The Netscape home page

SELECTING YOUR DEFAULT BROWSER

When you install Windows 98 SE, it automatically makes Internet Explorer your default browser. The default browser is the one that opens when, for example, you click a hyperlink in a document or an e-mail message. To see which browser is set as the default, open

CONTINUED ➤

Internet Explorer, choose Tools ➤ Internet Options to open the Internet Options dialog box, and click the Programs tab:

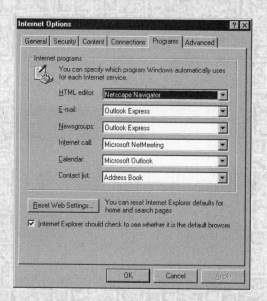

If you install Netscape Navigator after installing Internet Explorer, as we just did, some of the settings in this dialog box may have changed. To reestablish your original settings, click the Reset Web Settings button.

NAVIGATING THE NAVIGATOR

Netscape developers have made a concerted effort to keep you on the Netscape home page. Along with being a browser, Netscape is also a search engine, an entertainment center with multimedia links, and a starting point for finance and travel, among other things.

If you've used Internet Explorer or another browser, you can easily begin using Netscape. But you can also easily begin using Netscape even if you haven't used another browser. Simply click an underlined term or phrase to open that resource. If you've run across a Web address that interests you, simply select `http://home.netscape.com/` in the box at the top of the page, type your URL in its place, and press Enter to go to that site. It's just that easy.

To really use Netscape efficiently, however, you need to be familiar with some features of the interface, and in this section we'll look at several of those. If at any time you need help, you can get it. Click Help on the menu bar at the top of the screen (look back at Figure 20.4 if you need help finding the menu bar), and choose Help Contents to open NetHelp:

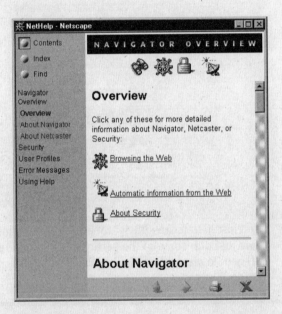

To search for a word or a phrase, you can click the Index or Find. Contents provides an overview. I have to mention that NetHelp is not exactly up-to-date, so you may search in vain for information on some features. In such a case, the information found at `http://help.netscape.com/products/client/pe/reflib/introcom.htm` may be of value.

Using the Menu Bar

As is the case with Windows, in Navigator you can get where you want to be or do what you want to do in several ways. You'll pick up on this quickly as we explore the menu bar and the toolbars. Which method you use depends on your personal preferences, sometimes the task at hand, and myriad other considerations. Near the top of the screen is the menu bar, which contains some of the most familiar Windows commands. Let's start by looking at the File menu.

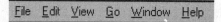

Using the File Menu

You'll probably use the commands on the File menu the most often, since it contains the commands for such tasks as opening, saving, and printing a file. Here's a brief explanation of what each does:

New Window   Opens a new browser window. To return to the previous window, click the Close button.

Open Page   Displays the Open Page dialog box, in which you can enter a URL or the name of a local file to open.

Save As   Opens the standard Windows Save As dialog box that you can use to save the current page or selection as a file.

Save Frame As   If the page you're viewing is in frames, choose this command to save the page as a file. This command will be grayed out if the current page is not in frames.

Send Page   If you installed the Communicator suite, this command opens Netscape Messenger with an e-mail message ready to go. The Web address will be in the message, so you only need to address to the sender.

Page Setup   Opens the Page Setup dialog box, which you can use to choose how the current page will be laid out when it prints.

Print Preview   Opens the page in a print preview window so that you can see how it will look when printed.

Print   Opens the standard Windows Print dialog box.

Close   Exits Navigator.

Exit   Exits Navigator.

Using the Edit Menu

You use the Edit menu when you want to manipulate individual elements on a Web page, find something, or configure Navigator. The Cut, Copy, Paste, and Select All commands work just as they do in any Windows program. Here's a brief description of what each of the other commands does:

Find In Page   Opens the Find dialog box, which you can use to search for a specific word or term on the current page.

Find Again   Lets you search once more for the term or phrase you previously searched on.

Search Internet   Opens the Net Search page, which you can use to specify a search engine and look for specific information on the Internet. We'll look at this feature in detail in a later section in this chapter.

Preferences   Opens the Preferences dialog box in which you can customize Navigator so that it looks and works the way you want. We'll look at this feature in detail in a later section in this chapter.

Using the View Menu

Although you'll use the Preferences dialog box to make major changes to Navigator, you can use the commands on the View menu to customize what appears on the screen and to view the source behind what appears on the screen. To hide or display the Navigation, Location, and Personal toolbars, use the first three commands on the View menu. Here's a description of what each of the other commands does:

Increase Font   Increases the size of the font on the screen. You'll see a brief flicker, and then the current page will reappear with the type in a bigger size.

Decrease Font   Decreases the size of the font on the screen. You'll see a brief flicker, and the current page will reappear with the type in a smaller size.

Reload   If a page is loading too slow, choose Reload to start the loading process again.

Show Images Displays images if you have previously turned them off.

Refresh Refreshes the screen display.

Stop Page Loading Halts the loading of a page. Handy if a page is coming up on the slow, slow side.

Stop Animations Calls a halt to those gyrating, pulsing, flickering images, banners, and so on.

Page Source Displays the HTML source code for the current page, as shown in Figure 20.5.

Page Info Displays the Document Info window, which provides information about the current page. Figure 20.6 shows information for the Netscape home page.

Encoding Displays a list of languages for which you can specify a character set to use when you haven't specified page encoding or when page encoding is not available.

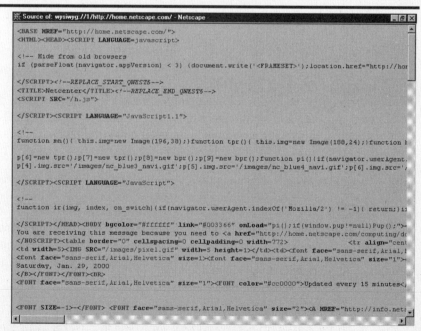

FIGURE 20.5: The HTML source code for a Web page

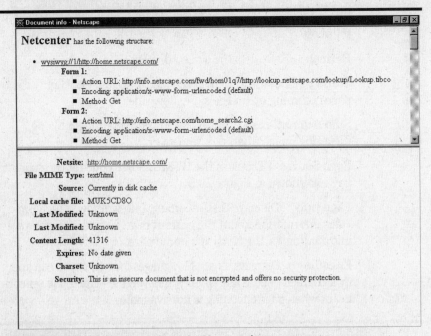

FIGURE 20.6: Information about the Netscape home page

Using the Go Menu

You probably won't use the Go menu frequently. It simply contains the Back, Forward, and Home commands, which are represented on the Navigation bar by icons that you can click much more quickly than choosing them from a menu. More useful is a list of previously viewed pages. Choose one of these to quickly retrace your steps.

Using the Window/Communicator Menu

If you installed the Communicator suite, you'll see a Communicator menu instead of a Window menu. If you installed only the Netscape browser, you'll see a Window menu. Here is a description of commands common to both:

Navigator   Opens a new browser window on your screen.

Bookmarks   Lets you add a favorite site to a list that you can use to quickly and easily access sites that you want to return to often. I'll discuss bookmarks in detail later in this chapter.

Security Info   Opens the Security Info dialog box, which contains information about whether the site is encrypted and establishes other security-related criteria.

Using the Navigation Toolbar

The Navigation toolbar contains buttons for some of the commands that are on the various menus, as well as buttons that have become common in Windows. For example, if you use Windows much at all, you've seen and used Back and Forward buttons in Windows Explorer and in Explorer-like folders. You've also most likely used the Print button in other Windows applications. Clicking the Reload button is the same as choosing View ➢ Reload.

Here's a description of the other buttons on the Navigation toolbar:

Home   Takes you to the Netscape home page or to a home page you have specified. We'll look at how to do this later in this chapter.

Search   Opens the Net Search page. We'll look at searching in detail later in this chapter.

My Netscape   Takes you to a page designed to be used as a home page default in your browser. You can customize this page according to your interests and needs.

Security   Opens the Security Info window. Clicking this button is the same as choosing Window ➢ Security Info.

Stop   Stops the loading of a page. Clicking this button is the same as choosing View ➢ Stop Page Loading.

Using the Location Toolbar

If you did as I suggested earlier and entered a URL to replace the Netscape home page URL, you've already used the Location toolbar, which contains the Bookmarks button, the Netsite field, and the What's Related button:

Bookmarks   Netsite: http://home.netscape.com/   What's Related

You enter a URL in the Netsite field and press Enter to go to a specific site. If you click the down arrow at the right of the Netsite field, you'll see a list of previously visited sites. To go to one of these, select it and press Enter.

Clicking the What's Related button displays a list of other places that are similar in content to the current page. We'll look at Bookmarks in detail in a later section.

The Personal Toolbar

The contents of the Personal toolbar depend on whether you are using the Communicator suite or stand-alone Netscape Navigator and on whether you have added any buttons to this toolbar.

Here's a description of the buttons common to both Communicator and Navigator. We'll look at how to add a button in the next section.

WebMail   Gives you access to a free Internet e-mail account. You'll be required to sign in with Netscape Center to use this feature, and if you aren't registered, you'll be required to register. Entering some of this information is tedious, but there's no charge.

People   Starts People Search, with which you can locate someone's phone number or e-mail address.

Yellow Pages   Starts the Netscape Yellow Pages, with which you can locate contact information for businesses and organizations.

Download   Opens the Download & Upgrade Page, from which you can download browsers, servers, shareware, updates, plug-ins, and so on.

Channels   Displays a list of bookmarked areas that exist on Netscape NetCenter.

KEEPING TRACK OF SITES WITH BOOKMARKS

The Netscape Navigator synonym for the Internet Explorer term *favorite* is *bookmark*. In Navigator, a bookmark is a link to a URL or some other Web page that you store in a file to use later. When you happen onto a site that you know you'll want to return to in the future, you put it in your bookmark list. You can then simply click the site's link to open the page. You don't have to remember the URL or even the name of the site. A bookmark, then, is simply a shortcut to a Web site.

Bookmarks are stored in folders in the Bookmarks folder, which is shown in Figure 20.7. To open the Bookmarks folder, choose Bookmarks ➢ Edit Bookmarks.

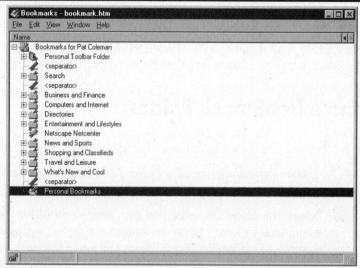

FIGURE 20.7:   Bookmarks are stored in a folder in the Bookmarks folder.

The Bookmarks folder works much like Windows Explorer. You can store bookmarks in the folders that Netscape provides, or you can create your own folders. Click the plus (+) sign next to a folder name to display its subfolders.

TIP

If you aren't up to speed using Windows Explorer, you're depriving yourself of a skill that is really essential to using Windows and Windows applications. See Chapter 6, earlier in this book, for the basics.

Creating and Opening a Bookmark

With the page open that you want to bookmark, you can add a bookmark in several ways:

▶ Click Bookmarks, and then choose Add Bookmark. This places a link in your Personal Bookmarks folder.

Part iv

▶ Right-click anywhere on a Web page, other than a link, and choose Add Bookmark from the shortcut menu. This places a link in your Personal Bookmarks folder.

▶ Click the down-pointing arrow to the left of the Bookmarks button to open the Bookmarks list, choose File Bookmark, and select a folder in which to store the link.

▶ Click the icon to the right of the Bookmarks button, and drag to a folder in the list of folders that is displayed in a shortcut menu.

Now, to use a bookmark you've created, click Bookmarks to open the Bookmarks list, click a folder, and then click the bookmark.

Creating a Bookmark Folder

You create a new folder in the Bookmarks folder in much the same way that you create a new folder in Windows Explorer. Follow these steps:

1. Choose Bookmarks ➤ Edit Bookmarks to open the Bookmarks folder.

2. Select the folder in which to put your new folder. For example, if you want your new folder to be a primary folder, select Bookmarks For *Your Name* at the top of the list.

3. Choose File ➤ New Folder to open the Bookmark Properties dialog box:

4. Type a name for the new folder, enter a description if you want, and click OK.

Adding a Button to the Personal Toolbar

You can also use the Bookmarks command to add a button to your Personal toolbar. Perhaps often, even several times a day, you need to check a particular site or sites. Create a button on the Personal toolbar. You can do so in a couple of ways:

- ▸ Open the page, click the icon immediately to right of the Bookmarks button, and drag it to the Personal toolbar.

- ▸ Choose Bookmarks ➢ File Bookmark ➢ Personal Toolbar Folder ➢ Personal Toolbar Folder.

When you no longer need that button on your Personal toolbar, follow these steps to delete it:

1. Choose Bookmarks ➢ Edit Bookmarks to open the Bookmarks folder.

2. Click the plus sign next to the Personal Toolbar Folder folder to expand its contents, if necessary.

3. Right-click the entry for your button, and choose Delete Bookmark from the shortcut menu.

Moving Bookmarks

Moving a bookmark from one folder to another is a bit tricky, though easy once you get the hang of it. Select the bookmark, drag it to just *beneath* the folder to which you want to move it, and then release the mouse button.

Deleting Bookmarks

You delete any bookmark in the same way that you delete a button from the Personal toolbar. Follow the steps in the previous section, "Adding a Button to the Personal Toolbar."

SEARCHING THE INTERNET

When you search for information on the Internet, you use a tool that has gathered lists of available files and documents and stored them in a database. This tool is known by various names, including search tool, search service, and search engine. Netscape Navigator uses the term *search engine*.

Part iv

You access the Navigator search engine in various ways. Let's start with the easiest, using the text box next to the Search The Web drop-down list on the Netscape home page. Simply enter a term or a phrase, and press Enter or click Go. Figure 20.8 shows the results I got when I searched on the phrase "Internet statistics." Click a link in the Search Results window to open that resource.

TIP

If you want to find an exact phrase, enclose it in quotation marks. If you don't do so and you enter multiple terms, your search results will include every resource that contains each of the words in your phrase.

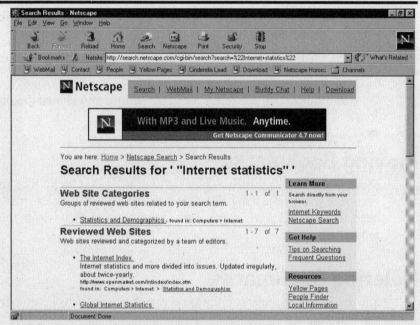

FIGURE 20.8: The results returned by searching the Internet for "Internet statistics"

To search using a search engine of your choice or to browse categories of information (such as people, games, software, and so on), follow these steps:

1. Click the Search button on the Navigator toolbar to open the Net Search page.

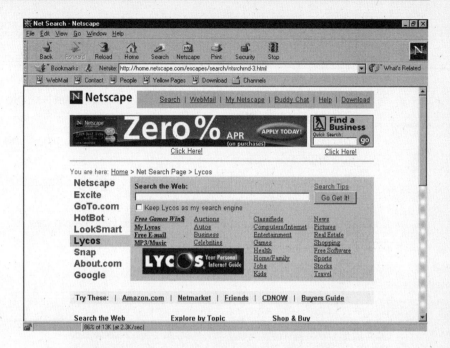

2. From the list on the left, select a search engine.

3. Press Enter, or click Go Get It.

Your results will be returned on the Web site of the search engine you selected.

To search by browsing categories of topics, scroll down to the bottom of the Net Search page, and click a link.

TIP

For a list of tips that you can use to improve the results of your searches, click the Tips link near the bottom of the Net Search page.

PERSONALIZING NETSCAPE

As promised earlier in this chapter, let's look in detail at the Preferences option on the Edit menu. When you choose Edit ➤ Preferences, the

Part iv

Preferences dialog box opens, as shown in Figure 20.9. You use the options in this dialog box to personalize Navigator. Here are just some of the ways that you can set up Navigator so that it works the way you want it to work:

- ▶ Change the appearance of toolbars to show pictures and text, pictures only, or text only.

- ▶ Change the font, font sizes, and colors in which Web pages and links appear.

- ▶ Specify that Navigator start with a page of your choosing rather than the Netscape home page.

- ▶ Specify the language in which you prefer to view Web pages.

- ▶ Specify helper applications for the various file types.

- ▶ Enable and disable the What's Related button.

- ▶ Set your name, e-mail address, and signature file.

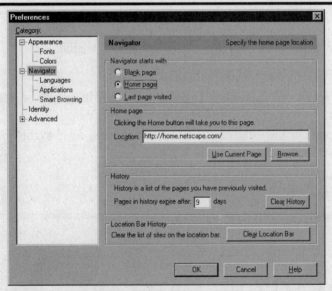

FIGURE 20.9: Personalize Navigator using the options in the Preferences dialog box.

To begin establishing your preferences, follow these steps:

1. Choose Edit ➤ Preferences to open the Preferences dialog box. By default, the Navigator category is selected in the list on the left, and the right part of this dialog box displays the options associated with Navigator.

2. Use the Navigator page to specify a start page and a home page, to specify the number of days that page will remain in the History list, and to clear the list of sites on the Location bar.

3. Click the Appearance category to display options that you can select to change the appearance of the display.

4. Click Fonts to display the dialog box shown in Figure 20.10. Use these options to change the font size on the screen.

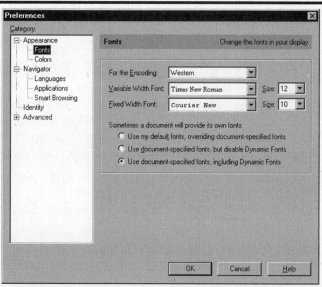

FIGURE 20.10:   Changing the font size of the display on the screen

5. Continue to select categories from the Category list to get an idea of the available customizations.

6. When you have made all your changes, click OK to apply them and to close the Preferences dialog box.

TIPS FOR GETTING THE MOST OUT OF NETSCAPE NAVIGATOR

The purpose of this chapter is to give you an overview of Netscape Navigator. The best way to get to know a browser is simply to use it. Along the way, you'll discover all sorts of tips and tricks that will make you a more efficient user and let you find what you're looking for faster. Here are some tips to start with:

▶ In addition to the search methods in the section "Searching the Internet," you can also search by entering a term or a phrase in the Netsite field and pressing Enter.

▶ The What's Related button isn't always active even if it isn't disabled. You'll see it primarily for the more popular sites.

▶ If you visit a page you like but forget to bookmark it and you can't remember the URL, you may still be able to find it. Click the down arrow next to the Netsite field to display a list of recently visited sites.

▶ If you have a slow Internet connection or pages just seem to be unusually slow to load, turn off the display of graphics. Choose Edit ≻ Preferences to open the Preferences dialog box, click Advanced, and clear the check mark from the Automatically Load Images check box. Large images will now be replaced with small icons. If you want to view an image, click the icon.

▶ Experiment with right-clicking. Often right-clicking opens a shortcut menu with choices appropriate for the object you clicked. And even if right-clicking does nothing, it will never do any harm.

▶ Clicking the Security indicator in the lower-left corner of the screen displays the Security Info folder with security information about the current page.

▶ If you're really new to the Internet and browsing, don't always follow the first instruction you might see at a site. For example, you'll find advertisements at the top of many pages, with a link that says, "Click Here!" If you want information about the advertiser, sure, go right ahead and click, but that's probably not what you were looking for when you navigated to the page.

CONTINUED ➡

> ▶ The Activity indicator, which is the Netscape logo in the top-right corner of a page, will be active when Navigator is working— locating a resource, loading an image, searching, and so on.
>
> ▶ If you find an image, text, or other object that you want to insert in another document, select it and use the Cut, Copy, and Paste commands as you would in any Windows program.
>
> ▶ If you find an image you'd like to use as wallpaper, right-click it, and choose Set As Wallpaper from the shortcut menu.

WHAT'S NEXT?

This chapter completes our look at the Internet, and now we turn to what many consider the raison d'être for a computer in the first place—playing games and playing and recording music. In the next chapter, Mark Cohen shows you how to equip your PC for the ultimate gaming experience and then fills you in on the hottest titles in the games field.

PART V
GAMING AND MUSIC

Chapter 21

AN INTRODUCTION TO GAMING AND YOUR PC

by Mark Cohen

Time for roll call. All those "power users" who bought their computers for the sole purpose of creating massive spreadsheets or designing multimedia business presentations, step out of line. There's plenty of useful information for you in the other chapters of this book. After all, you don't want to waste time reading about force-feedback joysticks, 3-D flight simulators, or online role-playing games.

Right. Let's face it: nothing justifies your latest computer upgrade better than a night mission in your F-14, a replay of your favorite Super Bowl game, or a trip back in time to meet Joan of Arc. So, even if you are one of the few, the proud, the people who actually do *work* on their computers, this chapter will bring you up to speed on the latest gaming hardware and software.

First, I'll give you a brief history lesson, to show how far computer entertainment has come since the days of *Pong*. Next, I'll move right into game hardware, with tips for putting together your dream system and guidelines for upgrading an aging rig. Once you get the lowdown on systems, accessories, and troubleshooting, you'll be ready for some serious playtime. In "The Games," I'll cover the hottest computer game genres, with capsule reviews of more than 35 games in the following categories:

- ▶ Action
- ▶ Adventure
- ▶ Military/strategy
- ▶ Multiplayer
- ▶ Online role-playing
- ▶ Puzzles/classics
- ▶ Role playing
- ▶ Simulations
- ▶ Sports

Finally, I'll introduce you to the world of online gaming in "You Are Not Alone." You'll thank me for this one, because just about the time that you finally beat the computer in your favorite game, you'll discover thousands of other gamers on the World Wide Web who are just waiting to blow you away.

And Then There Was *Spacewar!*

Although games first made their way to home computers in the mid-seventies, the early inspiration for digital entertainment came from mainframe gurus as early as 1961. In the same year that Roger Maris broke Babe Ruth's single season home-run record (kudos to Mark McGwire for breaking Maris's record in 1998), the Massachusetts Institute of Technology (MIT) received its first mainframe computer with a monitor. Of course, the computer science department had serious plans for their miracle machine, which was the size of a large closet. But to the brain trust at MIT, the monitor meant one thing: games, real games.

The following year, artificial intelligence expert Steve Russell, with the help of mathematician Wayne Witanen and mountain-climbing enthusiast J. Martin Graetz, grabbed hold of the new PDP-1 and programmed it to move two "spaceships" or, more accurately, clusters of dots around the tiny circular screen. Using wood, wire, and spare parts, Russell assembled two control boxes, each containing two levers and a button. One lever maneuvered the craft in a right or left rotation, and the other control accelerated the ship when moved back and sent it into hyperspace when pushed forward. The button, of course, fired the torpedoes.

The idea of firing at a moving shape on the computer screen was incredible enough, but Russell's cohorts had grander ideas. Additional features were added, including a backdrop of stars and constellations, gravitational pull from randomly placed stars, and even a fail-safe button that let the user launch a ship off the playing map into another galaxy. By the mid-sixties, Steve Russell's part-time programming project, dubbed *Spacewar!*, had made its way to college mainframes across the country (see Figure 21.1).

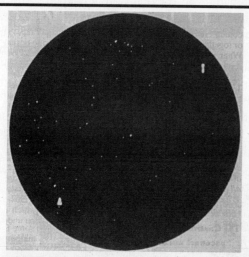

FIGURE 21.1: *Spacewar!* ready for action

Although *Spacewar!* is heralded as the first computer game, it was by no means the only mainframe-programmed computer game. Night programmers took advantage of their computer time to create games of all kinds, from baseball simulations to fantasy adventures. Amazingly, not all mainframes had monitors, so many of the games required players to print out the results of each turn.

Star Trek, or simply *Trek,* as it was called when copyright attorneys staked their claims, was another popular game during the sixties. Following the classic story line of the television show, players commanded their own starships and searched the galaxies for Romulans, who could cloak their ships, and Klingons, who were everywhere. Primitive graphics screens tracked the ships on multiple grids, while starship captains monitored their ships' vital signs and used quick reflexes to jump from galaxy to galaxy.

The First Video Game Systems

By the early seventies, a handful of engineers and programmers envisioned a self-contained home entertainment system that would use a regular television screen. Ralph Baer, an electrical engineer from New Hampshire, designed the first video game system in 1966. He sold his design to Magnavox in 1970, and two years later, the Odyssey 100—complete with 12 plug-in game modules—reached more than 100,000 homes.

During the same year, Nolan Bushnell, an engineer with Ampex Corporation, used the latest integrated circuits to develop *Computer Space,* a *Spacewar!* clone. Although it was the first commercial arcade system to use a television monitor, the project never achieved retail success, and Bushnell abandoned the project after making a grand total of five hundred dollars. However, Bushnell's profits were destined to grow substantially. In 1972, he invested his earnings in a new company, Atari, where he worked with computer programmer Allen Alcorn to develop a little game called *Pong* (see Figure 21.2). Using two paddles and a ball, *Pong*'s simplicity broke down the mysterious barrier between computers and the masses, and before long, the game made its way into thousands of restaurants, bars, and airports across the country.

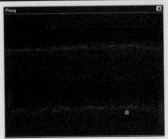

FIGURE 21.2: *Pong,* the first socially acceptable computer game

... You Are in the Kitchen of the White House

Spacewar! and *Pong* inspired the world to sit in front of a monitor and move their hands, but *Zork* was the first commercial computer game to challenge our brains. Developed by yet another group of MIT hackers in the late seventies, *Zork* was a text-based adventure game that greeted the user with screens like this:

> ... You are in the kitchen of the White House. A table seems to have been used recently for the preparation of food. A passage leads to the west, and a dark staircase can be seen leading upward. To the east is a small window which is open. On the table is an elongated brown sack, smelling of hot peppers. A bottle is sitting on the table. The glass contains: a quantity of water.

Zork was actually the second interactive game, inspired by the main-frame classic, *Adventure*. Designed by a Stanford programmer in 1970, *Adventure* recognized simple one- or two-word commands. However, *Zork* featured a more robust artificial intelligence that could understand full sentences. It was still only a text game, but the possible outcomes were so varied that it captivated gamers for months on end.

Zork first appeared as an Apple II title in 1981, as the debut game from Infocom. You can still find copies of the original *Zork* floating around; how-ever, if you just can't bring yourself to play a text game on your 350MHz Pentium II, pick up the latest incarnation, *Zork: The Inquisitor*, complete with 3-D graphics and hilarious voice and sound effects.

GEARING UP

Fortunately, computers have become much smaller and considerably more affordable than the machines used to create *Spacewar!* and *Pong*. Although the first IBM personal computers were costly by today's stan-dards, the popularity of PC clone machines in the mid-eighties triggered the first moderate wave of competitive pricing. An average AT class com-puter still cost three or four thousand dollars, but it was half the ticket of the first XT and boasted twice the power.

Emerging from the clone wars as the king of PC processors, Intel ruled the roost and garnered staggering profits as it boosted machine speeds with 286, 386, and 486 processors. However, by the time Intel rolled out its Pentium (586) processor, upstart chip manufacturers AMD and Cyrix had joined the market, and prices dropped again. Intel continued to dominate the business segment, but AMD established a majority share of the budget/home market with its K6 processors (Socket 7 motherboards). In response to AMD's success, Intel introduced its line of budget Celeron processors (based on the Socket 370 motherboard). Today, AMD and Intel continue to battle for the home PC market, and the result has been a boon to consumers.

At the high end of the market, AMD scored a major coup in 1999, unveiling the Athlon line of processors. With its debut 550MHz CPU, AMD equaled or surpassed Intel's fastest chip (at the time of release) in every test category. The sparring continued through the year, and as this book goes to press, Intel's 733MHz Coppermine CPU occupies the top spot. However, its title is already in jeopardy, as AMD prepares to roll out the 800MHz Athlon.

Techno-babble aside, the bottom line here is, it's a great time to buy a computer. Whether you are upgrading an existing rig, replacing an antique, or purchasing your first system, you are in a buyer's market. There is more good news for gamers. Unlike 10 years ago, when there was a clear distinction between a "game computer" and a serious business machine, today's PC buyer can take home the best of both worlds. Power, memory, storage, graphics, sound—it's all there for the buying. So, get out your wallet, and let's go shopping. For a guide to selecting a sensible, totally affordable game system, read on. If you've already decided the sky's the limit, skip the next section and go straight to "An Unreasonable, but Totally Cool Game Computer."

A Low-Cost (But Not Low-End) Game Computer

With today's rapidly changing market, it is difficult to quote specific prices that will remain meaningful even a few weeks after the release date of this book. However, I can establish general price ranges, so you won't be flying completely blind when you put your machine together. Don't let the word "component" scare you. It is not mandatory for you to build your own computer in order to save money. However, by familiarizing yourself with the parts that make up the whole, you can talk more intelligently with your vendor. More important, you can spot areas where less-than-honest retailers include inferior components in order to package a more profitable, budget-priced system. If, after reading the following sections, you decide to build your computer, check out "Yes, You Can Do It Yourself" for tips on putting together a system from scratch.

Motherboard/CPU

Although the motherboard and CPU are tightly linked, there are many possible combinations, and you will likely have several options, even in a prepackaged system. The most important point to remember is that every motherboard has a maximum processor speed. If you can't afford the fastest available processor, make sure that the motherboard has room for expansion (for example, a 450MHz Pentium III system, with a motherboard that can handle up to 650MHz). You can count on future games placing more and more demands on your CPU, so it's nice to have room for a quick upgrade.

WARNING

Although they represent outstanding values for general-purpose computing, stay away from 486 or Pentium I motherboard/CPU combinations. They will be unable to run many, if not all, of the most current games.

Thanks to the outstanding performance of AMD processors, you are no longer limited to an Intel CPU. In fact, the easiest way to save money on your game system, without suffering a serious performance hit, is to buy an AMD K6-2 or K6-3 processor. Compatibility is no longer an issue, so there is no reason to be nervous about straying from Intel. There is one important exception. If you plan to limit your game playing to Quake II and other games using the Quake engine, stay away from the "older" AMD K6 processor. It has trouble handling the considerable floating-point calculations required by Quake II. However, the K6-3 fares much better, and the high-end Athlon CPU even outperforms Intel in some areas.

Beyond the processor speed, every motherboard offers various features, some of which may be critical if you plan to use certain types of add-in cards or memory modules. The following list includes important requirements to keep in mind when choosing your motherboard/CPU combination:

▶ If you want to use an AGP (Accelerated Graphics Port) video card (see the "Video Card" section for more information), you must buy at least a Pentium II or Super Socket 7 motherboard; and you must install Windows 98/98 SE or Windows 95 OSR-2.

▶ If you want to enable the 100MHz bus on a Super Socket 7 (AMD K6 processor) motherboard, you must use PC-100 DIMM (dual inline memory module) memory modules.

▶ If you plan to use memory from an older computer, be sure that your new motherboard supports your existing format. Some of the popular memory formats are, from oldest to newest, EDO (extended data out), SDRAM (synchronous DRAM) DIMMs, and PC-100 DIMMs.

▶ If you plan on using USB (universal serial bus) devices with your new computer, you must install Windows 98/98 SE or Windows 95 OSR-2.

Recommended Motherboard	Estimated Price
Super Socket 7 ATX with AGP	$90

Recommended CPU	Estimated Price
AMD K6-3 450 3D	$155

If the thought of buying a non-Intel processor scares you to death, here is an alternative package with a similar price tag, but be forewarned: the K6-3 will outperform the Intel CPU.

Intel Motherboard/CPU	Estimated Price
BX Pentium II ATX-AGP/Intel Pentium II 450MHz	$250

Memory

Although some software publishers boast lower minimum requirements, today's games run best with at least 64MB of RAM (128MB is even better). For the best performance, use PC 100 memory instead of SDRAM. The difference in price is negligible, but the performance gain is substantial.

Memory	Estimated Price
64MB PC 100 DIMM	$75 (128MB: $145)

Video Card

Your motherboard and CPU may do most of the grunt work, but the video card grabs the glory. If you want to ensure a steady flow of *oohhs!* and *ahhs!* when you show off your latest game, buy the best 2-D/3-D AGP video card with the most onboard RAM that you can afford. With today's competitive pricing, it simply doesn't make sense to hang onto an aging 2-D card. However, if you must add a 3-D accelerator to work in tandem with your existing video card, you should opt for 3Dfx compatibility. The technical reasons for buying 3Dfx are not as important as the virtual guarantee of compatibility. It is less a factor when buying a combination card, thanks to Direct 3D support.

WARNING

When buying an AGP card for your Super Socket 7 motherboard, talk to your vendor about compatibility. Some older Super Socket 7 boards did not support video cards based on the Intel 740 chip set. However, you shouldn't have a problem locating a compatible AGP card manufactured by ATI, Matrox, Diamond, or Trident.

2-D/3-D Video Card	Estimated Price
Diamond Viper V770 32MB AGP	$110
3Dfx Voodoo 3 3000 16MB AGP	$120

Monitor

A few years ago, buying a 17-inch monitor was a privilege reserved for graphics designers with a big budget. Today, a 17-inch monitor is considered an entry-level display. In fact, you can purchase a 19-inch monitor for less than the 17-inch monitor listed in the previous edition of *PC Complete*. All the monitors listed below support up to 1280 by 1024 resolution, with a .27 dot pitch or better (the 19-inch Viewsonic E790 supports 1600 by 1200 at .26). If you opt for a monitor outside our recommended list, be sure that it meets or exceeds these specifications.

17-inch Monitor	Estimated Price
Optiquest Q71	$220
Mag Innovision XJ770	$250

19-inch Monitor	Estimated Price
Viewsonic E790	$350

Hard Drive

A typical game takes up an average of 75 to 150 megabytes of real estate on your hard drive and up to three times as much for a full installation.

Because hard drives are cheap these days, think big. Today's motherboards support the ATA-66 IDE (Integrated Drive Electronics) standard, which is almost as fast as more expensive SCSI-based hard drives. (SCSI is the acronym for Small Computer Systems Interface and is pronounced "scuzzy.") The suggested drives are bare-bones units, without installation kits. If you need extra mounting hardware, tack a twenty-dollar bill onto my prices.

Hard Drive	Estimated Price
Maxtor 13GB 7200RPM ATA-66	$135
Western Digital 13GB 5400RPM ATA-66	$125

CD-ROM/DVD Drive

It's hard to believe, but the first CD-ROM drive was a sizzling 1x unit that was known to induce sleep while graphics and sound files were loading. Since the early days, drive speeds have ramped up quickly, and prices have fallen. What a combination! If you don't plan to view DVD (digital video disc) movies or access massive DVD educational libraries on your PC, there is no need for DVD. However, be assured that a good combination DVD/CD drive will provide excellent performance for gaming (32X) as well as the added benefits of DVD.

NOTE
The CD-ROM drive listed below is a "drive only." You can pay more for an all-in-one drive/sound-card/game-title package. The recommended DVD drive is a kit that includes the drive and MPEG (Moving Pictures Experts Guide) decoder card that allows you to view DVD movies at maximum performance (cheaper DVD drives that provide only software support are *not* recommended).

CD-ROM Drive	Estimated Price
Toshiba 48X IDE	$58

DVD Drive	Estimated Price
Toshiba 6X DVD/32X CD-ROM	$165

NOTE
The X in a CD-ROM drive specification indicates speed and is calculated by comparison with the first CD-ROM drive, which was 1X. Therefore, a 48X drive is 48 times faster than a 1X drive.

Sound Card

This one's easy. For years, the game industry has adopted a SoundBlaster compatibility standard, so instead of looking for a card that is SoundBlaster compatible, just get a SoundBlaster. Creative Labs places a priority on its sound card bundles, packaging a card, CD-ROM drive, speakers, and several software titles. Don't bother. You can save money by purchasing the card and drive separately and then buying the games you really want.

Sound Card	Estimated Price
Creative Labs SoundBlaster Live! Value	$50

Modem

Artificial intelligence has reached amazing levels, but a time will come when you'll want to match your skills against a human opponent. You have a wide variety of 56Kbps modems that support the V.90 protocol. If you want an external model, plan to pay double the prices below.

NOTE

The V.90 protocol is also known as the 56K modem standard and provides download speeds up to 56Kbps and upload speeds up to 33.6Kbps.

56Kbps Modem	Estimated Price
Diamond Supramax PCI	$33
US Robotics PCI w/voice	$45

Etc., Etc.

You've got the basics covered, but you'll need a few odds and ends to complete your computer. Actually, I have a separate section devoted to game controllers ("Getting a Handle on the Action"), but to wrap things up, I've included a basic joystick in the following list:

Etc.	Estimated Price
Joystick	$50
Speakers	$40
Keyboard	$50
Mouse/trackball	$35
3½-inch floppy drive	$15
Mid-tower ATX case	$45

And the Total Is . . .

Well, here it is, a game system that you can be proud of, at about $200 less than the system I assembled in the previous edition of *PC Complete*. Even better than the savings, you have more power, speed, memory, and graphics performance! Remember, prices may vary, but Table 21.1 will give you a benchmark for putting your system together.

TABLE 21.1: A Sample Game System Price

COMPONENT	PRICE
Super Socket 7 motherboard	$90
AMD K6-3 3D 450MHz processor	$155
64MB PC-100 DIMM	$75
Viper 770 AGP 32MB video card	$110
Princeton EO75 17-inch monitor	$220
Maxtor 13GB hard drive	$135
Toshiba 48X CD-ROM drive	$58
SoundBlaster Live! Value	$50
US Robotics 56Kbps modem	$45
Etc.: joystick, keyboard, mouse/trackball, 3½-inch floppy drive, speakers, mid-tower ATX case	$235
TOTAL PRICE	**$1,173**

If the numbers don't work for you, Table 21.2 shows a few ways to trim the fat without suffering a substantial loss of performance.

TABLE 21.2: A Budget Game System

COMPONENT	BUDGET ALTERNATIVE	SAVINGS
Super Socket 7 motherboard		
AMD K6-3 3D 450MHz processor	AMD K6-3 3D 400MHz Processor	$70
64MB SDRAM (2 x 32MB)		
Viper 770 AGP 32MB video card		
Princeton EO75 17-inch monitor		
Maxtor 13GB hard drive	Western Digital 6.4GB hard drive	$35

TABLE 21.2 continued: A Budget Game System

COMPONENT	BUDGET ALTERNATIVE	SAVINGS
Toshiba 48X CD-ROM drive	Mitsumi 48X CD-ROM drive	$12
SoundBlaster AWE64 Value	SoundBlaster 128	$20
US Robotics 56Kbps modem		
Etc.: joystick, keyboard, mouse/ trackball, 3½-inch floppy drive, mid-tower ATX case	Economy models	$100
TOTAL SAVINGS		$237
ADJUSTED TOTAL PRICE		**$936**

How about that! Less than $1,000 for a high-quality gaming system.

WARNING
Don't be misled by promotional computer systems advertised for $500 or less. These "deals" frequently require long-term Internet service commitments. Even worse, they include inferior video and sound cards, smaller (and slower) hard drives, and smaller monitors.

An Unreasonable, but Totally Cool Game Computer

OK, we carefully selected our components and built a solid, high-performance game computer for $1,173. After a few adjustments, we even got the price down below $1,000. Now, it's time for a little fun. Throwing caution and our checkbooks to the wind, let's look at the mother of all game computers in Table 21.3.

TABLE 21.3: The Mother of All Game Computers

COMPONENT	DESCRIPTION	PRICE
Abit VA6	Upward compatible for faster Intel processors.	$90
Processor: Intel PIII 733MHz	A screamer.	$810
Memory: 256MB PC133	Fastest memory available.	$360

TABLE 21.3 continued: The Mother of All Game Computers

COMPONENT	DESCRIPTION	PRICE
Video Card: Guillemot 3D Prophet 32MB AGP	Direct X 7 compatible.	$275
Monitor: Mitsubishi Diamond-Pro 22-inch, .24 dot pitch	Flat screen, micro-fine dot pitch, and high refresh rates; not to mention a massive screen.	$1,250
Hard drive: Quantum Atlas 10K 36.4GB SCSI	Space is not a problem, and the 5.0ms seek times are stratospheric.	$1,100
Hard drive controller: Adaptec 2940 Ultra Wide SCSI 2	Atlas needs big shoulders.	$275
DVD/CD-ROM drive: Pioneer 303 SCSI 6X	Another drive for your SCSI chain. The 120ms access time rivals CD-ROM drives, and the slot load mechanism is cool.	$175
Sound card: SoundBlaster Live! Platinum	Connect four speakers for total immersion in your gaming fantasy.	$189
Modem: RoadRunner cable modem	For about $45 per month plus installation, you can say goodbye to latency problems.	$150 (initial outlay)
Joystick/flight controls: CH Products F-16 Combat-Stick USB, Pro Pedals USB	The F-16 CombatStick is near perfect, and the USB ends configuration woes. For the complete package, add CH Pro Throttle and Flight Sim Yoke when they become available.	$189
Speakers: MIDILand S2 4100	You'll be diving for cover when the shells start flying in *Battle Zone*. A 50-watt amplifier drives the subwoofer, while the two satellite speakers boast 25 watts each.	$349
Etc.: keyboard, trackball, 3½-inch floppy drive, case	Microsoft Internet Keyboard, Microsoft Intellimouse Explorer, TEAC floppy drive, ATX full tower w/450 watt power supply	$300
TOTAL PRICE		**$5,512**

Yes, You Can Do It Yourself

If you have yet to install a video card or change a hard-drive jumper, you are missing one of the great joys of life: denying your local computer repair person $48 an hour for turning a few screws. With all due respect, some jobs are best left to experienced computer technicians. But the reality of owning and operating a computer is that you can gradually acquire the necessary skills to maintain and upgrade your own system.

Having boosted your confidence level, let me say that the learning curve can be painful, especially if you rip open your computer and start yanking cables without doing your homework. Fortunately, the book you hold in your hands is a great place to start. However, gamers are by nature an impatient bunch. They like to open a new game, install it, and start firing within minutes of returning from the store. So, in the interest of speeding your learning process, I present the following list of red flags, warnings, and maintenance tips. It's sort of a "Do As I Say, not As I Did" list. Grab your screwdriver and follow me:

Keyboard   Your keyboard will eventually die or throw a key without semiregular cleaning. However, do not spray cleaning fluid directly on your keyboard. First, blast the area between the keys with compressed air. You won't believe what comes out. When you've excavated the debris, soak a cloth with isopropyl alcohol, and clean the tops of the keys.

Monitor   DO NOT SPRAY GLASS CLEANER DIRECTLY ON YOUR MONITOR! Forgive the caps, but I am recalling a painful life experience. The liquid runs down the glass and seeps into the monitor case, where it eventually finds all kinds of interesting high-voltage components. Can you spell *V-O-I-D-E-D W-A-R-R-A-N-T-Y*?

Motherboard   When installing a motherboard, remember that the board cannot come in contact with the metal computer case. If it does, the best you can hope for is a short that will prevent the computer from powering up. Worst case is a fried board and processor. If your case is new, it should have a bag of screws, clips, and washers. Pop the plastic spacer clips through the appropriate holes in your motherboard and then through the matching holes in the computer case. Newer boards use small brass spacers that screw into your case. After locating the spacers, line up the motherboard with the spacers, and screw the board down securely.

Power Supply   When connecting the two main power cables from an AT-style power supply to your motherboard, keep telling yourself *black on black*. The black wires on each cluster must be side by side in the middle of the connector. If you are connecting an ATX style power supply, don't worry. There is only one cable and only one way to connect it.

If you plan to build an AMD Athlon system, be sure to check the AMD Web site (www.amd.com) for an approved list of power supplies/cases. Don't worry—the cases are readily available; it's just that the Athlon has minimum power and voltage requirements.

Processor   A Pentium or AMD K-6 processor chip has a million (or so it seems) tiny pins on the bottom. If these pins become bent, you are in big trouble, so be sure to lower the chip gently into the motherboard. It can only go in one way. Rather than pushing it in to find the right orientation, look for the notch on the chip and for the matching holes on your motherboard. Once the alignment is correct, the chip drops in easily and locks down with the handle. For Pentium II, Pentium III, and AMD Athlon processors, spend the few extra bucks for the boxed set. It comes with the approved locking support for the processor, which insures a stable installation on any motherboard.

Add-In Cards   Most motherboards include three types of slots: PCI (Peripheral Component Interconnect), ISA (Industry Standard Architecture), and AGP. Each one is shaped differently, so there should be no mistake when you are installing a card. Confirm the type of card, and match it with the right slot. A card is designed to fit snugly into a slot, but you should not have to force it in. The gold card connectors should not be visible if the card is properly seated in the slot.

Hard Drives/CD and DVD Drives   It wasn't too long ago that a hard-drive installation was better left for a professional. These days, hard-drive manufacturers go to great lengths to include easy-to-follow instructions. The biggest potential problems are cable length, jumpering, and a shortage of power supply connectors. A typical motherboard includes standard-length hard-drive cables, which are usually too short for a large tower. You may need to rearrange your existing drives to make the cables fit or purchase a longer cable.

Depending on the number of hard drives/CD-ROM drives in your system, you may need to alter the jumper setting on the back of your new drive (see the next section for a detailed explanation of jumpers). The manufacturer typically ships a hard drive with the jumper set for a "master drive" in a 1-drive system. If you are adding a second drive, you will need to install the drive on a separate IDE connector or set the drive as a "slave" to your existing drive. Follow the manufacturer's instructions carefully for setting the jumpers. If you don't, your motherboard may not recognize the drive.

As your case becomes crowded, you may run out of power supply connectors. Not to worry; you can purchase inexpensive Y-connectors to accommodate your new drives.

Cables and Jumpers and Wires, Oh My!   The bane of most novice computer technicians is remembering which way the data cables go. If you are tackling a brand-new installation, read your manual for complete instructions. For hard drives and CD-ROM drives, the red stripe on the data cable should connect to the drive on the side closest to the power cable. This may not be the case on a floppy drive. However, in all instances, the red stripe should align with pin #1 on the drive connector. The best way to avoid problems when upgrading existing hardware is to label every wire and connection *before* you pull out the old device.

It's amazing how something as small as a jumper can cause so much confusion. Motherboards and drives use jumpers to enable or disable a connection. A jumper that slips over two pins closes the connection and therefore is in the "On" position. If there is no jumper, or if a jumper is attached to only one pin, the connection is open or in the Off position.

Figuring out how to connect all the colored wires from your case to the motherboard can be the most frustrating part of building a computer. Some of the wires, such as the Turbo switch, are obsolete and do not need to be connected. For the others, your best bet is to examine the coding on the motherboard and match the wires accordingly. However, motherboard connector coding is notorious for being inaccurate, so it becomes a process of trial and error. When you finally get it right, draw a little schematic for future reference.

Future Shock

Now that I have you all pumped up and ready to buy your dream system, it's time to prepare you for the agony of obsolescence. Even as you write your check at the store, manufacturers are already working on replacements for every component in your new computer. Processors get faster, hard drives get bigger, video cards add more features; the list goes on and on. However, this is not necessarily a bad thing.

A few short years ago, when processors made the big leap from 486 to Pentium, entertainment software designers experienced a major shift. Within months, games required the speed of a Pentium, and it became apparent that a 486 computer was not going to keep you on the cutting edge. Almost overnight, the Pentium II 266 became the next standard, and in the blink of a processor, software publishers began making games that required the Pentium III!

The best way to control upgrade fever is to stay a step or two behind the technology curve. This will guarantee that you are not paying rollout prices for the latest processors or peripherals, and it will let you take advantage of substantial price cuts when new versions are released.

Getting a Handle on the Action

In the early days of *Space Invaders* and *Centipede,* a gamer needed only the keyboard arrows to move a ship or vehicle and needed the spacebar to fire. Although many games still offer extensive keyboard controls, it is much more natural to use a joystick for fingertip access to important commands. However, there is no such luxury as a standard joystick, so you must consider the types of games that you play and then find a comfortable, durable controller that meets your needs. The following sections describe the different types of controllers and include my recommendations.

All-Purpose Joystick

If you play mostly strategy/military, role-playing, or adventure games, chances are you spend more time using your mouse and keyboard than you do using a joystick. If so, your best bet is to buy an all-purpose joystick that will provide just enough control to occasionally drive a car, fly a jet, or take out a few bad guys. Your joystick should include the following features:

▶ At least four buttons within reach when grasping the stick

▶ A "hat" switch for changing views

▶ A dedicated throttle on the base

▶ 3-D twisting

Logitech Wingman Extreme Digital 3D (Logitech; $40)   An outstanding, extremely versatile stick for the money that comes in gameport or USB models.

Gamestick 3D USB (CH Products; $49)   Programmable stick with excellent hat switch design, surprisingly precise handling and better than average response.

Flight Stick/Throttle/Rudder Pedals

If you are serious about flying, you need a true flight stick and dedicated throttle. In the heat of battle, a flight stick takes a serious pounding, so I recommend a "heavy" stick that will provide adequate resistance.

F-16 Combatstick (CH Products; $80)   Excellent flying stick that is also comfortable on the ground.

CH Pro Throttle (CH Products; $110)   Solidly built, great feel, and easily programmed with the CH Speedkeys program. Links with F-16 Combatstick and just about any brand of rudder pedals.

Thrustmaster Elite Rudder Pedals (Guillemot; $60)   Perfect foot placement, durable, and inexpensive.

Driving Wheel/Pedals

You can almost smell the oil when you grab the wheel and slam your foot on the pedal in your favorite racing simulation. However, you better clear your desk; a racing wheel and pedal assembly turn your organized workstation into a crowded cockpit.

Wingman Formula Force Wheel and Pedals (Logitech; $150)   The best force feedback effects of any racing wheel, with intelligent button and shifter placement. The pedals are durable and placed on a large, heavy-duty base. An added bonus is you'll never lose the fire-engine red wheel!

NASCAR Charger and Pedals (Guillemot; $50)   Excellent wheel design and driving response, with average pedals; but you can't beat the price.

3-D Shooter

When the computer action game took its first 360 degree turn, conventional joysticks seemed restricted and far too linear. If you want an alternative to keyboard controls in *Forsaken* or *Quake III,* you need a controller that lets you spin and fire on demand.

Hammerhead FX (Interact; $40)   This force-feedback gamepad took the action controller world by storm in 1999. With multiple control surfaces and 10 programmable buttons, the Hammerhead is equally adept at first person shooters, driving titles, and sports games.

Panther XL (Mad Catz; $79.95)   Similar to the Wingman in size, the Panther has 17 buttons and hat switches and uses a large control ball. The stick has a better feel than the Wingman, and the extra buttons make it a more versatile controller.

Force Feedback

If racing games, combat flight simulators, and action shooters aren't stressful enough, you can buy a game controller that will make you suffer with every hard turn or laser blast. Force feedback technology is spotty at best, with much of the responsibility for realism placed on the shoulders of software developers. However, when it works, force feedback adds to the gaming experience, and if the thrill wears off, you can always deactivate the effects.

Sidewinder Force Feedback Pro (Microsoft; $149)   The Sidewinder is a good all-around stick but not particularly well designed as a flight controller, so serious sim pilots will be disappointed. However, the force feedback implementation is widespread for action and racing games, and with each release of Microsoft Direct X, more games are supported.

Hammerhead FX (Interact; $40)   At only $40, this may be the best way to test the choppy waters of force feedback, and you get an outstanding 3-D gamepad to boot.

Gamepad

Once reserved for video game consoles, the gamepad has become a staple for PC gamers. The two-handed grip lends itself well to sports and fighting games, where you want immediate access to movement and action controls. With a standard design, there is considerably less distinction among gamepads than their joystick counterparts. However, the following products are worthy of your consideration. For maximum flexibility, connect your favorite joystick to your computer's gameport, and connect a gamepad to a USB port.

Gamepad Pro USB (Gravis; $15)   At $15, you can't afford not to have a Gamepad Pro. The original design is still functional, and USB connectivity is a snap.

Rage 3D, Thrustmaster (Guillemot; $15)   Heftier than the Gamepad Pro but just as easy to use and configure. The thumbpad is almost a trackball, and it is perfectly positioned. A 2-D/3-D switch lets you match the right range of motion to your favorite game.

Board the Universal Serial Bus

Despite a continuous wave of technology leaps since the introduction of the first PC, Macintosh owners have always had one advantage: the ability to plug and unplug devices while their computers are up and running. With the official activation of USB support in Windows 98, you can do the same with your PC. The USB port allows you to swap various devices without rebooting or configuring. These devices can include scanners, monitors, digital cameras, keyboards, speakers, and more.

However, the best use for your USB is to jam it full of game controllers. In the past, connecting more than one type of controller to your PC required an additional game card with two ports or a special multi-device connector. Not so with the USB. You can keep multiple devices plugged in, or you can swap controllers on demand. A standard Pentium II or III motherboard is equipped with two external USB connectors, and you can add two more by attaching an additional connector to the motherboard. However, the best solution for a USB logjam is to buy a third-party hub that plugs into one of your computer's USB ports and then supplies at least four more connections in a convenient desktop unit. Or, you can buy the Microsoft Internet Keyboard, which comes with two handy USB connectors on the back of the keyboard.

WHY DOESN'T MY GAME WORK?

We're almost ready to dive into the games, so this is a perfect time to prepare you for patchwork software. Thanks to the World Wide Web, we now have access to mass quantities of information and files. We can not only search millions of topics at the click of a mouse, we can visit software publisher Web sites and get the latest news on our favorite games. Unfortunately, this has provided a very soft cushion for software designers when it comes to meeting release deadlines. Unlike the past, when a software publisher was faced with a product recall or mass market mailing to replace a flawed product, today's problems can be fixed with a patch file, or two, or three. In fact, chances are the brand new game that you are about to install has already been patched.

The bad news is that a growing number of software companies knowingly release unfinished products. It is frustrating for the user, and ultimately it hurts the software publisher. However, having singled out the worst offenders, it is important to note that many software glitches are innocent mistakes, and the ability to download a patch is a painless way to solve your gameplay problems.

When you buy new software, check the company Web site for a patch *before* installing and playing the game. Also, take a few minutes to review the `readme.txt` file included with most games. It could contain information on known problems or hardware compatibility issues. With hundreds of motherboard and peripheral combinations available, it is impossible to make a game work with every configuration, so be patient if you uncover a problem that is being fixed. However, if a software company has no plans to fix a compatibility problem that affects your computer, do not hesitate to return a game.

One last reminder about patches—it is not uncommon for a game to have several patches in sequence over a period of time, so get in the habit of periodically checking for updates. Some companies are more diligent than others, and they take advantage of the patching process to not only fix problems, but to add requested features. Talonsoft, a publisher of military/strategy games, has an amazing reputation for supporting its games. Several of their titles, including *The Operational Art of War I & II* and *West Front*, have undergone several patches, each offering significant improvements over the last. This does not mean that the original games were failures. Along with bug fixes, the patches have introduced a steady stream of new features and artificial intelligence tweaks. When a software publisher provides this level of support, the end result is a game that continues to evolve long after it was purchased. For my money, that is the mark of a company that deserves my loyalty.

THE GAMES

I bet you thought "genre" was a term reserved for Hollywood types. Guess again. From its humble *Pong* and *Pac Man* beginnings, the computer game industry has evolved into a vast universe of categories, styles, and titles. Those who shake their heads at gamers who spend hours in mindless rapture have no idea of the breadth of knowledge and experiences that can be found in computer games. OK, so it is possible to get a little twitchy after a long session of *Half-Life*, but it's nothing that a little fresh air won't cure.

Now that I've justified my place in the universe, let's get back to *genres*. With so many distinctive game categories, it is a good idea to review the field before charging down to your favorite software store. Although some locations may vary, most retailers group their games into the following categories:

Action   If puzzles put you to sleep, this is the place for you. Here you will find plenty of first-person shooters, where it's just you and a whole bunch of bad guys. Because of increased animation frame rates, action titles stress your system to the max, so pay attention to each game's minimum specifications.

Adventure   There is still plenty of action here, although it may not be from a first-person perspective. The emphasis is on solving puzzles and mysteries as you progress through the story. Adventure games can also tax your hardware because of their reliance on interactive videos.

Military/strategy   These titles bring out the Patton in you. Selections range from fictitious worlds to historical re-creations of actual battles and campaigns. Either way, you must manage troops and resources as you move toward the victory objectives. Strategy games may also be nonmilitary in nature, challenging you to manage a multifaceted environment.

Multiplayer   With the improved speed and quality of Internet connections, a small collection of action games has garnered the lion's share of online play. In response to this popularity, software publishers have released customized versions of these games to take advantage of the online environment. The best of the best play these games online, so you had better hone your skills before stepping into the worldwide arena.

Online role playing   Take all the ingredients of role playing and multiply it by the vastness of the Internet, and you have a role-playing game that could go on forever.

Puzzles/classics   Chess, checkers, and backgammon are a few examples of this traditional category. If you long for the games of your youth, you will find digital versions of Risk, Monopoly, Battleship, and other table-top classics.

Role playing   Not as structured as an adventure game, an RPG presents a complex fantasy world in which your decisions and character development can twist the plot and your environment in many directions.

Simulations   Art imitates life in these highly realistic, wonderfully educational games. From flying a jet fighter to building a railroad, you can have a contemporary or historical experience that lets you live out your fantasy without the risks.

Sports   You may never feel what it's like to get leveled by a 250-pound linebacker, but you can still make it to the championship game in a computer sports game. Football, baseball, basketball, and hockey are just a few traditional sports covered, along with less-visible pursuits such as bass fishing, billiards, and miniature golf.

Action Games

Rainbow Six: Rogue Spear (Red Storm Entertainment, 1999)

When author Jack Clancy released his antiterrorist team to the computer in the original *Rainbow Six*, action gamers took to the title like a nightscope to an M-95. Now, the Rainbow team is back (see Figure 21.3), re-armed and reinforced for all-new missions, including a hostage situation at the Metropolitan Museum of Art and an airplane hijacking. The new game adds full sniper support, with special weapons, planning features, and controls. Team AI is much improved, for both friendly and enemy personnel; while weather factors, enhanced explosions, and new wound effects add even more tension to an already volatile environment.

FIGURE 21.3:   *Rainbow Six: Rogue Spear*

Battlezone II (Activision, 1999)

A sequel to the 1998 Action Game of the Year (Computer Gaming World), *Battlezone II* (see Figure 21.4) is even better than the original. If you like a variety of weapons and vehicles to control, *Battlezone II* fills your arsenal with more than 30 unit types, including tanks, walkers, infantry, air support, and mobile turrets. This game requires a 3-D-accelerator card, but the visual rewards are worth the investment, with special effects such as ground fog, lens flares, and rippling water. The game spans six unique planets, where you fight in the air, on the ground, and even hand-to-hand.

FIGURE 21.4: *Battlezone II*

Half-Life: Opposing Force (Sierra Studios, 1999)
Everyone's "Game of the Year" is back in *Opposing Force*, an official *Half-Life* expansion pack. You return to the Black Mesa Research Facility, but this time as one of the soldiers who made your life miserable in the original episode. The tables are turned, as your mission is to eliminate Gordon Freeman and his scientist cohorts who are roaming the facility. Along the way, you uncover a new alien race which is so terrifying that survival takes precedence over your mission to find Freeman. The aliens are out to destroy you, but an all-new collection of human characters is more difficult to figure out. To succeed, you need to gather weapons, determine who your friends are, and survive...just survive.

Swat 3: Close Quarters Battle (Sierra Studios, 1999)
In a year of outstanding squad-level action games, *Swat 3* (see Figure 21.5) is one of the best, with fully developed AI (artificial intelligence) that governs

teammates, enemies, and civilians. You are in command of a future (2005) L.A. SWAT team, and you have the unenviable task of sweeping terrorists from the city streets, as world governments prepare to sign a historic Nuclear Abolishment Treaty. Civilians are everywhere, and you must plan defensive strategies on tactical maps, as well as in the field, where you engage in combat and lead your five-man team. There is plenty of action as your men wield a variety of weapons and surveillance gear. However, you must also use your head and negotiate peaceful arrests whenever possible.

FIGURE 21.5: *Swat 3*

Heavy Gear II (Activision, 1999)   When Activision released *Mech-Warrior 2* back in 1994, they established a lofty standard for robotic combat games. After taking a step backward with *Heavy Gear*, Activision has once again moved to the top of the big metal heap with *Heavy Gear II*. If your hardware is up to speed, this game will deliver stunning 3-D animation and special effects. Once you step into your "gear," the action is hot and heavy; but thanks to a seemingly unlimited number of systems and weapons configurations, building your robot is just as much fun. Your ability to assemble the right robot for the job will determine your success in eight single missions or in a full campaign that includes a linked story line and full-screen video cut scenes.

Adventure Games

Gabriel Knight 3: Blood of the Sacred, Blood of the Damned (Sierra Studios, 1999)   Sierra Studios continues to suck the life out of the vampire-adventure category, but thanks to Gabriel Knight, the series retains its immortality. In the latest chapter, Gabriel, a freelance monster hunter, is asked to protect the son of a deposed prince, whose family has been haunted by vampires for generations. The boy is snatched on the first night of Gabriel's watch, and the trail leads to the ancient town of Rennes le Chateau (an actual town that some historians believe contains buried treasure and secret religious documents). Unlike the last video-based episode, *GKIII* (see Figure 21.6) is a 3-D, animated adventure that lets you choose between first- and third-person views. As you scan various clues into a laptop computer, Gabriel and his assistant Grace are asked to solve a series of increasingly challenging riddles that will help you to unravel the mystery.

FIGURE 21.6: *Gabriel Knight 3*

Omikron: The Nomad Soul (Eidos Interactive, 1999)   This real-time 3-D adventure takes you on a journey of "virtual reincarnation," as your character passes from person to person upon death. As you journey across a vast universe, you develop fighting, shooting, and investigating skills that will help you to unlock the mystery of Omikron. Although the game is largely a process of exploration and the acquisition of knowledge, the game switches to a first-person combat view when violence is your only option. The journey is long, but an unusual environment and excellent plot will keep you going. See Figure 21.7.

FIGURE 21.7: *Omikron*

Outcast (Infogrames Entertainment, 1999)   Cast in the *Tomb Raider* action/adventure mold, *Outcast* (see Figure 21.8) takes you on a fascinating journey to a parallel world, where you lead a group of scientists on a mission of mercy. Your character, Cutter Slade, is yet another sarcastic hero, à la Tex Murphy. However, he loses his stereotyped role upon arriving in Adelpha, where he is left alone, and the situation becomes far less amusing. This is where the story takes you away. The inhabitants of Adelpha agree to assist Slade, but on the condition that he helps rid the world of the evil Fae Rhan. You must interact with dozens of characters along the way, and each one is more entertaining than the last. When the situation calls for action, you control Cutter against a variety of challenging enemies. The action sequences are surprisingly good for an adventure game, but it is the joy of exploration that will keep bringing you back to Adelpha.

FIGURE 21.8: *Outcast*

Grim Fandango (Lucas Arts, 1998)   Lucas Arts has had their way
with the adventure category in recent years, and 1998 was another ban-
ner year. *Grim Fandango* is uncharacteristically dark for Lucas, taking
place in the Land of the Dead. The hero, Manny Calavera, is very dead
and hating his job as tour guide for the freshly deceased. He can't leave
until he sells his quota of underworld junkets, but try as he may, he
keeps coming up short. Finally, he steals a client and triggers a chain of
events that could keep Manny from his dream of salvation. While enjoying another terrific Lucas Arts music score, you travel to dozens of eerie
locations and meet more than 50 haunted cartoon characters, reminis-
cent of Tim Burton's animated movie, *Nightmare before Christmas*. A
twist on the traditional adventure game interface is that you can interact with Manny's total environment, rather than stop only at predetermined locations. *Fandango* brings a little death to a lively category, and
the results are grossly entertaining.

Military/Strategy Games

Age of Empires II: The Age of Kings (Microsoft, 1999)   This much
anticipated sequel introduces 13 great medieval civilizations, each pos-
sessing unique technological and military capabilities. A refined interface
is even easier to use than in the original game, and although the *AOEII* is

not 3-D, the expanded maps and beautifully rendered units and structures create a near-perfect strategy game environment. Military gamers will be impressed with the new combat system that includes garrisoning, formations, and true facing effects. In addition to attacking your enemies, you can now patrol, guard, or follow; and you can customize each command with several aggression levels. If you spent far too much time playing the original game, you had better start working on a new (and greatly expanded) set of excuses!

Freespace 2 (Interplay, 1999)   It has been 32 years since the Great War of *Freespace*, but peace is about to be shattered as the dreaded Shivans return to annihilate the Alliance in *Freespace 2* (see Figure 21.9). In the latest 3-D incarnation of the venerable *Descent* series, you command as many as 11 squad-mates in a 30-mission campaign. A new targeting system lets you plan coordinated attacks on specific subsystems such as engines, turrets, and fighterbays. The game features 70 different ships, including new Stealth fighters, Juggernauts, and AWACS radar vessels. Online play allows as many as 12 players to battle in a dogfight, while 8-player teams can square off or work cooperatively on a number of special multiplayer missions.

FIGURE 21.9: *Freespace 2*

Sid Meier's Antietam! (Firaxis, 1999)   The bloodiest single day in American history is re-created in *Sid Meier's Antietam!*, an odds-on favorite as the best military game of 1999. The original *Gettysburg!* engine has been refined from top to bottom. A streamlined interface makes it easier to monitor and direct your troops, while a greatly expanded AI places more emphasis on battlefield tactics. Some of the improvements include better line-of-sight factors, the ability to "hold" artillery fire, brigade retreat and fallback commands, and more realistic interaction with terrain and structures. History buffs can re-create the entire day's skirmishes and battles that produced more than 22,700 casualties on both sides. Additional variants offer more than 120 different battle situations, and a random scenario generator provides still more gameplay.

Homeworld (Sierra Studios, 1999)   Sierra Studios brings 3-D real-time strategy to deep space in the vast landscape of *Homeworld* (see Figure 21.10). The story line is familiar; a once glorious civilization is ravaged by a conquering race, and the survivors are relocated to a far-off, desolate planet. However, when an ancient tablet is discovered, the surviving members of this lost society build a giant ship and set off in search of their *Homeworld.* All the classic strategy elements are here: resource gathering, building, exploration, technology, and combat. However, unlike linear games, your ships and resources carry over from one mission to the next, so there is a need for long-term planning. And, once you experience *Homeworld's* real-time combat in 3-D, you just might banish your old 2-D games to the dark side of your shelf.

FIGURE 21.10: *Homeworld*

DungeonKeeper II (Bullfrog, 1999)   With so many PC games delivering seriously nasty characters and story lines, *DungeonKeeper II* distinguishes itself with a forked tongue-in-cheek approach to evil. Like the original, the latest version casts you as Master of the Underworld. Your challenge is to build a nightmarish dungeon, complete with traps and dead-ends, for the purpose of destroying the do-gooder adventurers who are bent on your destruction. Of course, the Master of the Underworld needs a support staff, so you are encouraged to recruit a gaggle of foul creatures including vampires, trolls, Black Knights, and Bile Demons (lunch anyone?). It is great fun and surprisingly challenging. A 3-D accelerator card makes the demons jump off the screen, but software 3-D is supported, so you don't need to upgrade your machine.

Multiplayer Games

Unreal Tournament (GT Interactive, 1999)   *Unreal Tournament* delivers a pure multiplayer environment, where you and a few of your closest (or soon to be ex) friends can exchange fire with Pulse Guns, Biorifles, Impact Hammers, and other tools of destruction. You'll find traditional multiplayer games, along with Botmatch, a fight to the death between one or more human players and computer-controlled enemies. This format lets you hone your skills before going online with the big boys. Another *Unreal* exclusive is Assault and Domination, which pits two teams against each other in a timed mission. One team attacks, and the other defends, and after the first team completes its objectives (or the clock runs out), the timer is reset to the time it took the first team to finish.

Quake 3: Arena (ID Software, 1999)   Although the multiplayer first-person shooter category is growing rapidly, all eyes were turned toward ID Software when they announced *Quake 3: Arena*. Of course, *Quake* fans have been enjoying multiplayer fragfests for years, but they yearned for a dedicated package. Ironically, one of the features that sets *Quake 3* apart from other multiplayer titles is a very strong and playable solo component that pits a human player against AI-driven Bots in more than 40 different deathmatches. The computer dynamically adjusts the Bots' capabilities so that you progress through an extended training period that prepares you for the online experience. Once you graduate to full-on deathmatches, you'll find an incredible collection of maps (including vertical structures), and dramatic fog and lighting effects.

Team Fortress Classic (Sierra Studios, 1999)   More than a half million people have downloaded *Team Fortress* (1996), and more recently *Team Fortress Classic* (see Figure 21.11), an enhanced version that utilizes the *Half-Life* engine. Using many of your favorite *Half-Life* characters, the latest release includes updated maps and graphics and a streamlined interface. Online play is further improved with the addition of new character classes, such as scouts, snipers, and spies, and team-based multiplayer formats, such as Capture the Flag and Assassin. *Half-Life* is required to run this game, and it will be automatically updated to version 1.0.0.9 upon installation.

FIGURE 21.11: *Team Fortress Classic*

Online Role-Playing Games

Asheron's Call (Microsoft, 1999)   Available only on MSN Gaming Zone, *Asheron's Call* is a vast online adventure that offers all the ingredients of a classic role-playing game, including character creation, alliances, strategic combat using real physics models, and a dynamic spell-casting system that evolves along with its players. The story begins on the Island of Dereth, where you join one of three human heritage groups that have been transported to the island by Lord Asheron of Empyrea. As you travel through the island's cities and underground passageways, you meet friend and foe, and each encounter is an opportunity to expand your knowledge and power. Your first month online is free with the purchase of the game, followed by a monthly fee (approx. $9.95) for continued play.

Everquest (Verant, 1999)   Although *Everquest* falls short of *Asheron's Call* in the areas of combat and enemy AI, stunning 3-D graphics (hardware accelerated), multiple environments, and outstanding cooperative play between adventurers combine for one of the most playable online games to date. With several dozen race and class combinations, *Everquest* offers a wide range of experiences for all levels of gamers. Beginners may want to start out as a human cleric and work up to more complex characters such as troll shadowknights. In either case, each character has a hometown in which you will spend the first few weeks of play. Once your character becomes strong enough to move freely about the maps, you'll want to link up with other characters to fully experience the delights of *Everquest*.

Ultima Online (Origin Systems, 1999)   After breaking all records as the number one role-playing series ever, *Ultima Online* debuted with mixed reviews. However, after a series of patches, it is second only to *Everquest* in active accounts. Using 3-D landscapes, advanced lighting effects, and day/night environments, *Ultima Online* allows thousands of gamers to share the same world. But although the map is vast, you will have no trouble finding other adventurers to share your journey. Unlike some online games in which character/class limitations are imposed, *Ultima* lets you change your character's appearance and skills at any time. The latest release, *Second Age*, contains all patches and enhancements, including an auto-translator that allows English-speaking, German, and Japanese players to communicate easily.

Puzzles/Classics

Chessmaster 7000 (Mindscape, 1999)   *Chessmaster 7000* has always catered to advanced players, but in the latest version, new features make it easier than ever to learn the game and progress to higher levels. The Kids Room includes special chess sets, younger opponents, and a more casual atmosphere. Of course, purists will want to dive into the database of more than 500,000 games to see how Kasparov or Fischer achieved their greatest victories. The Tournament Room includes 80 computer opponents, plus 35 more "grandmaster" adversaries. When your skills have been honed, go online with Chessmaster Live and find other players from around the world.

Pandora's Box (Microsoft, 1999)   When the pressures of first-person shooters and action games set your mouse hand a'twitching, take a break with *Pandora's Box*, a collection of virtual puzzles that will challenge your mind even more than your reflexes. Designed by Alexey Pajitnov, the creator of *Tetris*, *Pandora's Box* contains 10 types of puzzles with more than 350 variations. From unique twists on classic board games to visual recognition challenges that take you around the world, you can find just the right level of difficulty for your mood or abilities. And, when you've beaten the computer, try matching scores or completion times with friends and family.

Role-Playing Games

Final Fantasy VII (Eidos Interactive, 1999)   After a successful run on the *PlayStation* console, *Final Fantasy VII* is a strict translation, and this is good news for RPG fans. The story features Cloud, a mercenary who joins a plot to sabotage a corporation that plans to strip all the energy from the planet. The game's attraction lies in the complexity of Cloud's character and how he is revealed during his journeys. The system of magic, called Masteria, is a bit complicated because of seemingly limitless spell combinations; however, mastering its subtleties is critical to your success.

Baldur's Gate (Interplay Productions, 1998)   Advanced Dungeons and Dragons fans waited patiently for a new game, and they were duly rewarded with *Baldur's Gate*, a massive five-CD adventure that remains true to traditional AD&D rules. However, non-Dungeon players need not worry. The play system is easy to master, and the real-time combat is considerably less stressful than in *Diablo*. Maps are beautifully rendered in 16-bit color, and 3-D terrain is fully functional, with mountains, pits, and stairways. The lighting is very dramatic, with day/night transitions, rain, snow, fog, and lightning displayed in real-time. Adding to the impressive visuals of *Baldur's Gate* are dynamic characters whose appearances change as they acquire weapons. The adventure continues with *Baldur's Gate: Tales of the Sword Coast* and a new DVD containing all five original CDs, both released in 1999.

System Shock 2 (Electronic Arts, 1999)   In its second incarnation, *System Shock 2* has become the best science fiction/horror role-playing game ever made. Once again, you battle Shodan, a female cyber-being who uses an array of robots, cyborgs, and mutants to bring your adventure to a premature end. After signing on for an expedition to deep space, your character awakens from an induced sleep to find an alien infestation onboard the abandoned ship. Fortunately, you have also received mysterious implants that allow you to develop superhuman powers as you search the ship for clues. To survive, you'll need to develop advanced psionic powers such as kinetic redirection and remote electron tampering. Aside from a highly detailed character growth system, the game features outstanding 3-D effects, including variable lighting and translucency, 16-bit color, and realistic first-person weapons simulation.

Planescape Torment (Interplay/Black Isle Studios, 1999)   Set in the Advanced Dungeons and Dragons universe of Planescape, this role-playing game's strength lies in a complex story line, portrayed with the excellent *Baldur's Gate* graphics engine. In *Torment* (see Figure 21.12), you are a character who is unable to die, but also unable to remember his past. Don't expect a golden haired hero in this game. Instead, your character is dressed in bones and animal skins, and his skin is covered in tattoos. Nevertheless, you will become quite attached to him as you wander the dark landscape. Because of the large perspective used in *Torment*, most of the weapons are used at close range, so it can be especially challenging to select a spell and cast it before your enemy is upon you.

FIGURE 21.12: *Planescape Torment*

Darkstone (Delphine Software, 1999)   If you liked *Diablo*, you'll love *Darkstone* (see Figure 21.13). Culled from the same engine, *Darkstone* is a straightforward, hack-and-slash role-playing game, which is not such a bad thing, especially when your brain is sore from AD&D. Unlike most games, you can directly control two characters, although both must come from the same basic class (Warrior, Monk, Assassin, or Wizard). Rather than use predrawn maps, *Darkstone* generates a random map for every adventure, each with 37 levels. When you add in a combined 66 spells, skills, and weapons, you have a *Diablo* clone that offers even more gameplay than the original classic.

FIGURE 21.13: *Darkstone*

Simulations

Railroad Tycoon II (PopTop Software, 1998)   Anyone who played the original *Railroad Tycoon* back in 1990 will fall in love all over again, but this time you will find great looks to go along with an incredible personality. Make no mistake about it, this is a serious railroad simulation that includes route planning, track construction, station building, maintenance, and everything else related to keeping your Iron Horses on the track. Along with the nuts and bolts of railroad management is a robust economic model that even allows you to play with (or lose) your millions in the stock market. Adding to the realism are various historical events and technological developments that are introduced at the proper times. This game lacks the action of a first-person shooter or adventure game, but if you can live without your rocket launcher for a few hours, you will find an immersive simulation that will (gasp!) even teach you a few things.

Microsoft Flight Simulator 2000 (Microsoft, 1999)   The original flight simulator keeps getting better, although the latest release will stress your hardware to its limits. If you have a fast Pentium III, a 3-D accelerator, and at least 64MB of RAM (forget about the minimum specs on the box), *Flight Simulator 2000* (see Figure 21.14) will hum like a LearJet at full throttle. There are two retail versions, regular and professional. The flight models and graphics are identical, but the extras (two new planes, six high-res cities, flight dynamics editor, and instrument panel editor) are worth the investment for serious pilots. In either package, you can fly to more than 20,000 accurately modeled airports, and a new real-world weather option lets you download up-to-the-minute weather effects for any flight, to any destination.

FIGURE 21.14:   *Microsoft Flight Simulator 2000*

European Air Wars (Microprose, 1998)   One of several recent WWII flight simulators takes a historical campaign approach, with 20 British, American, and German fighters, along with 10 more computer-controlled aircraft, including the German V-1 Flying Bomb. The planes are superbly modeled with actual technical specifications for weight, weapons, ammunition loads, rate of fire, climbing rates, and more. You can fly single missions or one of three campaigns, including the Battle of Britain. Missions include ground targets, bomber escorts, fighter sweeps, and interdiction. Recent WWII flight sims may boast sharper graphics, but *EAW* still has the corner on realistic dogfights and a fully tuned (and adjustable) flight model. See Figure 21.15.

FIGURE 21.15:   *European Air Wars*

Flight Unlimited III (Looking Glass Studios, 1999)   *Microsoft Flight Simulator 2000* dazzles computer pilots with a massive number of airports and cities, but *Flight Unlimited III* (see Figure 21.16) focuses on a smaller universe and, in some ways, comes out on top. The graphics cover the western United States with razor sharp coverage of the Seattle area (the detail is amazing, even from 5,000 feet). If two-way air traffic control communications (ATC) is on the top of your flight list, this game is as real as it gets (*MFS 2000* does not have ATC). However, if instrument flying is your specialty, *Flight Unlimited III* will leave you wanting more, and you won't find extensive flight instruction. Despite a few deficiencies, *Flight Unlimited III* has a lot to offer the computer pilot and with less stringent hardware demands than *MFS 2000*.

FIGURE 21.16:   *Flight Unlimited III*

Janes USAF (Electronic Arts, 1999) *Janes USAF* (see Figure 21.17) gives you the opportunity to fly eight hot Air Force jets in training flights or historic air battles over Vietnam and the Middle East. You can even vault into the future and fly the F-117 Stealth Fighter and F-22 Raptor in a hypothetical future campaign over Europe. Nobody does modern military flight like Janes, and *USAF* is no exception. With full 3-D cockpits for every plane, up to 1280 by 1024 resolution, and detailed "real world" terrain, the combat flight environment is fully tuned and very demanding. You can also record your missions and play them back, and when you are ready for live fire, *USAF* is fully supported on `JanesCombat.Net` and local networks with as many as 16 players.

FIGURE 21.17: *Janes USAF*

Need for Speed: High Stakes (Electronic Arts, 1999) In one of the longest running driving simulations for the PC, Electronic Arts has stayed with a proven formula: hot cars and cops trying to catch you. In *High Stakes* (see Figure 21.18), you choose from 18 screamers, including the Aston Martin DB7, Ferrari 550 Maranello, Lamborghini Diablo SV, and other cars that appear regularly in our dreams. Additional cars are available for download from www.needforspeed.com. There are 19 courses from exotic locations around the world, including Scotland, Germany, and an icy roadway that winds treacherously around peaks and through fresh powder. Each course will do its best to separate your car from the road, and it takes quick reflexes to maintain a successful career, win a High Stakes Challenge, or simply outrun the police chopper.

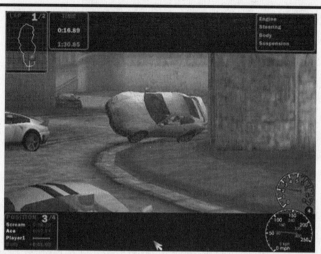

FIGURE 21.18: *Need for Speed: High Stakes*

Sports Games

High Heat 2000 (3DO Company, 1999)   In the ongoing battle of computer baseball games, there has been a bushel of foul balls, with only an occasional home run. However, in recent years, *High Heat* (see Figure 21.19) has dominated the category, and with version 2001 around the corner, there is serious talk of a dynasty. You will simply not find a more complete baseball game than *High Heat*, from stunning graphics to statistical depth. The batter/pitcher confrontation, which forms the foundation of any baseball game, is *High Heat's* strength. And after the ball is in play, it just gets better, with excellent base running and defensive play. If you haven't thrown out the first pitch with *High Heat*, don't delay, because this year's team will be even better.

FIGURE 21.19: *High Heat 2000*

NHL 2000 (EA Sports, 1999)   Although *NHL 2000* (see Figure 21.20) is certainly not the only hockey game for the PC, it might as well be. EA Sports' *NHL* franchise has ruled the ice for the past eight years, with the most exciting and, in recent years, the most realistic computer hockey game ever made. Ironically, *NHL 2000* goes back to the arcade style of earlier releases, and the end result is a faster, but less realistic game. However, the experience still captures the feel of professional hockey, complete with denture-rattling checks, acrobatic saves, sizzling slap shots, and comical fist fights. All the teams and players are here, and you can take your favorite team through an entire season or go straight to the playoffs.

FIGURE 21.20: *NHL 2000*

Madden 2000 (EA Sports, 1999)   It seems as if John Madden and EA Sports have been together since they stopped using leather helmets. Actually, that is only a slight exaggeration. One of the first graphical computer football games (there was an Apple II version!), *Madden* has aged well, and version *2000* is the most complete football package you can buy. The graphics and audio commentary are mainstays, but this year's game adds faster play, beautiful stadiums, game situation and player editors, and an exciting new route-based passing system. The best way to play *Madden 2000* is with your mitts wrapped around a gamepad. However, strategy fans should not hesitate to play this game in coaching mode. The playbook is vast, and the computer opponent will fight you for every yard until the final gun.

FIFA 2000 (Electronic Arts)   Despite the dominance of baseball and football in the United States, one of the best PC sports games you can buy is *FIFA 2000* (see Figure 21.21). Whether you are nuts about soccer or you're still trying to figure out what constitutes offsides, *FIFA 2000* is an absolute thrill to play, with stunning 3-D motion capture animation taken from MLS stars Eddie Pope, Zach Thornton, and Steve Ralston. Running, kicking, and throwing are smooth and fluid, and if you look closely, you'll even see players grimace after a nasty slide tackle or argue with the ref. *FIFA 2000* includes more than 110 teams, including all 12 MLS squads, 13 world teams, 45 national teams, and 40 great historic teams.

FIGURE 21.21: *FIFA 2000*

Part v

Jack Nicklaus 6: Golden Bear Challenge (Activision)

The *Jack Nicklaus Golf* series has long been touted for its powerful course design editor, and over the years, users have created hundreds of exceptional courses. However, it wasn't until *Jack Nicklaus 6* was released that the game engine caught up with *Links*, the reigning king of golf games. In fact, with a redesigned 3-D engine and ball physics, *Jack* finally has a slight edge. For the first time in any PC golf game, the feeling of depth has been accurately modeled, as well as the action of a ball that hits the side of a hill. Even ball spin, resulting from an inside-out or outside-in swing, is taken into account. When you add in a steady flow of user-created courses, you have a golf package that constantly reinvents itself.

NASCAR Racing 3 (Sierra/Papyrus, 1999)

If you have been trying to justify the purchase of that new racing wheel and pedal assembly, now is the time, because racing games just don't get any better than *NASCAR Racing 3* (see Figure 21.22). Your first challenge will be to stop watching the 3-D graphics and concentrate on driving your car. Speed and handling, smoking tires, collisions, and skids are modeled so accurately that you'll think you're watching an actual race. As usual with a Papyrus racing game, you have complete control over your car setup and performance, and you can even change its appearance with the built-in paint program. There are tracks galore, including the complete Winston Cup and Busch Grand National Series.

FIGURE 21.22:   *NASCAR Racing 3*

YOU ARE NOT ALONE

Thanks to constantly evolving computer AI, playing your favorite game against the computer has never been better. However, even at its best, a computer opponent is somewhat predictable. It is the introduction of a live adversary that brings out the true competitive nature in all of us, and it allows a computer game to free itself from most programming restraints.

In the early days of head-to-head competition, we had one option: a null modem cable connecting two computers via the serial port. Next came the parallel port connection, but it still required two computers within close proximity. Finally, the modem gave us unrestricted freedom, or so we thought. Unless our opponent was a local phone call away, we were faced with sobering long distance charges.

The final barrier came down when Internet providers delivered access to the World Wide Web for the cost of a local phone call. The ensuing explosion of online gaming has been massive. Dedicated gaming networks have bolstered gaming on the Internet by adding leagues, competitive ladders, and even technical support for a wide range of entertainment software. The news is all good if you're a gamer, and if you haven't jumped into online competition, you're only having half the fun.

In this section, I'll provide an overview of the online gaming experience, with tips on how to set up your system for maximum performance and a list of dedicated game networks. And, for those of you who are still unconnected, we offer a collection of excellent magazines for the latest reviews, technical information, and strategy tips.

Going Online

The quality of an online gaming session depends on four factors:

- ▶ Modem speed
- ▶ Quality of local telephone lines
- ▶ Quality of the Internet connection
- ▶ The speed of your computer in relation to the speed of your opponent's computer

Modem Speed

For occasional online gaming and good all-around performance and compatibility, buy a V.90 56Kbps modem. If you want maximum speed, invest in cable modem access (approximately $100 installation fee/$50 per month). Other high-speed options include ISDN (Integrated Services Digital Network) modems (dedicated line required), DSL (Digital Subscriber Line), or a satellite hookup (for example, DirecTV). However, keep in mind that when you play online, you are only half of a two-part connection. Hence, the speed of your game will always default to the slowest link in the chain. Whenever possible, link up with other gamers who have similar communications hardware.

Local Telephone Lines

About the most that you can do about local line quality, short of rewiring your house, is to check your wall jacks. One bad jack can cause interference throughout the system. You can check for loose wires and uncovered connectors. However, if you still hear static on any telephones in your house, call a repair person to check all the jacks. Unused lines can also cause problems. In an older house, it is not uncommon to have two active telephone lines and several other live lines that are not attached to active numbers. These additional open lines should be disabled.

Internet Connection

Unfortunately, this ends up as a trial-and-error exercise. Stay away from very small Internet providers that do not have a sufficient number of lines for their customer load. Ask a prospective provider about their ratio of callers to lines. If it's higher than ten to one, keep looking.

After signing up for service, keep a close watch on performance. Occasional busy signals are to be expected, but if you are constantly redialing even during off-peak hours, your provider may be overloaded. When you are having problems connecting, contact customer service for a status update. A good Internet provider should have up-to-the-minute knowledge of server problems, cut cables, and other disruptions.

Computer Speed

This is a no-brainer. Most games that support online play do a good job of balancing the communication between two computers. However, if one computer is dramatically slower than the other, the game may time out the connection due to inactivity. Your best bet is to limit your connections to computers within your processor category.

Online Gaming Networks

Although commercial game networks may have exclusive rights to certain titles, it is not uncommon to find your favorite game in several locations. Since most networks offer free basic services or, at the very least, a free trial period, you should sample several online companies before paying for premium titles. Also, check the Web site of your favorite software publisher for small dedicated networks devoted to one or two games. Table 21.4 includes several large gaming networks and a sampling of popular games. However, it is not uncommon for a large site to have 100 or more online games, so consult each site for a complete list.

TABLE 21.4: Online Gaming Networks

Network	Address	Key Games
Bezerk	www.won.net/channels/ bezerkwww.won.net/ channels/bezerk	*Half Life, Unreal Quake II, Starsiege Tribes, Interstate '82, Homeworld, Outpost 2,* and *Swat 2*
Gamestorm	www.gamestorm.com	*Air Warrior III, Warcraft II, Aliens Online, Multi-Player Battle Tech, Legends of Kesmai,* and *Magestorm*
Gamesville	www.bingozone.com	*Acey-Deucey, Bingo Zone, Gridiron Madness, Pictureama,* and *Crystal Ball*
Gameworld	www.gameworld.com	Currently in playtest mode for adventure and RPG games; a limited number of free beta test memberships are available
Heat	www.heat.net	*10Six, Quake II, Warcraft II, Kingpin, Quake, Baldur's Gate, Unreal, Battlezone,* and *Command & Conquer: Red Alert*
MSN Gaming Zone	www.zone.com	*Motocross Madness, Midtown Madness, Monster Truck Madness I & II, Age of Empires I & II, Close Combat I–IV, Allegiance, Asheron's Call, CyberStrike 2, Fighter Ace, Tanarus,* and *Rogue Spear*
MPlayer	www.mplayer.com	*Quake II Arena, Nerf Arena, Unreal Tournament, Half-Life, Rogue Spear, Rainbow Six, Aliens vs. Predator, Mech Commander, Mech Warrior, Gemstone III,* and *Dragon Realms*

TABLE 21.4 continued: Online Gaming Networks

NETWORK	ADDRESS	KEY GAMES
Professional Gamers League	www.pgl.com	Next season to begin: Spring 2000; games to be announced; $65,000 in cash and prizes awarded in first two seasons
The Station	www.station.sony.com	*Everquest, Fantasy War, Chron X, Tanarus,* and *Sovereign*
World Opponent Network	www.won.net	*Half-Life, Unreal Tournament, Quake II, Star-siege Tribes, Half-Life Opposing Force, Home-world, Lords of Magic, Birthright, NASCAR Racing 3,* and *Swat 2*

Magazines

For those rare times when you aren't playing games on your computer, you can follow your favorite PC software and hardware and stay current with the latest industry gossip by logging onto one of the Web sites listed in Table 21.5. Look for the subscriptions page for information on ordering a magazine subscription.

TABLE 21.5: Web 'Zines

MAGAZINE	WEB SITE
Computer Games Online	www.cdmag.com
Computer Gaming World	www.computergaming.com
	www.gamespot.com
PC Accelerator, PC Gamer, Next Generation, Maximum PC	www.imaginemedia.com
PC Gamer	www.pcgamer.com

WHAT'S NEXT?

After you return from your nearest software emporium, where you've gone to purchase some of the games Mark Cohen has mentioned in this chapter, you'll want to take a look at the next chapter. Guy Hart-Davis explains MP3, the newest compression format for audio files and a technology that is revolutionizing how you can play back and record at your computer.

Part v

Chapter 22

GETTING STARTED WITH MP3

In this chapter, we'll show you how to get started with MP3. You'll learn the following:

- ▶ What MP3 does
- ▶ What you can do with MP3
- ▶ What hardware and software you'll need to take advantage of MP3
- ▶ The legalities of downloading, creating, and distributing MP3 files
- ▶ How to use Winamp to play MP3 files
- ▶ How to use MusicMatch Jukebox to rip, play, and enjoy MP3

Adapted from *MP3! I Didn' t Know You Could Do That...*
by Guy Hart-Davis and Rhonda Holmes
ISBN 0-7821-2653-7   269 pages $19.99

UNDERSTANDING WHAT MP3 IS AND WHAT IT DOES

Put simply, MP3 is a highly compressed file format for storing digital audio in computer memory. MP3 takes up only a tenth of the space that was needed to store high-quality audio in previously available formats. The audio can be anything from the spoken word to soothing ocean sounds to the latest speed metal. If you can hear it, you can create an MP3 version of it.

Once you've recorded an MP3 file, you can store it on a computer—a laptop, a desktop, or a server—and play it back whenever you want, using MP3 player software (such as the applications included on the CD that comes with the book from which this chapter was adapted). You can also download an MP3 file to a portable MP3 hardware player (such as a digital Walkman) or a handheld computer or a palm-size PC and listen to it wherever you roam. In addition, you can get hardware MP3 jukeboxes that function more like stereo components than computers, and you can get MP3 players for your car—so with a little effort and a lot more money, you can have MP3 audio with you more or less wherever you go.

MP3 Turns Your Computer into a Jukebox

Computers have been able to record high-fidelity sound for many years now. But the resulting audio files have been far too large—from 35MB to 50MB for a typical music track of three to five minutes—to handle easily. So as recently as 1997, you could fit only a few hours of high-quality audio onto the largest hard drive that the average wallet could provide, which meant that it wasn't worth using a computer to store music unless you had a compelling reason.

Many recording studios have been using computers to record, process, and enhance audio, because computers let them record and manipulate the sound more easily, more accurately, and more cheaply than analog recording equipment. But once they'd finished processing the files, they stored them on tape and then duplicated them onto noncomputer technologies—cassettes, records, and CDs—that could easily be distributed to, and played by, the target audience.

The development of the MP3 format has changed all that. Compressed as MP3 files, high-quality audio takes up much less space than it used to. And because hard disks have grown dramatically over the last few years, you can fit several months' worth of music—playing 24/7—on a single hard disk.

Using a computer to record, store, and play music has become not only feasible but also advisable. With a little effort, you can put your entire CD collection on your computer and manage it effortlessly, turning your computer into an MP3 jukebox. From the computer, you can download MP3 tracks into your portable player or car player, burn them onto CDs, or simply pipe them to speakers in the various rooms of your house until your family or roommates have fled with their ears ringing.

Why Is MP3 Such a Breakthrough?

MP3 is a major breakthrough because it retains high audio quality while maintaining a small file size. MP3 works very well for both music and voice recordings such as radio shows, speeches, or audio books.

Before the MP3 standard was developed, downloading a single track of CD-quality audio over a modem took hours. For example, in the early 1990s, Aerosmith broke new ground by releasing a single as a WAV file on CompuServe, which at the time was an influential online service rather than a struggling subdivision of America Online. Because the file was so huge (something like 35MB) and the highest modem speed being used then was 28.8Kbps, downloading took the best part of four hours. Few people bothered: it simply wasn't worth the time (or the money—in those days, CompuServe charged by the minute).

MP3 files are far more compressed than WAV or other sound files. They consume only about 1MB of disk space per minute of music. Spoken-word audio, which typically doesn't need such high fidelity to sound okay, can fit several minutes into each megabyte of an MP3 file.

Not only have modem speeds increased, but an increasing number of people have better-than-modem access to the Internet. To start with, many homes in North America now have access to cable modems or digital subscriber lines (DSLs), which provide download speeds of several megabytes a minute—50 to 100 times faster than a modem. These high-speed connections give you the power to download an MP3-compressed track of average length in a minute or less. Some tech-heavy communities are now hooking up new residences with fiber-optic lines so fast that you'll be able to download a whole track in the time it takes to have a couple of good sneezes. And many colleges are way ahead of those tech communities in the bandwidth stakes, with dorms wired at blazingly fast speeds.

You can also play tracks directly off the Web without downloading them to your hard drive. This can come in handy when you're sampling new music and don't want to commit drive space to music you aren't sure of. When you do find something you like, just download it, and it will be available to you until your music tastes change or your hard drive dies.

A WORD ABOUT TERMINOLOGY

Unless we're missing it, there's really no appropriate word in English for "chunk of audio." For example, a "song" is usually understood to have words, and a "track" is usually understood as meaning one piece of music (or speech) from a CD, a cassette, or one of those black-vinyl Frisbees that nostalgic people call "records." In the absence of a better word, we'll refer to a chunk of audio as a "track," except when one of the applications chooses to refer to it as a "song."

While we're on the subject of words, the words "folder" and "directory" mean the same thing for Windows-based computers. We've used them interchangeably, trying to follow the terminology that the application being discussed uses.

Where Did MP3 Come From?

The MP3 format gets its name from having been created under the auspices of the Motion Picture Expert's Group (MPEG for short, pronounced *em-peg*). Dr. Karlheinz Brandenburg at the Fraunhofer Institute for Integrated Circuits IIS-A in Germany developed the coding method, thus ensuring himself a listing in the digital-music hall of fame.

MP is a shortened form of MPEG. But why 3? MP3 is the third compression method Fraunhofer developed. As you'd imagine, the first two methods were MP1 and MP2. They offered less compression than MP3 and didn't catch on widely, though a number of people did get kinda excited at the time.

How Does MP3 Work?

We mentioned that MP3 files are compressed, making them about 10 times smaller than equivalent CD audio files or WAV files. Let's look quickly at how this works. We won't get too technical here, but you need to understand a couple of points in order to create high-quality MP3 files that you'll enjoy hearing.

The key to the compression that MP3 uses is *sampling*. This isn't the same kind of sampling that techno artists use to achieve their musical effects—grabbing pieces of other artists' works and inserting mutated forms of them in their own creations. As far as MP3 is concerned, sampling is the process of examining the patterns of a sound to determine its characteristics and to record it from an analog format into a digital format.

NOTE

Tech moment: *Analog* is continuously variable, and *digital* is binary with two positions only—on or off. To create a digital version of an analog sound, you examine it at a sampling rate and a sampling precision and digitize the resulting data points. The higher the sampling rate and the sampling precision, the more accurate the sound is, the more data has to be stored, and the bigger the file is.

The *sampling rate* is the frequency with which the sound is examined, and the *sampling precision* (also called the *sampling resolution*) is the amount of information about the individual sample that is saved to the audio file.

CDs sample audio at a sampling rate of 44.1 kilohertz (kHz)—44,100 times a second—with a sampling precision of 16 bits (2 bytes) per sample. This high sampling rate is considered perfect as far as the human ear goes—the sampling is frequent enough, and the sampling precision stores enough information about the sound, that the human ear can't detect anything missing.

Is CD-quality audio perfect? Not really, but it's more than good enough for most people. If you look around hard enough, you can find a few people who claim to hear defects in CD-quality sound. Such people can probably hear dog whistles and see in the dark too.

Scientists call the study of what people can and can't hear *psychoacoustics*. In this case, *hear* doesn't refer to the ear's capacity to pick up the sound, but rather to the brain's capacity to identify it as a separate sound. You hear many things every day that your brain filters out, and there are whole sections of the spectrum of sound that you don't hear at all. (Ask dogs and bats.) An MP3 encoder trashes the frequencies and sounds that you won't be able to hear and saves only those that you will be able to hear. When a loud sound occurs at the same time as a quieter sound around the same frequencies, the encoder keeps only the loud sound because the loud sound masks the quieter sound.

Part v

Technically, MP3 is a *lossy* method of compression—it actually removes information from the source rather than just squashing the source down to its smallest possible size. (The opposite of lossy compression is *lossless* compression.) Because it's lossy, MP3 can compress audio to different degrees: the more you compress it, the more information is removed, and the worse the result sounds.

If you've ever listened to a CD on decent equipment, you know that CD-quality audio can—and should—sound great. But if you listen to CD-quality audio on poor equipment, you'll hear the defects in every measure.

So, CD-quality audio is basically excellent or at least good enough for 99.5 percent of the population. The only problem with it is that the files it produces are huge. If you sample at 44.1kHz and 16 bits, the files will run between 9MB and 11MB a minute. Because you can get about 650MB on a regular CD, most CDs can hold up to about 74 minutes of music. (Extended-capacity CDs, new at this writing, can hold 700MB and 80 minutes—a relatively trivial increase in capacity.) Not so coincidentally, most artists these days judge 50–70 minutes to be a CD's worth of music. (If you're old enough to have enjoyed vinyl before it became outmoded, you'll remember that most albums in those days were more like 30–45 minutes long—the amount that would comfortably fit on a vinyl LP.)

CD-quality audio is fine for CDs. But when a 4-minute track weighs in at a hefty 40MB, you don't want to try to transfer it over the Internet. At that size, you can put a couple of tracks on a 100MB Zip disk, but not enough music to entertain you for longer than a 40-ounce soda. Ten minutes of music isn't going to get you very far. These huge file sizes are great for the record companies because they amount to de facto copy protection—the files are too big for anyone to distribute easily. But for the audio fan, something smaller is needed.

Enter MP3. Providing almost CD-quality audio together with a decent rate of compression, MP3 solves both the quality problem and the file-size problem. Recorded at a decent sampling rate (as you'll see in a bit, you can use various sampling rates when recording MP3 files), MP3 provides the high-quality sound that audiophiles demand, but with enough compression that the resulting files can easily be transferred from one computer to another and from a computer onto palm-size PCs and dedicated hardware MP3 players.

That's the key feature of MP3—quality with portability. But wait, there's more.

In addition to the audio information stored in an MP3 file, there's also a *tag*—a container with various slots to hold key pieces of information about the MP3 files. A typical tag contains the artist's name, the title of the piece or audio item, the title of the album (if applicable), the genre, the year, and an optional comment.

Tags are great because they give you the power to sort your MP3 files by any of the pieces of information in the tags. So you can easily pull up everything in your Techno-Industrial, Nippon Pop, or Christian Metal collection.

Compare that to WAV files. WAVs have a filename and nothing else. You can sort them by filename, but you haven't a hope in hell of sorting them by genre or artist. And WAV files of a quality comparable to MP3 files are the same size as CD tracks. MP3 wins hands down.

What Can You Do with MP3?

Briefly put, you can easily create MP3 files from already-recorded music or audio (for example, from CDs) or audio you create yourself. You can save the files on your computer; play them back either on the computer or on portable players; sort them into collections or databases; and distribute them easily via the Internet (or other computer networks) or on conventional portable media such as CDs or removable disks (Zip, Jaz, Orb, and others). In essence, you can become a music creator *and* publisher. David Geffen, move over.

What Are the Advantages of MP3?

MP3 has massive advantages over conventional methods of distributing and listening to music. (Most of these advantages apply to other audio as well—for example, poetry or other spoken-word audio—but in this section, we'll assume you're mostly interested in music.)

For the Music Lover

The advantages of MP3 are clearest for the music lover. Now you can do the following:

Take your music with you   MP3 provides portable audio that you can play back on small players that don't skip, don't break, and are small enough to hide from view.

Store files on your electronic pal   You can store the files on computers.

Download and upload files easily   You can download or upload files without difficulty, even over a lame modem connection.

Create your own customized CDs   You can convert MP3 files to WAV format and burn them onto CDs. Better yet, if you use the MP3 format, you can fit between *100 and 200 tracks* onto one CD—up to a full night's worth of music, from seduction to regrets.

For the Artist

MP3 offers compelling advantages to artists too. Here's what you can do:

Publish and distribute your own music over the Internet
You no longer need to find a record company prepared to spend many thousands of dollars recording, packaging, and promoting you and your music. You can simply record the music, convert some tracks to MP3 format, and post them on the Web so that people can download them instantly and listen to them.

Promote your work by releasing samples of it   You can do this in any or all of several ways, including placing MP3 files on Web sites for distribution, posting them to MP3 newsgroups, distributing them as e-mail attachments, or sharing them via Napster.

Easily release different versions of a track rather than agonizing over which version to include on an album   You can even release work in progress and let your fans vote on which direction you should pursue.

Keep control of your destiny   No record company need be involved, whether you're releasing one track every decade or a couple of albums' worth of music every year.

As you might imagine, the point about the record company is where friction starts to set in. Until the mid-1990s, record companies decided which artists would be unleashed on the public, when the music would appear, and how it would be produced, packaged, presented, and priced.

Recording and producing an album took weeks or months—even years, if you were the Human League. The album then had to be manufactured (at great expense) and distributed in quantity to radio stations and record stores, preferably accompanied by an expensive promotional campaign and Bolivian Marching Powder to persuade the DJs to play the record and the stores to carry it.

Now an artist or a band can record high-fidelity sound with an affordable computer, mix it to professional quality, and then distribute it immediately and painlessly using MP3 files. If anyone likes the music, they can pay to download further songs or buy a CD directly from you.

You can see why the record companies weren't pleased when MP3 took off.

For the Record Company

MP3 seemed to pose a severe threat to record companies by bypassing first their control of the selection and recording process and then their expensively built production and distribution systems.

But MP3 cuts both ways: if it wants to, a record company can use MP3 to promote its songs and artists to customers—just as independent artists can, only more so. By using cross-promotion and the economies of scale, a record company can reap great benefits from MP3.

Here are the basic advantages for a record company using MP3:

Reduced production and distribution costs—*way* reduced   If a record company no longer needs to manufacture 100,000 CDs by its great new hope, print 100,000 inlay cards, buy 100,000 jewel cases, assemble them, and truck them around the world, it will save a huge amount of money.

Simple promotion   By offering a good selection of freely downloadable MP3 files, a record company can make its Web site a major destination for music fans. It can then move on to the next advantage—direct sales.

Direct sales to customers via the Web   What could be sweeter? The record company produces the music as usual and then sells it directly via the Web to the customer. Better yet, the record company can sell dozens of different mixes of any track—they've found out by now that people will pay for the Ultra Boonga-Chonka Techno remix as well as the Extended Boonga remix and the Techno remix. As a distribution mechanism, the Web allows far greater customer choice than physical stores can. The record company can also sell CDs—regular CDs and custom-made CDs—via mail order.

Simple cross-promotion   The record company can present information about related bands to customers, offering them free tracks to try. Customers can sign up for news (via, say, e-mail newsletters) on bands they're interested in, upcoming releases, concerts, and so on.

Seeding the market with low-fi tracks   The music company can release low-fidelity MP3 files of music they want to promote and then wait for people to buy the high-fidelity versions.

The advantages of MP3 for record companies are almost enough to make you want to start a record company yourself. And with MP3, there's little to stop you.

What Are the Disadvantages of MP3?

To go with its advantages, several disadvantages are associated with MP3. For most people, they're not too severe.

For the Music Lover

For the music lover, only a few disadvantages are associated with MP3. First of all, in most cases you must have a computer to download, record, and play MP3 files. You can now get portable MP3 players and MP3 players for cars, but you still need a computer to get and store the files. (There are hardware MP3 players that resemble stereo components, but inside, they're computers.)

Second, the music quality isn't quite as high as CD quality. Most people find the music quality good enough, and for most spoken-word recordings, quality isn't an issue. You can adjust the quality of MP3 files by choosing a higher or lower sampling rate when you create them.

And third, you may receive illegal MP3 recordings unwittingly. We'll examine the legal issues later in this chapter, but you need to know from the beginning that it's illegal to distribute someone else's MP3 files, and it's illegal to have illegally distributed MP3 files in your possession.

For the Artist

For the artist, the main disadvantage of MP3 is that any CDs they have released can be *ripped* (extracted and compressed) to MP3 files and distributed illegally, either directly (on CDs or other removable media) or via the Internet. Because MP3 files are digital, each copy retains the same quality of the original—unlike, say, audio tapes, for which each generation of duplication loses sound quality. In this way, an artist can lose money through piracy. New software such as Napster, which provides instant sharing of tracks by all members logged into a loose online community, can achieve savage levels of piracy within a period of hours.

At this writing, various artists groups, from the Recording Industry Association of America (RIAA) and downward, are working on ways to keep MP3 piracy to a tolerable level. *Tolerable* is hard to define in this context, but you'd think a good target would be a level analogous to the level of piracy tacitly accepted when people taped LPs and duped cassettes for their friends. Suggested "solutions" range from banning the MP3 format (which, even if it were not stupid and impractical, would be ineffective) to vigorously policing Web sites and newsgroups for illegal content, which is already happening to some extent.

For the Record Company

For the record company, the main disadvantage of MP3 is the same as that for the artist: the record company can lose money through piracy of released material.

When it comes to MP3, some record companies are in a more peculiar situation than others. For example, Sony Corp. is a top record label, with big-name artists such as Celine Dion and Fiona Apple—but it's also a major manufacturer of audio equipment. Sony's hardware division spent late 1998 and most of 1999 chafing at the bit to release a killer MP3 player and lock up a market that could be even more lucrative than the Walkman market it created in the 1970s. But Sony's music side has been scared spitless by the thought of its massive revenue stream from music dragging its mauled carcass into the desert to die after a cataclysmic showdown with MP3 hardware.

Toward the end of 1999, Sony finally released the VAIO Music Clip—externally exactly the kind of innovative MP3 player that you'd have expected to see from it about a year earlier. Longer and much thinner than most portable hardware MP3 players, the VAIO Music Clip handles MP3 and Atrac3 formats, is SDMI (Secure Digital Music Initiative) compliant, and is designed to be hung on a neck strap around the user's neck rather than clipping to the belt like most portable players. Unfortunately, the stringencies presumably exercised by Sony's music side have resulted in a truly grotesque software implementation that forces you to convert each MP3 file into a secure format before you can upload it to the Music Clip—a severe pain in the anatomy.

Part V

Where Is MP3 Heading?

MP4—of course. An MP4 Structured Audio format is currently under development, but it's far from mainstream deployment.

At this point, it's hard to say with any certainty what's going to happen with MP3 in the long term. The dramatic spread of MP3 has already started a tectonic shift in how music is distributed, at least among people who have computers. The three key groups involved with music—fans, artists, and record companies—can benefit greatly from MP3. Artists and record companies can also benefit from other audio-compression technologies that are less friendly to the consumer than MP3.

It should be no surprise to learn that—after a couple of years of denial—the music business and technology companies are working hard to neutralize the threats that MP3 presents to them. Initial efforts included a suit by the RIAA to prevent the release of the Diamond Rio hardware MP3 player. (It failed.) There has also been talk of trying to "ban" the MP3 format. Subsequent efforts have—more realistically—centered on securing the files so that you cannot play them at all or play them more than a few sample times without paying for them. And copying them without paying (more) is out of the question.

At this writing, several technologies have been developed for distributing music securely online, including a2b, ATRAC3, Liquid Audio, MS Audio, Mjuice, and VQF. We'll give you a short overview of each in the following sections, after these prefatory words of wisdom.

Reduced to the essentials, there are two problems for music formats competing with MP3. Neither problem is insurmountable, but each is huge, and together, they make a formidable roadblock.

▶ The first problem is that, from the consumer's point of view, none of the wannabe music formats has any compelling appeal. Each format is designed for secure distribution of music, which almost invariably means that consumers (a) get to pay for the music, preferably through the nose, and (b) are restricted from using the music as they want. (For example, some technologies can lock a particular track to the computer on which you first play it, so that you cannot then play it on another computer without paying more. Imagine how you'd react if your portable CD player prevented you from playing a CD on your car CD player.) The only advantages the wannabe music formats can claim for the consumer are a smaller file size (which is nice, but MP3 files are already plenty portable) and better audio quality (which is even nicer, but MP3 quality is more than good enough for most people).

▶ The second problem is that MP3 has such a massive lock on the market right now—because it's free, easy to use, and delivers more than acceptable audio quality—that it's hard for any other format to build any momentum behind it.

The wannabe formats are essentially aimed at commercializing the online distribution of music (or, to put it another way, enabling commercial online distribution of music). Because MP3 has such a head start over the other formats, is widespread if not rampant at this time, is open to everyone, is essentially free, and is easy to use, it's likely that MP3 will remain the dominant audio-compression technology for several years.

OK, enough general blather. Let's get into the formats.

a2b

The *a2b* format from AT&T stores audio in compressed and encrypted files. a2b claims better compression (2.25MB for a 3-minute song) and sound quality than MP3 and has the advantage of being able to store text and art with the audio. Therefore, a track can bring with it its lyrics, its credits, a brief enjoinder to save the whales, and a picture of the CD cover (or of a friendly whale). But these advantages are more than offset by a2b's minimal distribution so far—at this writing, a2b is more a curiosity than a valuable way of playing digital audio.

ATRAC3

ATRAC3 is a sound compression format developed by Sony for use with its OpenMG copyright-protection technology. Together, ATRAC3 and OpenMG enable secure distribution of digital music. At this writing, ATRAC3 has been implemented only in Sony hardware and software, making it a marginal player so far—but RealNetworks is currently integrating ATRAC3 into its RealJukebox ripper/player/jukebox, which will help bring ATRAC3 into the mainstream.

Liquid Audio

Liquid Audio (http://www.liquidaudio.com) makes a player that can play secured files and can also burn CDs. Liquid Audio has been used for several years on the Internet Underground Musical Archive (IUMA), which describes itself as "the granddaddy of all music Web sites." Liquid Audio is almost a major player in the digital music market, but it has yet to achieve widespread distribution. Not that it isn't trying—Liquid Audio made a splash in late 1999 by persuading Alanis Morissette to use Liquid Audio in the Internet marketing campaign for her CD *MTV Unplugged*.

MS Audio

Microsoft's Windows Media Technologies 4.0 has a secure compression scheme called *MS Audio* that claims to surpass MP3 in both compression and music quality. Problem is, Microsoft has been struggling to get enough music available in the MS Audio format for consumers to start taking them seriously. Several MP3 players, including Winamp and Sonique, can play MS Audio files, as can later versions of Windows Media Player.

Mjuice

Mjuice is a secure digital format that includes features such as an expiration date, allowing artists and record companies to release promotional files that will expire at a suitable point. For example, an artist promoting her forthcoming CD might release Mjuice versions of several tracks online, using an expiration date that coincided with the CD's release, a tactic used recently by bands such as Third Eye Blind (or, to be more precise, their record company, Elektra). A number of MP3 players (including Winamp) and jukeboxes (including RealJukebox) can play Mjuice files, so if you get them, you'll have no problem listening to them.

VQF

The *VQF* format (Transform-domain Weighted Interleave Vector Quantization, if you must ask) boasts better compression and higher sound quality than MP3, but almost nobody's using it at this writing. If you do decide to try VQF, you can download a Winamp plug-in to play the tracks, or you can use the MP3 player K-jofol. For information on the VQF format, visit http://www.vqf.com.

GET THE RIGHT HARDWARE

To record and play MP3 files, you need a moderately powerful computer. It doesn't matter if it's a PC, a Mac, or a Unix or Linux box—even a Be box is fine. What does matter is that it needs enough horsepower to process the MP3 files and play them back without faltering.

What does "moderately powerful" mean? Well, the computer doesn't have to be the latest screamer, though the faster chips with multimedia features will rip selections faster than older chips. For example, computers based on Pentium II, Pentium III, Celeron, K6-2, and Athlon chips rip at a goodly speed, as do PowerPC-based Macs. A 486 won't cut it. But if you're currently using your computer to play games involving sound and motion, and you haven't yet put a brick through your monitor in frustration at the lack of speed, you're probably in pretty good shape for playing MP3 music. If you have a CD-ROM as well, you'll also be able to rip MP3 files from CDs you own.

Let's look at the specifics of what you need in a computer to play, rip, and enjoy MP3 music.

NOTE

If your computer is generally underpowered, you'll probably do better to buy a new one rather than upgrade multiple components. Because computer prices have fallen dramatically in the last two years, and continue to fall, you can now buy a reasonably full-featured PC (not including a monitor, printer, and other accessories) for about $500—only a little more than it would cost to upgrade the processor, RAM, and hard drive of an older computer. Weigh your options carefully before putting any money down.

The Chip: Pentium 200MMX or Better; Mac G3

For most ripping programs, you need at least a Pentium 200MMX, though for older rippers you may be able to get by with an ancient Pentium 133 (that's the "classic" Pentium without the MMX extensions). But as you'd imagine, a faster chip will give you better performance.

For playing back MP3 files, you may be able to stagger along with a Pentium 75 or so (or even a 486DX4 with a high clock speed), depending on the program you're using. Be warned that if the computer is around this level, you may hear interruptions in the audio as it struggles to keep up, and you may not be able to run other applications without interrupting playback.

For the Macintosh, you'll want a PowerPC chip—preferably a G3. You'll get plenty of performance at 233MHz or above.

RAM: 32MB or More (Preferably Much More)

For ripping, you need 32MB of RAM—absolute minimum. For playback, you need 16MB of RAM—absolute, absolute minimum. As with almost any program, more RAM will make rippers and players run better. At this writing, RAM is once again nearing the historic low price it reached it mid-1999 (before an earthquake in Taiwan temporarily doubled prices). An extra 32MB or 64MB of RAM is a bargain that will give your computer a decent boost in performance. If you're buying a new PC, get 128MB to start with; you won't regret it.

CD or DVD Drive

For ripping CDs, you need a CD drive or a DVD drive. Most any CD speed above 2X will work, but one of today's drives (say 40X or better) will give far better performance. A SCSI (Small Computer Systems Interface) drive minimizes the load on the processor, whereas ripping with an IDE (Integrated Drive Electronics) drive imposes a significant load. If your chip is lame, a SCSI drive might help you out, but it'll be more expensive than an IDE drive.

The CD drive needs to support digital audio extraction in order to rip tracks digitally. (Most rippers offer an analog ripping option for CD drives that don't support digital audio extraction, but the results typically aren't as good as digital ripping.) If your CD drive isn't up to ripping, get another; it'll cost you anything from $35 and up.

NOTE
DVD speeds refer to the speed at which the DVD drive works with DVDs, not with CDs, which they read at a faster rate. For example, a 6X DVD drive typically delivers more like 24X performance for CDs—enough to rip at a goodly speed.

Sound Card

To produce any sound worth hearing, you need a decent sound card. All other things being equal, the better your sound card, the better the music will sound.

Choosing a sound card is about as personal as choosing underwear. But we'll give you a few pointers to help you avoid buying the digital equivalent of nylon briefs that are one size too small:

> ▶ Make sure the sound card will work with your computer and operating system. If your PC doesn't have a PCI (Peripheral Component Interconnect) slot free, a PCI sound card won't do you much good. If you *do* have PCI slots free, you probably don't want to get an ISA (Industry Standard Architecture) sound card. ISA cards

draw much more heavily on the computer's processor than PCI cards do, so go with PCI if it's an option. Many modern ATX motherboards have 16-bit SoundBlaster chips built into the motherboard, which may be enough to get you started with MP3. If you find yourself listening to a lot of music, you'll probably want to get something better pretty soon.

▶ Choose the number of *voices*—individually mixed tracks—that you'll need the sound card to produce. You'll need at least 64 voices to make music sound good because most music is mixed with 64 separate tracks. Advanced sound cards support several hundred voices. That'll probably be overkill—until you get seriously into MP3 and want your music to sound as good as it possibly can.

▶ Make sure you have the appropriate connectors for connecting your sound card to your speakers or your stereo. You'll think this is dumb advice until you find that you don't have the right connectors. If you want to connect your PC to your stereo, you'll usually need different connectors than if you're just going to plug a pair of speakers into the sound card. If you're buying connectors, make sure they're of an appropriate quality for your sound card—there's no sense in using Radio Shack's cheapest connectors with an advanced and expensive sound card, because chances are they'll lower the quality of the output.

▶ If you're making your own music, make sure that the sound card provides the MIDI (Musical Instrument Digital Interface) connections you need.

The following list mentions some sound cards you may want to consider, with approximate prices as of this writing. But because hardware companies are constantly bringing out new models, you'll probably want to do some research of your own.

▶ The SoundBlaster Live! from Creative Labs is a PCI card that can play as many as 512 voices at the same time—enough for professional-quality music playback. The SoundBlaster Live! MP3 costs $99, comes with a bundle of MP3-oriented software, and is a good value. If you want bells and whistles, the SoundBlaster Live! Platinum costs $199 and includes a Live! Drive—a drive bay that fits into the front of your computer like a CD-ROM drive and provides input and output jacks for S/PDIF (Sony/Phillips Digital Interface Format), headphones, line or microphone, and MIDI. Having the jacks right there is much handier than having them at the back of the PC, but you may not need to spend the extra money.

▶ The SoundBlaster AWE from Creative Labs is a 64-voice ISA card that costs about $199. It's also available in a Value Edition that costs $99.

▶ The Turtle Beach Montego II Quadzilla, which costs $79, is a 320-voice card that supports 4-speaker output for quadraphonic audio. If you want digital I/O, Voyetra Turtle Beach Inc. also makes the Montego II Plus, a $149 board that provides lossless digital signal transfer and 4-channel positional audio.

▶ The Diamond Monster Sound MX400 supports a maximum of 1,024 voices and costs about $79.

WARNING

Before you buy a sound card for a Linux box, make sure that drivers are available for it—otherwise, its voices will be silent. A good place to start looking for information on drivers is the sound card vendor's Web site, followed by the Linux distributor's site. For example, Red Hat Software keeps a list of supported hardware on its Web site at www.redhat.com. At this writing, leading sound cards such as the SoundBlaster Live! and Montego II Quadzilla do not have solid Linux drivers—though the folks at Creative are working hard to deliver them for the SoundBlaster Live!.

Now you need speakers (discussed in the next section) or headphones (discussed in the section after that). Alternatively, you can direct the output from your computer into your stereo system and use its speakers instead.

Speakers

Speakers come in a wide range of sizes, prices, and capabilities. This section discusses the key points that you need to keep in mind before opening your wallet.

Good Speakers Don't Come Free

Most every PC that's sold these days proudly advertises that it comes with "multimedia speakers." Most of these speakers aren't worth their weight in landfill. You can listen to spoken audio or to low-fi radio through them without annoyance, but music will suffer, along with your ears and your brain. Plan to invest some money in better speakers right from the start.

Anywhere from $60 to $400 will get you what you need, though you can easily spend more than that.

Tweeters, Woofers, and Subwoofers

Each speaker contains two or more *cones* or *drivers*. In a two-cone speaker, the *tweeter* plays the treble (high-frequency) sounds, and the *woofer* plays bass sounds. In a subwoofer system, the *subwoofer* plays the bass and very low-frequency sounds—those bass rumbles you feel reverberate in your body more than you hear in your ears. A subwoofer typically provides more bass sounds than a non-subwoofer setup and is considered a must by most gamers and many audiophiles. (Bear in mind that subwoofers have also been considered grounds for arrest, divorce, and eviction, not necessarily in that sequence.)

Passive or Amplified?

You need to choose between passive speakers—unpowered speakers—and amplified speakers. *Passive speakers* are typically used with an amplifier (which is often integrated into a receiver), as in a "normal" stereo system. The output from the CD, cassette deck, and radio goes into the amplifier into which you plug the speakers. The amplifier runs on AC and provides the heavy-duty lifting; the speakers just reproduce the sound. When you plug passive speakers into a sound card that's designed to work with amplified speakers, you get minimal volume.

Amplified speakers, as their name suggests, contain their own amplifier or amplifiers. Usually there's one amplifier in one of the speakers, which makes it much heavier than the other one. That speaker is the one that receives the power—usually from AC, because batteries won't get you far—and provides the boosting. In a subwoofer set, the subwoofer typically contains the amplifier and lives on the floor so that it doesn't break your furniture.

How Loud Are They?

Speaker volume is measured in watts, but the way manufacturers measure the wattage of speakers varies wildly. You'll see measurements in RMS watts (*root mean square* watts), which measures the wattage that the amplifier or speaker can deliver continuously rather than the wattage volume at which it maxes out. The peak wattage is sometimes referred to as *peak output* or *peak power*. The peak is basically the point beyond which the speaker blows up.

Unless you live for distortion and feedback or are the reincarnation of Jimi Hendrix, you'll seldom want to listen to music anywhere near your speakers' peak power, because it'll sound horrible. But many manufacturers of, uh, less expensive speakers list the peak wattage rather than RMS wattage so that the figure looks more impressive. So if you see inexpensive speakers advertised as delivering 100 watts, be on your guard: They probably can't sustain that volume, and if they can, you won't want to listen to it. At 100 watts RMS, the volume is enough to shake your house on its foundations and make the neighbors call the cops. Believe us, we *know*.

Passive speakers of 5 or 10 watts may be about right for discretion in an office cubicle; amplified speakers of the same power will give the feeling of a bit more punch, even if you keep the volume turned down.

If you want to rock out, you'll need a speaker system that delivers more like 20–50 watts. For example, the Altec Lansing ADA880R subwoofer system ($299) delivers 40 watts RMS through its satellites and 40 watts RMS through the subwoofer, giving a total of 80 watts RMS. The Creative Labs MicroWorks subwoofer system (built by Cambridge SoundWorks), which was one of the systems we used for everything from Morphine to the Chemical Brothers while writing this book, delivers 13 watts per channel on the satellites and 45 watts on the subwoofers. This is enough to disturb the rest of the household. A nice feature of the MicroWorks system is that it accepts twin inputs, so you can hook in two computers at the same time and play them simultaneously for bizarre mixing effects when the urge strikes you.

Choose Your Poison

Different speakers are designed for different types of uses: Some speakers are specifically designed for gamers, so they're better at reproducing shotgun blasts and roars of monstrous rage than delivering delicate violin passages. Some speakers are built for rock music; others, for classical music. Make sure the speakers you get are suited to your needs.

Some speakers succeed in being, if not all-purpose, at least multipurpose. For example, the MidiLand S2/4030 subwoofer set (about $200—you don't pay more for the catchy and memorable name) can comfortably both detonate the earth on *Armageddon* and deliver the details of your favorite Van Halen guitar solo. (We won't vouch for their fidelity on Chopin, though—our ears are still ringing.) The 4030s provide 30 watts; there's also an S4/4060 set that delivers 60 watts (30 from the subwoofer and 15 from each of the twin satellites).

Surround Sound and Home Theater

Surround sound uses four or five speakers to produce the effect of your being surrounded by the sound source. For example, when a car zips by in the background, you'll hear it go from left to right as you would with a normal stereo system, but you'll also hear that it's behind you rather than in front of you (or going straight through your head). Surround sound systems typically cost more than regular subwoofer systems, but if you like the effect, you may well find the expense justified.

If you have a DVD drive or a sound card that supports positional audio, you may want to consider a *home theater system*. Home theater systems typically use *5.1* setups—five satellite speakers with a powered subwoofer—to deliver realistic sound effects; some even use 7.1 setups. One example of a 5.1 setup is the DeskTop Theater 5.1 from Cambridge SoundWorks, which costs $299. DeskTop Theater is rated at 5 watts RMS to the main speakers and the surround speakers, 15 watts RMS to the center speaker, and 15 watts RMS to the subwoofer. The numbers may not seem impressive, but the sound is room filling. Other home theater systems cost upward of $1000 and are designed to hook into your TV and stereo system—into which you can hook your PC.

Listen to Them

It's an obvious suggestion—but if you can, listen to speakers before you buy them. Many stores display demonstration sets of speakers pulling from a common control panel that delivers samples of different types of audio so that you can test-drive the speakers with rock, classical, soothing sounds, or games to see if they meet your needs.

Known Brands

We've mentioned a couple of PC speaker brands: Altec Lansing and Creative Labs, which also distributes speakers made by Cambridge SoundWorks. Other well-known speaker brands include Bose (stunningly good, shatteringly expensive), Boston Acoustics, JBL, Yamaha, and Philips. Even Microsoft is getting in on the act, offering a speaker/subwoofer set that plugs into your computer's USB (Universal Serial Bus) port.

Headphones

If anything, headphones are even harder to choose than speakers: one person's dream set is another person's instrument of torture. So it's hard to give specific recommendations. But we can tell you this much: rather than buying headphones as an accessory to your stereo based largely on looks and price, you need to establish what you need in a pair of headphones and then find it.

Several styles of headphones are available:

Circumnaural, or over-the-ear, headphones   These are the headphones that completely enclose your ears. You can get either *open headphones*, which expose the back of the diaphragm to the air, providing better sound, or *sealed headphones*, which look and act more like a pair of ear defenders, insulating you somewhat from outside sound. As you'd guess, sealed headphones are good for noisy environments such as music studios or busy family rooms. If you've worn them, you'll know they're heavy enough for Ah-nold to use for neck presses. If you're looking for a recommendation, we can give you a couple to try: the Beyerdynamic DT831 headphones (about $200) deliver music pure enough to fry your brains if your ears don't melt from being clamped in; and the Sennheiser HD565 Ovations (about $220 street) are super-comfortable open circumnaural headphones that give a very civilized feel to all but the most raucous music while delivering exceptional punch and clarity.

Supra-aural, or on-the-ear, headphones   These are the ones that sit on your ears. They're lighter and smaller than circumnaural headphones, so they can be more comfortable to wear provided they don't press too hard against your ears. Like circumnaural headphones, most supra-aural headphones use a headband to keep them in place, but Koss makes a style of supra-aural headphones that use ear-clips to attach to your ears. This style frees you from a headband but makes you look like you're Spock using two old-fashioned hearing aids. A recommendation for standard supra-aurals? Check out the Grado 225s (about $200), which provide a good kick throughout rock ranges and whose leather headband snuggles sexily against your shaven skull.

Ear-bud headphones   These come in two styles: with a headband (buds that poke into your ears but don't wedge there) and without a headband (buds designed to wedge into your ear and stay there). Ear buds deliver an intense music experience but typically lower music quality and serve up less bass than circumnaural or supra-aural headphones. They're considered by some to carry a higher threat of hearing damage than circumnaural or supra-aural headphones. No recommendation here, because it will depend on the shape of your ears and the state of your brain—but anything real cheap is probably a bad idea. Because ear-bud headphones actually sit in your ear, you need to be especially alert for discomfort—it can indicate imminent damage.

You don't have to pay a huge amount for headphones. A $20 set of ear buds can sound great, and a $75 set of supra-aural or circumnaural headphones can sound better than a $300 set of speakers. But if you want to, you can drop the best part of a grand on headphones.

When buying headphones, don't overlook mundane concerns in your quest for the perfect sound for you. First, make sure that the headphone cord is long enough for your needs so that you can bop your head to the music without yanking the player off your belt or the stereo stand. (If the cord's not long enough, get an extension.) Second, make sure the headphones come with the right kind of plug for the output jack you're planning to use. Many headphones use the $1/4$-inch plug that slides into the $1/4$-inch jacks on stereo equipment rather than the mini-plug that most portable audio items use. You may need to get a $1/4$-inch-plug-to-mini-plug adapter. (The better headphones usually come with one.)

Big names in headphones include AKG, Beyerdynamic, Grado, Koss, and Sennheiser. (That's alphabetic order, not an order of recommendation.)

TIP

If you'll always be using headphones rather than speakers, you may want to invest in a headphone amplifier to help power your headphones. For home use, you may also want to get wireless headphones that will let you roam further from your sound source. *Try these out before you buy them.* Cheaper sets can seriously clip the top and bottom end of the frequencies, and even better sets tend to suffer in comparison to wired headphones.

As with speakers, you'll want to listen to headphones before buying them. Besides the obvious—to hear the sound quality—you should make sure they fit your ears and are comfortable enough to wear for your typical listening session.

Plenty of Storage

If you're going to store MP3 files (and we'll bet you are), you'll need plenty of storage space. Typically, this means space on your hard disk or disks, though you may also choose to use removable media as well. We'll discuss each in turn.

Hard Disk Storage

With MP3 providing roughly a 10:1 compression rate at almost CD quality, each minute of music takes up about 1MB of storage space. So a 4-minute piece of music consumes about 4MB in MP3 format, and each gigabyte (GB) of disk space can store about 250 pieces. At this writing, the biggest afford-able hard drives are in the 40GB range and cost about $300. (The biggest *unaffordable* hard drives are in the 73GB range and cost more like $1700.) You don't even need to do the math to know that this translates to a seri-ous boatload of music.

All IDE-controlled motherboards can take at least two drives; many can hold four; and if you have SCSI, you can chain a small horde of devices. Consult your friendly computer store for upgrade possibilities, or grab the *Complete PC Upgrade and Maintenance Guide* or *PC Upgrading and Main-tenance: No Experience Required* (both from Sybex, both good, the former three times the size of the latter) if you're prepared to roll up your shirt sleeves and get your hands dirty.

Removable Media Storage

If you're all maxed out for hard disk storage space, or if you need portable storage, you may want to fall back on removable media. These are the main candidates at this writing:

▶ Zip drives (made by Iomega Corp.) should need no introduction, because they've been around a number of years. Zip drives come in IDE, SCSI, parallel port, and USB versions. The basic Zip—the Zip Classic, if you think in marketing-speak—holds a marketer's 100MB, which translates to 95.7MB in the real world. (You'll recall that a megabyte is 1024 by 1024 bytes—1,048,576 bytes—rather than a million bytes clean.) The Zip 250 holds two-and-a-half times as much—250 marketing megabytes.

▶ The Jaz drive, as you probably know, is the bigger brother of the Zip, with the original Jaz holding 1GB and the Jaz 2GB packing twice that. (Again, these measurements are in millions—make that *billions*—of bytes rather than true gigabytes.)

▶ The Orb from Castlewood Technologies is a 2.2GB drive—a little bigger than the Jaz, and at a better price.

▶ CD-R and CD-RW media hold 650MB each (or 700MB for extended-capacity CDs).

▶ DVD-RAM discs hold 2.3GB a side. You can get single-sided or double-sided discs; as you'd guess, double-sided are more expensive. At this writing, DVD-RAM is too expensive for most people to use as a regular storage medium—but if you've got the bucks, it sure is fast and convenient.

Last, if you're hurting for disk space, consider external hard drives such as those made by LaCie. Various sizes of drives are available, from parallel port to USB, Firewire, and PC Card.

Port City: Parallel, Serial, USB, or Firewire?

If you'll be using a portable hardware MP3 player, you'll want to make sure that your computer has the right port or ports for it.

The first generation of hardware MP3 players relied on the parallel port, whereas the second generation tends toward USB. The main advantage of the humble parallel port is that it is almost as ubiquitous as the even more humble serial port (though not quite as slow). Almost every computer built since about 1990 has a parallel port.

The main disadvantage of the parallel port (apart from its lack of speed) is that the parallel port on many computers is already in use, either for a printer (the main beneficiary of the parallel port) or for one of the several technologies that have glommed on to the parallel port as the easiest way of connecting to a computer without adding hardware and expense, such as scanners, removable drives (such as external Zip drives, CD drives, and DVD drives), network adapters, and even some cameras. If you've got a device using your parallel port, you'd do well to look for an MP3 player with a better connection.

NOTE

Some MP3 players come with pass-through ports that theoretically pass through any data intended for devices other than the MP3 player. In practice, pass-through ports make many printers and scanners unhappy. Another possibility for attaching an MP3 player via a parallel port when your parallel port is already used is to add a PCI card that provides one or more additional parallel ports.

More recent MP3 players use the USB port to provide decent speed— USB can (and should) provide much faster throughput than the parallel port. If your computer already has USB and an operating system that can handle it, you're all set; if not, you can add USB to a computer with a PCI card easily enough. It'll cost a few bucks, but the installation procedure is straightforward.

For a desktop computer, get a PCI card with two or more USB ports. Siig makes an interesting PCI card that has five USB ports, but it's hard to find at this writing. In general, you'll probably do better to get a two-port USB card and plug into it a hub that has the number of ports you require. Unless you keep your computer front and center on your desk, a hub will usually be easier to plug USB devices into.

What lies in the future for hardware MP3 devices? For some, internal hard drives—the direction in which portable players such as the eGo are moving. For most, Firewire connections will provide savagely fast download speeds. Firewire—or IE1394, if you go for the technical number, or iLink, if you have a Sony machine—looks to be the wave of the future, offering bandwidth almost enough to meet the dreams of Croesus.

Also in the near future is USB 2, which promises far higher speeds than the 12Mbps of current USB devices. USB 2 will provide either 400Mbps or 800Mbps, depending on whom you listen to, and will be *totally free* of all the problems that have dogged the first generation of USB.

Will USB beat out Firewire for dominance of the next generation of local-machine connectivity, or will Firewire manage an end-around and take the prize? The contest will be academically interesting, but as a consumer, you don't have too much to worry at this point about the result of this battle. If you're one of the minority who now has Firewire available, you'll probably want to use it—at least until USB 2 makes its presence felt. And if you don't have Firewire, make the most of USB—it's your best bet.

Internet Connection: As Fast As Possible

Last, you'll want an Internet connection in order to be able to download MP3 files—and possibly to publish your own MP3 files as well.

Many books have been written about how and why to get on the Internet, so you probably know the basics. We'll confine ourselves to the key points:

▶ If cable modem access is available where you live, go for it. Cable provides the fastest affordable residential access—up to several megabits (millions of bits) a second—with some drawbacks, such as upload speed caps and some security concerns that you can deal with.

▶ If digital subscriber line (DSL) access is available and affordable where you live, get that. DSL typically offers between 384Kbps and 1.5Mbps downstream (to the consumer) and slower upstream (to the ISP) speeds. At this writing, the Baby Bells are vying with the cable companies for high-speed customers, so the cost of DSL is reasonable—from $35 to $50 a month for good service, including an account with their ISP.

▶ If you can't get cable or a DSL, try for ISDN (Integrated Services Digital Network)—a digital line that's not as fast as a DSL but is more widely available, especially for people outside major metropolitan areas. ISDN's *basic rate interface,* or *BRI,* provides two bearer channels that deliver 64Kbps each, plus a 16Kbps signaling channel, so it delivers decent speeds when both bearer channels are open. Check the prices before you order ISDN: it's traditionally been a business service, and it can be expensive (can you say *per-minute charges?*).

▶ If you're too rural to get ISDN, or if ISDN is too slow for you, consider one of the satellite solutions available, such as DirecPC. Satellite solutions have one major drawback: the satellite provides only downlink capabilities, so you have to use your phone line to send data to your ISP to tell them which information to deliver by satellite. But given that your only alternative is likely to be a modem connection, you may find this flaw quite sufferable. DirecPC currently offers plans starting at $19.99 a month for a truly miserable number of hours; make sure the plan you choose provides enough hours each month that you don't start incurring expensive extra hour charges.

▶ If you're stuck with modem access, try to get 56Kbps modem access—the fastest possible. Consider getting a *dual-line modem* (also known as a *shotgun modem*) that bonds together two conventional modems (on two separate phone lines) to increase your speed. You need an ISP that supports modem bonding for this to succeed—and two phone lines, of course.

▶ Whatever speed modem you have, make sure you're getting maximum performance out of it. Use a utility such as TweakDUN (DUN is the acronym for *dial-up networking*) or MTU Speed Pro (MTU is the abbreviation for *maximum transfer unit*). Both TweakDUN and MTU Speed Pro tune your TCP/IP settings to make sure that your connection is as efficient as possible. TweakDUN and MTU Speed are shareware and are available from many shareware archives. They're not infallible, but they're worth a try.

▶ If your connection is less speedy than you'd like, get a download-scheduling utility such as GetRight from Headlight Software

(http://www.getright.com) or AutoFTP from PrimaSoft
(http://www.primasoft.com) that will let you line up your
downloads to perform at a time when you don't need to do other
things on your computer. For example, you can arrange to download a hundred megs of music at an antisocial hour in the early
morning, when your corner of the Internet is likely to be less busy.

Get the Right Software

To record and play MP3 files, you need two types of applications: a *ripper*
to record MP3 files from existing sound sources, and a *player* to play them
back. As you'll see, some applications combine rippers and players.

To organize your collection of MP3 files, you may want some form of
jukebox software that enables you to catalog the tracks, arrange them by
category, and so on. Some applications combine a jukebox with a ripper.

Some of the main MP3 players have add-on features, including plug-
ins that create special audio and visual effects and *skins* (not drums but
alternative graphical interfaces for the player) that change the player's
appearance.

Go to Jail for Distributing MP3 Files

You need to read this section. It could save your ass. We'll keep it brief.

There's a lot of confusion about what's legal and what's illegal when creating, playing, and distributing MP3 files. The truth is really simple, but
you need to know what you're doing before you start creating and distributing MP3 files.

There's nothing inherently legal or illegal in MP3. It's just a file format
for compressed audio. MP3 is an ISO (International Organization for Standardization) standard, so it's not controlled by any one company in the
way Microsoft controls, say, the Word document file format.

For an MP3 file to be distributed legally, the copyright holder for the
music or other material in question needs to have granted permission for
the music or material to be downloaded or played. The copyright holder
might be the artist, their record company, or a distributor.

The Politically Correct Version

If you're downloading MP3 files from the Internet, make sure that the files you're downloading are being distributed legally.

Sites such as Riffage.com, MP3.com, and EMusic.com post only MP3 files that they have permission to distribute. Other sites, including many of those that blast you with porn banners and most all those that use the words "pirate" and "warez," are (how shall we put this?) less discriminating about the provenance of the files they make available for download.

The only way you'll be able to tell if a file is legal or not is from the source supplying it. You'll find plenty of files that look like someone has ripped them illegally but that are fully legal though incompetently labeled and delivered. (Some of the worst perpetrators of badly labeled MP3 files are the garage bands who stand to benefit most immediately from MP3.)

Most people agree that you can rip MP3 copies of music (or other material) for your personal use. That's legal, much the same way recording a CD onto a cassette tape for personal use is legal. What's not legal is distributing MP3 files that you make from your CD collection, records, or whatever—or selling MP3 files created from such sources. In other words, you can't distribute or sell MP3 files without the explicit written permission of the copyright holder.

That's the theory—the politically correct version. But we'd be doing you a disservice—read: *lying*—if we pretended that legal MP3 distribution is the only thing that's going on in the real world.

The Politically Incorrect Version

So what's *really* happening? *Weeeelll*, some people are ripping everything in sight to MP3 tracks, permission or no (that'd be mostly no), and either posting them to pirate MP3 sites on the Web for the world to download or just sharing them on-the-fly via Napster. Other people are chopping MP3 files up into manageable segments that can be sewn together again easily and posting them to MP3 newsgroups on the Internet for the world to download. Other people are e-mailing MP3 files directly to one another, much to the distress of their ISPs and of AOL, whose servers don't appreciate 5MB files piling through like semis hogging the carpool lane of the New Jersey turnpike.

So—where do *you* come into this? Are you a decent, moral, upstanding citizen, or are you going to be bending the copyright laws into a pretzel the moment you pick up your mouse?

Don't answer that—but know that the penalties for copyright infringement are savage. Under the No Electronic Theft Act (NET Act for short—a nice acronym) passed in 1997, you're committing a felony when you infringe a copyright by creating or distributing unauthorized copies of copyrighted work, *even if you're not doing it for commercial advantage or private financial gain*. The penalties include up to three years in jail for the first offense and six for the second—and fines, of course.

If you *are* infringing a copyright for commercial advantage or private financial gain, the penalties include up to five years in jail for the first offense. The definition of financial gain includes your receiving anything "of value" in return, specifically other copyrighted works. So trading or swapping MP3 files is not a good idea from a legal point of view.

If you're feeling cynical, the copyright laws are a bit like the speeding laws. The highway patrol tends to tolerate most people cruising a few miles per hour above the speed limit, only pulling over vehicles that blow past them at grossly illegal speeds, weave, or whose drivers flip them the bird. They're also only looking at a tiny minority of cars on the road at any given time.

Similarly, the forces of the law seem seldom to bother swinging the heavy hammer of copyright infringement law at relatively discreet individuals. In practical terms, the copyright police expend most of their effort on the gross violators, shutting down as soon as they can such pirate MP3 sites as they find. But Jane and Joe Sixpack with their 40GB hard drive stuffed with MP3 files, some legal and some perhaps not, are unlikely to find the feds busting down their front door. (Still, it could happen.)

Morally, the situation is clear: ripping off music is theft, and you know the seventh commandment (yeah, the one about not stealing). But because morality bends with the wind these days (ask Linda Tripp), you may be motivated more by practical concerns than morality.

The reason you shouldn't steal too much music is that if everyone steals music, nobody will be able to make a living creating it. All the artists (debate the word if you must) will be reduced to assembling Grande Meals and Big Macs for a living, and your only sources of music will be advertising jingles and such recycled '90s riffs as you can cobble together yourself.

Frightened enough to abide by most of the laws? Okay, good. Let's play some music.

PLAYING MUSIC WITH WINAMP

In this section, we'll show you how to use Winamp, one of the most popular and versatile MP3 players for Windows.

At this writing, Winamp is freeware and even comes distributed with recent versions of Netscape Navigator, so you shouldn't have any trouble getting hold of it.

Get and Install Winamp

To get Winamp, visit www.winamp.com and download the latest version. To install Winamp, follow these steps:

1. Double-click the Winamp distribution file. This is an executable file, so double-clicking it runs it. You'll see the Winamp Setup: License Agreement dialog box.

2. Read the license and click the Next button if you can handle the terms. You'll see the Winamp Setup: Installation Options dialog box, shown below:

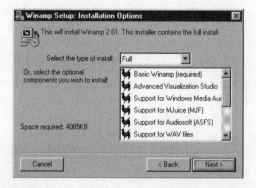

3. In the Select The Type Of Install drop-down list, choose Full, Lite, Minimal, or Custom to select a predefined package of the options shown in the list box:

   ▶ Full selects all options. We recommend this option unless you're severely short of disk space (at this writing, the full package takes a little less than 4MB), sure you won't want advanced visualizations, or are prejudiced against certain sound formats.

- ▶ Minimal selects only the Basic Winamp option.

- ▶ Lite adds to Basic Winamp support for the key music file types.

- ▶ Custom lets you select whatever you want by clicking its entry in the list box. When you select an item, the llama to its left turns from gray to black and dons a check mark.

TIP

You can also choose a custom setup by selecting and clearing llamas as you see fit—the Select The Type Of Install drop-down list will select Custom automatically when you select any group of options other than Minimal, Lite, or Full.

Select your install option, and click Next to proceed. Setup will display the Winamp Setup: Installation Directory dialog box.

4. If you don't like the directory that Winamp has chosen to install itself into, select a different directory. You can either type the directory's name into the text box or click the Browse button and use the resulting Select Install Directory dialog box to navigate to and select the folder you want to use. Click Next when you're ready to proceed.

5. Winamp will go ahead and install itself in the specified directory. You'll then see the Winamp Setup: Settings dialog box, shown below:

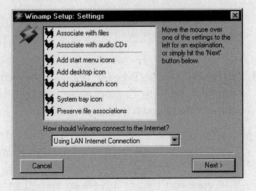

Here's what the items in this dialog box do. (If you've got a later version of Winamp, there may be additional features.) Again, select and clear the llamas as you see fit, and then click Next.

Associate With Files   Selecting this check box makes Winamp the default audio player for all files in formats that Winamp considers to be audio. This list of formats includes mp3 (of course) and most audio file formats. If you prefer to play some forms of audio through a different player, you can deselect them later. Alternatively, you can specify Winamp as the default audio player for specific formats after installation.

Associate With Audio CDs   Selecting this check box causes Winamp to spring to life when you insert an audio CD into your computer's CD drive. If you don't like autoplay, clear this check box. Note that this setting does not change the Auto Insert Notification setting on your PC. If Auto Insert Notification is off (in the CD drive's Properties dialog box), Winamp will not automatically play CDs even if you select the Autoplay Audio CDs option.

Add Start Menu Icons   Selecting this check box adds a Winamp group to the Start menu. Unless you prefer to have a Winamp icon on the Desktop or the Quick Launch bar and nowhere else, keep this check box selected.

Add Desktop Icon   Selecting this check box adds a Winamp icon to the desktop. Having the icon there is often handy.

Add Quicklaunch Icon   This option is available only if your computer is running Windows 98/98 SE or Internet Explorer 4 or 5. Because the Quick Launch bar is always accessible, it's usually the quickest way to get to Winamp.

System Tray Icon   This option adds a Winamp icon to the system tray so that you can quickly access Winamp and its bookmarks.

How Should Winamp Connect To The Internet drop-down list   This drop-down list lets you choose the way that Winamp will use the Internet. If the computer you're using doesn't have an Internet connection, or you don't want to use Winamp's Internet features, choose No Internet Connection Available. If your computer has a modem connection, choose Using Dial-Up Modem Internet Connection. If your computer connects to the Internet through a network (for example, a company's local area network or a home network, or a cable modem or DSL), choose Using LAN Internet Connection.

6. Winamp will install the icons and groups you chose and will display the Winamp Setup: User Information dialog box. Enter information here if you want to—there's no obligation.

> **Never Ask Me Again**   Select this check box if you don't want to be invited to register again.

> **Please Send Me Winamp Announcements**   Select this check box if you want Winamp announcements mailed to you. You may find it easier to visit the Winamp Web site periodically at your convenience to scan for new information rather than having it pushed out to you.

> **Allow Winamp To Report Simple, Anonymous Usage Statistics**   If you don't want Winamp to send back to Winamp.com anonymous statistics on how much you're using Winamp, clear this check box.

> If you fill in the user information, click the Next button to send it. Winamp will connect to the Internet using the connection you specified in the previous dialog box and will send the information to Nullsoft Winamp. If you don't fill in the user information, click the Later button.

7. You'll then see the Winamp Setup: Winamp Successfully Installed dialog box. Click the Run Winamp button to run Winamp.

Use the Winamp Interface

In this section, we'll examine the Winamp interface. If you're feeling impatient and have some MP3 files already, click the Open button, select a track or three, and listen to some tunes while you're playing with the interface.

Exploring the Winamp Windows

The illustration below shows Winamp's basic look. As you can see, it consists of four windows: the Main window, the Graphical Equalizer window, the Playlist Editor window, and the Browser window. Here's a brief overview of each window:

Main window   This window displays information about the track that's currently playing and provides CD-player–style controls. The Main window also provides quick access to the Playlist Editor window and the Graphical Equalizer window.

Graphical Equalizer window   This window provides a software graphical equalizer that you can use to tweak the sound that Winamp produces.

Playlist Editor window   This window contains the current playlist, buttons for creating and manipulating playlists, and a minimal set of play controls (so that you can dispense with the Main window if you want).

Browser window   This window provides a quick way of inputting information into your main Browser window for searching Amazon.com for music by the current artist. Whether you find the Browser window useful depends on your interests. We tend to find it annoying and recommend turning it off straightaway.

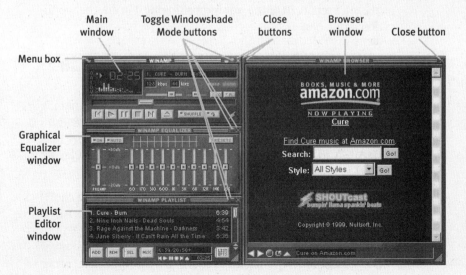

Arranging the Winamp Windows

Here's what you need to know about arranging the Winamp windows on screen. You can do the following:

▶ Close any Winamp window by clicking its Close button—the X button in its upper-right corner. Clicking the Close button on the Main window closes Winamp.

▶ Rearrange the Winamp windows any way you want by clicking the title bar of a window and dragging it to where you want it to appear.

▶ Move each Winamp window independently. When you move the edge of one of the satellite windows so that it touches any edge of the Main window, the satellite window sticks to the Main window. When you then move the Main window, any windows stuck to it will move along with it.

▶ Minimize all displayed Winamp windows by clicking the Minimize button on the Main window.

▶ Reduce any of the windows, except the Browser window, to a windowshade strip by clicking its Toggle Windowshade Mode button. In Windowshade mode (shown below), Winamp takes up very little space and provides only key information and controls. You can keep Winamp on top of other applications (as described next) and keep it out of the way by positioning it in another application's title bar.

▶ Keep Winamp on top of all other running applications so that it's always at hand. Press Ctrl+A to toggle the Always On Top feature for all Winamp windows except the Playlist Editor. Press Ctrl+Alt+A to toggle the Always On Top feature for the Playlist Editor.

▶ Toggle the display of the Winamp windows with keyboard short-cuts: press Alt+W to toggle the main Winamp window; press Alt+E to toggle the Playlist Editor window; press Alt+G to toggle the Graphical Equalizer window; and press Alt+T to toggle the Browser window. Alternatively, click the menu box in the upper-left corner of the Main window and select the entry for the window from the menu to toggle it on and off, as shown below:

NOTE

When you've hidden all the Winamp windows, make sure that the Winamp item is selected in the Taskbar when you try to restore a Winamp window by using the keyboard shortcut. If another application is selected, you can press these keyboard shortcuts all you want, but Winamp won't react. You may find it easier to right-click the Winamp item in the Taskbar, select the Winamp Menu item from the shortcut menu, and choose the window you want to restore from the submenu that appears.

▶ Display Winamp at double size by pressing Ctrl+D to make it easier to see what you're doing. When you need to reclaim your screen real estate, press Ctrl+D again to restore Winamp to its usual discreet size.

To exit Winamp, click the Control menu on the Main window (or press Alt+F), and choose Exit from the menu. Alternatively, click the Close button on the Main window.

TIP

If you chose during installation to add the Winamp icon to your system tray, you can also control Winamp from there when it's minimized. For example, right-click the system tray icon and choose Exit from the shortcut menu to close Winamp.

Play Tracks and SHOUTcast Streams with the Winamp Main Window

The Main window is dead easy to operate with the mouse, but it has many keyboard access features that you'll want to know as well. The illustration below shows the components of the Main window.

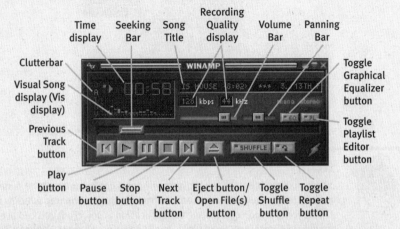

To open one or more tracks, click the Open File(s) button to display the Open File(s) dialog box. Navigate to the track or tracks you want, and select them. To select a contiguous list of tracks, click the first track; then hold down Shift, and click the last track. To select multiple individual tracks or to add them to a Shift-click–selected list, hold down Ctrl and click each track in succession. Click the Open button to open the files in Winamp. Winamp will add them to the current playlist and will start playing the first track. Usually Winamp decides that the last track you selected is the first track, so you may want to try selecting the tracks in reverse order.

Most of the buttons and displays in the Main window are easy to recognize because they look like those on a CD player or a cassette player. You click the Play button to play the current track, the Stop button to stop play, and so on. But you should know about a couple of mouse techniques for the Main window:

- ▶ Click the time in the Time display to toggle between time elapsed and time remaining on the track.

- ▶ Click the Visual Song display (the Vis display) to switch between visualization modes.

▶ Click the letters in the Clutterbar at the left side of the Time display window to perform common maneuvers. O displays the
Options menu; I displays the File Info dialog box; A toggles the
Always On Top feature; D toggles the double-size feature; and V
displays the Visualization menu, which contains options for the
visualization feature below the Time display.

▶ Right-click the Song Title to display a shortcut menu for moving
around the current track and current playlist. (More on these in
a moment.)

▶ Click the lightning-flash logo in the lower-right corner to display
the About Winamp dialog box.

As well as listening to music you've downloaded, you can play music
straight off the Web with Winamp—either MP3 files from a server or a
SHOUTcast server stream. *SHOUTcast* is streaming software created by
Nullsoft (the makers of Winamp) that allows you to broadcast music over
the Web.

To play music straight off the Web, follow these steps:

1. Press Ctrl+L, or choose Play Location from the main menu to
   display the Open Location dialog box, as shown here:

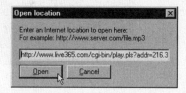

2. Enter the URL of a file or of a SHOUTcast stream.

3. Click the Open button. Winamp will start playing the file or
   the stream.

You can also add Web tracks or SHOUTcast streams to the Playlist Editor as follows:

1. Display the Playlist Editor if it's not already displayed.

2. Click the Add button to display the menu of buttons, and
   then choose the Add URL button to display the Open Location dialog box.

3. Enter the URL of a file or of a SHOUTcast stream.

4.   Click the Open button. Winamp will add the file or stream to the playlist. You can then play the file or stream by using the Winamp controls as usual.

NOTE
You won't always need to use this technique to play music directly off the Web because sites such as MP3.com include links that automatically start your MP3 player or browser plug-in playing the track.

Create and Use Winamp Playlists

Like most MP3 players, Winamp lets you build playlists—lists of tracks in the order in which you want to play them.

To work with playlists, you use the Playlist Editor. To display the Playlist Editor, click the Toggle Playlist Editor button in the Main window, or press Alt+E. The illustration below shows the Playlist Editor with a playlist loaded in it.

NOTE
Because you can control play by using the controls in the Playlist Editor, you may want to close the Main window to save space on screen. To toggle the Main window on and off, press Alt+W.

Creating a Playlist

To create a playlist, add tracks to it and arrange them in the order you want. You can add tracks to the playlist in several ways:

▶ Drag tracks from an Explorer window to the Playlist Editor.

▶ Double-click the Add button in the Playlist Editor to display the Add File(s) To Playlist dialog box, select the tracks, and click the Open button. (The first click of the Add button displays the menu of buttons, and the second selects the Add File button, which appears in place of the Add button—but you can perform the action as a double-click.)

▶ To add a whole directory to the playlist, click the Add button to display the menu of buttons, and then choose the Add Dir button. Winamp will display the Open Directory dialog box shown below. Navigate to and select the directory you want to add. If you want to add all the subdirectories under the directory you're selecting, make sure the Recurse Subdirectories check box is selected; if you don't, make sure it's cleared. Then click the OK button.

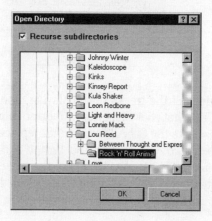

NOTE

To play a track more than once in a playlist, add two or more instances of it to the playlist.

Arranging and Sorting a Playlist

You can then rearrange or remove the tracks as follows:

▶ To remove a track from the playlist, select it and press the Delete key or click the Rem button. (The first click displays the button menu, and the second selects the Rem Sel button—Remove Selection—that replaces the Rem button.)

▶ To rearrange the tracks in the playlist easily, select tracks with the mouse and drag them up or down to where you want it or them to appear.

▶ To sort the playlist, click the Misc button, and choose Sort List from the menu of buttons, as shown below. You can sort a list by title, by filename, or by path and filename. You can also reverse the current order of the playlist—which can be good for variety—or randomize the playlist to produce something unexpected. There's nothing quite like the mind-jarring juxtaposition of Bach and Nine Inch Nails.

▶ To select all the tracks in the playlist, double-click the Sel button. (The first click displays the menu of buttons, and the second click selects the Sel All button that replaces the Sel button.) To deselect all tracks, click the Sel button and choose Sel Zero from the menu of buttons. To invert the selection (deselecting all selected tracks and selecting all unselected tracks), click the Sel button, and choose Inv Sel from the menu of buttons.

Saving a Playlist

To save a playlist, click the List Opts button, and choose Save List from the menu of buttons. Winamp will display the Save Playlist dialog box. Enter a name for the playlist—**Full Metal Morning**, **Dance into Bed**, whatever—and specify a different location if necessary. Then click the Save button to save the list. The default file format is M3U Playlist, but you can choose PLS Playlist in the Save As Type drop-down list if you want to save your playlists in the PLS format.

Opening a Saved Playlist

To open a playlist you've previously saved, double-click the List Opts button to display the Load Playlist dialog box. (The first click will display the menu of buttons, and the second will select the Load List button that replaces the List Opts button.) Navigate to the playlist, select it, and click the Open button.

Tips for Working with Playlists

Here's how to get around the current track and playlist quickly:

▶ To jump to a specific time in the track that is currently playing, press Ctrl+J, or right-click the Song Title display and choose Jump To Time from the shortcut menu to display the Jump To Time dialog box. Enter the time to which to jump in the Jump To text box in *minutes:seconds* format (for example, **2:15**), and click the Jump button. This is the precise way to skip lame intros.

▶ To move less precisely through a track, drag the Seeking Bar to the left or right.

▶ To jump to another track in the current playlist, press J, or right-click the Song Title display and choose Jump To File from the shortcut menu to display the Jump To File dialog box (shown below). The Jump To File dialog box lists the tracks in alphabetic order. Double-click the track to which you want to jump. To search for text in a track's name, you can enter the letters in the Search For Text text box. As you type, Winamp will reduce the list to tracks that have that sequence of letters in the title.

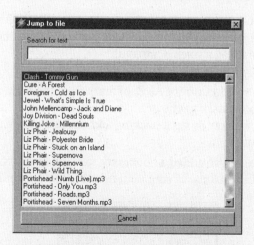

▶ You can also navigate the playlist by using the Playback submenu on the main Winamp menu (accessed by clicking the menu box in the upper-left corner of the Main window). This submenu offers navigation items including Stop W/ Fadeout, Back 5 Seconds, Fwd 5 Seconds, Start Of List, 10 Tracks Back, and 10 Tracks Fwd.

▶ You can control play by using the keyboard shortcuts listed below. These shortcuts aren't mnemonically obvious (though you can certainly make up some innovative mnemonics for them), but you'll notice that they're all on the bottom-left row of the keyboard, just where you can reach them most easily when you're lying wasted on the floor. (That's assuming you're using the QWERTY keyboard layout—if you're using a Dvorak keyboard layout, you'll need to get up off the floor to use the shortcuts.)

Keyboard Shortcut	Action
Z	Previous track
X	Play
C	Pause
V	Stop
B	Next

Use Winamp Bookmarks to Access Tracks Quickly

To enable you to quickly access a track or a SHOUTcast stream in your current playlist, Winamp provides *bookmarks*, virtual markers that you can use to tag a track or stream.

To bookmark the current track or stream, press Alt+I, or choose Bookmarks ➤ Add Current As Bookmark from the main menu. You can also add a bookmark to one or more selected tracks or streams in the Playlist Editor window by right-clicking and choosing Bookmark Item(s) from the shortcut menu.

Once you've added a bookmark, you can go to it by choosing its name from the Bookmarks submenu from the main menu, as shown below:

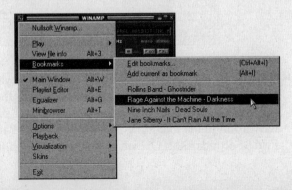

To edit a bookmark, press Ctrl+Alt+I with the Main window active, or choose Bookmarks ➤ Edit Bookmarks from the main menu. Winamp will display the Winamp Preferences dialog box with the Bookmarks page displayed, as shown below:

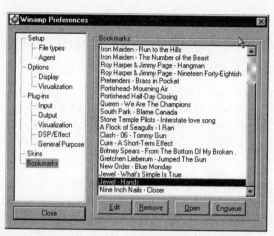

Select the bookmark you want to affect in the Bookmarks list box, and then take one of the following actions:

► Click the Edit button to display the Edit Bookmark dialog box, shown below. Change either the title of the bookmark or the file to which it refers, and then click the OK button to close the dialog box and apply the change.

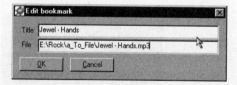

► Click the Remove button to remove the bookmark. Winamp doesn't ask you to confirm the deletion, so make sure you have the right bookmark selected before clicking the button.

► Click the Open button to open the bookmarked track in Winamp and start playing it.

► Click the Enqueue button to add the bookmarked track to your current playlist.

TIP

To go quickly to a bookmark, right-click the Winamp icon in the system tray, and then choose the bookmark from the Bookmarks shortcut menu.

Make Music Sound Good with the Winamp Graphical Equalizer

Winamp provides a full-featured graphical equalizer for adjusting the balance of the music. The graphical equalizer lets you increase or decrease ten different frequencies in the sound spectrum to boost the parts of the music you want to hear more of and reduce those you don't.

Graphical Equalizer Basics

To display the Graphical Equalizer window (shown below), click the Toggle Graphical Equalizer button in the Main window or press Alt+G. The frequencies are measured in hertz (Hz) and kilohertz (kHz)—the number of cycles per second. As you can see, the left end of the graphical equalizer controls the lower frequencies—from 60Hz booms and rumbles upward—and the right end controls the higher frequencies—up to 16kHz. You can increase or decrease each frequency up to 20 decibels (dB), enough to make a huge difference in the sound. (For example, boost all the bass frequencies and crank up Hole to knock all the ice off your bedroom window on snowy winter mornings.)

First, make sure the graphical equalizer is on. (It's off by default.) Click the On button to toggle the graphical equalizer on and off. When it's on, the On button will display a bright green light; when it's off, the light is a darker green. Guess it's lucky the Winamp guys didn't design traffic signals.

The PreAmp slider on the left side of the Graphical Equalizer window raises or lowers the preamplification of the graphical equalizer all at once. Usually you won't need to mess with the PreAmp slider because you can control the Winamp volume output through the Main window, through the Windows Volume Control (usually in the Taskbar's tray), or through the volume control on your amplifier or speakers. If you do adjust the Pre-Amp level, don't set it too high because that will distort the sound.

To adjust the sound, drag the sliders up and down. Winamp takes a second or two to implement the changes, so be patient. You'll notice that the equalizer display at the top of the Graphical Equalizer window changes shape to match the slider settings, as shown below with settings you might try for playing rap in a '65 Impala. This display helps you see when you've got a setting out of whack with the others.

Keep in mind that the graphical equalizer works with (or in some cases against) your sound card and your speakers. If your speakers are tinny and deliver too much treble, you can reduce the high frequencies on the graphical equalizer to help balance the music. And if your speakers are bass heavy, you can use the graphical equalizer to minimize the bass late at night when the folks next door start complaining—or crank it up if they tick you off.

NOTE

Don't expect the graphical equalizer to act as a panacea for a poor stereo system. If your audio hardware sucks, clever use of the graphical equalizer may make it suck less. But it won't make it sound like a $5000 Bang & Olufsen system.

Saving and Loading Preset Equalizations

The graphical equalizer's killer feature is its ability to save and auto-load preset equalizations. This means that you can create a custom equalization profile for any particular track and have Winamp automatically use it each time you play the track.

To create an auto-load preset equalization for a track, play the track and set the graphical equalizer sliders appropriately. Then click the Presets button to display its menu, highlight the Save menu to display its submenu, and choose Auto-Load Preset to display the Save Auto-Load Preset dialog box (shown next). The dialog box will suggest the title of the song as the name for the equalization; edit the name if necessary, and click the Save button to save the preset.

Then enable the auto-load presets by clicking the Auto button in the Graphical Equalizer window so that it displays a light-green light. (It's off by default.) From here on, Winamp will use your customized equalization whenever you play the track.

NOTE

When auto-load preset equalizations are enabled and Winamp finishes playing a track with a preset equalization, it will continue to use that equalization for the following track if that track does not have its own equalization.

Winamp comes with preset equalizations that you can load at will by clicking the Presets button, highlighting Load to display its submenu, and choosing Preset to display the Load EQ Preset dialog box, as shown here:

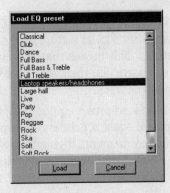

Select the equalization you want from the list box. Wait a couple of seconds and see how it sounds. To apply it, click the Load button. For example, you might select the Large Hall equalization to make Winamp sound as if it's playing in a large hall. Winamp's preset equalizations are well put together and demonstrate how different a graphical equalizer can make music sound. When you look at the slider positions for some of the equalizations, you may expect minimal changes in the sound—but your ears will tell you otherwise.

To add to the list of preset equalizations, set the sliders for the equalization, click the Presets button, and choose Save ➤ Preset to display the Save EQ Preset dialog box. Enter the name for the new preset, and click the Save button.

To delete a preset, click the Presets button, and choose Delete ➤ Preset or Delete ➤ Auto-Load Preset to display the Delete Preset dialog box or Delete Auto-Load Preset dialog box. Select the preset, and click the Delete button to delete it.

Check and Set Track Information with Winamp

Winamp lets you quickly view and change the track information, called *tag information*, that each MP3 file can store.

In the Playlist Editor, right-click a track, and choose File Info from the shortcut menu to display the MPEG File Info Box + ID3 Tag Editor dialog box (shown below) with the information for the track. (From the Main window, you can display this dialog box by double-clicking the track title.) Change the information as appropriate, and then click the Save button to save it to the MP3 file. You can also click the Remove ID3 button to remove the tag information from the MP3 file.

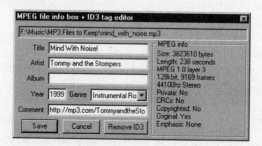

RIPPING AND PLAYING WITH MUSICMATCH JUKEBOX

In this section, we'll show you how to use MusicMatch Jukebox, one of the most popular ripper-jukeboxes. MusicMatch Jukebox offers a Standard version that you can download for free, but it is limited to recording at 96kbps (kilobits per second) or below—sampling rates that most people find unacceptable for sustained music listening. (It's a bit like listening to AM radio when you're used to FM.) MusicMatch is betting that, after listening to low-quality audio for a short while, you'll be prepared to register and cough up $29.99 for the full version of MusicMatch Jukebox that can record at 128kbps (the standard for "CD-quality" MP3 files) and higher speeds to make music sound good again.

Before we get started on MusicMatch Jukebox's features, we'll quickly discuss how to choose the right sampling rate for the MP3 files you'll create.

Choose the Right Sampling Rate

Minor alert: This section gets mildly technical. But as with the legal stuff earlier in this book, this is information you need to know—and we'll keep it short.

As we discussed earlier in this chapter, MP3 rocks because it compresses audio into a small file *and* it retains near-CD quality. To compress the audio, it uses sampling.

Before you start recording MP3 files, you need to set the sampling rate you'll use. To put it simply, the higher the sampling rate (within reason), the better the music will sound, and the larger the file size will be.

For example, a ripper such as MusicMatch Jukebox offers preset sampling rates of 64kbps, 96kbps, 128kbps, and 160kbps, together with custom sampling rates that you can choose for yourself. A rate of 64kbps is somewhat euphemistically termed "FM Radio Quality" (we reckon it's much worse), 96kbps is described as "near CD quality" (we'd say it's not within easy commuting distance of CD quality), and 128kbps and 160kbps are described as "CD quality" (which is almost true). Most people find music sampled at a rate below 128kbps to be unacceptable to listen to, but for spoken audio this high-capacity option is a good choice.

When recording music, you'll usually do best to use a sampling rate of 128kpbs. Using a higher sampling rate generally produces little improvement in sound quality, and the file sizes will of course be larger. Some people swear by 160kbps, and others by 192kbps, so try them yourself and see which suits you the best.

If you want to cram as much music as possible onto a device and are prepared to settle for poorer sound quality, then experiment with lower bit rates, and establish what you find tolerable for listening. But if you're looking to digitize any serious chunk of your music collection, be sure to do it at a sampling rate high enough that you'll enjoy the music for years rather than weeks.

Keep in mind that you won't be able to increase the sampling rate of any tracks you've already recorded. Though with certain specialized programs, you can decrease the sampling rate if you really want to do so.

NOTE

It doesn't take any more time to rip tracks at a higher sampling rate than at a lower sampling rate. (In fact, with most ripping programs, ripping at a higher sampling rate takes less time because it requires less compression and less processing power.)

Get, Install, and Configure MusicMatch Jukebox

To install MusicMatch Jukebox, double-click the distribution file. Install-Shield will walk you through a standard installation routine in which you accept a license agreement, are encouraged to register the software, and specify an installation folder, music folder, and Start menu group. We'll mention just the highlights here and leave you to handle the routine decisions.

The first thing to note is the Software Registration dialog box, in which you have to enter at least one character in the Name text box, the Email text box, and the Postal Code text box in order to enable the Next button, which is disabled by default. These entries are unavoidable, though they don't have to be honest; but think twice before you leave the Notify Me Of Software Upgrades check box selected, as it is by default.

Next, you get the Personalize Net Music dialog box, which invites you to let MusicMatch Jukebox upload to a MusicMatch server information on the music you listen to, save, and download. MusicMatch uses this information to deliver personalized recommendations to you, and assures you that "your personal music preferences... will never be sold or shared"—but the idea of MusicMatch Jukebox automatically uploading information about our listening habits creeps us out too much for us to recommend using this feature. However, your mileage will vary, so select the Yes (Recommended) option button rather than the No option button if you like. The option buttons are implemented a little strangely, and to access the No button via the keyboard, you'll need to press one of the arrow keys (for example, →) rather than the Tab key.

After you choose the destination location, your music folder, the program folder, and whether you want MusicMatch Jukebox icons on your Desktop, on your Quick Launch toolbar, and in your system tray, you get to a more serious decision in the Filetype Registration dialog box (shown below): for which file types do you want to use MusicMatch Jukebox?

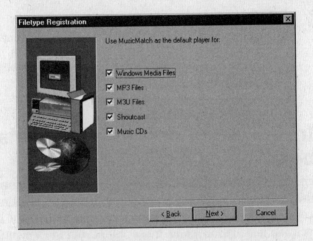

If you're using another MP3 player (such as Winamp, Sonique, or XingMP3 Player), you'll probably want to clear some or all of these check boxes. If you'll be using MusicMatch Jukebox primarily or exclusively, leave them selected.

If you do choose to make MusicMatch Jukebox your default MP3 player, it will monitor your file associations aggressively, even when you're not running it, to see if any have been stolen by another application. (Typically, this will happen when you install another MP3 player or jukebox after installing MusicMatch Jukebox; it may also happen when you run another player or jukebox that reclaims file associations it finds MusicMatch Jukebox has stolen.) If MusicMatch Jukebox detects that it no longer has its associations, it will display the MusicMatch Jukebox File Associations dialog box shown next.

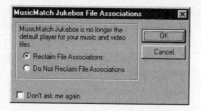

To restore the associations, leave the Reclaim File Associations option button selected (it's selected by default), and click the OK button. To leave the file associations with whichever application has stolen them, select the Do Not Reclaim File Associations option button, and click the OK button. You can prevent MusicMatch Jukebox from bugging you about this by selecting the Don't Ask Me Again check box before closing the MusicMatch Jukebox File Associations dialog box.

Once you're done with the file types, MusicMatch Jukebox will complete the installation and will display the Setup Complete dialog box. Click the Finish button to close this dialog box. You're just about ready to rock. Double-click the MusicMatch Jukebox icon on your Desktop or in your system tray, or click the icon on your Quick Launch toolbar, to get going.

The first time you run it, MusicMatch Jukebox will display the Search For Music dialog box, shown below. In the Look In drop-down list, select the drive or drives you want MusicMatch Jukebox to search. To limit the search to a particular folder, click the Browse button to display the Browse For Folder dialog box, navigate to and select the drive, and click the OK button.

MusicMatch Jukebox will automatically enter the appropriate drive in the Look In drop-down list. Make sure the Windows Media Files check box and the MP2/MP3 Files check box are selected or cleared as suits you, and then click the OK button. MusicMatch Jukebox will search for music and will display the Adding Songs To Music Library dialog box, shown below, until it has finished adding all the songs to its music database.

Next, you may see the Confirm Association dialog box, shown below, in which MusicMatch Jukebox is trying to grab some unspecified file associations from another application. You probably want to choose the Yes button in this dialog box, though it's tedious not to know which file associations MusicMatch Jukebox is after.

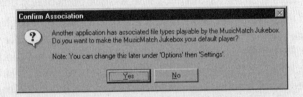

Finally, you'll be ready to start using MusicMatch Jukebox. The following images show the Main window and the Music Library window. You'll probably be seeing them joined together, but we've pulled them apart so that we could label them better. You'll also be seeing the Recorder window, which we'll show you how to use in a few pages' time, and a Welcome Tips window, which we'll let you explore on your own.

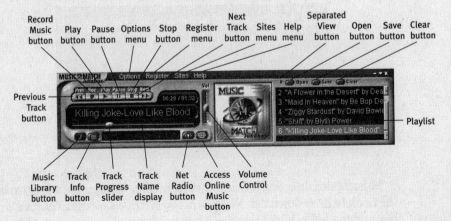

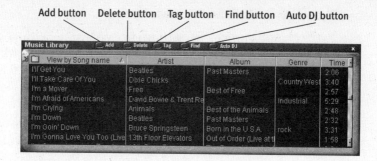

Add button   Delete button   Tag button   Find button   Auto DJ button

The MusicMatch Jukebox windows are easy to handle:

▶ You can drag the windows around as you want.

▶ You can click the Separated View button on the Main window to separate the Playlist window (on the right side of the Main window shown on the facing page) from the Main window. Click the resulting Integrated View button on the Playlist window to reunite the two.

▶ To make the Music Library window move with the Main window, drag the Music Library window so that one of its sides sticks to a side of the Main window.

▶ You can resize the Music Library window by clicking its border and dragging.

NOTE

To register your copy of MusicMatch Jukebox, choose Register ➢ Enter Key to display the MusicMatch Enter Key dialog box. Enter the key in the Enter The Key (Include Hyphens) text box, and click the OK button.

Configuring CDDB

If your computer has an Internet connection, make sure CDDB is configured correctly. You only need to configure CDDB once, and, as you'll see, it offers compelling benefits for most people.

CDDB is an online database of CD information from which PC CD-player applications (including MP3 players that play CDs) and rippers can download CD information—the artist's name, the CD title, track titles, and even lyrics for some tracks.

To configure CDDB, follow these steps:

1. Choose Options ➤ Settings to display the Settings dialog box, and then click the CDDB Preferences tab, which is shown below:

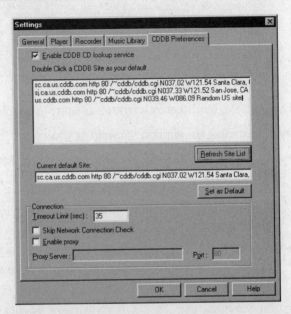

2. Make sure the Enable CDDB CD Lookup Service check box is selected. (If you don't want to use CDDB, clear this check box.)

3. Click the Refresh Site List button to get the latest CDDB sites available.

4. In the Double Click A CDDB Site As Your Default list box, double-click the CDDB site that you want to use. All other things being equal, you'll probably do best with one that's geographically close to you. But if your choice turns out to be slow or too busy, try another. Your selection will appear in the Current Default Site text box.

5. Click the Set As Default button to set the site as your default.

6. If you need to use a proxy server, select the Enable Proxy check box in the Connection group box, and enter the server's details in the Proxy Server text box and the Port text box. (Consult your network administrator for this information if you don't know it.) You can also select the Skip Network

Connection Check check box to prevent MusicMatch Jukebox from checking your network connection before contacting CDDB, and you can change the timeout limit from its default setting in the Timeout Limit text box.

7. Click the OK button to close the Settings dialog box.

Choosing the Sampling Rate

Next, choose the sampling rate to use for your recordings. Like CDDB, this is something you'll typically want to set and forget. Here's what to do:

1. Choose Options ➤ Recorder ➤ Settings to display the Recorder tab (shown below) of the Settings dialog box.

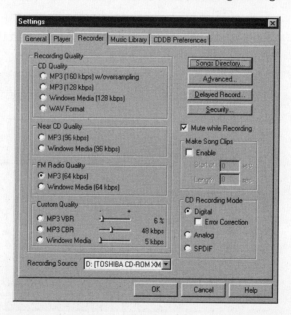

2. In the Recording Quality group box, select the sampling rate at which to record. For most music, you'll want to start with the MP3 (128kbps) setting, the default setting for the full version of MusicMatch Jukebox. (If you have the free version of MusicMatch Jukebox, you'll be able to record only at 96kbps or 64kbps.) If you find the quality not high enough, try the MP3 (160kbps) W/ Oversampling setting. For spoken audio, experiment with the MP3 (96kbps) and MP3 (64kbps) settings found in the Near CD Quality and FM Radio Quality group boxes, respectively. For special purposes,

you can use the VBR and CBR options found in the Custom Quality group box. Here's what you can do with them:

VBR   VBR stands for *variable bit rate* and lets you emphasize the quality of the audio; the amount of information recorded (the *bit rate*) varies according to the complexity of the music. Be warned that VBR can produce large files, and some MP3 players cannot play back VBR files successfully.

CBR   To squeeze even more audio into each megabyte of storage, select the CBR option button, and drag its slider to the left to reduce the bit rate. CBR stands for *constant bit rate* and is best used for reducing the size of the MP3 files you're recording.

3. In the Recording Source drop-down list, select the CD or DVD drive from which you want to record.

4. Click the Songs Directory button to display the New Songs Directory Options dialog box, as shown here:

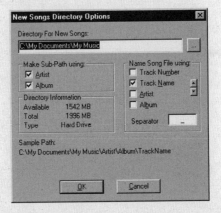

5. In the Directory For New Songs text box, enter the name of the folder in which to store the folders and tracks you rip. Click the ellipses (...) button to display the Browse For Folder dialog box, navigate to the folder you want to use, and click the OK button.

6. In the Make Sub-Path Using group box, select the Artist check box and Album check box as appropriate to include them in the name of the subfolders that'll be created. For example, if you're ripping the album *Exile On Coldharbour*

Lane by A3, selecting the Artist and Album check boxes produces the subfolder \A3\Exile On Coldharbour Lane\. The Sample Path label at the bottom of the New Songs Directory Options dialog box will show a generic path reflecting your choices.

7. In the Name Song File Using group box, select the information to include in the track file by selecting the check boxes for Track Number, Track Name, Artist, and Album as appropriate. You can change the order of these items by selecting one of them and using the up and down arrow buttons to move it. In the Separator text box, enter the separator character to use between these components. The default is an underscore, but you can use a different character (or several characters) if you prefer. For example, you might prefer to use two or three hyphens or a space, a hyphen, and a space (for readability).

8. Click the OK button to close the New Songs Directory Options dialog box.

9. Select the Mute While Recording check box to specify that MusicMatch Jukebox rip the tracks without playing them back at the same time. Using this option lets MusicMatch Jukebox record much faster—at least, on a fast computer.

10. Make sure that the Enable check box in the Make Song Clips group box is cleared. (This feature lets you make a clip from a song: you select the check box and specify a start second and a length—for example, a 29-second clip starting at second 10. The main reason for creating clips is to provide a quick sample that will allow the recipient to identify or judge the song—for example, for sharing a small part of a copyrighted song without transgressing too horribly against the law.)

11. In the Recording Mode group box, make sure that the Digital option button is selected. If you want to use error correction in your recordings, select the Error Correction check box. (Error correction helps reduce clicks and pops that occur when a CD disagrees with your CD drive's read head during the recording. Using error correction slows down the recording, so you probably won't want to use it unless you're experiencing quality problems with your MP3 files.)

12. Click the OK button to close the Settings dialog box.

TIP

You can also quickly change the sampling rate by choosing Options ➤ Recorder ➤ Quality and choosing the appropriate setting on the Quality submenu.

Rip Tracks with MusicMatch Jukebox

Now that you've got CDDB and your recording options set up, you're ready to rip tracks with MusicMatch Jukebox. Here's how to proceed:

1. Slot a CD into your CD drive (or DVD drive), and close it. MusicMatch Jukebox will read the CD. If you're using CDDB, MusicMatch Jukebox will retrieve the information for the CD from CDDB and will display the album's name, the artist's name, and the track titles. If CDDB can't decide between a couple of possible listings for the CD, it will display a dialog box such as the one shown below to let you decide. Do so.

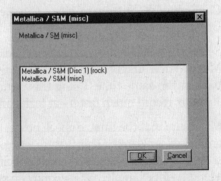

2. Click the Record Music CDs Into Digital Tracks button to display the Recorder window, as shown here:

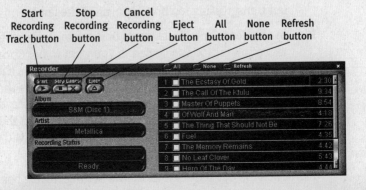

3. Select one or more tracks to record by selecting the check boxes for the tracks or by clicking the All button.

   ▶ Click the None button to deselect all currently selected tracks.

   ▶ Click the Refresh button if you want MusicMatch Jukebox to reread the CD's contents. (This button is mainly useful if you have auto-insert notification disabled for your CD drive and manage to insert a fresh CD without MusicMatch Jukebox's noticing.)

4. Click the Start Recording Track button to start ripping. The first time you go to rip tracks from a CD to MP3 files, MusicMatch Jukebox will configure your CD drive or drives. You'll see the CD-ROM Preparation dialog box, shown below. Make sure that each of your CD drives and DVD drives that you'll ever want to use for recording contains an audio CD, and then click the OK button. MusicMatch Jukebox will configure the drive for you and will then start recording.

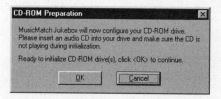

5. As MusicMatch Jukebox records the track, it displays a readout of its progress, as shown here:

6. When MusicMatch Jukebox has finished recording a track, it automatically adds the track to the music library.

Keeping Everything You Need to Know in a Track's Tag

MusicMatch Jukebox makes it easy to add tag information to all the tracks from the same album:

1. With a track selected in the Music Library, choose Options ➤ Music Library ➤ Edit Track Tag, or right-click the track in the Music Library window and choose Edit Track Tag from the shortcut menu, to display the Tag Song File dialog box, as shown here:

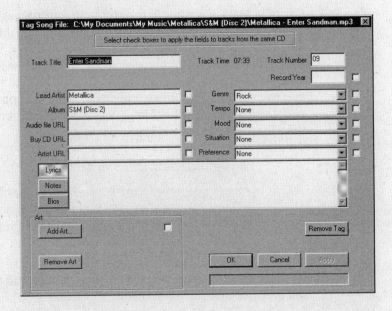

2. Enter information for the track by typing in the text boxes and by choosing items in the drop-down list boxes. If you want to apply the same information to all the tracks from the same CD, select the check box to the right of the text box or drop-down list box.

3. To add lyrics, notes, or bios to the track, click the Lyrics, Notes, or Bios button, and enter the information in the text box.

4. To add a bitmap or JPEG picture to the track, click the Add Art button to display the Open dialog box. Navigate to and select the picture file, and then click the Open button. The picture will appear to the right of the Remove button. Select

the check box to the right of the picture if you want to apply the picture to all the tracks from the CD. So if you gotta have pix of Shania or Ricky on all your MP3 files, it won't cost you much effort. (To remove a picture from a track, click the Remove Art button. To remove a picture from all the CD's tracks, select the check box to the right of the picture before clicking the Remove Art button.)

5. Click the Apply button to apply your changes to the tag or tags. The readout at the bottom of the dialog box will show you which file's tag MusicMatch Jukebox is currently updating. If you're applying tag info to all the tracks from the CD, it'll take a little while, and MusicMatch Jukebox will display an MMJB message box telling you the results when it has finished.

6. To remove a tag from the track, click the Remove Tag button.

7. Click the OK button to close the Tag Song File dialog box.

Build Music Libraries with MusicMatch Jukebox

MusicMatch Jukebox's key feature is its ability to create music libraries that you can use to store, organize, and retrieve your music files. By using music libraries, you can manage your music much more easily than schlepping thousands of individual files in and out of your MP3 player.

You can create as many music libraries as you want. If you prefer to have all your music in one music library, that's fine, but be warned that it may become unmanageably large. We suggest segmenting your music into the different themes, moods, or occasions by which you'll want to play it. You can put any individual track into multiple music libraries, so creating music libraries isn't exactly difficult.

If you don't have the Music Library window displayed, click the Music Library button in the Main window to display it.

Planning Your Music Libraries

Before you create a music library, choose options for the music libraries you'll create. (You can choose options for a music library after creating it, but you'll save time by setting things up right before creating any music libraries.) Here's what to do.

1. Choose Options ➤ Music Library ➤ Music Library Settings to display the Music Library tab of the Settings dialog box, as shown here:

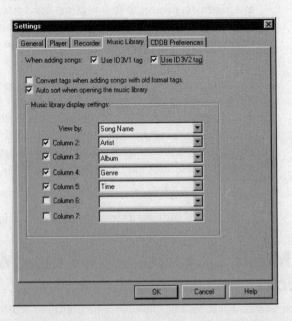

2. Make sure the Use ID3V1 Tag check box and the Use ID3V2 Tag check box are selected so that MusicMatch Jukebox adds all available tag information to the music library. (ID3V1 tags can contain title, artist, album, year, comment, and genre data; ID3V2 tags can add information, lyrics, and a picture.)

3. Select the Convert Tags When Adding Songs With Old Format Tags check box if you want to convert tags from older tag formats to new ones when you add them.

4. Select the Auto Sort When Opening The Music Library check box if you want MusicMatch Jukebox to automatically sort the tracks in the library each time you open it.

5. In the Music Library Display Settings group box, select the columns that you want to appear in the Music Library window. For each column, select the appropriate contents in the list box.

6. Click the OK button to close the Settings dialog box.

Now drag the dividers on the column headings in the Music Library window left or right to resize the columns to display the information you want to see. For example, you might want to narrow the Time column so that it takes the minimum amount of space possible and leaves more room for the track title and album names.

Creating a New Music Library

To create a new music library, choose Options ➤ Music Library ➤ New Music Library. In the Please Specify The Name And Location Of Your New Library dialog box (which is a Save As dialog box after a quick name-change operation), specify the filename and folder for the music library, and then click the Save button. MusicMatch Jukebox will save the music library with a .ddf extension.

Adding Tracks to a Music Library

MusicMatch Jukebox automatically adds to the current music library any new MP3 files you rip with it. But you'll need to add any existing MP3 files to the database so that you can work with them through MusicMatch Jukebox. The same goes for any MP3 files that you download.

Here's how to add files to the current music library:

1. Click the Add button in the Music Library window to display the Add Songs To Music Library dialog box, shown below:

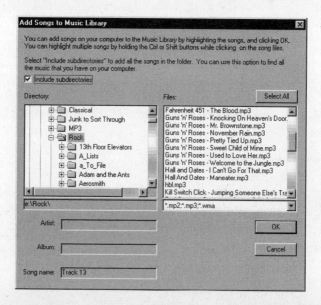

Part v

2. In the Directory list box, select the directory from which you want to add the MP3 files to the database.

3. If the directory contains subdirectories, select the Include Subdirectories check box.

4. In the Files list box, select the MP3 files you want to add to the database.

   ▶ To select all the files shown, click the Select All button.

   ▶ To view the information about a particular track (for example, to identify it more precisely), select it in the Files list box. The Artist, Album, and Song Name text boxes will display the information included for those categories in the file's tag.

5. Click the OK button to add the selected MP3 files to the database.

Deleting Tracks from a Music Library

To delete a track from a music library, select the track, and click the Delete button (or press the Delete key). MusicMatch Jukebox will display the MusicMatch Jukebox dialog box shown below:

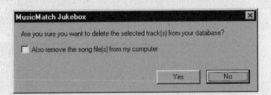

If you want to delete the file from your computer's hard disk, select the Also Remove The Song File(s) From My Computer check box. Then click the OK button.

WARNING

To nuke the contents of a music library, choose Options ➢ Music Library ➢ Clear Music Library. You won't usually want to do this, so MusicMatch Jukebox displays a confirmation dialog box to make sure you know what you're doing before it wipes out your carefully built library. Of course, if a well-meaning relative ripped the *Titanic* soundtrack into your music library, go right ahead and tear it out root and branch.

Opening a Music Library

To open a music library, choose Options ➤ Music Library ➤ Open Music Library to display the Open dialog box. Navigate to and select the music library; then click the Open button. MusicMatch Jukebox will open the music library, closing any music library that is currently open.

Dropping a Music Library on a Friend

To inflict a music library on friends, export it to a text file by choosing Options ➤ Music Library ➤ Export Music Library, entering a filename in the Save As dialog box, and clicking the Save button. You can then e-mail the text file to your friends, and they can import it by choosing Options ➤ Music Library ➤ Import Music Library.

Sharing a music library like this gives your friends only the list of tracks in the library. They need to have the MP3 files that the music library references in order to play them back—but you knew that already.

Rock Out with MusicMatch Jukebox

Once you've got your music organized into music libraries, you can create playlists, save them, and play them back. You can also use the Auto DJ feature to create automatic playlists for you.

Creating, Saving, and Opening Playlists

The Playlist window initially appears docked to the Main window. When you're working with it, you'll usually want to display it separately so that you can expand it to see more of its contents.

Click the Separated View button to display the Playlist window as a separate window. Click the Integrated View button to attach the Playlist window to the Main window again.

Creating a Playlist

Here's how to create a playlist:

▶ If you have tracks in the Playlist window that you don't want to include in the new playlist, click the Clear button to remove them all.

▶ Add tracks to the Playlist window by dragging them from the Music Library window or by selecting them in the Music Library window, right-clicking, and choosing Add Track(s) To Playlist from the shortcut menu.

▶ To preview a track, select it in the Music Library window, and choose Options ➤ Music Library ➤ Preview Track. MusicMatch Jukebox will start playing the track without adding it to the playlist.

▶ To rearrange the tracks in the playlist, drag them to where you want them. This is your opportunity to correct the crimes of the music publisher—now you can put all the best tunes up front and kill the abysmal tracks they only included to pump up the CD's total running time.

▶ To delete a track from the playlist, select it and click the Delete button.

Saving a Playlist   When you've assembled your playlist, save it by clicking the Save button to display the Save Playlist dialog box, entering a name, and clicking the Save button.

MusicMatch Jukebox supports really long names for playlists, but anything over about 40 characters tends to be hard to work with. Best types of titles: Guitars That Killed Cleveland; Psychedelic Psongs; Lame Ballads Babes Love. Keep it short but descriptive so you don't confuse yourself.

Opening a Playlist   To open a playlist, display the Playlist window in Separated View. In the Saved Playlists list, click the playlist to display its contents in the panel to the right, or double-click the playlist to add its contents to the Current Tracks list.

Having MusicMatch Jukebox DJ for You

MusicMatch Jukebox's AutoDJ feature lets you specify vague guidelines by which MusicMatch Jukebox should put together automatic playlists for you. The AutoDJ feature isn't for everyone. If you've ever sat out a dozen songs in a row at a party waiting for the one track to which you *can* dance, you'd do better to give MusicMatch Jukebox more specific instructions on how to please you.

If you want to chance your luck at the AutoDJ feature, here's how to start:

1. Click the AutoDJ button on the Main window to display the AutoDJ dialog box, shown below:

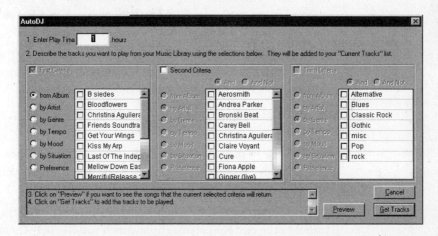

2. In the Enter Play Time text box, enter the number of hours that you want MusicMatch Jukebox to play. Keep this number low until you see what kind of effect AutoDJ produces with your pet music collection.

3. In the First Criteria group box, select the first set of criteria by which MusicMatch Jukebox should select the music. Choose From Album, By Artist, By Genre, By Tempo, By Mood, By Situation, or Preference, as appropriate. The first list box will display check boxes for the category. Select the check boxes for the items you want to include. For example, you might select the By Genre option button and the Techno, Trance, and Trip-Hop check boxes.

4. Define a second set of criteria if you want to by selecting the Second Criteria check box, selecting the And option button or the And Not option button as applicable, and making a choice from the same list. Select check boxes as appropriate. For example, you might select the And option button, select the By Artist option button, and select the check boxes for artists such as Massive Attack, the Chemical Brothers, and The Orb.

5. Define a third set of criteria if you want to by selecting the Third Criteria check box, selecting the And option button or the And Not option button, making another choice, and selecting from the resulting check boxes. For example, you might select the And option button, select the By Tempo option button, and select the Pretty Slow check box to find mellow music to get wasted by.

6. Click the Preview button to display information about how many tracks MusicMatch Jukebox has found matching those criteria (up to the play time you specified in step 2).

7. Adapt your criteria as necessary to produce the play time you want.

8. Click the Get Tracks button to close the AutoDJ dialog box. MusicMatch Jukebox will display a message box telling you how many tracks it has found and the total playing time.

9. Click the OK button. MusicMatch Jukebox will add the tracks to the current playlist, from which you can play them as usual.

What's Next?

Now that we've rocked through MP3, we are going to take a look at another hot topic—home networks. According to a recent estimate, soon close to 17 million households will be in the market for a home network. In the next chapter, Erik Sherman tells you how to set up a home network and what you can do with it when it's in place.

PART VI
HOME NETWORKING

Chapter 23

HOME
NETWORKING

***H**ome Networking* is part of the Sybex series, *I Didn't Know You Could Do That*. Books in this series cover the hottest computer topics in a lighthearted, irreverent tone and contain something for everyone, from the average user to the expert. In this chapter, we'll be looking at some tips and tricks culled from *Home Networking*. The book includes a CD that is loaded with antivirus software, games, household finance and phone message applications, home automation software, Internet utilities, and more.

Adapted from *Home Networking!*
I Didn' t Know You Could Do That... by Erik B. Sherman
ISBN 0-7821-2631-6   295 pages $19.99

Few things make it harder to use a home network than not having one. Luckily, networking technology available today makes installing a network an easy hurdle for most consumers. As you will learn, there are many networking choices that will suit homeowners and renters alike and are appropriate for mansions or one-bedroom apartments. There are solutions for those who can host a home remodeling show as well as those who find screwdrivers challenging.

BECOME THE NETWORK CABLE GUY

The typical image of a network is the type found at a business, with cables running through the walls and jacks conveniently placed near power sources. These networks may seem complicated, but they are actually fairly simple. Indeed, they are simple enough to use in your home network.

The basic building blocks of these business-class networks are the following:

Cables   The special wires that carry signals from one computer or printer to another.

Network devices   Anything attached to the network, including computers, printers, and fax machines.

Network interface cards (NICs)   Hardware that allows a network device to send and receive signals over the cables.

Hubs   Hardware that connects cables running from network devices and controls the physical communication between them.

Routers   Hardware that directs traffic between two networks or, for home users, between the network and the Internet.

Every computer, printer, or fax machine on the network has a NIC either internally installed as a card or externally installed through a connection to either the parallel port or a USB (universal serial bus) interface. Cables run from the NICs to a hub, with the router or perhaps a modem connected to the Internet, as in the image shown next.

Virtually all cable networks support *Ethernet*, which is an electrical standard for how networks communicate. Of the several network layouts, the best for a home network is a *star* network. As you see in the illustration above, all network devices connect to a central point, in this case the hub.

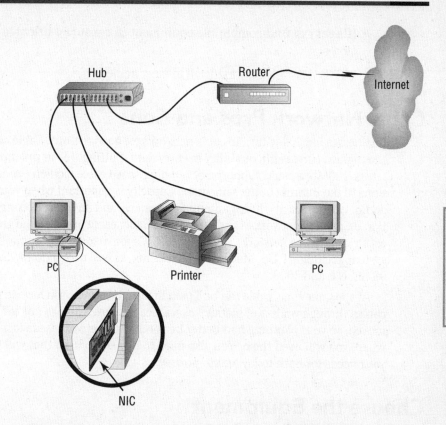

When it comes to the networking equipment available to consumers, a star cable network generally uses *10baseT, 100baseT,* or *10/100baseT* Ethernet products. This means that the network cable, called *unshielded twisted pair,* or UTP, is a special variation on the type of wire that telephones use. The cable attaches to the network equipment with *RJ-45 jacks,* which look like a wide version of the plastic jacks that your home phone uses. The initial number in an Ethernet product refers to the network bandwidth in millions of bits (megabits) per second (Mbps), so 10baseT carries 10Mbps, and 100baseT carries 100Mbps. The last type will work at either 10 or 100Mbps, depending on the speed of the equipment at the other end of the cable.

A star network is the best design for a home network for several reasons:

▶ UTP is the least expensive type of network cable.

▶ The network equipment and cable have a high capacity to carry data.

▶ It's easy to find compatible equipment in consumer-oriented stores.

▶ UTP is relatively easy to install in most homes.

Cable Network Pros and Cons

Businesses inevitably turn to cable networks for good reasons. Cable offers the highest *bandwidth*, or ability to carry data. Putting this in practical terms, 100Mbps could support a dozen high-speed cable modem connections to the Internet at the same time. Capacity is important when you use audio, video, security, home automation, games, and an Internet connection on a home network at the same time. Using cable provides the greatest flexibility to a network. You can find NICs for virtually any operating system, including DOS, Macintosh, and Linux, as well as Windows 95, 98, 98 SE, NT, and 2000.

At the same time, cable can be a pain to install, because you have to pull cables through walls and install jacks. Once in place, cable is not easily moved, so your planning had better be good, with network jacks located where you will need them. You also need to buy equipment that will fit your needs for both today and tomorrow.

Choose the Equipment

You have many choices in cable networks, from the cable itself to network interface cards, hubs, and even kits. Here's a simple rule for choosing network capacity: don't count the bits; just get the higher capacity. The 100Mbps products don't cost much more than the 10Mbps varieties, and they provide superior capabilities.

Cable

First select the cable to use. UTP cable comes in a variety of types—called *categories*—but the most common type for new networks is Category 5, or Cat 5 for short. This type of cable is less expensive and more bendable than most others—a very important feature when you are routing cable through your home. It also works with 100Mbps network equipment.

There are other good reasons to use UTP. Because the network is a star, with all devices connecting to hubs, it becomes relatively easy to trace a bad cable: the problem will affect only one device. You can't run UTP cable lengths longer than 100 meters, or a little more than 300 feet, but that shouldn't pose a problem for most homes.

NOTE

If you need to run cable farther than 300 feet, you can connect two hubs and place them up to 300 feet apart, effectively giving you more distance.

When buying cable, purchase in bulk. You will need lengths not usually found in precut cable, and it will be much cheaper. Be sure that the cable is rated Category 5. This will give you the best shielding from outside electrical interference. If you don't find the price differential too high, consider using Category 5 Enhanced, which has a maximum bandwidth of 1 gigabit per second, or ten times that of plain Category 5. You may not need it now, but if you ever want high-speed networking in the future, it's much easier to replace the network hardware than the cable.

NOTE

In addition to Cat 5, most vendors also carry a *plenum*-rated cable. Far more expensive, this cable has heavy thermal insulation for use inside false ceilings.

NOTE

If you are going to pull cable anyway, consider taking one more step and adding television cable and phone wires. Pulling multiple cables at the same time isn't much more work, and it makes use of any electronics in your house more flexible.

Network Interface Cards (NICs)

Network interface cards are specific in what they support. Most will work with Windows 95/98/98 SE, and some might support earlier versions of Windows or even DOS.

NICs will be 8-, 16-, or 32-bit. The 8-bit cards are an older style and much slower. Don't bother with them; stick to 32-bit, if possible, and get Plug-and-Play–compatible models if you are using Windows 95, 98, or 98 SE. As much as possible, plan on using the same card type in all your computers. Even Plug-and-Play cards might require some adjustments (as specified in the NIC installation instructions). Save yourself the trouble of dealing with two sets of idiosyncrasies.

PCs have different types of *buses*, which are the slots that hold sound cards, video cards, modems, and so on inside a computer. The drawing on the next page shows the two types of buses: ISA (Industry Standard Architecture) and PCI (Peripheral Component Interconnect). A NIC will work with one type or the other but not both.

NOTE

Newer computers usually have PCI connectors. If your computer has an open PCI connector, get a PCI NIC, because it will run much faster than an ISA NIC.

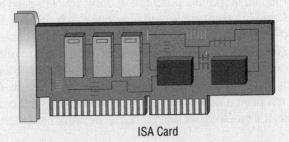

ISA Card

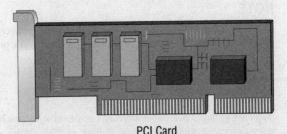

PCI Card

If you don't want to open the computer's case, you can choose devices that plug into a USB port or into the parallel port of a machine. Check specifications to be sure that the device will work with your hardware and operating system. There are also NICs that plug into the PC card slots of a laptop, notebook, or handheld.

Some printers have a NIC built into them to directly connect to the network, instead of attaching to the parallel port of a computer. If yours doesn't, you can buy hardware that will connect to the printer's parallel port and then to the network.

Hubs

Also known as concentrators, hubs become the center of your network. All devices on the network will connect to a hub. Besides the choice of 10, 100, or 10/100Mbps bandwidth, you must also choose the number of ports you want. The least expensive hubs have 4 to 5 ports, but they are available with a capacity of 16 ports and more. Virtually all hubs can connect to other hubs for expanded capacity. With some designs, you are limited to connecting three hubs. Other hubs with built-in switching technology have no limits on expansion.

When deciding on capacity, leave room for what may come in the future. You can connect hubs, but it is cheaper to purchase the higher capacity hub in the first place.

Home Network Starter Kits

Some vendors sell kits that have "everything" you need. That word is in quotes, because it's actually *almost* everything you need. Although you will get enough NICs and a hub to network some number of computers— typically two computers—the cables won't be long enough to run through the walls. But they will be adequate to connect the computers within the same room or to the wall jacks you installed.

WARNING

Because they usually have only two NICs and a 4- or 5-port hub, kits may be inadequate for your needs. You can solve this by purchasing additional NICs or by buying NICs, a larger capacity hub, and the cables separately.

Design Your Dream Network

Creating a cable-based network takes initial planning. In essence, you want to install a number of RJ-45 jacks, all cabled to a central point where they can connect to the hub. Computers, printers, and other network devices use short cables to plug into the jacks and, through them, the hub.

To plan how to run cable, first take a piece of paper and draw a floor plan of your house. Be sure to indicate room dimensions, including height. Mark the locations of electrical outlets, telephone jacks, cable television connectors, and furniture. Choosing the positions for network jacks becomes a matter of trade-offs. You want network jacks located where you might place a computer—by desks, at a telephone, in a convenient spot in your kitchen. Some rooms might be well served with more than one network jack, should you decide to rearrange the furniture.

WARNING

Though network devices will almost always be plugged into power outlets, you don't want to locate network jacks next to the plugs, which could cause some interference.

Remember that the total cable length between a network device and a hub—including both the cable between the jack and hub as well as the length of cable between the device and jack—must be under 328 feet (total length). The reason you include room heights in the floor plan is because the cable may have to travel up a wall. Each time a cable runs through a floor into the basement or through a ceiling into an attic in its wanderings, add a couple extra feet of cable.

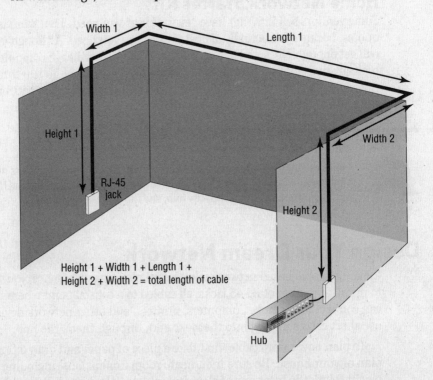

Height 1 + Width 1 + Length 1 + Height 2 + Width 2 = total length of cable

Next, locate your hubs. They should be in an out-of-the-way place, such as a closet or storage area, near a power outlet. If you have an exceptionally large house, or are exceptionally unlucky, you may find some jack or other that would require more than 328 feet of cable to reach the hub. You have three choices:

▶ Add another hub closer to the problem spot, and then connect the hubs.

▶ Reposition a single hub until all jacks are within the proper distance of it.

▶ Reconsider how badly you want a jack in that location.

Install the Cable

Installing cable takes some time, but it doesn't have to be too painful. You will need some tools to get the job done properly. Here is a list that you will find useful:

- ▶ Hammer
- ▶ Screwdrivers, both Phillips and flat head, of various sizes
- ▶ Stud finder, which locates the studs by finding the nails in them
- ▶ Keyhole saw
- ▶ Wire cutters
- ▶ Staple gun (for stapling cable in place in the attic or basement)
- ▶ Crimper, a special tool for stripping insulation from the cable and connecting an RJ-45 connector to a cable end
- ▶ Electric drill
- ▶ Flashlight
- ▶ Ladder

You have three options for running cable through your home: on the inside of the walls, on the outside of the walls, and along the outside of the building.

Good Cabling Practices

Cabling in a devil-may-care fashion will probably put you in hot water sometime in the future, from having loose wires to not knowing where cables lead. A little care at the outset will make life more pleasant.

WARNING

Cabling a house may fall under building codes, fire regulations, zoning, or other governmental constraint. Check with officials in your town about legal requirements.

When you run cables along joists or beams in the attic or basement, attach the cables to the joists or beams. The result is a neat appearance and cables stay out of the way of any additional projects. You can get special hardware for such purposes or even improvise with items such as small pipe clamps.

When running a number of cables to a hub, use cable ties where they meet. The ties are plastic strips that can wrap around several cables and secure them together. It keeps things neat.

WARNING

Label cable ends so you know where they lead. This will save you later aggravation.

Install Cables within the Wall

Installing cable in the walls of your home is definitely the way to go if it is possible. The principle is to open a hole in the wall where you want a jack. You push the cable up to the attic or down to the basement, whichever is easier. The cable then runs along and often across the beams, or joists, and finally up inside another wall to come out another jack.

For each jack location, you need an RJ-45 jack, which will probably include a face plate and a switch box, which sits in the wall and holds the jack and its face plate. Face plates are either metal or plastic; the latter can be fastened within a wall to hold the jack.

Buying a *fish tape* is worth the $20 to $30 investment. It is a long, stiff metal line used to pull cable. Unroll a length, put it into a hole in the wall, and then slide it until the end reaches another opening. Clip the cable to the hook on the end, and pull the fish tape and the cable through.

NOTE

A particularly good switch box for wiring existing homes is the Carlon model from Lamson & Sessions. Push the box into a properly sized hole in the wall, turn two screws, and plastic tabs bite into the inside of the wall, holding the box in place. For wiring, Ideal makes good crimpers and fish tapes.

You will probably find it easiest to bring the box or roll of cable into the attic or basement and pull the ends down (or up) to the proper locations.

1. Refer to your diagram, and locate the correct spots for the jacks in the actual rooms. Use the stud finder to be sure you have located the jack between studs.

2. Drill a pilot hole, and then use the keyhole saw to cut the right-size opening.

WARNING

Work carefully to avoid drilling into power cables, telephone lines, or pipes. If you meet resistance, stop!

3. Unroll 10 or 15 feet of fish tape, and then push it up to the attic (or down to the basement).

4. Attach a free end of cable to the clip on the end of the fish tape. (This is best done with two people, unless you like running up and down stairs.)

5. Pull on the fish tape to bring the cable into place.

NOTE

Be sure to leave a foot or two of cable sticking out from the wall. You can always push extra cable back up into the wall, but there are no cable stretchers to help you if a length is too short.

Follow the instructions included with the RJ-45 jack for connecting the wires in the cable. Because UTP relies on its wires being twisted to cut down outside interference with network traffic, don't untwist any more of an end than you need to connect to the jack—certainly no more than 2 inches.

Install Cables along the Wall

There are reasons to avoid cutting holes in the wall: not owning the property, avoiding installed pipes and wires, or laziness, to name three.

In such a situation, you can surface mount cable on the wall with special conduit. You cut lengths, fit them together with special connectors and elbows, and mount them to the wall. The cable runs through them. You can use surface mounted boxes (with a jack included) to complete a cable run.

Install Cables outside Your Home

In some older buildings, it may be difficult, if not impossible, to run cable through the walls. You can use surface mounting, but that doesn't help if you need to move from one floor to the next.

In such a case, you can use a cable TV installer's trick and drill though a ceiling (or floor). At times when this is not practical, you might consider drilling a hole in the wall, running a cable along the outside of the building, and pushing it through another drilled hole in another room. It's the least preferable way of cabling, but it may be the only choice in some situations.

NOTE

Check with your cable provider for cable that is UL rated for both indoor and outdoor use. General Cable has a special type of Cat 5 UTP called Command Links Plus for indoor or outdoor use.

Add Connectors to a Cable

Eventually you will need cables with RJ-45 connectors on them, either on one end for the cables running to the hub or on both ends to connect a network device to a wall jack. This is where you use the crimper and stripper.

To attach a connector to cable, follow these steps:

1. Cut the cable square at the end, and use the stripper to remove the outer insulation. You should now see four multicolored wires: one white with an orange stripe, one orange with a white stripe, one white with a green stripe, and one green with a white stripe.

2. The RJ-45 connector has one end with room for the cable to enter. The other end has eight pins that fit into the RJ-45 jack. Hold the jack so that the pins are facing up and the plastic tab that locks the jack into place faces away from you. The pins are numbered 1 through 8, from left to right.

3. Place the white wire with orange stripe into the pin 1 slot; the orange wire with white stripe into the pin 2 slot; and the white wire with green stripe into the pin 3 slot. Place the green wire with white stripe apart from the others into the pin 6 slot.

4. When the wires are in place, put the connector into the crimping tool, and squeeze the handle.

Wire the Hub

The other end of each cable running from a jack must attach to a hub. Instead of facing a mass of cables coming out of the wall, consider the professional's approach of a *patch panel*. A patch panel is a box that holds groups of wires that you want to connect.

Cables enter one side of the patch panel and connect via *punch down blocks*. Using a special tool, you quickly fasten the cable to the block. Each block is wired to a location on the patch panel. You run cables from the other side to the ports on the hub, adding RJ-45 connectors to the free ends so they can plug into the hub. By using patch cables, you can easily connect different ports to different cables in your house; if you then move a piece of equipment, it's easy to reconnect the equipment to its old port.

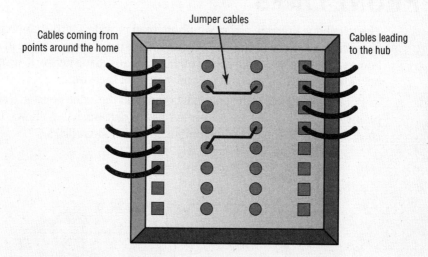

Jumper cables

Cables coming from points around the home

Cables leading to the hub

Part vi

Install a NIC in Each Computer

These are general instructions, but NICs may have their own peculiarities. Be sure to read the instructions that accompany them. Follow these steps to install an internal NIC card:

1. Turn off the computer, and unplug the power cord.

2. Open the computer case.

3. Prepare the NIC according to the manufacturer's instructions, if necessary, and insert it into an open bus slot.

4. Close the case.

5. Plug in the power cord, and turn the computer on.

6. Follow the manufacturer's directions for installing the device drivers for the NIC.

If you are using an external NIC, steps 1 through 5 are replaced by connecting a supplied cable from the NIC to either a USB port or the device's parallel port, depending on the type of NIC.

Once the NIC is installed, use a cable with RJ-45 connectors on each end to hook it to the jack.

RUN A NETWORK OVER YOUR PHONE LINES

The telephone lines already in your home can provide a terrific approach to installing a home network. Because many—if not most—rooms in a home will have a telephone jack, you have a ready-made network, waiting only for special NICs that can take advantage of the wiring.

Phone-line networks are possible because all the extensions on a single phone line in a building are connected, as the diagram below shows. Using special NICs, you connect your computers to the phone jacks.

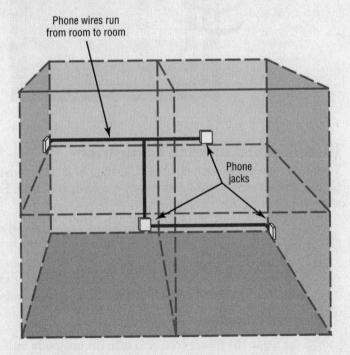

Phone wires run from room to room

Phone jacks

Phone wire with regular telephone connectors (type RJ-11) on each end connects a NIC to the telephone jack. Because the network operates at a different electrical frequency than telephones, the two can coexist on the same lines.

Phone Line Network Pros and Cons

The best reason to use phone networking is that it's easy. The phone wires are already in place; all you do is install the NICs and connect them to phone jacks. The Home Phoneline Networking Alliance (HomePNA) has defined standards for phone line networks. Theoretically, equipment from one vendor should work with the hardware from another.

NOTE

Most phone network equipment is available for Windows machines. Farallon's products support some Macintosh models, though older computers will not be supported.

NOTE

Phone line network capacities should be up to 10Mbps—or the low end of standard Ethernet speeds—by the time you read this. Because the telephone and network signals do not interfere with each other, you can take a telephone call while the network is running.

Telephone networking has limitations, though. Each device on the network must be near a telephone jack, which means that the number and location of appropriate jacks limit your network. You could add telephone cables throughout the house, but it would be just as easy to run UTP cable.

The related products have distance restrictions. The ActionTec model, for example, restricts the farthest distance between any two computers to 500 feet, which is shorter than the 200 meters, or almost 650 feet, possible with two UTP cables running to the same hub. For most homes, though, this should not be a problem. The main difficulty will be that you probably won't know the length of phone cord running inside the walls between jacks.

Install a Phone Line Network

Before installing hardware and software, give some thought to your phone lines. The network depends on all jacks being connected to the same phone line. If you have two or more separate phone lines, be sure the jacks you use are on the same line. Otherwise, your computers won't be able to communicate.

You don't want to put in a phone network at the price of being unable to connect your phones. Check the NICs. Some come with two phone jacks, so you can connect the NIC to the phone jack and then plug the phone into the NIC and still use it.

NOTE

If the NICs lack a second jack, buy some line splitters. These are little blocks that plug into a phone jack and turn it into two jacks, so you can plug in both the computer and the phone at the same time.

Installing the hardware for the phone line network is straightforward. Although these directions are for the ActionTec and Farallon products, others will be similar.

1. Turn off the computer, and unplug it.

2. Open the computer's case.

3. Find an open PCI slot, and insert the NIC.

4. Close the case again.

5. Take a cable, and plug one end into the NIC and the other into the phone jack.

6. If the computer does not use a modem and you have a phone, plug it into the appropriate jack on the NIC. (Some products will require a splitter at the wall jack.)

7. If the computer uses either an internal or external modem, connect another phone cable from the phone jack on the NIC to the line jack on the modem. Then you can connect a phone to the modem's telephone jack.

8. Turn on the computer, and follow the manufacturer's instructions for installing the device drivers.

NOTE

I used the phone network kits from ActionTec and Farallon, which include two NICs, two phone cables, and software for Windows 95, 98, or NT. Farallon's kit also supported Macs with open PCI slots.

ActionTec suggests unplugging any unused phones on the line, as excess equipment can cause electrical noise that can slow the network.

RUN A NETWORK OVER YOUR POWER LINES

Mention running a network over power lines, and many people react as though they were advised to speed through their morning by using a hair drier while sitting in a warm tub. Fear not. Power line networking is not only safe but often the only practical way of providing communications among your computers.

As the following graphic shows, power line networks work because the power outlets in a building are all connected. By using special equipment called *adapters*, the computers can send signals to each other through the house, turning the power lines into a network data transport mechanism.

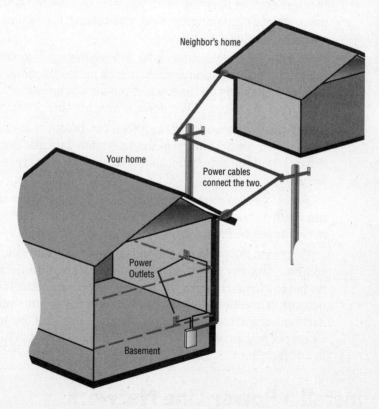

Neighbor's home

Your home

Power cables connect the two.

Power Outlets

Basement

Though the thought of plugging the back of a computer into an outlet may seem dangerous, it's not. Power line networking uses special adapters, which are network devices that plug into wall outlets and connect with a cable to a computer's or printer's parallel port. The adapters are designed to keep power wiring physically separate from the cable running to the computer or printer, so there is no chance of damaging equipment or getting a shock. Because the network generates signals that are much different than household current, they can coexist without problems.

Power Line Network Pros and Cons

Power line networks have some clear advantages at home. There's no need for cutting holes in walls and pulling cable—an important issue if you rent an apartment or house. Virtually any place you might use a computer will have a power outlet, which means you can get connected.

Because the network devices are outside your computer, you don't have to install cards or open the PC. If you want to move the location of a computer, instead of running more network cabling, just unplug the power-line adapter and bring it with you.

There are also some drawbacks. The technology is recent and focused on the largest computing markets, which means Windows 95, 98, 98 SE, and NT. Depending on the product vendor, you are out of luck if you use Macs, earlier versions of Windows, Linux, or other platforms.

This form of network has the lowest bandwidth of any network, which means you are more limited in the amount of data that can travel over the network, and you may find it slower than most other types of networking technologies.

You might also start running out of wall outlets faster than before: some outlets may not work because of electrical interference. Power line networks can be finicky.

Even with the potential problems, power line networking is a great solution for many people. You can share files and printers, devices connected to PCs on the network, and even Internet access. It's easy to add a network connection anyplace you suddenly decide you want another connection, even if it's temporary. For example, on a hot day you could set up a network and move from a stifling office to an air-conditioned bedroom in under an hour.

Install a Power Line Network

The mechanics of putting in a power line network are easy, as the following steps show:

1. Turn off the PCs and the printer.

2. Unplug the power cables of the PCs, and connect them to power conditioners, which are power strips that filter out any power line noise that could disrupt the network. Then plug the power conditioner into the power outlet.

3. Plug the network adapters into power outlets, and connect parallel cables from the adapter to a computer or printer. Be sure not to mix up the two types of adapters, one for computers and the other for printers.

4. Turn the PCs and printer back on.

5. Use the CD to install the configuration software on your computers. The CD will configure Windows networking for you.

6. Be sure to install printer drivers on all the PCs that will use the printer.

NOTE

I used Intelogis's PassPort power line networking kit, which works with Windows 95/98 and Windows NT. This kit comes with two adapters for PCs, two parallel cables, one printer adapter, a CD with software and drivers, and two power line conditioners. Similar products available from other vendors may be compatible with other operating systems.

You can add PCs and printers to the network with a few restrictions. There may be a limit on the total number of devices you can have in a network; for PassPort, the maximum number is 20. Also, printers using *bidirectional* communications—they send signals to a PC over the printer cable as well as receive printing jobs—don't work on PassPort and may not on similar products. You can get around this by disabling bidirectional communications as follows:

1. Either choose a PC with at least two parallel ports or add a parallel port card to one of the computers.

2. Plug the printer into the second parallel port. If the printer must be on LPT1, you can move the network adapter to the second parallel port.

3. Double-click Printers in My Computer on the Windows Desktop.

4. Right-click the printer in question, and select Properties.

5. Clear the Bidirectional check box.

Part vi

Set Up a Secure Power Line Network

It is also a good idea to create a *secure* network, which means that only specified machines can use that network. This is important with power line networks because the wires in one house or apartment are connected to those of neighboring units. Without secure networks, someone next door using equivalent equipment might be able to get access to the machines on your network.

With the PassPort product, setting up a secure network is easy. Open the PassPort Administrator program on one of the networked PCs, choose Security from the menu, and then click Secure Network Wizard. The program will walk you through the steps of choosing a network name and then selecting the PCs and printers that are in it.

NOTE

At the time of this writing, the most recent version of PassPort was version 1. Intelogis expects the maximum bandwidth in version 2 to almost triple to 1 million bits per second. The company was also considering support for other platforms.

SHARE FILES ON THE NETWORK

Saying that networks let you share files seems obvious, but sometimes the obvious is cool. By making it possible to share files, a network lets you do the following:

- ▶ Buy one copy of an application, and let everyone run it.

- ▶ Maintain a work-and-play schedule for multiple people.

- ▶ Have a single phone list that the whole family shares.

- ▶ Play music from any location from a central music server.

- ▶ Work on an important document from any location on the network, inside or outside.

All this is possible because networks let computers share their files, whether they are programs, music, phone lists, or images.

You have two considerations in file sharing: where to put the files and how to access them.

Designate a File Server

Choosing where to put the files depends on the type of your network operating system and how it's set up. Remember, there are two basic types of networks: client/server, on which a single computer controls the network, and peer-to-peer, on which all the PCs cooperate to control the network. Whichever you use, you can share files.

In a client/server network, files typically reside on the same computer running the NOS (network operating system). That's because it is the only computer to whose hard drives the other PCs have access. This machine is called the *file server* because it becomes a central repository of files and "serves 'em up" to the other computers.

In a peer-to-peer network, you can make a hard drive on any networked computer available to others. Yet you should still plan on thinking in terms of file servers. The reason is really organizational.

Having many drives available to you on a network becomes a potential problem if you actually use them, because you suddenly need to track which files are kept on which machine. Have you ever forgotten where you put a file on a single hard drive? Try looking on five. When you designate one computer as the file server, you know where to check.

Given the nature of home networks, you don't need to use the most powerful PC in the house for a file server. A more modest computer will do well. That may seem surprising. Corporations often favor fabulously fast machines, but that's because they have important applications running on the servers that all the employees use. Because you are looking to provide file access, speed of the CPU is less important.

Make Sure There's Enough Memory

For file sharing, you don't need hundreds of megabytes of RAM, but 32MB is good, and 64MB is better.

 NOTE
RAM memory is fairly inexpensive. Consider upgrading the memory of your file server from the 16MB or 32MB it had when you bought it to a more robust 64MB.

Make sure that the hard drive is large, which, depending on your situation and what you do with the computers, might mean 10 to 20 gigabytes. That may sound like a lot, but as you start storing multimedia files, especially audio and video, you will find it disappearing in no time.

NOTE

I turned a 120MHz, AMD-powered PC with 32MB of memory into a good file server by adding a 10.2GB Quantum Fireball hard drive.

Make Sure There's Enough Storage Space

You may decide that you don't have enough hard-drive space. Instead of buying a new computer, why not add another hard drive to your old one? Here's how to do it:

1. Turn off your computer, unplug it, and then open the case.

2. Check that there is an open *drive bay*. This is the part of the PC chassis that actually holds a hard drive in place.

3. Most home computers will have an IDE (Integrated Drive Electronics) drive, which connects to the computer with a ribbon cable terminated by a connector that has 40 holes in the end, as the following drawing shows. Another connector with four holes in the end provides the power. Your computer's manufacturer can tell you what sort of drive it has. When buying a new drive, you need to get the same type. One exception is when adding a SCSI (Small Computer Systems Interface) drive to a PC. I'll discuss SCSI drives later in this section.

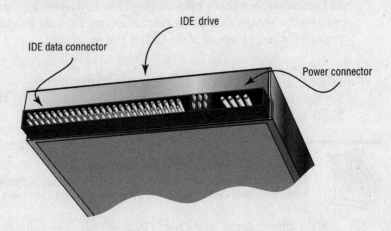

IDE drive

IDE data connector

Power connector

NOTE

Your computer has two types of bays: a 5.25-inch size and a 3.5-inch size. Hard drives are typically the 3.5-inch variety. If you only have a 5.25-inch open bay, purchase a set of *rails*. These metal attachments hold a smaller hard drive in the larger space.

4. Because you are adding the additional hard drive, you will need to configure the drive, probably by moving jumpers on the unit, to act as a *slave* to the original drive. See the directions that come with the hard drive for how to do this.

5. Slide the drive into the bay, and use four screws to hold it in place.

WARNING

Use only screws intended for mounting hard drives. A screw that is too long could poke through the mounting rail, touch electrical circuitry, and damage the drive.

6. The ribbon cable running to the first hard drive should have a second connector. Attach it to the new hard drive, and then attach a spare power connector.

7. Close the case, plug the PC in, and turn it on.

8. You now need to configure the BIOS to recognize the new drive. As your computer boots up, follow the instructions on the screen for how to start "setup." The menus on different BIOSs may vary. With an AMI BIOS, for example, the first menu item of Standard CMOS contains the hard-drive configuration information. If your BIOS contains an Auto Detect feature, run Auto Detect, and ensure the new drive has been detected. If it is detected properly, save your settings and exit BIOS.

9. Look for the spot to configure the primary slave hard drive. If your PC and hard drive are both Plug and Play, set the hard-drive type to Auto. Otherwise, set the hard-drive type to User, and enter the number of cylinders, sectors, and heads, provided in the information from the hard drive's vendor.

10. Follow the on-screen instructions to save the new BIOS values, and then let the machine restart.

Part vi

WARNING

If your server is an older PC, the BIOS may not support a large hard drive. In that case, you need a copy of Disk Manager DiskGo! by Ontrack (www .ontrack.com). It adds a special driver that will overcome the BIOS limitations and let an older machine use drives larger than two gigabytes.

11. You now have to format and partition the hard drive. *Partitions* are logical divisions within the hard drive. It is necessary to partition a hard drive because operating systems have limitations on the amount of contiguous hard-drive space they can recognize. You can partition and format the drive with the MS-DOS utility called fdisk, but Partition Magic from PowerQuest Corporation (www.powerquest.com) will also do the job and requires less knowledge and patience to partition. It graphically walks you through the process.

Add a SCSI Drive

If additional people in your home need access to large files, consider adding a SCSI drive. SCSI is a standard type of computer interface for many devices, including hard drives, CD-ROM drives, and scanners. Although more expensive than an IDE drive, a SCSI hard drive can run many times faster than the more usual IDE hard drive.

To run a SCSI drive, you need a SCSI interface card. This fits into the server the way any other add-in card would. To install the card, use this procedure:

1. Turn off the PC, and unplug it.

2. Open the PC's case.

3. Find an open slot, and insert the card.

4. Follow the vendor's directions for connecting cables from the SCSI hard drive to the interface card.

5. Close the case, plug the PC in, and turn it on.

6. Follow the vendor's installation directions to load a SCSI driver.

7. As with IDE drives, you have to format and partition the hard drive. You can do this with the MS-DOS utility called fdisk, but Partition Magic from PowerQuest Corporation (www .powerquest.com) makes the job easier.

Whether you have a client/server or peer-to-peer network, once you have selected the file server and added additional hard-drive space, if necessary, the next step to sharing files is to make sure different computers on the network have access to the server's drives. But setting the access depends on what you want to accomplish.

NOTE

Instead of adding hard drives and converting older machines, you could also buy a new computer. With the way prices have plummeted, consumer model PCs can come with lots of horsepower. I tried a Presario from Compaq that came with 64 megabytes of RAM as well as a 466MHz Intel Celeron processor. This should be fast enough for almost anything you will want to do. Another choice could be special hard drives that connect directly to your network, keeping you from opening the PC or even wondering what partitions are.

Plan File Access

Once you know where files are going to be, you should plan what you want to share. Look at the different file types you might want to keep on your network. They might include word-processing, spreadsheet, graphics, video, and audio files.

First, decide who should be able to use the files. You might, for example, let everyone have access to scanned photos or pictures taken with a digital camera but only allow yourself access to work-related documents. There are no hard and fast rules, only what works for your needs.

If you are using peer-to-peer networking and have decided against a single file server, decide where you want to store common files. Although not all your files would be on the same PC, it still makes sense to keep all files of one type together. Otherwise, you have to remember which PC contains the word-processing document you need or resign yourself to spending time browsing through directories on multiple machines.

Create a logical naming convention for folders. Having a Kids Pictures file listed under the Family Photos folder will help you rapidly narrow a search among all the graphics files (see the file structure shown on the next page). Similarly, long filenames under Windows or Macs let you provide descriptive titles. Use them to clearly indicate contents without forcing someone to open the file.

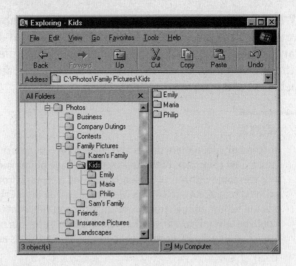

NOTE

You don't have to give everyone access to everything. If a person in your home is the only one who uses certain files, you can create a folder on a shared drive and give only that person access. This will prevent anyone from accidentally tampering with the file's content.

Machines need direction to make drives and files available to others. You can restrict access as you wish. In fact, you will likely need to actively provide availability, as an NOS often restricts access as its default. Windows 98/98 SE, for instance, initially makes drives read-only.

Access Files on a Client/Server Network

Setting up the file server is only half the battle. The other half is giving the PCs access to what is on a server. Although the details of different client/server network operating systems are too involved to cover in this chapter, here are some general steps to giving your PCs access:

1. Purchase whatever licenses you need. For example, owning a copy of Windows NT Server doesn't give you permission to connect a Windows 98 computer to it. In this case, you need to purchase a Windows NT Server Client Access License for each PC.

2. Install whatever software you need on the server. Linux can act as a file and print server for Windows machines if you run

the program called Samba. This lets Linux understand the SMB (Server Message Block) protocol that Windows networking uses.

3. Install whatever software you need on the PCs. If you are using a NetWare file server, every computer on the network needs to run special software to connect with it. NetWare has client software for Windows, DOS, and MacOS.

Once you have finished installing the software, the PC clients should have access to your server. Be aware that some client/server network operating systems require the clients to log onto the network each time they power up. Without the logon, the people using the machines will have no access to files and folders.

Access Files on a Peer-to-Peer Network

On a peer-to-peer network, you map a network drive. This means you create an alias drive letter that your system will use in referring to networked directories. If you had two PCs, called Office and Laptop, on your network, you could make the C drive on the Office machine appear as a different drive letter, say E, on the Laptop machine. Under Windows 98/98 SE, for example, you instruct your local PC to recognize a particular drive on the network:

1. Right-click the Network Neighborhood icon on the Desktop.

2. Click Map Network Drive to open the Map Network Drive dialog box.

3. The Drive list box at the top of the dialog box lets you select the local drive letter to use. It will only show drive letters not currently in use.

4. The Path list box lets you specify the network drive you want to map to the drive letter. Under Windows peer-to-peer networking, to specify the C drive on the Office machine, you would type **\\Office\C**. You can only map a drive to a resource that is already shared. In this format, the C drive is already shared.

5. Click OK.

The drive will now be available in all applications.

NOTE
The software included with the network kit you use may set up drive mappings with a different interface. Follow the vendor's directions in such cases.

PROTECT YOUR NETWORK FILES FROM DATA LOSS

Few sights are as pathetic as the face of people who have lost important information or files from their computer only to realize that they don't have copies. Luckily, a computer network gives you some terrific ways to avoid the problem.

You can lose files in many ways:

▶ You can accidentally delete them.

▶ You can uninstall software, including files needed by other programs.

▶ You can mistakenly overwrite a file, such as a word-processing document, with something else.

▶ You can sit helplessly as your computer crashes.

Whatever the cause, you are left sitting without something you want or need. It doesn't matter whether it is a file for work, a saved version of a computer game session in which you completed a difficult task, or your shopping list.

Undelete a Lost File with an Undelete Utility

Imagine accidentally deleting an important file and then emptying the Recycle Bin! If you catch the problem soon enough, you can always use an undelete utility.

An undelete utility actually goes into your hard drive and digs up a file whose space is now up for grabs. Programs such as FixIt Utilities 98 from Ontrack or Symantec's Norton Utilities have tools for recovering files emptied from a Windows Recycle Bin. Symantec also distributes a version of Norton Utilities for the Mac.

Because the operating system assumes it can overwrite a file once it's out of the Recycle Bin or Trash Can, time is of the essence. The sooner you try to recover the file, the more likely you will be successful.

Back Up Your Network Files on Offline Storage

Unhappily, many times you just can't undelete a file. That's why you should back up your files. With copies of files and applications safely squirreled away somewhere, it is always possible to restore them if you need them.

You can also create *offline storage*, where you keep files you don't need on the network all the time, such as archived documents. Think of it as a backup you know you will need one day rather than as a backup for an emergency.

Backup on a network can actually be easy, because you can automate the whole process and schedule it for the middle of the night, when it won't interfere with anyone. All you have to do is select the right hardware, configure the backup software, and let the network do the rest.

Select the Hardware

There is a range of backup choices to satisfy any need or budget. Although you could choose from types that include optical storage and digital audio tape (DAT), two particularly good ones for the home network are cartridge tape drives and CD or DVD drives. Each has its own strengths and weaknesses.

Tape drives are great for backing up a lot of material in one place. One tape can hold the content of your entire network. The ability to compress data provides even more capacity. The larger the capacity, however, the longer it takes to find a particular file when you want to restore it. Because a large capacity tape drive is a specialized item, you should need only one on the network.

Search times for a given file on a CD-ROM or DVD drive are far shorter. And because most computers on your network probably have a CD or DVD drive, if you want to restore a file to a particular machine, you can load it directly. But CDs and DVDs have limited capacity—about 600 megabytes for the former and a few gigabytes for the latter—which makes them more suitable for storing files offline. Look for a rewritable drive so you can reuse the disks and also add content over time, instead of having to record everything at one time.

NOTE

I have used a Tecmar tape drive to back up my PC for the last two years and have just switched to a 20 gigabyte model that can handle all the data on my network. An HP CD-RW, which reads CDs at 24X speed and records CDs at 4X, is helping store scanned photographs without cluttering hard drives.

Choose the Software

To make a backup, you need software that can run your hardware. Tape drives typically come with backup software, but not all such applications are made the same. For instance, some software can work while people are using the network.

If you are using a client/server network product, you will probably need a network backup product. If the network is peer-to-peer, you might get by with a regular backup package, such as Seagate Backup Exec, which is the full version of the backup software included in Windows 98. Be sure that the computer connected to the backup tape drive has full access to all the drives on all the PCs in your network.

Although some backup software may be able to write to CDs or DVDs, you really need recording software to take best advantage of them. The drives usually come with such software.

Run the Backup

Now it's time to configure the actual backup job. This example uses VER-ITAS Backup Exec because it can schedule the jobs to run in the middle of the night. Before you start, you have to work out a backup schedule. The following works well with two tapes, one for complete backups and one to back up files that have changed:

▶ One day a week, say Sunday, you back up everything on the full-backup tape.

▶ On Monday, you erase the changed file backup tape and then back up only the files that have changed since the last full backup.

▶ On Tuesday through Saturday, you back up only files that have changed since the last full backup. These backups get added to the end of the tape you used Monday.

With this approach, you can re-create anything on your network within the last week and need only two tapes to do so.

To make this work, first configure access on the network so the machine with the tape drive has full access to all the hard drives on all your PCs.

Here's how to create the Sunday job:

1. In Windows 98 SE, choose Start $\succ$ Programs $\succ$ Accessories $\succ$ System Tools $\succ$ Backup to open the Microsoft Backup dialog box.

2. Select Create A New Backup Job, and click OK to start the Backup Wizard.

3. Select Back Up Selected Files, Folders, And Drives, and click Next.

4. Check all the hard drives on the backup computer. Then click the plus sign next to Networks, and select all the other drives; then click Next.

5. Select All Selected Files, and click Next.

6. Select the tape drive, and click Next.

7. Make sure both the Compare Original And Backup Files and Compress The Backup Data To Save Space boxes are checked, and then click Next.

8. Type a name for the job, and click Start. Immediately click Cancel when the job starts.

9. Click Options to open the Backup Job Options dialog box.

10. Select the General tab, and be sure that Overwrite The Media With This Backup is selected.

11. Select the Report tab, and be sure that Perform An Unattended Backup is selected.

12. Select the Advanced tab, and be sure that Back Up Windows Registry is checked, and then click OK.

13. Click the Schedule button, and choose when to run the job.

14. Under the Job menu, select Save.

Now create the two jobs for Monday and the rest of the week. For both, you would select New And Changed Files in step 5. For the Tuesday through Saturday job, you would select Append This Backup To My Media in step 10.

Back Up Your Network Online

The problem with doing backups at home is that if anything happens to the tapes, you would be out of luck. Outside obvious acts of God—such as fire and tornadoes—pets, children, and accidents can render tapes useless.

For extra protection, consider using an online backup service. These companies let you upload backups over the Internet to their servers.

You won't want to back up everything on your system every night, but it's a great way of keeping your most vital records, information, and files some place safe.

NOTE
If your Internet account comes with storage space for a Web page, you could upload your most critical files there. Check with your ISP whether this would make your files available to people on the Internet.

Restore Your Data

Should you lose a file and need to restore it, you will use the restore portion of the backup software. Aside from recovering from a data loss, though, you can perform other tasks with restore:

▶ Move large blocks of files and folders from one system to another.

▶ Load data you have moved to offline storage.

▶ Move a Windows Registry and files to make one system act like another.

Restoring data is as easy as backing it up in the first place. With Microsoft Backup, which comes with Windows, you do the following:

1. Click Start ➤ Programs ➤ Accessories ➤ System Tools ➤ Backup to open the Microsoft Backup dialog box.

2. Select Restore Backed Up Files, and click OK.

3. Follow the instructions in the Wizard for selecting the files to restore and their destination.

Then all you have to do is wait for the files to be written to the hard drive you indicated.

TROUBLESHOOT NETWORK PROBLEMS

Nothing is perfect in this life, especially networks. Many things can go wrong, from small and annoying hardware errors to misconfigurations of software as well as major breakdowns that seem part and parcel with the use of computers.

When you have problems—and you will—it's important to know how to solve them. More important than a checklist of symptoms and possible causes, such as a car-repair manual, you need to concentrate on the right approach. The general steps are:

▶ Note what you know.

▶ Isolate the problem.

▶ Use diagnostic tools.

▶ Check the cables.

Although you can't predict potential problems, taking a methodical and planned approach will help solve them.

Note What You Know

Can you imagine playing poker and using only four of your five cards? It would be almost impossible to win. An equivalent event often happens when people face technical problems. Caught up by a problem, they forget all the information they actually have. Here are some practices that may help:

▶ Take a pad of paper and write down everything you can see about the problem. Don't dismiss the smallest piece of information.

▶ An error dialog box may offer a number or text that will assist you in finding help in a product reference book. The error message might even indicate which program is having the problem.

▶ Choose Start ➤ Settings ➤ Control Panel ➤ System to open the System Properties dialog box. Click the Device Manager tab, and look for any yellow exclamation points. They indicate a problem with hardware and provide an error message that can be helpful.

Part vi

▶ Make a list of any new hardware or software you may have installed into the machines having problems. If you added something, take it out, and see whether that improves the situation.

Having all the information at hand may provide you with a sudden insight or clue to the cure for your network's difficulty.

Isolate the Problem

Like a car, what often makes network problems difficult to diagnose is the number of interconnected elements involved. Aside from a phone number of an on-call expert, the best tool you can have is the habit of isolating a problem. Look at the problem and consider its potential causes. Then focus your investigation on those causes and not other issues. Take your list of information, and see what you can rule in or out.

For instance, say that one computer on a peer-to-peer network won't connect with the others, but the computer works fine on its own. Logically there follows three possible causes:

▶ All the other computers are incorrectly configured and won't recognize the one PC.

▶ The one PC is incorrectly configured and won't recognize the other PCs.

▶ Something is wrong with either the cables or connectors.

You can now investigate each area more methodically to find the actual cause of the problem. Sometimes the nature of the problem itself offers important information. Say you have set up a network; you go to one of your computers, start a word processor, and open a file on another PC. So far, so good. You make some changes, but suddenly find you can't save the file on the remote location. Because the file opens but you can't save a modification, the problem is likely on the remote system—either a problem with the drive or read-only permission to that directory.

Use Diagnostic Tools

Any mechanic has tools that can measure electrical output and resistance, compression in the engine, and tire pressure. If you are reading this section, you are probably the system administrator of your castle, if not the ruling monarch. To save time and find problems faster, use the diagnostic tools that some benign programmer left for you.

Both Windows NT and NetWare have sophisticated tools to measure performance of your network. A peer-to-peer system may or may not come with such tools.

Check the Cables

Cables and connectors can cause many network problems and should be the first item to check if a machine cannot connect to the network. You can separate this into three distinct areas:

- ▶ Cables that connect a computer to a jack
- ▶ Cables that run inside the walls
- ▶ Patch panels

Cables running from a computer to a wall jack often cause problems. Possible problems include wires that have worked loose from a connector after being pulled, or connectors that aren't crimped tightly enough, or flaws in the cable itself.

In any case, take a known good cable, such as one that is working on another computer, and use it to replace the one with a suspected fault. If the problematic PC seems cured, the cable is bad. See if either connector seems loose or damaged. If so, replace it, and test the cable again.

It is possible that a cable in the wall is a problem. A cable may not be well connected to the inside of the jack, or you may have bent the cable too sharply (more than 90 degrees) somewhere in its run. Special test equipment can inject a sound signal over two wires in the cable. By listening on the other end, you can literally hear whether the wires are providing a solid connection.

A cheaper way to test cables is to use a transistor radio. Open it, and disconnect the wires to the speaker. Attach the speaker wires to two of the cable wires at one end. Bring the speaker to the other end, and connect the far ends of the wires to the speakers. You should be able to hear the signal. By methodically testing pairs of wires, you can see whether all the wires are good. If so, the problem is elsewhere. If not, prepare to pull more cable.

The final place to check is the patch panel. It's easy to make a mistake and connect an unused cable to the hub, accidentally overlooking the cable that is actually connected to the computer in question. This is a good place to check if you are running the network for the first time or if you have just moved a device from one jack to another.

Part vi

Maintain Hard-Drive Performance

Your whole network works only as well as its hard drives do. By taking a little time, you can keep hard drives in top shape and keep an eye out for potential problems. Here are a few of the benefits you will see:

▶ Systems work faster.

▶ The network runs faster.

▶ You can catch hard-drive problems before you lose data.

You can split your time between defragmenting the hard drive to keep it performing well and using SMARTmonitor to catch problems before they occur.

Defragment Your Drive for Speed

In the normal course of operation, a computer writes data all over a hard drive. In the process, the operating system splits many files into pieces that can be scattered over the hard drive. When this happens, it takes longer to read and modify files.

Defragmentation programs analyze the hard drive and rearrange the blocks of data so that related blocks are next to each other. Windows 95, 98, 98 SE, NT, and 2000 all have defragmentation utilities built-in.

Because it must rearrange all the bits of files, the defragmentation program should have sole access to the hard drive. It's best to run defragmentation when you have nothing else to do, such as in the middle of the night. Once a week should be often enough for defragmenting. Here's how to do it.

1. Choose Start ➤ Programs ➤ Accessories ➤ System Tools ➤ Disk Defragmenter to open the Select Drive dialog box.

2. Choose the drive you want to defragment, and then click OK.

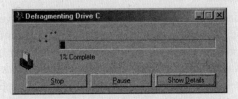

Depending on the size of the hard drive, defragmentation can take a good hour or more. To run it in the middle of the night, use Scheduled Tasks:

1. Click Start ➣ Programs ➣ Accessories ➣ System Tools ➣ Scheduled Tasks to open the Scheduled Tasks folder.

2. Double-click Add Scheduled Task to start the Wizard.

3. Click Next, and then scroll through the list of programs until you find Disk Defragmenter.

4. Select Disk Defragmenter, and click Next.

5. Choose the frequency for the task, and click Next.

6. Fill in the time and day to run the job.

7. Click Next, and then click Finish.

Now you will be able to defragment your drive without losing valuable time—or sleep.

Keep Problems in Check with SMARTmonitor

Hard drives keep precisely aligned, extremely flat platters spinning at ridiculously high speeds while metal arms slide in and out between them. This is equipment designed for eventual disaster. SMARTmonitor from SystemSoft is a program that keeps tabs on how well your hard drives are running. It works with S.M.A.R.T. (Self-Monitoring Analysis and Reporting Technology) drives, which can monitor their own performance. Virtually all new hard drives are S.M.A.R.T.-compliant.

The program monitors all the drives on your network periodically and warns you when a drive is close to failing, permitting you to save your data before you lose it. To install it, copy the SMARTmonitor file from the CD to your hard drive. Start Windows Explorer, highlight the file, and double-click it. It will install itself.

Here's how to use it:

1. Choose Start ➣ Settings ➣ Control Panel ➣ SMARTmonitor.

2. Select the Disks tab. It displays the drive letters and whether the drives are S.M.A.R.T.

3. Select the Settings tab. Be sure to check Always Run SMARTmonitor When Starting Windows and Display SMARTmonitor Disk Icons In The Taskbar.

Part vi

4. Click the Start SMARTmonitor button.

5. If any of the drives have monitoring turned off, the Monitor All Disk Drives button is active. Click it.

6. Click OK.

7. To check on drive status, right-click the SMARTmonitor icon, and choose Status Check.

In case of an imminent disk failure, SMARTmonitor will display a warning. If you see it, back up the data from that drive as quickly as you can.

Survive a Hard-Drive Crash

Despite care, hard drives sometimes crash. Hopefully, you have a backup. Even if you do, there may be times when you can't use the backup. You might be away from home with a crashed laptop, or the problem machine could be the one connected to the tape drive. In those circumstances, you can still take some steps:

1. Move the tape drive to another computer, and install the backup software. You can then replace the defective hard drive if necessary and run the restore part of the backup software.

2. Buy a new hard drive if necessary. If not, format a hard drive with the appropriate operating system, install it, and then reinstall the tape-drive software. You can now run the restore part of the backup software.

3. Use a data-recovery service. Some companies recover data from hard drives that have crashed or have had other problems.

But if you've been backing up the network regularly, the most data you will lose will be one day's worth.

ACCESS YOUR HOME NETWORK VIA THE INTERNET

You could use a dial-up server and phone into your network, but that might mean long-distance phone charges. Why not use the Internet for your connection? That means anywhere you can get onto the Internet, you can reach your home network.

If you have gone the client/server route, you could consider creating a *virtual private network,* or VPN, that generates a private network running through the Internet. Unfortunately, this can be rather complex. Refer to *Mastering Network Security,* by Chris Brenton (Sybex, 1999), for more information.

A much easier approach is to use Microsoft Personal Web Server (PWS) with Windows 98 or 98 SE and then give yourself access to all files through an Internet connection. PWS lets you run an actual Web server and connect it to the Internet. PWS can't handle more than a few people at one time, but if your intent is to provide remote access for your household and maybe a few close friends, that shouldn't be a problem. There are a few considerations:

► Your Web server has to be running when you need access. Either someone in your home must connect it at those times, or you need a continuous Internet connection, such as DSL or cable.

► You will want password security so that anyone stumbling across your Web site won't have unfettered access to your network. The PWS documentation contains instructions on how to add password support to PWS through Active Server Page *scripts* and instructions for the Web server.

► PWS will not publish a network drive's contents, so you can access only what is on the local hard drives of the computer hosting PWS. To get around the problem, run PWS from your file server.

► You will need a connection to an ISP from wherever you are to reach your Web server.

While your Web server is running, log in to an ISP, and start a browser. Enter the URL that you have from setting up the PWS. You now come to your Web server's home page. Provide your name and password, and you have access to your file server.

NOTE

Microsoft Personal Web Server is on your Windows 98/98 SE installation CD.

Part vi

GET YOUR E-MAIL WHILE ON THE ROAD

One of the main reasons you might want remote access to your network is to check your e-mail. Conveniently, you can do this in many ways, from dialing in to your network to having your e-mail follow you.

Use Remote Access to Get Your E-Mail

If you have a Dial-Up Server for your network, you can dial in for your e-mail. The trick is to have your e-mail client software get your e-mail for you. You can instruct software such as Eudora, Microsoft Outlook, and Microsoft Outlook Express to get your e-mail on a regular basis.

Follow these steps to use Outlook Express:

1. Choose Tools ➤ Options to open the Options dialog box.

2. Select the General tab.

3. Be sure there is a check mark next to Check For New Messages Every, and choose the number of minutes between checks. You can specify any number of minutes, up to 999, between e-mail checks. If you want to check your e-mail four times a day, have the program check four times a day, or every 360 minutes. To check every hour, set the time to 60.

4. Select the Connection tab, click Hang Up After Sending And Receiving, and click OK.

5. Now choose Tools ➤ Accounts to open the Internet Accounts dialog box.

6. Select the Mail tab, highlight your e-mail account, and then click Properties to open the Properties dialog box for this account.

7. Select the Connection tab.

8. If Outlook Express is using a modem on the PC running it, check Always Connect To This Account Using, and then select the dial-up account from the list. If, on the other hand, Outlook Express will use a networked Internet connection, select Local Area Network.

By configuring Outlook Express this way, you ensure that it will dial out to request e-mail on a regular basis and then hang up the phone after each session with the mail server is over.

If the e-mail client has to dial up an ISP, you need to take two steps. One is to configure the package to hang up the phone line after it sends and receives e-mail. Check the vendor's directions on how to set this. The other step, since you are probably using the Microsoft phone dialer, is to check the box that enables auto-dialing, as the image below shows.

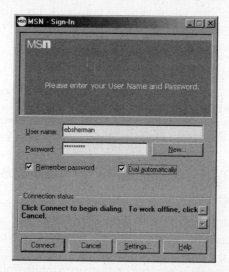

To get your mail when away from home, dial up the network, and synchronize your portable with your desktop, which will include your e-mail. Then read your e-mail, reply as necessary, dial a second time, and resynchronize so your outgoing mail is now in your desktop mail client. The next time the software checks with the mail server you use, it will send your messages.

Have Your E-Mail Follow You

You can have your e-mail follow you to another account where you can pick it up. That second account can be a Web-based free e-mail system, such as Hotmail (`www.hotmail.com`), or some other account, such as your e-mail account at work.

Some ISPs or e-mail servers will offer this capability of *redirecting* e-mails. Check with your e-mail service provider for more information. If such a service is not available, you can still effectively redirect your e-mail by forwarding the messages to the appropriate account. Major e-mail packages, such as Microsoft Outlook and Eudora, have tools to create rules for automatically handling e-mail. Besides directing e-mail to particular folders, you can also create a rule to forward all e-mail.

Next, configure the e-mail client to get mail on a regular basis according to the vendor's instructions. If the e-mail software has to call an ISP, have the software hang up the phone after sending and receiving mail. As you did for remote access to e-mail earlier in this section, set the phone dialer to auto-dial.

All you have to do to get your mail is to check the e-mail account to which you forwarded the e-mail.

WARNING

Replying to e-mails will require some thought if you have forwarded the message to yourself, because the return address will be your own. Be sure to check the e-mail for the address that originally sent the message to you, and manually insert that address into the recipient field of your return message.

Three Ways to Have a Computer Read Your E-Mail Aloud

It may sound like something out of a science-fiction television series, but with the current capabilities of voice synthesis, a computer can actually read your e-mail to you using software, such as Conversa Messenger from Conversational Computing or Mercury Mobile from CenturionSoft.

Conversa Messenger can take your phone call and read the contents of your e-mail over the phone. It also handles voice mail and faxes and offers many other features.

Mercury Mobile handles just e-mail, not the range of communications that Conversa Messenger can manage. However, Mercury Mobile can also telephone a number you give it, such as a cell phone, and read your e-mail to you. Combine that with voice-mail for the phone, and you know you will get your messages.

Shoutmail.com offers a free e-mail service. You can call it from a telephone, and the server will read your e-mail to you. It will even record a voice response to the e-mail. The server returns a note to the sender, telling the person to check a particular site on the Web to hear your answer. You can find the service at www.shoutmail.com.

Send E-Mail to Your Pager

If you can't wait to get your e-mail, consider a paging service that can send your e-mail to you. Such companies provide an e-mail address for you to use. Any e-mail the service receives is turned into an alphanumeric message and sent to your pager.

You don't have to have all your e-mail go to this address. Instead, use the directions earlier in this section for redirecting or forwarding your e-mail. Then, when you have regular access to your e-mail again, stop sending the e-mail to the pager.

NOTE

An example is the Motorola PageWriter 2000X using the SkyTel paging service. You can both send and receive e-mail from this pager as well as get both numeric and text pages.

SET UP A FAX SERVER

If you receive faxes at home, nothing is more convenient than a fax server. Instead of walking over to the fax machine to pick up piles of paper, you check the fax mailbox on the network server from wherever you are. If you need to send a fax from a program, just use the fax server. All this happens without additional phone lines or modems.

Various programs are available to create a network fax server. Call Center can provide a faxing service. Pressing the Send Fax button to start a Wizard that walks you through the fax-sending process.

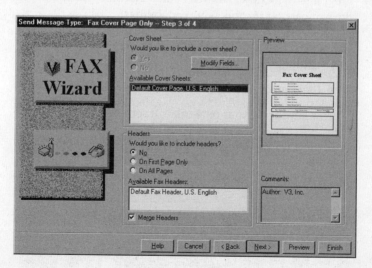

If you run a business out of your home, you might want to consider a package aimed more at network faxing. FaxMail Network for Windows from ElectraSoft is a shareware program that can run on any Windows computer on your network. Because it runs in the background, the program

Part VI

won't interfere with anything else the computer is doing. To install it, use this procedure:

1. Point a browser to www.electrasoft.com. Click the link to download FaxMail Network for Windows. Save the file fmn.zip to an empty directory on a network file server that has a fax modem.

2. Unarchive the file. You can download an evaluation version of Winzip, which handles archived files in Windows, from www.winzip.com.

3. Find the install.exe file, and double-click it.

4. Follow the directions in the installation program. You will have to provide a name and phone number for the faxes.

5. Once you have installed the program on the server, install it on your other PCs. The installation program will prompt you for a network drive to use. Give it the correct map letter for each PC.

Click Start ≻ Programs ≻ FaxMail Network For Windows ≻ FaxMail Tutor to learn how to use the system. To start the program, click Start ≻ Programs ≻ FaxMail Network For Windows ≻ FaxMail. This provides the work center the following capabilities:

▶ Sending and viewing faxes

▶ Monitoring activity

▶ Creating cover pages

Now anyone on your network can send and view faxes.

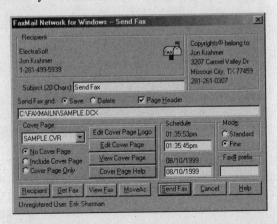

PROTECT YOUR NETWORK FROM POWER PROBLEMS

Anyone who has experienced it knows that losing power in the middle of doing something on a PC is extremely annoying. That annoyance can extend into mind-numbing aggravation when your entire network grinds to a halt, especially if you are using it for important things such as:

- ▶ Running your phone-answering system

- ▶ Monitoring household security

- ▶ Gaining access to your office

Keeping power available to your network can be important, indeed. You can take several steps to ensure that your network keeps running, depending on what causes an outage.

Guard against Loose Cords and Fumbling Feet

You can shut down a computer by tripping over a power cord and pulling it from an outlet. Though some may find the point inane, it becomes far less silly the first time your network loses power because you are not the reincarnation of Fred Astaire.

The easy fix is to route power cables out of the way of the non-nimble. Put cords behind desks and other furniture. Desks designed for computers will have openings in the rear to run cables.

When cords tangle together, you also increase the chance that moving one will accidentally pull out another. Try to keep all your cables neat and tidy by using cable ties to bundle them together.

Use Surge Suppressers

Because computers and networks involve multiple power outlets, you may consider using extension cords to provide more power. Don't succumb to temptation, because extension cords become something else to trip over.

Better you should use power strips, as professionals do. These devices typically have one cord running to a wall outlet and have space for five or six plugs.

Purchase the type that has *surge suppression*. In extraordinary circumstances, such as during a lightning strike, a surge of electricity travels along power lines. At those times, equipment operating and connected to the wall outlet can be damaged or even outright destroyed. A surge suppresser will shut down the circuit in the face of a power spike. You may lose data when the PC goes off, but better that than losing the data *and* the computer.

When plugging a combination surge suppresser and power strip into the wall, be sure the power circuit in your home can handle the load. The total amount of power a circuit can deliver is the product of the *amps* for which it's rated and the voltage of the house current, typically 120V. You can determine the power consumption of an electrical device in a similar manner: multiply the household voltage by the current consumed.

NOTE

For computer equipment, check the back of each device. You should see a plate that describes the number of amps the unit draws.

In the case of a typical 15-amp household circuit, the power capacity would be:

15 amps × 120 volts = 1800 watts

That sounds like a lot until you realize that a circuit may run through several rooms and must power *everything* connected to it. Power consumption adds up quickly, as shown in Table 23.1:

TABLE 23.1: Power Consumption

DEVICE	POWER CONSUMPTION
PC server	250 watts
Monitor	180 watts
Printer	120 watts
Scanner	100 watts
Air conditioner	500 watts
Six lights at 100 watts	600 watts
Total Power	**1750 watts**

Without planning ahead, you could find yourself pushing the power limits of a circuit in your home. Short of upgrading your home's circuitry, the best offense is a good defense. With a network, you can spread out the devices you use. For instance, connect the printer to another computer, and keep the scanner where it is. Another possibility is to be aware of what you use at the same time. For example, don't print and scan simultaneously, because that is when both consume the maximum amount of power.

Because telephone lines can direct lightning to your computer through an internal or external modem, look for surge suppressers that also offer telephone-line protection.

Keep Things Running with a UPS

You could glue cords in place and carefully plan how many electrical devices you can run at one time, but you are out of luck if the source of power goes out. A particularly virulent storm or excess demand during the summer can result in brown-outs or even a complete loss of electricity.

A type of device that is worth its weight in gold is an *uninterruptible power supply,* or UPS. Think of the device as a high-capacity battery with an intelligent switch. As long as an outlet provides power, the UPS passes the power to the PC while also charging its own battery.

On losing power into the home, the UPS senses the problem and flips its internal switch, powering the PC on the fully charged battery.

As with surge suppressers and electrical circuits in the home, a UPS has only so much capacity. The closer your devices get to the rated capacity, the less time you are likely to have in case of power loss. Here's how to select one:

1. Read the vendor's power rating for the UPS and the amount of time it can run off the battery.

2. List the equipment that you need to keep running. At the least, this would include a PC and a monitor.

3. Determine the power consumption of each.

4. Add the power consumptions together, and see how they compare with the UPS rating.

5. If the sum of the power consumptions is greater than the UPS rating, find a larger UPS.

A UPS won't solve all your potential power headaches. It can only run a short period of time, which is limited when power is out for an extended length of time. But that should be enough time to go around and let systems shut down gracefully, saving your data.

Many UPSs have a feature that will shut down a computer automatically and save whatever work was going on at the time. This is important because you won't be around the home all the time while your computer is on.

WHAT'S NEXT?

Now that you've read the last of this book's chapters, you can go directly to the "Vendor Guide" in Appendix A, which contains contact information for manufacturers, data recovery vendors, computer recycling centers, and so on. If you're still unclear about some of the terminology used in this book, you can check out Appendix B, "The Complete Hardware Dictionary." And if you'd like to know more about the books from which the chapters in this book were taken, you can go to our Web site at www.sybex.com. Happy computing!

PART VII
PC COMPLETE
USER'S REFERENCE

Appendix A

VENDOR GUIDE

The vendor listing in this appendix is divided into the following categories:

- ▶ Manufacturers of computers, peripherals, and components
- ▶ Data recovery vendors
- ▶ Memory vendors
- ▶ Storage device vendors
- ▶ Miscellaneous computer products vendors
- ▶ Older PC repair and exchange
- ▶ Computer recycling centers

Wherever possible, I have included non-800 numbers, as I recognize that my non-American readers cannot use 800 numbers.

Products, prices, and addresses change, so you may find some vendors listed here no longer exist or cannot be reached using the information given. I am not endorsing these particular vendors, but merely providing the information as a useful resource to you, the reader.

Adapted from *The Complete PC Upgrade & Maintenance Guide, 10th Edition* by Mark Minasi
ISBN 0-7821-2606-5   1620 pages $49.99

Manufacturers of Computers, Peripherals, and Components

Following are names, addresses, and phone numbers of various manufacturers of computers, peripherals, and components:

3Com Corporation
5400 Bayfront Plaza
Santa Clara, CA 95052-8145
(800) 638-3266, (408) 326-5000
http://www.3com.com

3DTV Corporation
1863 Pioneer Parkway East #303
Springfield, OR 97477
voicemail/fax (415) 680-1678
http://www.3dmagic.com
Hardware and software for 3-D (stereoscopic) video, computer graphics, and virtual reality

4Q Technologies
14425 Don Julian Road
City of Industry, CA 91746
(626) 333-6688
http://www.4qtech.com
Speakers

A4 Tech Corporation
20256 Apseo Robles
Walnut, CA 91789
(909) 468-0071
http://www.a4tech.com
Scanners

ABS Computer Technologies, Inc.
9997 Rose Hills Road
Whittier, CA 90601
(800) 876-8088
fax (562) 695-8923
http://www.buyabs.com

Abstract R&D, Inc.
120 Village Sq., Suite 37
Orinda, CA 94563
(510) 253-9588
Palmtop PCs

Acecad, Inc.
791 Foam St.
Monterey, CA 93940
voice (831) 655-1900
fax (831) 655-1919
http://www.acecad.com
Acecat III mouse replacement

Acer America Corporation
2641 Orchard Parkway
San Jose, CA 95134
(800) 733-2237
fax (408) 922-2933
http://www.acer.com

Acer Sertek Inc.
116 S. Wolfe Rd.
Sunnyvale, CA 94086
(408) 733-3174
www.ussertek.com
CD-ROMs, MPEG cards, and sound cards

ACL/Staticide
1960 E. Devon Avenue
Elk Grove Village, IL 60007
(800) 782-8420
http://www.aclstaticide.com
Antistatic equipment and cleaning kits

ACT-RX Technology Corporation
10F, 525, Chung Cheng Road
Hsin Tien, Taipei, Taiwan ROC
(886) 2-218-8000Booth I9025
CPU coolers

Action Electronics Co., Ltd.
198, Chung Yuan Road
Chung Li, Taiwan, ROC
(886) 3-4515494
http://www/action.com.tw
Axion monitors

Action Well Development Ltd.
Rm. 1101, 1103 and 4 Star Center
443-451 Castle Peak Road
Kwai Chung, NT, Hong Kong
(852) 2422-0010
http://www.actionwell.com
Fax modems, sound products, controller and VGA cards, and computer cases

ActionTec Electronics, Inc.
760 N. Mary Avenue
Sunnyvale, CA 94086
technical support (408) 752-7714
main (408) 752-7700
fax (408) 541-9003
http://www.actiontec.com
PC card (PCMCIA) products

Actown Corporation
8F, 527, Chung Cheng Road
Hsin Tien, Taipei, Taiwan ROC
(886) 2-2184612Booth S2050E
Opto-electronic products, including handheld
scanners, flatbeds, and sheet-fed scanners

Adaptec, Inc.
691 S. Milpitas Boulevard
Milpitas, CA 95035
(800) 934-2766, (408) 945-8600
http://www.adaptec.com

Addonics Technologies
48434 Milmont Drive
Fremont, CA 94538
(510) 438-6530
fax (510) 353-2020
http://www.addonics.com

Addtronics Enterprise Co.
43263 Osgood Road
Fremont, CA 94539
(510) 490-9898
fax (510) 490-7132
http://www.addtronics.com
Integrated computer cases

ADI Systems, Inc.
2115 Ringwood Avenue
San Jose, CA 95131
(800) 228-0530, (408) 944-0100
fax (408) 944-0300
http://www.adiusa.com
Multi-scanning color monitors

Adobe Systems Inc.
345 Park Avenue
San Jose, California 95110-2704
(800) 833-6687, (408) 536-6000
fax (408) 537-6000
http://www.adobe.com

ADPI (Analog and Digital Peripherals, Inc.)
P.O. Box 499
Troy, OH 45373
(937) 339-2241
(800) 758-1041
www.adpi.com
Backup devices

ADS Technologies (Advanced Digital Systems)
13909 Bettencourt Street
Cerritos, CA 90703
(800) 888-5244, (562) 926-1928
http://www.adstech.com
Multimedia specialty audio/video hardware

Advanced Gravis Computer Technology Ltd.
World Headquarters
2855 Campus Drive
San Mateo, CA 94403
(650) 572-2700, (800) 535-4242
fax (610) 231-1022
http://www.gravis.com
PC game interfaces

Advanced Integration Research, Inc.
2188 Del Franco Street
San Jose, CA 95131
(408) 428-0800
http://www.airwebs.com
486 and Pentium system boards based on
ISA, EISA, PCI, and VL-bus architectures

Advanced Matrix Technology, Inc.
747 Calle Plano
Camarillo, CA 93012-8598
(805) 388-5799
http://www.amtprinters.com
Dot matrix, laser, and ink-jet printers and
plotters

Advantage Memory
25A Technology Drive, building 2
Irvine, CA 92718
(800) 245-5299
http://www.advantagememory.com

AGFA (BAYER CORPORATION)

200 Ballardvale Street
Wilmington, MA 01887
(508) 658-5600
http://www.agfa.com

Scanners, film recorders, color management software, and digital cameras

AHEAD SYSTEMS, INC.

44244 Fremont Boulevard
Fremont, CA 94538
(510) 623-0900

3-D multimedia surround-sound, accelerator, and 3-D stereo vision products

AITECH INTERNATIONAL CORPORATION

47971 Fremont Boulevard
Fremont, CA 94538
(510) 226-8960
http://www.aitech.com

Multimedia and desktop video products

AIWA AMERICA, INC.

800 Corporate Drive
Mahwah, NJ 07430
(800) 920-2673
http://www.aiwa.com

Tape backup products

ALARIS, INC.

47338 Fremont Boulevard
Fremont, CA 94538
(510) 770-5700
http://www.alaris.com

Graphics acceleration and scalable full-motion video playback products

ALFA INFOTECH CO.

46600 Landing Pkwy.
Fremont, CA 94538
(510) 252-9300

Multimedia and communication products

ALI (ACER LABORATORIES, INC.)

1830-B Bering Drive
San Jose, CA 95112
(408) 467-7456
fax (408) 467-7474
http://www.acerlabs.com

Integrated circuits for personal computers and embedded systems

ALPHA & OMEGA COMPUTER

3041 E. La Jolla Street
Anaheim, CA 92806
(714) 632-0388
http://www.aocusa.com

486/Pentium CPU coolers

ALPHACOM ENTERPRISE, INC.

1407 Englewood Street
Philadelphia, PA 19111
(215) 722-6133

Joysticks, mice, trackballs, CPU cooling fans with built-in heat sinks, and removable hard disk drive kits

ALPS

3553 N. First Street
San Jose, CA 95134
(800) 825-2577, (408) 432-6000
fax (408) 432-6035
http://www.alpsusa.com

GlidePoint input devices and drive products

AMCC (APPLIED MICRO CIRCUITS CORPORATION)

6290 Sequence Drive
San Diego, CA 92121
(858) 450-9333
fax (858) 450-9885
http://www.amcc.com

Integrated circuits

AMD (ADVANCED MICRO DEVICES)

One AMD Place
P.O. Box 3453
Sunnyvale, CA 94088-3453
(408) 732-2400, (800) 538-8450
http://www.amd.com

CPUs

AMERICAN COVERS, INC.

102 W. 12200 S
Draper, UT 84092
(801) 553-0600
http://www.mousemat.com

Computer accessory products

AMI (AMERICAN MEGATRENDS, INC.)
6145F Northbelt Parkway
Norcross, GA 30071
(770) 246-8600
sales (800) 828-9264
fax (770) 246-8791
http://www.ami.com
Motherboards and AMIDiag software

AMPTRON INTERNATIONAL, INC.
1239 Etcher Ave.
City of Industry, CA 91748
(626) 912-5789
http://www.amptron.com
System boards

AMREL TECHNOLOGY, INC.
11801 Goldring Road
Arcadia, CA 91006
(800) 882-6735
http://www.amrel.com
Modular notebook computers

AMS TECH, INC.
12881 Ramona Boulevard
Irwindale, CA 91706
(800) 980-8889
http://www.amstech.com
Desktop and notebook computers

ANA PRECISION CO., LTD.
Suite 694, Kumjung-Dong, Kunp'O-shi
Kyunggi-Do, 435-050, Korea
(0343) 53-0813
Ink-jet and dot matrix printers

ANGIA COMMUNICATIONS
441 East Bay Boulevard
Provo, UT 84606
(800) 877-9159
fax (801) 373-9847
PCMCIA fax modem

AOC INTERNATIONAL
532 Valley Way
Milpitas, CA 95035
(408) 263-1567
http://www.aocltd.com
Visual display products

APC (AMERICAN POWER CONVERSION)
132 Fairgrounds Road
West Kingdom, RI 02892
(800) 800-4APC, (401) 789-5735
fax (401) 789-3710
http://www.apc.com
UPSs and phone line surge protectors

APEX DATA, INC. /SMART MODULAR TECHNOLOGIES, INC.
4305 Cushing Parkway
Fremont, CA 94538
(800) 841-APEX
tech support (510) 249-1605
fax (510) 249-1600
tech support fax (510) 249-1604
e-mail sales@smartm.com and support@smartm.com
BBS (510) 249-1601 (8 data bits, 1 stop bit, and no parity)
http://www.apexdata.com

APPLE COMPUTER, INC.
1 Infinite Loop
Cupertino, CA 95014
(408) 996-1010
http://www.apple.com

APS TECHNOLOGIES
6131 Deramus, Suite 4967
Kansas City, MO 64120
(800) 235-2753, (816) 483-1600
fax (816) 483-3077
http://www.apstech.com
Data storage and backup products

ARCADA SOFTWARE
Seagate Software
920 Disc Drive
Scotts Valley, CA 95067
(408) 438-6550
fax (408) 438-7612
http://www.arcada.com
Data protection and storage management software products

ARCHTEK AMERICA CORPORATION

18549 Gale Avenue
City of Industry, CA 91748-1338
(626) 912-9800
fax (626) 912-9700
http://www.archtek.com
Voice/data communications and network
products

ARCO COMPUTER PRODUCTS, INC.

2750 N. 29th Avenue, Suite 316
Hollywood, FL 33020
(954) 925-2688
http://www.arcoide.com
IDE busless, slotless, operating system-inde-
pendent mirroring adapter

ARKENSTONE, INC.

1390 Borregas Avenue
Sunnyvale, CA 94089
(800) 444-4443
http://www.arkenstone.org
Products that help individuals who are
blind, visually impaired, or learning disabled
to better access written information

ARTEK COMPUTER SYSTEMS

47801 Fremont Boulevard
Fremont, CA 94538
(510) 490-8492
fax (510) 490-8405
http://www.artek.com
High-end PC subsystems

ARTISOFT, INC.

One South Church Avenue, Suite 2200
Tucson, AZ 85701
(520) 670-7100
http://www.artisoft.com
Networking products suited to small businesses and workgroups

ARTMEDIA

2772 Calle del Mundo
Santa Clara, CA 95050
(408) 980-8988
http://www.artmedia.com

ASK LCD, INC.

100 West Forest Ave, Suite E
Englewood, NJ 07631
(201) 541-2424
tech support (888) 307-2561
fax (201) 541-2391
http://www.asklcd.com
LCD presentation products

ASK TECHNOLOGY LTD.

Unit 1, 4/F, Henley Ind. Ctr.,
9-15 Bute Street
Mongkok, Kowloon, Hong Kong
(852) 2398-3223
http://www.ask.com.hk
System boards, VGA cards, and sound cards

ASKEY INTERNATIONAL CORPORATION

47849 Fremont Boulevard
Fremont, CA 94538
http://www.askey.com
PCMCIA, external, and internal modem
cards and pocket models

ASOLID COMPUTER SUPPLY, INC.

(Biostar Manufacture Group)
4044 Clipper Court
Fremont, CA 94538
(510) 226-6678
http://www.biostar-usa.com
Motherboards

ASPEN SYSTEMS INC.

3900 Youngfield Street
Wheat Ridge, CO 80033-3865
(800) 992-9242, (303) 431-7196
http://www.aspsys.com
RISC (reduced instruction set computing)
systems

ASPEN TECHNOLOGY, INC.

Ten Canal Park
Cambridge, MA 02141-2200
(617) 949-1000
fax (617) 949-1030
http://www.aspentech.com
Internal, external, and PCMCIA fax modems

ASSMANN DATA PRODUCTS
  1849 W. Drake Drive, Suite 101
  Tempe, AZ 85283
  (877) ASSMANN (1-877-277-6266)
  fax (480) 897-7255
  http://www.usa-assmann.com
Ergonomic mice

AST COMPUTER
  AST Research, Inc.
  16225 Alton Parkway
  Irvine, CA 92618
  or
  P.O. Box 57005
  Irvine, CA 92619-7005
  (949) 727-4141
  tech support (800) 727-1278
  http://www.ast.com

ATI TECHNOLOGIES
  33 Commerce Valley Drive East
  Thornhill, Ontario, Canada L3T 7N6
  tech support (905) 882-2626
  tech support fax (905) 882-0546
  faxback (905) 882-2600 (press #2)
  CompuServe: GO ATITECH
  http://www.atitech.com
Graphics accelerators

ATLANTIC TECHNOLOGY
  343 Vanderbilt Avenue
  Norwood, MA 02062
  (781) 762-6300
  http://www
    .atlantictechnology.com
Speakers

ATronics INTERNATIONAL, INC.
  44700-B Industrial Drive
  Fremont, CA 94538-6431
  (510) 656-8400
  fax (510) 656-8560
  http://www.atronics.com
Advanced external storage products

ATTO TECHNOLOGY, INC.
  40 Hazelwood Drive, Suite 106
  Amherst, NY 14228
  (716) 691-1999
  fax (716) 691-9353
  http://www.attotech.com

VantagePCI Multi-Channel SCSI
accelerator card

AuraVISION CORPORATION
  47865 Fremont Boulevard
  Fremont, CA 94538
  (510) 252-6800
  fax (510) 428-9350
  http://www.liberty.com/
    home/auravision/Index1.htm
Multimedia IC devices

AUTUMN TECHNOLOGIES
  11705 69th Way N
  Largo, FL 34643
  (800) 837-8551
Test Bed Pro, a commercial PC testing,
assembly, and repair workbench

AVERMEDIA, INC.
  47923A Warm Springs Boulevard
  Fremont, CA 94538
  (510) 770-9899
  http://www.aver.com
PC-video multimedia hardware

AVM TECHNOLOGY, INC.
  Valencia Technology Park
  26074 Avenue Hall, Suite 15
  Valencia, CA 91355
  (800) 884-9399
  (805) 295-9399
  fax (805) 295-0692
  http://www.avmtech.com
Professional MIDI wavetable modules

AVNET TECHNOLOGY CO., LTD.
  6F-1, No. 102, Sung Lung Road
  Taipei, Taiwan ROC
  (886) 2-7607603
Audio-visual network card

AWARD SOFTWARE INTERNATIONAL
  (Phoenix Technologies)
  411 E. Plumeria Drive
  San Jose, CA 95134
  (408) 570-1000
  fax (408) 570-1001
  http://www.award.com
Desktop Plug-and-Play BIOS for 486, 586,
Pentium, and P6-based PC platforms

Axonix Corporation
844 S. 200 East
Salt Lake City, UT 84111
(800) 866-9797, (801) 521-9797
http://www.axonix.com
CD-ROMs

Axxon Computer Corporation
3979 Tecumseh Road E
Windsor, ON N8W 1J5, Canada
(519) 974-0163
http://www.softio.com/
Jumperless I/O cards

Aztech Labs, Inc.
45645 Northport Loop East
Fremont, CA 94538
(510) 623-8988
fax (510) 623-8989
BBS (510) 623-8933
tech support (510) 623-9037
tech support fax (510) 353-4327
http://www.aztechlabs.com
http://www.aztechca.com
ftp://ftp.aimnet.com/pub/users/
   aztech
CD-ROM drives

Belkin Components
501 West Walnut Street
Compton, CA 90220
(310) 898-1100
(800) 2-BELKIN (223-5546)
fax (310) 898-1111
http://www.belkin.com
Standard and custom computer cables,
printer-sharing devices, surge protectors,
and LAN cabling-related products

Benwin Inc.
Kwong Quest
1116 Coiner Court
City of Industry, CA 91748
(626) 935-8888
http://www.benwine.com
Multimedia products, specializing in
speakers

Best Data Products
19748 Dearborn Street
Chatsworth, CA 91311
(818) 773-9600
fax (818) 773-9619
http://www.bestdata.com

Best Power
General Signal
P.O. Box 280
Necedah, WI 54646
(800) 356-5794
fax (608) 565-2221
http://www.bestpower.com
UPSs and shutdown software

BIS Technology
13111 Brooks Drive, Suite A
Baldwin Park, CA 91706
(818) 856-5800
High-speed voice/fax/data modems

Boca Research
1377 Clint Moore Road
Boca Raton, FL 33478
(561) 997-6227
fax (407) 994-5848
http://www.bocaresearch.com

Borland International
Inprise Corporation
100 Enterprise Way
Scotts Valley, CA 95066
(831) 431-1000
http://www.borland.com
Products and services for software
developers

Bose Corporation
The Mountain
Framingham, MA 01701
(800) WWW-BOSE (800-999-2673)
http://www.bose.com

Brooks Power Systems, Inc.
1400 Adams Road
Bensalem, PA 19020
(800) 523-1551
Power Systems' SurgeStopper surge and
noise suppressors

BROTHER INTERNATIONAL CORPORATION
100 Somerset Corporate Boulevard
Bridgewater, NJ 08807-0911
(909) 704-1700
fax (909) 704-8235
http://www.brother.com
Multi-function products and laser printers

BRYSIS DATA, INC.
17431 Gale Ave.
City of Industry, CA 91748
(818) 810-0355
fax (818) 810-4555
Touch screen monitors

BSF COMPONENTS INC.
420 Third Street
Oakland, CA 94607
(510) 893-8822
Molded and assembled computer cables

C-CUBE MICROSYSTEMS
1778 McCarthy Boulevard
Milpitas, CA 95035
(408) 944-630
fax (408) 490-8590
http://www.c-cube.com
MPEG and JPEG decoders and encoders for
personal computers

CALIFORNIA PC PRODUCTS
205 Apollo Way
Hollister, CA 95023
(831) 637-2250, (800) 394-4122
fax (831) 637-7473
http://www.calpc.com
Computer chassis and power supplies

CALLUNA TECHNOLOGY LTD.
1 Blackwood Road
Eastfield, Glenrothes
Fife KY7 4NP, Scotland, UK
(44) 1592-630-810
fax (44)1592-630-920
http://www.calluna.com
PC card hard disk drives

CANON COMPUTER SYSTEMS
2995 Redhill Avenue
Costa Mesa, CA 92626
(800) 848-4123, (714) 438-3000
http://www.ccsi.canon.com

CANON U.S.A., INC.
1 Canon Plaza
Lake Success, NY 11042-1113
(516) 488-6700
http://www.usa.canon.com
Bubblejet CJ10 desktop color copier, scanner, and printer

CANOPUS
711 Charcot Avenue
San Jose, CA 95131
(408) 954-4500
fax (408) 954-4504
http://www.canopuscorp.com
High-performance multimedia products
for PCs

CARDINAL TECHNOLOGIES, INC.
1827 Freedom Road
Lancaster, PA 17601
(717) 293-3000
fax (717) 293-3055
http://www.cardtech.com
Fax modems

CASCO PRODUCTS, INC.
375 Collins Rd. NE, Ste. 115
Cedar Rapids, IA 52402
(319) 393-6960, (800) 793-6960
fax (319) 393-6895
http://www.casco.com
LightLink infrared, cordless keyboard

CD TECHNOLOGY, INC.
19160 Cozette Lane
Cupertino, CA 95014
(408) 863-4800
fax (408) 863-4801
http://www.w2.com/
    docs2/m/cdtech.html
CD-ROMs

CENTON ELECTRONICS, INC.
20 Morgan
Irvine, CA 92618
(800) 234-9292
fax (949) 855-6035
http://www.centon.com
Manufacturer of memory upgrades for desktops, workstations, laptops, notebooks,
portables, and printers

CERWIN-VEGA, INC.
555 E. Easy Street
Simi Valley, CA 93065
(805) 584-5300
fax (805) 526-3653
Digital audio-quality multimedia speaker systems

CH PRODUCTS
970 Park Center Drive
Vista, CA 92083
(619) 598-2518
http://www.chproducts.com
Joysticks, F-16 sticks, throttles, rudder pedals, flight yokes, trackballs, and gamecards

CHAINTECH COMPUTER U.S., INC.
509 Valley Way
Milpitas, CA 95035
(408) 935-6988
fax (408) 935-6989
http://www.chaintech.com.tw
Motherboards, VGA cards, multi-I/O cards, SCSI interfaces, and sound cards

CHAPLET SYSTEMS USA, INC.
252 N. Wolfe Road
Sunnyvale, CA 94086
(408) 732-7950
http://www.best.com/~chaplet/
    index.shtml
Notebook computers

CHARTERED ELECTRONICS INDUSTRIES
210A Twin Dolphin Drive
Redwood City, CA 94065
(415) 591-6617
PC PrimeTimeTV add-on board

CHASE ADVANCED TECHNOLOGIES
7 Manning Road
Billerica, MA 01821
(508) 670-0646
fax (508) 670-9025
http://www.chase-at.com
Computer peripheral products

CHEER ELECTRONICS (USA)
45 Ethel Road West
Piscataway, NJ 08854
(908) 572-5455
fax (908) 572-6698
http://www.allproducts.com
    .tw/cheer/
Monitors

CHERRY ELECTRICAL PRODUCTS
11200-88th Ave.
P.O. Box 581913
Pleasant Prairie, WI 53158
(414) 942-6500
http://www.cherrycorp.com
PC/POS keyboards, low-cost 101-key data entry keyboards

CHINON AMERICA, INC.
615 Hawaii Avenue
Torrance, CA 90503
(310) 533-0274
fax (310) 533-1727
Digital cameras, CD-ROM drives

CIRQUE CORPORATION
433 W. Lawndale Drive
Salt Lake City, UT 84115
(800) 454-3375, (801) 467-1100
http://www.cirque.com
GlidePoint trackpad

CIRRUS LOGIC, INC.
3100 W. Warren Avenue
Fremont, CA 94538
(510) 623-8300
http://www.cirrus.com

CITIZEN AMERICA CORPORATION
831 South Douglas Street, Suite 121
P.O. Box 1021
El Segundo, CA 90245-1021
(310) 643-9825
fax (310) 725-0969
http://www.citizen-america.com/
Printiva 600C near-photo-quality color printer

CLARY CORPORATION
1960 S. Walker Avenue
Monrovia, CA 91016
(800) 442-5279
http://www.clary.com/onguard/
UPSs

CMD TECHNOLOGY, INC.
19 Morgan
Irvine, CA 92618
(949) 454-0800
http://www.cmd.com
SCSI RAID and PC host adapters

COLORGRAPHIC
5980 Peachtree Road
Atlanta, GA 30341
(770) 455-3921, (877) 943-3843
fax (770) 458-0616
http://www.cologrfx.com

COM2001 CORPORATION
12250 El Camino Real, Ste. 160
San Diego, CA 92130
(858) 314-2001
fax (858) 314-2002
http://www.com2001.com
Video and audio conferencing software

COMBYTE, INC.
4424 Innovation Drive
Fort Collins, CO 80525
(970) 229-0660
Doubleplay dual-mode drive, which reads
and writes both floppy disks and minicartridge tapes

COMDIAL CORP.
1180 Seminole Trail
Charlottesville, VA 22906-7266
(800) 347-1432, (804) 978-2200
faxback (800) COMDIAL
http://www.comdial.com
PC and telephone interfaces

COMMAND SOFTWARE SYSTEMS
1061 E. Indiantown Road, Suite 500
Jupiter, FL 33477
(561) 575-3026, (800) 423-9147
fax (561) 575-3200
http://www.commandcom.com
F-Prot Professional antivirus software

COMPAQ COMPUTER CORPORATION
P.O. Box 692000
Houston, TX 77269-2000
(800) 345-1518, (281) 370-0670
product information (800) 345-1518
http://www.compaq.com

COMPUTER CONNECTIONS AMERICA
19A Crosby Drive
Bedford, MA 01730
(617) 271-0444
http://www.storagecompany.com
Peripheral equipment for backup and data
storage

COMPUTER FUN
8250 Valdosta Avenue
San Diego, CA 92126-2130
e-mail garyo@computerfun.com
(619) 271-9090
http://www.computerfun.com/
Manufacturer of mouse pads and computer toys

CONNECTIX CORPORATION
2955 Campus Drive, Suite 100
San Mateo, CA 94403
(800) 950-5880, (650) 571-5700
fax (650) 571-5195
http://www.connectix.com
QuickCam video camera

CONNER PERIPHERALS, INC.
1650 Sunflower Avenue
Costa Mesa, CA 92626
(800) 4-CONNER
http://www.conner.com

COPAM DYNAMIC SYSTEMS, INC.
46560 Fremont Boulevard, Suite 409
Fremont, CA 94538
(510) 770-0149
CPU cooling kits and memory-related
components

COPPER LEAF TECHNOLOGY

2233 Paragon Drive
San Jose, CA 95131
(408) 452-9288
Motherboards

**CORNERSTONE PERIPHERALS
TECHNOLOGY, INC.**

225 Hammond Avenue
Fremont, CA 94539
(800) 562-2552, (510) 580-8900
fax (510) 580-8998
http://www.bigmonitors.com

CREATIVE LABS, INC.

1523 Cimarron Plaza
Stillwater, OK 74075
(800) 998-1000
fax (405) 624-6780
http://www.creative.com

CREATIX POLYMEDIA, L.P.

3945 Freedom Cir., Suite 670
Santa Clara, CA 95054
(408) 654-9300
http://www.creatix.com
Multimedia products, high-speed modems,
and PCMCIA cards

CRYSTAL SEMICONDUCTOR

3100 W. Warren Avenue
Fremont, CA 94538
(510) 623-8300

CTX INTERNATIONAL, INC.

20955 Pathfinder Rd.
Diamond Bar, CA 91765
(909) 610-2520, (800) 888-2012
http://www.ctxintl.com
Monitors

CYBERMAX COMPUTER, INC.

133 North 5th Street
Allentown, PA 18102
(888) 566-1313, (610) 770-1808
from Canada (800) 695-4991
http://www.cybmax.com

CYRIX CORPORATION

2703 N. Central Expressway
Richardson, TX 75080
(800) 462-9749, (972) 968-8387
e-mail tech_support@cyrix.com
BBS (214) 968-8610
http://www.cyrix.com

DAEWOO ELECTRONICS

120 Chubb Ave.
Lyndhurst, NJ 07071
(201) 460-2501
fax (201) 460-2651
http://www.daewoo.com
Monitors

DARKHORSE SYSTEMS, INC.

Tanisys Technology
12201 Technology Blvd., Suite 130
Austin, Texas 78727-6101
(512) 335-4440, (800) 533-1744
fax (512) 257-5310
http://www.tanisys.com
Memory test systems

DATA DEPOT, INC.

1301 Seminole Blvd.
Largo, FL 33770
(727) 585-7678
fax (727) 518-9300
http://www.datadepo.com
PC diagnostic test products, including hardware and software products

DATALUX CORP.

155 Aviation Dr.
Winchester, VA 22602
(800) DATALUX, (703) 662-1500
fax (540) 662-1682
faxback (540) 662-1675
e-mail info@datalux.com
http://www.datalux.com
Space-saving PC hardware

DATASONIX CORPORATION

5700 Flatiron Pkwy.
Boulder, CO 80301
(303) 545-9500
Portable gigabyte storage devices

DELL COMPUTER CORPORATION
One Dell Way
Round Rock, TX 78682
(800) 915-3355, (888) 560-2384
http://www.dell.com

DELRINA CORPORATION
Symantec Corp.
175 West Broadway
Eugene, OR 97401
(541) 334-6054 (outside the U.S. and
    Canada)
(800) 268-6082
fax (541) 984-8020
http://www.delrina.com
PC fax, communications, and electronic
forms software

DELTA PRODUCTS CORPORATION
4405 Cushing Pkwy.
Fremont, CA 94538
(510) 668-5173
Video display products

DELTEC
2727 Kurtz Street
San Diego, CA 92110
(619) 291-4211
http://www.deltecpower.com
Uninterruptible power systems and power
management software

DENON ELECTRONICS
222 New Road
Parsippany, NJ 07054
(201) 575-7810
http://www.del.denon.com
CD-ROM jukebox that houses 200 discs

DFI (DIAMOND FLOWER, INC.)
47923 Warm Springs Blvd.
Fremont, CA 94539
(510) 623-5010
fax (510) 623-5020
http://www.dfi.com
Motherboards, video cards, notebooks,
desktop systems, and multimedia
components

DIAGSOFT, INC.
5615 Scotts Valley Drive, Suite 140
Scotts Valley, CA 95066
(408) 438-8247
fax (408) 438-7113
http://www.diagsoft.com
Diagnostic software

DIAMOND MULTIMEDIA SYSTEMS, INC.
S3 Incorporated
2841 Mission College Blvd.
Santa Clara, CA 95054-1838
(408) 588-8000
fax (408) 980-5444
http://www.diamondmm.com

DIGITAL EQUIPMENT CORPORATION (DEC)
20555 State Hwy 249
Houston, TX 77070
(281) 370-0670
http://www.compaq.com
PCs, servers, and workstations for 32- and
64-bit computing

DPT-DISTRIBUTED PROCESSING TECHNOLOGY
140 Candace Drive
Maitland, FL 32751
(407) 830-5522
http://www.dpt.com
SmartCache SCSI host adapters

DTC DATA TECHNOLOGY, INC.
1222 Alderwood Dr.
Sunnyvale, CA 94086
(408) 745-9320
fax (408) 745-9316
http://www.datatechnology.com
Drives and SCSI devices

DTK COMPUTER, INC.
770 Epperson Drive
City of Industry, CA 91748
(818) 810-0098
Pentium-based systems

EDEK TECHNOLOGIES, INC.

Div. of Elite Computer, Taiwan
1212 John Reed Ct.
City of Industry, CA 91745
(818) 855-5700
fax (626) 855-0365

Manufacturer and distributor of computer
motherboard and VGA card products

ELSA, INC.

1630 Zanker Rd
San Jose, CA 95112
(408) 961-4600
fax (408) 919-9120
http://www.elsa.com

2-D and 3-D graphics accelerators and ISDN
products

ENHANCE MEMORY PRODUCTS, INC.

18730 Oxnard Street, Suite 201
Tarzana, CA 91356
(818) 343-3066
fax (818) 343-1436
http://www.enhance3000.com

Memory systems

ENSONIQ

155 Great Valley Parkway
Malvern, PA 19355
(610) 647-3930
fax (610) 647-8908
http://www.ensoniq.com

EPS TECHNOLOGIES

8877 S. 137th Circle
Omaha, NE 68138
(800) 447-0921
fax (402) 891-9383
http://www.epstech.com

EPSON AMERICA, INC.

20770 Madrona Avenue
Torrance, CA 90509
(800) 463-7766, (310) 782-5174
fax (310) 782-5220
http://www.epson.com

ESS TECHNOLOGY, INC.

48401 Fremont Blvd
Fremont, CA 94538
(510) 492-1088
fax (510) 492-1098
http://www.esstech.com

ES689 Wavetable Music Synthesizer, ES938
3D Audio Effects Processor

EVERGREEN TECHNOLOGIES, INC.

808 W. Buchanan Ave.
Corvallis, OR 97330
(541) 757-0934
http://www.evertech.com

CPU upgrades for 386- and 486-based
computers

EXABYTE CORPORATION

1685 38th St.
Boulder, CO 80301
(800) 445-7736, (303) 417-7511,
(303) 417-7792
fax (303) 417-7890
EXAFAX (fax-on-demand system) (201)
946-0091
e-mail support@exabyte.com
http://www.exabyte.com

EXP COMPUTER, INC.

141 Eileen Way
Syosset, NY 11791
(516) 496-2914
http://www.expnet.com

Memory and PCMCIA products for notebooks and palmtops

EXPERT COMPUTER INTERNATIONAL, INC.

12951 166 Street
Cerritos, CA 90703
(562) 407-1719
http://www.expertcom.com

Generic and name-brand VGA cards in
DRAM/VRAM ISA, VL-bus, and PCI
configurations

FAST MULTIMEDIA U.S., INC.

15029 Woodinville Redwood Rd.
Woodinville, WA 98072
(800) 249-FAST, (425) 354-2002
fax (425) 354-2002
http://www.fastmultimedia.com

FPS60 video compression board for multi-media production

FOCUS COMPUTER PRODUCTS, INC.
35 Pond Park Road
Hingham, MA 02043
(617) 741-5008

Anti-glare glass screen filters, anti-radiation glass screen filters, wraparound screen filters, cleaning products for screen filters

FOCUS ELECTRONIC CORPORATION
21078 Commerce Pointe Drive
Walnut, CA 91789
(909) 468-5533

Signature Series keyboards

FORMOSA USA, INC.
9400 Lurline Avenue, Suite B
Chatsworth, CA 91311
(818) 407-4956

MPEG decoding cards, video capture boards, TV tuners, video conference products, 16-bit sound cards, and wavetable modules

FUJITSU PERSONAL SYSTEMS, INC.
5200 Patrick Henry Drive
Santa Clara, CA 95054
(408) 982-9500

FUJITSU COMPUTER PRODUCTS OF AMERICA
2904 Orchard Parkway
San Jose, CA 95134
(408) 432-6333, (800) 626-4686
http://www.fujitsu.com
http://www.fcpa.com

Peripherals including hard disk drives, optical disk drives, tape drives, laser and dot matrix printers, and document imaging scanners

FUJITSU MICROELECTRONICS, INC.
3545 N. First Street
San Jose, CA 95134
(408) 922-9000, (800) 626-4686
http://www.fujitsu.com

Memory cards, LAN cards, and multimedia and communications cards

GATEWAY2000
610 Gateway Dive
N. Sioux City, SD 57049-2000
(888) 888-0244, (605) 232-2230
from Canada (800) 846-3609
fax (605) 232-2023
faxback (800) 846-4526
http://www.gw2k.com

GVC TECHNOLOGIES
GVC Canada Headquarters
485 Millway Ave.
Concord ON L4K 3V4
(905) 738-9300
fax (905) 738-5563
http://www.gvc.ca

Modems

HAYES MODEM EXPRESS.
2800 Vicksburg Lane
Plymouth, MN 55447
(612) 857-1501
fax (612) 553-1964
http://www.hayes.com

Modems

HEI
1495 Steiger Lake Lane
P.O. Box 5000
Victoria, MN 55386
(612) 443-2500
http://www.heii.com

Fast Point light pens

HERCULES COMPUTER TECHNOLOGY, INC.
3839 Spinnaker Court
Fremont, CA 94538
(800) 323-0601, (510) 623-6030,
(510) 623-6050
fax (510) 623-1112
tech support fax (510) 490-6745
faxback (800) 711-HERC (800-711-4372)
e-mail support@hercules.com
CompuServe: GO HERCULES,
    71333,2532
BBS (510) 623-7449
http://www.hercules.com

Hewlett-Packard

Personal Information Products Group
5301 Stevens Creek Boulevard
Santa Clara, CA 95052
(800) 762-0900
http://www.hp.com

Hewlett-Packard Co.

Information Storage Group
800 S. Taft Avenue
Loveland, CO 80537
(970) 679-6000
http://www.hp.com
HP Colorado tape products, HP DAT tape
products, and HP optical products, disk
drives, and disk array systems

Hewlett-Packard Co.

North American Hardcopy Marketing
16399 W. Bernardo Drive
San Diego, CA 92127
(800) 752-0990
customer information center
    (800) 752-0900
http://www.hp.com
Printers

Hilgraeve, Inc.

111 Conant Avenue, Suite A
Monroe, MI 48161
(734) 243-0576
fax (734) 243-0645
http://www.hilgraeve.com
32-bit communications software, including
HyperTerminal

Hitachi America, Ltd.

50 Prospect Avenue
Tarrytown, NY 10591-4698
(800) HITACHI, (914) 332-5800
fax (914) 332-5555
http://www.hitachi.com
http://www
    .internetworking.hitachi.com
Computer peripherals and components,
including storage products

HTP International

1620 South Lewis Street
Anaheim, CA 92805
(714) 937-9300

Hyundai Electronics America

1955 Lundy Avenue
San Jose, CA 95131
(408) 232-8000
fax (408) 232-8146
http://www.hea.com
Components, including memory devices for
DRAM and SRAM

I/OMagic Corporation

6B Autry
Irvine, CA 92618
(949) 727-7466
customer support (949) 597-2462
fax (949) 727-7467
customer support fax (949) 380-0696
http://www.iomagic.com

IBM PC Co.

1 Orchard Road
Armonk, NY 10504
(800) IBM 4YOU, (914) 499-1900
http://www.ibm.com
http://www.pc.ibm.com

Iiyama North America, Inc.

575 Anton Blvd, Ste. 590
Costa Mesa, CA 92626
(714) 437-5111
fax (714) 437-5982
http://www.iiyama.com

Integrated Technology Express, Inc.

1557 Centre Pointe Drive
Milpitas, CA 95035
(408) 934-7330
http://www.ite.com.tw
PC core logic chip sets, I/O peripheral chips,
and custom ASIC design services on $x86$ and
PowerPC architectures

Intel Corporation

2200 Mission College Boulevard
Santa Clara, CA 95052
(408) 765-8080
customer service (800) 321-4044
fax (408) 765-9904
http://www.intel.com

INTERACT ACCESSORIES, INC.

(formerly STD Entertainment)
10999 McCormick Road
Hunt Valley, MD 21031
(410) 785-5661
http://www.interact-acc.com
Multimedia gaming products such as joysticks, control pads, game cards, speakers, woofers, mice, storage cases, and cleaning kits

IOMEGA CORPORATION

1821 West Iomega Way
Roy, UT 84067
(800) MY-STUFF, (801) 332-1000
http://www.iomega.com

IPC PERIPHERALS

48041 Fremont Boulevard
Fremont, CA 94538
(510) 354-0800
Sound cards, 24- and 32-speed CD-ROM drives, three- and seven-disc changers, PCMCIA sound and Ethernet cards, audio/fax/modem telephony products, and multimedia upgrade kits

IPC TECHNOLOGIES, INC.

7200 Glen Forest Drive
Richmond, VA 23228
(804) 285-9300
http://www.ipctech.com

J-MARK COMPUTER CORPORATION

480 E. Arrow Hwy.
San Dimas, CA 91773
(909) 385-8800
fax (909) 305-4856
http://www.j-mark.com
Motherboards, fax modems, SVGA cards, PCMCIA devices, and network cards for notebooks and PCs

JAZZ SPEAKERS

1355 Darius Court.
City of Industry, CA 91745
(626) 336-2689
fax (626) 336-2489
http://www.jazzspeakers.com

JBL CONSUMER PRODUCTS, INC.

Harmon Consumer Group
80 Crossways Pk. W
Woodbury, NY 11797
(516) 496-3400, (800) 336-4JBL
www.jbl.com
Multimedia speakers, both satellites and subwoofers

JOSS TECHNOLOGY LTD.

No. 20, Lane 84, San Min Road
Hsin Tien City
Taipei Hsien, Taiwan ROC
(886) 2-9102050
Motherboards, 4MB/16MB 72-pin SIMM modules

JVC INFORMATION PRODUCTS OF AMERICA

#2 JVC Road
Tuscaloosa, AL 35405
(205) 556-7111
authorized service centers (800) 537-5722
http://www.jvc.com
http://www.jvcdiscusa.com
CD-ROM products and software

KEYSONIC TECHNOLOGY, INC.

A Div. of Powercom America
2229 Paragon Dr.
San Jose, CA 95131
(408) 436-8688
MPEG video and audio decoding cards

KINESIS CORPORATION

22121 17th Avenue SE, Suite 107
Bothell, WA 98021-7404
(206) 402-8100
fax (206) 402-8181
http://www.kinesis-ergo.com/
Ergonomic keyboards

KINGSTON TECHNOLOGY CORPORATION

17600 Newhope Street
Fountain Valley, CA 92708
(877) 544-7866, (714) 435-2600
fax (714) 424-3939
http://www.kingston.com

KONICA BUSINESS MACHINES U.S.A., INC.
725 Darlington Ave
Mahwah, NJ 07430
(800) 285-6422, (201) 574-4010
http://www.konica.com
Multifunctional printers, cameras, and
scanners

KOSS CORPORATION
4129 N. Port Washington Ave
Milwaukee, WI 53212
(800) USA-KOSS, (414) 964-5000
http://www.koss.com
Stereo audio accessories for computers

LABTEC ENTERPRISES, INC.
1499 SE Tech Center Place, Ste. 350
Vancouver, WA 98683
(360) 896-2000
http://www.labtec.com

LAVA COMPUTER MFG., INC.
LSMI Division
28A Dansk Ct.
Rexdale, ON M9W 5V8, Canada
(800) 241-5282
http://www.lavalink.com
High-speed I/O boards

LEXMARK INTERNATIONAL, INC.
2275 Research Boulevard
Rockville, MD 20850
(301) 212-5900
(800) LEXMARK (800-539-6275)
http://www.lexmark.com

LG ELECTRONICS
1000 Sylvan Avenue
Englewood Cliffs, NJ 95131
(201) 816-2000
http://www.lgeus.com
Goldstar monitors

LIBERTY SYSTEMS, INC.
120 Saratoga Avenue, Suite 82
Santa Clara, CA 95051
(408) 983-1127
http://www.libertyinc.com
CD-ROMs, hard drives, and backup devices

**LION OPTICS CORPORATION
(LIKOM SDN BHD)**
1001 South Lawson Street
City of Industry, CA 91748
(626) 935-0200
fax (626) 935-0202
http://www.likom.com.my/
CD-ROM drive products

LOGITECH, INC.
6505 Kaiser Drive
Fremont, CA 94555
(510) 795-8500
http://www.logitech.com
Pointing devices

MAG INNOVISION CO., INC
20 Goodyear
Irvine, CA 92618
(800) 827-3998, (949) 855-4930
fax (949) 855-4535
http://www.maginnovision.com
Monitors

MAGNAVOX
Philips Consumer Electronics Company
One Philips Drive
Knoxville, Tennessee 37914-1810
(800) 531-0039, (423) 521-4316
http://www.philipsmagnavox.com

MATROX GRAPHICS, INC.
1055 St. Regis Boulevard
Dorval, Quebec
Canada H9P 2T4
(514) 685-7230
fax (514) 685-2853
http://www.matrox.com
Video boards

MAXELL CORPORATION OF AMERICA
22-08 Rt. 208
Fair Lawn, NJ 07410
(800) 533-2836
http://www.maxell.com
Data storage media

Maximus Computers
5817 Martin Road
Irwindale, CA 91706
(800) 888-6294
fax (626) 969-2775
http://www.maximuspc.com

Maxi-Switch
2901 East Elvira Road
Tucson, AZ 85706
(520) 294-5450
Keyboards

MaxTech Corporation
13915 Cerritos Corporate Drive
Cerritos, CA 90703
(562) 921-1698
http://www.maxcorp.com

Maxtor Corporation
510 Cottonwood Dr.
Milpitas, CA 95035
(800) 2-MAXTOR, (408) 432-1700
fax (408) 922-2050
tech support fax (303) 678-2260
http://www.maxtor.com

McAfee Associates
2805 Bowers Av.
Santa Clara, CA 95054
tech support (972) 855-7044
http://www.mcafee.com/
VirusScan antivirus software

Mediatrix Peripherals, Inc.
4229 Garlock Street
Sherbrooke, PQ J1L 2C8, Canada
(819) 829-8749
fax (819) 829-5100
http://www.mediatrix.com
Audiotrix Pro 16-bit sound board

Memory Card Technology
2721 Loker Ave. West
Carlsbad, CA 92008
(760) 603-0150, (888) 480-2273
fax (760) 603-0250
http://www.memory-card-
    technology.com/
Memory upgrades and PCMCIA products

Micro 2000, Inc.
1100 E. Broadway
Glendale, CA 91205
(818) 547-0125
tech support (800) 864-8008
http://www.micro2000.com
Universal Diagnostics Toolkit

Micro Accessories, Inc.
6086 Stewart Avenue
Fremont, CA 94538
(510) 226-6310
http://www.micro-a.com
Computer interface cables and terminators

Micro Solutions
132 West Lincoln Hwy
DeKalb, IL 60115
(815) 754-4500
sales (800) 890-7227
fax (815) 756-4986
faxback (815) 754-4600
BBS (815) 756-9100
http://www.micro-solutions.com

MicroClean, Inc.
2050 S. Tenth Street
San Jose, CA 95112
(408) 995-5062
http://www.microclean.com
Computer care cleaning products

Microlabs
204 Lost Canyon Court
Richardson, TX 75080
(972) 234-5842

Micron Electronics, Inc.
8000 S. Federal Way
P.O. Box 6
Boise, ID 83707-0006
(208) 368-4000
tech support (800) 336-8916,
(208) 368-5083
sales (800) 209-9686
fax (208) 368-2536
http://www.micron.com
Computer systems and WinBook notebook
computers

MICROSOFT CORPORATION
One Microsoft Way
Redmond, WA 98052-6399
(206) 882-8080, (800) 426-9400
http://www.microsoft.com

MICROSTAR INTERNATIONAL
47800 Fremont Boulevard
Fremont, CA 94538
(510) 623-8818
fax (510) 623-8585
http://www.msicomputer.com
PC-based motherboards, Ethernet cards,
and video accelerators

MICROTEK LAB, INC.
3715 Doolittle Drive
Redondo Beach, CA 90278
(800) 654-4160, (310) 297-5000
tech support (310) 297-5100
fax (310) 297-5050
BBS (310) 297-5102
AutoTech faxback (310) 297-5101
CompuServe: GO GRAPHSUP, library 6
http://www.mteklab.com

MINDFLIGHT TECHNOLOGY, INC.
608 Weber Street North
Waterloo, Ontario N2V 1K4
(519) 746-8483
fax (519) 746-3317
http:// www.mindflight.com
Portable data products that connect to a PC
parallel port or a SCSI port

MINOLTA CORPORATION
101 Williams Drive
Ramsey, NJ 07446
(201) 825-4000
http://www.minolta.com
Graphics-specific input and output devices

MIRO COMPUTER PRODUCTS, INC.
Pinnacle Systems, Inc.
280 N. Bernardo Avenue
Mountain View, CA 94043
(650) 526-1600
fax (650) 526-1601
http://www.miro.com
Multimedia products

MITA COPYSTAR AMERICA, INC.
225 Sand Road
Fairfield, NJ 07004-0008
(800) ABC-MITA, (973) 808-8444
http://205.216.100.152/home/
index.cfm
Multifunctional printers

MITSUBA CORPORATION
1925 Wright Avenue
Laverne, CA 91750
(800) 648-7822, (909) 392-2000
http://www.mitsuba.com
Custom file servers, PCs, and notebooks

MITSUBISHI ELECTRONICS AMERICA, INC.
Americas Corporate Office
5665 Plaza Drive
Cypress, CA 90630-0007
(714) 220-2500
http://www.mitsubishielectric-
usa.com/

MITSUMI ELECTRONICS CORPORATION
5808 West Campus
Circle Drive
Irving, TX 75063
(800) 648-7864, (800) 801-7927
(972) 550-7300
fax (972) 550-7424
http://www.mitsumi.com
Keyboards, mice, floppy disk drives, and
CD-ROM drives

MOTOROLA PCMCIA PRODUCTS DIVISION
1501 Woodfield Road
Suite 120 North
Schaumburg, IL 60173
(847) 240-7700
http://www.mot.com

MTC AMERICA, INC.
(800) MTC-CDRS
Mitsui Gold CD-R device

MULTI-TECH SYSTEMS, INC.
2205 Woodale Drive
Mounds View, MN 55112
(800) 328-9717, (612) 785-3500
tech support (800) 972-2439
fax (612) 785-9874
http://www.multitech.com

MULTIWAVE TECHNOLOGY, INC.
17901 E. Ajax Circle
Industry, CA 91748
(800) 234-3358
(626) 912-9285
fax (626) 912-9495
http://www.mwave.com

MUSTEK, INC.
121 Waterworks Way, #100
Irvine, CA 92618
(949) 788-3600
fax (949) 788-3670
http://www.mustek.com
Scanners

MYLEX CORP.
34551 Ardenwood Boulevard
Fremont, CA 94555
(510) 796-6100
http://www.mylex.com
SCSI host adapters

NANAO USA CORPORATION
EIZO NANAO Technologies, Inc.
5710 Warland Drive
Cypress, CA 90630
(562) 431-5011
fax (562) 431-4811
http://www.nanao.com
Monitors

NATIONAL SEMICONDUCTOR
Personal Systems Div.
2900 Semiconductor Drive
Santa Clara, CA 95051
(408) 721-5000
http://www.nsc.com
Silicon products and systems for personal
computers and peripherals

NCE STORAGE SOLUTIONS
1973 Friendship Drive, Suite B
El Cajon, CA 92020
(800) 767-2587, (619) 452-7974
fax (619) 212-3036
http://www.ncegroup.com
Emerald System backup devices

NCR CORP.
1334 South Patterson Blvd.
Dayton, OH 45479
(937) 445-5000
fax (937) 445-4184
http://www.ncr.com

NEC TECHNOLOGIES, INC.
8 Corporate Center Dr.
Melville, NY 11747
(516) 753-7000, (800) 338-9549
http://www.nec.com

NEW MEDIA CORPORATION
6 Cromwell, Suite 102
Irvine, CA 92618
(949) 597-0888, (800) CARDS-4-U
fax (949) 609-1788
http://www.newmediatechcorp.com

NOKIA DISPLAY PRODUCTS
123 Second St.
Sausalito, CA 94965
(415) 331-4244
fax (415) 331-6211
http://www.nokia.com

NOKIA MOBILE PHONES
Corporate Communications
6000 Connection Drive
Irving, Texas 75039
(972) 894-4573
fax (972) 894-4831
http://www.nokia.com

NSA/HITACHI
200 Lowder Brook Drive, Suite 2200
Westwood, MA 02090
(800) 441-4832, (781) 461-8300
tech support (800) 536-6721
http://www.hitachidisplays.com/

NUMBER NINE COMPUTER CORPORATION
18 Hartwell Avenue
Lexington, MA 02173
(781) 674-0009, (800) GET-NINE
fax (781) 869-7230
http://www.nine.com

Ocean Information Systems Inc. (Octek)

50 Airport Parkway
San Jose, CA 95110-1011
(408) 487-3221
fax (408) 487 3227
http://www.oceanhk.com
http://www.ocean-usa.com
PC computer systems, motherboards, cases,
power supplies, multimedia products, and
peripherals

Okidata Corporation

2000 Bishops Gate Blvd.
Mt. Laurel, NJ 08054
(609) 235-2600
(800) OKIDATA (800-654-3282)
http://www.okidata.com

Olivetti Office USA

765 US Highway 202
Bridgewater, NJ 08807
(908) 526-8200
http://www.olivetti.com/

Orchestra MultiSystems, Inc.

12300 Edison Way
Garden Grove, CA 92841
(800) 237-9988, (714) 891-3861
fax (714) 891-2661
http://www.orchestra.com

Orevox USA Corporation

248 N. Puente Avenue
P.O. Box 2655
City of Industry, CA 91746
information (626) 336-0516
orders (800) 237-0700
fax (626) 336-3748
www.dynavox.com
Computer cases and multimedia speakers

Padix Co. Ltd.

Rockfire
18F-3, No. 75, Sec. 1, Hsin Tai Wu Road
Hsih-Chih, Taipei, Taiwan ROC
(886) 2-698-1478
http://www.padix.com
PC-compatible game controllers and
joysticks

Panasonic Communications & Systems Co.

1 Panasonic Way
Secaucus, NJ 07094
(201) 348-7000, (800) 742-8086
http://www.panasonic.com

Pantex Computer, Inc.

10301 Harwin Drive
Houston, TX 77036
(713) 988-1688, (888) PANTEX-1
fax (713) 988-2838
http://pantexcom.com/
Motherboards and bare-bones systems

Pathlight Technology, Inc.

9 Brown Road
Ithaca, NY 14850
(800) 334-4812, (607) 266-4000
fax (607) 266-4010
http://www.pathlight.com
Storage I/O and networking interface technologies and products

PC Cables and Parts

One-Up Computer
2331 NE 50th Court
Lighthouse Point, FL 33064
(954) 418-0817
fax (954) 418-0835
http://www.pccables.com

PC Concepts, Inc.

511 Fifth Street, Unit B
San Fernando, CA 91340
(818) 837-9495, (800) 735-6071
http://www.pcconcepts.com
Computer accessories including color-coded
cables, manual and auto data switches,
printer network devices, surge protectors,
and multimedia products

PC Power & Cooling, Inc.

5995 Avenida Encinas
Carlsbad, CA 92008
(760) 931-5700
CPU cooler for Intel's P6 processor

PCMCIA (Personal Computer Memory Card Int'l. Association)
2635 N. First St., Suite 209
San Jose, CA 95134
(408) 433-2273

Pengo Computer Accessories
16018-C Adelante Street
Irwindale, CA 91702
(888) PENGO99, (626) 815-9885
fax (626) 815-9964
http://www.pengo.com/
Floppy disks, dust covers, keyboard drawers, disk file boxes, tool kits, and various workstation accessories

Phillips Consumer Electronics Co.
1 Phillips Drive
Knoxville, TN 37914
(423) 521-4316, (800) 531-0039
http://www.philipsmagnavox.com

Phoenix Technologies, Ltd.
411 East Plumeria Dr.
San Jose, CA 95134
(408) 570-1000
fax (408) 570-1001
http://www.ptltd.com
PhoenixBIOS for desktops, NoteBIOS for notebook computers, and PhoenixPICO for handheld and embedded systems

Pioneer New Media Technologies, Inc.
Multimedia & Mass Storage
2265 E. 220th Street
Long Beach, CA 90810
(310) 952-2111, (800) 527-3766
fax (310) 952-2990
http://www.pioneerusa.com
CD-ROM and CD-R products for multimedia and mass storage applications

Pixie Technologies
3225 Laurel View Ct.
Fremont, CA 94538
(510) 440-9721
fax (510) 440-9356
http://www.pixie.com
Monitors

PKWare, Inc.
9025 N. Deerwood Drive
Brown Deer, WI 53223
(414) 354-8699
fax (414) 354-8559
http://www.pkware.com
PKZIP compression utilities

Play, Inc.
2890 Kilgore Road
Rancho Cordova, CA 95670-6133
(916) 851-0800, (800) 306-PLAY
fax (916) 851-0801
http://www.play.com
Snappy Video Snapshot software

Plextor USA
4255 Burton Drive
Santa Clara, CA 95054
(800) 886-3935, (408) 980-1838
fax (408) 986-1010
http://www.plextor.com
CD-ROM drives

Portrait Display Labs
5117 Johnson Drive
Pleasanton, CA 94588
(925) 227-2700
fax (925) 227-2700
http://www.portrait.com
Monitors

Powercom America, Inc.
1040A S. Melrose Street
Placentia, CA 92870-7119
(714) 632-8889
fax (714) 632-8868
http://www.powercom-usa.com/
Modems and UPSs

PowerQuest Corporation
1359 N. Research Way
Building K
Orem, UT 84057
(800) 379-2566, (801) 437-8900
http://www.powerquest.com
Manufacturer of Partition Magic, a software utility for creating and managing disk partitions

PRINCETON GRAPHIC SYSTEMS
2801 South Yale Street
Santa Ana, CA 92704
(800) 747-6249, (714) 751-8405
fax (714) 751-5736
http://www
  .princetongraphics.com/
Monitors

PROCOM TECHNOLOGY, INC.
1821 E. Dyer Road
Santa Ana, Calif. 92705
(800) 800-8600, (949) 852-1000
fax (949) 261-7380
http://www.procom.com
Hard drives and backup devices

PROLINK COMPUTER
15336 East Valley Blvd.
City of Industry, CA 91746
(626) 369-3833, (800) 686-8110
fax (626) 369-4883
http://www.prolink-usa.com/

QLOGIC CORPORATION
3545 Harbor Blvd.
Costa Mesa, CA 92626
(714) 438-2200, (800) 662-4471
fax (714) 668-5008
http://www.qlc.com

RAVISENT TECHNOLOGIES, INC.
1 Great Valley Parkway
Malvern, PA 19355
(800) 700-0362
tech support (610) 251-9999
fax (610) 695-2592
e-mail qi-tech@quadrant.com
http://www.ravisent.com
Video editing and capture products

QUANTEX MICROSYSTEMS, INC.
400B Pierce Street
Somerset, NJ 08873
(800) 864-9022
fax (888) 665-1656
http://www.quantex.com

QUANTUM CORPORATION
500 McCarthy Boulevard
Milpitas, CA 95053
(800) 624-5545, (408) 894-4000
fax (408) 894-5217
http://www.quantum.com

QUATECH, INC.
662 Wolf Ledges Pkwy.
Akron, OH 44311
(330) 434-3154, (800) 553-1170
fax (330) 434-1409
http://www.quatech.com
Communication, data acquisition, industrial
I/O, and PCMCIA products

QUICKPATH SYSTEMS, INC.
220 Stanford Ave
Fremont, CA 94539-6094
e-mail quickpath@addcom.com
http://www.quickpath.com/

QUICKSHOT TECHNOLOGY, INC.
QuickShot Technology, Inc.
950 Yosemite Drive
Milpitas, CA
(408) 263-4163
fax (408) 263-4005
http://www.quickshot.com

QVS, INC.
2731 Crimson Canyon Drive
Las Vegas, NV 89128
(800) 344-3371
http://www.qvs.com
Computer cables and computer electronic
products

REGAL ELECTRONICS, INC.
4251 Burton Drive
Santa Clara, CA 95054
(408) 988-2288, (800) 882-8086
fax (408) 988-2797, (800) 345-2831
http://www.regalusa.com/
Plug-and-Play CD-ROM changers and multimedia speakers

RELISYS (TECO)

48329 Fremont Boulevard
Fremont, CA 94538
(510) 413-3000
http://www.relisys.com
Video monitors, scanners, and multifunctional facsimile products

ROLAND CORPORATION U.S.

5100 S. Eastern Avenue
Los Angeles, CA 90040-2938
(323) 890-3700
fax (323) 890-3701
http://www.rolandus.com
Sound cards, PCMCIA cards, MIDI keyboards, powered speakers, and music software

ROSE ELECTRONICS

10707 Stancliff
Houston, TX 77099
(281) 933-7673, (800) 333-9343
fax (281) 933-0044
http://www.rosel.com
Keyboard and video control products, print servers, and data switches

NETWORK ASSOCIATES

3965 Freedom Circle
Santa Clara, CA 95054
(972) 308-9960
fax (408) 970-9727
http://www.drsolomon.com
Dr. Solomon's Anti-Virus Toolkit

S. T. RESEARCH CORP.

8419 Terminal Rd.
Newington, VA 22122
(703) 550-7000
http://www.sensytech.com
Palmtop computers

S3, INC.

2841 Mission College Blvd.
Santa Clara, CA 95054
(510) 651-2300
http://www.diamondmm.com
Graphics acceleration products

SAGER COMPUTER

18005 Cortney Court
City of Industry, CA 91748
(800) 669-1624, (626) 964-2381
fax (626) 964-2381
http://www.sager-midern.com
Notebook computers

SAMPO TECHNOLOGY, INC.

5550 Peachtree Ind. Boulevard
Norcross, GA 30071
(888) 321-4100, (770) 449-6220
fax (770) 447-1109
http://www.sampotech.com
Monitors

SAMSUNG AMERICA, INC.

14251 E. Firestone Boulevard
La Mirada, CA 90638
(562) 802-2211
http://www.samsung.com
CPU cooler for the Pentium and P6

SAMSUNG ELECTRONICS AMERICA, INC.

Information Systems Div.
105 Challenger Road
Ridgefield Park, NJ 07660
(800) 933-4110, (201) 229-4000
http://www.samsung.com
Notebook PCs, color monitors, hard disk drives, and laser printers

SAMTRON

A Div. of Samsung Electronics America
18600 Broadwick Street
Rancho Dominguez, CA 90220
(310) 537-7000
Monitors

SANYO ENERGY (USA) CORPORATION

2055 Sanyo Avenue
San Diego, CA 92173
(619) 661-4888
fax (619) 661-6743
Batteries and amorphous solar cells

SANYO FISHER (USA) CORPORATION
Office Automation Products
21605 Plummer Street
Chatsworth, CA 91311
(818) 998-7322
http://www.sanyo.com
Multifunctional fax machines, CD-ROM
drives, notebooks, desktop personal computers, and monitors

SEAGATE SOFTWARE
920 Disc Drive
Scotts Valley, CA 95067
(831) 438-6550, (800) 877-2340
fax (831) 438-7612
http://www.seagatesoftware.com
Hard drives

SEATTLE TELECOM & DATA, INC.
4556 150th Ave. N.E. Building E1
Redmond, WA 98052
(425) 883-8440
http://www.seamem.com
PS/2-compatible accelerator boards for
most Micro Channel models

SHARP ELECTRONICS CORPORATION
Sharp Plaza
Mahwah, NJ 07430
(201) 529-8200, (800) BE-SHARP
fax (201) 529-8425
http://www.sharp-usa.com
LCDs and LCD-based products

SHINING TECHNOLOGY, INC.
10533 Progress Way, Suite C
Cypress, CA 90630
(714) 761-9598
http://www.shining.com
Parallel I/O products to EIDE (supporting
hard disk drives and CD-ROMs)

SHUTTLE TECHNOLOGY
160 Knolls Dr.
Los Gatos, CA 95032
(408) 370-4888
Parallel port interfacing technology

SICOS PRODUCTS
SICOS Computer
01805/959995
fax 06021/570849
http://www.sicos.com
Scanners

**SIGMA INTERACTIVE SOLUTIONS
CORPORATION**
335 Fairview Way
Milpitas, CA 95035
(408) 262-9003
http://www.sigmadesigns.com

SIMPLE TECHNOLOGY
3001 Daimler Street
Santa Ana, CA 92705
(949) 476-1180
(800) 4-SIMPLE (800-474-6753)
http://www.simpletech.com
Memory and PC card products

SL WABER
520 Fellowship Road, Suite 306
Mount Laurel, NJ 08054
(800) 634-1485, (609) 866-8888
fax (609) 866-1945
http://www.waber.com
Uninterruptible power supplies

SMART AND FRIENDLY
20520 Nordhoff Street
Chatsworth, CA 91311
(800) 542-8838, (818) 772-8001
fax (818) 772-2888
http://www
    .smartandfriendly.com/
CD recording devices

SMART MODULAR TECHNOLOGIES, INC.
4305 Cushing Pkwy.
Fremont, CA 94538
(510) 623-1231, (800) 956-7627
fax (510) 623-1434
http://www.smartm.com
DRAM, SRAM, and Flash memory modules
and upgrade cards

SMILE INTERNATIONAL, INC.
23 Hubble Drive
Irvine, CA 92618
(949) 753-8899
fax (949) 753-8999
http://www.smilekfc.com

SONY CORPORATION
1 Sony Drive
Park Ridge, NJ 07645
(201) 930-1000
sales (800) 352-7669
tech support (800) 326-9551
http://www.sony.com
Digital technologies for computers, communications, audio, and video

SRS LABS, INC.
2909 Daimler Street
Santa Ana, CA 92705
(949) 442-1070, (800) 243-2733
fax (949) 852-1099
http://www.srslabs.com
3-D sound technology

STAC ELECTRONICS
12636 High Bluff Drive, Suite 400
San Diego, CA 92130-2093
(619) 794-4300, (800) 522-7822
fax (619) 794-4575
http://www.stac.com
Backup and disaster recovery products

STB SYSTEMS, INC.
3400 Waterview Parkway
Richardson, TX 75080
(800) 234-4334
e-mail support@3dfx.com
http://www.stb.com

STORAGE TECHNOLOGY CORPORATION
One StorageTek Drive
Louisville, CO 80028
(719) 536-4055, (800) 786-7835
fax (719) 536-4053
http://www.storagetek.com
StorageTek storage products

STRACON, INC.
1672 Kaiser Avenue
Irvine, CA 92714
(949) 851-2288
http://www.superpc.com
Memory upgrades for PCs, laptops, and workstations

SYMANTEC CORPORATION
175 West Broadway
Eugene, OR 97401
(800) 441-7234, (541) 334-6054
outside the U.S. and Canada
(541) 334-6054
fax (541) 334-7400
http://www.symantec.com
Norton Utilities and Norton Anti-Virus software

SYNNEX INFORMATION TECHNOLOGIES, INC.
3797 Spinnaker Court
Fremont, CA 94538
(510) 656-3333, (800) 756-9888
http://www.synnex.com

TAGRAM SYSTEM CORPORATION
3170 Pullman Street
Costa Mesa, CA 92626
(800) TAGRAMS, (714) 979-8900
tech support (800) 443-5761
http://www.tagram.com

TAHOE PERIPHERALS
5301 Longley Lane Suite A-2
Reno, NV 89511
(800) 288-6040
fax (775) 832-2200
http://www.tahoeperipherals.com

TANDBERG DATA
2685-A Park Center Drive
Simi Valley, CA 93065
(805) 579-1000, (800) 826-3237
fax (805) 579-2555
http://www.tandberg.com
SCSI QIC tape backup drives and kits

TANISYS TECHNOLOGY CORPORATION

12201 Technology Boulevard
Austin, TX 78727-6101
(512) 335-4440, (800) 533-1744
http:// www.tanisys.com
Memory products

TATUNG COMPANY OF AMERICA, INC.

2850 El Presidio Street
Long Beach, CA 90810
(310) 637 2105, (800) 827-2850
fax (310) 637 8484
http://www.tatung.com
Monitors

TDK ELECTRONICS CORPORATION

12 Harbor Park Drive
Port Washington, NY 11050
(516) 625-0100, (800) TDK-TAPE
fax (516) 625-0171
http://www.tdk.com
Optical and magnetic recording media

TEAC AMERICA, INC.

Data Storage Products Div.
7733 Telegraph Road
Montebello, CA 90640
(323) 726-0303
fax (323) 727-7656
http://www.teac.com
CD-ROM, tape, and floppy drives

TEKTRONIX, INC.

14200 SW Karl Braun Drive
Beaverton, OR 97077
(800) 835-9433
fax (503) 682-2980
http://www.tek.com

TEMPEST MICRO

18760 E. Amar Road, Suite 188
Walnut, CA 91789
(929) 595-0550, (800) 818-5163
fax (929) 595-5025

THRUSTMASTER, INC.

700 Ygnacio Valley Road, Suite 200
Walnut Creek, CA 94596
(925) 943-2059
fax (925) 943-2006
http://www.thrustmaster.com

THUNDER MAX CORPORATION

15011 Parkway Loop, Suite A
Tustin, CA 92780
(714) 259-8800, (888) 852-8898
http://www.thundermax.com

TMC RESEARCH CORPORATION

48550 Fremont Boulevard
Fremont, CA 94538
(510) 262-0888
http://www.mycomp-tmc.com
Celeron and Pentium motherboards

TOSHIBA AMERICA INFORMATION SYSTEMS, INC.

9775 Toledo Way
Irvine, CA 92718
(800) 457-7777, (714) 455-2000
sales (800) 867-4422
http://www.toshiba.com
CD-ROMs and hard drives

TOUCHSTONE SOFTWARE CORPORATION

1538 Turnpike St.
North Andover, MA 01845
(978) 686-6468
fax (978) 683-1630
http://www.checkit.com
CheckIt Pro and WinCheckIt 4 diagnostic
software

TREND MICRO DEVICES

10101 N. DeAnza Boulevard, Second Floor
Cupertino, CA 95014
(408) 257-1500, (800) 228-5651
fax (408) 257-2003
http://www.trendmicro.com
PC-cillin antivirus software

TRIDENT MICROSYSTEMS, INC.

2450 Walsh Avenue
Santa Clara, CA 95051-1303
(408) 496-1085
http://www.trid.com
32- and 64-bit integrated graphics and multimedia video processing controllers for PC
compatibles

TRUEVISION, INC.
Pinnacle Systems
280 N. Bernardo Avenue
Mountain View, CA 94043
(650) 526-1600
fax (650) 526-1601
http://pinnaclesys.com

TYAN COMPUTER
3288 Laurelview Court
Fremont, CA 94538
sales (510) 651-8868
tech support (510) 440-8808
fax (510) 651-7688
http://www.tyan.com
High-end motherboards and add-on cards

U&C AMERICA
3016 Gainsborough Drive
Pasadena, CA 91107
(626) 319-1938
http://www.superpen.com
SuperPen

U.S. ROBOTICS CORP.
3Com Corp
5400 Bayfront Plaza
Santa Clara, CA 95052
(408) 326-5000
fax (408) 326-5001
http://www.3com.com

UMAX TECHNOLOGIES
3561 Gateway Boulevard
Fremont, CA 94538
(510) 651-4000
fax (510) 651-8834
http://www.umax.com

UNISYS CORPORATION
Personal Computer Div.
2700 N. First Street
San Jose, CA 95134-2028
(408) 434-2848, (800) 448-1424
http://www.unisys.com
Notebook and desktop systems

VALITEK
100 University Drive
Amherst, MA 01102
(413) 549-2700, (800) 825-4835
fax (413) 549-2900
http://www.valitek.com
Backup devices

VERBATIM CORPORATION
1200 W.T. Harris Boulevard
Charlotte, NC 28262
(704) 547-6500, (800) 538-8589
http://www.verbatimcorp.com
Optical discs, tape products, floppy disks,
CD-Rs and CD-ROMs, and imaging products

VIDEO ELECTRONICS STANDARDS ASSOCIATION (VESA)
920 Hillview Court, Suite 140
Milpitas, CA 95035
(408) 957-9270
http://www.vesa.org

VIEWSONIC CORPORATION
381 Brea Canyon Rd.
Walnut, CA 91789
(800) 888-8583, (909) 869-7976
http://www.viewsonic.com
ViewSonic and Optiquest monitors

VOYETRA-TURTLE BEACH SYSTEMS
Voyetra Turtle Beach
5 Odell Plaza
Yonkers NY 10701-1406
(914) 966-0600, (800) 233-9377
fax (914) 966-0600
http://www.voyetra-turtle-
    beach.com
Multimedia sound products

WACOM TECHNOLOGY CORPORATION
1311 SE Cardinal Court
Vancouver, WA 98683
(800) 922-9348
fax (360) 896-9724
e-mail sales@wacom.com,
    support@wacom.com
http://www.wacom.com
Pen tablets

WESTERN DIGITAL

8105 Irvine Center Drive
Costa Mesa, CA 92718
(949) 932-5000
tech support (800) 275-4932
http://www.wdc.com
IDE hard drives, integrated circuits, and
board-level products for the microcomputer
industry

WILLOW PERIPHERALS

P.O. Box 5058
Stanton, NY 11937-6073
(631) 329-4222, (800) 444-1585
fax (631) 329-4221
http://www.willow.com
Video output and video capture products

WINNER PRODUCTS (USA) INC.

21128 Commerce Pointe Drive
Walnut, CA 91789
(909) 595-2490
fax (909) 595-1483
http://www.joystick.com
Joysticks and other peripherals

WYSE TECHNOLOGY

3471 N. First Street
M/S 618-3
San Jose, CA 95134
(408) 473-1200, (800) GET-WYSE
http://www.wyse.com
Advanced video display terminals

XEROX CORPORATION

800 Phillips Road
Webster, NY 14425
(800) ASK-XEROX
tech support (800) 821-2797
http://www.xerox.com
Printers

XIRCOM

2300 Corporate Center Drive
Thousand Oaks, CA 91320-1420
(800) 438-4526
tech support (805) 376-9200
fax (805) 376-9311
http://www.xircom.com

YAMAHA CORPORATION OF AMERICA

CBX Group
6600 Orangethorpe Avenue
Buena Park, CA 90620
(714) 522-9011
http://www.yamaha.com
Computer sound products

ZENITH DATA SYSTEMS

http://www.zds.com
Desktops and wireless technology

ZOOM TECHNOLOGIES

207 South Street
Boston, MA 02111
(617) 423-1072
sales (800) 631-3116
fax (617) 423-3923
http://www.zoomtel.com

DATA RECOVERY VENDORS

The following vendors specialize in products
for recovering data from damaged hard drives:

AA COMPUTECH

28170 Avenue Crocker, Suite 207
Valencia, CA 91355
(661) 257-5717
http://www.scvnet.com

DATA RECOVERY LABS

85 Scarsdale Road, Suite 100
Toronto, Ontario
M3B 2R2, Canada
(800) 563-1167, (416) 510-6990
fax (416) 510-6992
e-mail admin@datarec.com
http://www.datarec.com

DATA RECOVERY LABS, INC.

29269 US 19 North, Suite 101
Clearwater, Florida 34623
(727) 772-7455, (800) 577-8360
http://www.drlabs.com

DATA RETRIEVAL SERVICES

1040 Kapp Drive
Clearwater, FL 34625
(727) 461-5900, (800) 952-7530
fax (727) 461-5668

DISKTEC
> 5875 W. 34th Street
> Houston, TX 77092
> (713) 681-4691
> fax (713) 681-5851

DRIVE SERVICE COMPANY
> 3303 Harbor Blvd., Suite E-7
> Costa Mesa, CA 92626
> (714) 549-DISK, (888) 272-8332
> fax (714) 549-9752
> e-mail mark@driveservice.com
> http://www.driveservice.com

DRIVESAVERS DATA RECOVERY
> 400 Bel Marin Keys Blvd.
> Novato, CA 94949
> (800) 440-1904, (415) 382-2000
> fax (415) 883-0780
> e-mail recovery@drivesavers.com
> http://www.drivesavers.com

ELECTRONIC RENAISSANCE
> 105 Newfield Avenue
> Edison, NJ 08837
> (732) 417-9090
> fax (732) 471-9099

EXCALIBUR DATA RECOVERY, INC.
> 101 Billerica Avenue, Bldg. #5
> N. Billerica, MA 01862-1256
> (800) 466-0893, (978) 663-1700
> fax (978) 670-5901
> e-mail recover@excalibur.ultra-
> net.com
> http://www.excaliburdr.com

EXPRESS POINT
> 1101 National Drive
> Sacramento, CA 95834
> (800) 767-9281, (916) 928-1107
> fax (916) 928-1006
> http://www.expresspoint.com

LAZARUS
> 381 Clementina Street
> San Francisco, CA 94103
> (415) 495-5556, (800) 341-DATA
> fax (415) 495-5553
> http://www.lazarus.com

MICRO COM
> 20802 Plummer Street
> Chatsworth, CA 91311
> (800) 469-2549, (818) 718-1200
> fax (818) 718-1485
> http://www.data-master.com

NORTHWEST COMPUTER SUPPORT, INC.
> 975 Industry Drive, Bldg. 31
> Seattle, WA 98188
> (206) 575-3181
> fax (206) 575-3128
> http://www.nwcsupport.com

ONTRACK DATA RECOVERY, INC.
> 9023 Columbine Road
> Eden Prairie, MN 55347
> (800) 872-2599, (612) 937-5161
> fax (612) 937-5750
> http://www.ontrack.com

VANTAGE TECHNOLOGIES, INC.
> 4 John Tyler Street
> Merrimack, NH 03054
> (800) ITS-LOST (800-487-5678),
> (603) 429-3019, (603) 883-6249
> fax (603) 883-1973
> e-mail recovery@vantagetech.com
> http://www.vantagetech.com

MEMORY VENDORS

Here are a number of computer memory dealers. Many will also buy your old memory; however, call and check first before sending anything.

BLUESTAR, INC. DBA MEMORY WORLD
> 47410 Warm Springs Blvd.
> Fremont, CA 94539
> (510) 438-4460, (800) 839-5762
> fax (510) 438-4490
> http://www.memoryworld.net/

DMS (DATA MEMORY SYSTEMS)
> 24 Keewaydin Drive
> Salem, NH 03079
> (800) 662-7466, (603) 898-7750
> fax (603) 898-6585
> e-mail sales@datamem.com
> http://www.datamem.com

H&J ELECTRONICS INTERNATIONAL, INC.

5233 Powerline
Ft. Lauderdale, FL 33309
(800) 275-2447, (954) 971-7750
fax (954) 979-9028
http://www.askchip.com
Laptop, printer, and PC memory for name-brand computers

MCDONALD AND ASSOCIATES: THE MEMORY PLACE

2544 South 156th Circle
Omaha, NE 68130
(800) 306-8901, (402) 691-8548
fax (402) 691-8548
e-mail info@memoryplace.com
http://www.buymemory.com

MEMORY 4 LESS

2622 West Lincoln, Suite 104
Anaheim, CA 92801
(800) 821-3354, (714) 826-5981
fax (714) 821-3361
http://www.memory4less.com

THE MEMORY MAN

5440 Mounes St. #112
Jefferson, LA 70123
(800) 634-2298, (504) 818-2717
fax (504) 818-2820
http://www.memory-man.com

BIOS UPGRADE VENDORS

These are vendors who sell upgrade BIOS ROM to support new hard and floppy drive types, solve some compatibility problems, or add a new feature (such as built-in Setup).

If you've got a clone, your clone may have a compatible BIOS written by Phoenix Technologies. Phoenix periodically updates their BIOS to speed them up, support new devices, and fix bugs. The person from whom you bought the clone, however, may have gone on to selling land in Florida. You can buy upgrades for your Phoenix ROM from Wholesale Direct.

ALLTECH ELECTRONICS CO.

2618 Temple Heights
Oceanside, CA 92056
(760) 724-2404
fax (760) 724-8808
e-mail allelec.com
http://www.allelec.com

TTI TECHNOLOGIES, INC.

2101 Autocenter Drive, Suite 150
Oxnard, CA 93030
(800) 541-1943

UNICORE SOFTWARE

1538 Turnpike Street
N. Andover, MA 01845
(800) 800-2467, (978) 686-6468
fax (978) 683-1630
http://www.unicore.com

STORAGE DEVICE VENDORS

In case you're looking specifically for a new hard drive or tape drive, here are a few vendors who specialize in storage devices:

AA COMPUTECH

28170 Avenue Crocker, Suite 207
Valencia, CA 91355
(661) 257-5717
http://www.scvnet.com
Hard drives and data recovery

BASON HARD DRIVE WAREHOUSE

20500 Plummer St.
Chatsworth, CA 91311
(800) 238-4453, (818) 727-9054
fax (818) 727-9066
http://www.basoncomputer.com

DIRT CHEAP DRIVES

3716 Timber Drive
Dickinson, TX 77539
(800) 786-1170, (281) 534-4140
fax (281) 534-6452
http://www.dirtcheapdrives.com
Hard drives, CD-ROMs, optical drives, and tape backup units

MEGAHAUS HARD DRIVES

2201 Pine Drive
Dickinson, TX 77539
(800) 786-1157, (281) 534-3919
fax (281) 534-6580
http://www.MegaHaus.com/
Drives, controller cards, and drive accessories

STORAGE USA

2400 Reach Road
Williamsport, PA 17701
(800) 538-DISK, (570) 323-6737
http://www.storageusa.com

MISCELLANEOUS COMPUTER PRODUCTS VENDORS

Many manufacturers also sell their own products. Here, however, are the dealers who sell a wide range of useful computer parts and peripherals:

1ST COMPU CHOICE

740 Beta Drive, Suite G
Mayfield Village, OH 44143
(800) 345-8880, (440) 460-1002
fax (440) 460-1741
http://www.1stcompuchoice.com

A MATTER OF FAX

105 Patterson Avenue
Patterson, NY 07029
(800) 433-3FAX
Fax machines, printers, scanners, and other components and peripherals

A2Z COMPUTERS

325 Harris Drive
Aurora, Ohio 44202
(800) 983-8889
http://www.a2zcomp.com
Computer components and peripherals

ABC DRIVES

8717 Darby Ave.
Northridge, CA 91325
(818) 885-7157
http://www.abcdrives.com/
Sale and service of most major storage devices, including hard-to-find or obsolete drives

ALLSOP COMPUTER ACCESSORIES

4201 Meridian
Bellingham, WA 98226
(800) 426-4303
(360) 734-9858
http://www.allsop.com
Ergonomic enhancements (drawers and glare filters)

ALPHA SYSTEMS, INC.

5070 Brandin Court
Fremont, CA 94538
(510) 249-9280
fax (510) 259-9288
e-mail compu@alphasys.com
http://www.alphasys.com

AMERICAN COMPUTER RESOURCES, INC.

88 Long Hill Cross Road
Shelton, CT 06484-4703
(203) 944-7333
fax (203) 944-7370
http://www.the-acr.com/

AMERICAN RIBBON AND TONER CO.

2895 West Prospect Road
Ft. Lauderdale, FL 33309
(954) 733-4552, (800) 327-1013
http://www.ribbontoner.com
Printer ribbons, toner cartridges, and so on

ARLINGTON COMPUTER PRODUCTS

851 Commerce Court
Buffalo Grove, IL 60089
(800) 548-5105, (847) 541-6583
fax (847) 541-6881

ARM COMPUTER INC.

998 Rock Avenue
San Jose, CA 95131
(888) 824-5709, (408) 964-2500
fax (408) 935-9192
http://www.armcomputer.com

ASI

48289 Fremont Boulevard
Fremont, CA 94538
(510) 226-8000
Computer hardware, peripherals, and private-label Nspire personal computers and multimedia kits

ASPEN IMAGING INTERNATIONAL, INC.

1500 Cherry Street, Suite B
Louisville, CO 80027-3036
(800) 955-5555, (303) 666-5750
fax (303) 665-2972

Computer printer supplies including printer ribbons, printbands, and laser toner and ink-jet supplies

ASSOCIATES COMPUTER SUPPLY CO., INC.

275 West 231st Street
Riverdale, NY 10463
(718) 543-8686
fax (718) 548-0343
http://www
    .associatescomputer.com

Motherboards, cases, video cards, hard drives, keyboards, memory, and CD-ROMs

ATRONICS INTERNATIONAL INC.

44700-B Industrial Drive
Fremont, CA 94538
(800) 488-7776, (510) 656-8400
fax (510) 656-8560
http://www.atronicsintl.com

Parallel port CD-ROM adapter, BIOS enhancement card for IDE hard drive controllers

AURA INDUSTRIES, INC.

6352 N. Lincoln Avenue
Chicago, IL 60659
(312) 588-8722

CPUs, hard drives, memory, multimedia products, and computer accessories

AUTOMATED TECH TOOLS

3301 E. Royalton Road
Broadview Heights, OH 44147
(800) 413-0767
http://www.autott.com

AUTOTIME CORPORATION

6605 S.W. Macadam Avenue
Portland, OR 97201
(503) 452-8577
http://www.autotime.com

Memory recycling services and products

BARNETT'S COMPUTERS

417 Fifth Avenue
New York, NY 10017
(212) 252-0099, (800) 931-7070
http://www.compdirect.com

BATTERY NETWORK

955 Borra Place
Escondido, CA 92029
(800) 327-0814
http://www.battnet.com

Assembly, sales, and service of rechargeable batteries

BATTERY TECHNOLOGY, INC.

16500 E. Gale Ave
City of Industry, CA 91745
(626) 336-6878
fax (626) 336-5657
http://www.batterytech.com

Battery products for laptop computers and portable peripherals

BATTERY-BIZ INC.

31352 Via Colinas, Suite 101
Westlake Village, CA 91362
(800) 848-6782, (818) 706-0635
fax (818) 706-3234
http://www.battery-biz.com

Batteries for desktops, laptops, and notebooks, as well as for UPS systems and utility meters

BIGCITY EXPRESS

96 Hobart Street
Hackensack, NJ 07601
(201) 457-9044, (888) 243-2489
fax (201) 457-9576
http://www.bigcityexpress.com

BLACK BOX CORPORATION

1000 Park Drive
Lawrence, PA 15055
(877) 877-2269
http://www.blackbox.com

Networking and data communication products

BNF ENTERPRISES
134R Rt.1 South Newbury St.
Peabody, MA 01960
(978) 536-2000
fax (978) 536-7400
http://www.bnfe.com

CABLE CONNECTION
102 Cooper Ct.
Los Gatos, CA 95032
(408) 395-6700
fax (408) 354-3980
http://www.cable-connection.com
Cable products and interconnect accessories

CABLES AMERICA
(800) 348-USA4
fax (800) FAX-USA4

CABLES TO GO
1501 Webster Street
Dayton, OH 45404
(937) 224-8646, (800) 506-9607
fax (937) 496-2666, (800) 331-2841
http://www.cablestogo.com/
Cables, test equipment, and toolkits

CAD WAREHOUSE
6703 International Avenue
Cypress, CA 90630
(714) 816-2200, (800) 811-3265
fax (714) 816-2297
http://www.cadwarehouse.com

CENTURY MICROELECTRONICS, INC.
4800 Great America Parkway
Santa Clara, CA 95054
(408) 748-7788
fax (408) 748-8688
http://www.century-micro.com/
Memory upgrades, with products ranging
from industry-standard SIMMs and DIMMs
to proprietary modules and memory cards

CHEMTRONICS
8125 Cobb Centre Drive
Kennesaw, GA 30152
(770) 424-4888, (800) 645-5244
fax (770) 424-4267
http://www.chemtronics.com

Ozone-safe compressed gas for cleaning
inside PCs

CIRCO TECHNOLOGY CORPORATION
222 South 5th Avenue
City of Industry, CA 91746
(626) 369-5779, (800) 678-1688
fax (626) 369-2769
http://www.circotech.com
Cases, power supplies, removeable hard
drive kits, and motherboards

CMO CORPORATION
2400 Reach Rd.
Williamsport, PA 17701
(800) 417-4580

COMPAQ DIRECTPLUS
P.O. Box 69200
Houston, TX 77269-2000
(281) 370-0670
http://www.compaq.com

COMPUSA DIRECT
14951 North Dallas Parkway
Dallas, TX 75240
(800) COMPUSA
http://www.compusa.com

COMPUTABILITY
7271 N. 51st Boulevard
Milwaukee, WI 53223
(800) 554-2184, (414) 357-8181
fax (414) 357-7814
http://www.computability.com

COMPUTER DISCOUNT WAREHOUSE (CDW)
200 North Milwaukee Avenue
Vernon Hills, Illinois 60061
(847) 465-6000, (800) 826-4239
fax (847) 465-6800
http://www.cdw.com

COMPUTER GATE INTERNATIONAL
2960 Gordon Avenue
Santa Clara, CA 95051
(408) 730-0673, (888) 437-0895
fax (408) 730-0735
e-mail cgate@computergate.com
http://www.computergate.com
Testers, cleaning products, cables, switches,
and computer assembly products

COMPUTER PARTS OUTLET, INC.

33 S.E. First Avenue
Delray Beach, FL 33444
(561) 265-1206, (800) 475-1655

Buys all types of memory, including large or small quantities of working or nonworking modules

DALCO ELECTRONICS

425 S. Pioneer Boulevard
P.O. Box 550
Springboro, OH 45066
(800) 489-0075, (513) 743-8042
fax (513) 743-9251
CompuServe: GO DA
http://www.dalco.com

DATA IMPRESSIONS

13180 Paramount Blvd
South Gate, CA 90280
(562) 630-8788, (800) 677-3031
fax (562) 634-5033
http://www.di-wave.com

Computer supplies and printer supplies

DATAVISION

445 Fifth Avenue
New York, NY 10016
(888) 888-2087
http://www.datavis.com

Computers and multimedia components

DIRT CHEAP DRIVES

3716 Timber Drive
Dickinson, TX 77539
(800) 786-1170, (281) 534-4140
fax (281) 534-6452
http://www.dirtcheapdrives.com

Hard drives, CD-ROMs, optical drives, and tape backup units

DIGITAL MICRO, INC.

901 S. Fremont Avenue, Suite 118
Alhambra, CA 91803
(626) 300-0620

DISKETTE CONNECTION

P.O. Box 1674
Bethany, OK 73008
(800) 654-4058, (405) 789-0888
fax (405) 495-4598
http://www
    .disketteconnection.com

Disks, tapes, and drive cleaning kits

DISKETTES UNLIMITED

6206 Long Drive
Houston, TX 77087
(713) 643-9939
fax (713) 643-2722

Disks

EDMUND SCIENTIFIC CORPORATION

101 E. Gloucester Pike
Barrington, NJ 08007
(856) 573-6250
fax (856) 573-6295

Dual Function Digital Lab Thermometer

ENVISIONS SOLUTIONS TECHNOLOGY, INC.

47470 Seabridge Drive
Fremont, CA 94538
(800) 365-SCAN, (510) 360-8300
fax (510) 623-7349
http://www.envisions.com

Scanners, printers, and graphics/OCR software

EXPERT COMPUTERS

2495 Walden Avenue
Buffalo, NY 14225
(716) 681-8612

FAIRFAX

145 West 45th Street, Suite 1010
New York, NY 10036
(800) 932-4732, (212) 768-8300

FIRST COMPUTER SYSTEMS, INC.

665 Highway 120, Suite 804
Lawrenceville, GA 30045
(770) 441-1911
fax (770) 441-1856
e-mail sales@fcsnet.com
http://www.fcsnet.com

Motherboards, computers, and peripherals

FIRST SOURCE INTERNATIONAL
3511 W. Sunflower Avenue, Suite 210
Santa Ana, CA 92704
(800) 858-9866
e-mail sales@firstsource.com
http://www.firstsource.com

FRY'S ELECTRONICS
600 E Brokaw Rd
San Jose, CA 95112
(408) 487-4500

GALAXY COMPUTERS, INC
332c Dante Court
Holbrook, NY 11741
(516) 467-0800
http://www.galaxyusa.com/
Motherboards

GIFI INC.
20814 Aurora Road
Cleveland, OH 44146
(216) 662-1910
http://www.gifi.com

GLOBAL COMPUTER SUPPLIES
921 W. Artesia Blvd., Dept. WB
Compton, CA 90220
310) 603-2266, (888) 8-GLOBAL
fax (310) 637-6191
http://www.globalcomputer.com

GLOBAL MICROXPERTS
6230 Cochran Road
Solon, OH 44139
(800) 875-6973
http://www.microx.com

GRAPHICS WAREHOUSE
8515 Freeway Drive, unit C & D
Macedonia, OH 44087
(216) 487-0485

HARMONY COMPUTERS
1801 Flatbush Avenue
Brooklyn, NY 11210
(800) 441-1144, (718) 692-3232
http://www.shopharmony.com/

HARTFORD COMPUTER GROUP, INC.
1610 Colonial Parkway
Inverness, IL 60067
(800) 680-4424
fax (847) 934-0157
http://www.hcgi.com

HDSS COMPUTER PRODUCTS
6225 Jarvis Ave
Newark, CA 94560

HI-TECH COMPONENT DISTRIBUTERS, INC.
59 S. La Patera Lane
Goleta, CA 93117
(800) 406-1275, (805) 967-7971
fax (805) 681-9971

HI-TECH USA
1582 Centre Pointe Drive
Milpitas, CA 95035
(800) 831-2888, (408) 262-8688,
(408) 956-8285
fax (408) 262-8772
BBS (408) 956-8243
http://www.hitech-usa.com

HYPERDATA DIRECT
809 South Lemon Avenue
Walnut, CA 91789
(800) 786-3343, (800) 985-8228,
(909) 468-2933
fax (909) 468-2954
BBS (909) 594-3645
http://www.hyperdatadirect.com
Laptops and accessories

INSIGHT COMPUTERS
6820 South Harl Ave.
Tempe, AZ 85283
(480) 902-1001, (800) 467-4448
fax (480) 902-1180
http://www.insight.com

INTERPRO MICROSYSTEMS, INC.
44920 Osgood Road
Fremont, CA 94539
(510) 226-7226, (800) 226-7216
fax (510) 226-7219
http://www.interpromicro.com

JADE COMPUTER
18511 Hawthorne Boulevard
Torrance, CA 90504
(800) 421-5500, (310) 370-7474
fax (310) 370-1328
http://www.jadecomputer.com
Parts and peripherals

JINCO COMPUTERS
5122 Walnut Grove Avenue
San Gabriel, CA 91776
(800) 253-2531, (626)309-1108
tech support (626) 309-1103
fax (626) 309-1107
e-mail jinco@pacbell.net
http://www.jinco.com
Cases and power supplies

KAHLON, INC.
23255 La Palma Ave.
Yorba Linda, CA 92887
(888) KAHLON-C, (714) 694-0006
fax (714) 694-0003
http://www.kahlon.com
IBM and Compaq parts and memory

KENOSHA COMPUTER CENTER
9809 So. Franklin Dr. Suite 100
Franklin, WI 53132
(800) 255-2989, (414) 304-3200
fax (414) 304-3210
http://www.kcc-online.com

KREX COMPUTERS
9320 Waukegan Road
Morton Grove, IL 60053
(800) 222-KREX, (847) 967-0200
fax (847) 967-0276
http://www.krex800.com

LAITRON COMPUTER
1550 Montague Expressway
San Jose, CA 95131
(408) 888-4828

LAMBERTH COMPUTER SERVICES
3837 Northdale Blvd, #113
Tampa, FL 33624
fax (800) 876-0762
e-mail john-lcs@intnet.net

LEGEND MICRO
3200 South Arlington Rd
Akron, OH 44312
(800) 935-9305, (330) 644-7955
fax (330) 644-7960
http://www.legendmicro.com
Motherboards and components

M.B.S.
7466 Early Drive
Mechanicsville, VA 23111
(804) 944-3808

MACRO TECH INC.
23151 Verdugo Drive, Suite 102
Laguna Hills, CA 92653
(714) 580-1822
http://www.macropc.com/

MAGIC PC
5400 Brookpark Road
Cleveland, OH 44129
(800) 762-4426, (216) 661-7218
fax (216) 661-2454
Motherboards, systems, and components

MAIN STREET COMPUTER CO.
1720 Oak Street
Lakewood, NJ 08701-9885
(800) 333-9899
fax (908) 905-5731

MARINE PARK COMPUTERS
3126 Avenue U
Brooklyn, NY 11229
(719) 262-0163

MEGACOMP INTERNATIONAL, INC.
261 N.E. 1st Street, #200
Miami, FL 33132
(888) 463-4226, (305) 372-0222
fax (305) 374-5040

MEGATECH INC.
3070 Bristol Pike
Bensalem, PA 19020

MERRITT COMPUTER PRODUCTS, INC.
5565 Red Bird Center Drive, Suite 150
Dallas, TX 75237
(800) 627-7752, (214) 339-0753
fax (214) 339-1313
SafeSkin keyboard cover

MICRO ASSIST
50 Harrison Street
Hoboken, NJ 07030
(888) 97-MICRO, (201) 459-0233
fax (201) 459-0283

MICRO TIME, INC.
35375 Vokes Drive, Suite 106
Eastlake, OH 44095
(440) 954-9640
CPUs, memory, motherboards, and peripherals

MICRO X-PRESS
5646-48 West 73rd Street
Indianapolis, IN 46278
(317) 334-5640, (800) 875-9737
fax (317) 334-5639
http://www.microx-press.com

MICRONIX USA, INC.
23050 Miles Road
Cleveland, OH 44128
(800) 580-0505, (216) 475-9300
fax (216) 475-6610
Motherboards, memory, and other hardware

MICROSENSE, INC.
370 Andrew Avenue
Leucadia, CA 92024
(800) 544-4252, (800) 246-7729, (909)
    688-2735
fax (619) 753-6133
e-mail docdrive@microsense.com
http://www.microsense.com

MICROSUPPLY, INC.
(800) 535-2092
http://www.microsupply.com

MICRO-X
6230 Cochran Road
Solon, OH 44139
(800) 642-1266, (216)498-3517

MIDLAND COMPUTERMART
5699 West Howard
Niles, IL 60714
(800) 407-0700, (847) 967-0700
fax (847) 967-0710
e-mail sales@midlandcmart.com
CompuServe 102404,327
http://www.midlandcmart.com

MIDWEST COMPUTER WORKS
600 Bunker Ct.
Vernon Hills, IL 60061
(800) 770-4341, (847) 367-4700
fax (847) 459-6933
http://www.mcworks.com

MIDWEST MICRO
6910 St., Rt. 36
Fletcher, OH 45326
(800) 626-0544, (937) 368-2309
fax (800) 562-6622
http://www.mwmicro.com

MIDWESTERN DISKETTE
509 West Taylor
Creston, IA 50801
(800) 221-6332
fax (515) 782-4166
e-mail salesinfo@mddc.com
http://www
    .midwesterndiskette.com
Bulk disks

MILLENIUM TECHNOLOGIES
35 Cherry Hill Drive
Danvers, MA 01923
(800) 814-5681
Motherboards and additional components

MMI CORPORATION
New MMI Corporation
2400 Reach Road
Williamsport, PA 17701
(570) 327-9200
http://www.newmmi.com

MOTHERBOARD DISCOUNT CENTER
670 N. Arizona Ave., Ste 11
Chandler, AZ 85224
(800) 486-2026
fax (602) 857-4369
Motherboards, video boards, and other
hardware

MOTHERBOARD EXPRESS
333-B West State Road
Island Lake, IL 60042
(888) 440-1617
fax (888) 487-4637
http://www.motherboardx.com
Motherboards and drives

MOTHERBOARD SUPERSTORE

Motherboard SuperStore
26 Center Avenue
Sulphur, LA 70663
  (318) 625-9592, (800) 364-7232
fax (318) 625-4830
http://www.motherboards.com
Motherboards and cases

NATIONWIDE COMPUTERS DIRECT (NWCD)

110A McGaw Drive
Edison, NJ 08837
(800) 747-NWCD, (908) 417-4455
fax (800) 329-6923
Notebook computers, PCMCIA cards, printers, modems, and scanners

NCA COMPUTER PRODUCTS

1202 Kifer Road
Sunnyvale, CA 94086
(800) 622-9444, (408) 739-9010
fax (800) 622-1666
http://www.ncacomputer.com

NECX DIRECT

4 Technology Drive
Peabody, MA 01960
(800) 961-9208
http://www.necx.com

NETWORK EXPRESS

1720 Oak Street
P.O. Box 301
Lakewood, NJ 08701-9885
(800) 333-9899
fax (908) 905-5731
e-mail netexp@netline.net
Computers, peripherals, and test equipment

NEXT INTERNATIONAL

13622 Neutron Road
Dallas, TX 75244
(800) 730-NEXT, (214) 404-8260
fax (214) 404-8263
e-mail next@fastlane.net

NORTH AMERICAN CAD COMPANY

8515 Freeway Dr. Suite B
Macedonia, OH 44056
(800) 704-3337, (330) 468-4751
fax (330) 467-3668
http://www.nacad.com

Graphics-related peripherals, including printers, monitors, video boards, digitizers, and scanners

NOVA COMPUTERS, INC.

5245 North Harlem Ave.
Chicago, IL 60656
(888) 797-NOVA, (773) 774-9915
fax (773) 774-9918
http://www.novacomputers.com
Computers, parts, accessories, and motherboards

ODYSSEY TECHNOLOGY

5590 Lauby Road, Suite 70B
Canton, OH 44720
(800) 683-2808, (330) 497-2444
fax (330) 497-3156
http://www.odysseypc.com

PC CONNECTION

Rte. 101A, 730 Milford Rd.
Merrimack, NH 03054-4631
(888) 213-02600, (603) 335-6005
http://www.pcconnection.com

PC IMPACT

(800) 853-9337, (800) 698-3820
fax (216) 487-5242
http://www.pcimpact.com

PC IMPORTERS

290 Lena Drive
Aurora, OH 44202
(800) 886-5155
fax (216) 487-5242
Parts, systems, and components

PC UNIVERSE

2302 North Dixie Highway
Boca Raton, FL 33431
(800) 728-6483, (561) 447-0050
fax (407) 447-7549
e-mail sales@pcuniverse.com
http://www.pcuniverse.com
Computers, peripherals, and accessories

PCL COMPUTER, INC.

636 Lincoln Highway
Fairless Hills, PA 19030
(215) 736-2986
Cases

PCOMPUTER SOLUTIONS
130 West 32nd Street
New York, NY 10001
(212) 629-8300

PERIPHERALS UNLIMITED, INC.
1500 Kansas Avenue, Suite 4C
Longmont, CO 80501
(303) 772-1482
Computer-related hardware and software
products, specializing in mass storage and
connectivity

POWER PROS, INC.
6307-A Angus Drive
Raleigh, NC 27613
(919) 782-9210, (800) 788-0070
http://www.powerpros.com
Power protectors and UPSs

PRICE POINTE
3 Pointe Drive
Brea, CA 92621
(800) 840-7860
fax (800) 840-7861
Computers, peripherals, and software

PUBLISHING PERFECTION
21155 Watertown Road
Waukesha, Wisconsin 53186-1898
(262) 717-0600
http://www
    .publishingperfection.com
Digital cameras, scanners, and multimedia
hardware

QUARK TECHNOLOGY
5275 Naiman Parkway, Unit C
Solon, OH 44139
(440) 974-8807
fax (440) 974-8857

QUICK-LINE DISTRIBUTION
26001 Miles Road, Unit 8
Warrensville Heights, OH 44128
(800) 808-3606, (216) 514-9800
fax (216) 514-9805

ROYAL COMPUTER
1208 John Reed Court
Industry, CA 91745
(800) 486-0008, (818) 855-5077
fax (818) 330-2717
http://www.goroyalpc.com
Multimedia/graphics monitors

SEATTLE DATA SYSTEMS
746 Industry Drive
Seattle, WA 98188
(206) 575-8123
fax (206) 575-8870
e-mail sdsinc@seadat.com
http://www.seadat.com

SKY 1 TECHNOLOGIES
437 Chestnut Street
Philadelphia, PA 19106
(800) 294-5240, (215) 922-2904
fax (215) 922-6920
Motherboards, memory, drives, and
peripherals

STARQUEST COMPUTERS
4491 Mayfield Road
S. Euclid, OH 44121
(800) 945-0202, (216) 691-9966
fax (216) 691 9968
http://www.starquest-pc.com
Systems, parts, and peripherals

SUNSHINE COMPUTERS
1240 East Newport Center Drive
Deerfield Beach, FL 33442
(305) 422-9680

SUNWAY INC.
Sunway 1103 East Pine Street
St. Croix Falls, WI 54024
(715) 483-1179
fax (715) 483-1757
http://www.sunwayinc.com
Ergonomically designed computer accessories

SWAN TECHNOLOGIES
313 Boston Post Road
Marlborough, MA 01752
(800) 446-2499, (508) 460-1977
fax (508) 480-0156

TC Computers

TC Computers Corporate Sales
6820 South Harl Ave.
Tempe, AZ 85283
(800) 723-9491
http://www.tccomputers.com
Motherboards, cases, and peripherals

Technological Innovations, Inc.

26 Main Street
East Haven, CT 06512
(800) 577-1970, (203) 488-7867

Technology Distribution Network

1000 Young Street, Suite 270
Tonawanda, NY 14150
(800) 420-3636, (716) 743-0195
fax (716) 743-0198
http://www.tdn.com
Motherboards and components

The PC Zone

Multiple Zones International, Inc.
Corporate Headquarters
707 South Grady Way
Renton, WA 98055-3233
(425) 430-3000, (800) 408-9663
http://www.pczone.com

Tiger Software

800 Douglas, Executive Tower
Coral Gables, FL 33134

Top Data

574 Wedell Drive, #5
Sunnydale, CA 94089
(800) 888-3318, (408) 734-9100

Tri-State Computers

650 6th Avenue
New York, NY 10011
(800) 433-5199, (212) 633-2530
fax (212) 633-7718

USA Flex

444 Scott Drive
Bloomingdale, IL 60108
(800) 944-5599, (708) 582-6206
fax (708) 351-7204
http://www.usaflex.com

Vektron

2100 N. Highway 360, Suite 1904
Grand Prairie, TX 75050
(800) 660-0314, (972) 606-0280
fax (972) 606-1278
http://www.vektron.com

Older PC Repair and Exchange

For those of you with older PCs, there are
vendors who will repair and/or exchange
parts for these PCs. Many vendors will not
service all brands, so call to confirm that the
vendor actually services your specific model
of hard drive, motherboard, floppy drive,
and so on, before sending it off. Typically,
vendors will not exchange damaged parts
(for example, the board is in two pieces or
is water or fire damaged).

Computer Commodity, Inc.

1405 SW 6th Court, Suite B
Pompano Beach, FL 33069
(305) 942-6616
fax (305) 946-7815
e-mail computer@gate.net
www.commodityinc.com
A full service dealer/broker/distributor of new,
used, and refurbished computer hardware

Computer Recycle Center, Inc.

303 East Pipeline
Bedford, TX 76022
(817) 282-1622
fax (817) 282-5944
e-mail bert@recycles.com
http://www.recycles.com/
A world-wide trading site and recycling center for used and surplus computer equipment and materials; provides upgrades for
users of older equipment

Computer Recycler

670 West 17th Street
Costa Mesa, CA
(714) 645-4022
e-mail maurer44@wdc.net
http://www
    .computerrecycler.com/

Buyer, seller, and trader of new and pre-owned Mac and PC equipment

COMPUTER RECYCLERS

4119 Lindberg Road
Addison, TX 75244
(214) 774-0366
fax (214) 774-1161
http://www.comp-recycle.com

CPAC (COMPUTERS, PARTS, AND COMMODITIES)

22349 La Palma Ave, #114
Yorba Linda, CA 92687
(800)778-2722, (714) 692-5044
fax (714) 692-6680
e-mail cpac@wavenet.com
http://remarketing.com/
   broker_html/cpac/

CROCODILE COMPUTERS

360 Amsterdam Avenue
New York, NY 10023
(212) 769-3400
http://www.crocs.com/

DAKTECH

4025 9th Ave. SW
Fargo, ND 58103
(800) 325-3238, (717) 795-9544
fax (717) 795-9420
e-mail daktech@ix.netcom.com
http://www.daktech.com
Specializing in IBM and COMPAQ parts

DATA EXCHANGE CORPORATION

3600 Via Pescador
Camarillo, CA 93012
(800) 237-7911, (805) 388-1711
fax (805) 482-4856
http://www.dex.com
A leading full-service company specializing in contract manufacturing, end-of-life support, depot repair, logistics services, and worldwide inventory management services for all high-technology industries; has an extensive inventory of spare parts for sale

ERITECH INTERNATIONAL, INC.

213 N. Orange St, Unit C
Glendale, CA 91203
(818) 244-6242, (888) 808-6242
fax (818) 500-7699
http://www.eritech.com
Buyers of old CPUs and memory

NIE INTERNATIONAL

3000 E. Chambers
Phoenix, AZ 85040
(800) 797-8717
fax (602) 470-1540
e-mail nie@nieint.com
http://www.nieint.com/
A leading supplier of microcomputer parts and systems to companies that maintain and support PC installations

NORTHSTAR

221 Jackson Avenue North
Minneapolis, MN 55343
(612) 908-0616
fax (612) 908-0615
http://www.northstar-mn.com/
A complete PC repair service

OAK PARK PERSONAL COMPUTERS

130 South Oak Park Avenue, Suite #2
Oak Park, IL 60302
(708) 848-1553
fax (708) 524-9791
e-mail mlund@oppc.com
http://www.oppc.com/

ONLINE COMPUTING

3550-L SW 34th Street
Gainesville, FL 32608
(352) 372-1712
fax (352) 335-8192
e-mail online@gnv.fdt.net

THE USED COMPUTER MARKETPLACE

(part of the Affiliated ReMarketing Web)
http://www.remarketing.com
A place where you can list for-sale or wanted items for free in their confidential classifieds, which are then accessed by subscribing dealers

UNITED COMPUTER EXCHANGE

1690 Enterprise Way, Suite A
Marietta, GA 30067
(770) 612-1205
fax (770) 612-1239
http://www.uce.com/

A global clearinghouse for buyers and sellers of new and used microcomputer equipment

COMPUTER RECYCLING CENTERS

After upgrading your PC, you might prefer to donate the older parts to needy organizations rather than sell them. Here are some organizations that help with the redistribution:

COMPUTER RE-USE NETWORK (CoRN)

P.O. Box 1078
Hollywood, SC 29449
(803) 889-8247
e-mail corn2000@juno.com
http://www.awod.com/gallery/
    probono/corn/

COMPUTER RECYCLING PROJECT, INC.

Dale M. Tersey
San Francisco, California 94110
(415) 695-7703
e-mail dale@wco.com
http://www.wco.com/~dale/
    crp.htmml

A listing of additional organizations that deal with accepting old computers and funneling them to nonprofit groups/individuals in need

LAZARUS FOUNDATION, INC.

East Coast:
10378 Eclipse Way
Columbia, MD 21044
Donald Bard, President
(410) 740-0735
e-mail lazaruspc@aol.com
West Coast:
30 West Mission Street, #4
Santa Barbara, CA 93101
Kenneth M. Wyrick, Western Regional
    Director
(805) 563-1009
e-mail Recycle@west.net
http://www.lazarus.org

This is a computer recycling center that accepts donated computers which they, in turn, refurbish. These computers are then donated to individuals, schools, and other nonprofit organizations.

Appendix B

COMPLETE HARDWARE DICTIONARY

Adapted from *The Complete PC Upgrade and Maintenance Guide, Tenth Edition* by Mark Minasi
ISBN 0-7821-2606-5   1620 pages $49.99

A: The identifier used for the first floppy disk drive; the second floppy disk is designated as B:, and the first hard disk is known as C:. Unless instructed differently in the ROM-BIOS settings, the operating system always checks drive A for start-up (or bootstrap) instructions before checking the hard disk, drive C.

a-b box A switching box designed to share a peripheral between two or more computers. It can be switched manually or under program control.

accelerator board An add-in printed circuit board that replaces the main processor with a higher-performance processor, so you can upgrade your system without replacing monitor, case, keyboard, and so on.

Using an accelerator board can reduce upgrade costs substantially. However, there are other factors to consider, such as disk access time, in determining the overall performance of your system.

access mechanism In a floppy or hard disk drive, the component that positions the read/write head over the surface of the disk so that data can be read from or written to the disk.

access time The period of time that elapses between a request for information from disk or memory and the information arriving at the requesting device. Memory access time refers to the time it takes to transfer a character from memory to or from the processor; disk access time refers to the time it takes to place the read/write heads over the requested data. RAM may have an access time of 60 nanoseconds or less, and hard-disk access time could be 10 milliseconds or less.

active-matrix screen An LCD display mechanism that uses an individual transistor to control every pixel on the screen. Active-matrix screens are characterized by high contrast, a wide viewing angle, vivid colors, and fast screen refresh rates, and they do not show the streaking or shadowing that is common with passive matrix LCD technology.

active partition That part of the hard disk containing the operating system to be loaded when you start or restart the computer.

You can install two different operating systems (perhaps Windows 98 SE and Windows 2000 Professional) on your hard disk, but each must be in its own separate area, or partition. Only one partition can be active at any given time, and to change from, for example, Windows 98 SE to Windows 2000 Professional, you have to reboot.

ActiveX The name given by Microsoft to a set of object-oriented programming technologies. The main product of this technology is the ActiveX control, a piece of code that programmers can use over and over again in many applications.

adapter A printed circuit board that plugs into a computer's expansion bus to provide added capabilities. Common adapters for the PC include display adapters, memory expansion adapters, input/output adapters that provide serial, parallel, and games ports, and other devices such as internal modems, CD-ROMs, or network interface cards. One adapter can often support several different devices; for example, an input/output adapter may support one parallel port, a games or joystick port, and several serial ports. Some PC designs incorporate many of the functions previously performed by these individual adapters on the motherboard.

address **1.** The precise location in memory or on disk where a piece of information is stored. Every byte in memory and every sector on a disk has its own unique address.

2. To reference or manage a storage location.

address bus The electronic channel, usually from 20 to 32 separate lines wide, used to transmit the signals that specify locations in memory. The number of lines in the address bus determines the number of memory locations that the processor can access, as each line carries one bit of the address. An address bus of 20 lines (used in early Intel 8086/8088 processors) can access 1MB of memory, one of 24 lines (as in the Intel 80286) can access 16MB, one of 32 lines (as used by the Intel 80386, 80486, and later processors, or the Motorola 68020) can access more than 4GB, and one of 36 lines (used by the Pentium II Xeon) can access a maximum of 64GB of RAM.

advanced run-length limited encoding

Abbreviated ARLL. A technique used to store information on a hard disk that increases the capacity of run-length limited (RLL) storage by more than 25 percent and increases the data-transfer rate to 9 megabits per second.

AGP

Short for Accelerated Graphics Port, AGP is a video specification that enhances and accelerates the display of three-dimensional objects.

algorithm

A formal set of instructions that can be followed to perform a specific task, such as a mathematical formula or a set of instructions in a computer program.

Altair 8800

The first commercially successful microcomputer, based on the Intel 8080, introduced in 1975 by Micro Instrumentation Telemetry Systems of New Mexico. More than 10,000 were sold, mostly in kit form, and the Altair was packaged with the Microsoft MBASIC interpreter, written by Paul Allen and Bill Gates. The Altair 8800 had 256 bytes of memory, received input through a set of switches on the front panel, and displayed output on a row of LEDs.

alternating current

Abbreviated AC. An electrical current that reverses its polarity or direction of flow at regular intervals. AC is usually represented by a sine wave. In the United States, domestic wall plugs provide AC at 60 hertz, or 60 cycles per second.

alt newsgroups

A set of Usenet newsgroups that often contain articles on controversial subjects usually considered outside the mainstream.

These newsgroups were originally created to avoid the rigorous process required to create a normal Usenet newsgroup. Some alt newsgroups contain valuable discussions on subjects that range from agriculture to wolves, others contain sexually explicit material, and still others are just for fun. Not all service providers and online services give access to the complete set of alt newsgroups.

American National Standards Institute

Abbreviated ANSI. A nonprofit organization of business and industry groups, founded in 1918, devoted to the development of voluntary standards. ANSI represents the United States on the International Organization for Standardization (ISO). In the PC world, ANSI committees have developed recommendations for the C programming language, for the C++ programming language, for the Fortran programming language compiler, for the SCSI interface, for the ANSI.SYS device driver, and for FDDI (Fiber Distributed Data Interface).

America Online

One of the most popular and fastest-growing of the commercial online services, often abbreviated AOL.

America Online provides a well-designed and easy-to-use service that includes a wide range of content, e-mail services, and basic Internet-access services. Many hardware and software vendors maintain software libraries and well-moderated technical-support forums, and news and weather information is available through Reuters and UPI. Sports, hobbies, games, and online shopping are also available.

analog

Describes any device that represents changing values by a continuously variable physical property such as voltage in a circuit, fluid pressure, liquid level, and so on.

An analog device can handle an infinite number of values within its range. By contrast, a digital device can manage only a fixed number of possible values. For example, an ordinary mercury thermometer is an analog device and can record an infinite number of readings over its range. A digital thermometer, on the other hand, can only display temperature in a fixed number of individual steps.

analog-to-digital converter Abbreviated ADC or A-D converter. A device that converts continuously varying analog signals into discrete digital signals or numbers by sampling the analog signal at regular intervals. Once analog signals have been converted into digital form, they can be processed, analyzed, stored, displayed, and transmitted by computer. The key to analog-to-digital conversion lies in the amount of digital data created from the analog signal. The shorter the time interval between samples, and the more data recorded from that sample, the more closely the digital signal will reproduce the original analog signal. Many of today's sound boards can sample and play back at a maximum of 44.1kHz using a 16-bit analog-to-digital converter.

anonymous FTP A method of accessing an Internet computer with the FTP (File Transfer Protocol) that does not require that you have an account on the target computer system. Just log in to the Internet computer with the user name *anonymous*, and use your e-mail address as your password.

anonymous posting In a Usenet newsgroup, a public message posted via an anonymous server in order to conceal the identity of the original author. This server removes all the information from the message that could identify the sender and forwards the message to its destination. If you ever use an anonymous server, don't forget to remove your signature from the bottom of your posting.

antivirus program An application program you run to detect or eliminate a computer virus or infection. Some antivirus programs are terminate-and-stay-resident programs that can detect suspicious activity on your computer as it happens; others must be run periodically as part of your normal housekeeping activities.

applet A small application program, limited in scope to one small but useful task. A

calculator program or a card game might be called an applet.

AppleTalk A suite of protocols used by Apple computers to communicate with one another over a network.

application layer The seventh, or highest, layer in the International Organization for Standardization's Open Systems Interconnect (ISO/OSI) model for computer-to-computer communications. This layer uses services provided by the lower layers, but is completely insulated from the details of the network hardware. It describes how application programs interact with the network operating system, including database management, e-mail, and terminal emulation programs.

application program interface Abbreviated API. The complete set of operating system functions that an application program can use to perform tasks such as managing files and displaying information on the computer screen.

An API is a complete definition of all the operating system functions available to an application program, and it also describes how the application program should use those functions.

In operating systems that support a graphical user interface, the API also defines functions to support windows, icons, drop-down menus, and other components of the interface.

In network operating systems, an API defines a standard method that application programs can use to take advantage of all the network features.

application-specific integrated circuit Abbreviated ASIC. A computer chip developed for a specific purpose, designed by incorporating standard cells from a library, rather than designed from scratch. ASICs can be found in VCRs, microwave ovens, automobiles, and security alarms.

arbitration The set of rules used to manage competing demands for a computer resource, such as memory or peripheral devices, made by multiple processes or users.

Archie   A shortened form of *archive,* Archie is a system used on the Internet to locate files available by anonymous FTP. Archie was written by students and volunteers at McGill University's School of Computer Science in Montreal, Canada, and is available worldwide.

Once a week, special programs connect to all the known anonymous FTP sites on the Internet and collect a complete listing of all the publicly available files. This listing is kept in an Internet Archive Database, and when you ask Archie to look for a file, only this database is searched rather than the whole Internet; you can then use anonymous FTP to retrieve the file.

architecture   The overall design and construction of all or part of a computer, particularly the processor hardware and the size and ordering sequence of its bytes. Also used to describe the overall design of software.

array processor   A group of special processors designed to calculate math procedures at very high speeds, often under the control of another central processor. Some computers use array processors to speed up video operations or for fast floating-point math operations.

ASCII   Pronounced "askee." Acronym for American Standard Code for Information Interchange. A standard coding scheme that assigns numeric values to letters, numbers, punctuation marks, and control characters to achieve compatibility among different computers and peripherals.

In ASCII each character is represented by a unique integer value. The values 0 through 31 are used for nonprinting control codes, and the values 32 through 127 are used to represent the letters of the alphabet and common punctuation symbols. The entire set from 0 through 127 is referred to as the standard ASCII character set. All computers

that use ASCII can understand the standard ASCII character set.

The extended ASCII character set (from code 128 through code 255) is assigned variable sets of characters by computer hardware manufacturers and software developers and is not necessarily compatible between different computers. The IBM extended character set includes mathematical symbols and characters from the PC line-drawing set.

ASCII file   A file that contains only text characters from the ASCII character set. An ASCII file contains letters, numbers, and punctuation symbols, but does not contain any hidden text-formatting commands. Also known as a text file and as an ASCII text file.

Association for Computing Machinery Abbreviated ACM. A membership organization, founded in 1947, dedicated to advancing computer science through technical education of computing professionals and through technical publications. ACM also sponsors several special interest groups (SIGs).

Association of PC User Groups   Abbreviated APCUG. A nonprofit affiliation of local PC user groups, dedicated to fostering communications between personal-computer user groups, and acting as an information network between user groups and software publishers and hardware manufacturers.

asynchronous transmission   In communications, a method of transmission that uses start and stop bits to coordinate the flow of data so that the time intervals between individual characters do not have to be equal. Parity may also be used to check the accuracy of the data received.

ATA   The first IBM PC had no hard disk storage capability. When the 80286-based AT was developed, it included a hard disk as a major feature, and the hard disk controller interface (ATA or AT Attachment) became a de facto industry standard from that day to this. As PCs have grown up, however, the controller interface has also evolved, and we do mean evolution rather than revolution. Everything still leads back to that original interface, in one way or another. The children of ATA are now quite various, and the family tree currently looks like this:

ATA (Advanced Technology Attachment) is the original interface and is the same as the Integrated Device Electronics interface (IDE) for disk drives. ATA (thus IDE) was designed as a way to integrate the controller onto the hard disk drive itself and to lower manufacturing costs, as well as make firmware implementations easier.

ATA-2 is an extension of ATA that was beefed up to include performance enhancing features such as fast PIO (Programmed Input/Output) and DMA (direct memory access) modes. The ATA-2 interface also got an improved Identify Drive command. This particular feature lets a hard drive tell the software exactly what its characteristics are and is the basis for both Plug-and-Play hard drive technology and compatibility with any new version of the standard that may come down the road in the future.

ATAPI (ATA Packet Interface) is a standard that is still being worked out. It has been designed for devices such as CD-ROMs and tape drives that plug into an ordinary ATA (IDE) port. The major benefit of ATAPI hardware is that it's cheap and works on your current adapter. For CD-ROMs, ATAPI also uses fewer CPU resources than proprietary adapters, but is not otherwise any faster. For tape drives, ATAPI could potentially be both faster and more reliable than interfaces that are driven by the floppy drive controller.

Fast ATA is what people are calling the technology and products that support the high-speed data transfers specified by ANSI-standardized Programmed Input/Output (PIO) Mode 3 and multi-word direct memory access (DMA) Mode 1 protocols. Fast ATA enables the drive to transfer data at speeds as high as 13.3MBps.

Fast ATA-2 is like Fast ATA, but is a standard that will allow manufacturers to create products that support ANSI PIO Mode 4 and multi-word DMA Mode 2 protocols. With Fast ATA-2, we should be able to get data transfers as high as 16.6MBps.

AT command set   A set of standard instructions used to activate features on a modem. Originally developed by Hayes Microcomputer Products, the AT command set is now used by almost all modem manufacturers.

The code AT is short for ATtention and precedes most of the modem commands. On a Hayes or Hayes-compatible modem, the ATDP (ATtention Dial Pulse) command initiates pulse (rather than touch-tone) dialing, and the ATDT (ATtention Dial Tone) command initiates touch-tone (rather than pulse) dialing.

attenuation   In communications, the decrease in power of a signal transmitted over a wire. Attenuation is measured in decibels and increases as the power of the signal decreases. In a local area network, attenuation can become a problem when cable lengths exceed the stated network specification; however, the useful length of a cable can often be extended by the use of a repeater.

ATX   A type of computer case that uses a different power connector and rotates the processor 90 degrees on the motherboard, physically placing it and the slots in a different position. The ports on the motherboard (i.e., the keyboard, serial, and mouse ports) are all stacked on top of one another. An ATX motherboard will not fit in a standard case and vice versa.

A20   The A20 line is a microprocessor address line on Intel processors that controls access to the 64K of address space known as the high memory area. This is managed automatically by Windows. On DOS machines, this area was managed by HIMEM.SYS on IBM AT and compatible computers. You specified the A20 handler you wanted to use on your computer with the appropriate code value for the HIMEM .SYS /MACHINE switch in CONFIG.SYS; the default setting for IBM ATs and compatible computers is AT or 1.

AUTOEXEC.BAT   A contraction of AUTOmatically EXECuted BATch. A special DOS batch file, located in the root directory of older DOS systems, that would run automatically every time the system was booted up or rebooted.

B: In Windows, the identifier used for the second floppy disk drive; the first floppy disk is designated as A:, and the first hard disk is known as C:.

backbone   In communications, that portion of the network that manages the bulk of the traffic. The backbone may connect several locations or buildings and may also connect to other, smaller networks.

back-end processor   A secondary processor that performs one specialized task very effectively, freeing the main processor for other, more important work.

background noise   In communications, any unwanted signal that enters a line, channel, or circuit.

backplane   A printed circuit board containing slots or sockets, into which expansion boards are plugged.

backup   An up-to-date copy of all your files that you can use to reload your hard disk in case of an accident. It is an insurance against disk failure affecting the hundreds or possibly thousands of files you might have on your system hard disk or on your local area network hard disk.

backward-compatible   Fully compatible with earlier versions of the same application program or computer system.

bad sector   An area on a hard disk or floppy disk that cannot be used to store data, because of a manufacturing defect or

accidental damage. One of the tasks an operating system performs is finding, marking, and isolating bad sectors. Almost all hard disks have some bad sectors, often listed in the bad track table, as a result of the manufacturing process, and this is not usually anything to worry about; the operating system will mark them as bad, and you will never even know that they are there. If you see these appear regularly during routine maintenance, usually running Scandisk, you may need to consider replacing your hard drive.

bad track table   A list of the defective areas on a hard disk, usually determined during final testing of the disk at the factory. Some disk-preparation programs ask you to enter information from this list to reduce the time that a low-level format takes to prepare the disk for use by an operating system.

bandwidth   In communications, the difference between the highest and the lowest frequencies available for transmission in any given range.

In networking, the transmission capacity of a computer or a communications channel, stated in megabits or megabytes per second; the higher the number, the faster the data transmission takes place.

bank switching   A method of switching between two sets (or banks) of memory in a computer, only one of which can be active at a time. Because of the overhead involved in switching between banks, memory-intensive tasks can take much longer to perform using bank-switched memory than when using contiguous memory.

batch file   An ASCII text file containing operating system commands and possibly other commands supported by the batch processor. The commands in the file are executed one line at a time, just as if you had typed them at the system prompt. You can include program names, operating system commands, batch language commands, and other variables in your batch files. Batch files are used to automate repetitive tasks; almost all DOS users placed regularly used setup commands in a batch file called AUTOEXEC.BAT, which executes every time the computer is started. A DOS batch file must have the filename extension .BAT.

baud   A measurement of data-transmission speed. Originally used in measuring the speed of telegraph equipment, it now usually refers to the data-transmission speed of a modem or other serial device.

baud rate   In communications equipment, a measurement of the number of state changes (from 0 to 1 or vice versa) per second on an asynchronous communications channel.

Baud rate is often mistakenly assumed to correspond to the number of bits transmitted per second, but because in today's high-speed digital communications systems, one state change can be made to represent more than one data bit, baud rate and bits per second are not always the same. A rate of 300 baud is likely to correspond to 300 bits per second, but at higher baud rates, the number of bits per second transmitted can be higher than the baud rate, as one state change can represent more than one data bit. For example, 2400 bits per second can be sent at 1200 baud if each state change represents two bits of information.

On the PC, the MODE command is used to set the baud rate of a serial device, perhaps a modem or a printer. Both the sending and the receiving devices must be set to the same baud rate, and in times past, mismatched baud rates were one of the most common reasons for communications failures. These days, intelligent modems can lock onto one of a range of rates and can even change rates in response to changing line conditions during the course of a transmission.

benchmark   A test that attempts to quantify hardware or software performance—usually in terms of speed, reliability, or accuracy. One of the major problems in determining performance is deciding which of the many benchmarks available actually reflects how you plan to use the system. For best results, you should evaluate performance using the same mix of applications and system commands that you expect to use in your day-to-day work.

Bernoulli box   A high-capacity data-storage device featuring a removable cartridge, developed by Iomega Corporation.

beta software   Software that has been released to a cross-section of typical users for testing before the commercial release of the package.

B channel   Two of the three channels that make up an ISDN (Integrated Services Digital Network) line. The B channels (or bearer channels) are used for sending data and use 64Kbps of bandwidth each. Each B channel can be used as a separate connection or combined to give a full 128Kbps connection.

binary   Any scheme that uses two different states, components, conditions, or conclusions. In mathematics, the binary, or base-2, numbering system uses combinations of the digits 0 and 1 to represent all values. The more familiar decimal system has a base of 10 (0–9).

Computers and other digital devices are designed to work with information (internally) in the form of binary numbers, because it is relatively simple to construct electronic circuits that generate two voltage levels ("on" and "off," corresponding to 1 and 0).

Unlike computers, people find binary numbers that consist of long strings of 0s and 1s difficult to read, so most people who work at this level use hexadecimal (base-16) numbers instead.

binary-coded decimal   Abbreviated BCD. A simple system for converting decimal numbers into binary form; each decimal digit is converted into binary and then stored as a single character.

In binary numbers, the largest value that can be stored in a single 8-bit byte is 255, and this obviously represents a severe limitation to storing larger numbers. BCD is a way around this limitation that stays within the 8-bit storage format. For example, the decimal number 756 can be broken down so that the numbers 7, 5, and 6 are represented by one byte each. In BCD, each decimal digit occupies a byte, so 3 bytes are needed for a 3-digit decimal number. There is no limit to the size of the stored number; as the number increases in size, so does the amount of storage space set aside to hold it.

BIOS   Acronym for basic input/output system, pronounced "bye-os." In the PC, a set of instructions, stored in read-only memory (ROM), that let your computer's hardware and operating system communicate with application programs and peripheral devices such as hard disks, printers, and video adapters. These instructions are stored in nonvolatile memory as a permanent part of your computer. They are always available at specific addresses in memory, so all programs can access them to perform their basic input and output functions.

IBM computers contain a copyrighted BIOS that only their computers can use; however, other companies such as Phoenix, Award, and American Megatrends have developed BIOSs for other manufacturers' computers that emulate or mimic the IBM instructions without using the same code. If you use a non-IBM computer, the BIOS company's copyright message and BIOS version number are displayed every time you turn on your computer.

BIOS extensions   In the PC, extensions to the main BIOS (basic input/output system) that enable the computer to work with add-on devices such as hard disk controllers and EGA (Enhanced Graphic Adapter) or VGA (Video Graphics Adapter) adapters. The ROM chips containing these extensions do not have to be located on the motherboard; they can also be on expansion boards plugged into the expansion bus. Any BIOS extensions needed to run these expansion boards are loaded automatically when you boot your computer.

BIOS parameter block   Abbreviated BPB. In the PC, a part of the boot record contained on every formatted disk that contains information about the disk's physical characteristics. This information includes the version number of the operating system used to format the disk, the number of bytes per sector, and the number of sectors per cluster, per track, and per disk. This information is provided for use by device drivers.

bit   Contraction of *Binary digit*. A bit is the basic unit of information in the binary numbering system, representing either 0 (for off) or 1 (for on). Bits can be grouped together to make up larger storage units, the most common being the 8-bit byte. A byte can represent all kinds of information including the letters of the alphabet, the numbers 0 through 9, and common punctuation symbols.

bit-mapped font   A set of characters in a specific style and size, in which each character is defined by a pattern of dots. The computer must keep a complete set of bitmaps for every font you use on your system, and these bitmaps can consume large amounts of disk space.

bit-mapped graphic   A graphic, created with a paint program such as MacPaint or PC Paintbrush, composed of a series of dots, or pixels, rather than a set of lines or vectors. Resizing a bit-mapped image without distortion or aliasing is very difficult, and bit-mapped graphics consume large amounts of disk and memory space. Color bit-mapped graphics often require many times the amount of control information that a monochrome bit-map needs. Scanners and screen-capture programs may also produce bit-mapped images.

bits per inch   Abbreviated bpi. The number of bits (binary digits) that a tape or disk can store per inch of length.

bits per second   Abbreviated bps. The number of binary digits, or bits, transmitted every second during a data transfer. A measurement of the speed of operation of equipment such as a computer's data bus or a modem connecting a computer to a transmission line.

BNC connector   A small connector with a half-turn locking shell used with coaxial cable.

boot   The loading of an operating system into memory, usually from a hard disk, although occasionally from a floppy disk. This is an automatic procedure begun when you first turn on or reset your computer. A set of instructions contained in ROM begin executing, first running a series of power-on self tests (POST) to check that devices such as hard disks are in working order, then locating and loading the operating system, and finally, passing control of the computer over to that operating system.

The term is supposed to be derived from the expression "pulling yourself up by your own bootstraps."

bootable disk   Any disk capable of loading and starting the operating system, although most often used when referring to a floppy disk. In these days of larger and larger operating systems, it is less common to boot from a floppy disk. In some cases, all the files needed to start the operating system will not fit on a single floppy disk, which makes it impossible to boot from a floppy.

boot record   That part of a formatted disk containing the operating system loading program, along with other basic information needed by the computer when it starts running.

bridge   A device working at the data-link layer of the Open Systems Interconnect (OSI) model used to connect local area networks and thus form one larger network. A limitation of bridges is that they rely heavily on broadcast traffic, meaning that all traffic goes to all computers on all networks connected by a bridge.

broadband network   In communications, a technique for transmitting a large amount of information, including voice, data, and video, over long distances.

The transmission capacity is divided into several distinct channels that can be used concurrently, normally by using frequency-division multiplexing, and these individual channels are protected from one another by guard channels of unused frequencies. A broadband network can operate at speeds as high as 20 megabits per second and is based on the same technology that cable television uses.

brouter   In networking, a device that combines the attributes of a bridge and a router. A brouter can route one or more specific protocols, such as TCP/IP (Transmission Control Protocol/Internet Protocol), and bridge all others.

brownout   A short period of low voltage often caused by an unusually heavy demand for power. A brownout may cause your computer to crash, and if your area experiences frequent brownouts, you should consider purchasing an uninterruptible power supply (UPS).

browser   1. An application program used to explore Internet resources. A browser lets you wander from node to node without concern for the technical details of the links between the nodes or the specific methods used to access them, and presents the information—text, graphics, sound, or video—as a document on the screen.

2. In networking, a service that keeps a list of all available resources on a network and disseminates that list to clients.

buffer   An area of memory set aside for temporary storage of data, often until some external event completes. Many peripherals, such as printers, have their own buffers. The computer transfers the data for printing from memory into the buffer, and the printer then processes that data directly from the buffer, freeing the computer for other tasks.

bug   A logical or programming error in hardware or software that causes a malfunction of some sort. If the problem is in software, it can be fixed by changes to the program. If the fault is in hardware, new circuits must be designed and constructed. Some bugs are fatal and cause the program to hang or cause data loss, others are just annoying, and many are never even noticed. The term apparently originates from the days of the first electro-mechanical computers, when a problem was traced to a moth caught between two contacts inside the machinery.

bug-fix   A release of hardware or software that corrects known bugs but does not contain additional new features. Such releases are usually designated only by an increase in the decimal portion of the version number; for example, the revision level may advance from 2.0 to 2.01 or 2.1, rather than from 2.0 to 3.0.

bulletin board system   Abbreviated BBS. A computer system, equipped with one or more modems, acting as a message-passing system or centralized information source, usually for a particular special interest group. Bulletin board systems are often established by software vendors and by PC user groups. For the most part, the BBS has been replaced by the World Wide Web.

bus   An electronic pathway along which signals are sent from one part of a computer to another. In the PC, several buses are available:

- ISA (Industry Standard Architecture)
- EISA (Extended Industry Standard Architecture)
- VL bus (VESA [Video Electronics Standards Association] local bus)
- PCI (Peripheral Component Interconnect local bus)

Because you may want to add a new function to your computer, most PC buses allow for this through one or more expansion slots; when you plug an expansion board into an expansion slot, you are actually plugging the board into the bus and making it part of the system.

bus mastering   A technique that allows certain advanced bus architectures to delegate control of data transfers between the central processing unit (CPU) and associated peripheral devices to an add-in board. This gives greater system bus access and higher data-transfer rates than conventional systems.

- Today's buses such as MCA (Microchannel Architecture), EISA (Extended Industry Standard Architecture), VL bus (Video Electronics Standards Association local bus), and PCI (Peripheral Component Interconnect) all support some form of bus mastering, but older systems such as ISA (Industry Standard Architecture) do not.

bus mouse   A mouse connected to the computer using an expansion board plugged into an expansion slot, instead of simply connected to a serial port as in the case of a serial mouse.

byte   Contraction of *binary digit eight*. A group of 8 bits that in computer storage terms usually holds a single character, such as a number, a letter, or a symbol.

Because bytes represent a very small amount of storage, they are usually grouped into kilobytes (1,024 bytes), megabytes (1,048,576 bytes), or even gigabytes (1,073,741,824 bytes) for convenience when describing hard disk capacity or computer memory size.

C: In the PC, the drive designation for the first hard disk.

cache   Pronounced "cash." A special area of memory, managed by a cache controller, that improves performance by storing the contents of frequently accessed memory locations and their addresses. When the processor references a memory address, the cache checks to see if it holds that address. If it does, the information is passed directly to the processor; if not, a normal memory access takes place instead. A cache can speed up operations in a computer whose RAM access is slow compared with its processor speed, because the cache memory is always faster than normal RAM.

cache controller   Pronounced "cash controller." A special-purpose processor, such as the Intel 82385, whose sole task is to manage cache memory. On newer processors, such as the Intel Pentium, cache management is integrated directly into the processor.

cache memory   Pronounced "cash memory." A relatively small section of very fast memory (often static RAM) reserved for the temporary storage of the data or instructions likely to be needed next by the processor. For example, the Intel Pentium II has a 16K code cache as well as a 16K data cache built into the processor. The Pentium III has either a 512K level two cache or a 256K Advanced Transfer cache built into the processor.

caddy   A flat plastic container used to load a compact disc into older CD-ROM drives.

Canon engine   The combination of laser mechanism and toner cartridge, first produced by Canon, used as the heart of Hewlett-Packard's popular line of laser printers.

card   A printed circuit board or adapter that you plug into your computer to add support for a specific piece of hardware not normally present on the computer.

cardcage   An enclosure designed to hold printed circuit boards or cards. Most PCs have an area with edge connectors and mounting plates designed to receive expansion boards. The term originally referred to an external box that held rack-mounted cards.

card services   Part of the software support needed for PCMCIA (PC Memory Card International Association) hardware devices in a portable computer, controlling the use of system interrupts, memory, or power management.

When an application wants to access a PC card, it always goes through the card services software and never communicates directly with the underlying hardware. For example, if you use a PCMCIA modem, card services establishes which communications port and which interrupts and I/O addresses are in use, not the application program.

carpal tunnel syndrome   A form of wrist injury caused by holding the hands in an awkward position for long periods of time. A narrow tunnel in the wrist—the carpal tunnel—contains tendons and the median nerve, which conducts sensation from the thumb, index, and middle fingers and parts of the hand up the arm to the central nervous system. Burning sensations and tingling occur when the median nerve is compressed as it passes through the narrow tunnel of bone and ligature at the wrist. Keyboard operators, musicians, dental hygienists, meat packers, and other workers who perform repetitive motions for long periods of time may be prone to this sort of injury. Improvements in the work environment, more frequent breaks, and even job modification can all help alleviate this problem, which is costing industry millions of dollars each year, according to National Institute for Occupational Health figures.

carrier signal   In communications, a signal of chosen frequency generated to carry data, often used for long-distance transmissions. The data is added to this carrier signal by modulation, and it is decoded on the receiving end by demodulation.

CBIOS   Acronym for Compatibility Basic Input/Output System. Firmware service routines built into the IBM PS/2 series of computers with the Microchannel Architecture (MCA), generally considered a super-set of the original IBM PC BIOS.

CCITT   Abbreviation for Consultative Committee for International Telephony and Telegraphy. An organization, based in

Geneva, that develops worldwide data communications standards. CCITT is part of the ITU (International Telecommunications Union).

Three main sets of standards have been established:

▸ CCITT Groups 1–4 standards apply to facsimile transmissions.

▸ The CCITT V series of standards apply to modems and error detection and correction methods.

▸ The CCITT X series standards apply to local area networks.

Recently, the trend has been to refer to these standards as ITU standards rather than CCITT standards; you will see both. Recommendations are published every four years, and each update is identified by the color of its cover.

CCITT Groups 1–4   A set of four CCITT-recommended standards for facsimile transmissions. Groups 1 and 2 defined analog facsimile transmissions and are no longer used. Groups 3 and 4 describe digital systems, as follows:

Group 3 specifies a 9600bps modem to transmit standard images of 203 dots per inch (dpi) horizontally by 98dpi vertically in standard mode, and 203dpi by 198dpi in fine mode.

Group 4 supports images up to 400dpi for high-speed transmission over a digital data network such as ISDN, rather than a dial-up telephone line.

CCITT V Series   A set of recommended standards for data communications over a telephone line, including transmission speeds and operational modes, issued by CCITT.

CCITT X Series   A set of recommended standards issued by CCITT to standardize protocols and equipment used in public and private computer networks, including the transmission speeds, the interfaces to and

between networks, and the operation of user hardware.

CD-I   Abbreviation for Compact Disc–Interactive, pronounced "see-dee-eye." This older hardware and software standard disk format encompasses data, text, audio, still video images, and animated graphics. The standard also defines methods for encoding and decoding compressed data, as well as displaying data.

CD-R   Abbreviation for Compact Disc–Recordable. A type of CD device that brings CD-ROM publishing into the realm of the small business or home office. From a functional point of view, a CD-R and a CD-ROM are identical; you can read CD-R discs using almost any CD-ROM drive, although the processes that create the discs are slightly different. Low-cost CD-R drives are available from many manufacturers, including Kao, Kodak, Mitsui, Phillips, Ricoh, Sony, TDK, 3M, and Verbatim.

CD-ROM   Abbreviation for Compact Disc–Read-Only Memory, pronounced "see-dee-rom." A high-capacity, optical storage device that uses compact disc technology to store large amounts of information, up to 650MB (the equivalent of approximately 300,000 pages of text), on a single 4.72-inch disc.

A CD-ROM uses the constant linear velocity encoding scheme to store information in a single, spiral track, divided into many equal-length segments. To read data, the CD-ROM drive must increase the rotational speed as the read head gets closer to the center of the disc and decrease as the head moves back out. Typical CD-ROM data access times are much slower than hard disk data access times.

CD-ROM drive   A disk device that uses compact disc technology for information storage. CD-ROM drives are manufactured to much higher tolerances than audio CD players. If a CD player misreads a small amount of data, the human ear will probably not detect the difference; if a CD-ROM drive misreads a few bytes of a program, the program simply will not run. Many CD-ROM drives also have headphone jacks, external speaker jacks, and a volume control because they can also read audio CD discs. CD-ROM drives come in a variety of transfer speeds from the most common 32× up to 50× used in large networks. The two most popular CD-ROM drive interface cards are IDE/EIDE and SCSI. Other CD-ROM drives may use the computer's parallel port or a PCM-CIA connection.

CD-ROM Extended Architecture Abbreviated CD-ROM/XA. An extension to the CD-ROM format, developed by Microsoft, Phillips, and Sony, that allows for the storage of audio and visual information on compact disc so that you can play the audio at the same time you view the visual data.

CD-ROM/XA is compatible with the High Sierra specification also known as ISO standard 9660.

Celeron The Intel Celeron processor is specifically designed for the sub-$1200 market segment to handle the Internet, educational programs, interactive 3-D games, and productivity applications.

central processing unit Abbreviated CPU. The computing and control part of the computer. The CPU in a mainframe computer may be contained on many printed circuit boards; the CPU in a minicomputer may be contained on several boards; and the CPU in a PC is contained in a single extremely powerful microprocessor.

Centronics parallel interface A standard 36-pin interface in the PC world for the exchange of information between the PC and a peripheral such as a printer, originally developed by the printer manufacturer Centronics, Inc. The standard defines eight parallel data lines, plus additional lines for status and control information.

CGA Abbreviation for Color/Graphics Adapter. A video adapter introduced by IBM in 1981 that provided low-resolution text and graphics. CGA provided several text and graphics modes, including 40- or 80-column by 25 line 16-color text mode, and graphics modes of 640 horizontal pixels by 200 vertical pixels with 2 colors, or 320 horizontal pixels by 200 vertical pixels with 4 colors. CGA has been superseded by later video standards, including EGA (Enhanced Graphics Adapter), VGA (Video Graphics Adapter), SuperVGA, and XGA (Extended Graphics Array).

charge-coupled device Abbreviated CCD. A special type of memory that can store patterns of changes in a sequential manner. The light-detecting circuitry contained in many still and video cameras is a CCD.

checksum A method of providing information for error detection, usually calculated by totaling a set of values.

The checksum is usually appended to the end of the data that it is calculated from, so that data and the checksum can be compared. For example, Xmodem, the popular file transfer protocol, uses a 1-byte checksum calculated by adding all the ASCII values for all 128 data bytes and ignoring any numeric overflow. The checksum is added to the end of the Xmodem data packet. This kind of checksum will not always detect all errors, and in later versions of the Xmodem protocol, it was replaced by a cyclical redundancy check (CRC) for more rigorous error control.

circuit A communications channel or path between two devices capable of carrying electrical current. Also used to describe a set of components connected together to perform a specific task.

Class A certification An FCC (Federal Communications Commission) certification for computer equipment, including mainframe and minicomputers destined for use in an industrial, commercial, or office setting, rather than for personal use at home. The Class A commercial certification is less restrictive than the Class B certification for residential use because it assumes that most residential areas are more than 30 feet from any commercial computer equipment.

Class B certification   An FCC (Federal Communications Commission) certification for computer equipment, including PCs, laptops, and portables destined for use in the home rather than in a commercial setting. Class B levels of radio frequency interference (RFI) must be low enough so that they do not interfere with radio or television reception when there is more than one wall and 30 feet separating the computer from the receiver. Class B certification is more restrictive than the commercial Class A certification.

clock speed   Also known as clock rate. The internal speed of a computer or processor, normally expressed in MHz.

The faster the clock speed, the faster the computer will perform a specific operation, assuming the other components in the system, such as disk drives, can keep up with the increased speed. Current clock speeds vary with processor type. The Pentium II is capable of running at 400MHz while the DEC Alpha RISC processor is able to run at 533MHz. The Pentium III can run at 600MHz, 667HMz, 733MHz, and 800MHz.

clone   Hardware that is identical in function to an original. Usually used in the sense of, for example, an "IBM clone," a PC that uses an Intel (or similar) microprocessor and functions in the same way as an IBM computer. Although most clones do perform as intended, minor internal differences can cause severe problems in some clones that can be solved only by the intervention of the manufacturer.

Companies have offered clones of IBM-compatible computers for many years, but Apple waited until early 1995 to announce that they too would license the Macintosh operating system and related technology to other manufacturers.

cluster   The smallest unit of hard disk space that DOS can allocate to a file, consisting of one or more contiguous sectors.

The number of sectors contained in a cluster depends on the hard disk type.

CMOS   Acronym for Complementary Metal-Oxide Semiconductor, pronounced "see-moss." A type of integrated circuit used in processors and for memory. CMOS devices operate at very high speeds and use very little power, so they generate very little heat. In the PC, battery-backed CMOS is used to store operating parameters such as hard disk type when the computer is switched off; in the Macintosh, PRAM performs this same function.

coaxial cable   Often shortened to coax, pronounced "co-ax." A high-capacity cable used in networking. It contains an inner copper conductor surrounded by plastic insulation and an outer braided copper or foil shield. Coaxial cable is used for broadband and baseband communications networks. Coax is also used by cable television because the cable is usually free from external interference, and it permits very high transmission rates over long distances.

cold boot   The computer startup process that begins when you turn on power to the computer. A cold boot might be needed if a program or the operating system crashes in such a way that you cannot continue. If operations are interrupted in a minor way, a warm boot may suffice.

color printer   A general term for all printers, including dot-matrix, ink-jet, thermal-transfer, and laser printers that can create color as well black-and-white output.

command processor   Also called the command interpreter. The command processor is that part of the operating system that displays the command prompt on the screen, interprets and executes all the commands and filenames that you enter, and displays error messages when appropriate.

The command processor also contains the environment, a memory area that holds values for important system definitions or defaults that are used by the system and which can be changed by the user.

compact disc   Abbreviated CD. A non-magnetic, polished, optical disc used to store large amounts of digital information. A CD can store approximately 650MB of information, equivalent to more than 450 floppy disks. This translates into approximately 300,000 pages of text or 72 minutes of music, all on a single 4.72-inch disc.

Digital information is stored on the compact disc as a series of microscopic pits and smooth areas (called lands) that have different reflective properties. A beam of laser light shines on the disc so that the reflections can be detected and converted into digital data.

compatibility   The extent to which a given piece of hardware or software conforms to an accepted standard, regardless of the original manufacturer.

In hardware, compatibility is often expressed in terms of certain other widely accepted models, such as a computer described as IBM-compatible or a modem described as Hayes-compatible. This implies that the device will perform in every way just like the standard device.

In software, compatibility is usually described as the ability to read data file formats created by other vendors' software or as the ability to work together and share data.

complex instruction set computing   Abbreviated CISC, pronounced "sisk." A processor that can recognize and execute more than 100 different assembly-language instructions. CISC processors can be very powerful, but there is a price for that power in terms of the number of clock cycles these instructions take to execute.

This is in contrast to reduced instruction set computing (RISC) processors, for which the number of available instructions has been cut to a minimum. RISC processors are common in workstations and can be designed to run as much as 70 percent faster than CISC processors.

COM port   The device name used to denote a serial communications port.

Modems, mice, and printers are commonly connected to these ports.

composite video   A method of combining all the elements of video information, including red, blue, and green components, horizontal synchronization, and vertical synchronization, into one signal. Televisions and video recorders require an NTSC (National Television Standards Committee) composite-video signal.

CompuServe   An online PC information service, CompuServe (a subsidiary of America Online) provides a tremendous range of information and services, including online conferences, hundreds of vendor-specific forums, file downloading, weather and stock market information, e-mail and other messaging services, and travel and entertainment information. CompuServe also offers Internet access, as well as access to Usenet newsgroups.

computation bound   A condition in which the speed of operation of the processor actually limits the speed of program execution. The processor is limited by the number of arithmetic operations it must perform.

CONFIG.SYS   In DOS, a special text file containing settings that control the way the operating system works. CONFIG.SYS must be located in the root directory of the default boot disk, normally drive C, and is read by the operating system only once as the system starts running.

Some application programs and peripheral devices require you to include special statements in CONFIG.SYS, while other commands may specify the number of disk-read buffers or open files on your system, specify how the disk cache should be configured, or load any special device drivers your system may need.

configuration   The process of establishing your own preferred setup for an application program or computer system. Configuration information is usually stored in a configuration file so that it can be loaded automatically the next time you start your computer.

configuration file   A file, created by an application program or by the operating system, containing configuration information specific to your own computing environment.

Application program configuration files may have a filename extension of CFG or SET; older Windows configuration files use the INI filename extension (newer programs use the Registry). If you accidentally erase an application's configuration file, the program will return to using its default settings and so will continue to function, but these settings may not be suitable for your use.

connectivity   In networking, the degree to which any given computer or application program can cooperate with other network components, either hardware or software, purchased from other vendors.

constant angular velocity   Abbreviated CAV. An unchanging speed of rotation. Hard disks use a constant angular velocity encoding scheme in which the disk rotates at a constant rate. This means that sectors on the disk are at the maximum density along the inside track of the disk; as the read/write heads move outward, the sectors must spread out to cover the increased track circumference, and therefore the data transfer rate declines.

constant linear velocity   Abbreviated CLV. A changing speed of rotation. CD-ROM drives use a constant linear velocity encoding scheme to ensure that the data density remains constant. Information on a compact disc is stored in a single, spiral track, divided into many equal-length segments. To read the data, the CD-ROM drive must increase the rotational speed as the read head gets closer to the center of the disc and decrease as the head moves back out. Typical CD-ROM data access times are in the order of 0.3 to 1.5 seconds; much slower than a hard disk.

conventional memory   The amount of memory accessible by DOS in PCs using an Intel processor operating in real mode, normally the first 640K. The Intel 8086 and 8088 processors can access 1MB of memory; the designers of the original IBM PC made 640KB available to the operating system and application programs and reserved the remaining space for internal system use, the BIOS, and video buffers. 640KB may not seem like much memory space now, but it was 10 times the amount of memory available in other leading personal computers available at the time. Since that time, operating systems have broken through the conventional memory barrier, and we no longer need to worry about configuring our systems to surpass it.

convergence   The alignment of the three electron guns (one each for red, blue, and green) in a monitor that create the colors you see on the screen. When all three of the electron guns are perfectly aligned and used at full power, the result is pure white. Deviation from this alignment gives poor convergence, leading to white pixels showing some color at the edges and to a decrease in image sharpness and resolution.

cooperative multitasking   A form of multitasking in which all running applications must work together to share system resources. Microsoft Windows 3.11 and lower supports cooperative multitasking by maintaining a list of the active applications and the order in which they execute. When Windows transfers control to an application, other applications cannot run until that application returns control to Windows once again. Windows' cooperative multitasking system differs from a preemptive multitasking system such as that used in Windows 95/98/98 SE, Windows NT, and Windows 2000. In these systems, the operating system executes each application in turn for a specific period of time before switching to the next application, regardless of whether the applications themselves return control to the operating system.

coprocessor   A secondary processor used to speed up operations by taking over a specific part of the main processor's work. The most common type of coprocessor is the math or floating-point coprocessor, designed to manage arithmetic calculations many times faster than the main processor.

crash   An unexpected program halt, sometimes due to a hardware failure, but most often due to a software error, from which there is no recovery. You will probably have to reboot your computer to recover after a crash.

cross-posting   In Usenet, to post the same article to more than one newsgroup. Sometimes it may make sense to post the same message to more than one newsgroup, but in general, the practice is frowned upon as it wastes network resources.

CRT   Abbreviation for cathode ray tube. A display device used in computer monitors and television sets. A CRT display consists of a glass vacuum tube that contains one electron gun for a monochrome display or three (red, green, and blue) electron guns for a color display. Electron beams from these guns sweep rapidly across the inside of the screen from the upper left to the lower right.

The inside of the screen is coated with thousands of phosphor dots that glow when they are struck by the electron beam. To stop the image from flickering, the beams sweep at a rate of between 43 and 87 times per second, depending on the phosphor persistence and the scanning mode used—interlaced or noninterlaced. This is known as the refresh rate and is measured in Hz. The Video Electronics Standards Association (VESA) recommends a vertical refresh rate of 72Hz, noninterlaced, at a resolution of 800 by 600 pixels.

cyberspace   A descriptive term for the virtual geography of the online world. This term first appeared in print in William Gibson's novel *Neuromancer*, published in 1984, in which it describes the online world of computers and the elements of society that use these computers.

cylinder   A hard disk consists of two or more platters, each with two sides. Each side is further divided into concentric circles known as tracks; and all the tracks at the same concentric position on a disk are known collectively as a cylinder.

daisy-wheel printer   An impact printer that uses a plastic or metal print mechanism with a different character on the end of each spoke of the wheel. As the print mechanism rotates to the correct letter, a small hammer strikes the character against the ribbon, transferring the image onto the paper. Changing to a different font is a matter of changing the daisy wheel; this means that you cannot change fonts in the middle of a document as you can with a laser printer. Daisy-wheel printers have two main drawbacks; they are relatively slow in printing, and they can be very noisy.

data   Information in a form suitable for processing by a computer, such as the digital representation of text, numbers, graphic images, or sounds. Strictly speaking, "data" is the plural of the Latin word "datum," meaning an item of information; but it is commonly used in both plural and singular constructions.

data area   In DOS, that part of a floppy disk or hard disk that is available for use after the boot record, partition table, root directory, and file allocation table have been established by the formatting program. This area is the largest part of a disk and is where programs and data files are located.

data bits   In asynchronous transmissions, the bits that actually constitute the data; usually 7 or 8 data bits make up the data word.

data compression   Any method of encoding data so that it occupies less space than in its original form. Many different mathematical techniques can be used, but the overall purpose is to compress the data so that it can be stored, retrieved, or transmitted more efficiently. Data compression is used in facsimile and many other forms of data transmission, CD-ROM publishing, still image and video image manipulation, and database management systems.

data encoding scheme   The method used by a disk controller to store digital information onto a hard disk or floppy disk. Common encoding schemes used in the PC world include modified frequency modulation (MFM) encoding, run-length limited (RLL) encoding, and advanced run-length limited (ARLL) encoding.

Data Encryption Standard   Abbreviated DES. A standard method of encrypting and decrypting data, developed by the U.S. National Bureau of Standards.

DES is a block cipher that works by a combination of transposition and substitution and was developed after years of work at IBM, rigorously tested by the National Security Agency, and finally accepted as being free of any mathematical or statistical weaknesses. This suggests that it is impossible to break the system using statistical frequency tables or to work the algorithm backward using standard mathematical methods. DES has remained unbroken despite years of use; it completely randomizes the information so that it is impossible to determine the encryption key even if some of the original text is known. DES is used by the federal government and most banks and money-transfer systems to protect all sensitive computer information.

data-link layer   The second of seven layers of the International Organization for Standardization Open Systems Interconnect (ISO/OSI) model for computer-to-computer communications. The data-link layer validates the integrity of the flow of data from one node to another by synchronizing blocks of data and by controlling the flow of data.

data packet   In networking, a unit of information transmitted as a discrete entity from one node on the network to another. More specifically, in packet-switching networks, a packet is a transmission unit of a fixed maximum length that contains a header, a set of data, and error control information.

data transfer rate   The speed at which a disk drive can transfer information from the drive to the processor, usually measured in megabits or megabytes per second. For example, a SCSI drive can reach a transfer rate of about 40 megabytes per second.

data type   **1.** The kind of data being stored or manipulated. In some databases, for example, data types include numeric (numbers), alphanumeric (text characters), date, logical (true or false), memo (used for larger pieces of text), formatted memo, short number, currency, OLE, graphic, and binary (all other types of data). Once the data type has been specified for a field, it cannot be changed to another data type, and the type also determines the kind of operation that can be performed on the data. For example, you cannot perform a calculation on alphanumeric data or separate the digits in a numeric field.

2. In programming, the data type specifies the range of values that a variable or constant can hold and how that information is stored in computer memory. For example, the floating-point data type can hold a different range of values from the integer data type and should be manipulated differently; and the character or string data type is different again.

daughter board   A printed circuit board that attaches to another board to provide additional functions. For example, a multimedia PC video adapter may accept a frame grabber daughter board to add freeze-frame video processing.

DB connector   Any of several types of cable connectors used for parallel or serial cables. The number following the letters DB (for data bus) indicates the number of pins that the connector usually has; a DB-25 connector can have a maximum of 25 pins, and a DB-9 connector, a maximum of 9. In practice, not all the pins (and not all the lines in the cable) may be present in the larger connectors. If your situation demands, for example, that all 25 lines of a serial cable be present, be sure you buy the right cable. Common DB connectors include DB-9, DB-15, DB-19, DB-25, DB-37, and DB-50.

DCE Abbreviation for Data Communications Equipment. In communications, any device that connects a computer or terminal to a communications channel or public network, usually a modem.

D-Channel One of three separate channels that compose an ISDN (Integrated Services Digital Network) line. The D-Channel uses 16Kbps of bandwidth and is used for control and signaling information.

DCI Abbreviation for Display Control Interface. A device-driver specification from Intel and Microsoft intended to speed up video playback in Microsoft Windows.

For this device driver to work, your hardware must support DCI; if it does, a Windows application can send video information directly to the screen and so bypass any holdups in the Windows graphics device interface (GDI).

Multimedia applications and programs that manage digital video can benefit from using DCI.

DC-2000 A quarter-inch tape minicartridge used in some tape backup systems with a capacity of up to 250MB when some form of data compression is used.

DEC Alpha A 64-bit microprocessor from Digital Equipment Corporation (DEC), introduced in 1992. The Alpha is a superscalar design, which allows the processor to execute more than one instruction per clock cycle. The fastest Alpha runs at an incredible 533MHz.

decibel Abbreviated dB. One-tenth of a bel, a unit of measurement common in electronics that quantifies the loudness or strength of a signal.

decimal The base-10 numbering system that uses the familiar numbers 0–9.

dedicated line A communications circuit used for one specific purpose. Like the phone line in your house; your neighbors do not use the same line that is dedicated to you.

defragmentation The process of reorganizing and rewriting files so that they occupy one large continuous area on your hard disk rather than several smaller areas.

When a file on your hard disk is updated, especially over a long period of time, it may be written into different areas all over the disk. This file fragmentation can lead to significant delays in loading files, but its effect can be reversed by defragmentation. Windows 95/98/98 SE come with a defragmentation program (Disk Defragmenter), and the Norton Utilities package contains an excellent defragmentation program.

defragmenter Any utility program that rewrites all the parts of a file into contiguous clusters on a hard disk. As you update your data files over time, they may become fragmented, or divided up into several widely spaced pieces. This can slow down data retrieval if the problem becomes severe. Using a defragmenter (such as the Windows 98 SE utility Disk Defragmenter) can restore that lost performance.

demand paging A common form of virtual memory management in which pages of information are read into memory from disk only when required by the program.

desktop In a graphical user interface, an on-screen version of a desktop containing windows, icons, and dialog boxes that represent application programs, files, and other desktop accessories. As you work, you open files, put them away, move items around on the desktop, and perform other day-to-day tasks. The analogy to a real desktop breaks down fairly quickly, but it is useful in understanding how the graphical user interface helps you to organize your activities.

device   A general term used to describe any computer peripheral or hardware element that can send or receive data. For example, modems, printers, serial ports, disk drives, and monitors are all referred to as devices. Some devices may require special software, known as a device driver, to control or manage them.

device-dependence   The requirement that a specific hardware component be present for a program to work. Device-dependent software is often very difficult to move or port to another computer due to this reliance on specific hardware.

device driver   A small program that allows a computer to communicate with and control a device. Each operating system contains a standard set of device drivers for the keyboard, the monitor, and so on, but if you add specialized peripherals such as a CD-ROM drive or a network interface card, you will probably have to add the appropriate device driver so that the operating system knows how to manage the device.

device-independence   The ability to produce similar results in a wide variety of environments, without requiring the presence of specific hardware.

The Unix operating system and the PostScript page-description language are both examples of device-independence. Unix runs on a wide range of computers, from the PC to a Cray, and PostScript is used by many different printer manufacturers.

device name   The name used by the operating system to identify a computer-system component. For example, LPT1 is the device name for the first parallel port.

DHCP   An abbreviation for Dynamic Host Configuration Protocol. On a network using the TCP/IP protocol suite, computers must have settings such as an address and default gateway to communicate. Ordinarily you would have to configure this manually at each machine, but with the Windows NT Server program DHCP or its Unix counterpart BootP, this information can be assigned to a computer automatically each time it starts.

diagnostic program   A program that tests computer hardware and peripherals for correct operation. In the PC, some faults, known as "hard faults," are easy to find; the diagnostic program will diagnose them correctly every time. Others, such as memory faults, can be difficult to find; these are called "soft faults" because they do not occur every time the memory location is tested but only under very specific circumstances.

Most PCs run a simple set of system checks when the computer is first turned on; in the IBM world these tests are stored in ROM, and are known as the power-on self-tests (POST). If the POST detects an error condition, the computer will stop and you will see an error message on the screen. AMIDiag from American Megatrends is an excellent diagnostics program.

digital   Describes any device that represents values in the form of binary digits.

digital audio   Analog sound waves stored in a digital form; each digital audio file can be decomposed into a series of samples.

digital audio tape   Abbreviated DAT. A method of recording information in digital form on a small audio tape cassette, originally developed by Sony and Hewlett-Packard. More than a gigabyte of information can be recorded on a cassette, and so a DAT can be used as a backup medium. Like all tape devices, however, DATs are relatively slow.

digital-to-analog converter   Abbreviated DAC or D-A converter. A device that converts discrete digital information into a continuously varying analog signal.

Many of today's sound boards can sample and play back at up to 44.1kHz using a 16-bit digital-to-analog converter that produces spectacular stereo sound. Compact disc players use a digital-to-analog converter to convert the digital signals read from the disc to the analog signal that you hear as music.

Digital Video Interactive   Abbreviated DVI. A proprietary technique from Intel Corporation used to store highly compressed, full-motion video information onto compact discs. DVI is usually available as a chip set and uses a form of compression that saves only the changes between images, rather than saving each individual frame. This form of data compression can reduce memory requirements by a factor of 100 or more.

On a CD-ROM, DVI provides more than 70 minutes of full-screen video, 2 hours of half-screen video, 40,000 medium-resolution images, or 7000 high-resolution images.

DIP switch   A small switch used to select the operating mode of a device, mounted as a *dual in*-line *package*. DIP switches can be either sliding or rocker switches and are often grouped together for convenience. They are used on printed circuit boards, dot-matrix printers, modems, and other peripherals.

direct access storage device   Abbreviated DASD, pronounced "daz-dee." A storage device such as a hard disk, whose data can be accessed directly, without having to read all the preceding data (as with a sequential device such as a tape drive).

direct current   Abbreviated DC. Electrical current that travels in one direction only and does not reverse the direction of flow. The PC's power supply converts AC line voltage from a wall outlet into the various DC voltages that the internal components of the computer need to operate.

direct memory access   Abbreviated DMA. A method of transferring information directly from a mass-storage device such as a hard disk or from an adapter card into memory (or vice versa), without the information passing through the processor. Because the processor is not involved in the transfer, direct memory access is usually very fast.

DMA transfers are controlled by a special chip known as a DMA controller; the 8237A (or its equivalent) is used in most PCs. Generally, most PCs use two of these chips to provide eight DMA channels numbered 0 through 7; only seven of these channels are available, as channel 4 is used to connect—or cascade—the two controllers together. Channels 0 through 3 are 8-bit channels and can manage a maximum of 64K of data in a single DMA operation; channels 5 through 7 transfer data 16 bits at a time and can manage a maximum of 128K of data. Channel 3 is reserved for the floppy disk drive controller, and channel 5 is used by the hard-disk controller in PS/2 systems.

DirectX   A set of predefined code, called an application programming interface (API), written by Microsoft. Programmers can use it to create graphic images or other multimedia effects in their applications. It is divided into five distinct parts: DirectDraw manages two-dimensional images, Direct3D manages three-dimensional images, DirectSound coordinates sound with images, DirectPlay speeds game play, and DirectInput manages input devices such as a joystick.

disable   To turn a function off or prevent something from happening. In a graphical user interface, disabled menu commands are often shown in gray to indicate that they are not available.

discrete component   Any electronic component or hardware device that can be treated as a separate and distinct unit.

disk cache   An area of computer memory where data is temporarily stored on its way to or from a disk.

When an application needs data from a hard disk, it asks the operating system to find it. The data is read and passed back to the application. Under certain circumstances, such as when updating a database, the same information may be requested and read many times over. A disk cache mediates between the application and the hard disk, and when an application asks for information from the hard disk, the cache program first checks to see if that data is already in the cache memory. If it is, the disk cache program loads the information from the cache memory rather than from the hard disk. If the information is not in memory, the cache program reads the data from the disk, copies it into the cache memory for future reference, and then passes the data to the requesting application.

disk capacity   The storage capacity of a hard or floppy disk, usually stated in kilobytes (KB or K), megabytes (MB), or gigabytes (GB).

disk controller   The electronic circuitry that controls and manages the operation of floppy or hard disks installed in the computer.

A single disk controller may manage more than one hard disk; many disk controllers also manage floppy disks and compatible tape drives. In the Macintosh, the disk controller is built into the system. In IBM-compatible computers, it is part of the hard disk drive itself, as in the case of an IDE (Integrated Drive Electronics) drive.

disk drive   A peripheral storage device that reads and writes magnetic or optical disks. When more than one disk drive is installed on a computer, the operating system assigns each drive a unique name—for example A and C.

Three types of disk drives are in common use; floppy disk drives, hard disk drives, and compact disc drives. Floppy disk drives accept removable 5.25 inch or 3.5 inch media, although you won't see many 5.25-inch disk drives unless you run into a really old PC. Hard disk drives usually have much greater capacity and are considerably faster than floppy disk drives, and they are contained inside a protective sealed case. Compact disc drives can be either internal or external to the system unit; they can contain a great deal more than a floppy disk yet less than a hard disk and are generally used for read-only files.

disk duplexing   In networking, a fault-tolerant technique that writes the same information simultaneously onto two hard disks. Each of the hard disks uses a different disk controller to provide greater redundancy. In the event of one disk or disk controller failing, information from the other system can be used to continue operations. Disk duplexing is offered by most of the major network operating systems and is designed to protect the system against a single disk failure; it is not designed to protect against multiple disk failures and is no substitute for a well-planned series of backups.

diskless workstation   A networked computer that does not have any local disk storage capability.

The computer boots up and loads all its programs from the network file server. Diskless workstations are particularly valuable when very sensitive information is processed; information cannot be copied from the file server onto a local disk, because there isn't one.

disk mirroring   In networking, a fault-tolerant technique that writes the same information simultaneously onto two different hard disks, using the same disk controller. In the event of one disk failing, information from the other can be used to continue operations. Disk mirroring is offered by most of the major network operating systems and is designed to protect the system against a single disk failure; it is not designed to protect against multiple disk failures and is no substitute for a well-planned series of disk backups.

distributed processing   A computer system in which processing is performed by several separate computers linked by a communications network. The term often refers to any computer system supported by a network, but it more properly refers to a system in which each computer is chosen to handle a specific workload and the network supports the system as a whole.

DLC   An abbreviation for Data Link Control. This is a point-to-point protocol that functions at the data-link layer of the Open

Systems Interconnect networking model. On the Windows operating system, DLC is used to connect printers and mainframes to PCs over a network.

DLT An abbreviation for digital linear tape, DLT is a tape storage medium that is used to back up 20 to 40GB of data at speeds of as fast as 800KB per second.

DMI An abbreviation for Desktop Management Interface. A standard method of identifying PC hardware and software components automatically, without input from the user.

At a minimum, DMI will identify the manufacturer, product name, serial number, and installation time and date of any component installed in a PC. DMI was developed by the Desktop Management Task Force, a consortium of computer equipment manufacturers.

DNS Abbreviation for Domain Name System. The method used when naming Internet host computers, and the directory services used when looking up those names. Each of these host names (such as pd .zevon.com) corresponds to a long decimal number known as the IP address (such as 199.10.44.8). Domain names are much easier to remember than the long IP addresses.

docking station A hardware system into which a laptop computer fits so that it can be used as a full-fledged desktop computer.

Docking stations vary from simple port replicators that allow you access to parallel and serial ports and a mouse, to complete systems that give you access to network connections, CD-ROMs, even a tape backup system or PCMCIA ports.

domain 1. The general category to which a computer on the Internet belongs. The most common high-level domains are:

.com a commercial organization

.edu an educational establishment

.gov a branch of the U.S. government

.int an international organization

.mil a branch of the U.S. military

.net a network

.org a nonprofit organization

Most countries also have unique domains named after their international abbreviation. For example, .UK for the United Kingdom and .CA for Canada.

2. In networking, this is a logical grouping of users and resources collected together for ease of administration and security purposes.

domain name The easy-to-understand name given to an Internet host computer, as opposed to the numeric IP address.

DOS 1. Acronym for Disk Operating System, an operating system originally developed by Microsoft for the IBM PC. DOS exists in two similar versions: MS-DOS, developed and marketed by Microsoft for use with IBM-compatible computers, and PC-DOS, supported and sold by IBM for use only on computers manufactured by IBM.

2. A DOS CONFIG.SYS command that loads the operating system into conventional memory, extended memory, or into upper memory blocks on computers using the Intel 80386 or later processor. To use this command, you must have previously loaded the HIMEM.SYS device driver with the DEVICE command in CONFIG.SYS. This command is not used on Windows 95 or later, since Windows configures the high memory area for you.

DOS prompt A visual confirmation that the DOS operating system is ready to receive input from the keyboard. The default prompt includes the current drive letter followed by a greater-than symbol; for example, C>. You can create your own custom prompt with the PROMPT command.

dot-matrix printer An impact printer that uses columns of small pins and an inked ribbon to create the tiny pattern of dots that form the characters. Dot-matrix printers are available in 9-, 18-, or 24-pin configurations, but they are very noisy and produce relatively low quality output. They are especially useful when you must print on carbon duplicates.

dot pitch In a monitor, the vertical distance between the centers of like-colored phosphors on the screen of a color monitor, measured in millimeters (mm). As the dot pitch becomes smaller, the finer detail appears on the screen; straight lines appear sharper, and colors appear more vivid. Today's monitors often have a dot pitch of between 0.31mm and 0.28mm.

dots per inch Abbreviated dpi. A measure of resolution expressed by the number of dots that a device can print or display in one inch. Laser printers can print at up to 1200dpi, while Linotronic laser imagesetters can print at resolutions of 1270 or 2450dpi.

drift In a monitor, any unwanted motion or undulation in a line drawn on the screen.

drive bay An opening in the system unit into which you can install a floppy disk drive, hard disk drive, or tape drive. Today's computers usually accommodate half-height drive bays.

drive letter A designation used to specify a particular hard or floppy disk. For example, the first floppy disk is usually referred to as drive A, and the first hard disk as drive C.

DSL Abbreviation for Digital Subscriber Line, DSL is a remote access connection technology that provides data rates from 16Kbps to 52Mbps, as opposed to the current 56Kbps limitations seen with standard modems.

DSP Abbreviation for digital signal processor. A specialized high-speed chip, used for data manipulation in sound cards, communications adapters, video and image manipulation, and other data-acquisition processes in which speed is essential.

DSR Abbreviation for Data Set Ready. A hardware signal defined by the RS-232-C standard to indicate that the device is ready.

DTE Abbreviation for Data Terminal Equipment. In communications, any device, such as a terminal or a computer, connected to a communications channel or public network.

DTR Abbreviation for Data Terminal Ready. A hardware signal defined by the RS-232-C standard to indicate that the computer is ready to accept a transmission.

dual in-line package Abbreviated DIP. A standard housing constructed of hard plastic commonly used to hold an integrated circuit. The circuit's leads are connected to two parallel rows of pins designed to fit snugly into a socket; these pins may also be soldered directly to a printed-circuit board. If you try to install or remove dual in-line packages, be careful not to bend or damage their pins.

dual in-line memory module Abbreviated DIMM, it is actually best described as a double SIMM (single inline memory module). SIMMs are small circuit boards that contain RAM chips and can be snapped into SIMM slots on a motherboard. One drawback is that they use a 32-bit data path, which means that SIMMs must be installed in pairs on newer systems. DIMMs use a 64-bit data path, and therefore only one DIMM is needed where two SIMMs would ordinarily be used.

dumb terminal A combination of keyboard and screen that has no local computing power, used to input information to a large, remote computer, often a minicomputer or a mainframe. This remote computer provides all the processing power for the system.

duplex In asynchronous transmissions, the ability to transmit and receive on the same channel at the same time; also referred to as full-duplex. Half-duplex channels can transmit only or receive only.

One popular use for this is in a Fast Ethernet network. Some 100MBps hubs are not capable of transmitting at 100MBps and full-duplex. If you have such a network configuration, configure your network cards to transmit at half-duplex.

duplex printing   Printing a document on both sides of the page so that the appropriate pages face each other when the document is bound.

DVD   Abbreviation for digital video disc; sometimes called digital versatile disc. A type of CD that is capable of holding as much as 4.7GB of data as opposed to the standard 600MB. DVD can also be used to store video or audio recordings.

Dvorak keyboard   Pronounced "di-vor-ack." A keyboard layout invented by August Dvorak in 1936 as a faster alternative to the QWERTY typewriter keyboard. The Dvorak keyboard groups all vowels and punctuation marks on the left side of the keyboard and common consonants together on the right. Studies have shown that typists make 70 percent of all keystrokes on the second or home row on the Dvorak keyboard compared with 32 percent on the QWERTY keyboard. The Dvorak keyboard, despite its advantages, has not found wide acceptance, mostly because of the retraining costs involved in switching.

DX4   A 32-bit chip, based on the 80486, from Intel. Despite the name, the DX4 is not a clock-quadrupled chip; it is a clock-tripled chip. For example, the 75MHz version of the chip completes three CPU cycles for each cycle of the 25MHz motherboard. The DX4 is available in 75, 83, and 100MHz versions, and fills the performance gap between the existing chips in the 80486 set and the Pentium processor.

dynamic link library   Abbreviated DLL. A program module that contains executable code and data that can be used by application programs, or even by other DLLs, in performing a specific task.

The DLL is linked into the application only when you run the program, and it is unloaded when no longer needed. This means that if two DLL applications are running at the same time and both of them perform a particular function, only one copy of the code for that function is loaded, making for a more efficient use of limited memory. Another benefit of using dynamic linking is that .EXE files are not as large, since frequently used routines can be put into a DLL rather than repeated in each EXE that uses them. This results in saved disk space and faster program loading.

DLLs, which are used extensively in Windows, may have filename extensions of .DLL, .DRV, or .FON.

dynamic RAM   Abbreviated DRAM, pronounced "dee-ram." A common type of computer memory that uses capacitors and transistors storing electrical charges to represent memory states. These capacitors lose their electrical charge and so need to be refreshed every millisecond, during which time they cannot be read by the processor.

DRAM chips are small, simple, cheap, and easy to make and hold approximately four times as much information as static RAM (SRAM) chips of similar complexity. However, they are slower than static RAM. Processors operating at clock speeds of 25MHz or more need DRAM with access times of faster than 80 nanoseconds (80 billionths of a second); SRAM chips can be read in as little as 15 to 30 nanoseconds.

edge connector   A form of connector consisting of a row of etched contacts along the edge of a printed circuit board that is inserted into an expansion slot in the computer.

EEPROM   Acronym for electrically erasable programmable read-only memory, pronounced "ee-ee-prom" or "double-ee-prom." A memory chip that maintains its contents without electrical power, and whose contents can be erased and reprogrammed either within the computer or from an external source.

EGA   Abbreviation for Enhanced Graphics Adapter. A video adapter standard that provides medium-resolution text and graphics, introduced by IBM in 1984. EGA can display

16 colors at the same time from a choice of 64, with a horizontal resolution of 640 pixels and a vertical resolution of 350 pixels. EGA has been superseded by VGA and SVGA.

EIDE   Abbreviation for Enhanced Integrated Drive Electronics, EIDE is an interface between your computer and your mass storage devices, such as a hard drive or CD-ROM. The EIDE standard allows access to drives larger than the standard IDE (Integrated Drive Electronics) limitation of 528MB. It is also faster than IDE and allows up to four drives to be connected, as opposed to the standard IDE two-drive limit.

8-bit color   A method of representing a graphical image as a bitmap containing 256 colors.

80286   Also called the 286. A 16-bit microprocessor from Intel first released in February 1982 and used by IBM in the IBM PC/AT computer. Since then it has been used in many other IBM-compatible computers.

The 80286 uses a 16-bit data word and a 16-bit data bus, uses 24 bits to address memory, and has the following modes:

▶ Real mode effectively limits performance to that of an 8086 microprocessor and can address 1MB memory.

▶ Protected mode prevents an application program from stopping the operating system due to an inadvertent error and can address 16MB of memory.

The 80286 is equivalent to approximately 134,000 transistors and can execute 1.2 million instructions per second. The floating-point processor for the 80286 is the 80287.

80287   Also called the 287. A floating-point processor from Intel, designed for use with the 80286 CPU chip. When supported by application programs, a floating-point processor can speed up floating-point and transcendental math operations by 10 to 50 times.

The 80287 conforms to the IEEE 754–1985 standard for binary floating-point

operations and is available in clock speeds of 6, 8, 10, and 12MHz.

80386DX   Also called the 80386, the 386DX, and the 386. A full 32-bit microprocessor introduced by Intel in October 1985 and used in many IBM and IBM-compatible computers. Available in 16, 20, 25, and 33MHz versions, the 80386 has a 32-bit data word, can transfer information 32 bits at a time over the data bus, and can use 32 bits in addressing memory. It has the following modes:

▶ Real mode effectively limits performance to that of an 8086 microprocessor and can address 1MB of memory.

▶ Protected mode prevents an application program from stopping the operating system due to an inadvertent error and can address 4GB of memory.

▶ Virtual 8086 mode allows the operating system to divide the 80386 into several 8086 microprocessors, all running with their own 1MB space and all running separate programs.

The 80386 is equivalent to about 275,000 transistors and can perform 6 million instructions per second. The floating-point processor for the 80386DX is the 80387.

80386SX   Also called the 386SX. A lower-cost alternative to the 80386DX microprocessor, introduced by Intel in 1988. Available in 16, 20, 25, and 33MHz versions, the 80386SX is an 80386DX with a 16-bit data bus. This design allows systems to be configured using cheaper 16-bit components, leading to a lower overall cost. The floating-point processor for the 80386SX is the 80387SX.

80387   Also called the 387. A floating-point processor from Intel, designed for use with the 80386 CPU chip. When supported by application programs, a floating-point processor can speed up floating-point and transcendental math operations by 10 to 50 times.

The 80387 conforms to the IEEE 754–1985 standard for binary floating-point operations and is available in clock speeds of 16, 20, 25, and 33MHz.

80387SX   Also called the 387SX. A floating-point processor from Intel, designed for use with the 16-bit data bus of the 80386SX CPU chip only. When supported by application programs, a floating-point processor can speed up floating-point and transcendental math operations by 10 to 50 times.

The 80387SX conforms to the IEEE 754–1985 standard for binary floating-point operations and is available only in a 16MHz version.

80486DX   Also called the 486 or i486. A 32-bit microprocessor introduced by Intel in April 1989. The 80486 represents the continuing evolution of the 80386 family of microprocessors and adds several notable features, including on-board cache, built-in floating-point processor and memory management unit, as well as certain advanced provisions for multiprocessing. Available in 25, 33, and 50MHz versions, the 80486 is equivalent to 1.25 million transistors and can perform 20 million instructions per second.

80486DX2   Also known as the 486DX2. A 32-bit microprocessor introduced by Intel in 1992. It is functionally identical to, and 100 percent compatible with, the 80486DX, but with one major difference: the DX2 chip adds what Intel calls speed-doubling technology—meaning that it runs twice as fast internally as it does with components external to the chip. For example, the DX2-50 operates at 50MHz internally, but at 25MHz while communicating with other system components, including memory and the other chips on the motherboard, thus maintaining its overall system compatibility. 50 and 66MHz versions of the DX2 are available. The 486DX2 contains 1.2 million transistors and is capable of 40 million instructions per second.

80486SX   Also called the 486SX. A 32-bit microprocessor introduced by Intel in April 1991. The 80486SX can be described as an 80486DX with the floating-point

processor circuitry disabled. Available in 16, 20, and 25MHz versions, the 80486SX contains the equivalent of 1.185 million transistors and can execute 16.5 million instructions per second.

80487   Also called the 487. A floating-point processor from Intel, designed for use with the 80486SX CPU chip. When supported by application programs, a floating-point processor can speed up floating-point and transcendental math operations by 10 to 50 times.

The 80487 is essentially a 20MHz 80486 with the floating-point circuitry still enabled. When an 80487 is added into the coprocessor socket of a motherboard running the 80486SX, it effectively becomes the main processor, shutting down the 80486SX and taking over all operations.

The 80487 conforms to the IEEE 754–1985 standard for binary floating-point operations.

8080   An 8-bit microprocessor, introduced by Intel in April 1974, that paved the way for the 8086 family of microprocessors that followed. The 8080 contained 6000 transistors and was capable of 0.64 million instructions per second.

8086   A 16-bit microprocessor from Intel, first released in June 1978, available in speeds of 4.77MHz, 8MHz, and 10MHz. The 8086 was used in a variety of early IBM-compatible computers as well as the IBM PS/2 Model 25 and Model 30. The 8086 contains the equivalent of 29,000 transistors and can execute 0.33 million instructions per second.

8087   A floating-point processor from Intel, designed for use with the 8086 and 8088 CPU chips. When supported by application programs, a floating-point processor can speed up floating-point and transcendental math operations by 10 to 50 times.

The 8087 conforms to the IEEE 754–1985 standard for binary floating-point operations and is available in speeds of 5MHz, 8MHz, and 10MHz.

8088   A 16-bit microprocessor from Intel released in June 1978 that was used in the first IBM PC, as well as the IBM PC/XT, Portable PC, PCjr, and a large number of IBM-compatible computers. The 8088 uses a 16-bit data word but transfers information along an 8-bit data bus; the 8086 uses a 16-bit data word and a 16-bit data bus. Available in speeds of 4.77MHz and 8MHz, the 8088 is approximately equivalent to 29,000 transistors and can execute 0.33 million instructions per second.

8514/A   A video adapter from IBM, providing up to 256 colors or 16 shades of gray, on an interlaced display of 1024 by 768 pixels in the highest resolution mode. The IBM monitor used with this adapter is also known as an 8514/A.

88000   A family of 32-bit RISC microprocessors from Motorola, introduced in 1988 and used in workstations. The 88000 chip set includes one 88100 CPU and usually two 88200 cache memory management units. One of the units is used to cache data, the other to cache instructions. The 88100 CPU also includes a floating-point processor.

The 88000 is a true 32-bit computer, with 32-bit internal registers and a 32-bit data bus. Up to four chip sets can be configured to work together in a multiprocessor system.

EISA   Acronym for Extended Industry Standard Architecture, pronounced "ee-sah." A PC bus standard that extends the traditional AT-bus to 32 bits and allows more than one processor to share the bus.

EISA was developed by the so-called Gang of Nine (AST Research, Compaq Computer Corporation, Epson, Hewlett-Packard, NEC, Olivetti, Tandy, Wyse Technology, and Zenith Data Systems) in 1988 in reply to IBM's introduction of their proprietary Microchannel architecture (MCA).

EISA maintains compatibility with the earlier Industry Standard Architecture (ISA) and also provides for additional features introduced by IBM in the MCA standard. EISA accepts ISA expansion cards, and so,

unlike the Microchannel architecture, it is compatible with earlier systems.

EISA has a 32-bit data path and, at a bus speed of 8MHz, can achieve a maximum throughput of 33 megabytes per second.

electromagnetic interference   Abbreviated EMI. Any electromagnetic radiation released by an electronic device that disrupts the operation or performance of any other device.

e-mail   Also called electronic mail. The use of a network to transmit text messages, memos, and reports. Users can send a message to one or more individual users, to a predefined group, or to all users on the system. When you receive a message, you can read, print, forward, answer, or delete it.

emoticon   A set of characters commonly used in e-mail and Usenet newsgroups to signify emotions. An emoticon can be as simple as including <> or <grin> in the text, meant to indicate that the writer is joking, to some of the complex smiley faces, such as the wink ;-) or the frown :-(which are all meant to be read sideways.

emulator   A device built to work exactly like another device, either hardware, software, or a combination of both. For example, a terminal emulation program lets a PC pretend to be a terminal attached to a mainframe computer or to certain of the online services or bulletin boards by providing the control codes that the remote system expects to see.

Encapsulated PostScript   Abbreviated EPS. The file format of the PostScript page description language. The EPS standard is device independent so that images can easily be transferred between different applications and can be sized and output to different printers without any loss of image quality or distortion. Many high-quality clip art packages store images in EPS form.

The EPS file contains the PostScript commands needed to re-create the image, but the image itself cannot be displayed on a monitor unless the file also contains an optional preview image stored in TIFF or PICT format.

The EPS file can be printed only on a PostScript-compatible laser printer, and the printer itself determines the final printing resolution; a laser printer might be capable of 1200dpi, whereas a Linotronic printer is capable of 2450dpi.

encryption   The process of encoding information in an attempt to make it secure from unauthorized access. The reverse of this process is known as decryption.

One of the most popular encryption programs is Pretty Good Privacy (PGP), written by Phil Zimmermann, available at no charge from certain Internet sites.

end user   During the mainframe computer era, the end user was always a person who received output from the computer and used that output in their work. They rarely, if ever, even saw the computer, much less learned to use it themselves.

Today, the term more often refers to the person who uses the application program to produce their own results. End users today often write macros to automate complex or repetitive tasks and sometimes write procedures using command languages.

Enhanced Expanded Memory Specification   Abbreviated EEMS. A revised version of the original Lotus-Intel-Microsoft Expanded Memory Specification (LIM EMS), which lets DOS applications use more than 640KB of memory space.

enhanced keyboard   A 101- or 102-key keyboard introduced by IBM that has become the accepted standard for PC keyboard layout. Unlike earlier keyboards, it has 12 function keys across the top, rather than 10 function keys in a block on the left side, has extra Ctrl and Alt keys, and has a set of arrow keys between the main keyboard and the numeric keypad.

Enhanced Small Device Interface   Abbreviated ESDI. A hard disk, floppy disk,

and tape drive interface standard, capable of a data transfer rate of 10 to 20 megabits per second.

enterprise   A term used to encompass an entire business group, organization, or corporation, including all local, remote, and satellite offices. Most often used with reference to large networked systems.

entry-level system   A computer system that meets the basic requirements for a specific task. As computers become both cheaper and more capable, the definition of an entry-level system changes. Also, application developers continue to create new and more complex programs, which in turn demand more capability from the hardware.

EPP/ECP   An acronym for Enhanced Parallel Port/Enhanced Capabilities Port. EPP/ECP is a parallel port standard defined in IEEE standard 1284 that allows computer systems to communicate with parallel port devices at faster speeds than standard parallel ports. It also allows for bidirectional communication. EPP ports are for nonprinter devices, such as scanners, and ECP ports are suited for printers. The two technologies can be combined into one port called an EPP/ECP port.

EPROM   Acronym for erasable programmable read-only memory, pronounced "ee-prom." A memory chip that maintains its contents without electrical power, and whose contents can be erased and reprogrammed by removing a protective cover and exposing the chip to ultraviolet light.

erasable CD   A standard format that allows users to store and revise large amounts of data. The standard is supported by Sony, Phillips, IBM, Hewlett-Packard, and other leading companies. One of the major advantages of this standard is that it is completely compatible with existing compact discs, and makers of CD-ROM disk drives only have to make minor manufacturing changes to existing drives to meet the standard.

error   The difference between the expected and the actual. In computing, an error is not necessarily the same as a mistake, but is often the way that the computer reports unexpected, unusual, impossible, or illegal events. Errors range from trivial, like a disk drive that does not contain a disk, to fatal, as when a serious operating system bug renders the system useless.

error detection and correction A mechanism used during a file transfer to determine whether transmission errors have occurred and to correct those errors, if possible. Some programs or transmission protocols request a retransmission of the affected block of data if such an error is detected. More complex protocols attempt to both detect and correct transmission errors.

error message A message from the program or the operating system, informing you of a condition that requires some human intervention.

Error messages can indicate relatively trivial problems, such as a disk drive that does not contain a disk, all the way to fatal problems, as when a serious operating system bug renders the system useless and requires a system restart.

Ethernet A widely used local area networking technology defined in IEEE standard 802.3. Ethernet uses the Carrier Sense Multiple Access with Collision Detection (CSMA/CD) protocol to ensure that data can move between computers without getting in an accident on the wire (called a collision). Standard Ethernet will transmit at speeds of 10Mbps, and Fast Ethernet will transmit at speeds of 100Mbps.

exa- Abbreviated E. A prefix meaning 1 quintillion, 10^{18}. In computing, this translates into 1,152,921,504,606,846,976; the power of 2 closest to 1 quintillion (1060).

exabyte Abbreviated EB. 1 quadrillion bytes, or 1,152,921,504,606,846,976 bytes.

expandability The ability of a system to accommodate expansion. In hardware, this may include the addition of memory, more or larger disk drives, and new adapters, and in software it may include the ability of a network to add users, nodes, or connections to other networks.

expanded memory A DOS mechanism by which applications can access more than the 640KB of memory normally available to them.

The architecture of the 8086 and 8088 processors restricted the original IBM PC to accessing 1MB of memory, 640KB of which was available for application programs, and the remaining 384KB was reserved for system use, the BIOS, and the video system. At that time, 640KB was more than 10 times the amount of memory available in other personal computers. However, as both applications and DOS grew larger, they began to run out of room.

expanded memory manager Abbreviated EMM. A device driver that supports the software portion of the expanded memory specification in an IBM-compatible computer.

Expanded Memory Specification Abbreviated EMS. The original version of the Lotus-Intel-Microsoft Expanded Memory Specification (LIM EMS), which lets DOS applications use more than 640KB of memory space.

expansion bus An extension of the main computer bus that includes expansion slots for use by compatible adapters, such as memory boards, video adapters, hard disk controllers, and SCSI (Small Computer Systems Interface) cards.

expansion slot One of the connectors on the expansion bus that gives an adapter access to the system bus. You can add as many additional adapters as there are expansion slots inside your computer.

expansion unit An external housing available with certain portable computers designed to contain additional expansion slots and maintain a connection to the main expansion bus in the computer's system unit.

extended ASCII character set The second part of the ASCII character set from decimal code 128 through decimal code 255. This part of the ASCII character set is not standard and will contain different characters on different types of computer. In IBM-compatible computers, it includes special mathematical symbols and characters from the PC line-drawing set. The Apple extended ASCII character set uses a different set of characters.

extended DOS partition   A further optional division of a hard disk, after the primary DOS partition, that functions as one or more additional logical drives. A logical drive is simply an area of a larger disk that acts as though it were a separate disk with its own drive letter. Creating an extended partition allows you to install a second operating system; in early DOS versions it was the only way to use disk space above 32MB.

DOS partitions are created and changed using the FDISK command.

extended memory   Memory beyond 1MB on computers using the Intel 80386 and later processors, not configured for expanded memory.

Computers based on the Intel 8086 and 8088 processors can access only 1MB of memory, of which 640KB is available for application programs, and the remaining 384KB is reserved for DOS, the BIOS, and video settings.

Later processors can access more memory, but it was the 80386 with its ability to address 4GB of memory that really made extended memory usable, along with the DOS memory manager HIMEM.SYS that lets DOS use all of the extended memory installed in your computer. Windows 95/98/98 SE, all versions of Windows NT, and Windows 2000 do not require HIMEM.SYS because memory management is built into the operating system.

extended memory manager   A device driver that supports the software portion of the extended memory specification in an IBM-compatible computer in older operating systems such as DOS.

extended memory specification   Abbreviated XMS. A standard developed by Microsoft, Intel, Lotus, and AST Research that has become the preferred way of accessing extended memory in the PC running older operating systems such as DOS. DOS and Windows 3.x include the extended memory device driver HIMEM.SYS, and this command or an equivalent must be present in your CONFIG.SYS file before you can access extended memory successfully.

external hard disk   A hard disk packaged in its own case, with cables and an independent power supply, rather than a disk drive housed inside and integrated with the computer's system unit.

extremely low-frequency emission   Abbreviated ELF. Radiation emitted by a computer monitor and other very common household electrical appliances such as televisions, hair dryers, electric blankets, and food processors.

ELF emissions fall into the range of 5Hz to 2000Hz and decline in signal strength with the square of the distance from the source. Emissions are not constant around a monitor; they are higher from the sides and rear, and weakest from the front of the screen. Low-emission models are available, and laptop computers with an LCD display do not emit any ELF fields.

FAQ   Pronounced "fack," a document that answers frequently asked questions. If you have just purchased new hardware or software and have some questions, check the manufacturer's Web site for a FAQ page before calling tech support.

fatal error   An operating system or application program error from which there is no hope of recovery without rebooting (and thus losing any unsaved work).

fault tolerance   A design method that ensures continued system operation in the event of individual failures by providing redundant elements.

At the component level, designers include redundant chips and circuits and add the capability to bypass faults automatically. At the computer system level, they replicate any elements likely to fail, such as processors and large disk drives.

Fault-tolerant operations often require backup or UPS (uninterruptible power supply) systems in the event of a main power failure and may imply the duplication of entire computer systems in remote locations to protect against vandalism, acts of war, or natural disaster.

fax   Short for facsimile. The electronic transmission of copies of documents for reproduction at a remote location.

The sending fax machine scans a paper image and converts the image into a form suitable for transmission over a telephone line. The receiving fax machine decodes and prints a copy of the original image. Each fax machine includes a scanner, fax modem, and printer.

fax modem   A modem that includes fax capabilities, providing many of the functions of a full-sized fax machine in addition to standard modem operation.

There are three main classes of fax modems:

SendFax   Originally developed by Sierra Semiconductor, these fax modems are send-only and date from the days when a single-function fax modem was much cheaper than one that could both send and receive.

Class 1   An early fax-modem standard that specified that most of the processing of the fax document should be performed by the application software.

Class 2   A more recent standard that shifts the task of preparing the fax document to the fax modem itself. In this standard, the modem hardware manages all data-compression and error-correction functions.

FCC   Abbreviation for Federal Communications Commission. A U.S. government regulatory body for radio, television, all interstate telecommunications services, and all international services that originate inside the United States.

All computer equipment must be certified by the FCC before it can be offered for sale in the United States to ensure that it meets the legal limits for conductive and radio frequency emissions, which could otherwise interfere with commercial broadcasts.

FCC certification   Approval by the FCC that a specific computer model meets its standards for radio frequency interference emissions.

There are two levels of certification. Class A certification is for computers used in commercial settings, such as mainframes and minicomputers, and the more stringent Class B certification is for computers used in the home and in home offices, such as PCs, laptops, and portables.

female connector   Any cable connector with receptacles designed to receive the pins on the male part of the connector.

Fiber Distributed Data Interface
Abbreviated FDDI. A specification for fiber-optic networks transmitting at a speed of up to 100 megabits per second over a dual, counter-rotating, token-ring topology. FDDI is suited to systems that require the transfer of very large amounts of information, such as medical imaging, 3-D seismic processing, oil reservoir simulation, and full-motion video.

fiber-optic cable   A transmission technology that sends pulses of light along specially manufactured optical fibers. Each fiber consists of a core, thinner than a human hair, surrounded by a sheath with a much lower refractive index. Light signals introduced at one end of the cable are conducted along the cable as the signals are reflected from the sheath.

Fiber-optic cable is lighter and smaller than traditional copper cable, is immune to electrical interference, and has better signal-transmitting qualities. However, it is more expensive than traditional cables and more difficult to repair.

file   A named collection of data stored on disk, appearing to the user as a single entity. A file can contain a program or part of a program, may be a data file, or can contain a user-created document. Files may actually be fragmented or stored in many places across the disk; the operating system manages the task of locating all the pieces when the file is read.

file allocation table   Abbreviated FAT, pronounced "fat." A table maintained by the operating system that lists all the clusters available on a disk. The FAT includes the location of each cluster, as well as whether it is in use, available for use, or damaged in some way and therefore unavailable.

Because files are not necessarily stored in consecutive clusters on a disk, but can be scattered all over the disk, the FAT also keeps track of which pieces belong to which file.

FAT comes in two sizes, 16 and 32 bit. FAT16 is capable of supporting a 2GB drive, and FAT32 is capable of supporting up to 2TB on a single drive.

file compression program   An application program that shrinks program or data files so that they occupy less disk space. The file must then be extracted or decompressed before you can use it.

Many of the most popular file compression programs are shareware, such as PKZIP, LHA, and StuffIt for the Macintosh.

file fragmentation   The storage of a file in several noncontiguous areas of a disk, rather than as one single unit.

When you store a file on a disk, the operating system looks for the first available free cluster on the disk and stores the file there. If the file is too large for one cluster, the operating system looks for the next free cluster and stores the next part of the file

there. These clusters may not be next to one another and may be widely scattered over the disk.

This fragmentation can slow down data retrieval if the problem becomes severe, but by using a defragmenter, you can restore that lost performance. The defragmenter program removes file fragmentation by rewriting all files and directories into contiguous areas of your disk.

file recovery   The process of recovering deleted or damaged files from a disk. In many operating systems, a deleted file still exists on disk until the space it occupies is overwritten with something else. A file can be deleted accidentally, or it can become inaccessible when part of the file's control information is lost.

Many utility packages offer excellent file recovery programs that guide the user through the recovery process, including Norton Utilities from Symantec, PC Tools from Central Point Software, and the Mace utilities from Fifth Generation Systems. If damage is extreme, the program may only be able to recover some of the damaged file, and substantial editing may be necessary before the file can be used; indeed the best way to recover a damaged program file is to restore it from a backup copy. You must, of course, recover the deleted or damaged files before you add any new files or directories to the disk.

file server   A networked computer used to store files for access by other client computers on the network. On larger networks, the file server may run a special network operating system; on smaller installations, the file server may run a PC operating system supplemented by peer-to-peer networking software.

file sharing   In networking, the sharing of files via the network file server. Shared files can be read, reviewed, and updated by more than one individual. Access to the file or files is often regulated by password protection, account or security clearance, or file locking, to prevent simultaneous changes from being made by more than one person at a time.

filespec   A contraction of *file* spec*ifica-tion*, commonly used to denote the complete drive letter, path name, directory name, and filename needed to access a specific file.

file system   In an operating system, the structure by which files are organized, stored, and named. Some file systems are built-in components of the operating system, and others are installable. In Windows 98 SE, you can select either the FAT16 or the FAT32 file system.

finger   A Unix utility program found on many Internet systems and online services that displays information about a specific user, including full name, login time, and location.

Finger may also display the contents of the user's .plan or .project file, and many users exploit this in a rather novel way, in order to display such varied information as instructions for using a university's comput-erized Coke-vending machine, sports scores, and earthquake information.

firewall   A method of preventing unau-thorized access to a computer system, often found on networked computers. A firewall can be hardware, software, or both. A fire-wall is designed to provide normal service to authorized users, while at the same time preventing unauthorized users from gaining access to the system.

FireWire   Apple Computer Corporation's implementation of IEEE standard 1394 for High Performance Serial Bus. It is supposed to function a great deal like Universal Serial Bus. FireWire will allow up to 63 devices chained together on a single serial to com-municate at up to 400Mbps.

firmware   Any software stored in a form of read-only memory—ROM, EPROM, or EEPROM—that maintains its contents when

power is removed. The BIOS used in IBM-compatible computers is firmware.

first in, first out   Abbreviated FIFO, pro-nounced "fi-foe." A method used to process information in which the first item in the list is processed first. FIFO is commonly used when printing a set of documents; the first document received in the queue is the first document to be printed.

5.25-inch disk   A floppy disk, enclosed in a flexible 5.25-inch jacket, used in IBM and IBM-compatible computers.

The 5.25-inch disk can contain either 360KB or 1.2MB of information, depending on the type of disk. Because the disks are flexible, and because part of the recording surface is exposed through the read/write slot, 5.25-inch floppy disks should be han-dled with care and always stored in their paper jackets when not in use.

You'll seldom see one of these disks today because they have been replaced by the 3.5-inch floppy disk.

fixed-frequency monitor   A monitor designed to receive an input signal at just one frequency. This is in contrast to a multi-sync monitor, which can detect and adjust to a variety of different input signals.

flame   A deliberately insulting e-mail mes-sage or post to a Usenet newsgroup, usually containing a personal attack on the writer of an earlier post. Flames are often generated by established newsgroup members when a newbie posts a question that is answered in the newsgroup's FAQ.

flame war   A prolonged series of flames in a Usenet newsgroup, which may begin as a creative exchange of views but which quickly degenerates into personal attacks and crude name-calling.

flash memory   A special form of non-volatile EEPROM that can be erased at sig-nal levels normally found inside the PC, so that you can reprogram the contents with whatever you like without pulling the chips out of your computer. Also, once flash memory has been programmed, you can remove the expansion board it is mounted on and plug it into another computer if you wish.

flatbed scanner   A device used to transfer paper copies of documents or pictures into a file that can be stored and used on a computer.

flat-panel display   In laptop and notebook computers, a very narrow display that uses one of several technologies, such as electroluminescence, LCD, or thin film transistors.

flicker   On a monitor, any form of unwanted rapid fluctuation in the image that occurs when the refresh rate is too slow to maintain an even level of brightness.

floating-point calculation   A calculation of numbers whose decimal point is not fixed but moves or floats to provide the best degree of accuracy. Floating-point calculations can be implemented in software, or they can be performed much faster by a separate floating-point processor.

floating-point processor   A special-purpose secondary processor designed to perform floating-point calculations much faster than the main processor.

Many processors have matched companion floating-point processors, for example, the 80386 and the 80387. The current trend in processor design is to integrate the floating-point unit onto the main processor, as in the 80486 and the Pentium.

floppy disk   A flat, round, magnetically coated plastic disk enclosed in a protective jacket.

Data is written on to the floppy disk by the disk drive's read/write heads as the disk rotates inside the jacket. The advantage of the floppy disk is that it is removable and so can be used to distribute commercial software, to transfer programs from one computer to another, or to back up files from a hard disk. But compared with a hard disk, floppy disks are slower,

offer relatively small amounts of storage, and can be easily damaged.

Floppy disks in personal computing are of two physical sizes, 5.25 inches and 3.5 inches, and have a variety of storage capacities. The 5.25-inch floppy disk has a stiff plastic external cover, and the 3.5-inch floppy disk is enclosed in a hard plastic case. The 5.25-inch floppy is no longer in use today, and even the 3.5-inch floppy is being used less and less. The proliferation of networks obviates the need for floppies, and a great deal of software is distributed on CD-ROMS.

floppy disk drive   A device used to read and write data to and from a floppy disk.

floptical disk   A removable optical disk much like a compact disc that has a storage capacity of between 20 and 25 megabytes.

font cartridge   A plug-in module available for certain printers that adds new fonts to those already available in the printer. The font information for bit-mapped or outline fonts is stored in ROM in the cartridge.

footprint   The amount of desktop or floor space occupied by a computer or display terminal.

foreground   In an operating system, a process that runs in the foreground is running at a higher level of priority than a background task.

Only multitasking operating systems support true foreground and background processing; however, some application programs can mimic background and foreground processing. For example, many word processors will print a document while still accepting input from the keyboard.

formatting   **1.** To apply the page-layout commands and font specifications to a document to produce the final printed output.

2. The process of initializing a new, blank floppy disk or hard disk so that it can be used to store information.

form feed Abbreviated FF. A printer command that advances the paper in the printer to the top of the next page. This can be done by pressing the form feed button on the printer, or an application can issue the command. In the ASCII character set, a form feed has the decimal value of 12.

forum A feature of online services and bulletin boards that allows subscribers to post messages for others to read and to reply to messages posted by other users.

Most forums are devoted to a specific subject such as working from home or photography, while others are run by hardware and software vendors providing what amounts to online technical support.

free memory An area of memory not currently in use.

Free-net Sometimes Freenet. An organization that provides free Internet access, usually through public libraries or local universities.

freeware A form of software distribution in which the author retains copyright of the software but makes the program available to others at no cost. Freeware is often distributed on Web sites or through user groups. The program may not be resold or distributed by others for profit.

frequency modulation encoding Abbreviated FM encoding. A method of storing digital information on a disk or tape. FM encoding is inefficient in its use of disk space and has been replaced by the more efficient method advanced run length limited (ARLL) encoding.

friction feed A paper-feed mechanism that uses pinch rollers to move the paper through a printer, one page at a time.

Friction feed is usually available on those printers that use paper with pin-feed holes or that use a tractor feed, so that they can also print on single sheets of paper. Manually loading more than just a few sheets of paper using friction feed can become tedious very quickly.

front-end processor A specialized processor that manipulates data before passing it on to the main processor. In large computer-to-computer communications systems, a front-end processor is often used to manage all aspects of communications, leaving the main computer free to handle the data processing.

FTP Abbreviation for File Transfer Protocol. The protocol used to access a remote Internet host and then transfer files between that host and your own computer. FTP is also the name of the program used to manage this protocol.

FTP is based on client/server architecture; you run an FTP client program on your system and connect with an FTP server running on the Internet host computer. The FTP program originated as a Unix utility, but versions are now available for almost all popular operating systems. The traditional Unix FTP program starts a text-based command processor; today's versions use a graphical user interface with drop-down menus instead. The general consensus seems to be that the graphical versions are easier to use, but once you get the hang of things, the command processor versions, while not as pretty, are usually faster.

full backup A backup that includes all the files on your hard disk. If you have a large hard disk, this process can consume a lot of time and a large number of floppy disks, and one way to speed up the process is to use a tape drive system.

function keys The set of programmable keys on the keyboard that can perform special tasks assigned by the current application program.

Most keyboards have 10 or 12 function keys, and they are used by an application as shortcut keys. For example, many programs use F1 to gain access to the help system; in other programs the use of function keys is so complex that special plastic key overlays are needed just so you can remember how to use them.

G   Abbreviation for giga-, meaning 1 billion, or 10^9.

gateway   In networking, a shared connection between a local area network and a larger system, such as a mainframe computer or a large packet-switching network. Usually slower than a bridge or router, a gateway typically has its own processor and memory and can perform protocol conversions. Protocol conversion allows a gateway to connect two dissimilar networks; data is converted and reformatted before it is forwarded to the new network.

gender changer   A special intermediary connector for use with two cables that both have male or both have female connectors.

General-Purpose Interface Bus   Abbreviated GPIB. A 24-pin parallel interface bus that conforms to the IEEE 488 interface definition standard, often used to connect scientific instruments together or to a computer. Originally developed by Hewlett-Packard, GPIB is also known as the Hewlett-Packard Interface Bus (HPIB).

genlocking   A contraction of generator lock. The synchronization and superimposition of computer-generated text or graphics onto a video signal so that the two images can be combined into the same signal and displayed at the same time.

In the PC, a board containing the circuitry required for genlocking often plugs into the display adapter. It converts the VGA signal into a standard NTSC video signal, which it then synchronizes with an external video signal.

giga-   A prefix meaning 1 billion, or 10^9.

gigabyte   Pronounced "gig-a-bite." Strictly speaking, a gigabyte would be 1 billion bytes; however, bytes are most often counted in powers of 2, and so a gigabyte becomes 2^{30}, or 1,073,741,824 bytes.

GPF   Abbreviation for General Protection Fault, which occurs in an operating system when a program tries to use RAM that it is not supposed to use.

graphical user interface   Abbreviated GUI, pronounced "gooey." A graphics-based user interface that allows users to select files, programs, or commands by pointing to pictorial representations on the screen rather than by typing long, complex commands from a command prompt.

Application programs execute in windows, using a consistent set of drop-down menus, dialog boxes, and other graphical elements such as scroll bars and icons. This consistency among interface elements is a major benefit for the user, because as soon as you learn how to use the interface in one program, you can use it in all other programs running in the same environment.

graphics accelerator board   A video adapter that offloads most of the graphics processing from the CPU. By offloading most of the graphics processing tasks from the main processor onto the graphics accelerator board, you can improve the performance of your system considerably, particularly if you are a Windows user.

graphics coprocessor   A fixed-function graphics chip, designed to speed up the processing and display of high-resolution images. Popular graphics coprocessors include the S3 86C9xx accelerator chips.

grayscale monitor   A monitor and video adapter that uses a set of gray shades from black to white instead of using colors. Grayscale monitors are expensive and are used in medical and photographic imaging systems.

half-height drive   A space-saving drive bay that is half the height of the 3-inch drive bays used in the original IBM PC. Most of today's drives are half-height drives.

hand-held computer   A portable computer that is small enough to be held in one hand.

hand scanner   An optical device used to digitize a relatively small image or piece of art.

hard card   A single expansion board that contains a small hard disk and associated controller circuitry. A hard card allows you to add another hard disk, even when all your drive bays are occupied, as long as there is still a single expansion slot available. Hard cards were brought to prominence by Plus Development Corporation.

hard disk controller   An old-technology expansion board that contains the necessary circuitry to control and coordinate a hard disk drive. Many hard disk controllers are capable of managing more than one hard disk, as well as floppy disks and even tape drives.

hard disk drive   A storage device that uses a set of rotating, magnetically coated disks called platters to store data or programs. In everyday use, the terms "hard disk," "hard disk drive," and "hard drive" are all used interchangeably, because the disk and the drive mechanism are a single unit.

A typical hard disk platter rotates at up to 3600rpm, and the read/write heads float on a cushion of air from 10 to 25 millionths of an inch thick so that the heads never come into contact with the recording surface. The whole unit is hermetically sealed to prevent airborne contaminants from entering and interfering with these close tolerances.

Hard disks range in capacity from a few tens of megabytes to several gigabytes of storage space; the bigger the disk, the more important a well-thought-out backup strategy becomes. Hard disks are very reliable, but they do fail, and usually at the most inconvenient moment.

hard disk interface   A standard way of accessing the data stored on a hard disk. Several hard disk interface standards have evolved over time, including IDE (Integrated Device Electronics), EIDE (Enhanced Integrated Device Electronics), and SCSI (Small Computer System Interface).

hard reset   A system reset made by pressing the computer's reset button or by turning the power off and then on again. Used only when the system has crashed so badly that a Ctrl+Alt+Delete reboot doesn't work.

hardware   All the physical electronic components of a computer system, including peripherals, printed circuit boards, displays, and printers.

hardware dependence   The requirement that a specific hardware component be present for a program to work. Hardware-dependent software is often very difficult to move or port to another computer.

hardware independence   The ability to produce similar results in a wide variety of environments, without requiring the presence of specific hardware.

The Unix operating system and the PostScript page-description language are both examples of hardware independence. Unix runs on a wide range of computers, from the PC to a Cray, and PostScript is used by many printer manufacturers.

hardwired   Describes a system designed in a way that does not allow for flexibility or future expansion. May also refer to a device or computer connected directly to a network.

Hayes-compatible modem   Any modem that recognizes the commands in the industry-standard AT-command set, defined by Hayes Microcomputer Products, Inc.

head   The electromagnetic device used to read and write to and from magnetic media such as hard and floppy disks, tape drives, and compact discs. The head converts the information read into electrical pulses sent to the computer for processing.

head crash   An unexpected collision between a hard disk head and the rapidly rotating magnetic recording surface of the disk, resulting in damage to the disk surface and in some severe cases resulting in damage to the head itself.

A head crash in the file allocation table (FAT) area of a disk can be especially devastating, because the FAT contains instructions for the operating system on how to find all the other directories and files on the disk, and if it is damaged, the other files and directories may become completely inaccessible.

Recent hard disk design has done much to eliminate this problem.

hertz   Abbreviated Hz. A unit of frequency measurement; 1 hertz equals one cycle per second.

hexadecimal   Abbreviated hex. The base-16 numbering system that uses the digits 0 through 9, followed by the letters A through F (equivalent to the decimal numbers 10 through 15).

Hex is a very convenient way to represent the binary numbers computers use internally, because it fits neatly into the 8-bit byte. All the 16 hex digits 0 to F can be represented in 4 bits, and so 2 hex digits (1 digit for each set of 4 bits) can be stored in a single byte. This means that 1 byte can contain any one of 256 different hex numbers, from 0 through FF. Hex numbers are often labeled with a lowercase h (for example, 1234h) to distinguish them from decimal numbers.

HGC   Abbreviation for Hercules Graphics Card. A video adapter for DOS computers, introduced by Hercules Computer Technology. HGC provides monochrome graphics with 720 horizontal pixels and 348 vertical pixels.

high-density disk   A floppy disk with more recording density and storage capacity than a double-density disk. In the Macintosh, high-density disks contain 1.44MB. In IBM-compatible computers, high-density 5.25-inch floppy disks contain 1.2MB, while high-density 3.5-inch floppy disks contain either 1.44MB or 2.88MB of storage space.

high-level format   The process of preparing a floppy disk or a hard disk partition for use by the operating system. In the case of DOS, a high-level format creates the boot sector, the file allocation table (FAT), and the root directory.

high memory area   Abbreviated HMA. In an IBM-compatible computer, the first 64K of extended memory above the 1MB limit of 8086 and 8088 addresses. Programs that conform to the extended memory, specification can use this memory as an extension of conventional memory, although only one program can use or control HMA at a time—DOS, Windows, or an application. If you load DOS into the HMA, you can recover approximately 50K of conventional memory for use by your applications.

high-persistence phosphor   In a monitor, a phosphor that glows for a relatively long time after being energized by electrons. This can lead to ghost images on the screen.

high resolution   In monitors and printers, a description of high-quality output; resolution refers to the sharpness and detail of the image.

What actually constitutes high resolution is in the eye of the beholder; high resolution to one person represents a bad case of the jaggies to another. On a 12-inch monitor, a realistic-looking display requires a grid of approximately 1000 by 1000 pixels. Laser printers can manage a resolution of 1200dpi, but Linotronic typesetters can print at up to 2540dpi.

HIMEM.SYS   The DOS and Windows 3.x device driver that manages the use of extended memory and the high memory area on IBM-compatible computers. HIMEM .SYS not only allows your application programs to access extended memory, it also oversees that area to prevent other programs from trying to use the same space at the same time.

HIMEM.SYS must be loaded by a DEVICE command in your CONFIG.SYS file; do not use DEVICEHIGH.

home page   On the Internet, an initial starting page. A home page may be related to a single person, a specific subject, or to a corporation and is a convenient jumping-off point to other pages or resources.

horizontal scanning frequency   In a monitor, the frequency at which the monitor repaints the horizontal lines that make up an image. Horizontal scanning frequency is measured in kHz and is standardized at 31.5kHz for a VGA. For SuperVGA, this frequency ranges from 35 to 85kHz, depending on the refresh rate of the video adapter.

host   The central or controlling computer in a networked or distributed processing environment, providing services that other computers or terminals can access via the network.

Computers connected to the Internet are also described as hosts and can be accessed using FTP, Telnet, Gopher, or a World Wide Web browser.

HP LaserJet   A family of very popular desktop laser printers launched in 1984 and manufactured by Hewlett-Packard Company.

HTML   Abbreviation for Hypertext Markup Language. A standardized hypertext language used to create Web pages and other hypertext documents.

When you access an Internet HTML document using a Web browser, you will see a mixture of text, graphics, and links to other documents. When you click a link, the related document will open automatically, no matter where on the Internet that document is actually located. Normally, you don't see the individual elements that make up HTML when you view a document, although certain browsers have a special mode that displays both the text and the HTML in a document.

HTTP   Abbreviation for Hypertext Transfer Protocol. An application layer protocol included with the TCP/IP protocol suite on most operating systems. Used to transfer HTML documents, files, sound, graphics, and anything else linked to the Web page.

hub   In networking, a hub is the junction for all of the cables coming from the networked computers, thus allowing the systems to communicate.

hypertext   A method of presenting information so that it can be viewed by the user in a nonsequential way, regardless of how the topics were originally organized.

Hypertext was designed to make a computer respond to the nonlinear way that humans think and access information—by association, rather than according to the linear organization of film, books, and speech.

In a hypertext application, you can browse through the information with considerable flexibility, choosing to follow a new path each time you access the information. When you click a highlighted word, you activate a link to another hypertext document that may be located on the same Internet host or can be on a completely different system thousands of miles away.

IAB   Abbreviation for Internet Architecture Board. A technical advisory group of the Internet Society.

IBM-compatible computer   Any personal computer compatible with the IBM line of personal computers. Also referred to as a clone.

IBM PC   A series of personal computers based on the Intel 8088 processor, introduced by IBM in mid-1981.

The specifications for the IBM PC seem puny in comparison to current computer systems; the PC was released containing 16K of memory, expandable to 64K on the motherboard, and a monochrome video adapter incapable of displaying bit-mapped graphics. The floppy disk drive held 160K of data and programs. There was no hard disk on the original IBM PC; that came later with the release of the IBM PC/XT.

In 1983, IBM released an improved version of the PC, the IBM PC-2, which came with 64K of memory, expandable to 256K on the motherboard, and a double-density floppy disk drive capable of storing 360K of programs and data. The Color/Graphics Adapter (CGA) and an RGB (red-green-blue) color monitor were also introduced at the same time.

IBM PC/AT   A series of personal computers based on the Intel 80286 processor, introduced by IBM in 1984.

The AT represented a significant performance increase over previous computers, up to 75 percent faster than the PC/XT, and the AT bus standard is used in many clones or IBM-compatible computers.

IBM PC/XT   A series of personal computers based on the Intel 8088 processor, introduced by IBM in 1983.

The PC/XT was the first IBM personal computer to offer a built-in hard disk and the capability to expand memory up to a whopping 640K on the motherboard. The original PC/XT used an Intel 8088 running at a clock speed of 4.77MHz—very slow when compared with today's clock speeds in the neighborhood of 450MHz.

IBM PS/2   A series of personal computers using several different Intel processors, introduced by IBM in 1987.

The main difference between the PS/2 line and earlier IBM personal computers was a major change to the internal bus. Previous computers used the AT bus, also known as ISA (Industry Standard Architecture), but IBM used the proprietary MCA (Microchannel Architecture) in the PS/2 line instead. MCA expansion boards will not work in a computer using ISA.

IBM RS/6000   A set of seven or nine separate 32-bit chips used in IBM's line of RISC (reduced instruction set computing) workstations. With up to 7.4 million transistors depending on configuration, the RS/6000 uses a superscalar design with four separate 16K data cache units and an 8K instruction cache.

The venture announced between IBM, Apple, and Motorola in late 1991 specified the joint development of a single-chip version of the RS/6000 architecture called the PowerPC.

IBM ThinkPad   A series of innovative and popular notebook computers from IBM.

The ThinkPad first introduced the touch-sensitive dual-button pointing stick, or TrackPoint, the pencil-eraser-like device between the G, H, and B keys that replaces the mouse, which is now found on many portable computers.

The ThinkPad 701C, also known as the "Butterfly," introduced another innovative concept, that of the expanding keyboard. When the 701C case is closed, the TrackWrite keyboard is completely concealed inside the case; the right half sits above the left. When the case is opened, the two parts of the full-sized keyboard automatically unfold and overhang the edges of the case. The 701C, based on the Intel DX2 50MHz processor, also contains an internal 14,400bps fax/data modem with built-in speaker phone and digital answering machine, infrared wireless file transfer, and two PCMCIA Type I or Type II PC cards or one Type III card.

IBM 3270   A general name for a family of IBM system components—printers, terminals, and terminal cluster controllers—that can be used with a mainframe computer by an SNA (Systems Network Architecture) link. Terminal emulation software that emulates a 3270 terminal is available for both DOS and Microsoft Windows.

imagesetter   A large, professional-quality typesetter capable of high-resolution output on paper or film.

Linotronic imagesetters can print at resolutions of 1225 to 2450dpi; compare this with the 300 to 600dpi produced by most desktop laser printers.

impact printer   Any printer that forms an image on paper by forcing a character image against an inked ribbon. Dot-matrix, daisy-wheel, and line printers are all impact printers, whereas laser printers are not.

impedance   An electrical property that combines capacitance, inductance, and resistance. Impedance can be described as the apparent resistance to the flow of alternating current at a given frequency; mismatches in impedance along a cable cause distortions and reflections.

incremental backup   A backup of a hard disk that consists of only those files created or modified since the last backup.

infection   The presence of a computer virus.

Information Superhighway   Sometimes abbreviated I-Way. An imprecise albeit popular term often applied to the Internet or to the National Information Infrastructure.

ink-jet printer   A printer that creates an image by spraying tiny droplets of ink from the printhead. Although many dot-matrix printers have 9 to 24 pins, most ink jets have printheads with somewhere between 30 and 60 nozzles, and this allows them to create high-resolution images in a single pass over the paper. Both color and black-and-white ink-jet printers are available.

input/output   Abbreviated I/O. The transfer of data between the computer and its peripheral devices, disk drives, terminals, and printers.

input/output bound   Abbreviated I/O bound. A condition in which the speed of operation of the I/O port limits the speed of program execution; getting the data into and out of the computer is more time-consuming than processing that same data.

install   To configure and prepare hardware or software for operation.

Many application packages have their own install programs—programs that copy all the required files from the original distribution floppy disks or CDs into appropriate directories on your hard disk and then help you to configure the program to your own operating requirements. Microsoft Windows programs are usually installed by a program called SETUP.

installation program   A program whose sole function is to install (and sometimes configure) another program.

The program guides the user through what might be a rather complex set of choices, copying the correct files into the right directories, decompressing them if necessary, and asking for the next disk when appropriate. This program may also ask for a person's name or a company name so that the start-up screen can be customized.

Some older IBM-compatible installation programs may change your CONFIG.SYS or AUTOEXEC.BAT files without letting you know; others will ask your permission and add their statements to the end of the existing commands.

Institute of Electrical and Electronics Engineers   Abbreviated IEEE. Pronounced "eye-triple-ee." A membership organization, founded in 1963, including engineers, students, and scientists. IEEE also acts as a coordinating body for computing and communications standards, particularly the IEEE 802 standard for the physical and data-link layers of local area networks, following the ISO/OSI model.

integer   Also referred to as INT, an integer is a whole number, one in which there is no decimal portion.

integrated circuit   Abbreviated IC, also known as a chip. A small semiconductor circuit that contains many electronic components.

Integrated Drive Electronics interface   Abbreviated IDE. A popular hard-disk interface standard, used for disks in the range of 40MB to 1.2GB, requiring medium to fast data transfer rates. IDE gets its name from the fact that the electronic control circuitry needed is actually located on the drive itself, thus eliminating the need for a separate hard-disk controller card.

Intel OverDrive   The original Intel OverDrive microprocessor was designed as a user-installable upgrade to an 80486SX or 80486DX-based computer, while the Pentium OverDrive chip is designed as a replacement for 486-based systems. OverDrive chips boost system performance by using the same clock-multiplying technology found in the Intel 80486DX-2 and DX4 chips. Once installed, an OverDrive processor can increase application performance by an estimated 40 to 70 percent.

interface   That point where a connection is made between two different parts of a system, such as between two hardware devices, between a user and a program or operating system, or between two application programs.

In hardware, an interface describes the logical and physical connections used, as in RS-232-C, and is often considered synonymous with the term "port."

A user interface consists of all the means by which a program communicates with the user, including a command line, menus, dialog boxes, online help systems, and so on. User interfaces can be classified as character-based, menu-driven, or graphical.

Software interfaces are application program interfaces, the codes and messages used by programs to communicate behind the scenes.

interface standard   Any standard way of connecting two devices or elements having different functions.

Many different interface standards are used in the PC world, including SCSI (Small Computer System Interface), IDE (Integrated Drive Electronics), and the ESDI (Enhanced Small Device Interface) for hard disks, RS-232-C and the Centronics parallel interface for serial devices and parallel printers, and the ISO/OSI model for computer-to-computer communications over a network.

interlacing   A display technique that uses two passes over the monitor screen, painting every other line on the screen the first time and then filling in the rest of the lines on the second pass. Noninterlaced scanning paints all the lines on the display in a single pass.

interleave factor   The order in which the sectors were arranged on your hard disk by the initial low-level format.

Introduced as a compensation for slow computers, interleaving eliminates the delay that results when a drive is not ready to read or write the next sector as soon as it has read or written the previous one. With a 3:1 interleave factor, sequentially numbered sectors are located three sectors apart on the disk. An interleave that is either too high or too low can lead to a severe degradation in performance, because the computer spends its time waiting for the next sector to arrive at the read/write heads. Thanks to increases in PC speed, interleaving is obsolete, and most of today's disks use a 1:1 interleave factor (which actually indicates a noninterleaved drive).

interleaved memory   A method of speeding up data access by dividing dynamic RAM (DRAM) memory into two separate banks so that the processor can read one bank while the other is being refreshed. DRAM requires that its contents be updated at least every thousandth of a second, and while it is being refreshed, it cannot be read by the processor; interleaving memory speeds up access times. Of course, if the processor needs to read from the same bank of RAM repeatedly, it must wait for the full DRAM cycle time.

The introduction of static RAM (SRAM) has removed the need for interleaved memory, because SRAM memory can retain its contents without the need for refreshment.

internal hard disk   A hard disk drive housed inside the computer's system unit and integrated with it, rather than an external drive packaged with its own case, cables, and independent power supply.

International Organization for Standardization   Sometimes mistakenly referred to as the International Standards Organization and commonly referred to as

ISO. ISO is not an abbreviation, but a derivation of the Greek word *isos*, which means equal. This is an international standard-making body, based in Geneva, that establishes global standards for communications and information exchange. ANSI is the U.S. member of ISO.

The seven-layer International Organization for Standardization Open Systems Interconnect (ISO/OSI) model for computer-to-computer communications is one of the ISO's most widely accepted recommendations.

internet   Abbreviation for internetwork. A set of computer networks, made up of a large number of smaller networks.

Internet   The world's largest computer network, consisting of millions of computers supporting millions of users around the world. The Internet is growing at a phenomenal rate—between 10 and 15 percent per month—so any size estimates are quickly out-of-date.

The Internet was originally established to meet the research needs of the U.S. defense industry, but it has grown into a huge global network serving universities, academic researchers, commercial interests, and government agencies, both in the United States and overseas. The Internet uses TCP/IP protocols, and Internet computers run a variety of operating systems, including Windows 2000 and Unix.

Internet access can be via a permanent network connection or by dial-up through one of the many service providers.

Internet address   An IP (e.g., 131.107 .2.200) or domain (e.g., www.microsoft .com) address that identifies a specific node on the Internet.

interprocess communication   Abbreviated IPC. A term that describes all the methods used to pass information between two programs running on the same computer running a multitasking operating system, or between two programs running on a network, including pipes, shared memory, queues, the Clipboard, DDE (Dynamic Data Exchange), and OLE (Object Linking and Embedding).

interrupt   A signal to the processor generated by a device under its control (such as the system clock) that interrupts normal processing.

An interrupt indicates that an event requiring the processor's attention has occurred, causing the processor to suspend and save its current activity and then branch to an interrupt service routine. This service routine processes the interrupt, whether it was generated by the system clock, a keystroke, or a mouse click; and when it's complete, returns control to the suspended process. In the PC, interrupts are often divided into three classes: internal hardware, external hardware, and software.

interrupt controller   A chip, used to process and prioritize hardware interrupts. In IBM-compatible computers, the Intel 8259A Programmable Interrupt Controller responds to each hardware interrupt, assigns a priority, and forwards it to the main processor.

interrupt handler   Special software invoked when an interrupt occurs. Each type of interrupt, such as a clock tick or a keystroke, is processed by its own specific interrupt handler. A table, called the interrupt vector table, maintains a list of addresses for these specific interrupt handlers.

interrupt request   Abbreviated IRQ. Hardware lines that carry a signal from a device to the processor.

A hardware interrupt signals when an event has taken place that requires the processor's attention and may come from the keyboard, the input/output ports, or the system's disk drives. In the PC, the main processor does not accept interrupts from hardware devices directly; instead interrupts are routed to an Intel 8259A Programmable Interrupt Controller. This chip responds to each hardware interrupt, assigns a priority, and forwards it to the main processor.

interrupt vector table   A list of addresses for specific software routines known as interrupt handlers. In a DOS computer, the interrupt vector table consists of 256 pointers located in the first megabyte of memory.

intranet   An interconnected collection of networks that is contained within an enterprise. Intranets can be connected to the Internet, with people from the outside being given limited access to the intranet.

IP   Abbreviation for Internet Protocol. The underlying communications protocol on which the Internet is based. IP allows a data packet to travel across many networks before reaching its final destination.

IPSEC   Most current methods of securing network transmission work at the application layer of the Open Systems Interconnect networking model. IPSEC is a developing security standard that is designed to work at the network layer of the OSI model where the packets are actually processed. At this layer, it is possible to encrypt the packet and digitally sign the packet so that its origin can be verified.

IPv6   The next version of IP, IPv6 lengthens the IP address from 32 to 128 bits, thereby creating a much larger address pool. IPv6 is faster than IP and allows for security as well as other enhancements.

IPX/SPX   A suite of networking protocols created by Novell Corporation to allow Novell Netware systems to communicate over local and wide area networks.

IRC   Abbreviation for Internet Relay Chat. An Internet client/server application that allows large groups of users to communicate interactively. Specific channels are devoted to one particular topic, from the sacred to the profane, and topics come and go regularly as interest levels change.

ISA   Abbreviation for Industry Standard Architecture. The 16-bit bus design was first used in IBM's PC/AT computer in 1984. ISA has a bus speed of 8MHz and a maximum throughput of 8 megabytes per second.

EISA (Extended Industry Standard Architecture) is a 32-bit extension to this standard bus.

ISDN   Abbreviation for Integrated Services Digital Network. A worldwide digital communications network emerging from existing telephone services. Computers and other devices connect to ISDN via interfaces called terminal adapters or ISDN modems. ISDN systems are capable of transmitting voice, video, music, and data.

ISO/OSI model   Abbreviation for International Organization for Standardization Open System Interconnect. In networking, a reference model defined by the ISO that divides computer-to-computer communications into seven connected layers, known as a "protocol stack."

ITU   Abbreviation for International Telecommunication Union. The United Nations umbrella organization that develops and standardizes telecommunications worldwide. The ITU also contains the CCITT, the International Frequency Registration Board (IFRB), and the Consultative Committee on International Radio (CCIR). Popular usage is starting to refer to the CCITT standards as ITU standards.

Java   An object-oriented programming language designed specifically for use in large distributed networks such as the Internet. It is designed to look and feel like C++ and yet be easier to use. Programs written in Java are portable, which means that they can run on any computer with any operating system that has a Java virtual machine.

joystick   A popular multidirectional pointing device, used extensively in many computer games, as well as in certain professional applications such as computer-aided design (CAD).

Jughead   An Internet search mechanism used to construct an index of high-level Gopher menus. Once a search is complete, you interact with the Jughead-built menu in the same way that you use a Gopher menu.

jumper   A small plastic and metal connector that completes a circuit, usually to select one option from a set of several user-definable options. Jumpers are often used to configure older pieces of hardware that do not support Plug and Play.

kernel   The most fundamental part of an operating system. The kernel stays resident in memory at all times, often hidden from the user, and manages system memory, the file system, and disk operations.

keyboard   The typewriter-like set of keys used to input data and control commands to the computer. Most keyboards use a QWERTY layout and may also have a calculator-like numeric keypad off to one side, as well as a set of arrow keys.

keyboard buffer   A small amount of system memory used to store the most recently typed keys, also known as the type-ahead buffer. Some utility programs let you collect a number of keystrokes or commands and edit or reissue them.

keyboard layout   Most computers use a keyboard based on the traditional QWERTY typewriter-like keyboard.

The most common keyboard currently used has 101 keys, with 12 function keys in a row above the other keys.

keyboard template   A plastic card that fits over certain keys (usually the function keys) on the keyboard to remind you how to use them. These templates are specific to an application and can be very useful if you are an occasional user or are learning to use the program.

kilo-   A prefix indicating 1000 in the metric system. Because computing is based on powers of 2, in this context kilo usually means 2^{10}, or 1024. To differentiate between these two uses, a lowercase k is used to indicate 1000 (as in kHz), and an uppercase K to indicate 1024 (as in KB).

kilobit   Abbreviated Kb or Kbit. 1024 bits (binary digits).

kilobits per second   Abbreviated Kbps. The number of bits, or binary digits, transmitted every second, measured in multiples of 1024 bits per second. Used as an indicator of communications transmission rate.

kilobyte   Abbreviated K, KB, or Kbyte. 1024 bytes.

L1 and L2 cache   Cache memory is much faster for a processor to access than RAM. Level one cache, which is built right into the processor, is checked first for required data, and if it is not present, the processor checks level two cache, which is usually on a separate chip or chips.

laptop computer   A small portable computer light enough to carry comfortably, with a flat screen and keyboard that fold together.

Laptop computers are battery-operated and often have a thin, backlit or sidelit LCD display screen. Some models can even mate with a docking station to perform as a full-sized desktop system back at the office. Advances in battery technology allow laptop computers to run for many hours between charges, and some models have a set of business applications built into ROM.

laser printer   A high-resolution nonimpact printer that uses a variation of the electrophotographic process used in photocopying machines to print text and graphics onto paper.

A laser printer uses a rotating disc to reflect laser beams onto a photosensitive drum, where the image of the page is converted into an electrostatic charge that attracts and holds the toner. A piece of charged paper is then rolled against the drum to transfer the image, and heat is applied to fuse the toner and paper together to create the final image.

latency   The time that elapses between issuing a request for data and actually starting the data transfer.

In a hard disk, this translates into the time it takes to position the disk's read/write head and rotate the disk so that the required sector or cluster is under the head. Latency is just one of many factors that influence disk access speeds.

layout   In printed-circuit board design, the arrangement of the individual components on the circuit board.

LCD monitor   A monitor that uses liquid-crystal display technology. Many laptop and notebook computers use LCD displays because of their small size and low weight.

LDAP   Abbreviation for Lightweight Directory Access Protocol, LDAP is used to search for individuals, companies, and the like on large networks and display e-mail address, phone number, city, state, zip code, and just about any other information that the systems administrator has seen fit to include in their directory.

letter quality   A printer mode that produces text higher in quality than draft mode. As the name suggests, letter-quality printing is supposed to be good enough to be used in business letters and therefore comparable to typewriter output. Laser printers, some ink-jet printers, and all daisy-wheel printers produce letter-quality output; certain high-end dot-matrix printers can produce letter-quality output, but most do not.

light-emitting diode   Abbreviated LED. A small semiconductor device that emits light as current flows through it. LEDs are often used as activity lights on computer peripherals such as hard disk drives and modems.

light pen   A light-sensitive input device shaped like a pen, used to draw on the computer screen or to make menu selections. As the tip of the light pen makes contact with the screen, it sends a signal back to the computer containing the x,y coordinates of the pixels at that point.

line adapter   In communications, a device such as a modem that converts a digital signal into a form suitable for transmission over a communications channel.

line printer   Any printer that prints a complete line at a time, rather than printing one character at a time (as a dot-matrix or daisy-wheel printer does) or one page at a time (as a laser printer does). Line printers are very high-speed printers and are common in the corporate environment where they are used with mainframe computers, minicomputers, and networked systems.

line sharing device   A small electronic device that allows a fax machine and a telephone answering machine to share the same phone line. The device answers the call and listens for the characteristic high-pitched fax carrier signal. If this signal is detected, the call is routed to the fax machine; if it is not present, the call is sent to a telephone or answering machine instead.

Linux   A Unix-style operating system developed by Linus Torvalds at the University of Helsinki. Linux is free or very low cost and extensible by anyone who feels like doing some programming. Linux has a reputation of being a stable and efficient operating system.

liquid crystal display   Abbreviated LCD. A display technology common in portable computers that uses electric current to align or misalign crystals, allowing light to pass or not to pass as needed.

The rod-shaped crystals are contained between two parallel transparent electrodes, and when current is applied, they change their orientation, creating a darker area. Many LCD screens are also backlit or sidelit to increase visibility and reduce the possibility of eyestrain.

local area network   Abbreviated LAN. A group of computers and associated peripherals connected by a communications channel capable of sharing files and other resources between several users.

local bus   A PC bus specification that allows peripherals to exchange data at a rate faster than the 8 megabytes per second allowed by the ISA (Industry Standard

Architecture) and the 32 megabytes per second allowed by the EISA (Extended Industry Standard Architecture) definitions. Local bus can achieve a maximum data rate of 133 megabytes per second with a 33MHz bus speed, 148 megabytes per second with a 40MHz bus, or 267 megabytes per second with a 50MHz bus.

To date, the Video Electronics Standards Association (VESA) video cards have been the main peripheral to benefit from local bus use.

local disk In networking, a disk attached to a workstation rather than to the file server.

local printer In networking, a printer attached to a workstation rather than to the file server or a print server.

logical drive The internal division of a large hard disk into smaller units. One single physical drive may be organized into several logical drives for convenience.

long filename The ability of a file system to take advantage of multiple-character filenames. Several operating systems are not limited to the DOS 8.3 filenaming convention of eight characters before a period and three more optional characters forming the filename extension. Unix, Windows 95/98/ 98 SE, Windows NT, Windows 2000, and the Macintosh file systems can all manage long filenames, even those containing spaces, more than one period, and mixed upper- and lowercase letters.

lost chain A part of a file, consisting of one or more clusters, that no longer has an entry in the file allocation table and so cannot be reconnected to the rest of the file. The Windows program Scandisk detects these lost chains and converts them into files so that you can delete them and recover the disk space they occupy. You can also examine the contents of these lost chains after Scandisk has recovered them, but the chance of the contents being usable is very slim indeed.

lost cluster A cluster, originally part of a file, for which there is now no file allocation table entry. Use the Windows program Scandisk to convert lost clusters into files. You can then examine the contents of the cluster and decide if you want to keep it or delete it and recover the disk space that it occupies.

low-level format The process that creates the tracks and sectors on a blank hard disk or floppy disk; sometimes called the physical format. Most hard disks are already low-level formatted; however, floppy disks receive both a low- and a high-level format (or logical format) when you format them in Windows.

low resolution In monitors and printers, a description of low-quality output, lacking sharpness or definition. Resolution is determined by the technology used to create the output.

What actually constitutes low resolution is in the eye of the beholder; what one person may consider low resolution may be quite acceptable to another.

LPT Abbreviation for Line Printer Terminal, LPT is the device name used to denote a parallel communications port, often used with a printer.

lurking The practice of reading an Internet mailing list or Usenet newsgroup without posting anything yourself. In the online world, lurking is not considered particularly antisocial; in fact, it is a good idea to lurk for a while when you first subscribe so you can get a feel for the tone of the discussions in the group and come up to speed on recent history.

magneto-optical drive Abbreviated MO drive. An erasable, high-capacity, removable storage device similar to a CD-ROM drive.

Magneto-optical drives use both magnetic and laser technology to write data to the disk and use the laser to read that data back. Writing data takes two passes over the disk, an erase pass followed by the write pass, but reading can be done in just one pass and, as a result, is much faster.

mailing list   On the Internet, a group of people who share a common interest and who automatically receive all the mail posted to the listserver, or mailing-list manager program. Contributions are sent as e-mail to the listserver and then distributed to all subscribers. Most listserver programs include a command that will send you a complete list of all the subscribers' e-mail addresses by return e-mail.

mainframe computer   A large, fast multi-user computer system, designed to manage very large amounts of data and very complex computing tasks. Mainframes are normally installed in large corporations, universities, or military installations and can support hundreds, even thousands, of users.

maintenance release   A software upgrade that corrects minor bugs or adds a few small features, distinguished from a major release by an increase in only the decimal portion of the version number—for example, from 3.0 to 3.1, rather than from 3.1 to 4.0.

male connector   Any cable connector with pins designed to engage the sockets on the female part of the connector.

Maltron keyboard   An alternative keyboard designed to eliminate carpal tunnel syndrome that arranges the keys in two concave areas conforming to the shape of the hand, allowing better alignment of the forearm and wrist.

MBONE   Abbreviation for *m*ulticast *bone*. A method of transmitting digital video over the Internet in real time.

The TCP/IP protocols used for Internet transmissions are unsuitable for real-time audio or video; they were designed to deliver text and other files reliably, but with some delay. MBONE requires the creation of another backbone service with special hardware and software to accommodate video and audio transmissions; the existing Inter-

net hardware cannot manage time-critical transmissions.

MCA   Abbreviation for Microchannel Architecture. A 32-bit proprietary expansion bus first introduced by IBM in 1987 for the IBM PS/2 range of computers and also used in the RS/6000 series.

MCA is incompatible with expansion boards that follow the earlier 16-bit AT bus standard, physically because the boards are about 50 percent smaller, and electronically as the bus depends on more proprietary integrated circuits.

MCA was designed for multiprocessing, and it also allows expansion boards to identify themselves, thus eliminating many of the conflicts that arose through the use of manual settings in the original bus.

MCGA   Abbreviation for Multi-Color Graphics Array. A video adapter included with certain IBM PS/2 computers that provides 64 gray shades with a palette of 16 colors at a resolution of 640 by 350 pixels.

MDA   Abbreviation for Monochrome Display Adapter. A video adapter introduced in 1981 that could display text but not graphics, in one color, at a resolution of 640 pixels horizontally by 350 vertically. MDAs were replaced in many cases by the Hercules Graphics Card (HGC).

mean time between failures   Abbreviated MTBF. The statistically derived average length of time that a system component operates before failing.

mean time to repair   Abbreviated MTTR. The average length of time that it takes to repair a failed component.

Media Control Interface   Abbreviated MCI. A standard interface used for controlling multimedia files and devices. Each device has its own device driver that implements a standard set of MCI functions such as stop, play, or record.

meg   A common abbreviation for megabyte or megahertz.

mega- Abbreviated M. A prefix meaning 1 million in the metric system. Because computing is based on powers of 2, in this context mega usually means 2^{20} or 1,048,576; the power of 2 closest to 1 million.

megabit Abbreviated Mbit. Usually 1,048,576 binary digits or bits of data. Often used as equivalent to 1 million bits.

megabits per second Abbreviated Mbps. A measurement of the amount of information moving across a network or communications link in 1 second, measured in multiples of 1,048,576 bits.

megabyte Abbreviated MB. Usually 1,048,576 bytes. Megabytes are a common way of representing computer memory or hard-disk capacity.

megahertz Abbreviated MHz. One million cycles per second. A processor's clock speed is often expressed in MHz. The original IBM PC operated an 8088 running at 4.77MHz; the Pentium III processor runs at speeds of up to 800MHz.

membrane keyboard A pressure-sensitive keyboard covered by a protective plastic sheet used in a hostile environment where operators may not always have clean hands. Since it is very difficult to type quickly and accurately on a membrane keyboard, they are most often used for occasional data entry in factories or in fast-food restaurants. They do not work well for touch typing.

memory The primary RAM installed in the computer.

The operating system copies application programs from disk into memory, where all program execution and data processing takes place; results are written back out to disk again. The amount of memory installed in the computer can determine the size and number of programs that it can run, as well as the size of the largest data file.

memory address The exact location in memory that stores a particular data item or program instruction.

memory board A printed circuit board containing memory chips. When all the sockets on a memory board are filled, and the board contains the maximum amount of memory that it can manage, it is said to be "fully populated."

memory cache An area of high-speed memory on the processor that stores commonly used code or data obtained from slower memory, replacing the need to access the system's main memory to fetch instructions.

The Intel 82385 cache controller chip was used with fast static RAM on some systems to increase performance, but more modern processors include cache management functions on the main processor. The Intel 80486 contains a single 8KB cache to manage both data and instruction caching; the Pentium contains two separate 8K caches, one each for data and instructions. The Pentium II has two 16KB caches built into the chip. The Pentium III has a 512KB level two cache or 256KB of advanced transfer cache.

memory chip A chip that holds data or program instructions. A memory chip may hold its contents temporarily, as in the case of RAM, or permanently, as in the case of ROM.

memory management unit Abbreviated MMU. The part of the processor that manages the mapping of virtual memory addresses to actual physical addresses.

In some systems, such as those based on early Intel or Motorola processors, the MMU was a separate chip; however, in most of today's processors, the MMU is integrated into the CPU chip itself.

memory map The organization and allocation of memory in a computer. A memory map will give an indication of the amount of memory used by the operating system and the amount remaining for use by applications.

message channel A form of interprocess communication found in multitasking operating systems. Interprocess communications allow two programs running in the same computer to share information.

metafile   A file that contains information about other files, particularly those used for data interchange. For example, a graphics metafile contains not only a graphical image of some kind, but also information on how the image should be displayed. This allows the image to be output to a variety of display devices. Metafiles often have the filename extension .MET.

metropolitan area network   Abbreviated MAN. A public high-speed network, operating at 100 megabits per second, capable of voice and data transmission over a distance of up to 50 miles. A MAN is smaller than a wide area network (WAN) but larger than a local area network (LAN).

microcomputer   Any computer based on a single-chip processor. Many of today's microcomputers are as powerful or even more powerful than mainframe computers from a few years ago.

microkernel   An alternative kernel design developed by researchers at Carnegie-Mellon University and implemented in the Mac and Windows NT operating systems.

Traditionally, the kernel has been a monolithic piece of the operating system, resident in memory at all times, taking care of operations as varied as virtual memory management, file input/output, and task scheduling. The microkernel, on the other hand, is a kernel stripped down to the point where it is only concerned with loading, running, and scheduling tasks. All other operating system functions (virtual memory management, disk input/output, and so on) are implemented and managed as tasks running on top of the microkernel.

micron   A unit of measurement. One millionth of a meter, corresponding to approximately 1/25,000 of an inch. The core diameter of fiber-optic network cabling is often specified in terms of microns, 62.5 being a common size.

microprocessor   Often shortened to processor. A CPU on one single chip. The first microprocessor was developed by Intel in 1969. The microprocessors most often used in PCs are the Motorola 680 × 0 series (in the Apple Macintosh computers), and the Intel 80 × 86 family (in IBM and IBM-compatible computers).

Besides computers, microprocessors are used in applications ranging from microwave ovens, VCRs, and automobiles to pocket calculators and laser printers.

Microsoft Diagnostics   A PC diagnostic and technical information program first released along with MS-DOS 6.

MIDI   Pronounced "middy." Acronym for Musical Instrument Digital Interface. A standard protocol that describes communications between computers, synthesizers, and musical instruments.

Instead of transcribing a composition by hand, a musician can play the piece at a piano-style keyboard and record it on a computer as a series of musical messages. These messages include the start of a note, its length, tempo, pitch, attack, and decay time. Once this information is recorded on disk, it can be edited very easily using appropriate software; for example, transposing a piece from one key to another is an easy task for a computer, but a long, laborious task to perform manually.

MIDI port   A port that allows the connection of a Musical Instrument Digital Interface (MIDI) device to a personal computer.

The three types of ports described in the standard are MIDI In, MIDI Out, and MIDI Thru. A synthesizer receives MIDI messages via its MIDI In port and forwards messages to other devices using the MIDI Thru port. A synthesizer can send its own messages to the computer using the MIDI Out port.

milli-   Abbreviated m. A prefix meaning one thousandth in the metric system.

millisecond   Abbreviated ms or msec. A unit of measurement equal to one thousandth of a second. In computing, hard disk and CD-ROM drive access times are often described in terms of milliseconds; the higher the number, the slower the disk system.

millivolt   Abbreviated mv. A unit of measurement equal to one thousandth of a volt.

MIME   Abbreviation for Multipurpose Internet Mail Extensions. A set of extensions that allows Internet e-mail users to add non-ASCII elements such as graphics, PostScript files, audio, or video to their e-mail. Most of the common e-mail client programs include MIME capabilities.

minicomputer   A medium-sized computer system capable of managing more than 100 users simultaneously, suitable for use in a small company or single corporate or government department.

minihard disk   A hard disk mounted on a Type III PCMCIA card.

MIPS   Acronym for million of instructions per second. A measure of the processing speed of a computer's CPU.

MIPS R4000 and R4400   A family of 64-bit microprocessors developed by MIPS Computer Systems. The R4000 has a 1.3 million transistor design, with both an 8K data cache and an 8K instruction cache, as well as a floating-point processor. Internally, the R4000 runs at 100MHz, double its external 50MHz clock output. The R4400, with 2.2 million transistors, is based on the R4000 but has larger cache units (16K data cache and 16K instruction cache) and runs internally at 150MHz, externally at 75MHz.

MMX   A series of 57 commands built into the Pentium II and higher processors from Intel that accelerate processing of multimedia applications.

modem   Contraction of *modulator/demodulator*, a device that allows a computer to transmit information over a telephone line.

The modem translates between the digital signals that the computer uses, and analog signals suitable for transmission over telephone lines. When transmitting, the modem modulates the digital data onto a carrier signal on the telephone line. When receiving, the modem performs the reverse process and demodulates the data from the carrier signal.

Modems usually operate at speeds ranging from 2,400 to about 53,000 bits per second over standard telephone lines and can use even faster rates over leased lines. A suitable communications program is needed to operate the modem. Modems come in internal and external versions; the internal version plugs into an expansion slot inside the computer while the external is connected via a serial cable and sits outside the system.

moderated newsgroup   On the Internet, a Usenet newsgroup or mailing list that is managed by one or more people in an attempt to maintain standards for the newsgroup. All posts to the newsgroup are reviewed by the moderator to make sure that they meet the standards the newsgroup has set for subject and commercial content before being passed on to the whole group. Moderation is not censorship, but an attempt to avoid some of the more extreme antics of those who enjoy flaming and flame wars.

moderator   A person or small committee of people who review the contents of all posts to a Usenet newsgroup or mailing list in an attempt to ensure that the postings meet the standards set by the group. Moderators are almost always volunteers.

modified frequency modulation encoding   Abbreviated MFM encoding. An obsolete method of storing data on a hard disk. Based on an earlier technique known as frequency modulation (FM) encoding, MFM achieves a two-fold increase in data storage density over standard FM recording, but it is not as efficient a space saver as run-length limited encoding.

modulation   In communications, the process used by a modem to add the digital signal onto the carrier signal so that the signal can be transmitted over a telephone line.

The frequency, amplitude, or phase of a signal may be modulated to represent a digital or analog signal.

monitor   A video output device capable of displaying text and graphics, often in color.

monochrome monitor   A monitor that can display text and graphics in one color only. For example, white text on a green background or black text on a white background.

motherboard   The main printed circuit board in a computer that contains the central processing unit, appropriate coprocessor and support chips, device controllers, memory, and also expansion slots to give access to the computer's internal bus.

mouse   A small input device with one or more buttons used for pointing or drawing.

As you move the mouse in any direction, an on-screen mouse cursor follows the mouse movements; all movements are relative. Once the mouse pointer is in the correct position on the screen, you can press one of the mouse buttons to initiate an action or operation; the way a mouse click is interpreted depends on the user interface and the file program.

MS-DOS   Acronym for Microsoft Disk Operating System, pronounced "em-ess-dos." MS-DOS, like other operating systems, allocates system resources such as hard and floppy disks, the monitor, and the printer to the applications programs that need them.

MS-DOS is a single-user, single-tasking operating system, with either a command-line interface or a shell interface.

multilayer   A printed circuit board that contains several layers of circuitry. The layers are laminated together to make a single board, onto which the other discrete components are added.

multimedia   A computer technology that displays information using a combination of full-motion video, animation, sound, graphics, and text with a high degree of user interaction.

multimedia personal computer   Abbreviated MPC. The Multimedia PC Working Group, formerly the Multimedia PC Marketing Council, consisting of several hardware and software vendors, including Microsoft, Zenith Data Systems, Video Seven, Media Vision, and NEC Technologies, sets standards for multimedia PCs and the software that runs on them.

The Council's original Level 1 minimum requirements for a multimedia PC included an 80386SX running at 16MHz, 2MB of memory, a hard disk with 30MB of free space, a CD-ROM capable of a 150K/second transfer rate and an 8-bit sound card.

Level 2 requirements specify an 80486SX running at 25MHz, 8MB of memory, a hard disk with 160MB of free space, a double-speed CD-ROM capable of a 300K/second transfer rate, and a 16-bit sound card.

Level 3 requirements, released in February 1996, require at least a 75MHz Pentium processor, 8MB RAM, 3.5-inch floppy drive, 540MB hard disk, CD-ROM with 250-millisecond access time, 16-bit stereo sound card with 44.1 sample rate, 3-watt speakers, and a video card capable of 30 frames per second with MPEG playback capabilities.

multiplexing   In communications, a technique that transmits several signals over a single communications channel.

Frequency-division multiplexing separates the signals by modulating the data into different carrier frequencies. Time-division multiplexing divides the available time between the various signals. Statistical multiplexing uses statistical techniques to dynamically allocate transmission space depending on the traffic pattern.

multiplexor   Often abbreviated mux. In communications, a device that merges several lower-speed transmission channels into one high-speed channel at one end of the link. Another multiplexor reverses this process at the other end of the link to reproduce the low-speed channels.

multiprocessing   The ability of an operating system to use more than one CPU in a single computer. Symmetrical multiprocessing refers to the operating system's ability to assign tasks dynamically to the next available processor, whereas asymmetrical multiprocessing requires that the original program designer choose the processor to use for a given task at the time of writing the program.

multisync monitor   A monitor designed to detect and adjust to a variety of input signals. By contrast, a fixed-frequency monitor must receive a signal at one specific frequency.

multitasking   The simultaneous execution of two or more programs in one computer.

multithreading   The concurrent processing of several tasks or threads inside the same program. Because several tasks can be processed in parallel, one task does not have to wait for another to finish before starting.

multiuser   Describes a computer system that supports more than one simultaneous user.

DOS, OS/2, Windows, and Windows NT are all single-user operating systems; Unix and its derivatives are all multiuser systems.

nano-   Abbreviated n. A prefix meaning one-billionth.

nanosecond   Abbreviated ns. One-billionth of second. The speed of computer memory and logic chips is measured in nanoseconds.

Processors operating at clock speeds of 25MHz or more need dynamic RAM with access times of faster than 80 nanoseconds (60 nanoseconds is the current speed of choice); static RAM chips can be read in as little as 10 to 15 nanoseconds.

narrowband   In communications, a voice-grade transmission channel of 2400 bits per second or less.

NetBEUI   Acronym for NetBIOS Extended User Interface; pronounced "net-boo-ee." A network device driver for the transport layer supplied with Microsoft operating systems.

NetBIOS   Acronym for Network Basic Input/Output System; pronounced "net-bye-os." In networking, a layer of software, originally developed in 1984 by IBM and Sytek, that links a network operating system with specific network hardware. NetBIOS provides an application program interface (API) with a consistent set of commands for requesting lower-level network services to transmit information from node to node.

Netiquette   A contraction of "network etiquette." The set of unwritten rules governing the use of e-mail, Usenet newsgroups, and other online services.

network   A group of computers and associated peripherals connected by a communications channel capable of sharing files and other resources between several users.

A network can range from a peer-to-peer network connecting a small number of users in an office or department, to a local area network connecting many users over permanently installed cables and dial-up lines, to a wide area network connecting users on several networks spread over a wide geographic area.

network file system   Abbreviated NFS. A distributed file sharing system developed by Sun Microsystems, Inc.

NFS allows a computer on a network to use the files and peripherals of another networked computer as if they were local. NFS is platform-independent and runs on mainframes, minicomputers, RISC-based workstations, diskless workstations, and personal computers. NFS has been licensed and implemented by more than 300 vendors.

network interface card   Abbreviated NIC. In networking, the PC expansion board that plugs into a personal computer or server and works with the network operating system to control the flow of information over the network. The network interface card is connected to the network cabling (twisted-pair, coaxial- or fiber-optic cable), which in turn connects all the network interface cards in the network.

network layer   The third of seven layers of the International Organization for Standardization Open Systems Interconnect (ISO/OSI) model for computer-to-computer communications.

The network layer defines protocols for data routing to ensure that the information arrives at the correct destination node.

newsgroup   A Usenet e-mail group devoted to the discussion of a single topic. Subscribers post articles to the newsgroup that can then be read by all the other subscribers. Newsgroups do not usually contain hard news items.

newsreader   An application used to read the articles posted to Usenet newsgroups.

Newsreaders are of two kinds; threaded newsreaders group the newsgroup posts into threads of related articles, and unthreaded newsreaders simply present the articles in their original order of posting. Of the two types, threaded newsreaders are much more convenient to use.

NeXT   A Unix-based workstation from NeXT, Inc., using a 24MHz Motorola 68040 processor, a high-resolution color display, stereo sound, and an erasable optical disk.

NeXT computers had the reputation for being well manufactured and providing good value for money; however, the hardware part of the company was sold to Canon in 1993, and NeXT now concentrates on marketing the software development environment known as NeXTStep, a windowed, object-oriented programming environment for creating graphics-based applications.

9-track tape   A tape storage format that uses 9 parallel tracks on half-inch reel-to-reel magnetic tape. Eight tracks are used for data, and one track is used for parity information.

node   In communications, any device attached to the network.

noise   In communications, extraneous signals on a transmission channel that degrade the quality or performance of the channel. Noise is often caused by interference from nearby power lines, from electrical equipment, or from spikes in the AC line voltage.

nonimpact printer   Any printer that creates an image without striking a ribbon against the paper.

Nonimpact printers include thermal printers, ink-jet printers, and laser printers. These printers are all much quieter in operation than impact printers, and their main drawback is that they cannot use multi-part paper to make several copies of the same printout or report.

noninterlaced   Describes a monitor in which the display is updated (refreshed) in a single pass, painting every line on the screen. Interlacing takes two passes to paint the screen, painting every other line on the first pass, and then sequentially filling in the other lines on the second pass.

non-preemptive multitasking   Any form of multitasking in which the operating system cannot preempt a running task and process the next task in the queue.

The cooperative multitasking scheme used in Microsoft Windows 3.x is non-preemptive, and the drawback to this method is that although programs are easy to write for this environment, a single badly written program can hog the whole system. By refusing to relinquish the processor, such a program can cause serious problems for other programs running at the same time. Poorly written non-preemptive multitasking can produce a kind of stuttering effect on running applications, depending on how well (or badly) programs behave.

nonvolatile memory   Any form of memory that holds its contents when power is removed. ROM, EPROM, and EEPROM are all nonvolatile memory.

Norton Utilities   A popular package of small utility programs from the Peter Norton Computing Group of Symantec Corporation that run on DOS computers, the Macintosh, and Unix-based systems.

The utilities include UnErase, the famous file-recovery program; Speed Disk, the disk defragmenting program; and Norton Disk Doctor, a program that finds and fixes both logical and physical problems on hard and floppy disks.

notebook computer   A small portable computer, about the size of a computer book, with a flat screen and a keyboard that fold together.

A notebook computer is lighter and smaller than a laptop computer, and recent advances in battery technology allow them to run for as long as 9 hours between charges. Some models use flash memory rather than conventional hard disks for program and data storage; other models offer a range of business applications in ROM. Many offer PCMCIA expansion slots for additional peripherals such as modems, fax modems, or network connections.

NTSC   Abbreviation for National Television System Committee, founded in 1941 to establish broadcast-television standards in North America.

NTSC originally defined a picture composed of 525 horizontal lines, consisting of two separate interlaced fields of 262.5 lines each, refreshed at 30Hz, or 30 times a second. The modern broadcast signal carries more information, including multichannel television sound (MTS) and second audio program (SAP). Many personal computer video controllers can output an NTSC-compatible signal in addition to or instead of their usual monitor signal.

null   A character that has all the binary digits set to zero (ASCII 0) and therefore has no value.

In programming, a null character is used for several special purposes, including padding fields or serving as delimiter characters. In the C language, for example, a null character indicates the end of a character string.

null modem cable   A short RS-232-C cable that connects two personal computers so that they can communicate without the use of modems. The cable connects the two computers' serial ports, and the send and receive lines in the cable are crossed over so that the wires used for sending data by one computer are used for receiving data by the other computer, and vice versa.

numeric keypad   A set of keys to the right of the main part of the keyboard, used for numeric data entry.

object-oriented   A term that can be applied to any computer system, operating system, programming language, application program, or graphical user interface that supports the use of objects.

octet   The Internet's own term for 8 bits or a byte. Some computer systems attached to the Internet have used a byte with more than 8 bits, hence, the need for this term.

OEM   Abbreviation for original equipment manufacturer. The original manufacturer of a hardware subsystem or component. For example, Canon makes the print engine used in many laser printers, including those from Hewlett-Packard; in this case, Canon is the OEM and HP is a value-added reseller (VAR).

offline   Describes a printer or other peripheral that is not currently in ready mode and is therefore unavailable for use.

offline reader   An application that lets you read postings to Usenet newsgroups without having to stay connected to the Internet.

The program downloads all the news-group postings you have not read into your PC and disconnects from your service provider. You can then read the postings at your convenience without incurring online charges or tying up your telephone line. If you reply to any of these postings, the program will automatically upload them to the right newsgroup the next time you connect to your service provider.

off-the-shelf   Describes a ready-to-use hardware or software product that is packaged and ready for sale, as opposed to one that is proprietary or has been customized.

online   **1.** Most broadly, describes any capability available directly on a computer, as in "online help system," or any work done on a computer instead of by more traditional means.

2. Describes a peripheral such as a printer or modem when it is directly connected to a computer and ready to operate.

3. In communications, describes a computer connected to a remote computer over a network or a modem link.

online service   A service that provides an online connection via modem for access to various services. Online services fall into four main groups:

Commercial services   Services such as America Online, CompuServe, and MSN charge a monthly membership fee for access to online forums, e-mail services, software libraries, and online conferences.

Internet   The Internet is a worldwide network of computer systems containing a wealth of information that is easily accessible to most computer users today. To gain access, all one needs is an account with an Internet Service Provider and an Internet browser.

Specialist databases   Specific databases aimed at researchers can be accessed through online services such as Dow Jones News/Retrieval, for business

news, and Lexis and Nexis, the legal information and news archives.

Local bulletin boards   There are thousands of small, local bulletin board systems (BBS), often run from private homes, by local PC users groups or by local schools. Some BBS offer software libraries, e-mail, online conferences, and games, while others may be devoted to a specific subject. Look for listings in local computer-related publications, or ask at your local PC users group.

Exploring the world of online services is a fascinating pastime that can eat up all your spare time; it can also quickly increase your phone bill.

open architecture   A vendor-independent computer design that is publicly available and well understood within the industry. An open architecture allows the user to configure the computer easily by adding expansion cards.

operating system   Abbreviated OS. The software responsible for allocating system resources, including memory, processor time, disk space, and peripheral devices such as printers, modems, and the monitor. All application programs use the operating system to gain access to these system resources as they are needed. The operating system is the first program loaded into the computer as it boots, and it remains in memory at all times thereafter.

Popular PC operating systems include DOS, Windows, and Unix.

optical character recognition   Abbreviated OCR. The computer recognition of printed or typed characters. OCR is usually performed using a standard optical scanner and special software, although some systems use special readers. The text is reproduced just as though it had been typed. Certain advanced systems can resolve neat hand-written characters.

output   Computer-generated information that is displayed on the screen, printed, written to disk or tape, or sent over a communications link to another computer.

packet   Any block of data sent over a network. Each packet contains information about the sender and the receiver and error-control information, in addition to the actual message. Packets may be fixed- or variable-length, and they will be reassembled if necessary when they reach their destination.

packet switching   A data transmission method that simultaneously sends data packets from many sources over the same communications channel or telephone line, thus optimizing use of the line.

paged memory management unit
Abbreviated PMMU. A specialized chip designed to manage virtual memory. High-end processors, such as the Motorola 68030 and 68040 and the Intel 80386, 80486, and later, have all the functions of a PMMU built into the chip itself.

page-mode RAM   A memory-management technique used to speed up the performance of dynamic RAM.

In a page-mode memory system, the memory is divided into pages by specialized dynamic RAM chips. Consecutive accesses to memory addresses in the same page result in a page-mode cycle that takes about half the time of a regular dynamic RAM cycle. For example, a normal dynamic RAM cycle can take from 130 to 180 nanoseconds, but a typical page-mode cycle can be completed in 30 to 40 nanoseconds.

pages per minute   Abbreviated ppm. An approximation of the number of pages that a printer can print in one minute. This number often represents the rate that the printer can reach when printing the simplest output; if you combine text with complex graphics, performance will degrade.

palmtop computer   A very small battery-powered portable computer that you can hold in one hand. Many palmtop computers have small screens and tiny keyboards. A growing number of these come with the Windows CE operating system and scaled-down versions of Microsoft software such as Word and Internet Explorer.

parallel communications   The transmission of information from computer to computer or from computer to a peripheral, in which all the bits that make up the character are transmitted at the same time over a multiline cable.

parallel port   An input/output port that manages information 8 bits at a time, often used to connect a parallel printer.

parallel printer   Any printer that can be connected to the computer using the parallel port.

parallel processing   A computing method that can be performed only on systems containing two or more processors operating simultaneously.

Parallel processing uses several processors, all working on different aspects of the same program at the same time, in order to share the computational load. Parallel processing computers can reach incredible speeds. The Cray X-MP48 peaks at 1000 million floating-point operations per second (1000MFLOPS) using just four extremely powerful processors; parallel-hypercube systems first marketed by Intel can exceed 65,536 processors with possible speeds of up to 262 billion floating-point operations per second (262GFLOPS). What is this mind-boggling speed used for? Applications such as weather forecasting in which the predictive programs can take as long to run as the weather actually takes to arrive, 3-D seismic modeling, and groundwater and toxic flow studies.

parameter RAM   Abbreviated PRAM and pronounced "pee-ram." A small part of the Macintosh RAM that holds information, including the hardware configuration, the date and time, which disk is the startup disk, and information about the state of the desktop. The contents of PRAM are maintained by a battery, and so the contents are not lost when the Mac is turned off or unplugged at the end of your session.

parity   In communications, a simple form of error checking that uses an extra, or redundant, bit, after the data bits but before the stop bit(s).

Parity may be set to odd, even, mark, space, or none. Odd parity indicates that the sum of all the 1 bits in the byte plus the parity bit must be odd. If the total is already odd, the parity bit is set to 0; if it is even, the parity bit is set to 1.

In even parity, if the sum of all the 1 bits is even, the parity bit must be set to 0; if it is odd, the parity bit must be set to 1.

In mark parity, the parity bit is always set to 1, and is used as the eighth bit.

In space parity, the parity bit is set to 0, and is used as the eighth bit.

If parity is set to none, there is no parity bit, and no parity checking is performed.

The parity setting on your computer must match the setting on the remote computer for successful communications. Most online services use no parity and an 8-bit data word.

parity bit   An extra, or redundant, bit used to detect transmission errors.

parity checking   A check mechanism applied to a character or series of characters that uses the addition of extra, or redundant, bits known as parity bits. Parity checking is used in situations as diverse as asynchronous communications and computer memory coordination.

parity error   A mismatch in parity bits that indicates an error in transmitted data.

park   To move the hard disk read/write heads to a safe area of the disk (called a landing zone) before you turn your system off, to guard against damage when the computer is moved. Most of today's hard disks park their heads automatically, and so you do not need to run a special program to park the heads.

partition   A portion of a hard disk that the operating system treats as if it were a separate drive. Information about these partitions, including which of them is the active partition, is contained in the partition table.

partition table   An area of the hard disk containing information on how the disk is organized.

passive-matrix screen   An LCD display mechanism that uses a transistor to control every row of pixels on the screen. This is in sharp contrast to active-matrix screens, in which each individual pixel is controlled by its own transistor. Passive-matrix displays are slower to respond, have weaker colors, and have a narrower viewing angle, but they are much cheaper to make than active-matrix displays.

PC   Abbreviation for personal computer. A computer specifically designed for use by one person at a time, equipped with its own central processing unit, memory, operating system, keyboard and display, hard and floppy disks, as well as other peripherals when needed.

When written in capital letters, the abbreviation usually indicates a computer conforming to the IBM standard rather than a Macintosh computer. The spelled-out capitalized form, Personal Computer, indicates that the computer was made by IBM.

PC Card   A term describing add-in cards that conform to the PCMCIA (Personal Computer Memory Card International Association) standard.

PC Card slot   An opening in the case of a portable computer intended to receive a PC Card; also known as a PCMCIA slot.

PC-DOS   The version of the DOS operating system supplied with PCs sold by IBM.

PC-DOS and MS-DOS started out as virtually identical operating systems, with only a few very minor differences in device driver names and file sizes, but after the release of MS-DOS 6, the two grew much further apart.

PC-DOS 7 was released by IBM in early 1995 and includes the REXX programming language, enhanced PCMCIA support, Stacker file compression, and FILEUP, an application used to synchronize files between portable and desktop PCs.

PCI   Abbreviation for Peripheral Component Interconnect. A specification introduced by Intel that defines a local bus that allows as many as 10 PCI-compliant expansion cards to be plugged into the computer. One of these 10 cards must be the PCI controller card, but the others can include a video card, network interface card, SCSI interface, or any other basic input/output function.

The PCI controller exchanges information with the computer's processor as 32- or 64-bits and allows intelligent PCI adapters to perform certain tasks concurrently with the main processor by using bus mastering techniques.

PCI can operate at a bus speed of 32MHz and can manage a maximum throughput of 132 megabytes per second with a 32-bit data path or 264 megabytes per second with a 64-bit data path.

PCMCIA   Abbreviation for Personal Computer Memory Card International Association. A nonprofit association formed in 1989 with more than 320 members in the computer and electronics industries that developed a standard for credit-card-size plug-in adapters aimed at portable computers.

A PCMCIA adapter card, or PC Card, uses a 68-pin connector, with longer power and ground pins, so they always engage before the signal pins. Several versions of the standard have been approved by PCMCIA:

Type I   The thinnest PC Card, only 3.3mm thick; used for memory enhancements including dynamic RAM, static RAM, and EEPROM.

Type II   A card used for modems or LAN adapters, 5mm thick.

Type III   A 10.5mm card, used for mini-hard disks and other devices that need more space, including wireless LANs.

In theory, although space is always a major consideration, each PCMCIA adapter can support 16 PC Card sockets, and up to 255 adapters can be installed in a PC that follows the PCMCIA standard; in other words, PCMCIA allows for up to 4080 PC Cards on the same computer.

The majority of PCMCIA devices are modems, Ethernet and Token Ring network adapters, dynamic RAM, and flash memory cards, although mini-hard disks, wireless LAN adapters, and SCSI adapters are also available.

PDA   Abbreviation for Personal Digital Assistant. A tiny pen-based palmtop computer that combines fax, e-mail, PCMCIA support, and simple word processing into an easy-to-use unit that fits into a pocket. PDAs are available from several manufacturers, including Apple, Casio, Tandy, Toshiba, Motorola, Sharp, Sony, and AT&T.

pen-based computer   A computer that accepts handwriting as input. Using a pen-like stylus, you print neatly on a screen, and the computer translates this input using pattern recognition techniques. You can also choose selections from on-screen menus using the stylus.

Pentium   A 32-bit microprocessor introduced by Intel in 1993. After losing a courtroom battle to maintain control of the *x*86 designation, Intel named this member of its family the Pentium rather than the 80586 or the 586. The Pentium represents the continuing evolution of the 80486 family of microprocessors and adds several notable features, including 8K instruction code and data caches, built-in floating-point processor and memory management unit, as well as a superscalar design and dual pipelining that allow the Pentium to execute more than one instruction per clock cycle.

Available in a whole range of clock speeds, from 60MHz all the way to 200MHz versions, the Pentium is equivalent to an astonishing 3.1 million transistors, more than twice that of the 80486.

Pentium Pro   A microprocessor in the 80x86 family from Intel. The 32-bit P6 has a 64-bit data path between the processor and cache, and is capable of running at clock speeds up to 200MHz. Unlike the Pentium, the Pentium Pro has its secondary cache built into the CPU itself, rather than on the motherboard, meaning that it accesses cache at internal speed, not bus speed. The Pentium Pro contains the equivalent of 5.5 million transistors.

Pentium II   The Pentium II is a Pentium Pro with MMX technology built in, as well as a 512KB L2 cache and 32KB L1 cache (16KB data and 16KB instruction). The clock speed is currently at 333MHz.

Pentium II Xeon   Same as the Pentium II with the ability to access 64GB of RAM and a 100MHz system bus. The clock speed is currently at 400MHz.

Pentium III   The latest member of the Pentium family. Its features include new floating-point instructions, new registers to speed scientific and engineering calculations, and new multimedia instructions. Clock speeds range from 450MHz to 500MHz.

peripheral   Any hardware device attached to and controlled by a computer, such as a monitor, keyboard, hard disk, floppy disk, CD-ROM drives, printer, mouse, tape drive, and joystick.

permanent swap file   A swap file that, once created, is used over and over again. This file is used in virtual memory operations, where hard disk space is used in place of random-access memory (RAM).

A permanent swap file allows Windows to write information to a known place on the hard disk, which enhances performance over using conventional methods with a temporary swap file. The Windows permanent

swap file consists of a large number of consecutive contiguous clusters; it is often the largest single file on the hard disk, and of course this disk space cannot be used by any other application. If you have plenty of unused hard disk space, consider a permanent swap file to boost performance. If disk space is at a premium, use a temporary swap file to conserve disk space, at the cost of a slight loss in performance.

peta-   Abbreviated P. A prefix for 1 quadrillion, or 10^{15}. In computing, based on the binary system, peta has the value of 1,125,899,906,842,624, or the power of 2 (2^{50}) closest to 1 quadrillion.

petabyte   Abbreviated PB. Although it can represent 1 quadrillion bytes (10^{15}), it usually refers to 1,125,899,906,842,624 bytes (2^{50}).

phosphor   The special electrofluorescent coating used on the inside of a CRT screen that glows for a few milliseconds when struck by an electron beam. Because the illumination is so brief, it must be refreshed constantly to maintain an image.

Photo CD   A specification from Kodak that allows you to record and then display photographic images on CD. Originally, only single-session recordings could be made. However, several CD-ROM players are now compatible with multi-session Photo CD, where images can be loaded onto the CD several times over several different recording sessions.

physical drive   A real device in the computer that you can see or touch, rather than a logical drive, which is a part of the hard disk that functions as if it were a separate disk drive but is not. One physical drive may be divided into several logical drives.

physical layer   The first and lowest of the seven layers in the International Organization for Standardization Open Systems Interconnect (ISO/OSI) model for computer-to-computer communications. The physical layer defines the physical, electrical, mechanical, and functional procedures used to connect the equipment.

pica   A unit of measure used to measure type size. One pica (12 points) is equivalent to 1/6 inch.

pincushion distortion   A type of distortion that usually occurs at the edges of a video screen where the sides of an image seem to bow inward.

pipelining   1. In processor architecture, a method of fetching and decoding instructions that ensures that the processor never needs to wait; as soon as an instruction is executed, another is waiting.

2. In parallel processing, the method used to pass instructions from one processing unit to another.

pixel   Contraction of *pic*ture *el*ement. The smallest element that display software can use to create text or graphics. A display resolution described as being 640 by 480 has 640 pixels across the screen and 480 down the screen, for a total of 307,200 pixels. The higher the number of pixels, the higher the screen resolution.

A monochrome pixel can have two values, black or white, and this can be represented by one bit as either zero or one. At the other end of the scale, true color, capable of displaying approximately 16.7 million colors, requires 24 bits of information for each pixel.

platter   The actual disk inside a hard disk enclosure that carries the magnetic recording material. Many hard disks have multiple platters, most of which have two sides that can be used for recording data.

plotter   A peripheral used to draw high-resolution charts, graphs, layouts, and other line-based diagrams, and often used with CAD (computer aided design) systems. Plotters generally print very large documents up to 36 inches wide as opposed to 11 inches wide for a laser printer.

Plug and Play   Abbreviated PnP. A standard from Compaq, Microsoft, Intel, and Phoenix that defines automatic techniques designed to make PC configuration simple and straightforward. Currently, ISA and PCI expansion boards are covered by the specification, but the standard may soon also cover SCSI and PCMCIA buses.

PnP adapters contain configuration information stored in nonvolatile memory, which includes vendor information, serial number, and checksum information. The PnP chipset allows each adapter to be isolated, one at a time, until all cards have been properly identified by the operating system.

PnP requires BIOS changes so that cards can be isolated and identified at boot time; when you insert a new card, the BIOS should perform an auto-configuration sequence enabling the new card with appropriate settings. New systems with flash BIOS will be easy to change; older systems with ROM BIOS will need a hardware change before they can take advantage of PnP.

Plug and Pray   What most of us will do when our Plug-and-Play systems do not work automatically.

plug-compatible   Describes any hardware device designed to work in exactly the same way as a device manufactured by a different company.

For example, external modems are plug-compatible, in that you can replace one with another without changing the cabling or connector.

POP3   A protocol used for receiving e-mail on a TCP/IP network. In a POP3 environment, your mail is received at a POP3 server and held there until you connect and download the mail.

port   1. A physical connection, such as a serial port or a parallel port.

2. To move a program or an operating system from one hardware platform to another. For example, Windows NT portability refers to the fact that the same operating system can run on both Intel and RISC architectures.

3. A number used to identify a specific Internet application (location).

post An individual article or e-mail message sent to a Usenet newsgroup or to a mailing list, rather than to a specific individual. Post can also refer to the process of sending the article to the newsgroup.

posting The process of sending an individual article or e-mail message to a Usenet newsgroup or to a mailing list.

PostScript A page-description language developed by Adobe Systems, Inc., used for designing and printing one kind of high-quality text and graphics. Desktop publishing or illustration programs that create PostScript output can print on any PostScript printer or imagesetter, because PostScript is hardware independent. An interpreter in the printer translates the PostScript commands into commands that the printer can understand. This means that you can create your document and then take it to any print shop with a PostScript printer to make the final printed output.

PostScript uses English-like commands to scale outline fonts and control the page layout; because of this, users have a great deal of flexibility when it comes to font specification.

PostScript printer A printer that can interpret PostScript page-description language commands. Because the PostScript page-description language is complex and computer intensive, PostScript printers often contain as much computing power as the PC you originally used to create the output, and they are often much more expensive than standard printers.

power-on self test Abbreviated POST. A set of diagnostic programs, loaded from ROM, designed to ensure that the major system components are present and operating. If a problem is found, the POST software writes an error message in the screen, sometimes with a diagnostic code number indicating the type of fault located. These POST tests execute before any attempt is made to load the operating system.

PowerPC A family of microprocessors jointly developed by Apple, Motorola, and IBM. The 32-bit 601 houses 2.8 million transistors, runs at 110MHz, and is designed for use in high-performance, low-cost PCs. The 66MHz 602 is targeted at the consumer electronics and entry-level computer markets. The low-wattage 603e is aimed at battery-powered computers, the 604 is for high-end PCs and workstations, and the top-of-the-line 620 is designed for servers and very high-performance applications. The 620 is a 64-bit chip.

PCs based on the PowerPC chip usually include a minimum of 16MB of memory, a 540MB hard disk, PCI bus architecture including a local-bus-based graphics adapter, and a CD-ROM.

power supply A part of the computer that converts the AC power from a wall outlet into DC in the lower voltages (typically 5 to 12 volts DC) required internally in the computer. PC power supplies are usually rated in watts, ranging from 200 watts at the low end to 300 watts at the high end. The power supply is one of the main sources of heat in a computer and usually requires a fan to provide additional ventilation; it is also a sealed unit with no operator-serviceable parts, and you should make sure it stays that way.

power surge A brief but sudden increase in line voltage, often destructive, usually caused by a nearby electrical appliance such as a photocopier or elevator, or when power is reapplied after an outage.

power user A person who is proficient with many software packages and who understands how to put the computer to work quickly and effectively. While not necessarily a programmer, a power user is familiar with creating and using macros and other command languages.

PPP Abbreviation for Point-to-Point Protocol. One of the most common protocols used to connect a PC to an Internet host via high-speed modem and a telephone line.

PPP establishes a temporary but direct connection to an Internet host, eliminating the need for connecting to an interim system. PPP also provides a method of automatically assigning an IP address, so that remote or mobile systems can connect to the network at any point.

preemptive multitasking   A form of multitasking in which the operating system executes an application for a specific period of time, according to its assigned priority. At that time, it is preempted, and another task is given access to the CPU for its allocated time. Although an application can give up control before its time is up, such as during input/output waits, no task is ever allowed to execute for longer than its allotted time period. Unix, Windows, Windows NT, and Windows 2000 all use preemptive multitasking.

presentation layer   The sixth of seven layers of the International Organization for Standardization Open Systems Interconnect (ISO/OSI) model for computer-to-computer communications. The presentation layer defines the way that data is formatted, presented, converted, and encoded.

primary DOS partition   In DOS, a division of the hard disk that contains important operating system files.

printed-circuit board   Abbreviated PCB. Any flat board made of plastic or fiberglass that contains chips and other electronic components. Many PCBs are multilayer boards with several sets of copper traces connecting components together.

printer   A computer peripheral that presents computer output as a printed image on paper or film.

Printers vary considerably in price, speed, resolution, noise level, convenience, paper-handling abilities, printing mechanism, and quality, and all of these points should be considered when making a selection.

printer emulation   The ability of a printer to change modes so that it behaves just like a printer from another manufacturer.

Many dot-matrix printers offer an Epson printer emulation in addition to their own native mode. This means you can use the printer as an Epson printer just by changing some switches—a useful feature if the software you are using does not have a device driver for your printer, but does have the appropriate Epson driver. Many non-HP laser printers support an HP LaserJet emulation.

printhead   That part of a printer that creates the printed image. In a dot-matrix printer, the printhead contains the small pins that strike the ribbon to create the image, and in an ink-jet printer, the printhead contains the jets used to create the ink droplets as well as the ink reservoirs. A laser printer creates images using an electrophotographic method similar to that found in photocopiers and does not have a printhead.

privileged mode   An operating mode supported in protected mode in 80286 (or later) processors that allows the operating system and certain classes of device driver to manipulate parts of the system including memory and input/output ports.

PRN   In DOS, the logical device name for a printer, usually the first parallel port, which is also known as LPT1.

process   In a multitasking operating system, a program or a part of a program.

program   A sequence of instructions that a computer can execute. Synonymous with software.

programmable   Capable of being programmed. The fact that a computer is programmable is what sets it apart from all other instruments that use microprocessors; it is truly a general-purpose machine.

PROM   Acronym for programmable read-only memory, pronounced "prom." A chip used when developing firmware. A PROM can be programmed and tested in the lab, and when the firmware is complete, it can be transferred to a ROM for manufacturing.

protected mode   In Intel 80286 and higher processors, an operating state that supports advanced features.

Protected mode in these processors provides hardware support for multitasking and virtual memory management, and prevents programs from accessing blocks of memory that belong to other executing programs.

In 16-bit protected mode, supported on 80286 and higher processors, the CPU can directly address a total of 16MB of memory; in 32-bit protected mode, supported on 80386 and higher processors, the CPU can address up to 4GB of memory.

Windows and most versions of Unix that run on these processors execute in protected mode.

protocol   In networking and communications, the specification that defines the procedures to follow when transmitting and receiving data. Protocols define the format, timing, sequence, and error-checking systems used.

protocol stack   In networking and communications, the several layers of software that define the computer-to-computer or computer-to-network protocol. For example, the protocol stack on a Novell NetWare system will be different from that used on a Banyan VINES network.

public-domain software   Software that is freely distributed to anyone who wants to use, copy, or distribute it.

Pulse Code Modulation   Abbreviated PCM. A method used to convert an analog signal into noise-free digital data that can be stored and manipulated by computer. PCM takes an 8-bit sample of a 4kHz bandwidth 8000 times a second, which gives 16K of data per second. PCM is often used in multimedia applications.

quadrature amplitude modulation   A data-encoding technique used by modems operating at 2400 bits per second or faster.

Quadrature amplitude modulation is a combination of phase and amplitude change that can encode multiple bits on a single carrier signal. For example, the CCITT V.42 bis standard uses four phase changes and two amplitude changes to create 16 different signal changes.

quarter-inch cartridge   Abbreviated QIC. A set of tape standards defined by the Quarter-Inch Cartridge Drive Standards, a trade association established in 1987.

queue   Pronounced "Q." A temporary list of items waiting for a particular service. An example is the print queue of documents waiting to be printed on a network print server; the first document received in the queue is the first to be printed.

QWERTY keyboard   Pronounced "kwertee." The standard typewriter and computer keyboard layout, named for the first six keys at the top left of the alphabetic keyboard.

quoting   To include a relevant portion of someone else's article when posting a follow-up to a Usenet newsgroup or online forum. It is considered poor Netiquette to quote more of the original post than is absolutely necessary to make your point.

radio frequency interference   Abbreviated RFI. Many electronic devices, including computers and peripherals, can interfere with other signals in the radio-frequency range by producing electromagnetic radiation; this is normally regulated by government agencies in each country.

RAID   Acronym for Redundant Array of Inexpensive Disks. In networking and truly critical applications, a method of using several hard disk drives in an array to provide fault tolerance in the event that one or more drives fail catastrophically.

The different levels of RAID, 0 through 5, are each designed for a specific use; each having its own advantages in a particular situation. The correct level of RAID for your installation depends on how you use your network.

RAM   Acronym for random access memory. The main system memory in a computer, used for the operating system, application programs, and data.

RAM chip   A semiconductor storage device, either dynamic RAM or static RAM.

RAM disk   Used in older operating systems such as DOS, a RAM disk is an area of memory managed by a special device driver and used as a simulated disk.

Because the RAM disk operates in memory, it works very quickly, much faster than a regular hard disk. Remember that anything you store on your RAM disk will be erased when you turn your computer off, so you must save its contents onto a real disk first. RAM disks may also be called virtual drives.

random access   Describes the ability of a storage device to go directly to the required memory address without having to read from the beginning every time data is requested.

There is nothing random or haphazard about random access; a more precise term is direct access. Unfortunately, the word "random" is used as part of the abbreviation RAM and is obviously here to stay. In a random access device, the information can be read directly by accessing the appropriate memory address. Some storage devices, such as tapes, must start at the beginning to find a specific storage location, and if the information is toward the end of the tape, access can take a long time. This access method is known as "sequential access."

raster device   A device that manages an image as lines of dots. Television sets and most computer displays are raster devices, as are some electrostatic printers and plotters.

read   To copy program or data files from a floppy or a hard disk into computer memory; to run the program or process the data in some way. The computer may also read your commands and data input from the keyboard.

README file   A text file placed on a set of distribution disks by the manufacturer at the last minute that may contain important information not contained in the program manuals or online help system. You should always look for a README file when installing a new program on your system; it may contain information pertinent to your specific configuration.

The filename may vary slightly; READ .ME, README.TXT, and README.DOC are all used. README files do not contain any formatting commands, so you can look at them using any word processor.

read-only   Describes a file or other collection of information that may only be read; it may not be updated in any way or deleted.

Certain important operating system files are designated as read-only files to prevent you from deleting them by accident. Also, certain types of memory (ROM) and certain devices such as CD-ROM can be read but not changed.

read-only attribute   A file attribute that indicates the file can be read but cannot be updated or changed in any way; nor can you delete the file.

read/write head   That part of a floppy or hard disk system that reads and writes data to and from a magnetic disk.

reboot   To restart the computer and reload the operating system, usually after a crash.

Red Book audio   The standard definition of compact disc digital audio as a 16-bit stereo pulse code modulation waveform at 44.1kHz. So called because of the cover color used when the definition was first published.

reduced instruction set computing   Abbreviated RISC, pronounced "risk." A processor that recognizes only a limited number of assembly-language instructions.

RISC chips are relatively cheap to produce and debug, as they usually contain fewer than 128 instructions. CISC (complex instruction set computing) processors use a richer set of instructions, typically somewhere between 200 to 300. RISC processors are commonly used in workstations and can be designed to run up to 70 percent faster than CISC processors.

reformat   To reinitialize a disk and destroy the original contents.

refresh   **1.** In a monitor, to recharge the phosphors on the inside of the screen and maintain the image.

2. In certain memory systems, dynamic RAM must be recharged so that it continues to hold its contents.

refresh rate   In a monitor, the rate at which the phosphors that create the image on the screen are recharged.

Registry   In Windows, the Registry is the heart of the system. It is a database that contains all user, software, and machine settings. Everything that is done on the computer requires the Registry for configuration.

relative addressing   In programming, the specification of a memory location by using an expression to calculate the address, rather than explicitly specifying the location by using its address.

removable mass storage   Any high-capacity storage device inserted into a drive for reading and writing, then removed for storage and safekeeping. This term is not usually applied to floppy disks, but to tape- and cartridge-backup systems and to Bernoulli boxes.

rendering   In computer graphics, the conversion of an outline image into a fully formed, three-dimensional image, by the addition of colors and shading.

repeater   In networking, a simple hardware device that moves all packets from one local area network segment to another. The main purpose of a repeater is to extend the length of the network transmission medium beyond the normal maximum cable lengths.

Repetitive stress injury   Abbreviated RSI. A common group of work-related injuries. Computer operators performing repetitive tasks can suffer pins-and-needles and loss of feeling in their wrists and hands, and pains in their shoulders and necks. Carpal tunnel syndrome, common among people who use a keyboard all day, is one form of RSI.

reserved word   Any word that has a special meaning and therefore cannot be used for any other purpose in the same context. For example, the words that make up a computer language (if, printf, putchar), and certain device names in an operating system (COM1, LPT1), are all different kinds of reserved word.

reset button   The small button on the front of many computers used to reboot the computer without turning off the power.

resolution   The degree of sharpness of a printed or displayed image, often expressed in dpi (dots per inch).

Resolution depends on the number of elements that make up the image, either dots on a laser printer or pixels on a monitor; the higher the number per inch, the higher the resolution of the image appears.

resource   Any part of a computer system that can be used by a program as it runs. This can include memory, hard and floppy disks, and printers.

In some programming environments, items such as dialog boxes, bitmaps, and fonts are considered resources, and they can be used by several application programs without requiring any internal changes to the programs.

response time   The time lag between sending a request and receiving the data. Response time can be applied to a complete computer system, as in the time taken to look up a certain customer record, or to a system component, as in the time taken to access a specific cluster on disk.

reverse engineering   The process of disassembling a hardware or software product from another company to find out how it works, with the intention of duplicating some or all of its functions in another product.

reverse video   In a monochrome monitor, a display mode used to highlight characters on the screen by reversing the normal background and foreground colors; for example, if the normal mode is to show green characters on a black background, reverse video displays black characters on a green background.

RGB   Abbreviation for red-green-blue. A method of generating colors in a video system that uses the additive primaries method. Percentages of red, blue, and green are mixed to form the colors; 0 percent of the colors creates black, 100 percent of all three colors creates white.

RGB monitor   A color monitor that accepts separate inputs for red, blue, and green color signals and normally produces a sharper image than composite color monitors, in which information for all three colors is transmitted together.

ring network   A network topology in the form of a closed loop or circle.

RJ-11/RJ-45   Short for registered jack, RJs are commonly used modular telephone connectors. RJ-11 is a 4- or 6-pin connector used in most connections destined for voice use. RJ-45 is the 8-pin connector used for data transmission over twisted-pair wiring.

ROM   Acronym for read-only memory. A semiconductor-based memory system that stores information permanently and does not lose its contents when power is switched off. ROM is used for firmware such as the BIOS in the PC; in some portable computers, application programs and even the operating system are being stored in ROM.

root directory   In a hierarchical directory structure, the directory from which all other directories must branch.

The root directory is created by the FORMAT command and can contain files as well as other directories. It is wise to store as few files as possible in the root directory, because the number of entries (files or directories) that the root directory can hold is limited to 512 in most operating systems. Also, you cannot delete the root directory.

The backslash (\) character represents the root directory, and you can use this character to make the root directory the current directory in a single step, if you type **CD ** from the system prompt.

roping   In a monitor, a form of image distortion that gives solid straight lines a twisted or helical appearance. This problem is caused by poor convergence.

ROT-13   A simple encryption scheme often used to scramble posts to Usenet newsgroups. ROT-13 makes the article unreadable until the text is decoded and is often used when the subject matter might be considered offensive. Many newsreaders have a built-in command to unscramble ROT-13 text, and if you use it, don't be surprised by what you read; if you think you might be offended, don't decrypt the post.

router   In networking, an intelligent connecting device that can send packets to the correct local area network segment to take them to their destination. Routers link local area network segments at the network layer of the International Organization for Standardization Open Systems Interconnect (ISO/OSI) model for computer-to-computer communications.

RS-422/423/449   In asynchronous transmissions, a recommended standard interface established by the Electrical Industries Association for distances greater than 50 feet but less than 1000 feet. The standard defines the specific lines, timing, and signal characteristics used between the computer and the peripheral device.

RS(recommended standard)- 449 incorporates RS-422 and RS-423; serial ports on Macintosh computers are RS-422 ports.

RS-232-C In asynchronous transmissions, a recommended standard interface established by the Electrical Industries Association. The standard defines the specific lines, timing, and signal characteristics used between the computer and the peripheral device and uses a 25-pin or 9-pin DB connector.

RS-232-C is used for serial communications between a computer and a peripheral such as a printer, modem, digitizing tablet, or mouse. The maximum cable limit of 50 feet can be extended by using very high quality cable, line drivers to boost the signal, or short-haul modems.

RS is the abbreviation for recommended standard, and the C denotes the third revision of that standard. RS-232-C is functionally identical to the CCITT V.24 standard.

RTS Abbreviation for request to send. A hardware signal defined by the RS-232-C standard to request permission to transmit.

run-length limited encoding Abbreviated RLL encoding. An efficient method of storing information on a hard disk that effectively doubles the storage capacity of a disk when compared with older, less efficient methods such as modified frequency modulation encoding (MFM).

RXD Abbreviation for receive data. A hardware signal defined by the RS-232-C standard to carry data from one device to another.

save To transfer information from the computer's memory to a more permanent storage medium such as a hard disk.

As you work with your computer, you should save your work every few minutes. Otherwise, if you suffer a power failure or a severe program error, all your work will be lost because it is stored in memory, which is volatile, and when the power is removed, the contents of memory are lost.

scan code In IBM-compatible computers, a code number generated when a key on the keyboard is pressed or released. Each key

and shifted key is assigned a unique code that the computer's BIOS translates into its ASCII equivalent.

scanner An optical device used to digitize images such as line art or photographs so that they can be merged with text by a page-layout or desktop publishing program or incorporated into a CAD drawing.

SCSI Acronym for Small Computer System Interface, pronounced "scuzzy." A high-speed, system-level parallel interface defined by the ANSI X3T9.2 committee. SCSI is used to connect a personal computer to several peripheral devices using just one port. Devices connected in this way are said to be "daisy-chained" together, and each device must have a unique identifier or priority number.

Today, SCSI is often used to connect hard disks, tape drives, CD-ROM drives, and other mass storage media, as well as scanners and printers.

SCSI bus Another name for the SCSI interface and communications protocol.

SCSI terminator The SCSI interface must be correctly terminated to prevent signals echoing on the bus. Many SCSI devices have built-in terminators that engage when they are needed; with some older SCSI devices you have to add an external SCSI terminator that plugs into the device's SCSI connector.

sector The smallest unit of storage on a disk, usually 512 bytes. Sectors are grouped together into clusters.

seek time The length of time required to move a disk drive's read/write head to a particular location on the disk. The major part of a hard disk's access time is actually seek time.

segmented addressing An addressing scheme used in Intel processors that divides the address space into logical pieces called segments.

To access any given address, a program must specify the segment and also an offset within that segment. This addressing method is sometimes abbreviated to "segment:offset" and is used in Intel processors in real mode; most other processors use a single flat address space.

semaphore   In programming, an interprocess communication signal that indicates the status of a shared system resource, such as shared memory.

Event semaphores allow a thread to tell other threads that an event has occurred and that it is safe for them to resume execution. Mutual exclusion (mutex) semaphores protect system resources such as files, data, and peripherals from simultaneous access by several processes. Multiple wait (muxwait) semaphores allow threads to wait for multiple events to take place or for multiple resources to become free.

semiconductor   A material that is halfway between a conductor (which conducts electricity) and an insulator (which resists electricity), whose electrical behavior can be precisely controlled by the addition of impurities called dopants.

The most commonly used semiconductors are silicon and germanium, and when electrically charged, they change their state from conductive to nonconductive or from nonconductive to conductive. Semiconductor wafers can be manufactured to create a whole variety of electronic devices; in personal computers, semiconductors are used in the processor, memory, and many other chips.

Easily the most significant semiconductor device is the transistor, which acts like an on/off switch and is incorporated into today's microprocessors by the millions.

serial communications   The transmission of information from computer to computer or from computer to peripheral, one bit at a time.

Serial communications can be synchronous and controlled by a clock, or they can be asynchronous and coordinated by start and stop bits embedded in the data stream.

It is important to remember that both the sending and the receiving devices must use the same baud rate, parity setting, and other communications parameters.

serial mouse   A mouse that attaches directly to one of the computer's serial ports.

serial port   A computer input/output port that supports serial communications, in which information is processed one bit at a time.

RS-232-C is a common serial protocol used by computers when communicating with modems, printers, mice, and other peripherals.

serial printer   A printer that attaches to one of the computer's serial ports.

server   In networking, any computer that makes access to files, printing, communications, or other services available to users of the network. In large networks, a server may run a special network operating system; in smaller installations, a server may run a personal computer operating system.

service provider   A general term used to describe those companies providing a connection to the Internet for private and home users. Several of the online services such as CompuServe and America Online are providing access to the Internet as a part of their basic services.

session layer   The fifth of seven layers of the International Organization for Standardization Open Systems Interconnect (ISO/OSI) model for computer-to-computer communications. The session layer coordinates communications and maintains the session for as long as it is needed, performing security, logging, and administrative functions.

settling time   The time it takes a disk's read/write head to stabilize once it has moved to the correct part of the disk. Settling time is measured in milliseconds.

setup string   A short group of text characters sent to a printer, modem, or monitor, to invoke a particular mode of operation.

SGML   Abbreviation for Standard Generalized Markup Language. A standard (ISO 8879) for defining the structure and managing the contents of any digital document. HTML (Hypertext Markup Language), used in many World Wide Web documents on the Internet, is a part of SGML.

shadow memory   In PCs based on the 80386 (or later) processor, the technique of copying the contents of the BIOS ROM into faster RAM when the computer first boots up; also known as shadow RAM or shadow ROM.

RAM is usually two to three times faster than ROM, and the speedier access cuts down the time required to read a memory address so that the processor spends more time working and less time waiting.

shared memory   An interprocess communications technique in which the same memory is accessed by more than one program running in a multitasking operating system. Semaphores or other management elements prevent the applications from "colliding," or trying to update the same information at the same time.

shareware   A form of software distribution that makes copyrighted programs freely available on a trial basis; if you like the program and use it, you are expected to register your copy and send a small fee to the program creator. Once your copy is registered, you might receive a more complete manual, technical support, access to the programmer's bulletin board, or information about upgrades. You can download shareware from the Internet and from many bulletin boards and online services including CompuServe, and it is often available from your local PC user group.

silicon   A semiconductor material used in many electronic devices. Silicon is a very common element found in almost all rocks and in beach sand that, when "doped" with chemical impurities, becomes a semiconductor. Large cylinders of silicon are cut into wafers and then etched with a pattern of minute electrical circuits to form a silicon chip.

Silicon Valley   A nickname for the area around Palo Alto and Sunnyvale in the Santa Clara Valley region of Northern California, noted for the number of high-technology hardware and software companies located there.

single-density disk   A floppy disk that is certified for recording with frequency modulation encoding. Single-density disks have been superseded by double-density disks and high-density disks.

single in-line memory module   Abbreviated SIMM. Individual RAM chips are soldered or surface mounted onto small, narrow circuit boards called carrier modules, which can be plugged into sockets on the motherboard. These carrier modules are simple to install and occupy less space than conventional memory modules.

single in-line package   Abbreviated SIP. A plastic housing containing an electronic component with a single row of pins or connections protruding from one side of the package.

16-bit color   A method of representing a graphical image as a bitmap containing 65,536 different colors.

68000   A family of 32-bit microprocessors from Motorola, used in Macintosh computers and many advanced workstations.

The 68000 uses a linear addressing mode to access memory, rather than the segmented addressing scheme used by popular microprocessors from Intel; this makes it more popular with programmers.

6845   An early programmable video controller chip from Motorola, used in IBM's Monochrome Display Adapter (MDA) and Color/Graphics Adapter (CGA). Because of the extensive use of the 6845, later and more capable video adapters like the EGA contained circuitry to emulate the functions of the 6845.

SLIP   Acronym for Serial Line Internet Protocol. A communications protocol used over serial lines or dial-up connections. SLIP has been almost entirely replaced by PPP because it lacks a great deal of the functionality that PPP provides.

SMARTDRV.SYS   The DOS device driver that provides compatibility for hard-disk controllers that cannot work with EMM386 and Windows 3.x running in enhanced mode. Use the DEVICE command to load this device driver in CONFIG.SYS.

This command does not load the DOS disk cache; use the SMARTDRV command for that. Neither SMARTDRV.SYS or command files are used with Windows 95 or later operating systems.

socket services   Part of the software support needed for PCMCIA (Personal Computer Memory Card International Association) hardware devices in a portable computer, controlling the interface to the hardware.

Socket services is the lowest layer in the software that manages PCMCIA cards. It provides a BIOS-level software interface to the hardware, effectively hiding the specific details from higher levels of software. Socket services also detect when you insert or remove a PCMCIA card and identify the type of card it is.

software   An application program or an operating system that a computer can execute. Software is a broad term that can imply one or many programs, and it can also refer to applications that may actually consist of more than one program.

SOHO   Abbreviation for small office/ home office. That portion of the market for computer services occupied by small offices and home-based businesses rather than the large corporate buyers. SOHO is a growing market sector characterized by well-informed buyers.

Millions of Americans run a small business or work from home. This is a result of many factors in the economy, including corporate downsizing and cheaper and more

capable computers and office equipment, and is a trend that is likely to continue.

Solaris   A Unix-based operating system from SunSoft that runs on Intel processors and supports a graphical user interface, e-mail, the Network File System, and Network Information Service. Solaris brings a common look and feel to both SPARC and Intel platforms.

sound board   An add-in expansion board for the PC that allows you to produce audio output of high-quality recorded voice, music, and sounds through headphones or external speakers. In the Macintosh, digital stereo sound reproduction is built into the system.

Almost all multimedia applications take advantage of a sound board if one is present; the MPC Level 2 specification requires the inclusion of a 16-bit sound card.

source   The disk, file, or document from which information is moved or copied.

source code   The original human-readable version of a program, written in a particular programming language, before the program is compiled or interpreted into a machine-readable form.

spaghetti code   A slang expression used to describe any badly designed or poorly structured program that is as hard to unravel (and understand) as a bowl of spaghetti.

SPARC   Acronym for Scalar Processor ARChitecture. A 32-bit RISC processor from Sun Microsystems.

SPARCstation   A family of Unix workstations from Sun Microsystems, based on the SPARC processor. SPARCstations range from small, diskless desktop systems to high-performance, tower SPARCservers in multiprocessor configurations.

special interest group   Abbreviated SIG. A group that meets to share information about a specific topic—hardware, application software, programming languages, even operating systems. A SIG is often part of a larger organization such as a users group or the ACM (Association for Computing Machinery).

stack   A reserved area of memory used to keep track of a program's internal operations, including functions' return addresses, passed parameters, and so on. A stack is usually maintained as a "last in, first out" (LIFO) data structure, so the last item added to the structure is the first item used.

stand-alone   Describes a system designed to meet specific individual needs that does not rely on or assume the presence of any other components to complete the assigned task.

star network   A network topology in the form of a star. At the center of the star is a wiring hub or concentrator, and the nodes or workstations are arranged around the central point representing the points of the star. Wiring costs tend to be higher for star networks than for other configurations, as very little cable is shared; each node requires its own individual cable.

start bit   In asynchronous transmissions, a start bit is transmitted to indicate the beginning of a new data word.

static RAM   Abbreviated SRAM, pronounced "ess-ram." A type of computer memory that retains its contents as long as power is supplied; it does not need constant refreshment like dynamic RAM chips. A static RAM chip can store only about one-fourth of the information that a dynamic RAM of the same complexity can hold.

Static RAM, with access times of 15 to 30 nanoseconds, is much faster than dynamic RAM, at 60 nanoseconds or more, and is often used in caches; however, static RAM is four to five times as expensive as dynamic RAM.

S3 86Cxxx   A family of fixed-function graphics accelerator chips from S3 Corporation. These chips, the 86C801, 86C805, 86C924, and 86C928, are used in many of the accelerated graphics adapters that speed up Windows' video response.

stop bit(s)   In asynchronous transmissions, stop bits are transmitted to indicate the end of the current data word. Depending on the convention in use, one or two stop bits are used.

streaming tape   A high-speed tape backup system, often used to make a complete backup of an entire hard disk.

A streaming tape is designed to optimize throughput so that time is never wasted by stopping the tape during a backup; this also means that the computer and backup software also have to be fast enough to keep up with the tape drive.

stylus   A pen-like pointing device used in pen-based systems and personal digital assistants.

substrate   The base material used in the construction of a disk, tape, printed circuit board, or integrated circuit.

supercomputer   The most powerful class of computer. The term was first applied to the Cray-1 computer. Supercomputers can cost more than $50 million each. They are used for tasks such as weather forecasting, complex three-dimensional modeling, and oil reservoir modeling.

superscalar   A microprocessor architecture that contains more than one execution unit, or pipeline, allowing the processor to execute more than one instruction per clock cycle.

For example, the Pentium processor is superscalar and has two side-by-side pipelines for integer instructions. The processor determines whether an instruction can be executed in parallel with the next instruction in line. If it doesn't detect any dependencies, the two instructions are executed.

SuperVGA   Abbreviated SVGA. An enhancement to the Video Graphics Adapter (VGA) video standard defined by the Video Electronics Standards Association (VESA).

SuperVGA video adapters can display at least 800 pixels horizontally and 600 vertically (the VESA-recommended standard), and up to 1600 horizontally and 1200 vertically, with 16; 256; 32,767; or 16,777,216 colors displayed simultaneously. Most SuperVGA boards contain several megabytes of video RAM for increased performance.

surface mount technology   Abbreviated SMT. A manufacturing technology in which integrated circuits are attached directly to the printed circuit board, rather than being soldered into pre-drilled holes in the board. This process also allows electronic components to be mounted on both sides of a board.

surge   A sudden and often destructive increase in line voltage. A regulating device known as a surge suppressor or surge protector can protect computer equipment against surges.

surge suppressor   Also known as a surge protector. A regulating device placed between the computer and the AC line connection that protects the computer system from power surges.

swap file   On a hard disk, a file used to store parts of running programs that have been swapped out of memory temporarily to make room for other running programs.

A swap file may be permanent, always occupying the same amount of hard disk space even though the application that created it may not be running, or temporary, only being created as and when needed.

swapping   The process of exchanging one item for another. In a virtual memory system, swapping occurs when a program requests a virtual memory location that is not currently in memory; the information is then read from disk and displaces old information held in memory.

Swapping may also refer to changing floppy disks as needed when using two disks in a single floppy disk drive.

synchronization   The timing of separate elements or events to occur simultaneously.

1. In a multimedia presentation, synchronization ensures that the audio and video components are timed correctly and so actually make sense.

2. In computer-to-computer communications, the hardware and software must be synchronized so that file transfers can take place.

3. The process of updating files on both a portable computer and a desktop system so that they both have the latest versions is also known as synchronization.

synchronous transmission   In communications, a transmission method that uses a clock signal to regulate data flow. Synchronous transmissions do not use start and stop bits.

system area   The part of a disk that contains the partition table, the file allocation table, and the root directory.

system attribute   The file attribute that indicates that the file is part of the operating system and should not appear in normal directory listings. There are also further restrictions on a system file; you cannot delete, copy, or display the contents of such a file.

system date   The date and time as maintained by the computer's internal clock. You should always make sure that the system clock is accurate, because the operating system notes the time that files were created; this can be important if you are trying to find the most recent version of a document or spreadsheet.

system disk   A disk that contains all the files necessary to boot and start the operating system. In most computers, the hard disk is the system disk; indeed, most of today's operating systems are too large to run from a floppy disk.

system file   A file whose system attribute is set. In IBM's PC-DOS, the two system files are called IBMBIOS.COM and IBMDOS.COM; in

Microsoft's MS-DOS, they are called IO.SYS and MSDOS.SYS. These files contain the essential routines needed to manage devices, memory, and input/output operations.

SYSTEM.INI In Windows, an initialization file that contains information on your hardware and the internal Windows operating environment. These files are used primarily in Windows 3.*x* and are used in Windows 95 or later for backward compatibility only.

Systems Application Architecture Abbreviated SAA. A set of IBM standards, first introduced in 1987, that define a consistent set of interfaces for future IBM software. Three standards are defined:

Common User Access (CUA) A graphical user interface definition for products designed for use in an object-oriented operating environment. Windows implements certain CUA features, but by no means all of them.

Common Programming Interface (CPI) A set of Application Programming Interfaces (APIs) designed to encourage independence from the underlying operating system. The standard database query language is SQL.

Common Communications Support (CCS) A common set of communications protocols that interconnect SAA systems and devices.

system software The programs that make up the operating system, along with the associated utility programs, as distinct from an application program.

system time The time and date maintained by the internal clock inside the computer.

This internal clock circuitry is usually backed up by a small battery so that the clock continues to keep time even though the computer may be switched off. The system time is used to date-stamp files with the time of their creation or revision, and you can use this date stamp to determine which of two files contains the latest version of your document. The system time can also be inserted into a document as the current time by a word processor or a spreadsheet program.

system unit The case that houses the processor, motherboard, internal hard and floppy disks, power supply, and expansion bus.

tap 1. A connector that attaches to a cable without blocking the passage of information along that cable.

2. In communications, a connection onto the main transmission medium of the network.

tape cartridge A self-contained tape storage module, containing tape much like that in a video cassette. Tape cartridges are primarily used to back up hard disk systems.

tape drive A computer peripheral that reads from and writes to magnetic tape. The drive may use tape on an open reel or may use one of the small, enclosed tape cartridges. Because tape-management software has to search from the beginning of the tape every time it wants to find a file, tape is too slow to use as a primary storage system, but tapes are frequently used to back up hard disks.

T-connector A T-shaped connector, used with coaxial cable, that connects two thin Ethernet cables and also provides a third connector for the network interface card.

TCP Abbreviation for Transmission Control Protocol. The connection-oriented, transport-level protocol used in the TCP/IP suite of communications protocols.

TCP/IP Abbreviation for Transmission Control Protocol/Internet Protocol. A set of computer-to-computer communications protocols first developed for the Defense Advanced Research Projects Agency (DARPA) in the late 1970s. The set of TCP/IP protocols encompass media access, packet transport, session communications, file transfer, e-mail, and terminal emulation.

TCP/IP is supported by a very large number of hardware and software vendors and is available on many different computers from PCs to mainframes. Many corporations, universities, and government agencies use TCP/IP, and it is also the foundation of the Internet.

Telnet   That part of the TCP/IP suite of protocols used for remote login and terminal emulation; also the name of the program used to connect to Internet host systems.

Originally a Unix utility, Telnet is available these days for almost all popular operating systems. You will find that most versions of Telnet are character-based applications, although some contain the text inside a windowed system.

temporary swap file   A swap file that is created every time it is needed. A temporary swap file will not consist of a single large area of contiguous hard disk space, but may consist of several discontinuous pieces of space. By its very nature, a temporary swap file does not occupy valuable hard disk space if the application that created it is not running. In a permanent swap file the hard disk space is always reserved and is therefore unavailable to any other application program. If hard disk space is at a premium, choose a temporary swap file.

tera-   Abbreviated T. A prefix meaning 10^{12} in the metric system, 1,000,000,000,000; commonly referred to as 1 trillion in the American numbering system, and 1 million million in the British numbering system.

terabyte   Abbreviated TB. In computing, usually 2^{40}, or 1,099,511,627,776 bytes. A terabyte is equivalent to 1000 gigabytes, and usually refers to extremely large hard-disk capacities.

terminal   A monitor and keyboard attached to a computer (usually a mainframe), used for data entry and display. Unlike a personal computer, a terminal does not have its own central processing unit or hard disk.

terminate-and-stay-resident program   Abbreviated TSR. A DOS program that stays loaded in memory, even when it is not actually running, so that you can invoke it very quickly to perform a specific task.

Popular TSR programs include calendars, appointment schedulers, calculators, and the like that you can invoke while using your word processor, spreadsheet, or other application. TSRs occupy conventional memory space that becomes unavailable for use by your applications programs; however, if you have a recent version of DOS and an 80386 (or later) processor, you can load your TSRs into upper memory blocks and therefore recover that conventional memory for other uses.

TSRs are no longer in general use thanks to Windows 95, which allows multiple programs to run at the same time without being preloaded into memory.

terminator   A device attached to the last peripheral in a series or to the last node on a network.

For example, the last device on a SCSI bus must terminate the bus; otherwise the bus will not perform properly. A resistor is placed at both ends of an Ethernet cable to prevent signals from reflecting and interfering with the transmission.

text editor   In computer programming, software used to prepare program source code. Text editors do not have all the advanced formatting facilities available in word processors, but they may have other features that particularly relate to programming, like complex search-and-replace options and multiple windows.

text file   A file that consists of text characters without any formatting information. Also known as an ASCII file, a text file can be read by any word processor. The README file, containing late-breaking news about an application, is always a text file.

thermal printer   A nonimpact printer that uses a thermal printhead and specially treated paper to create an image. The main advantage of thermal printers is that they are virtually silent; the main disadvantage is that they usually produce poor quality output that is likely to fade with time. They are used in calculators and in terminals to provide a local printing capability.

thick Ethernet   Connecting coaxial cable used on an Ethernet network. The cable is 1cm (approximately 0.4 inch) thick and can be used to connect network nodes up to a distance of approximately 3300 feet. Primarily used for facility-wide installations.

thin Ethernet   Connecting coaxial cable used on an Ethernet network. The cable is 5mm (approximately 0.2 inch) thick, and can be used to connect network nodes up to a distance of approximately 1000 feet. Primarily used for office installations.

thrashing   An excessive amount of disk activity in a virtual memory system, to the point where the system is spending all its time swapping pages in and out of memory and no time executing the application. Thrashing can be caused when poor system configuration creates a swap file that is too small, or when insufficient memory is installed in the computer. Increasing the size of the swap file and adding memory are the best ways to reduce thrashing.

thread   **1.** A concurrent process that is part of a larger process or program. In a multitasking operating system, a program may contain several threads, all running at the same time inside the same program. This means that one part of a program can be making a calculation while another part is drawing a graph or chart.

2. A connected set of postings to a Usenet newsgroup or to an online forum. Many newsreaders present postings as threads rather than in strict chronological sequence.

386 enhanced mode   In Microsoft Windows 3.x, the most advanced and complex of the different operating modes. 386 enhanced mode lets Windows access the protected mode of the 80386 (or higher) processor for extended memory management and multitasking for both Windows and non-Windows application programs.

3.5-inch disk   A floppy disk, originally developed by Sony Corporation, that encloses the recording media inside a rigid plastic jacket.

TMS34020   A graphics chip from Texas Instruments used in high-end PC graphics adapters. The older 34010 uses a 16-bit data bus with a 32-bit data word, while the 34020 uses 32 bits for both.

Both are compatible with the Texas Instruments Graphical Architecture (TIGA) used in some IBM-compatible computers. TIGA video adapters and monitors display 1024 pixels horizontally and 786 pixels vertically, using 256 colors.

token-ring network   A local area network with a ring structure that uses token-passing to regulate traffic on the network and avoid collisions.

On a token-ring network, the controlling computer generates a "token" that controls the right to transmit. This token is continuously passed from one node to the next around the network. When a node has information to transmit, it captures the token, sets its status to busy, and adds the message and the destination address. All other nodes continuously read the token to determine if they are the recipient of a message; if they are, they collect the token, extract the message, and return the token to the sender. The sender then removes the message and sets the token status to free, indicating that it can be used by the next node in sequence.

Token Ring network   IBM's implementation of the token-ring network architecture; it uses a token-passing protocol transmitting at 4 or 16 megabits per second.

Using standard telephone wiring, a Token Ring network can connect up to 72 devices; with shielded twisted-pair wiring, the network can support up to 260 nodes. Although it is based on a closed-loop ring structure, a Token Ring network uses a star-shaped cluster of up to eight nodes all attached to the same wiring concentrator or MultiStation Access Unit (MSAU). These MSAUs are then connected to the main ring circuit.

A Token Ring network can include personal computers, minicomputers, and mainframes. The IEEE 802.5 standard defines Token Ring networks.

T1   A long-distance, point-to-point 1.544-megabit-per-second communications channel that can be used for both digitized voice and data transmission; T1 lines are usually divided into 24 channels, each transmitting at 64 kilobits per second.

toner cartridge   The replaceable cartridge in a laser printer or photocopier that contains the electrically charged ink to be fused to the paper during printing.

touch screen   A special monitor that lets the user make choices by touching icons or graphical buttons on the screen.

Touch-screen systems are popular for interactive displays in museums and in automatic teller machines, where input is limited. They never achieved much popularity in the business world, because users have to hold their hands in midair to touch the screen, which becomes tiring very quickly.

tower case   A vertical system unit case designed to have more drive bays and expansion slots than the desktop units.

track   A concentric collection of sectors on a hard or floppy disk.

The outermost track on the top of the disk (or platter) is numbered track 0 side 0, and the outermost track on the other side is numbered track 0 side 1. Numbering increases inward toward the center of the disk. Tracks are created during the disk formatting process.

On tapes, tracks are parallel lines down the axis of the tape.

trackball   An input device used for pointing, designed as an alternative to the mouse.

A trackball is almost an upside-down mouse; it stays still and contains a movable ball that you rotate using your fingers to move the mouse cursor on the screen. Because a trackball does not need the area of flat space that the mouse needs, trackballs are popular with users of portable computers; Apple PowerBook computers include a trackball as part of the keyboard case, and Microsoft has released a small trackball that clips onto the side of a laptop computer.

tracks per inch   Abbreviated TPI. The number of tracks of sectors on a hard or floppy disk. TPI is an indication of the density of data that you can store on any given disk; the larger the TPI, the more data the disk can hold. Among floppy disks, high-density 5.25-inch disks have 96 TPI; most 3.5-inch disks have 135 TPI.

track-to-track access time   An indication of hard disk speed; the amount of time it takes the disk's read/write heads to move from one track to the next adjacent track.

transistor   A contraction of *trans*fer re*sistor*. A semiconductor component that acts like a switch, controlling the flow of an electric current. Transistors are incorporated into modern microprocessors by the million.

transport layer   The fourth of seven layers of the International Organization for Standardization Open Systems Interconnect (ISO/OSI) model for computer-to-computer communications. The transport layer defines protocols for message structure, and supervises the validity of the transmission by performing some error checking.

Trojan horse   A type of virus that pretends to be a useful program, such as a game or a utility program, when in reality it contains special code that will intentionally damage any system onto which it is loaded.

true color   A term used to indicate that a device, usually a video adapter, is capable of displaying 16,777,216 different colors; you will also see this number abbreviated to simply 16 million.

T3   A long-distance point-to-point 44.736-megabit-per-second communications service that can provide up to 28 T1 channels. A T3 channel can carry 672 voice conversations and is usually available over fiber-optic cable.

TWAIN   Generally thought to be an acronym for Technology Without An Important Name, TWAIN is the name given to the technology that allows you to scan images directly into any application without the use of a dedicated scanning program.

24-bit color   A method of representing a graphical image as a bitmap containing 16,777,216 different colors.

24-bit video adapter   A video adapter that uses 24 bits to define the color used for an individual pixel. Each of the three color channels (red, green, blue) is defined by one 8-bit byte; this means that each channel can be defined in terms of 256 different intensities for each of the three primary colors. This adds up to a total of 16,777,216 different gradations of colors; probably at least as many as the human eye can distinguish.

twisted-pair cable   Cable that consists of two insulated wires twisted together at six twists per inch. In twisted-pair cable, one wire carries the signal and the other is grounded. Telephone wire installed in modern buildings is often twisted-pair wiring.

TXD   Abbreviation for transmit data. A hardware signal defined by the RS-232-C standard that carries information from one device to another.

UART   Abbreviation for Universal Asynchronous Receiver/Transmitter. An electronic module that combines the transmitting and receiving circuitry needed for asynchronous transmission over a serial line.

Asynchronous transmissions use start and stop bits encoded in the data stream to coordinate communications rather than the clock pulse found in synchronous transmissions.

Ultra DMA/33   A protocol that allows a hard drive to transfer information directly to random access memory at up to 33.3Mbps without passing the information through the central processor.

undelete   To recover an accidentally deleted file. DOS 5 (and later) provides the UNDELETE command, but many of the popular utility program packages also contain similar undelete programs, which often have a much better user interface and are therefore easier to use.

undelete program   A utility program that recovers deleted or damaged files from a disk. A file can be deleted accidentally, or it can become inaccessible when part of the file's control information is lost.

Many utility packages offer excellent file recovery programs, including Norton Utilities from Symantec. DOS 5 (and later) also offers undelete programs. These programs guide the user through the recovery process or, if damage is extreme, attempt to recover as much of the damaged file as possible. In this case, substantial editing may be necessary before the file can be used; the best way to recover a damaged file is to restore it from a backup.

unformat   The process of recovering an accidentally formatted disk. DOS 5 (and later) provides the UNFORMAT command, but many of the popular utility program packages also contain similar programs, which often have a much better user interface and so are easier to use.

unformat program   A utility program that recovers files and directories after a disk has been formatted by accident.

Many utility packages offer excellent unformat programs, including Norton Utilities from Symantec. DOS 5 (and later) and Windows 95 (and later) also offer unformat utilities. These programs guide the user through the recovery process, offering advice and assistance as they go. You must, of course, recover the original information on the disk before you add any new files or directories to the disk.

uninterruptible power supply   Abbreviated UPS, pronounced "you-pea-ess." An alternative power source, usually a set of batteries, used to power a computer system if the normal power service is interrupted or falls below acceptable levels.

A UPS can often supply power for just long enough to let you shut down the computer in an orderly fashion; it is not designed to support long-term operations.

Unix Pronounced "you-nix." A 32-bit, multiuser, multitasking, portable operating system originally developed by AT&T.

Unix was developed by Dennis Ritchie and Ken Thompson at Bell Laboratories in the early 1970s. It has been enhanced over the years, particularly by computer scientists at the University of California, Berkeley.

Networking, in the form of the TCP/IP set of protocols, has been available in Unix from the early stages. During the 1980s, AT&T began the work of consolidating the many versions of Unix. In January 1989, the Unix Software Operation was formed as a separate AT&T division, and in November 1989, that division introduced a significant new release, System V Release 4.0. In June 1990, the Unix Software Operation became known as Unix System Laboratories (USL), which was bought by Novell in 1993.

Unix is available on a huge range of computational hardware, from a PC to a Cray, and is also available in other, related forms. For example, AIX runs on IBM workstations; A/UX is a graphical version that runs on powerful Macintosh computers, and Solaris from SunSoft runs on Intel processors. Many of the computers that make up the Internet run Unix.

unmoderated newsgroup A Usenet newsgroup or mailing list in which posts are not subject to review before distribution. You will find the discussions in unmoderated newsgroups to be wildly spontaneous, but they will also contain more than their fair share of flames and flame wars.

upgrade 1. The process of installing a newer and more powerful version; for example, to upgrade to a newer and more capable version of a software package or to upgrade from your current hard disk to one that is twice the size. In the case of hardware, an upgrade is often called an upgrade kit.

2. A new and more powerful version of an existing system, either hardware or software, is also known as an upgrade.

upgradable computer A computer system specifically designed to be upgraded as technology advances.

Upgradable computers differ in how much of the PC's circuitry must be changed when you make the upgrade and also in how you actually make the upgrade. At minimum, you must replace the processor; at most, some upgrades come close to changing all the circuitry installed in the computer.

upload In communications, sending a file or files from one computer to another over a network or using a modem. For example, a file could be uploaded to a bulletin board. In this case, the remote computer stores the uploaded file on disk for further processing when the transmission is complete. Files can also be uploaded to a network file server.

upper memory blocks Abbreviated UMB. The memory between 640KB and 1MB in an IBM-compatible computer running DOS was originally reserved for system and video use; however, not all the space is used, and the unused portions are known as upper memory blocks.

If you have an 80386 (or later) processor, you can gain up to 120K of additional memory by accessing these UMBs, and you can use this space to load device drivers and terminate-and-stay-resident programs.

upward compatibility The design of software so as to function with other, more powerful, products likely to become available in the short term. The use of standards makes upward compatibility much easier to achieve.

URL Abbreviation for Uniform Resource Locator. A method of accessing Internet resources.

URLs contain information about both the access method to use and also about the resource itself and are used by Web browsers to connect you directly to a specific document or page on the World Wide Web, without you having to know where that resource is located physically.

The first part of the URL, before the colon, specifies the access method. On the Web, this is usually `http` (for Hypertext Transmission Protocol), but you might also see `file`, `ftp`, or `gopher` instead. The second part of the URL, after the colon, specifies the resource. The text after the two slashes usually indicates a server name, and the text after the single slash defines the directory or individual file you will connect to. If you are linking to a document, it will usually have the filename extension .html, the abbreviation for Hypertext Markup Language.

URLs are always case-sensitive, so pay particular attention to upper- and lowercase letters, and to symbols as well. One example of a URL is `http://www.sybex.com`.

USB   An abbreviation for Universal Serial Bus, a peripheral bus "standard" that was jointly developed by Compaq, DEC, IBM, Intel, Microsoft, NEC, and Northern Telecom to allow computer peripherals to be automatically configured as soon as they are physically attached. USB will also allow up to 127 devices to run simultaneously on a computer, with peripherals such as monitors and keyboards acting as additional plug-in sites, or hubs. USB was specified to have a 12 megabit/second data rate and to provide a low-cost interface for Integrated Services Digital Network (ISDN) and digital PBXs.

One of the benefits of having Microsoft as part of the development effort is that Windows 95/98/98 SE can already let your PC recognize USB peripherals. Once you get the drivers installed for the new drive or whatever, Windows will take care of the rest. Almost all new PC designs from major vendors shipping today already have USB connections on the motherboard and the correct Windows operating system to make them work.

USB and FireWire (IEEE 1394) may appear similar in their goals of automatic configuration of peripherals (what FireWire calls "hotplugging") without the need to reboot or run SETUP, but they are not really the same, and the developers point out that they have different applications. USB is slower than FireWire but is supposed to address traditional PC connections, like keyboards and mice. Conversely, FireWire targets high-bandwidth consumer electronics connections to the PC, like digital camcorders, cameras, and digital videodisc players. The two technologies target different kinds of peripheral devices and are supposed to be complementary. USB proponents feel that future PCs probably will have both USB and FireWire connection ports.

Usenet   Contraction of *user network*. An international, non-commercial network, linking many thousands of Unix sites.

Although there is a very close relationship between the Internet and Usenet, they are not the same thing by any means. Usenet predates the Internet; in the early days, information was distributed by dial-up connections. Not every Internet computer is part of Usenet, and not every Usenet system can be reached from the Internet.

Like the Internet, Usenet has no central governing body; Usenet is run by the people who use it. With thousands of newsgroups, Usenet is accessed by millions of people every day around the world.

Usenet newsgroups   The individual discussion groups within Usenet.

Usenet newsgroups contain articles posted by other Internet and Usenet subscribers; very few of them contain actual hard news. Most newsgroups are concerned with a single subject; the range of subjects available through Usenet is phenomenal—there are thousands of newsgroups from which to choose. If people are interested in a subject, you are sure to find a newsgroup for it somewhere.

Newsgroups are like the online forums found on CompuServe or America Online; you can post your own articles and browse through similar items posted by others. When you reply to a post, you can reply to the newsgroup so that other subscribers can read your reply, or you can respond directly to the originator in a private e-mail message.

user group   A voluntary group of users of a specific computer or software package, who meet to share tips and listen to industry experts. Some PC user groups hold large, well-attended monthly meetings, run their own bulletin boards, and publish newsletters of exceptional quality.

utility program   A small program or a set of small programs that supports the operating system by providing additional services that the operating system does not provide.

In the PC world, there are many tasks routinely performed by utility programs, including hard disk backup, disk optimization, file recovery, safe formatting, and resource editing.

uudecode   Pronounced "you-you-de-code."

1. To convert a text file created by the Unix uuencode utility back into its original binary form. Graphical images and other binary files are often sent to Usenet newsgroups in this form, because the newsgroups can only handle text and don't know how to manage binary files.

2. The name of the utility program that performs a text-to-binary file conversion. Originally a Unix utility, uudecode is now available for most operating systems.

uuencode   Pronounced "you-you-en-code."

1. To convert a binary file such as a graphical image into a text file so that the file can be sent over the Internet or to a Usenet newsgroup as a part of an e-mail message. When you receive a uuencoded text file, you must process it through the Unix uudecode utility to turn it back into a graphical image that you can view.

2. The name of the utility that performs a binary-to-text file conversion. Originally a Unix utility, uuencode is now available for most operating systems.

vaccine   An application program that removes and destroys a computer virus.

The people who unleash computer viruses are often very accomplished programmers, and they are constantly creating new and novel ways of causing damage to a system. The antivirus and vaccine programmers do the best they can to catch up, but they must always lag behind to some extent.

vaporware   A sarcastic term applied to a product that has been announced but has missed its release date, often by a large margin, and so is not actually available.

VAR   Abbreviation for value-added reseller; a company that adds value to a system, repackages it, and then resells it to the public. This added value can take the form of better documentation, user support, service support, system integration, or even just a new nameplate on the outside of the box. For example, Canon makes the print engine used in many laser printers, including those from Hewlett-Packard; in this case, Canon is an original equipment manufacturer (OEM) and HP is the value-added reseller.

VDT   Abbreviation for video display terminal. Synonymous with monitor.

vendor   The person or company that manufactures, supplies, or sells computer hardware, software, or related services.

Veronica   A search service built into the Gopher Internet application. When you use Veronica to search a series of Gopher menus (files, directories, and other items), the results of the search are presented as another Gopher menu, which you can use to access the resources your search has located. Veronica supposedly stands for Very Easy Rodent-oriented Net-wide Index to Computer Archives.

version number   A method of identifying a particular software or hardware release.

The version number is assigned by the software developer and often includes numbers before and after a decimal point; the higher the number, the more recent the release. The number before the decimal point indicates the major revision levels, while the part after the decimal indicates a minor revision level, which in some cases can produce a significant difference in performance.

vertical scanning frequency   In a monitor, the frequency at which the monitor repaints the whole screen; sometimes called the vertical refresh rate.

Vertical scanning frequency is measured in Hz (cycles per second), and higher rates are associated with less flicker. VGA has a vertical scanning frequency of 60 or 70Hz, and SuperVGA rates vary from the VESA guidelines of 56Hz (which is about the minimum tolerable) and 60Hz, to the official recommended standard of 72Hz or higher.

very low-frequency emission   Abbreviated VLF. Radiation emitted by a computer monitor and other very common household electrical appliances such as televisions, hair dryers, electric blankets, and food processors. VLF emissions fall into the range from 2kHz to 400kHz and decline with the square of the distance from the source. Emissions are not constant around a monitor; they are higher from the sides and rear and weakest from the front of the screen.

VGA   Abbreviation for Video Graphics Array. A video adapter introduced by IBM along with the IBM PS/2 line of computers in 1987.

VGA supports previous graphics standards and provides several different graphics resolutions, including 640 pixels horizontally by 480 pixels vertically. A maximum of 256 colors can be displayed simultaneously, chosen from a palette of 262,114 colors.

Because the VGA standard requires an analog display, it is capable of resolving a continuous range of gray shades or colors, in contrast to a digital display, which can only resolve a finite range of shades or colors.

video adapter   An expansion board that plugs into the expansion bus in a DOS computer and provides the text and graphics output to the monitor.

Some later video adapters, such as the VGA, are included in the circuitry on the motherboard, rather than as separate plug-in boards.

Video CD   A compact disc format standard developed by Sony, Phillips, JVC, and Matsushita that allows up to 74 minutes of video to be stored on one compact disc.

Compact discs recorded in Video CD format can be played on CD-I, Video CD, and CD-ROM drives and on CD players that have digital output and an add-on video adapter.

videodisc   An optical disk used for storing video images and sound. A videodisc player can play back the contents of the videodisc on a computer or onto a standard television set. One videodisc can contain up to 55,000 still images or up to 2 hours worth of full-frame video.

video RAM   Abbreviated VRAM, pronounced "vee-ram." Special-purpose RAM with two data paths for access, rather than just one as in conventional RAM. These two paths let a VRAM board manage two functions at once—refreshing the display and communicating with the processor. VRAM doesn't require the system to complete one function before starting the other, so it allows faster operation for the whole video system.

virtual DOS machine   Abbreviated VDM. A DOS emulation that takes advantage of the virtual 8086 mode of 80386 (or later) processors.

Windows NT uses this feature of the processor to create multiple multitasking DOS and Windows sessions, and each VDM runs as a single-threaded, protected-mode process.

virtual 8086 mode   A mode found in the 80386 and later processors that lets the processor emulate several 8086 environments simultaneously.

The operating system controls the external elements, such as interrupts, and input and output; and applications running in this mode are protected from the applications running in all the other virtual 8086 environments, and behave as though they have control of the whole 8086 environment. To the user, this looks like several 8086 systems all running side-by-side, but under the control of the operating system.

virtual machine   An environment created by the operating system that gives each executing application program the illusion that it has complete control of an independent computer and can access all the system resources that it needs.

For example, the Intel 80386 (and higher) processor can run multiple DOS applications in completely separate and protected address spaces using a processor mode known as virtual 8086 mode.

virtual memory   A memory-management technique that allows information in physical memory to be swapped out to a hard disk. This technique provides application programs with more memory space than is actually available in the computer.

True virtual memory management requires specialized hardware in the processor for the operating system to use; it is not just a question of writing information out to a swap file on the hard disk at the application level.

In a virtual memory system, programs and their data are divided into smaller pieces called pages. At the point where more memory is needed, the operating system decides which pages are least likely to be needed soon (using an algorithm based on frequency of use, most recent use, and program priority), and it writes these pages out to disk. The memory space that they used is now available to the rest of the system for other application programs. When these pages are needed again, they are loaded back into real memory, displacing other pages.

virtual reality   Abbreviated VR. A computer-generated environment that presents the illusion of reality. The user wears a head-mounted display (HMD) that displays a three-dimensional image of the environment and uses an instrumented glove to manipulate objects within the environment.

A whole range of applications are emerging to exploit VR; architects can present clients with a VR walk-through of a proposed structure, and biologists can seem to get inside a human cell. Undoubtedly, the most lucrative avenues for VR will be computer games.

virus   A program intended to damage your computer system without your knowledge or permission.

A virus may attach itself to another program or to the partition table or the boot track on your hard disk. When a certain event occurs, a date passes, or a specific program executes, the virus is triggered into action. Not all viruses are harmful; some are just annoying.

VL bus   Also known as VL local bus. Abbreviation for the VESA local bus, a bus architecture introduced by the Video Electronics Standards Association (VESA), in which up to three adapter slots are built into the motherboard. The VL bus allows for bus mastering.

The VL bus is a 32-bit bus, running at either 33 or 40MHz. The maximum throughput is 133 megabytes per second at 33MHz, or 148 megabytes per second at 40MHz. The most common VL bus adapters are video adapters, hard disk controllers, and network interface cards.

voice recognition   Also known as speech recognition. Computer recognition and analysis of human language is a particularly difficult branch of computer science. Background noise, different voices, accents and dialects, and the ability to recognize and add new words to a computer vocabulary all contrive to complicate the problem.

Systems that work with only one speaker must be trained before they can be used, and systems that can work with any speaker have extremely restricted vocabularies. In the future, voice recognition will find wide applications from the phone companies to credit card authorizations to automatic voice-mail systems.

volatile memory   Any memory system that does not maintain its contents when power is lost. Normal computer memory, whether dynamic RAM or static RAM, is volatile; flash memory and ROM are not volatile.

volume **1.** A unit of physical storage, such as a floppy disk, a hard disk, or a tape cartridge. A volume may hold a number of complete files or may just hold parts of files.

2. In networking, a volume is the highest level of the file server directory and file structure. Large hard disks can be divided into several different volumes when the network operating system is first installed.

volume serial number A unique number assigned to a disk during the formatting process and displayed at the beginning of a directory listing.

In the Macintosh, System 7 assigns a similar number, known as a "volume reference number," that programs can use when referring to disks.

VRML Abbreviation for Virtual Reality Modeling Language, VRML is used to design three-dimensional, interactive worlds on the Internet. In a VRML world, it is possible for a user to interact with objects just as if they were in real space.

wafer A flat, thin piece of semiconductor material used in the construction of a chip. A wafer goes through a series of photomasking and etching steps to produce the final chip, which has leads attached and is finally packaged in a ceramic, plastic, or metal holder.

wait state A clock cycle during which no instructions are executed because the processor is waiting for data from a device or from memory.

Static RAM chips and page-mode RAM chips are becoming popular because they can store information without being constantly refreshed by the processor and so eliminate the wait state. A computer that can process information without wait states is known as a zero wait state computer.

warm boot A reboot performed after the operating system has started running.

Web browser A World Wide Web client application that lets you look at hypertext documents and follow links to other HTML documents on the Web. When you find something that interests you as you browse through a hypertext document, you can click your mouse on that object, and the browser automatically takes care of accessing the Internet host that holds the document you requested; you don't need to know the IP address, the name of the host system, or any other details.

wideband In communications, a channel capable of handling more frequencies than a standard 3kHz voice channel.

window In a graphical user interface, a rectangular portion of the screen that acts as a viewing area for application programs.

Windows can be tiled or cascaded and can be individually moved and sized on the screen. Some programs can open multiple document windows inside their application window to display several word processing or spreadsheet data files at the same time.

Windows accelerator An expansion card or a chip containing circuitry dedicated to speeding up the performance of PC video hardware so that Windows appears to run faster. Standard display adapters do not handle the throughput required by Windows particularly well and rapidly become input/output bound. An accelerator card specifically "tuned" for Windows can improve overall performance considerably.

Windows application Any application program that runs within the Windows environment and cannot run without Windows. All Windows applications follow certain conventions in their arrangement of menus, the use and style of dialog boxes, as well as keyboard and mouse use.

Windows 95/98 The replacement for the DOS and Windows 3.1 operating systems, from Microsoft Corporation.

Windows 95/98 is a 32-bit, multitasking, multithreaded operating system capable of running DOS, Windows 3.1, and Windows 95/98 applications, supports Plug and Play (on the appropriate hardware), and adds an enhanced FAT file system in the Virtual FAT, which allows long filenames of up to 255 characters while also supporting the DOS 8.3 filenaming conventions.

Applets include WordPad (word processor) and Paint, and System Tools such as Backup, ScanDisk, Disk Defragmenter, and DriveSpace. Access to Microsoft Network is available directly from the Windows 95/98 Desktop. A Start button and Desktop taskbar make application management easy and straightforward.

Windows 98 Second Edition   The successor to Windows 98; an evolutionary upgrade that takes better advantage of new technologies.

Windows 2000   A family of operating systems based on Windows NT. The family includes Windows 2000 Professional for workstations; Windows 2000 Server, Windows 2000 Advanced Server, and Windows 2000 Datacenter Server.

Windows NT   A 32-bit multitasking portable operating system developed by Microsoft and first released in 1993.

Windows NT was designed as a portable operating system, and initial versions ran on Intel 80386 (or later) processors and RISC processors such as the MIPS R4000, and the DEC Alpha.

Windows NT contains the graphical user interface from Windows 3.1 and can run Windows 3.1 and DOS applications as well as new 32-bit programs specifically developed for Windows NT.

Multitasking under Windows NT is preemptive, and applications can execute multiple threads. Security is built into the operating system at the U.S. government-approved C2 security level. Windows NT supports the DOS FAT file system, installable file systems such as CD-ROM systems, and a native file system called NTFS. Windows NT also supports multiprocessing, OLE, and peer-to-peer networking.

WIN.INI   In Windows 3.*x*, an initialization file that contains information to help customize your copy of Windows.

When Windows starts, the contents of WIN.INI are read from the hard disk into memory so that they are immediately available. WIN.INI contains sections that define the use of colors, fonts, country-specific information, the desktop, and many other settings.

word   A computer's natural unit of storage. A word can be 8 bits, 16 bits, 32 bits, or 64 bits in size.

workgroup   A group of individuals who work together and share the same files and databases over a local area network. Special groupware such as Lotus Notes coordinates the workgroup and allows users to edit drawings or documents and update the database as a group.

workstation   **1.** In networking, any personal computer (other than the file server) attached to the network.

2. A high-performance computer optimized for graphics applications such as computer-aided design, computer-aided engineering, or scientific applications.

World Wide Web   Abbreviated WWW, W3, or simply the Web. A huge collection of hypertext pages on the Internet.

World Wide Web concepts were developed in Switzerland by the European Laboratory for Particle Physics (known as CERN), but the Web is not just a tool for scientists; it is one of the most flexible and exciting tools in existence for surfing the Internet.

Hypertext links connect pieces of information (text, graphics, audio, or video) in separate HTML pages located at the same or at different Internet sites, and you explore these pages and links using a Web browser such as Netscape Navigator or Microsoft Internet Explorer.

You can also access a WWW resource directly if you specify the appropriate URL (Uniform Resource Locator).

worm   A destructive program that reproduces itself to the point where a computer or network can do nothing but manage the worm. Eventually, your computer memory or hard disk will fill up completely.

WORM   Acronym for Write Once Read Many. A high-capacity optical storage device that can be written to only once, but can be read any number of times. WORM devices can store from 200 to 700MB of information on a 5.25-inch disk and so are well suited to archival and other non-changing storage.

write   To transfer information from the processor to memory, to a storage medium such as a hard or floppy disk, or to the display. In the PC world, the term usually refers to storing information onto disks.

write-back cache   A technique used in cache design for writing information back into main memory.

In a write-back cache, the cache stores the changed block of data but only updates main memory under certain conditions, such as when the whole block must be overwritten because a newer block must be loaded into the cache or when the controlling algorithm determines that too much time has elapsed since the last update. This method is rather complex to implement but is much faster than other designs.

write-protect   To prevent the addition or deletion of files on a disk or tape. Floppy disks have write-protect notches or small write-protect tabs that allow files to be read from the disk but prevent any modifications or deletions.

Certain attributes can make individual files write-protected so they can be read but not altered or erased.

write-through cache   A technique used in cache design for writing information back into main memory.

In a write-through cache, each time the processor returns a changed bit of data to the cache, the cache updates that information in both the cache and in main memory. This method is simple to implement but is not as fast as other designs; delays can be introduced when the processor must wait to complete write operations to slower main memory.

XGA   Abbreviation for Extended Graphics Array. A high-resolution video adapter introduced by IBM in 1991 to replace the 8514/A standard.

XGA is available as a microchannel architecture expansion board or in certain laptops; it is not available in ISA or EISA form. XGA supports resolution of 1024 horizontal pixels by 768 vertical pixels with 256 colors, as well as a VGA mode of 640 pixels by 480 pixels with 65,536 colors, and like the 8514/A, XGA is interlaced. XGA is optimized for use with graphical user interfaces, and instead of being very good at drawing lines, it is a bit-block transfer device designed to move blocks of bits like windows or dialog boxes.

Yellow Book   The definition of the standard storage format for compact disc data, also referred to as the CD-ROM format. So called because of the cover color used when the specification was first published.

zero wait state   Describes a computer that can process information without wait states. A wait state is a clock cycle during which no instructions are executed because the processor is waiting for data from a device or from memory.

Static RAM chips and page-mode RAM chips are becoming popular because they can store information without being constantly refreshed by the processor, and so they eliminate the wait state.

ZIF socket   Abbreviation for Zero Insertion Force socket. A specially designed chip socket that makes replacing a chip easier and safer.

INDEX

Note to Reader: In this index, **boldfaced** page numbers refer to primary discussions of the topic; *italicized* page numbers refer to figures.

EXCEL 2000: NO EXPERIENCE REQUIRED™

Gene Weisskopf
0-7821-2374-0
448 pp.
$19.99 US

Here is a guide that teaches you all the essential skills you need to become a truly proficient Excel user. Real-world exercises and projects test your mastery and ensure that you are able to complete the tasks at hand. Just like a training course, the chapters are broken into skills, and the material is presented in manageable bite-sized chunks—you learn by doing, rather than by simply reading theory. With this book, you are certain to get up to speed in a hurry and become an efficient Excel user.

HOME NETWORKING!
I DIDN'T KNOW YOU COULD DO THAT...™

Erik B. Sherman
0-7821-2631-6
320 pp.
$19.99 US

Of American homes, 98% have a TV, 89% have a VCR, 45% have a computer, 40% have a printer, 28% have Internet access, and 22% have multiple computers. Finally, the technologies to put these components together easily into a usable network are available. This book explains how and why to network your computers and home electronics. The dozens of home-networking projects covered include connecting Macs to PC networks, connecting your TV, creating a DVD movie server, hosting your own Web site, collaborating on school projects, and monitoring your babysitter. The CD provides valuable home-networking software, including friendly proxy servers, parental-control software, and multiplayer games.